HARVARD STUDIES IN BUSINESS HISTORY

· XVII ·

*Edited by Henrietta M. Larson, Associate Professor of Business History
and Thomas R. Navin, Assistant Professor of Business History
Graduate School of Business Administration
George F. Baker Foundation
Harvard University*

HARVARD STUDIES IN BUSINESS HISTORY

A HISTORY OF
THE BIGELOW–SANFORD
CARPET COMPANY

BROADLOOMS and BUSINESSMEN

JOHN S. EWING and NANCY P. NORTON

HARVARD UNIVERSITY PRESS

1955 | Cambridge, Massachusetts

Copyright, 1955, by the President and Fellows of Harvard College

Distributed in Great Britain by Geoffrey Cumberlege, Oxford University Press, London

Library of Congress Catalog Card Number 54–12236

Printed in the United States of America

TO OUR MOTHERS

CONTENTS

APPENDICES

ILLUSTRATIONS

TABLES

CONTENTS

CHARTS

Editors' Introduction

In the closing months of 1945 President James D. Wise of the Bigelow-Sanford Carpet Company, Inc., inquired if the Harvard Graduate School of Business Administration would be interested in writing a history of his company. Since the invitation included free access to the company's records and to the company's executive personnel, and since the company had a long history and a reputation for leadership in its industry, the opportunity seemed attractive. A survey conducted by Professor N. S. B. Gras indicated, however, that the company's records were incomplete and that a worth-while study would be difficult to complete even if supplemented by printed materials and the memories of men. To this difficulty was added the further disadvantage that the members of the business history faculty were already committed to other tasks and, with the war just over, it was likely that there would be for several years a shortage of personnel at all academic levels.

There the matter stood until the summer of 1950 when the publication of Professor Navin's history of the Whitin Machine Works came to President Wise's attention and reminded him to reopen the question of a Bigelow-Sanford history. Meanwhile, Professor Gras had retired and his work was being carried on by his successors, Professors Larson and Navin. There followed a series of conferences between representatives of the Harvard Business School and the company. It was ascertained that two authors with experience in the business history field were available. The question of inadequate records was still regarded as a serious handicap —and indeed it was to plague the authors throughout the project, causing them to hunt for bits of evidence after the manner of the archaeologist— but offsetting this handicap was the confirmation which Professors Larson and Navin received from many quarters that President Wise was the kind of business leader who could be counted on to assure to the project the scholarly detachment which would be essential to a successful undertaking. It was therefore decided to go ahead with the project. The research and writing were to be under the direction of Professor Larson.

The Bigelow-Sanford Carpet Company agreed to make a gift to Harvard University to finance the study and accepted the stipulation that there should be no restriction on publication except that nothing should be published that might impair the company's current business relationships in individual instances. The early records of the company and its predecessors were to be deposited at the Harvard Business School * and

---

* These records have been placed on permanent deposit in Baker Library of the Harvard Business School.

later records were to be available in the company offices. It was understood that company executives would read the manuscript and suggest
changes or corrections but that the final decision as to fact, generalization,
or interpretation should be the authors'. One responsibility of the director
of the project was to help to resolve any issues that might arise.

To participate in such a project is to participate in an experimental
type of scholarly effort. The student, who traditionally has sought knowledge in library or study, here enters the factory, the market place, and the
central office to observe men at work, in reality and in records. Here
assumptions and theories, while useful and important tools, give preced-
ence to direct observation. Here the challenges, the efforts, the conflicts,
the failures and successes which are a part of the life of business must be
considered and evaluated.

Working in the records of a living company involves serious responsibilities. No easy generalizations or interpretations can be made where the
interests of many individuals are concerned; nor, indeed, is it simple to
arrive at conclusions where many factors in a dynamic environment are
seen to bear upon the decisions and efforts of men. The task of the re-
searcher is, moreover, complicated by the fact that no two persons remem-
ber a given past experience in the same way and that loyal employees
unconsciously see their company in a somewhat rosy light.

To write from a company's records would, in fact, be impossible if the
company's executives responsible for the undertaking did not see that to
be worth while to both company and outside readers a company history
must be as factual and objective as possible. Success can come only where
executive and scholar understand and agree that, in order to contribute
to an understanding of the historical background of contemporary business, research and writing on the history of business must not abandon
the accepted canons of historical scholarship.

The editors of this study find satisfaction in recording their observation that Bigelow-Sanford has co-operated fully in every way. Executives
in the head offices in New York and at the plants in Thompsonville and
Amsterdam responded generously whenever called on for help. Several
directors and many active and retired employees contributed information
from their memory of the past. A number of executives have read parts
or all of the manuscript and have made valuable suggestions. Firm in
pointing out where they have differed with the manuscript, they have in
no respect tried to press the acceptance of their recommendations.

Of the many who have given of their time and interest, only one will
be mentioned here. We wish to acknowledge our grateful appreciation
of the warm interest and courteous and generous help of the late Bruce K.
MacLaury, who was our liaison with the company until his untimely
death in 1953.

The editors and not the authors decided to undertake this study on a two-part basis. At the time the decision was made to go ahead with the project, the United States had just become involved in the Korean war. Since one of the prospective authors, Dr. Ewing, had served as an officer in World War II, there was no certainty that he would be able to complete an extended study such as was contemplated. Because the Harvard Business School was reluctant to commit itself to a project it might not be able to finish, it was decided that Dr. Ewing's part in the effort would be limited in time to the events occurring after 1914. By that means it was hoped that the project could be finished in a relatively short period; if, however, Dr. Ewing should be called away it was expected that Dr. Norton would be able to complete the work.

Because of the individual training of the two authors, this division of responsibility had a certain inherent logic. In writing her thesis for a doctorate, Dr. Norton had studied the history of a predecessor of today's United States Rubber Company and had familiarized herself with the nineteenth-century business history of New England. In his study for the master's and doctor's degrees at the Harvard Business School and in his research in the history of an oil company, Dr. Ewing had focused his interest more especially on contemporary business and its recent historical background. The director of the project did not attempt to shape the writing or thinking of the authors into a common mold but rather encouraged both to employ their special talents in their own ways. The unity in this volume is, therefore, that of subject rather than of form.

The editors resolved the problem of the order of authors' names in a simple way by placing them alphabetically. Since no order would be wholly fair to both authors, this was chosen as a reasonable compromise.

In view of the initial concern that the study might suffer from a lack of records, the results proved unexpectedly rewarding. The authors found themselves observing a company which, before their very eyes, was struggling to resolve two of the most perplexing, yet age-old, problems confronting modern business: the problems of management succession and of product diversification in a highly specialized economy. These problems were not new to the company in recent years, as the authors soon found; they had periodically recurred over a span of more than half a century. What was new was the vigorous way they were being met by the company's current management team.

In a sense these problems were the heritage of an industrial growth so rapid that productive capacities outran administrative organization and practices. By the end of the nineteenth century industrial development in the carpet industry had created managerial complications of pressing concern.

A series of mergers followed, as one result. Occurring at the turn of the century (and on two occasions thereafter), these mergers point to the possibility that the merger movement in this country has been, not only in the recent past as is now recognized but from the beginning, a reaction in part to the stresses which many companies experience sooner or later when problems of management succession arise.

For Bigelow-Sanford, however, merger did not provide a long-run answer to the need for management continuity. Again in 1944 the need recurred, this time in a form as critical as any it had previously taken. Against this background the present management set itself the task of making certain, from within its own ranks, that if possible no future crisis of this type would recur.

Meanwhile, another problem born of nineteenth-century industrial development was reaching a critical stage in the Bigelow-Sanford company. So rapidly had the markets for goods expanded in the nineteenth century that it had been possible for numerous companies to grow large on the basis of exceedingly high specialization of product. In Bigelow-Sanford's industry, for instance, few companies produced anything but carpets; carrying this specialization still further, many carpet companies produced only certain carpet weaves, some no more than two out of the six or more basic types. Unfortunately for the carpet industry, however, buying habits changed, leaving carpet producers in a vulnerable position.

For a specialized producer with a product that is losing ground in competition with other products, the only long-range solution is diversification. But successful diversification is difficult to achieve in a company of moderate size, like Bigelow-Sanford. It requires large capital resources, skill in applied research, and exceptionally able executives. These advantages are not obtained quickly and not without a dramatic increase in overhead expenses. Bigelow-Sanford is now engaged in an experiment which will throw some light on the question whether a company of moderate means can quickly enough earn a return on its diversification to pay for the increased costs.

Whatever the outcome, it should be evident to the readers of this book that a study of Bigelow-Sanford's history is a study of broad and enduring problems in our business system. To those interested in Bigelow-Sanford and the carpet industry, particularly, this study should help to bring meaning to the present efforts of the company to solve old problems while adjusting to changed and changing conditions.

HENRIETTA M. LARSON

THOMAS R. NAVIN

Authors' Preface

Since the Bigelow-Sanford Carpet Company is the end product of four distinct mergers, its history has descended from many directions out of the past. Its predecessor companies have been so numerous and so different in many respects that there was no easy solution to the means by which their stories should be presented.

Furthermore, strictly comparable data was not always available for the several companies which went to make up the Bigelow-Sanford organization. During the period of the mergers much material in the local offices of the predecessor companies was destroyed or abandoned. Some of the data, stored at Thompsonville, Connecticut, was in a basement that suffered periodic floods. In addition the company's head office was moved several times and each move led to the destruction of what would have been valuable material for the purposes of this study.

It has therefore been necessary to supplement company material with interviews and with published information. *The American Carpet & Upholstery Journal* was selected as the principal trade publication used because its coverage of industry affairs seems to have been the most nearly complete. Other magazines and newspapers have been drawn on as is shown in the cited sources.

The organization of the book has been in terms of corporate and internal changes and not on the basis of industry-wide developments, such as technological advances or shifts in marketing. Thus the first part covers the years from the beginnings of the carpet industry in America until the predecessors of Bigelow-Sanford had taken on the corporate forms under which they were to do business for the next forty or fifty years. This latter event occurred sometime in the mid-1850's. The second period comes to a close at the turn of the century with the first two mergers. The third period ends in 1914 with the third merger, and the next period in 1929 with the final amalgamation which was to produce the present company name: Bigelow-Sanford Carpet Company, Inc. The final period brings the history down to 1953. In its original form the manuscript was much longer than here appears. The uncut version is on deposit in Baker Library of the Harvard Business School.

The last two chapters of the book represent an effort to record history in the making. So many changes occurred while the book was in preparation that it was not always possible to distinguish the significant from the transient. These chapters should be regarded, therefore, as tentative reports on recent developments, for they have not had the benefit of the perspective that time alone can bring.

Throughout our study we have been fortunate in the assistance we have received. For over a year Mrs. Elizabeth Bricker Currier worked with us. Not only did her research uncover important material, but her critical suggestions on the main areas of investigation and her pertinent comments on the problems of the company contributed much to our analysis of the company's past.

Associate Professor Henrietta M. Larson, of the business history group at the Harvard Business School, gave us the full benefit of her inquiring mind and her extensive knowledge of business problems. In addition to commenting on subject matter, Assistant Professor Thomas R. Navin reviewed the manuscript for continuity and conciseness. Miss Josepha M. Perry read the entire manuscript and gave us the benefit of her skills in gracious wording. Miss Hilma Holton patiently undertook a wide range of tasks from correcting footnotes and arranging tables to seeing the manuscript through the press and preparing the index.

Bigelow-Sanford directors, executives, and employees have been highly co-operative. In interviews they have talked fully, frankly, and helpfully. In the course of their business schedules they have taken time to assist us in finding records and uncovering facts. Every question was answered if it was possible to do so; nowhere were we conscious of any attempt at concealment.

It is impossible to acknowledge all those in the company who have assisted us, but some should receive special mention: Mr. Neal Rantoul, Mr. Frank Deknatel, and Mr. Samuel A. Welldon of the board of directors; President James D. Wise; Vice-president E. I. Petersen, Secretary John J. Kenny, and Advertising Director Bruce K. MacLaury of the New York office; Mr. Willard Furey and Mr. Leon Salley of the Thompsonville plant; Mr. James J. Delaney, Mr. Gerald C. Denebrink, Mr. Richard G. Knowland, and Mr. Julius Roth. We are especially indebted to Mr. James M. Donnelly for allowing us to use the many materials which he had gathered on the history of the Bigelow Carpet Company.

JOHN S. EWING
NANCY P. NORTON

BROADLOOMS and BUSINESSMEN

A HISTORY OF
THE BIGELOW–SANFORD
CARPET COMPANY

CHAPTER 1

PIONEERING AN INDUSTRY:

The Lowell Manufacturing Company, 1828–1852

From a purely corporate point of view, the Bigelow-Sanford Carpet Company dates only from 1951. In that year the company was rechartered as a diversified enterprise engaged in a number of activities outside the textile field. Technically, therefore, the corporation is young in years. But a corporation is more than a legal entity. It is an aggregate of administrative experience and technical know-how, of physical properties, of contacts and goodwill. All of these require years to create. All were in a stage of advanced development as early as 1929 when the Bigelow-Sanford name came into being. Behind the 1929 merger were eleven predecessor companies (Chart I), which properly traced their lineage more than one hundred years back to the date 1825.

Leaders in point of time, leaders in scale of operations, leaders in mechanization, in market extension, and in integration, the predecessors of Bigelow-Sanford literally made carpet history. This study of their development is therefore more than an exercise in the background of a single firm; it is a survey of the origins and growth of an important American industry.

INDUSTRY BACKGROUND

As every book on carpet-making quickly points out, the cradle of the carpet industry lay in distant times and distant places. Carpetings were made in the Near and Middle East a thousand or more years before Christ, and even today the product of this area is respected the world over for its high quality and exceptional colors.

The introduction into Europe of these carpeting products was soon followed by the development of the necessary manufacturing skills. Par-

CHART I

CORPORATE GENEALOGY OF THE BIGELOW–SANFORD CARPET COMPANY

(Dates Indicate When Companies Were Started)

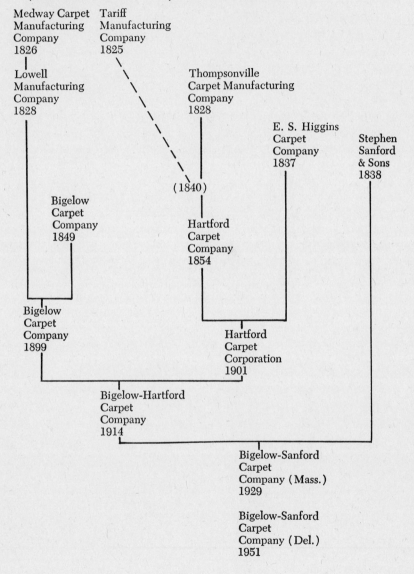

Medway Carpet Manufacturing Company 1826

Tariff Manufacturing Company 1825

Lowell Manufacturing Company 1828

Thompsonville Carpet Manufacturing Company 1828

E. S. Higgins Carpet Company 1837

Stephen Sanford & Sons 1838

(1840)

Bigelow Carpet Company 1849

Hartford Carpet Company 1854

Bigelow Carpet Company 1899

Hartford Carpet Corporation 1901

Bigelow-Hartford Carpet Company 1914

Bigelow-Sanford Carpet Company (Mass.) 1929

Bigelow-Sanford Carpet Company (Del.) 1951

ticularly in France and in the Low Countries the laborious process of fashioning and tying-in the carpeting tufts was cultivated, but more as an art than as an industry.

For five hundred years the making of carpets remained a skilled and restricted trade. Then, with the Industrial Revolution, first the British and thereafter the Americans lent their business genius to the creation of the modern system of carpet manufacture. The British, by putting carpet-making on a systematized, large-scale production (though still hand-operated) basis, converted an *objet d'art,* gracing the castles of the nobility, into a furnishing of upper-class homes. The Americans, by inventing and perfecting the power carpet loom, in turn transformed the luxury of the elite into the common necessity of all classes.

The American power loom with its cost-cutting advantages soon came to be used by other technically advanced countries. In France, Germany, and Canada, sizable industries developed behind protective tariff walls. In Britain the already established carpet industry was quick to see the cost advantages of power operation and, on converting to the new type of loom, continued to grow as the great world exporter of carpet products. The American carpet industry, with an output which came to be the largest in the world, sold almost exclusively to the home market. Meanwhile, the rise of a luxury market in America in the twentieth century has buttressed the hand-operated industry of the Middle East.

At the time the United States began to produce carpets, the basic styles and weaves of carpet-making had already been developed and perfected. Witness the fact that many weave patterns were named after European cities: brussels, axminster, wilton, and kidderminster. Subjected to American ingenuity these weaves were so greatly modified, however, in the effort to produce new effects, that it became impossible to describe them in a way that would be accurate for all times and all manufacturers. Nevertheless, in the interests of the lay reader, Chart II has been constructed to reduce, in so far as possible, the complexities of weave patterns to a simple schematic arrangement. Though not without defects, the chart should help to identify the leading weaves and the general relationship among them.

Historically, carpet weaves have been of three basic types: the flat ingrain weave with its smooth surface; the wire-formed pile weave with its loops either cut or uncut; and the loom-formed pile weave used in axminster carpetings. Generally speaking it is the type of fiber and the amount of fiber used per square inch that determines the relative price of machine-woven carpets. The now-obsolete ingrain was an inexpensive product compared with the wool-rich pile fabrics of axminster or wilton design. But the most expensive carpet of all is still the hand-woven, hand-knotted imported article known as the oriental rug.

CHART **II**

Basic Carpet Weaves in Four Periods of History, Arranged in Descending Order of Market Value per Yard, with Shaded Areas Indicating Market Dominance

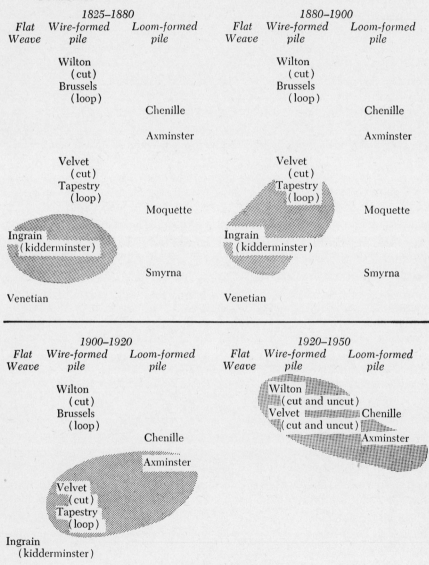

		1825–1880			1880–1900	
Flat Weave	*Wire-formed pile*	*Loom-formed pile*	*Flat Weave*	*Wire-formed pile*	*Loom-formed pile*
	Wilton (cut) Brussels (loop)			Wilton (cut) Brussels (loop)	
		Chenille			Chenille
		Axminster			Axminster
	Velvet (cut) Tapestry (loop)			Velvet (cut) Tapestry (loop)	
		Moquette			Moquette
Ingrain (kidderminster)			Ingrain (kidderminster)		
		Smyrna			Smyrna
Venetian			Venetian		

		1900–1920			1920–1950	
Flat Weave	*Wire-formed pile*	*Loom-formed pile*	*Flat Weave*	*Wire-formed pile*	*Loom-formed pile*
	Wilton (cut) Brussels (loop)			Wilton (cut and uncut) Velvet (cut and uncut)	Chenille
		Chenille			Axminster
		Axminster			
	Velvet (cut) Tapestry (loop)				
Ingrain (kidderminster)					

Gradually over the last century and a quarter, the mass demand for carpeting shifted upward as more and more Americans became able to afford the costlier weaves. This upward movement constantly left whole sections of the carpet industry equipped with obsolete machinery. Some companies replaced their machinery rapidly enough to stay solvent; others did not. Among the successful firms were those that ultimately formed Bigelow-Sanford, but even they had their vicissitudes.

From the beginning of the American carpet industry until after the Civil War, ingrain was virtually the only type of carpeting produced in this country. When Americans spoke of carpeting in the first half of the nineteenth century, they meant ingrain. For the rest of the century ingrain was able to retain a certain dominance, but during those years its position of leadership was seriously challenged by the slightly more expensive and considerably better-appearing fabrics. Axminster-type fabrics were slow to take hold, for the intricacy of the tying-in process defied mechanization for many years. With the turn of the century, however, axminster fabrics came into their own, and ingrain rapidly disappeared from carpet showrooms. For the decade and a half before World War I axminsters and moderately priced pile fabrics held the field. Then, with rising labor costs the pile fabrics with lower profit margins bowed out of the market struggle and left the competition to axministers and the higher-margin pile fabrics such as wiltons.

This constant upgrading of market demand during the last century naturally has had a profound effect on the structure of the carpet industry. Before the Civil War, when ingrain was the principle product, the industry had two geographical centers: Philadelphia with its small-scale handweavers working on the domestic putting-out system; and southern New England, with its large, power-driven mills at Lowell, Thompsonville, and Clinton. After the Civil War a number of medium-sized firms grew rapidly as specialized producers of pile carpetings. With the exception of M. J. Whittall Associates, Incorporated, of Worcester, these new companies were firms located in eastern New York State: Shuttleworth Brothers Company and McCleary, Wallin & Crouse (predecessors of the Mohawk Carpet Mills Incorporated); Firth Carpet Company; Alexander Smith Incorporated; E. S. Higgins Carpet Company; and Stephen Sanford & Sons.

The collapse of the ingrain market after the turn of the century wiped out a large segment of the highly specialized and inflexible Philadelphia industry. Then two decades later nearly all the rest of the Philadelphia industry, the part that had specialized in narrow seamed wilton fabrics, also disappeared as consumer demand shifted to broadloom carpets. Of the five largest firms today, only James Lees & Sons Company has a Philadelphia heritage, although some of the smaller ones, such as Magee Carpet Company, have prospered recently.

Among the southern New England firms an earlier effort to diversify the carpeting line was enough to cushion the loss of the ingrain business, but not enough to prevent declining profits. About the same time, moreover, severe internal strains within several of these companies brought on a series of management crises. It made no difference, apparently, what the corporate structure of the companies was; the problems of passing control from one generation of executives to the next occurred nonetheless. Some of the companies were corporations whose ownership was so widely spread that few of the stockholders participated in management. Others, while incorporated, were closely held and owner-managed. Still others were partnerships run by one or two men. The solution in each case proved to be a merger. All but one of the leading New England firms eventually became involved, as did two of those in New York State. Out of these mergers came a company with a fully diversified carpet line and the promise of greater organizational stability: the Bigelow-Sanford Carpet Company.

FOUNDING FACTORS

The Bigelow history, and with it the history of the carpet industry in the United States, may be said to have taken its start in the decade between 1825 and 1835. In that ten-year span well over a dozen carpet concerns of substantial size made their bow, including three of the predecessors of Bigelow-Sanford: the Tariff Manufacturing Company, the Lowell Manufacturing Company, and the Thompsonville Carpet Manufacturing Company.

Among the many factors which made that decade so favorable to the establishment of American carpet companies, the market demand was clearly the catalytic agent. In colonial dwellings the homemade rug had been a prized possession, but it was by no means a universal floor covering. Those who could afford to, imported carpeting from England. By the early part of the nineteenth century several decades of European warfare had helped to build up a moneyed class in this country—a class which bought not only the amenities of life but the luxuries as well.

After the War of 1812—and contrary to the postwar conditions of our own time—the backlog of consumer demand was immediately supplied by a plethora of manufactured goods, including carpets, which Great Britain shipped to the American market. This oversupply was a temporary phenomenon, however. The continuing development of the American continent provided the basis of an expanding and wealthier nation, and growing urbanization increased the number of style-conscious families in the country. Between 1790 and 1850 the percentage of population living in towns tripled. Most of the city dwellers were concentrated in the Northeast, but transportation improvements constantly extended the westward limits of the market.

To supply this market, foreign manufacturers, mainly British, were sending in a half-million yards of carpeting annually by 1825. American businessmen searching for profits were unlikely to leave such a field long uncultivated. Besides, many new projects which were being undertaken in the woolen industry at that time created an interest in manufacturing wool carpets and also led to improvements in the wool machinery used in such preparatory processes as spinning.

Even more immediately important, the tariff of 1824, while permitting the burden on imported raw wool to remain at 15 per cent, nearly doubled the duty on imported carpets by increasing it to 25 cents a yard. Then, four years later, the Tariff of Abominations, while increasing slightly the cost of imported carpet wools, nearly doubled again the duty on carpets themselves.

Whatever the real or psychological advantages of protection, the year 1824 seems to have been a turning point. Within a twelvemonth Alexander Wright of the future Lowell company and the three partners of the future Tariff Manufacturing Company had decided to enter the carpet business. With them the American carpet industry made its permanent start.

BEGINNING OF THE LOWELL MANUFACTURING COMPANY

During the formative years of the American carpet industry, the out-standing name was Lowell.[1] For years the Lowell Manufacturing Company was the largest and best-known producer of American carpetings. It was especially famous for the "high standing, socially and in a business point of view," of its projectors, for the Lowell company was created by that distinguished group of Boston merchants whose capital and energies were to make New England the textile center of the United States. Moreover, the Lowell mill produced goods of such "high character" that they became the standard of excellence by which the output of other American carpet mills was rated. Most important of all, however, it was at Lowell that the first significant innovations in the American carpet industry oc-curred, innovations which were to reduce the costs and increase the ca-pacity of production in this country to a point where few imported carpets could compete.

True to the pattern of the New England textile industry during the era of the Industrial Revolution, the Lowell company represented the coming together in fruitful union of the wealthy merchant and the talented me-chanic. The merchant in this case was Frederick Cabot, member of a famed and wealthy Boston family; the mechanic, a Scottish immigrant, was Alexander Wright, nephew and namesake of the American ornithologist, Alexander Wilson. Cabot was the financial backer and general administrator; Wright was the man with new ideas.

Wright's decision to manufacture carpets was taken in 1825, at a time when he was manufacturing coach lace in Medway, Massachusetts, a small village southwest of Boston. His desire to take up carpet-making was probably influenced by the fact that many of his kin in the old country were carpet weavers. Going abroad in 1826 he obtained, with the aid of these relatives, three looms and some twenty workmen, including Peter Lawson, John Turnbull, and two cousins of the Wright family, William and Claude Wilson.

Despite a shipwreck, Wright succeeded in getting men and equipment back to this country and soon he had a mill in operation on Chicken Brook in Medway. This first establishment suffered a fate common among early New England mills; it burned down. The looms, however, were salvaged and were soon operating again with the aid of capital provided by a new partner, Henry Burdett, a Boston hardware merchant. For $2,900 Burdett acquired a nearby woolen mill to which the partners added a single-story building, 60 by 18 feet, with a basement into which the hand looms were put.[2] Shortly thereafter, in September, 1827, an advertisement appeared for Medway carpets, inviting purchasers and others who took an interest in the success of American manufactures to examine the carpets to see for themselves that they were "equal in every respect, if not superior to the best [English] kidderminster carpetings."[3]

But Wright and his workers had scarcely settled down when Burdett withdrew from the venture. The reason for this sudden withdrawal can only be surmised. Indications are that the factory at Medway, while technically successful, was not profitable. To make it so required more ample financing than Burdett was able or willing to give and more extensive power than the Chicken Brook could afford.

It was at this time that Frederick Cabot became interested in the project. Believing he could solve the money and power difficulties by interesting his Boston associates in the project and by moving the equipment of the carpet mill to the excellent water-power site which he and his friends were developing at Lowell, Cabot bought Burdett's interest for $12,000.[4] Inherent in Cabot's investment was a conviction that carpet manufacture could be carried on in this country in competition with the imported products of England and Scotland.

Born in 1786, Frederick Cabot had started his career in the British and Far Eastern trades.[5] After the War of 1812 he had specialized as a commission merchant, importing carpets and wool among other things. After several other partnerships, he had joined with William Whitney and with his cousin and brother-in-law, Richard Clarke Cabot, in July, 1825, to form Whitney, Cabot & Company. Early in 1826 the firm appeared as agent for the Elliot Manufacturing Company, a cotton textile concern which Frederick had organized in 1823 in association with, among others, his cousin, Samuel Cabot, and of which Frederick was treasurer.[6]

Closely associated with Cabot in the purchase of the Medway mill was Patrick Tracy Jackson, a former merchant in the India trade. Jackson had joined his brother-in-law, Francis Cabot Lowell, in 1813, to establish at Waltham, Massachusetts, the famous Boston Manufacturing Company, the first American cotton textile factory to have all the processes in one plant. Enthusiastic about the possibilities of Lowell, Jackson resigned as treasurer of the pioneering Waltham firm in 1827 and in September purchased the land for a new concern at Lowell.

For this new undertaking Jackson wished to select a product which would not compete with any of those of the other Lowell corporations in which he had interests.[7] With this in mind he and Cabot purchased Wright's carpet enterprise, stipulating that they were to receive not only the plant and equipment but the services of the skilled workmen as well.

Having acquired the property, Cabot and Jackson turned to their relatives and close friends among the leading mercantile capitalists of Boston and the North Shore to procure additional funds. Thomas H. Perkins and his brother James, the Thorndikes, father and son, Thomas Lee, Jr., George W. Lyman, and the partnership of Bryant & Sturgis joined Whitney, Cabot & Company and Patrick Tracy Jackson in subscribing $30,000 each to the new venture. Jackson's two brothers, James and Charles, completed the list with pledges of $15,000 each.[8]

Before actually launching the firm the subscribers reached an agreement covering the scope and management of the business. Concluding that the carpet business alone would require so little capital that the resulting profit would not afford a "sufficient Compensation to persons possessing the requisite talents to conduct the affairs of the Company," they decided to manufacture coarse cotton goods also and appointed Whitney, Cabot & Company to run the concern. Because of Frederick Cabot's connections with the Elliot Manufacturing Company, the machinery for the cotton branch of the business was ordered from the machine shop maintained by that firm.[9] Machinery for the manufacture of carpets was, of course, to be moved up from Medway.

With the major decisions made, Frederick Cabot, William Whitney, and Richard C. Cabot secured a special act of incorporation from the Massachusetts legislature on February 4, 1828, and by the end of the month the Lowell Manufacturing Company was organized with a capital stock of 300 shares of $1,000 each. At the first meeting the owners elected Frederick Cabot treasurer, Richard Cabot clerk, and William Sturgis, Patrick Tracy Jackson, George W. Lyman, and Israel Thorndike, Jr., directors, the treasurer being a director ex-officio.[10] To complete their business,

they voted to reimburse Jackson and Cabot for previous expenses at cost
plus interest. The next day the directors chose Sturgis as president, voted
an assessment of $150 on each $1,000 share, and appointed a committee to
effect a management arrangement with Whitney, Cabot & Company.

Terms were soon settled. In the five-year contract signed on March 1,
Whitney, Cabot & Company agreed to superintend the affairs of the
Lowell Manufacturing Company as its agent. In addition to erecting the
buildings, procuring the machinery, and hiring the personnel, Whitney,
Cabot was responsible for purchasing and selling—for all of which the
manufacturing concern paid at the rate of $2,500 a year for the first 18
months and thereafter 2 per cent on all sales, not to exceed $6,500 a year.[11]

Immediately Frederick Cabot went to work. On March 15, 1828, he
bought from the Proprietors of Locks & Canals in Lowell one and one-
eighth mill privileges at the Middle Falls for $10,503 and an annual
rental.[12] Soon the main building—four stories high and 200 feet long—was
under way. By the end of the year the agent had expended some $63,000
on real estate and buildings and $58,000 on cotton machinery,[13] a very
creditable achievement and one which surpassed that of the other corporations of Lowell of the same period.[14]

During most of that year the factory at Medway was kept in operation
under the supervision of Alexander Wright with Whitney, Cabot & Company supplying the wool yarns and dyestuffs and handling sales of $9,996
worth of ingrain and brussels carpeting and finger rugs.[15] By the end of
the year carpet machinery and supplies worth $34,000 had been trans-
ferred to the building at Lowell—the spinning equipment was abandoned
—and the workers were settled in new quarters. Thus, in his first report to
the stockholders on January 7, 1829, Cabot could announce that the preliminary tasks were completed and that the factory was ready to proceed
in what was hoped would be a profitable venture. Beginning as a small
operation, strong in production, but weak in finance and without market
connections, Alexander Wright's enterprise, through the misfortune of fire
and shortage of funds, had been thrown into the rushing development of
New England's first great textile center where capital was plentiful and
skills in marketing highly developed. But for this turn of destiny the Medway mill would almost certainly have ended in bankruptcy and important
pioneering work in the carpet industry would have been done at some
other place and perhaps at a considerably later time.

MANAGERS OF THE LOWELL MILL: 1829–1852

The management responsibilities of the Lowell Manufacturing Company were laid out in the bylaws adopted by the stockholders at the first
meeting. Under these rules the powers of the stockholders were limited
to control of the capital structure, amendment of the bylaws, and election

Erastus Brigham Bigelow (1814–1879); one of America's outstanding inventors of 19th century; revolutionized carpet industry by inventing first loom to weave carpets by power

Bigelow's Loom; an improved model of the inventor's ingrain loom; patented in 1846; now on display at Smithsonian Institution

of the directors, clerk, and treasurer. Since the original stockholders had many other interests and since the dispersion of holdings soon began, owner influence on the actual conduct of the business was sporadic at best, at least as registered through official channels.

In the directors resided the "general control" of the company, a control which consisted mainly of broad policy formulation, since nearly all the routine work was delegated to the officers. Throughout the period the board was dominated by Boston merchants. At the end of the period the seven members were: George W. Lyman; the incumbent treasurer, Israel Whitney; the lawyer, William H. Gardiner; the merchants, Samuel Cabot and William Appleton; the industrialist, William Amory; and the merchant-manufacturer, Samuel Lawrence. Gardiner and Cabot were sons-in-law of Thomas Perkins.

The president, selected by the directors, was merely a figurehead, a presiding officer. In the northern New England tradition the real executive officer of the Lowell Manufacturing Company was the treasurer. The actual delineation of executive duties was complicated in the first two years by the fact that an outside agency, Whitney, Cabot & Company, had a contract to manage the firm. This was but a temporary expedient and in reality the situation was simple enough. Frederick Cabot, whether viewed as Lowell's treasurer or as the interested partner of Whitney, Cabot, was the chief executive. Because of his dual role, however, his responsibilities at first were greater than those of succeeding treasurers. During his tenure practically all the company's operational and supervisory functions were heaped upon his shoulders, since he served as the mill's builder, buyer, salesman, and what we today would call vice-president in charge of manufacturing. In addition he also served as the financial head.

For reasons not now known, Cabot's term as treasurer lasted only three years. It may be that the brevity of his tenure was somehow connected with personal financial difficulties, for in 1829 the partnership of Whitney, Cabot & Company was dissolved and Cabot was granted a $15,000 loan from the Lowell company, with his Lowell stock as collateral. At that time his duties changed considerably. Since he had been unable previously to find a person "fit for the charge" of the mill, he moved to Lowell, taking over the "agency" directly. The change in headquarters forced him to give up the functions of purchasing and selling which could be done more efficiently in Boston. Therefore these tasks, which had been associated with the office of treasurer, were temporarily handled by Patrick Tracy Jackson.[16] Under these conditions, financial and functional, it is easy to imagine that Cabot's continuation as treasurer was not looked upon with enthusiasm by the other stockholders. On April 8, 1831, when he asked the board of directors for instructions on certain additions and alterations in the mills, the board designated George Williams Lyman to help him. A

little over a month later Frederick Cabot, founder and organizer of the
Lowell Manufacturing Company, stepped out.[17]

On July 11, 1831, the board elected Lyman as Cabot's successor. As
the only director to serve continuously from 1828 to 1852, as treasurer from
1831 to 1841, and later as president of the firm, Lyman was to exercise more
influence than any other single person in the first half century of the company's existence. His father, son of a Maine clergyman, had prospered in
trade with the Northwest Coast and Canton. Educated at Harvard, George
had been a partner of his father and brother, but after 1824 he had put
his money and his time into textile projects, first at Lowell and later in
Lawrence and Holyoke. In character he had more than his share of reserve. To his business responsibilities he brought great imagination and
daring as well as prosaic hardheadedness.[18]

Under Lyman the office of treasurer took on the duties which it was
to retain, with minor exceptions, for the remainder of the life of the corporation. In addition to exercising general control over policy and its execution, the treasurer was directly responsible for purchasing and financing.
The supervision of manufacturing and sales was delegated to others.

After Lyman's resignation in 1841 the treasurer was not typically an
important stockholder. Of the three men who followed Lyman in the next
seven years—Nathan W. Appleton, William C. Appleton, and J. Thomas
Stevenson—none can be said to have left a strong imprint on the business.
The next treasurer of note was Captain Israel Whitney, who commenced
his long term in office in January, 1848. Already Whitney was old in the
service of Boston capitalists. Though just before coming to the Lowell
company he had briefly engaged in the Calcutta and Canton trades on his
own account, for most of his life he had been employed as an agent by
the Boston financiers, either in trade or in manufacturing operations.
While no great changes occurred in the nature of the treasurer's job, the
size of the firm increased rapidly, and in recognition of this the board
raised the treasurer's salary to $5,000.[19]

While the capitalists of Boston concerned themselves with finance and
general policy, Alexander Wright continued to serve as production manager. His responsibilities grew greatly under George Lyman who, after
1832, put him in charge of the cotton mill as well as the carpet mill. His
twenty-four years as head of manufacturing and his manifest ability made
him a vital architect in the building of the corporation's success. Wright
displayed both imaginative and practical talent. He saw opportunities and
translated them into realities. One goal reached, he did not rest on his oars,
but rather sought others. Gifted with both administrative and technical
proficiency, he was outstanding in three roles: initiator, adapter, and
organizer.

This then was the administrative team which gave life to the chartered corporation: a not uncommon team of men skilled in management, mechanics, and mercantile affairs. Among the Boston policy makers, George Lyman was the outstanding figure, not only because of his long service but because he was the driving force behind the two major policy decisions: in the early 1830's he favored continuing and expanding the carpet business, and at the end of the decade he sponsored the introduction of the power loom. Wright's role was equally significant. Indeed because of his importance, initially in the founding of the carpet branch of the business and later in the revolutionizing of manufacturing through his successful adaptation of the Bigelow power loom, the first period in the history of the Lowell Manufacturing Company may logically be limited to the span of his service.

THE PRODUCT AND THE POWER LOOM

The first decisions incumbent on Wright and his Boston employers were those pertaining to the product. The crucial nature of product determination is vividly illustrated in the case of the Lowell Manufacturing Company, since the Boston capitalists had plans for a corporation before they had a product. Even after the decision to go into carpets was reached, there was still the question of type. Among the possibilities were ingrains, venetians, brussels, wiltons, and axminsters.

Ingrain carpeting, a cheap construction with some durability, substance, and firmness, supplied the mass market of that time, and indeed for the rest of the century. It was composed of two or three webs—or layers of material—each of which had a worsted warp and a woolen weft. The warp provided the body; the weft carried the colors.[20] These two or three webs were bound into one compact fabric by a process of interweaving, which at the same time produced the design.[21] Thirty-six inches was the standard width. Venetian carpetings, strictly of two-ply texture, were cheaper still, but, since in venetian the warp carried the colors, fewer designs were possible, and so they were less popular.[22]

The other possible selections, brussels, wilton, and axminster, were known as pile fabrics. More expensive to manufacture, requiring more skilled labor, they were also more vulnerable to foreign competition. Brussels had from three to six alternate warps of worsted, or frames as they were called, only one of which appeared on the surface at any one time. In weaving, as each warp appeared at the top surface it was formed into loops over thin wires, temporarily inserted during the process. The wilton technique was similar, except that the surface loops were cut by a sharpened edge as the wires were withdrawn. Axminster was tufted fabric requiring a great deal of hand labor. All three were made 27 inches wide, or three-quarters of a yard, hence the name "three-quarter goods." [23]

With these possibilities the Lowell management, in order to take advantage of the large-volume market, selected ingrain as the primary carpet product, although it did turn out some brussels and venetian. In the cotton branch of the business, in which the larger part of the capital was invested in the early years, osnaburgs, coarse cloth for which there was little domestic competition, were selected.[24]

To turn out these fabrics, the original four-story mill was soon supplemented by a dyehouse, drying shed, storeroom, and countinghouse or office. The cotton machinery from the Elliot company was undoubtedly the standard equipment of the day. The fifty-odd carpet looms brought from Medway were essentially a heavier version of the ordinary hand-operated textile loom. With their jacquard attachments, harnesses, and other appurtenances, they cost about $80 or $90.[25] Though Claude Wilson, one of Wright's cousins, adapted the jacquard for the looms of the Lowell company by simplifying the construction and making it more reliable,[26] this first carpet equipment was truly foreign in its conception.[27]

Late in 1830 the first additions to the original equipment were made. The board voted to acquire six brussels looms, four venetian looms, and one three-ply loom as well as some more cotton machinery. Mindful of the fire at Medway, the agent purchased a fire engine, but the requirements of the Proprietors of the Locks & Canals, which specified that all buildings above ten feet high had to be of stone or brick with roofs of slate,[28] reduced the hazards considerably. In contrast to many other carpet concerns, the Lowell firm never experienced a major conflagration.

In the next year came a re-evaluation of the company's carpet business. It had not been immediately profitable and the directors considered abandoning it. After a survey a committee headed by Lyman reported favorably on Wright's operation, concluding that "In the Carpet Mill a good knowledge of the business and skill in its management has been acquired which may in future, if well directed, give good profits." To insure these profits the committee made two suggestions: first, that separate buildings be provided for the carpet works, these buildings to be large enough for turning out "more work . . . as greater economy would result in the details and general management."[29] Secondly, it proposed that the company undertake the manufacture of its own yarns. For the first few years, in contrast to the procedure at Medway, the factory had bought all its carpet yarns, including about 50,000 pounds of imported worsted warps;[30] but shipping distances and the difficulty of quality control had made such an arrangement unsatisfactory. To gain the advantages of an integrated process the directors voted to erect a spinning mill. Additional land and water power, equaling 2⅝ mill privileges, east of the original site, were also purchased for $21,341,[31] but the proposed carpet-weaving mill did not materialize at that time.

Following the rounding out of the enterprise in these early years, no construction work of major importance was undertaken or major product decision made until the 1840's; then the manufacture of brussels was temporarily abandoned, the power loom was installed, and to all intents and purposes the factory was rebuilt on an entirely different scale.

The successful introduction of a carpet loom driven by power was an epoch-making step for the company and for the whole industry. This achievement was the result of a high order of inventive genius.[32] But the contribution of businessmen was also important, for Wright and the Lowell capitalists, grasping the possibilities of a power-driven instrument, actively stimulated inventors and finally financed the project.

Why were these men so innovation-conscious? With the business under way, with so many other interests, why were they so aware of the need for improvements? It may have been that the carpet mill, though firmly established and prosperous, was not rendering adequate returns to satisfy the profit-conscious merchants of Boston. Possibly after their experience with other textiles, mechanization seemed a natural approach to the problem of greater profitability, offering as it did the possibilities of larger scale, and hence more economical, operation. Then too, the quest for power equipment was a natural reaction to high labor costs, especially in the carpet industry where it was necessary to rely on highly skilled and independent foreign hand weavers. Not only did the use of power stimulate the hope of using the less skilled, but it also promised the substitution of the more tractable female.

Finally there was the matter of foreign competition. The achievement of the twenties and thirties, that is, the establishment of a hand industry here in competition with the greater skill and lower costs of British labor, was remarkable. However, the fact remained that the British still dominated the market. While Lowell production was under 200,000 yards of carpeting a year, British imports during the thirties ranged as high as 1,300,000 yards and averaged about 660,000. Compounding the dissatisfaction of Lyman and Wright with their competitive position, were the low carpet prices during the long depression from 1837 to 1842.

On his first trip to Scotland in 1826, Alexander Wright had made "particular inquiries as to power looms." The replies he received told of forty years of failure, yet he continued the search for a machine that offered a chance for successful development, and in this effort he was encouraged by Jackson and Lyman. Later, in 1837 the Scotsman suggested to Erastus Brigham Bigelow, the inventor of a mechanized coach-lace loom, that he, Bigelow, turn his attention to the invention of a power loom for weaving carpets.[33]

This remarkable man, who was to make a contribution to the weaving of almost every type of fancy goods, was born on April 2, 1814, in West Boylston, Massachusetts. His father, a farmer in the summer and a wheelwright and chairmaker in the winter, eventually became owner of a small cotton factory. Though early in his youth Bigelow devised an improved method of making piping cord which was adopted by his father, his ambitions were not mechanical but medical. However, his ambitions were to be thwarted. Money was the problem. Following a brief interval with S. F. Morse & Company, commission merchants in Boston, he went on the road selling his own book on stenography. This proving unremunerative, he tried manufacturing, first twine and then cotton. Neither project was successful, but teaching penmanship in New York brought him sufficient funds for at least one year at school. On completion of this year, he turned to inventing to obtain more money. Though he was successful in producing a power model of a counterpane loom, his backers, Freeman, Cobb & Company, were temporarily pressed for funds and unable to continue with the project. Bigelow thereupon switched his attention to a power loom for the manufacture of coach lace, a fabric which was used as a trimming on upholstery in stage coaches. Within forty days after his preliminary discussions with Fairbanks, Loring & Company, the largest distributors of coach lace in the Boston area, he produced the power loom. Commenting on this and similar remarkable achievements, Bigelow said, "I find no difficulty in effecting that concentration of thought which is so necessary in pursuits like mine. . . ." In more detail he discussed his inventing process.[34]

My first step toward an invention has always been to get a clear idea of the object aimed at. I learn its requirements as a whole, and also as composed of separate parts. . . . I ascertain the character of the several motions required, and the relations which these must sustain to each other in order to effect a combined result. Secondly, I devise means to produce these motions; and thirdly, I combine these means, and reduce them to a state of harmonious cooperation. . . . To conduct . . . an invention through its last or practical stage, constitutes the chief labor.

Once the coach-lace loom was launched, Bigelow, as requested by the Lowell management, turned his attention to the ingrain loom. To succeed where others had failed, Bigelow had to solve five problems: (1) the mechanical interweaving of two or three plies, (2) the provision of an accurate take-up of the fabric, (3) the production of an even and firm selvage, (4) the fabrication of a smooth surface with figures of such uniform length as to match perfectly when the strips were sewed together, and (5) the handling of the numerous shuttle boxes.

Within a few weeks he submitted drawings of sufficient excellence for Lyman to order an experimental loom. After an inspection tour by the directors in April, 1840, the Lowell Manufacturing Company agreed to bear the expenses of further experiments and patenting, provided it was given exclusive rights to the new device. To maintain these rights the company had to give notice before July 1, 1841, that it would install the looms and then put in enough of them by July 1, 1842, to weave 400 yards a day and by July 1, 1843, 1,000 yards a day. Royalty payments to the inventor were set at 2 cents a yard, and until they reached $18 a week, Bigelow was to receive that amount as a salary.[35]

With Wright's help the work of improving and adapting went forward, but it was May, 1842, before patents were received.[36] The following month the directors appointed Lyman, William Appleton, and the treasurer as a committee to examine the looms and "to make enquiry concerning their utility for the purposes of this Company." [37] Though the loom was still too slow and could produce only the simplest patterns,[38] the committee recommended further investment. Despite the gloomy business outlook,[39] the directors agreed, and on October 8, 1842, authorized the construction of sufficient power machinery to produce the 1,000 yards of carpeting a day required by the agreement.

Work was soon under way on a small two-story brick building of fifty-loom capacity. On January 2, 1843, the Lowell mill contracted with the Amoskeag Manufacturing Company to have the machine shop of the latter concern build looms according to Bigelow's specifications. The first order was for 24 two-ply ingrain looms at from $200 to $400 each and 26 three-ply at $300 to $350. Since these machines were so specialized Lowell agreed to pay an additional $550 for making the wooden patterns.

The first looms were still imperfect and workmen in the Amoskeag machine shop had to aid Bigelow in ironing out the difficulties.[40] Alterations delayed the delivery of the first loom until December, 1843, and another eleven months elapsed before all the looms were in the factory. Changes also increased the cost, the final bill being $31,771, or $653 a loom. All told, expenditures on the buildings, machinery, and an additional mill privilege totaled $127,000.[41]

In the meantime, on April 4, 1843, the company had reached a new agreement with Bigelow whereby the inventor conveyed to it all ingrain patents granted or to be granted to him. The date for the production of 1,000 yards was set for October 1, 1846, and the royalty was reduced to 1½ cents per square yard—an amount based on the assumption that the output of a loom was 20 square yards a day of two-ply and 14 square yards of three-ply.[42]

The original power looms rapidly proved their worth. An initial reckoning estimated an operating profit of about $1,000 per loom for the first year, and savings on weaving of 6 cents a yard on two-ply and 12 cents on three-ply. This favorable outlook, in conjunction with generally improving business conditions, led to a consideration not only of expanding the ingrain production but also of installing some of the brussels power looms which Bigelow had also invented. After two committees had made careful reviews of the cost figures and estimates for future returns, the directors voted to increase ingrain capacity to 4,070 yards a day and to use the new brussels power loom to step up the output of that line to 500 yards a day, a program involving the addition of 150 ingrain and 50 brussels power looms. In more detail the plan, which Bigelow himself drew up for the concern, called for the following, including estimated cost: [43]

A new weaving mill	$ 50,000
A new spinning mill	30,000
Machinery	194,079
Shafting	15,000
Buildings for Pattern room, Cloth room & Counting room	6,000
Waterwheels	20,000
Boiler house & steam apparatus. The present mode of heating the mills & dyehouses requires a large number of fires on different parts of the premises. It is thought that a more economical & safe arrangement can be effected by erecting a building to contain all the boilers required for drying and warming the mills	35,000
Water pipes, Force pumps	10,000
Wool washing establishment	37,500
	$397,579

Upon getting approval of the stockholders at the annual meeting, the treasurer signed a contract with Bigelow whereby the latter agreed "to render his service . . . as the agent . . . in perfecting said plans and in superintending and directing the construction of building and machinery." In return he was to receive $5,000, plus office and traveling expenses.[44]

Preliminary to the actual construction was the job of filling the swampland and driving piles, a process which proved to be considerably more expensive than anticipated. To offset this unexpected cost the directors decided to forego the brussels expansion, explaining: [45]

The Company is entirely occupied in building and making the preparations for a large increase of two-ply carpet manufacture and to the extent which will more than use up all its capital. . . . If Brussels carpeting is made in the mill, a part of the two or three ply must be omitted.

.   .   .   .

It [Brussels] cannot now be considered so certain of sale as the two-ply, and the market for it may be more easily overstocked.

Thus the management again decided to stay with the mass market.

In December, 1846, with the foundations complete, another crisis arose when the recently reorganized Proprietors of Locks & Canals planned to raise the water level in the canals. A stern protest eliminated this threat, and the summer of 1847 saw bricks laid for the 138-by-281-foot two-story building, which had been designed by Bigelow especially for his power looms. The pillars were part of the framework of the looms and the floors were made as rigid as possible, to prevent any settling which might interfere with the action of shuttles.[46]

In the spring of 1847 certain machinery contracts were given to the Providence Machine Company and the Amoskeag Manufacturing Company on the basis of cost plus 25 per cent. These contracts authorized all expenses, covering material and labor and an equitable proportion of general expenses, such as the salaries of foremen, clerks, engineers, and watchmen, insurance on stock and tools, and fuel. The Providence concern promised to deliver twelve shuttle boxes on December 1, 1847, if it received the patterns four months in advance.[47] Amoskeag agreed to deliver the carders, combers, warpers, and quilling and spinning frames between October 1, 1848, and April 1, 1849.[48] Reuben Daniels of Woodstock, Vermont, supplied the wool pickers.[49] It was decided that the looms themselves should be built by the Lowell company in its own machine shop—a practical measure in view of continuing modifications.

Before all the contracts were fulfilled, however, the whole program was again up for reassessment. Expenses had been higher and business duller than anticipated. The first committee appointed to review the situation in January, 1849, reached no conclusion. The second admitted perplexity: [50]

They doubt not that Carpets can be made by the Lowell Company when in full operation for less than by hand looms or any other establishment in this country. They have reason to believe for less than can be imported. . . . [Bigelow] fully believes in the ultimate success of the business. Although he was mistaken in the cost, nothing has been done not essential to carrying out the enterprise.

Still the committee felt it had to reduce the number of new looms from 150 to 100.

Returning prosperity, accelerated by the California Gold Rush, eased general financial conditions. Late in 1850 with 102 new and 24 old looms turning out carpets, the directors concluded: [51]

It is indispensable to the profitable and economical manufacture of Carpets that the whole, or nearly the whole, of the machinery originally contemplated should be put into operation as soon as possible, thus enabling us to increase the production 50% without materially adding to the General expenses.

The treasurer considered this allowed him to install looms up to the original joint brussels and ingrain authorization of 200. Since by that time the loom had been standardized, the order for 35 three-ply and 35 two-ply looms with jacquard attachments was given to Amoskeag at a contract price of $500 a loom.[52]

By 1852 the fixed assets at Lowell had grown to $1,448,161 from $377,-

427 in 1845, the new carpet looms alone accounting for $219,446 of the increase. Other woolen and worsted machinery was listed at $171,809. Cotton and pantaloon machinery and repair tools brought the total machinery investment to $520,775. Buildings valued at $685,378 and land, water and steam power carried at $242,008, rounded out the fixed assets.[53] But more significant than this growth in the capacity of the mill had been the revolutionary effect of the first successful mechanization of the carpet-weaving process, a mechanization long actively sought by the management and brought to fruition through the genius of Erastus Brigham Bigelow.

RAW MATERIALS

Though the decisions on product and on the power loom were the most crucial in the early company history, the management also faced the many recurring problems that face any business operation. The purchasing of materials, the training and co-ordination of labor, the distribution of finished goods, and underlying all, the provision of adequate funds, repeatedly called for fresh considerations.

The procurement of raw materials was, except for a brief interval during the Cabot regime, the direct responsibility of the treasurer, though Wright took care of small local purchases. As the size of the establishment increased, and as carpets accounted for a larger proportion of the firm's output, the shrewd purchase of wool became vital. As the amount used by the concern grew from 3,500 pounds a week in the early thirties to 36,000 pounds in 1850,[54] the extent of a year's profit—or loss—rode on the careful analysis of conditions in the wool market.

In its dependence upon an imported commodity the carpet industry differed from the typical American business which used our own abundant domestic raw materials. Though Wright at one time hoped to use coarse western wools, such grades were never as remunerative to the American farmer as the better grades and therefore were left to be supplied by shepherds of harsher climates and more backward regions. Thus, in 1832 Lyman reported his sources of raw wool as Smyrna, South America, and the north of Europe. In the early years Smyrna wool predominated, but imports of the still cheaper Buenos Aires wool increased—its use perhaps aided by the introduction about 1850 of improved machinery for removing burrs.[55]

Though the source of supply was remote, the Lowell treasurers were fortunate in having a relatively well-established wool market in Boston.[56] This they supplemented with their own agents in South America and the Near East. A report of 1846 shows some of the difficulties which beset the treasurer: [57]

The Company had funds in South America, remitted for purchase of Wool, the shipment of which was prevented by the War in the Rio de la Plata. Voted

that the Treasurer instruct his Agent in South America to invest the funds remitted, in Wool, and to take measures to divide as much as possible the risk
upon the property until it can be shipped.

WORKMEN

The Lowell entrepreneurs had valued Wright's group of skilled Scotsmen even more highly than they had valued his machinery. And rightly
so, for on the know-how of the workers the business was built. Their existence not only eliminated the need for an immediate recruiting program
but gradually attracted other workers to Lowell. Even with these initial
advantages skilled workmen were always scarce—a factor which was duly
considered at the time of the adoption of the power loom.[58]

The installation of the power loom increased the proportion of women
in the carpet mill. In 1832, with 153 operatives in the carpet division,
the ratio of men to women had been four to one. The introduction of the
spinning processes first had altered this proportion, and in 1850, with the
program for the mechanization of the weaving process still incomplete,
women comprised about 47 per cent of the carpet workers. Total employment for the whole establishment grew from 443 in 1832 to 975 in 1850.[59]

Following the policy of other corporations in Lowell the company
assumed responsibility for establishing boardinghouses for the women,
who were recruited mainly from New England farms. It also took care of
its Scottish colony. The first detailed annual report in October, 1829, listed
ten cottages for the carpet-mill employees as well as ten houses for those
of the cotton mill. After this provision, the management evidently considered local facilities adequate, for during the expansion of the forties,
the mill investment in housing did not increase.

Along with the other concerns in town, the company contributed to
a library and the Mechanics Institute and in 1839 helped to establish the
Lowell Hospital Association. While this association did not offer free
medical services, the Lowell corporations agreed to take care of deficits
and to defray the expenses in cases where employees did not pay.[60]

On the lighter side, the executives associated with the operatives at
"blow-out frolics." Many of these were picnics or musicals organized by
the workers,[61] but in 1848 at the opening of the new Bigelow-designed
carpet mill, the management itself put on the biggest entertainment of the
period. On that occasion the huge weaving room of the new building was
lit by three or four hundred lamps. "When we first entered, a soft, sub-
duing influence fell upon us, for we were reminded of our childhood ideas
of heaven," wrote one guest.[62] Two bands entertained three or four thousand mill workers and their families, who ate their fill of corned beef,
cold ham, bread, cheese, pies, tarts, apples, oranges, and raisins.[63] A visitor
from Thompsonville, Connecticut, commented, "It seemed to me that old

Millers prophecy was actually fulfilled for they all seemed of one heart and one mind—such dancing I never expect to see again this side of Heaven." [64]

This new mill also represented the best in working conditions, with methods of drainage, lighting, and ventilation which excited great admiration.[65] A shift from gas to oil lighting in the mid-thirties and a reduction in the work week from 72 to 66 hours were the only other major changes in labor conditions during the period.[66]

While hours were declining, wage rates were fluctuating with the times. In 1832 Lyman had reported that men in the cotton mill were averaging 90 cents a day while those in the carpet branch were receiving $1.00. Women and boys were being paid $3.00 a week.[67] Business had been very bad in the mid-thirties, and the carpet company probably reduced wages along with the others. During the 1837–1843 depression the matter had been serious enough to be brought before the directors who declared in 1840 that it was "absolutely necessary from the present depressed prices of our manufactured goods that the wages of the operatives be reduced." Accordingly the agent was instructed to give notice that after payday in April wages would be lowered.[68]

By 1842, the first date for which there is any record of Lowell wage rates, the piece rates for hand-loom weaving of ingrain were approximately 10 cents a yard. Since 1842 was a year of deep depression, it is not surprising to find, in the two succeeding years, a return of piece rates to higher levels. By early 1844 weavers were earning from 20 to 50 per cent more per yard than in the worst of the depression.[69] But it is evident that the cut in piece rates, following the shift from hand to power weaving was drastic. From a level of 12 to 15 cents the piece rate per yard fell to 4 and 5 cents.

The first record of weekly wages dates from 1849. In that year weavers were receiving $5.00 or $6.00 a week, depending on whether they were women or men. The lowest paid employees of the mill were women helpers who received $3.00 a week; the highest—the overseer of the worsted yarn room—received $18.[70]

For wage earners, continuity of employment was as important as rates, but no estimate of the days worked is possible. Nevertheless it is clear that in 1842 and 1843 when business was very slow, the mills were shut down for a considerable period.

The task of co-ordinating the work of the men and women from Scotland, England, Ireland, and the New England hills, some of them skilled, some unskilled, some craft trained, all industrially ignorant, was the function of Alexander Wright, a few "staff" officials, and the line supervisory personnel. Among the staff officials were countinghouse personnel, designers, the head of the machine shop and a chemist. The latter, a specialist from abroad, was paid $2,000 a year to conduct tests on oiling, scouring, and dyeing. A French designer was also brought over on a five-year contract at $2,000 to $2,500 a year.[71] The head of the machine shop, Ezekial K. Davis, had helped Bigelow develop the power loom, transferring to Lowell when the power looms were installed. In 1841 Bigelow himself was hired on an advisory basis by all the Lowell cotton mills to install methods which he had observed on a trip to Great Britain.[72]

The overseers came primarily from two sources: those in the cotton mill were usually New Englanders, while those in the carpet mill were typically from Scotland. Turnover was high in both divisions. Some of the replacements came from outside the mill; others, including one William Murkland, came up from the ranks.

Murkland has left a description of his duties at various stages. Coming to this country at the age of twenty-one after training in Scotland as a weaver of fancy goods, he worked as a hand- and power-loom weaver for four years, as a section hand for a similar period, and as a second hand (assistant to the overseer) for three years before reaching the top post. His responsibilities as section hand consisted of keeping 16 to 19 looms in proper order, assisting the women loom tenders, and setting up or changing all designs. When he was overseer, besides his general supervisory functions he looked after the patterns, changing from one to another and arranging them so that each was applied to a suitable loom. He also kept the time and web books. The time books contained the records of employees paid by the day, while the web books recorded the number of webs produced by the weavers who were on piece rates.[73] Murkland was virtually supreme as far as dealings with his workers were concerned. Hiring, firing, and disciplinary action all were in his province.

With such a system the climate of each division depended upon the personality of the overseers. Some of Murkland's contemporaries in the Lowell company were tyrants, but they were dealing with undisciplined workers. In these years when the tightening control of the factory system was slowly being established, sparks flew as adjustments were gradually made. Management might seem arbitrary, labor might seem unreasonably fractious under a far looser rein than is now taken for granted, but both were moving across unmapped countryside.

THE MANUFACTURING PROCESS

Product determination, buildings, machinery, raw materials, and a labor force are all prerequisites to starting the production line. While the disciplining of labor under the factory system was largely a new field for management, the merchant capitalists of Boston had had long experience with general administrative and accounting methods which could be applied to the control of the manufacturing process. Twice a year Wright submitted statements on production costs. No complete record of these survive, but scattered references give some idea of the items included. Thus, the cost per pound of clean wool was computed from the pounds of wool used by the mill, the price per pound of the raw wool, and the cost of cleaning it.[74] Labor costs were recorded separately for each stage of the process. Other items included repairs—embracing both labor and materials —and such general expenses as those for freight, insurance, steam power, watchmen, outdoor labor (chiefly maintenance), oil, burlap, and the chemist's salary.[75]

The general expenses were usually allocated on a fixed ratio between the carpet and cotton mills, according to their percentage of the fixed investment. In a special plant study comparing weaving costs in the hand-loom, first power-loom, and second power-loom plants, interest at 8 per cent on the cost of the buildings and machinery was also included. Annual depreciation was not considered. Wright's successor explained the depreciation policy as follows: [76]

It is my purpose and practice to keep the machinery, fixtures, and buildings in such a state of repair as to have the depreciation as slight as possible. . . .
In making up the accounts at the close of each six months, there is no allowance made for depreciation in calculating the cost of the carpets. Whether this system . . . was adopted on account of the depreciation being so slight, I can not state. . . .

Of the actual steps in the process, designing came first. The designer was faced with two major problems: technical and aesthetic. The designs for ingrains required careful planning to eliminate any large spaces unoccupied by pattern, since such space made "pockets" between the plies which were not good for wearing purposes. Fortunately the tastes of the public were in line with these technical requirements; the large, floriated scroll designs were ideal for this weave because the many serrations in the leaf and flower motifs, requiring an interchange of colors, held the two layers of woven web firmly together.[77] In keeping with this happy concurrence of consumer demand and technical necessity, the patterns of Lowell's carpet designer, Peter Lawson, were composed of great blossoms with sweeping foliage, asymmetrically arranged. Even when some magazines in the early fifties were denouncing the unnaturalness of walking on flowers and were recommending formal geometric patterns,[78] Lawson continued in the old style, perhaps because he was catering to a middle-class market which was a trifle behind the latest trend.

Once the pattern was determined, the wool could begin its long process of transformation. Dirty and full of burrs, often shrinking 40 to 50 per cent,[79] raw wool required thorough "scouring" to produce good wearing and dyeing qualities. To overcome presumed European superiority in these matters, Wright worked continually on the cleaning problem and by 1839 had attained considerable success.[80] Still efforts did not slacken, for in 1850 Wright wrote, "I am at present experimenting, with a view to ascertain a better way of scouring Syrian wool than I have practiced heretofore," [81] and the chemist was ordered to learn what he could in Europe about the most advanced cleaning techniques.

After the washing and drying came the picking, carding, and spinning. The picker, composed of a spiked drum rotating at high speed in one direction while smaller spiked cylinders revolved more slowly in the other, untangled and blended the wool. From the attic where this was done, the wool dropped to the room below, where by 1845 some ten sets of cards were in operation.[82] There the long fibers used for the worsted warp were separated from the short, called noils, which were used for the filling. Most wool yielded too high a proportion of noils, so the surplus was used for linseys, or for a short period in the mid-forties for a "Union" superfine carpet. The roving from the cards was then fed into the spinner where, by drawing and twisting, it was made into the finished yarn.

In the critical dyeing operation, which followed, the skeins of yarn were moved by means of poles through open vats, filled with a hot solution of carefully weighed dyestuff. Next, the dyed yarn was wound onto bobbins and then onto the warp beam by a method improved by Bigelow. During the hand-loom days the weaver tied in the warp, drawing the ends until the right tension was achieved. A three-ply weaver was assisted in this operation by a treadboy or drawboy, but the others worked alone. Once the weaving had begun, the outcome depended on the accuracy of the weaver's eye and his sensitivity to the strain upon the yarn. If the weaver mismatched patterns by more than an inch, he was subject to a reduction in wages. On completion of the actual weaving process, he was responsible for several finishing operations, such as trimming the selvage and darning his own tangles.[83]

With the introduction of the power loom the assignment of duties changed. The girl who tended the loom did none of the preliminary or subsequent tasks. Small boys tied in the warps and section hands were responsible for technical aspects. As the fabric was woven it passed through to the floor below, and when the amount reached about 100 to 110 yards the cloth was gathered in irregular folds and tied with ropes to await the time when it would be drawn over a table for picking, darning, shearing, rolling and measuring.[84]

PRODUCT, SALES, AND FINANCIAL RETURN

The product of the Lowell factory was from the beginning well received, being aided to some extent by the generally good reputation of all textiles produced by the Boston capitalists. In 1837 the Committee at the Massachusetts Charitable Mechanic Association wrote, "The Superfine In-

grain Carpeting is all of good, and some of superior fabric, and of handsome fashionable colors and patterns." [85] Commenting for the first time
on power-loom samples in 1841, the committee declared, "They are firm,
heavy goods, well-woven, of bright and apparently fast colors, and of
good patterns." At the same time they said that the three-ply ingrain was
of superior quality, and excelled in fabric, colors, and style, any that the
committee had before seen manufactured in this country. This ingrain
was generally regarded as the equal of the best imported from Scotland.[86]

Total output of the Lowell Manufacturing Company in 1832 was 101,-
500 yards of ingrain, 7,500 yards of brussels and brussels rugs, and 1,500
tufted rugs.[87] After the first expansion project of the mid-forties the annual
capacity was 338,000 yards of ingrain and 2,080 rugs, the brussels line
having been eliminated.[88] The completion of the second expansion raised
this amount to 1,300,000 yards of ingrain in 1853. Shifts in imports illustrate the significance of this growth: in 1832 over a half-million yards of
ingrain were imported, in 1853 only 239,000. Thus in twenty years Lowell's
ratio jumped from one-fifth of the yardage imported to over five times
the imports. Meantime, however, the importation of better-grade fabrics
had shot up from just under 150,000 yards to over 800,000.[89]

With the finished product the task of the Lowell Manufacturing Company was over. Since the firm had no sales department, once the goods
were completed they passed into other hands for distribution. This sepa-
ration of the manufacturing function from selling was typical of the age,
an age in which the marketing mechanism, like the industrial system
which it served, was in a state of flux. The sedentary merchant, long the
chief figure in the economic order, was not capable of coping with the
ever-increasing output of the factories, and gradually, after a period of
dumping by auctions, the more specialized businessman selling on commission replaced him.

This specialized commission agent usually worked through a partnership. While the old sedentary merchants had correspondents or perhaps
an associated partnership in another city or cities, the new selling houses
gradually established branches as certain localities became known as the
center for marketing a particular type of product.

The nature of the product (carpeting in those days fell into the luxury
class), the customs inherited from the mercantile capitalists, and the current stage of industrial and distributional development all influenced the
marketing structure. The agents sold principally to wholesalers, making
no special effort to reach either the retailer or the consumer. They did
not even cultivate the wholesalers with any aggressiveness. They sent out
no traveling salesmen. They advertised only by displaying their wares at
industrial expositions or by running in newspapers small boxed announce-
ments which did little more than give the Lowell name and list the carpets

available, with perhaps reference to an award or citation won by a Lowell product.

These advertisements did, however, attract the "country" wholesalers who visited the leading textile marketing centers once or twice a year to select merchandise. Furthermore, since many of the selling houses handled the goods of several manufacturers producing a wide variety of fabrics, a large number of buyers were reached who might not otherwise have considered carrying carpets.

Once the wholesaler was within the gates he might order from patterns or he might select from the large stock on hand in the warehouse. With transportation slow and communication difficult, the stock-in-being in Boston and New York was important, and carpet warehouses, in contrast with the situation in most other textile lines, soon made their appearances in these centers.

Besides the routine handling of sales and advertising the sales agent had other duties, some of which approached the production side of the business. The selling firm eventually took over the responsibility for supervising the designing staff and on occasion advised on the over-all production level. In addition it took the credit risks, secured insurance, helped to determine selling prices and provided financial support.

While the first designers had worked right at the mill, as the pattern demands grew more rigorous, and as special artists were brought over from Europe, the design staff was finally moved to the New York branch of the selling house. On matters of output the sales agent was consulted most frequently in the depression years of the early forties when inventories began to pile up. It was in this period also that the management decided to pay the selling firm 1 per cent extra on sales for assuming the credit risks.[90]

Though the selling house never actually took ownership of the goods, it was an important factor in determining the selling price. On several occasions the directors ordered the treasurer to consult with the marketing men before setting the price level, and in some instances the marketers were evidently given a free hand since they wrote the company announcing the figures set. There is record of the average prices per yard charged by the Lowell concern for its various lines every six months from May, 1842. Despite the fact that 1842 was a depression year, the figures for that year, as shown in Table 1, are practically the highest of pre-Civil War days, illustrating the savings in costs brought about thereafter by the power loom and passed on to the ultimate consumer.

The importance of the selling agent in the supply of funds is highlighted by several incidents in these early years. In 1840 the treasurer of the carpet company was ordered "to draw on the selling Agents for payrolls and funds required in conducting his business,"[91] and later in the decade the terms for financial support were the crucial clauses in one agreement. Support might be in the form of advances for goods on hand, discounts on bills receivable, endorsements of company notes, or stock subscriptions. According to the terms of the 1849 agreement, the paper received for the sales was to be made payable to the treasurer and handed over to him, and in addition to an existing endorsement of $100,000 the

TABLE 1

LOWELL MANUFACTURING COMPANY

Average Net Prices of Ingrain per Yard   1842 to 1852

Six Months Ending	Fine Two-Ply	Superfine Two-Ply	Superfine Three-Ply
May 31, 1842	$.64	$.80	$1.23
November 30, 1843	.56	.66	.96
November 30, 1844	.65	.78	1.14
May 31, 1847	.60	.70	.90
May 31, 1848	.61	.74	.99
May 31, 1852	.55	.63	.83

Source: "Statement of Case and Evidence," *Application of Erastus B. Bigelow to the Commissioner of Patents for an Extension of His Letters-Patent, for Improvements in the Power-Loom for Weaving Ingrain Carpets* (Boston, 1860), pp. 255, 353.

selling house was to guarantee a like note for a three-year term and a $50,000 note for a shorter period.

After the dissolution of Whitney, Cabot & Company and the resignation of Frederick Cabot as treasurer of the Lowell mill, the selling account had been divided between J. W. Paige & Company and A. & A. Lawrence, with the former seemingly handling the larger volume of goods. The partners in both these houses, like Frederick Cabot, had had experience as sedentary merchants, importing primarily British goods, and then had successfully made the transition to the commission handling of domestic goods. Although Frederick Cabot was so closely associated with all phases of the company's management that it almost seemed as if the old sedentary merchant had integrated a step further in taking over the control of factory production, this situation was deceptive, as the position of the later agents proved. Their stock ownership was minor, they held no offices, and often they were not even represented on the board.

This lack of complete identity of interests was frequently a basis for friction; "reformers" of the early forties even asserted that the concern was being milked by the marketing firm. For this reason, but also as was natural in a time when distribution practices were undergoing rapid change, relations with the selling agents were constantly under observation and frequently up for a detailed review. During a crisis which arose in the early forties, from losses on bad debts during the depression,[92] the

Lowell management gave some consideration to establishing its own sales force, but upon a review of the situation it found that, if the treasurer had undertaken the task of selling all the goods, even without any increase in salary, the saving in relation to the company's sales volume would have been only ⅝ of 1 per cent semiannually, hardly enough to compensate for the risks of breaking with old and well-tried houses.[93] As a conciliatory measure, in August, 1843, the Lawrences offered several alternatives: [94]

a. To sell cottons for 1 per cent commission and carpets for 1¼ per cent.
b. To sell all for 1 per cent if the amount of all commissions reached $4,500 per annum, otherwise, charging 1½ per cent on carpets.
c. To charge 1 per cent on cottons and 1½ per cent on carpets, returning one-half of the amount of commissions on carpets exceeding $3,000.

Evidently the second proposition was accepted and the Lawrence house was made sole agent.

By 1847, however, the Lawrences discovered that the terms of the 1843 agreement were too burdensome. They suggested commissions of 1¼ per cent for cotton goods and 1½ per cent for carpets, but the directors voted that it was inexpedient to raise the commissions. It was another two years before a new agreement was reached. Then, in return for promises of large loans to ease the shortage of capital during the great expansion program, the carpet company agreed to pay a commission of 1 per cent on cottons and 1½ per cent on carpets and other woolens.[95]

Satisfaction with these new arrangements also was short-lived, and June, 1851, saw another directors' committee considering the "general disposition of the Company's goods." Perhaps the issue this time was the establishment of a branch in New York, for by the fifties New York had become the important center for the sale of carpetings,[96] an eminence due in large measure to the increasing market west of the Alleghenies. Whatever the bone of contention, a *modus vivendi* was reached and a Lawrence partner was ensconced in New York.

Despite such frequent discontents, the selling house played a vital role in the days of infant industry. With its trained and specialized personnel, with its wide contacts before modern methods of advertising were available, the selling house performed its tasks far more efficiently than a newly established manufacturing concern could have hoped to do—especially when the executives of these manufacturing firms had to cope not only with technical innovations but also with the problems of labor management and process organization entailed in the adoption of the factory system of production. Furthermore by enabling several relatively small production units (in terms of modern corporate size) to share in a single marketing organization, the institution of the selling house made the process of distribution much less expensive to each. Indeed it is questionable how much of a selling organization a $1,000,000 or $2,000,000 firm, with so many demands on its funds, could have financed—certainly not one which could compete with foreign importations over a wide market. Finally the selling agent provided financial support, primarily in the form of a loan of working capital, but to some extent, through stock purchase, in the form of long-term investments.

The sales agent, though important, was but one of many sources from which the funds for financing the business were obtained. Suppliers, company shareholders, Boston merchants with surplus cash, and banks, all contributed money for current operating requirements and for the acquisition of fixed assets.

Loans from the Massachusetts Hospital Life Insurance Company, an incipient investment trust in which many of the Lowell stockholders were interested, played an important role in the mill's pioneering years. The initial loan of $30,000 in 1832 grew to $100,000 by 1845 and by 1848 the original eighteen-month term had been lengthened to three years. Interest, which at first had been 5 per cent rose to 6 per cent after the panic of 1837.

Among the commercial banks, the Railroad Bank in Lowell allowed drafts by Wright up to $20,000 a month, and in 1848 the Merchants Bank in Boston advanced $150,000, due in eight, ten, and twelve months. In this instance the carpet company had to take $100,000 of the loan in United States 5 per cent scrip at par, payable June 30, 1853. Later in 1848 a committee of directors considered getting a large loan to help finance the expansion of capacity, but the responses from the money market were not encouraging. Reluctantly they were forced to advise an increase in capitalization.[97]

The proprietors, of course, supplied the major portion of the long-term funds. It was the general policy of the Boston entrepreneurs to keep one-third of the capital available for current operating expenses,[98] for which requirement the initial Lowell capitalization of $300,000 was inadequate. At first no steps were taken to rectify this situation and Lyman, Jackson and others temporarily advanced funds or, when they did not lend directly, endorsed notes of the corporation. In 1830, however, the directors sponsored a scheme to tap the resources of the other shareholders. Instead of immediately increasing the capitalization they decided to borrow from each stockholder an amount ranging up to 20 per cent of his interest in the company in the form of a twelve-month loan at 6 per cent. This loan was convertible if new stock was issued before the expiration date—a contingency which materialized in 1831. In 1836 additional capital was provided when $100,000 worth of stock was sold at auction. Three years later a $100,000 stock dividend brought the capitalization of the concern to $600,000.[99]

The first expansion program of the forties drew chiefly on accumulated earnings, but the second and bigger project, the heavy investment in

power weaving, forced the company to negotiate for large loans from
A. & A. Lawrence, as already related, and to seek new capital investment.
In February, 1846, the charter was amended to permit an additional
capital of $900,000 of which only $300,000 was offered immediately.
Though the subscription was payable 20 per cent in cash and the rest in
notes, the 300 shares were not all taken and the treasurer had to dispose
of some at auction. The next year when the treasurer reported that the
newly raised capital had already been spent and a like sum was needed,
the investors were even less willing to take shares. By the closing date
only 100 of the shares had been subscribed for at $1,000.[100] These subscrip-
tions were then canceled and the $300,000 was successfully raised by offer-
ing 400 shares at $750 each, in effect allowing participation in the venture
at a cut-rate price.

The demands for funds continued. In January, 1849, after their futile
attempt to negotiate a loan, the directors called for the remaining $300,000
and asked for authorization of a new maximum capitalization of $2,000,-
000. Though the stockholders voted to issue 600 new shares at $500 each,
payable in fifths over the next year, they balked at the proposal to increase
the capitalization beyond $1,500,000.[101] Apparently they were reluctant
or unable (since many other Lowell mills were expanding also) to contribute the additional capital themselves. Yet the public market for industrial shares was limited and in any event they did not wish to dilute their
own interest, at the low price necessary to attract new investors. Faced
with the prospect of insufficient capital, the officials tried to cut back
construction.

Two years later, in January, 1851, with improved business conditions,
a stronger appeal to the stockholders and a threat of no dividends elicited
the desired response. The capitalization was increased to the suggested
figure, but the additional $500,000 again had to be issued in $500 par
shares. Ten per cent of the subscription was payable in cash, the rest in
three notes due in one, two, and three years. With this flotation the capital structure of the Lowell Manufacturing Company reached a point of
stability. After trebling within a decade the stockholders' investment arrived at the figure from which it was not to depart for the remainder of
the life of the firm (see Appendix 1).[102]

A rough estimate of the changes in the financial condition of the company is shown in Table 2 under three headings: the initial years from
1831 to 1836, the depression years from 1837 to 1842, and the years of
expansion from 1843 to 1852. Further analysis might be made of two
points indicated in this table: the relation of profits to capitalization and
the relation of dividends to profits.

While on the average, annual profits were maintained and even slightly
increased over the three periods, they did not keep pace with the growing

investment and capitalization, as is shown in Table 3. From 1841 through 1843, the company lost money in three consecutive years, yet the only year in which dividend payments were passed was 1840. Dividends were relatively high. Even in poor years almost half the net profit was disbursed and in ordinary times the stockholders received around 85 per cent of the

TABLE 2

LOWELL MANUFACTURING COMPANY

Estimate of changes in Financial Structure

1831 to 1836, 1837 to 1842, and 1843 to 1852

	From 1831 to 1836	From 1837 to 1842	From 1843 to 1852
Total profits a	$300,000	$286,000	$ 576,000
New capital b	200,000		1,194,000
Total dividends	252,000	157,000	512,000
Additions to net working capital	235,000	96,000	115,000
Additions to plant	13,000	33,000	1,143,000

a Average annual profits: 1st period, $50,000; 2nd, $47,000; 3rd, $57,000.
b Stock dividend of $100,000 in 1839.

Source: Lowell Manufacturing Company, Directors' and Stockholders' minutes. Balance sheets for final years of this period are reproduced in Appendix 1.

TABLE 3

LOWELL MANUFACTURING COMPANY

Financial Returns   1831 to 1852

	Average Profit on Stated Capital a	Average Dividend on Stated Capital a
1831–1836	12 per cent	10 per cent
1837–1842	8 " "	4 " "
1843–1852	7 " "	5 " "

a Stated capital did not at any time exceed paid-in capital by more than 15 per cent.

Source: Lowell Manufacturing Company, Directors' and Stockholders' minutes, *passim*.

earnings. Generally it seems that the amount paid depended on the cash on hand.

Obviously the growth of the company did not depend on the profits returned. Indeed it is improbable that the concern could have undertaken the expensive power-loom expansion program from retained earnings, even if no dividends had been paid. Only in the early forties did the increase in facilities come out of profits; for the rest of the time the management procured additional funds from outside. In the early years of the firm's existence (1831 to 1836), a need for greater working capital was met by raising $200,000 in new capital, and during the years from 1843 to 1852 when the power loom was being introduced, more than a million dollars in new funds were brought into the venture, with some difficulties, to be sure, as would be expected in a financial undertaking of that magnitude.

On the surface it may seem strange that conservative Boston capitalists should have followed what today would be considered as a far from conservative dividend policy and should have relied so heavily on outside resources. Partly this policy may have been a carry-over of partnership mentality when profits were withdrawn in the present, yet a man's whole fortune was at the disposal of the business in the future. Undoubtedly the policy was predicated upon the availability of capital funds in the Boston area and on the readiness with which the Boston associates were able to find new money for investment. Such a situation allowed greater flexibility than if it had been necessary to rely on company earnings exclusively, but the availability of funds in the community was not without its competitive aspects. Many other corporations were making demands on the same moneyed group, and the more generous the dividends the more attractive Lowell stock must have appeared to new investors.

Despite these objectives the dividend rate was not comparable with that of some of the more important among other New England textile concerns.[103] By the end of the first twenty-five years, anyone who had acquired a $1,000 share in 1828 would have received a return of $1,770 in dividends (including the amount paid on the one-fifth of a new share distributed in 1839). The market value of this share-and-a-fifth would have fallen, meanwhile, to $570.[104] The net return would therefore have been an average of about 5½ per cent a year.

Though the Lowell stockholders had not received as much as those in some other firms, yet in the first years dividends had been adequate, and, with the introduction of more efficient methods of production, the owners of the Lowell mill could look forward to a period of greater profits. Quite apart from the financial return of the first quarter-century, the owners had accomplished much in the years from 1828 to 1852. Not merely had they established an institution, not merely had they put a complex organization into running order, but they had initiated a technological revolution. To their laurels as pioneers in starting the carpet industry on a large scale, they had added luster by leading in the shift from hand to machine methods. In so doing and in solving the difficult tasks of construction and financing, they had built on firm foundations. At the death of the founder, Alexander Wright, in 1852, they were well prepared to enjoy the prosperity of the next few years and to withstand the economic storms of the decades following the Civil War.

CHAPTER 2

PIONEERING AN INDUSTRY:

The Connecticut Companies, 1825–1854

In Connecticut as in Massachusetts businessmen were looking for new opportunities for investment. In the years following the War of 1812 Connecticut's declining trade in agricultural products with the West Indies and with metropolitan New York not only was forcing the merchants of that state to shift their funds but also was a factor in creating a surplus of population on the worn-out farms of the state. The Industrial Revolution provided an answer both for the merchant and for the excess rural population. The merchant, the farm boy with a mechanical or business bent, and the ordinary farm folk, urban-bound with their willing hands, combined their assets and jointly solved their problems by creating a new industrial society.

Among the new ventures were two carpet companies: the Tariff Manufacturing Company, the earliest ancestor of the present Bigelow-Sanford Carpet Company, and the Thompsonville Carpet Manufacturing Company. In many aspects the general development of these two companies followed that of the Lowell firm. Yet the sophisticated procedures and large resources of the Massachusetts enterprise were quite foreign to the small beginnings of the Connecticut companies. Principally because of this difference in origin, the Connecticut concerns had a character and a denouement quite at variance with that of the Lowell Manufacturing Company.

THE TARIFF MANUFACTURING COMPANY

The smaller of the two Connecticut companies was the one with its mill at Tariffville. In 1824 three Hartford businessmen decided to look into wool manufacturing, and from their interest this company sprang. By tracing its ancestry back through direct and collateral lines to this company, the Bigelow-Sanford Carpet Company may claim to be the oldest carpet company in the country today.

Of the three Hartford business men William H. Knight evidently was the experienced mechanic. Henry Leavitt Ellsworth, son of a Chief Justice of the United States, had studied law, but his "spirit of enterprise" had led him into important executive positions in many new ventures, including insurance companies, banks, and steamboat concerns.[1] Nathan Allen, the third member of the trio, was an important real-estate owner in Hartford[2] and in Tariffville, a community within the town of Simsbury, Connecticut. He had been using the power of the Farmington River at Tariffville to manufacture iron, wire, and cards for over a decade when, in 1824, and 1825, he bought additional property in the village, evidently with a specific project in mind.[3]

The nature of this project was soon revealed. On April 19, 1825, *The Connecticut Courant* reported, "The corner stone of the *'Tariff Woolen Factory'* . . . was laid on the 14th inst. in the presence of above an hundred spectators, and an elegant address was delivered by *William H. Knight, Esq.*"[4]

The four-story stone building, 85 by 46 feet, was designed for the manufacture of a hundred yards of superfine broadcloth per day. A charter received a month later by Ellsworth, Knight and Allen provided for a maximum capitalization of $300,000 with the right to begin operations as soon as $20,000, at $500 a share, was subscribed.[5] With the transfer of the properties held by Allen for $20,000 on May 24, 1825, the new corporation got under way.[6]

Though the first product was broadcloth, carpeting was soon added to the factory's line. The demand for this article was obvious, and raw material was available in the wool discarded from the broadcloth process.[7] On December 5, 1826, the *Boston Daily Advertiser* reported: [8]

We have just seen a piece of Carpeting woven at Tariffville . . . by which it appears that Carpets can be made there of any colours, and to any pattern, durable, cheap, and elegant. Colouring can be done as well in this country as in any other, and the weaving by this loom is of the right sort. The public will in a short time become acquainted with their carpets, and we only claim the credit of being the first to mention them.

Making broadcloth and carpets was not the sole object of the Tariff Manufacturing Company. The directors also had developed plans "to establish at this place every branch of Mechanical business."[9] To that end they bought several neighboring properties with manufacturing facilities[10] and tried to find someone who would take a lease on the machine shop which came with one of the acquisitions.

Such an ambitious scheme required money, and Boston capital soon supplemented, and then displaced, the local investment. From early 1828, if not before, Freeman, Cobb & Company of Boston had been selling Tariffville ingrain, and in the next year Nathaniel R. Cobb became treasurer of the Connecticut corporation. At the same time another Bostonian, Thomas Kendall, brother of the wool broker, Hugh Kendall, loaned the firm $20,000 on six notes running from six months to three years.

The new management, under the direction of Cobb, decided to concentrate on the manufacture of superfine and common ingrain. According to the McLane Report of 1832—a report to Congress on manufactures in the United States—the carpet factory produced an average of 114,000 yards of carpeting worth $120,000 annually from 237,000 pounds of wool worth $65,000. The output was sold principally in New York, Philadelphia, and Baltimore, though some goods were shipped to Boston and Hartford. About half was sold for cash, the rest on six months' credit. At that time the firm had a capital of $123,000, of which $80,000 was invested in real estate and equipment and $40,000 in materials. It had a total of 136 employees: 81 men, who were paid an average of $1.00 a day, 38 women at 35 cents, and 17 children at 25 cents.[11]

Despite this impressive start the next few years were to be full of trouble. In July, 1834, the treasurer sold the property to the Kendalls, who in turn disposed of it to Thomas Brewer of Boston and Elbridge Roberts of New York. These men, with Charles Roberts, a member of the firm of Freeman, Cobb & Company, formed a partnership, the New England Carpet Company, in 1836. Charles Roberts became the agent in Tariffville and John Turnbull of Lowell was employed to direct the manufacturing there.

Though the product was highly praised,[12] the partnership did not prosper. In August, 1837, the partners mortgaged the property to Hugh Kendall for his endorsement on some $74,115 of notes payable to Freeman, Cobb & Company. When the notes came due in 1838, the title passed to Kendall. Phelps, Beach & Company, of Hartford, which also had rights to the property because of credit extended to the firm, challenged Kendall's position and his disposition of the assets. After two years the court decided in favor of Kendall, who then promptly sold out in December, 1840, to George Beach and his son. Thereupon the Beaches and Orrin Thompson, who had bought a two-thirds interest, transferred the property on June 18, 1841, to a revived Tariff Manufacturing Company.[13]

Orrin Thompson already was interested in carpet manufacturing, having started in 1828 the Thompsonville Carpet Manufacturing Company in Enfield, Connecticut, a town on the Connecticut River, north of Hartford. As the Tariff Manufacturing Company came under his management also, its subsequent history, except for the introduction of a line of tweeds and jeans in the mid-forties, paralleled that of the Thompsonville Carpet Manufacturing Company.

THE THOMPSONVILLE CARPET MANUFACTURING COMPANY

The Thompsonville Carpet Manufacturing Company, which has contributed not only its traditions but also some of its buildings to the present Bigelow-Sanford plant in Thompsonville, Connecticut, was very much the creation of one man, Orrin Thompson. Like his contemporaries in the Lowell company, he was a merchant. Unlike them, he was a specialized carpet importer and wholesaler. Manifesting great energy and tenacity of purpose, exuding self-confidence and daring, he dominated his concern to an extent unparalleled by any owner of the Lowell company.[14]

Orrin Thompson was a partner in the New York carpet-importing firm of Andrews, Thompson & Company when he decided to become a carpet manufacturer. Born in Suffield, Connecticut, March 28, 1788, the son of a trader and successful land speculator, Thompson grew up across the Connecticut River in Enfield. After working as an apprentice in a store in Hartford and as a clerk in a manufacturing company in Jewett City, he established his own store in Enfield in 1814. His ambitions and abilities outstripping Enfield's possibilities, he went to New York in 1821 where he joined the firm of Austin & Andrews. Two years later he became a partner, having bought out Austin.[15] A third partner, James Elnathan Smith, spent most of his time in Europe selecting and forwarding carpeting and rugs to the New York house. Owing to his judicious selections and to Thompson's energy and tact, the house obtained its share of the growing market and increased its business fivefold within a few years.[16]

The existence of such a market obviously set Thompson to thinking about manufacturing carpets in this country. Perhaps the tariff of 1824 had some effect. Its increased duty on finished carpets may have persuaded the Scottish carpet manufacturers, Gregory, Thomson & Company, who were one of Thompson's large suppliers, to contribute their very essential capital and know-how to Thompson's scheme. Early in 1828 the Scottish house agreed to a project whereby the yarn would be manufactured in the old country and the weaving done in the United States.

Upon receiving approval of his plans, Thompson purchased a power site around a fall of 50 feet on Freshwater Brook in the town of Enfield, and commissioned a Massachusetts firm to build for $1,000 a stone dam 118 feet long, 14 feet high, and 15 feet thick at the bottom and 4 feet at the top.[17] The charter, which Orrin Thompson, his brother Henry, his brother-in-law, Sylvester Lusk, and David Andrews obtained from the Connecticut legislature in May, 1828, set the capitalization at $150,000 but allowed the owners to commence business once $30,000 was subscribed.[18]

Under the bylaws adopted at the organization meeting in November, 1828, stockholder participation was virtually limited to the election of the directors, who in turn chose the president, secretary, and treasurer. In this company the president was a more important figure than in the Lowell company, while the treasurer was also the agent superintending all the business of the company in Enfield. The corporate skeleton was given life with the election of the two Thompsons, Andrews, and Lusk as directors, Andrews as president, Lusk as secretary, and Henry Thompson as treasurer and agent at $300 a year. The fact that Orrin Thompson did not become one of the officers may be explained by his location in New York and his deference to Andrews as the senior partner. On the day of organization, land valued at $34,000 was deeded by the directors to the Thompsonville Carpet Manufacturing Company; and Andrews, Orrin Thompson, and James Elnathan Smith subscribed for a total of 71 shares of stock at $500 a share. On June 24, 1829, Gregory, Thomson & Company took ten shares.

Meanwhile Gregory, Thomson had sent over machinery. Included in this was spinning equipment for woolen yarn since the important decision had been made that splitting the processes would not be practicable. The Scottish manufacturers also helped supply workers, most of whom signed at an initial bonus of 6 pence sterling to work for the Thompsonville managers for two years at the same price they paid to "other Weavers in their employ, or the usual price paid in the country for Weaving," the money advanced for passage to be deducted in weekly installments.[19]

The harbingers of what was to be Thompsonville's famous Scottish colony arrived in the fall of 1828, long before the village or factory was ready to receive them. Boarded in taverns used by the river boatmen, they helped to complete the dam and worked on the houses known as Scotch Row and on the factory buildings. The most important of the latter, the White Mill, a three-story frame building built with the brook running through its basement, might have been mistaken for a New England church with its white paint, clerestory lighting for the attic and its cupola and bell. Sometime in the spring of 1829 it was completed. A second group of Scottish weavers arrived, spinners were acquired from the surrounding countryside and management and weavers conducted a survey of wages in other mills. In June or July the first piece of carpet was woven.

Though the business was under way and workers continued to come from Scotland, the path of the new enterprise was not smooth. As with the Lowell company, there soon arose debate over the question of abandoning the enterprise. In addition to the problem of profitability, the concern experienced internal difficulties. Robert Thomson, who had come to Thompsonville to represent the Scottish interests, retired from the management in 1831 after two dissension-wracked years. At the same time Orrin

Thompson and David Andrews agreed to buy out Lusk and other Enfield stockholders who were alarmed at the showing of the balance sheet.[20]

This increased burden had just been assumed when Andrews died, thrusting all business and financial responsibilities on Thompson. The New York mercantile partnership was reconstituted as Thompson & Company by taking in Thaddeus Phelps, a shipping merchant with experience and capital, and two young salesmen in the store.

This change did not affect the ownership of the manufacturing corporation to any great extent, since the new firm purchased the shares of the old, and Orrin Thompson took over Andrews' personal interest. Thompson and his partners likewise absorbed the shares of Gregory, Thomson & Company when it decided to sell out in 1835. Not until the mid-forties did new names begin to appear on the list of stockholders. Thompson and his associates still owned 61 per cent of the stock, but Henry W. and John H. Hicks, New York wool merchants, had 24 per cent and there were several other small holders. Thus matters stood until the fifties.

Major changes in ownership were reflected in the membership of the board and in the succession of officers. From the date of Lusk's leaving in 1831 until the year 1845, the directorate was comprised of Henry Thompson, Elizur Wolcott, the overseer of the carding department, and members of the New York partnership. In 1846 Henry Hicks was elected to the board, in 1849 William Wetmore, a New York iron merchant, and then in 1851, James Brown.

On the death of Andrews, Orrin Thompson had become president and George W. Martin, a Scotsman who had worked as bookkeeper in the New York store and later in Thompsonville, had filled the vacancy left when Lusk had resigned as secretary. Henry Thompson had continued as agent until 1847 when he resigned because of his disapproval of the program to install power looms. At that time Martin became the agent while Jabez Taylor, an elderly local politician, became treasurer.

THE INPUT: EQUIPMENT

The administrators at Thompsonville faced the same problems as their counterparts at Lowell in the continuing operation of the economic unit they had created. Decisions on product and equipment were made and made again. Purchasing, managing the labor, and co-ordinating an integrated manufacturing operation continually called for new evaluations, flexibility, and constructive action, however routine and repetitive the activities might seem. In their capacity as partners of Thompson & Company, Thompson and his associates received a fresh challenge with each shipment of carpeting to be marketed. And behind the whole operation, was the never-ending flow of funds.

To the men of the Thompsonville Carpet Manufacturing Company, unlike those of Lowell and Tariffville, the product was obvious. They were carpet marketers—integrating backwards. As such they had selected the article they knew and had decided to manufacture it alone—no osnaburgs, no broadcloth to hedge the risks. In contrast to most other carpet mills of the day, the Thompsonville factory would stand or fall on carpet profits.

To provide as broad a base as possible, the management selected in-grains, venetians, and rugs as their first offerings. Ingrain, however, throughout the entire history of the concern was the major product. About 1833 Thompson began to upgrade the line, introducing three-ply ingrain and a heavier two-ply, possibly for the first time in this country.[21] Early in the forties, Orrin's son, Henry G. Thompson, went to Great Britain to study the manufacture of brussels, and shortly thereafter the Thompson-ville mill began production of this type of pile fabric. Next came chenille rugs and axminsters. A price list in 1846 on the eve of mechanization car-ried the following items: [22]

Three-ply ingrain	Fine rugs
Fine venetian	Super rugs
Twilled venetian	Small rugs
Damask venetian	Chenille rugs
Superfine two-ply ingrain	Tuft matts
Brussels	Chenille matts
Axminster	

Each major decision to introduce or expand a product line had its concomitant undertaking in new buildings and equipment. The White Mill initially housed eight to ten looms on the upper floors and cards and jacks on the first two floors. Almost at once the Long Weave Shop was built, and the ingrain looms in the White Mill were replaced by venetian and rug looms. A machine and blacksmith shop, a shed covering three washtubs with a wooden platform for drying, a flour mill converted into a dyehouse, and a sixth building containing a baling room and storeroom completed the original layout. All told, this establishment had a capacity of 100 looms.[23]

The first major addition to this original layout was the "Black Mill," a four-story "brick and stone building . . . for carding, spinning and weav-ing," constructed on the lower water privileges in 1832 and 1833 in order to provide capacity for three-ply carpeting.[24] Shortly after this building was completed, the dyehouse went up in flames in June, 1834, despite a night watch, a fire engine, and the best efforts of the neighboring farmers summoned by the bell atop the White Mill.[25] To reduce such disasters to a minimum in the future, stockholders at the next meeting voted the money to set up a regular fire department, and soon many of the local citizenry were sporting new titles and new uniforms.

At the same meeting the stockholders surveyed the scene and according to a local historian [26] professed themselves satisfied. With the replacement of the dyehouse the company had all the buildings necessary to carry on the work and the owners felt that "Their heavy expenditures of money must cease, and, from this time forth, peace and prosperity must be the result of heretofore uphill work." [27]

The acquisition of the Tariffville factory by Thompson and his associates at the beginning of the forties precluded the necessity of augmenting ingrain capacity at Thompsonville, but the directors added a brussels shop with 41 looms. Thompson had been importing the small quantities of worsted yarn which he had needed, but with a brussels line and two factories he decided to spin his own worsted at Thompsonville. Henry G. Ellsworth, who owned patents on the desired machinery, was hired to supervise the construction of a worsted spinning mill and to provide the yarn on contract. In addition to his machinery, which was made by the Ames Manufacturing Company, Ellsworth introduced a Clark, Fairbanks & Company steam engine to supply power to the spindles. Two factors were behind this move. The limit of power afforded by Freshwater Brook had been reached, and the use of the exhaust steam in the dyehouse would eliminate the need for large quantities of wood for fuel.

The following inventory of buildings and machinery at Thompsonville gives a picture of what in 1846 was probably at the time the largest hand-loom carpet establishment in the country: [28]

Buildings with value:

Factory Number 1—White Mill—dam and water wheel	$ 7,500
Factory Number 2—Black Mill—dam and water wheel	13,000
Steam and worsted mill—three-story, brick	9,000
Long Weaving Shop—two story, 100 feet long	2,500
Baling and Weaving Shop—two-story frame	2,000
Old dye house—frame	300
New dye house	1,000
Brussels shop—three-story, brick	6,000
First sorting house—two-story, brick	1,200
Second sorting house	2,000
Large wool storage house—two-story, brick	3,000
Winding room and yarn room—two-story frame	1,500
Drying house—two-story, brick	800
Machine shop—two-story, brick	2,000
Blacksmith shop—one-story, brick	400
Venetian shop	1,200
Office	1,200
Four storehouses	9,000

Machinery with value:

50 three-ply looms at $250	12,500
78 superfine two-ply looms at $125	9,750
40 brussels looms at $250 [sic]	9,000
13 chenille looms at $25	325

6	broad chenille looms at $30	180
37	rug and venetian looms at $20	740
9	burring machines	2,700
4	wool pickers	825
12	sett carding machines	12,000
9	combing machines	2,600
13	spinning jacks at $250	3,250
9	spinning frames with 96 spindles each	6,912

All told, the assets reached about $400,000, a considerable investment to be endangered by competition arising from the Lowell company's decision to install power looms on a larger scale. How to counter this development was the critical problem in the history of the Thompsonville Carpet Manufacturing Company. In the exchange of opinions concerning this issue, Orrin Thompson's brother, Henry, the agent and treasurer, withdrew from the concern; he is reported to have said that "he was too old to undergo the labor, and was also opposed to the immense outlay which he saw would be required to carry on the work to completion." [29] Yet Orrin Thompson did not feel that his business could survive such a negative approach. He was not competing with the lower-quality and lower-priced ingrain produced in the Philadelphia area by the putting-out or domestic system; such cheap hand-woven ingrain was to continue to find a market for another forty years. After having gathered his working force into a central workshop, a factory, Thompson was turning out a better grade of fabric, the chief rival of which was the ingrain manufactured under similar conditions at the Lowell Manufacturing Company. Thus when the Lowell company cut costs and prices through the introduction of a power loom, Thompson, if he wanted to remain in business, had no alternative but to do likewise. While contemporary opinion attributed Thompson's move to either labor troubles or impending tariff reductions, in retrospect it seems apparent that he was forced into power production by the action of his competitor.

To meet the immediate threat from Lowell, Thompson cut wages 25 per cent in 1846.[30] Then began his search for a power loom. At first he pinned his hopes on the invention of a competing loom, but he was soon disabused of this notion by his experience with two would-be inventors. He thereupon went to Lowell in the summer of 1847 to inspect the Bigelow loom. Impressed with what he saw, he signed a contract on August 31, 1847, by which the Lowell Manufacturing Company sold to the Thompsonville Carpet Manufacturing Company the right to own and to use for weaving two- and three-ply ingrain carpeting, 125 to 150 power looms until August 18, 1860, with provision for additional extension of the patents. In return, Thompsonville was to pay a royalty of 2 cents a square yard on two-ply and 4 cents on three-ply. John Turnbull, Thompson's

Stephen Sanford (1826–1913) and Orrin Thompson (1788–1873); the men responsible for establishing at Amsterdam, New York, and Thompsonville, Connecticut, the two plants that served for many years as Bigelow-Sanford's principal manufacturing units

White Mill; original handloom mill at Thompsonville, Connecticut; built in 1829; torn down in 1902

Sanford Mill; crenelated building erected by Stephen Sanford in 1854 after second disastrous fire had destroyed earlier mill

uncle and agent at the Tariff Manufacturing Company, negotiated a similar agreement for that branch of Thompson's carpet-making enterprise.[31]

The machinery contracts called for delivery late in 1848, though the actual start waited on completion by the Lowell company of a new and improved model loom. William Mason of Taunton successfully bid for 50 of the looms at $500 each, plus 4 cents a pound for pillars and framework. The contract for 75 more looms and an order for carding and spinning equipment went to Amoskeag. The terms were cost plus 25 per cent, plus 7 per cent for delivery and setting up, and 3¼ cents a pound for castings.[32] An order for seven additional sets of cards at $1,000 and 10,000 power-loom bobbins at a penny apiece was assigned to John Boynton & Son of South Coventry, Connecticut.[33]

New machinery at Thompsonville, as at Lowell, meant new buildings, especially because the old wooden weave shop could not stand up under power looms. Even before the final terms were settled, plans were completed for a new brick mill, 330 feet long and 60 feet wide, with a 110-foot ell on the eastern end.[34] The building (which is still in use) had two stories except where the west end, because of the slope to the river, had three.[35]

Though the management had wasted no time in letting the contracts for looms, deliveries were slow. As late as November, 1850, over three years after the original power-loom contracts had been signed, production was on such a small scale that Thompsonville and Tariffville together had only paid $5,000 in royalties to the Lowell company. Such delays, though attributable to the constant modification of the loom, eventually brought a note of discord into what had been originally very happy relations between the Massachusetts and Connecticut firms.

When the architect of the new Thompsonville mill had visited Lowell in September, 1847, to study the construction of the iron beams, he had found the agent and overseers helpful; [36] a year later, a machinist, sent to Lowell by Martin to learn the business, had been welcomed by Wright but had found some of the underlings less cordial.[37] Subsequently Wright had sent some of his ablest men to Connecticut to aid in setting up the machinery. Furthermore, he had given Martin and Turnbull permission to hire Lowell employees. But this gesture of co-operation had boomeranged.

When several attempted arrangements fell through, Martin accused Wright of raising wages and otherwise privately discouraging the Lowell men from leaving. This imputation the Lowell agent bitterly denied. "I assure you, sir," wrote Alexander Wright, "I am now and from the commencement of our connexion in this business have been anxious to do everything in my power to facilitate and forward everything belonging to your concern for the reason that it is for the interest of the Lowell Company that I should do so." [38] As for Martin's complaints that the delivery of machinery was slow, Wright insisted that it was in the interest of the Thompsonville company that the machinery be as modern and the work as nearly perfect as possible, so that there would be no chance of failure. But George Martin, harassed by financial pressures, privately expressed the belief that Lowell management was purposely dilatory.

Tooling up was also more expensive than had been expected. The loom shown Thompson had cost $650; the improved model cost over $1,000. When the amounts laid out on the buildings and incidentals were included, Turnbull estimated the charge per loom at three times the original calculations. All told, machinery expenditures from July 1, 1848, to July 1, 1851, were $351,717. Mason, who had contracted to build looms at a fixed rate, suffered a $50,000 loss. The cost-plus agreement protected Amoskeag, leaving Orrin Thompson to strain his resources in order to meet the unexpected drain. By September, 1850, he had almost cleared up his indebtedness to Amoskeag with payments of about $150,000, but other accounts remained outstanding and the company's capital structure was overburdened.

On completion of this ambitious program the whole establishment at Thompsonville was carried on the books at over $600,000. An inventory of the property made about this time starts with the Old White Mill at the head of the street, with its dam, pickers, cards and jacks. Next to it were wool-washing and drying quarters. Down Main Street on the north side stood the new power-loom mill with 127 ingrain looms, 8 venetian looms, and shearing machines. Next door was the worsted mill with its cards and combs, pickers and twisters, and 20 brussels looms. Closely connected were two small structures for dyeing and winding, and further down on Main Street was the yarn storehouse. At the back of the lot was the chenille and brussels shop, the venetian shed, the warping and winding building, the machine and blacksmith shop, another carding and spinning mill, and a collection of small buildings for sorting and storage purposes. Across the street were the office, the dyehouse, and the Black Mill, in which the three-ply looms had been replaced with cards.

THE INPUT: RAW MATERIALS

As the establishment grew from its small beginnings in 1828 and 1829 to the sizable proportions of 1850 and 1851, as the hand looms were replaced by the more productive power models, the quantity of raw materials consumed rose to over $300,000 annually. Wool, as is shown in Table 4, was the largest item.

Andrews, Thompson & Company—and its successor, Thompson & Company—situated in the greatest market in the country, was responsible for procurement of these supplies. Following Orrin Thompson's policy, the mercantile house bought heavily during financial crises when prices were low, on the assumption that finished goods would be sold on a rising market, a procedure predicated upon good credit, and one which could result in considerable inventories.[39]

In the first agreement in 1829 the New York firm received a 1 per cent commission if it used the factory's credit for the purchases and

TABLE 4

THOMPSONVILLE CARPET MANUFACTURING COMPANY

Amount and Value of Raw Materials Used   1850

Material	Amount	Value
Wool	1,000,000 lbs.	$250,000
Dyestuffs	400,000 "	40,000
Linen yarn	48,000 "	10,000
Oil	11,000 gals.	7,000
Coal	2,500 tons	15,000
		$322,000

Source: Products of Industry, Original Returns of the Assistant Marshals in Connecticut, Seventh Census of the United States, in the Connecticut State Library at Hartford.

2½ per cent, if its own. These commissions were adequate for items acquired in this country, but additional compensation was necessary for buying wool overseas. To take care of such purchases the terms of the contract were modified in 1830. Andrews, Thompson & Company were given 2½ per cent for all purchases made by their resident partner in England, James Elnathan Smith. In addition they were reimbursed for any expenses in "paying W. & J. Brown & Co. for advancing payments for the same." [40]

Three years later the carpet company made more ambitious plans. The stockholders authorized Andrews, Thompson & Company "to send an agent to Smyrna or elsewhere on the Continent of Europe for the purpose of purchasing wool for the company and establishing a regular correspondence in that part of the World and that they be allowed for such services a commission of 5 per cent . . . should their agent succeed in finding wool that will give answer, and in case he can not find it the Company are to pay the traveling expenses." [41] Thus matters stood until 1844, when the terms of wool buying abroad were changed to 2½ per cent for the purchase and 2½ per cent for cash advance, an arrangement extended to domestic procurement in 1847. In addition the carpet company reimbursed Thompson & Company whenever the latter paid more than 7 per cent per annum for moneys for its account.

Though under these arrangements the New York partnership did purchase some of the wool for the carpet company abroad, most of the supply

came from dealers in Boston and New York. "Smyrna" was the variety
bought most frequently in the 1830's. A decade later "Cordova"—a type of
wool produced in several countries, the most important of which came to
be Argentina—was used in equal amounts. While the latter cost about the
same as Smyrna in 1840—9 cents a pound—it soon was much more expensive, selling for 18 cents by the end of the decade as compared with
Smyrna's 11 cents. However, the weight lost in cleaning Cordova was only
15 to 20 per cent, about one-half the loss on Smyrna.

The prices quoted above did not include freight from New York to
the factory. Raw materials were brought from New York to Hartford by
water. From there in the early years they went on to the mill either by
boat or cart, but by the end of the period they were transshipped by rail.
According to an 1849 agreement with a shipping firm, transportation by
water from New York to Hartford cost $1.90 a ton for wool, $1.65 a ton
for dyestuffs, and 43 cents a bale for cotton. For the last eighteen-mile
haul the Hartford and New Haven Railroad charged 95 cents a ton.

THE INPUT: LABOR

In the early years the Thompsonville mill used highly skilled imported
workers and less skilled workers drawn from the native labor supply.
Weavers, dyers, and machinists were typically Scotsmen, recruited with
the help of the Scottish firm, Gregory, Thomson & Company. For the spinning process, which was mechanized from the beginning and which had
less demanding requirements, Americans were used. Later in the forties,
when the worsted spinning mill was built, Englishmen were brought over,
and about this time the Irish began to drift in. In 1848, before the installation of the power loom, 65 per cent of the employees were English, Scottish, and Irish. Such figures, however, underestimate the importance of
these national groups since the first two at least tended to be concentrated
in the skilled operations.

The first Scots were especially influential. When they landed at Warehouse Point, they started a movement significant not only in company
history but for all American labor relations. More vital than sheer numbers
was the fact that they were first to arrive, that they were recruited from a
closely knit community or group of communities in the old country, and
that they retained an unusual cohesiveness. While Wright's Scottish weavers were, figuratively speaking, lost among the larger industrial population
at Lowell, in Thompsonville a host of men, women, and children moved
into a village where the total population—overwhelmingly Yankee in composition—did not exceed forty in number. Though today the restrained
Puritan and the dour Presbyterian might be considered two of a kind,
they were perhaps too much alike in inflexibility and seriousness and

shrewdness to gloss over their differences in custom and religious observ-
ances. An early bone of contention was the Scottish habit of merrymaking
on New Year's Day. Later the two groups clashed in politics inasmuch as
the old farming interests remained Democrats and free traders, while the
newcomers became Whigs. The breach was not narrowed when the Scots
hired a cannon from Springfield to celebrate the first victory of a protec-
tionist at the polls. The economic advantages of a growing market, however, softened the first bitterness, and by the mid-forties the community
had achieved a certain unity—from a Scottish point of view—whether from
amalgamation or domination is not clear.[42]

To such a people New England paternalism did not appeal. The corporation might provide the housing—an essential service in a new industrial development then as now—but the workers struck successfully in
1831 against an increase in board, and a decade later they were buying
their own homes. The corporation might extend helpful aid to the Presbyterian Church, the night school for treadboys, and the Odd Fellows, but,
for the rest, the employees would brook little interference. Orrin Thompson might be "greatly interested in the welfare and comfort of those in his
employ," [43] but the latter were quick to sense any condescension, and
gifts after the fashion of the lord of the manor were not well received.
When Thompson gave fine broadcloth to the men and silk to the women
for Christmas, the spirited workers returned it with the comment, "If ya
gae us our proper wages, we'll buy our own suits and dresses." [44]

The same independence was exercised by the Scots in their business
relations with their employers. Not only did the group have a skill monopoly, which in early years was in no danger of being overthrown, but
each individual weaver had his own, for no other could duplicate his
touch on an unfinished piece of goods. To bolster these advantages they
brought a tradition of unionism from the old country which abated not
one whit when they were thrown together in one factory in one small
town. The aim of these workers was as much financial return and as much
independence of action as possible. The objective of the management, directors, superintendent, and overseers, all of whom participated directly
in the formulation of labor policy, was more production and at as low
cost as possible.

With these purposes in the background, battle was joined on two main
fronts: wages and working conditions. Wages were a matter of great and
recurring importance, not only as to level but also because the Scots tried
to establish the principle of negotiation as a group. The original rates
were set after industry-wide surveys by both management and labor, but,
as new grades of carpet were manufactured, the company established rates
unilaterally, despite the protests of the weavers, thus providing one of the
issues in the great strike of 1833.

Under the first wage list weavers received 14½ cents a yard for super-fine and 10½ cents for fine ingrain.[45] Since a minimum production was about six yards a day and an average eight, the worker could earn from $4.00 to $7.00 a week—and this at a time when room and board cost $2.00. Records do not extend to annual earnings. The worker was subjected to periodic shutdowns, but a manufacturer who had gone to considerable effort to gather a skilled staff was reluctant to risk its dispersal by prolonged layoffs.

Equally as important as wage rates to labor-management peace was satisfaction with working conditions. And in this field, harmony was even more difficult to achieve. To the handworker, restraint was the aspect of the industrial system most strange and alarming. To the management, with little experience from the prefactory era upon which to draw, problems of discipline were crucial in attaining production. Attempts at control varied from prohibitions, to time pressures, to incentives. In the first category were bans on smoking, on reading newspapers, and on unauthorized absences of more than 15 minutes. Under the rules in the second class the workers were required to give a web's, or piece's, notice before leaving, and two consecutive failures to finish a piece within the prescribed time could result in dismissal. As to incentives, a system of fines and premiums was superimposed upon the piece-rate structure. Failure to weave a piece—90 yards—of fine carpeting in 12 days or superfine in 15 days cost the worker a shilling for each extra day. For completing a piece of fine in 10 days or superfine in 12, the weaver received a bonus of 50 cents. How effective these various rules were is not clear. The rule on absences was revoked after a strike. In 1832 the agent increased the fines, bringing on a wave of protest. According to one worker Henry Thompson frankly told the men "he wanted more work done, and he wished to know what means he could take to accomplish it." Equally frank was the reply, "When a man did not suit him he had always discharged him, and it was the only proper remedy," [46] a remedy equivalent in a tight labor market, to burning down the barn to get rid of the mice.

The outlook for the company did not improve in 1833. Money was tight in New York and the new tariff dropped rates on imported ingrain. Early in the year the agent stopped paying premiums. A few weeks later he refused to pay a weaver who had not given a web's notice. At a mass meeting he agreed to pay the worker, but before the meeting could be adjourned someone brought up the question of the rates on new goods. At the suggestion of Henry Thompson the men petitioned the board. "The introduction of new and fancy fabrics are alike beneficial to all the employed as well as the employer. But when there is additional labor, it is right the laborer should have remuneration for his extra work." [47] Rejecting the directors' pleas of inability to pay, the weavers demanded an increase in the three-ply rate from 29 to 30 cents a yard, in the superfine two-ply from 14½ to 15 cents, and in the fine from 10½ to 11 cents.[48]

Management's reply was to shut down the plant and to announce reduced wage rates.[49] So that there might be no misunderstanding, a set of "conditions of work" was printed and posted for all to see:

Notice of leaving must be given before commencing the last piece. All weavers keeping a piece of Fine Carpeting over 12 days, Superfine over 15, three-ply over 21 shall be liable to a fine of 25 cents per day.
No reading of newspapers or other publications.
No smoking.
Notice must be given for an absence of more than one day.

With these developments in July, 1833, the weavers decided to "stand permanently." After hearing a plea to conduct themselves with propriety and to keep away from rum barrels, they set up a committee to write to other carpet centers and to pay each weaver from $2.00 to $3.00 a week from benefit funds. Presently, contributions came from the other centers, while the company was blocked in its efforts to obtain replacements by the refusal of weavers in other localities to come to Thompsonville.

Despite the boast of one participant that the Scots had broken companies in the old country and would break this one,[50] the strike was peaceful. Personal relations were so good that some of the strikers were employed by the agent on his farm. After three weeks the management acted to break the impasse. The president of the union was won over by the offer of a supervisory position, and the other leaders were arrested. Still the men stayed out. Finally the company enlisted some strikebreakers from its warehouse crew in New York and from immigrant linen weavers who were friends of the crew. Failing to dissuade the new arrivals, the Thompsonville weavers, after some maneuvering to obtain the release of the leaders, went back to work at lower rates.

Naturally the event was not immediately forgotten. For a time some feeling existed between the old and the new workers, and for several years disputes dragged on in the courts. Upon instruction from a judge that an agreement to work only for certain rates was not an indictable offense, a Hartford county jury refused to convict the strikers of conspiracy. Another decision denied the leaders any damages. So the matter was dropped. By this time the more discontented had drifted off with testimonials from the company as to their "honesty, sobriety, and industry." [51]

The rest of the decade was quiet, despite a 20 per cent wage cut in 1837 and a partial payment in the form of carpets in 1839; [52] the forties were more turbulent. After one strike for an undisclosed reason in 1843, there was another in 1846 which was part of an industry-wide movement. In that year Orrin Thompson led a movement for a 25 per cent piece-rate reduction. According to the *Voice of Industry*, a contemporary paper: [53]

> One large manufacturer, Mr. Thompson, . . . exercises a controlling influence over others less wealthy. . . . He is a rich nabob in the city of New York, . . . and he jumps at every opportunity to cut down the wages of his operatives, for the sole purpose of putting into his own pockets money that should of right belong to them.

Though the low Walker Tariff may have influenced Thompson, the main reason for his action was the successful introduction of the power loom. As initially used, the power loom cut direct weaving costs from 12 cents to 4½ cents a yard; but, since the expenses of supervision, repairs, and interest on equipment increased, the over-all economies were only about 25 per cent.

To combat the 1846 rate revision, 34 delegates from 31 factories assembled in New York in August, 1846, with Thompson employees dominating the gathering. They—and in this they were joined by such "informed sources" as the newspapers—failed to see the main issue: that of the power loom. Nor did they regard the tariff as a source of their troubles. Instead, they blamed overproduction in the domestic market. Denouncing the wage cut as unnecessary, unjust, and pauperizing, as a remedy they suggested that the just and proper action for the manufacturers to take was to withhold the supply until the demand caused a return to remunerative prices.[54] An attempt to get an industry-wide agreement with the employers failed, and a proposed constitution for a permanent national labor organization was never put into operation, with the result that each mill was left to deal with the problem as it saw fit. At Thompsonville work stopped, though on whose initiative is not clear. Newspaper reports suggest that the employers "after mature deliberation" closed down to "await the effect of the new tariff and other contingencies."[55] At Lowell the directors were not sure whether the suspension was "in consequence of the low price or partly because their operatives would not submit to a reduction of wages."[56] On the other hand *The New York Journal of Commerce* termed it a strike and denounced the foreigners who had not "been here long enough to have their ideas of liberty and individual rights much enlightened."[57] The outcome is equally unclear—though both sides were sufficiently stubborn to prolong the struggle for eight or nine weeks.[58]

With the advent of the power loom the days of the weavers' monopoly were numbered. In 1847 the Thompsonville agent reported, "the girl goes nicely on the first loom."[59] The next year the hand weavers made a defiant stand. That strike petered out, and as more power looms were set up, some workers drifted away, others moved into supervisory and semisupervisory jobs, and the first epoch of union activity at Thompsonville was over. The unskilled men and women who replaced the hand weavers had neither training nor the bargaining strength to continue an active organization.

With the weaver went the treadboy whom he trained and for whom he was responsible. "A jolly, good-natured, romping boy," he passed into Thompsonville legend not as the waif, exhausting himself for a mere pittance, but as the prankster, who between tours of duty had pelted the Shaker farmers with their own produce, or transformed the packing boxes into cages for a menagerie. While a few may have been sufficiently studious to read as they trod, for many, night school had been another arena for pleasurable and violent activity. With the teacher cast in the role of another adult to be outwitted, the company had found it wise to select the master of the night school for his strong arm.[60] The treadboy's passing eased the educational responsibilities of the company.

THE OUTCOME: PRODUCT AND PROFITS

The process of making carpets was in many respects the same in Thompsonville as in Lowell. In the writings of James Wallace, company bookkeeper and local historian, appear descriptions of washing the wool, spreading it on the hill to dry, turning it, gathering it—often in a rush before impending rain or wind—tying it in sheets, and storing.[61] Meanwhile the designers, Scotsmen all, were readying the patterns. Customers supplied some of the ideas, Smith sent others from Europe. So prompt was he in forwarding three-foot copies of the latest patterns and styles, that the Thompsonville line was ordinarily in the market ahead of that of other producers, both domestic and foreign. On the other hand the factory did not blindly follow British leads. Wallace claimed that Thompsonville's patterns were better suited to the taste and style of the home trade.[62]

The Connecticut factory apparently differed from the one in Lowell, paying for much more work on contract. In 1840 Ellsworth took the worsted spinning contract at 6½ cents a pound for number 12, 13, and 14 yarns. His successors charged less but were not satisfactory. One forfeited his contract for indifferent quality, another for drinking.[63] The head dyer, John Houston, also worked periodically on contract.

Total costs of production declined considerably during these years, even before introduction of the power loom as shown by Table 5. The decline from 1833 to 1847 represented a reduction of 23 per cent in costs for two-ply ingrain and 24 per cent for three-ply. Since the purchase price of clean wool was about 22 cents in the early thirties and 21 cents in the late forties, the saving occurred primarily in the manufacturing processes —particularly in the cost of making warp and filling.[64] With weaving costs still 19 per cent of the total of superfine two-ply and 26 per cent of superfine three-ply, any appreciable cut through the use of the power loom would more than offset royalty payments. The Connecticut firm also thought that as a more efficient plant it could remain competitive with Lowell despite the license fee.[65] Whether right or wrong in this belief, the

Thompsonville company paid over $35,000 in royalties from 1849 through 1852, and Tariffville contributed another $25,000.

As the power looms came into operation, output grew rapidly. In 1832 output may have been around 150,000 yards. Early in 1850 when the full complement of looms was not yet fully installed, Thompsonville was producing at the rate of about 250,000 yards per year, of which about a third

TABLE 5

THOMPSONVILLE CARPET MANUFACTURING COMPANY

Cost and Price of Ingrain Carpeting Produced   1833 and 1847

(Per Yard)

	Superfine Two-Ply 1833	1847	Superfine Three-Ply 1833	1847	Brussels 1847
Cost					
Warp	$ .28	$.13	$ .43	$ .21	$ .25 [a] .30 [b]
Filling	.417	.32	.489	.38	.11
Weaving	.145	.13	.29	.25	.325
Winding	.033	.02	.038	.02	.04
General	—	.07	—	.09	.055
Total	$ .875	$.67	$1.247	$ .95	$1.08
Selling					
Price	$1.12	$.875	$1.68	$1.25	$1.50

[a] Foreign
[b] Domestic

Source: Thompsonville Carpet Manufacturing Company, Cost Book.

was two-ply ingrain and two-thirds was three-ply. A year later production had doubled.

By breakfast time on a Monday morning carpeting made the previous week was ready for shipment. At midnight of Sunday the six employees of the baling room would have hastened to their tasks: two to unroll and fold the goods and four to work the press and sew up the square bales. In the early years the bales went by boat to Thompson & Company in New York, but later the railroad took them to Hartford for 95 cents a ton, from whence they were forwarded by boat at 2¾ cents a foot.

During the entire active life of the Thompsonville Carpet Manufacturing Company the partners in the sales agency were almost identical with the officers and directors of the manufacturing firm. Sometime in the midforties the New York business was reorganized, Orrin Thompson withdrew to concentrate on the problems of the factory, and Henry G. Thompson and Joseph A. Dean became the new partners. This change did not make the relationship between mill and store any less close, and conflict of interest remained small.

Thompson & Company's functions as purchasing agent and product advisor have already been discussed. For its selling activities it received a 5 per cent commission plus 2½ per cent for the guarantee of credit. The latter was dropped in 1837 but the commission remained the same until a supplementary agreement in 1851 provided a 2½ per cent commission on auction sales and 5 per cent on private sales, the New York firm guaranteeing all transactions.

In disposing of the goods, the partnership followed the usual channels. Originally the New York house sold the Thompsonville carpets at both wholesale and retail, but after the partnership moved from 180 Broadway to a larger store on Spruce Street in 1836 retailing was abandoned, possibly because the relative returns were too small or perhaps because the original prejudice of New York merchants against American goods had been overcome.

Much of the early business seems to have been on a contract basis, the carpeting being made chiefly to fill orders. The bookkeepers said of the procedure, "We keep patterns and merchants come to the office and select." At the time of the strike in July, 1833, orders for some 530 to 540 pieces were on the books.[66] In later years Thompson & Company insisted on customers taking an assortment—two-ply along with three-ply.[67] By this time capacity had expanded so considerably that goods were made up in advance of orders. To take care of these it was necessary to maintain a large warehouse in New York—an unusually early appearance for such an investment—and to resort periodically to auctions.

In addition to the routine mechanics of selling, the agent was responsible for what little advertising was done. Besides exhibiting at the various fairs and presenting samples to institutions, on one occasion Thompson & Company took prospective buyers through the plant. Though the Connecticut firm did not have the initial advantage of big names like the Lowell company, it soon established an enviable reputation for its goods.

In the role of financier the New York store made the customary advances on sales. But it went beyond the normal. It was the financial foundation on which the corporation stood. Turnbull later commenting on the situation in Tariffville declared: "As a company I do not suppose we had then any working capital at all. It was all supplied by arrangement, I believe, with Thompson & Company."[68] The same was probably true of the companion concern.

Besides supporting the current operations of the mill, the selling house, directly and through its members, furnished permanent capital. The original charter of the firm allowed a capitalization of $150,000, of which $45,000 was paid in during the first year and a half. Needing more capital, the management authorized the issue of $30,000 of stock in 1830, but only $10,000 was actually sold. The remainder of the money was obtained in

1831 when the Hartford Bank, for a mortgage, agreed to accept drafts of $40,000 against Andrews, Thompson & Company.[69] For the next sixteen years no new capital funds were brought in, and the increase in capitalization stemmed from stock dividends: in 1836, 1844, and 1845. By 1845 the capital account stood at $250,000, a figure which was revised upward to $500,000 in 1848 to allow for financing of the power-loom construction. Despite the fact that the additional $250,000 was offered as a 7 per cent preferred security, subscription was so slow that only half had been taken by the fall of 1851. Six months later, however, and in spite of increasing financial difficulties—Orrin Thompson reported that all but $2,000 had been paid in.[70]

Of the $498,000 in the capital stock account in 1852, at least $195,000 represented stock dividends—profits plowed back from 1828 to 1846. Starting with its first profit of $3,847 in 1830, the company had made $386,388 in that period, with $60,000 in 1844 and again in 1845 as the peak in earnings. An "Interest" account added $215,975 more. Against this was a loss of $15,521 in 1841 and bad debts of $42,070, leaving a gain for the period of $544,762. This compares with the $888,000 made by the Lowell company from 1828 to 1846—a very creditable record when it is considered that the Lowell profits included those from the cotton line and were made on a capitalization of from $500,000 to $600,000. Besides the $195,000 in stock dividends, given by the Thompsonville Carpet Manufacturing Company, some $77,200 was distributed in cash—in 1836, 1844, 1845, and 1846. By 1846 the owner of two original $500 shares had received stock dividends of 5% new shares and had received $1,314 in cash dividends—or slightly less than 7 per cent per year.

The story of the next few years was quite different. From 1847 to 1852 the good years brought the company profits of $38,000. Against these must be set operating losses of $17,000 and bad debts of $215,000 in the same period. While the Thompsonville company thus lost around $194,000, the Lowell company showed profits of $274,000. With this deficit eating away at the surplus at a time when so much was being expended on the mechanization program, the resources of Orrin Thompson, the corporation, and the New York house were strained to the breaking point. To this load was added the burden of a similar program for the Tariff Manufacturing Company.

When the sales of stock went slowly after 1848, the immediate burden of meeting payments fell on Thompson & Company. By the fall of 1850 the factory was in debt to the selling house for $481,000. To cover partially this indebtedness, the Thompsonville Carpet Manufacturing Company had issued 375 bonds of $1,000 each at 6 per cent interest—in three equal installments in six, eight, and ten years. These bonds, secured by a mortgage on the company's real estate and machinery, were held in trust by

John H. Hicks, the New York wool-merchant stockholder; William S. Wetmore, New York iron merchant; and James M. Brown, member of the New York banking house of Brown Brothers.

The bond issue was but a temporary palliative, however. While the growing demand for ingrain eventually absorbed the output of the expanded capacity of the American industry, the adjustment took time and Thompson did not have enough liquid capital to survive the period of adaptation. On January 1, 1851, the New York partners had to advance another $150,000 against the mill's promissory note, secured by a second mortgage. During the summer of that year discussions "respecting mutual interests" were held with the Lowell company, but nothing concrete or helpful materialized.[71] A few weeks later when Thompson & Company was embarrassed by the failure of several of its debtors, it tried to get money by selling the Thompsonville bonds. The taking price was ruinously low. With no alternative but to close doors, on September 20, 1851, Henry G. Thompson and Joseph A. Dean, comprising the firm of Thompson & Company, conveyed to Henry W. Hicks and James M. Brown all their property in trust for the benefit of creditors.[72]

The failure of the Thompson-Dean partnership sealed the fate of the Connecticut corporations. When the directors met at Thompsonville on September 25 they executed a mortgage of all goods, merchandise, and personal property belonging to the company to Henry Thompson, Elizur Wolcott, and Brown Brothers. A second mortgage on the real estate and machinery was given to Brown Brothers for the $150,000 note due Thompson & Company. At that time the balance sheet of the Thompsonville Carpet Manufacturing Company stood as shown in Table 6.

The bankruptcy naturally brought about the breakup of the Thompson holdings with the creditors of the company taking over as the new owners. An 1852 stockholder list shows twenty owners of 485 shares, of which Brown and his banking house held 314. As a rule Brown Brothers did not invest heavily in industrials, but large advances to Thompson & Company, probably to finance the purchase of wool abroad, had involved it so inextricably in the affairs of the carpet plant that it had been forced to acquire a direct interest.

After Martin, as agent for Brown Brothers, had disposed of the materials on hand, the new stockholders appointed several committees to prepare an exact statement of the condition of the firm and to devise some plan to get it into operation.[73] Efforts to raise sufficient new capital proving fruitless, James Brown and William Wetmore wrote the Lowell company in January, 1853, that as trustees of the bondholders they were desirous that the properties should be sold to a new and responsible company. Indeed they hoped that the proprietors of the Lowell company would "join them in the purchase of the Thompsonville and Tariff concerns' property." [74] Though the Massachusetts manufacturers declined this overture, they agreed to transfer the Bigelow loom contract to a successor firm, provided that "arrangements with reference to the sales of goods, purchases of wool, etc. likely to be mutually advantageous to both parties," could be previously made. [75]

TABLE **6**

THOMPSONVILLE CARPET MANUFACTURING COMPANY

Balance Sheet, September, 1851

Assets:			
Current			
Receivables	$12,385.90		
Receivables in abeyance from			
Thompson & Company	75,415.43		
Steam Boating Company's stock	1,000.00		
Inventory	160,560.74		
		$249,362.07	
Fixed:			
Real estate—factories	245,181.58		
Real estate—houses, lands	115,540.04		
Machinery	433,121.67		
		793,843.29	
			$1,043,205.36
Liabilities:			
Short-term			
Debts secured by mortgages assigned			
to Brown Brothers,			
Thompson & Company	150,000.00		
Henry Thompson	5,000.00		
Elizur Wolcott	2,500.00		
Lowell Manufacturing Co.	4,653.37		
Outstanding obligations—payable	184,401.10		
		346,554.47	
Long-term			
Bonds	375,000.00		
Capital stock			
Common	250,000.00		
Preferred	125,000.00		
		750,000.00	
			$1,096,554.47

Source: Bigelow-Sanford Manuscript Collection.

Reassured on this important point, Orrin Thompson incorporated a new concern, the New England Carpet Company, in an effort to raise funds to buy the properties. He soon dropped this venture, however, deciding instead to co-operate with a group of Hartford business and professional men, headed by Timothy Mather Allyn, Edmund Grant Howe, and William R. Cone. These men had their own plans for acquiring the property and reviving the business. From this collaboration came the Hartford Carpet Company. With the organization of the Hartford Company the history of carpet-making in Thompsonville entered its second phase.

Though, as a corporation, the Thompsonville Carpet Manufacturing Company had not continued long in the history of the carpet industry, its achievements had been considerable and its contributions toward future success substantial. The staggering total of bad debts in the late forties was a serious drain on the company resources at a critical moment, but financing had been the Achilles heel of Thompson's company. While its resources were adequate for the routine transaction of business, they could not support the major overhauling of the factory and equipment and at the same time carry the concern through the postinstallation period when the temporarily flooded market was not adjusted to the increased capacity. Though the Lowell owners had similarly miscalculated the cost of mechanization, their wealth allowed a larger margin of error. With smaller means Thompson had undertaken a larger program—considering that he also was responsible for Tariffville. His uncle, John Turnbull, thought that he might have been able to swing 50 power looms in each factory.[76] Perhaps it was Lowell which had insisted on his taking the larger number to ensure an adequate return but the scope of the project was quite in keeping with Thompson's optimistic temperament.

Thompson's was an enterprising spirit—bolder than most in the carpet industry. While in the end, because of very special circumstances, he had lost his own equity and his bondholders had received only 50 cents on the dollar and his other creditors had received nothing, he had proved that the American market could support a business devoted solely to carpets and he had shown that with a moderate amount of protection the American industry could compete with the British. Though he had overreached himself financially, he had created a manufacturing unit. There remained only the need to make adequate financial arrangements and the two Connecticut mills could be placed in operation again. The knowhow, the skill of working men, the most modern machinery, the intricate relationships with the economic and noneconomic community, all were there, ready to meet and prosper on the great increase in carpet consumption which the future was confidently expected to bring.

CHAPTER 3

PIONEERING AN INDUSTRY:

Three Younger Companies, 1837–1856

Three more of the predecessors of the Bigelow-Sanford Carpet Company were established in the late 1830's and 1840's, including the two that supplied the name of the present concern: A. & E. S. Higgins Company, John Sanford & Company, and the Bigelow Carpet Company. Though none of them reached the scale of operations or attained the importance of the Thompsonville and Lowell firms in this first period, they laid the foundations for future fame, and two of them were to make early and significant innovations in the industry.

A. & E. S. HIGGINS COMPANY

The first of these, the A. & E. S. Higgins Company, like the Thompsonville company, was started by carpet merchants reaching backward for supplies. Its founders selected the environs of New York City for their factory. Like Thompsonville and Lowell this company originally concentrated on ingrains, but unlike them it pioneered in tapestry before the mid-century. Finally, like its counterparts, Higgins remained competitive by adopting the power loom in the weaving process.

Elias Higgins, the son of a Maine shipbuilder, brought to New York traits of shrewdness and industry which he applied to the objective of amassing wealth. For a few years after his arrival in 1833 at the age of eighteen, he worked as a clerk; then he was joined by his brother Alvin, who induced him to invest in a one-loom venture of making rag rugs. On February 6, 1837, the two took a major step by opening a store for wholesaling and retailing carpets and other floor coverings at 438 Pearl Street, New York. During the first month, sales of $310.91—about equally divided between cash and credit—netted the young merchants $33.44. Among the items sold to customers, at such points as Boston, Geneseo in New York,

Williamsburg in Virginia, Zanesville in Ohio, and Hillsborough in North Carolina, were plain, fine, and superfine ingrain and brussels carpetings. For the first year sales totaled $52,000, with profits of $6,213—and this notwithstanding the panic in the fall.[1]

Continued success led to notable growth in the next ten years. Sales and profits more than doubled in 1838 and 1839 despite the depression, and by 1840 these petty capitalists had tucked away enough to invest in seven ingrain hand looms. The first factory was in Jersey City, but the manufacturing plant was soon moved to Brooklyn where 30 looms were in operation when fire struck in 1844. In this emergency the Higgins brothers rented, for the season, buildings and equipment in Poughkeepsie and Astoria, New York, and Paterson, New Jersey. As a more nearly permanent solution they leased a former ironworks in Haverstraw, New York, and put up a new building for one hundred ingrain looms.[2] During the same time they rented a large carpet warehouse on Broadway at $3,000 a year. Finally, in 1847, the brothers acquired the site where their factory was to stand for fifty years, obtaining at an auction 34 lots of land at 43rd and 44th Streets along the Hudson River in New York City for $16,400.[3]

With the transfer of the manufacturing facilities to New York came new products. Previously the Higginses had concentrated on ingrain; now they branched into tapestry and velvet. Tapestry represented an attempt to produce the same effect as brussels, but with one frame of warp instead of the cost-consuming three to five frames. Velvet was a similar variation of wilton. Drum printing of yarn was essential for these fabrics; and, when in the mid-forties such a process was introduced into this country, the alert Higgins partners saw its possibilities. By 1849 the company was winning gold medals.[4]

With the line established, the Higginses signed a contract with Bigelow to use the brussels power loom which he had invented after the ingrain and which the Lowell company had decided not to install. This loom was easily adaptable to tapestry weaving and it was for the manufacture of this product that the Higgins brothers obtained rights. On June 11, 1849, the Clinton Company (the coach-lace company in whose machine shop many of Bigelow's looms were perfected and built), agreed to construct 50 tapestry looms for $320 each—half in cash and the balance in six months' notes, 25 looms to be delivered within four months and the rest in six.[5]

Though these tapestries were to become the Higginses most famous product, the firm continued to make ingrains, developing their own power loom. Less efficient and more expensive to operate than the Bigelow loom, this new power loom produced about one-third less per day at a cost of about one-third more per yard and carried only a limited number of shuttles.[6]

Meanwhile annual sales, which had been $143,000 in 1840, exceeded a million in 1851. Profits which had started at $10,000 in 1840, rose—with fluctuations—to $40,000 a decade later. For some reason they dropped off 50 per cent in 1851, and did not approach the previous high again until 1855.[7]

A large part of the profits received from the business was put into New York real estate. In 1856 Alvin Higgins, deciding to concentrate on this form of investment, sold to Elias and another brother, Nathaniel, his share in the firm for $30,000. With the new partnership of E. S. Higgins & Company, Elias definitely became the dominant figure, guiding his concern to an important place in the industry.

JOHN SANFORD & COMPANY

Upstate in New York a similar story of a one-man company was unfolding. Again the roots were in selling—this time the general country store instead of the specialized city house. John Sanford, who had migrated from Connecticut to Amsterdam in the Mohawk Valley just as the Erie Canal was bringing prosperity to the region, had amassed a considerable competence from mercantile and real-estate ventures and had risen to the dignity of Congressman when, in the early forties, a new local enterprise, the Greene carpet factory, offered an outlet for his surplus capital.

William K. Greene, Jr., also a native of Connecticut, was working in the silk mills in Poughkeepsie, as a bookkeeper, when in 1836 a fellow worker named Douglas, whose father had owned an ingrain mill in Scotland, suggested a similar undertaking in this country. Answering an advertisement in the *New York Herald*, Greene and his father rented an old satinette mill and dwelling at Hagaman's Mills (now a part of Amsterdam) for $100 a year. Six hand looms, sent by sloop up the Hudson and then 50 miles overland by sleigh, and three experienced weavers completed the assets. After a few years of varied success, the Greenes moved the business to Amsterdam,[8] and John Sanford became a partner.

Possibly the Greene-Sanford firm had had a small shop before August, 1843,[9] but in that month it bought for $1,000, plus a $500 mortgage, a planing mill on Chuctenunda Creek. In the following month an advertisement in the *Evening Recorder* announced: "Wm. K. Greene & Son . . . have established their carpet factory . . . and will receive yarn and color and weave the same into fine and superfine carpeting." [10] A few months later William K. Greene, Sr., sold his share to Sanford for $1,600; and the following year his son followed suit for $3,800.[11]

It was in this year, 1844, that John Sanford's son Stephen entered the business. How active the father, John, had been in the actual management of the carpet works is not known, but his son was to be the directing hand and driving force for nearly seventy years. Born in 1826, Stephen Sanford

was educated at the Amsterdam academy and for two years at George-
town College. Returning home in 1844, he started his career by learning
the carpet-making process from the bottom up. Four years later, when
he became a partner of John Sanford & Son, he was the thorough master of
every detail from raw material to finished goods.

To one biographer, he was the military man. Outwardly his bearing
was that of the soldier; inwardly his soldierly instinct was shown in his
appreciation of the value of subordination, his insistence on the honor of
a gentleman, and his strong strategic sense in expanding his business and
in adopting new products.[12] Cautious in determining the mode of action,
he was bold in execution.[13] With his simple business methods, detailed
knowledge of all phases of his business, intense concentration, imperious
will, and insistence on personal liberty, he was an excellent representative
of his time.[14] Although he married a sister of a future president of Alexander Smith & Sons Carpet Company, Sanford remained to the end of his
days, a lone operator, indifferent to the vast possibilities of joint action.

Shortly after his admission to the firm, a spectacular fire in the winter
of 1849 destroyed the mill as it stood among blazing evergreens.[15] Unde-
terred, father and son immediately moved the business to a new upstream
site, the present location of the plant.[16] Here, according to *Hunt's Merchants' Magazine* in 1850, John Sanford & Son in a year turned out carpet
yarn, worsted warp, three-ply ingrain, and chenille carpets and rugs worth
$133,000.[17]

But the days of blazing buildings were not yet past. In 1853 fire again
swept the works. This time the father was unwilling to rebuild, but the
son, confident of the future, took over the ruins. In a one-story crenelated
gray stone building, covering three times the area of the previous plant,
with some machinery acquired at a public auction at Utica,[18] and with an
ingrain power loom invented by William Greene, Jr., Stephen Sanford
faced a future which was to reward richly his industriousness and confidence.

THE BIGELOW CARPET COMPANY

If ingrains were the floor covering of middle-class America through
most of the nineteenth century, pile carpeting was making steady progress
toward the pre-eminent position it occupies today. Here again Erastus
Bigelow showed the way. His brussels loom, a modification of the coach-
lace loom with carefully controlled wires over which the warp was looped,
produced 20 to 25 yards a day as compared with 7 yards turned out by a
man and a boy on the hand loom.[19]

Though the savings on labor were high, domestic brussels faced severe
competition from the British, who had the required skill to cater to the
more discriminating market for higher quality goods. Potentially the qual-

ity of power-made goods excelled the best hand-woven carpets, but time was needed to acquire skills and to overcome consumer prejudices. Notwithstanding the advance in the standard of living, the immediate demand for brussels was negligible compared with ingrain. Because of this situation and because of the cost involved in perfecting the loom, the Lowell Manufacturing Company had not, as we have seen, exercised its option for the brussels loom in 1846. After further improvements Bigelow and his older brother, Horatio Nelson Bigelow, decided to set up in Clinton, Massachusetts, their own factory to produce pile carpetings on a power basis.

Born in 1812, the brother of the inventor had served an apprenticeship in several Massachusetts cotton factories before adding his small funds to those of Erastus to start the manufacture of coach lace. As the managing executive of the coach-lace concern, he had shared the credit for many of the improvements made in his brother's inventions. In 1842 he also had become agent of a mill in Clinton which had been formed to use Erastus Bigelow's counterpane loom. Two years later he had assumed responsibility for a still larger project, the Lancaster Mills, formed to exploit Erastus' gingham-loom patent. Thus by the time he had relinquished these many offices to devote himself to the new carpet project, Horatio Bigelow had already shown his creative ability and his skill in day-to-day management.

In the summer of 1848 Erastus Bigelow obtained the use of the brussels loom from the Clinton Company, to which he had earlier assigned his rights. There was no initial charge, but he promised to pay 1 cent a yard royalty on an output which was expected to reach 300 yards a day in three years, and 1,000 yards in five.[20] Erastus transferred this license to the partnership of H. N. & E. B. Bigelow for an additional 3-cent royalty, and Horatio, who had erected a brick building 42 by 200 feet on a plot of land on Chestnut Street, in Clinton, sold a half share in the property to Erastus for $14,000.[21]

With the addition of a second story to the building, the fitting up of a small wooden building in the rear with dye tubs,[22] and the installation of looms made by the Clinton Company and a 30-horsepower engine, the manufacturing facilities, limited to weaving, dyeing, and finishing, were complete. On July 11, 1849, a Worcester newspaper announced: "Those enterprising gentlemen, E. B. and H. N. Bigelow, are about putting in operation a new mill at Clintonville. . . . No man has done more than he who is now about to launch his fourth great invention, to extend the fame and prosperity of the manufactures of the union."[23] Soon the first brussels were woven and early the next spring advertisements of brussels, American-made on Bigelow power looms, were appearing in Boston and Worcester newspapers.[24]

By this time the project was sufficiently tested to warrant expansion. To supply his original share of capital Erastus Bigelow had sold some of his Lowell Manufacturing Company stock and had reached a lump-sum settlement with that concern for other moneys due. The savings of his brother had completed the investment. Now for additional capital the brothers turned to outsiders—to the Fairbanks family.

Stephen Fairbanks, born in Dedham in 1784, had gone to Boston just before the turn of the century. By the mid-thirties he had prospered sufficiently in the saddlery and hardware business to be elected president of the Massachusetts Charitable Mechanics Association and to be the leading figure in the marketing of coach lace. It was this reputation that had first brought Erastus Bigelow to Fairbanks, Loring & Company. With its encouragement he had gone ahead with his invention of the coach-lace loom and Stephen Fairbanks, in turn, had become a large stockholder and president of the coach-lace company in Clinton. In 1844 Fairbanks had been an incorporator and first president of the Lancaster Mills at Clinton. Soon thereafter he had left the saddlery and hardware business to his son, Henry, to become a director and treasurer of the Western Railway Corporation.

It was his son, Henry, who first joined the Bigelows in their carpet venture. On April 1, 1850, a new partnership, the Bigelow Carpet Company, composed of Horatio and Erastus Bigelow and Henry P. Fairbanks, paid $31,658 for the Bigelow brothers' carpet factory and business.[25] Not quite two years later another partner was added when Henry Kellogg of Hartford bought a quarter interest for $25,000. Kellogg agreed that whenever the interest of the firm required, he would devote his whole time to the concern's affairs,[26] but his influence on the business proved to be slight.

With the growth of the partnership went the physical expansion of the plant. The first looms, purchased from the Clinton Company in August, 1848, were supplemented by a second order in June, 1849, and a third in May, 1850, bringing the total to 50. Under the contract for the first looms, the Bigelow firm had paid cost plus 12½ per cent for general expenses, plus a profit of 20 per cent. The second group had cost $500 apiece. A year later the price had risen to $618, payable 10½ months after delivery.[27] With the increasing equipment went the need for an expanded plant. An assessment of July, 1852, listed the mill, dyehouse, drying house, counting room, forge shop, boiler house, waste house, storehouse, reservoir, and well, with a total value of $30,000. Machinery and fittings added another $47,000.[28]

At no time in the early years did the concern make its own yarn. In the first six months of 1850 it purchased 25,000 pounds of worsted yarn and 15,000 pounds of linen; in the similar period in 1854, 127,000 pounds of worsted yarn, 62,000 pounds of linen, and 971 pounds of cotton were going into 90,820 yards of carpet.[29]

The work force was composed of 50 men and 100 women. Many of the men had been recruited from Great Britain for the Lancaster Mills; others drifted to this carpet center. As in other industrial villages the company provided the housing, probably following the high standards set by the Lancaster Mills. By 1852 the Bigelow Carpet Company had invested $19,000 in brick houses. Records of rent do not survive, but room and board for women cost $1.34 a week.[30]

Since the women served as the unskilled loom tenders, most of the men held highly skilled or supervisory positions. Horatio Bigelow, whose quick step was heard daily throughout the factory as well as in the office, was assisted by William Eaton, the plant superintendent, who had worked with him on an earlier venture. A Scot, John Neil, was the designer. In his first contract Neil agreed to work for $83.33 a month, but the next year he was changed to a piece-rate basis, receiving 6 cents a card for copying patterns, 8 cents a card for cutting and adapting them to the cutting machine and looms, and 9 cents for new designs.[31] His first creations were simple geometrical figures in plain reds, greens, blues, and blacks, with little shading.[32] James Craig, in charge of the dyehouse, was given $1,200 a year and a house rent-free for his services. Scots also supervised the winding and weaving rooms.

Horatio Bigelow and his assistant kept careful records of costs and production, from which they prepared semiannual statements. For the six months ending July 1, 1851, the average cost per yard of all carpeting woven (67,135 yards) was $1.07; three years later it had risen to $1.25 (see Appendix 3). Individual items had risen in cost, but part of the increased cost was the reflection of higher priced items in the line; for example, wiltons had been introduced and more five-frame brussels were produced. Despite this introduction of new items, five-frame three-fourths brussels accounted for 86 per cent of the 195,000 yards produced in 1854.

Probably much of the Bigelow power-woven product was still inferior in quality to the British. One authority states that the face did not come out to the selvage, which left a distinct line when two strips were sewed together;[33] yet the increase in output, almost sixfold from 1850 to 1854, and the expanding line show that the partners were supplying an effective demand. Their methods of impressing the public consciousness were the same as the other manufacturers'—through exhibitions at fairs. The high praise from the judges at the 1851 Exhibition in London was the best of advertising, since patriotic and proud Americans attentively absorbed the favorable reports from the home of the Industrial Revolution.[34]

Henry Fairbanks acted as sales agent for the partnership. Headquarters for sales were in his Boston Office, but he soon established a branch in

New York. This, with a large business, from W. & J. Sloan, enabled the Bigelow Carpet Company to serve the ever-growing New York market.[35] Besides his marketing services, for which he received a 3¾ per cent commission, Fairbanks made the usual advances of funds.

A $52,000 increase in the partners' investment during 1852 was the result of $25,000 furnished by Kellogg as his share in the partnership and $27,000 in profits returned to the business. By 1854, reinvested earnings had brought the total net worth of the partnership to an estimated $160,000.

This reckoning was made in March, 1854, preparatory to the incorporation of the Bigelow Carpet Company.[36] While the adoption of the corporate form indicated that the business had achieved a degree of stability which augured well for a long existence, the immediate spur to action was the dissolution of the partnership due to the premature death from scarlet fever of Henry Fairbanks on February 14, 1854. Since he had no heir of age, his father assumed his interest, becoming president of the new corporation. H. N. Bigelow became the treasurer and agent, while Erastus Bigelow and Henry Kellogg retained their quarter interest but took no official posts. In continuing as a closely held firm, despite the change in legal form, the Bigelow Carpet Company over the next half century was much more akin to the Sanford and Higgins concerns than to the Hartford and Lowell.

SUMMARY OF THE PIONEERING PERIOD

To draw generalizations from the records of six different firms is not an easy task. The sample is small and the disparities are many; the very differences in origin, development, and personalities reflect the kaleidoscopic character of American industrial life during a revolutionary era. Yet despite variations in experience and development, many common traits stand out in the histories of the six predecessors of the Bigelow-Sanford Carpet Company.

For instance, all of these ventures were fed primarily by mercantile capital. Even where initially, as in the case of the Bigelows and Wright, the funds may have come from some other source, mercantile capital soon entered and proved the galvanizing force.

Then too, in all of these companies the merchants who invested their capital also supplied their abilities and training, although the techniques of the great merchants in the China trade would be somewhat different from the methods of the small upstate merchant in Amsterdam. Though the accounting precepts of the Lowell directors had their shortcomings, as in ideas on depreciation, and though their standards often did not equal modern ones as in profits returned or liquidity, generally these former sedentary merchants led in adopting conservative financial policies by insisting on the importance of working capital, paying dividends only from earnings, by financing unusual expansion only with stock issues, and by keeping detailed cost and production records. In many aspects Thompson and the Bigelows were not far behind, but the former failed when he tried to erect his mechanized mill without adequate stock subscriptions and the latter adopted a less conservative, if more modern, feature of bookkeeping, including such intangibles as patent rights in the balance sheet.

While all these merchants knew how to buy and sell and keep records of the transactions when they entered the carpet business, none knew how to manufacture. Like many other early American textile magnates, they remedied this by borrowing foreign ideas, foreign skills, and foreign machinery. And, as in other fields, American businessmen of the second generation with the aid of American mechanics threw off this tutelage. Indeed, Bigelow's achievements in the carpet industry were original contributions of unusual magnitude. The close connection of the Lowell company with Bigelow's first invention, the ingrain loom—the inspiration, money, and technical assistance it provided—and its rejection of the second, the brussels power loom, supply an interesting study in motivation in the process of invention.

The principal motivation seems to have been the attainment of a secure competitive position vis à vis the foreign manufacturer who had lower labor costs. Actually the carpet industry had already been successfully established here on a hand basis—a rare instance in American industrial history.[37] Yet such an achievement did not mean that the venture had attained the degree of security or profitability required by industrial leaders like those in Lowell and Boston. The large imports of the thirties rather than the depression of the forties furnished the original impetus toward mechanization. Then the declining prices of those hard years intensified the efforts to reduce costs by this means. Once the power loom was an actual fact, competitors like Orrin Thompson, producing goods of comparable quality, had to fall into line.

Not only was the carpet factory as originally established unusual in its use of the hand loom, but also in its Athena-like genesis. Unlike other branches of the woolen industries in this country, the development of the carpet factory was completely disassociated from any slow evolutionary process. It sprang full-fledged into being. There are several possible explanations for this phenomenon. First it may have been a matter of timing, since carpet manufacture was established later than other textile branches. Again it may have been a matter of individual experience: the Lowell magnates at least were only interested in the factory form of organization and anything they undertook would naturally be on this basis. Finally perhaps the labor supply was a factor. In Great Britain and in the Philadelphia area there were skilled workers to whom the work could be distributed at home. In New England no such reservoir of craftsmen existed. Rather the concerns had to import workers and, once weavers and dyers were gathered from across the ocean, to assemble them under one roof was easier and more efficient than to disperse them in a system of domestic manufacture already becoming archaic.

Once the dyeing and weaving processes were set up in the factory, problems of quality control and reliability dictated that the preliminary processes should be brought into the same establishment. At Lowell, Thompsonville, Tariffville, and Amsterdam, at least, an integrated production line appeared almost immediately, covering the many stages of cleaning, spinning, weaving, and finishing, and requiring considerable managerial and capital resources.

Setting up such a production line is more than an arrangement of tools and a scheduling of materials. It includes the problem of co-ordinating individuals—and this in the days before even the roughest disciplinary code had been drawn up by management and labor. In these and many plants like them was accomplished the task of instituting the standards of social and economic co-ordination for the new age. Because of the nature of the labor force at Thompsonville—skilled, independent yet cohesive Scottish workers, with a tradition of unionism—the friction engendered was spectacular and became famous in the annals of early American labor history. Clashes between management and labor provide the records which illustrate the problems of adjustment of men to new systems, but these collisions are the exception. Beneath the pyrotechnics of conflict is a story of reasonable co-operation, of effective relationships in a complex process, and of the slow evolution of economic institutions.

In getting its labor from abroad, the carpet industry was typical of many others, though its experiences in handling labor may have differed. In getting its staple abroad its path diverged from the usual American infant industry, which was buttressed against foreign competition by a cheap and ready supply of raw materials. Not only were carpet manufacturers more vulnerable to superior European skills, but they faced greater purchasing problems, need for more managerial co-ordination, and greater expense.

While purchasing was usually the direct responsibility of one of the officers, the selling function more typically was handled by a separate legal entity. The Higgins firm was the exception—an exception explained possibly by its location in New York City. Yet in the other cases marketing was often integrated with manufacturing by strong personal connections. Nothing is known of the early Sanford outlets, but for Thompsonville and for Bigelow the leading men were both manufacturers and salesmen, and even in the case of Lowell there were close ties between factory and commission house. Since the men behind the mills were merchants, this unity was natural. Since as merchants, they already controlled an available distribution system, common sense dictated its use rather than the creation of another selling organization within the newly established manufacturing concern at a time when there were so many other pressing problems. In addition there were certain financial advantages and possibilities of spreading risks over a broader base.

The commission houses might sell to retailers or consumers; but primarily they sold to wholesalers. The Thompson house at least resorted to the auction in hard times. Advertising announced the existence of a stock of goods; the chief statements to influence purchasers were mere claims of equality with the imported article.

The licensees of the Bigelow loom were, on the whole, in a good position to make these claims. The Lowell, Thompsonville, and Bigelow firms, especially, had a reputation for product leadership. In the case of the first two, this existed even before the adoption of power machinery because of concentration on better-grade goods and because the factory system turned out better qualities of ingrain than the domestic system of the Philadelphia area. Mechanization merely increased the stature of the mills at Lowell and Thompsonville. But leadership was not only a matter of technical performance. The Bigelow Carpet Company itself "led the van among educators of public taste in the matter of floor decoration," [38] as well it might since it was producing for an upper-middle-class market.

The furnishing of American-made goods to an upper-middle-class clientele is representative of the strides made by the industry as it emerged from infancy at the end of thirty years. At first a tentative answer to a vague and aspiring demand, the carpet industry by the end of the fifties could count over a hundred establishments with an invested capital of over $4,000,000 and a product for American homes of floor coverings worth $6,000,000 annually.[39] The successful transition from hand looms to power had been made by a significant segment of the industry, thus assuring future growth. The conquest of the American market for ingrain had been completed; the installation of the Bigelow brussels loom foretold future inroads into the market for better grade goods.

Since the concerns which later formed the Bigelow-Sanford Carpet Company accounted for a large proportion of the total output of American-made carpets and were prominent among the leaders toward new manufacturing methods, a large measure of the carpet industry's achievement is theirs. As these firms solved the problems of an infant industry, they defined the formative years of the trade. By the mid-fifties the days of experimentation were over. The days when technical production problems bulked largest had passed. Major policy decisions had been taken. Financial foundations had been laid, and the corporate and legal structures and ownership patterns of the firms had attained the forms in which they were to remain for forty or fifty years. With technical competence and administrative experience, the companies were ready to compete among themselves and with the foreigner for all levels of the American market— a market growing ever larger and more discriminating.

CHAPTER 4

YEARS OF ADAPTATION:

The Lowell Manufacturing Company, 1852–1899

The problems of the founders, the struggles to launch infant concerns, the first successes, these stir the imagination. Less dramatic are the repeated adjustments of the individual firm, which by its very continuity of existence seems a natural part of the community and the nation. But every decade brings its difficulties, and the quest for the right solution is usually just as rigorous for the current generation as for the preceding, and the achievement just as serviceable.

In their search for a profit, the men of the various carpet companies—Bigelow, Lowell, Hartford, Higgins, and Sanford—reacted like their fellow industrial capitalists. As patent protection ended, energetic domestic rivals with low overhead costs and up-to-date methods competed aggressively for old customers and new consumer groups. Pursuing their independent ways, the old companies added new products, improved equipment, cut prices, and flooded the market with the outpourings of an expanded capacity. Despite competitive pressures, they eschewed any detailed program of co-operation until internal problems of management forced four of the firms—Bigelow and Lowell, Hartford and Higgins—to merge. Though these mergers took place at the turn of the century when the consolidation movement in the United States was at a peak, there is no suggestion of economic inevitability. No other amalgamations occurred in the carpet industry. Still, it is reasonable to assume that reliance on mergers as the solution of internal problems was a form of remedy dictated by the temper of the times. At some other time, in some other milieu, these problems of internal stress might have been solved in some other way. With the mergers, new corporate histories began, and old institutions regained some of the vigor which is associated with a young firm.

These developments within the industry were taking place against an economic background of violently contrasting conditions. The prosperity of the 1850's was succeeded by a short depression at the outbreak of the Civil War. Hectic war activity and a mild postwar boom were followed by a major depression, extending from 1873 to 1878, and then by two decades with a few bright spots amidst general economic gloom.

In spite of the general economic malaise with which many of the years in the last half of the century were afflicted, several developments increased the demand for carpets. Prices fell faster than wages, thereby increasing consumer purchasing power,[1] and adding to the number of potential buyers. Furthermore, the growing population multiplied the number of prospective customers. Again the urban areas, where most carpets were sold, developed more rapidly than the nation as a whole—increasing fivefold in fifty years.[2] Finally while the city dweller remained the chief customer, the Middle Western farmer became more important as the railroad, which enabled him to shift from a subsistence to a cash economy, also brought the carpet to his local market.

While population and purchasing power grew, the service and consumers goods industries were developing, but more slowly. Thus, though nineteenth-century incomes seem low, there was not the modern plethora of goods and services to compete for the consumer dollar. With the rage for conspicuous consumption spreading from the war-enriched, carpets came to be regarded as a necessity down through many levels of society. By 1890 Americans were using more carpets than all the rest of the civilized world.[3] Statistically 23,500,000 yards worth $24,700,000 were produced domestically and imported in 1870; at the end of the century the figures were 77,000,000 yards, valued at $50,000,000. This represented a yardage gain of 228 per cent. Since population over the same period grew but 145 per cent, per capita consumption of carpeting rose from four-tenths to one full yard. Contrary to what a glance at the above figures on volume and value might suggest, the quality of carpets increased remarkably.

Of the total yardage put on the American market, the foreign share shrank from 15 per cent in 1869 to 1 per cent in 1899. How much the virtual disappearance of the foreign carpet manufacturer from the American market was due to the postwar tariff is not clear. As early as 1854 American producers were dominating the low-priced ingrain market—despite the reduced tariff after 1846. Still, great importance was attached to excluding the foreigner from the higher priced pile-carpet market as well, and in the post-Civil War years the tariff issues absorbed the energies of the carpet industry to a degree equaled in few other businesses.

Though the carpet manufacturers imported dyes and jute, these presented no tariff problem, since there was no domestic industry. But wool was another matter. Since the American farmer was a negligible factor as a supplier of cheap carpet wools, carpet mills drew on South American, Turkish, and in later years Russian and Far Eastern wools.[4] But the task of framing a tariff to permit free, or virtually free, entry of carpet wool and yet exclude other better grades was far more difficult than the obvious value formula would seem to indicate. The wool growers seeking tariff protection were determined—and powerful—throughout most of the period. Carpet manufacturers, with wool accounting for 50 per cent of their total costs, could not afford to be less aggressive. Yet, they were placed in an awkward position. While arguing for lower raw wool duties on the one hand, they were lobbying for higher carpet duties on the other.

The tariff of 1857, enacted by free-trade Southern Democrats, favored the carpet men by providing for free entry of cheap wool. Though the duty on the finished goods was reduced to 24 per cent, the directors of the Hartford Carpet Company reported, "the free admission of carpet wools into this country will enable us to make our goods at as low a rate as our foreign competitors can furnish them, and with the protection secured by the duties being retained upon imported carpet, it is confidently believed the future promises well." [5]

The victory of the Republicans in 1860 cut short the life of this tariff, and Civil War necessities spawned several transitory measures. As the war progressed, wool manufacturers—inspired by Erastus Bigelow—became interested in setting up a more nearly permanent system. Through the agency of the National Association of Wool Manufacturers, founded in 1864 with Bigelow as president, an arrangement was reached with the wool growers. The system of compensatory duties, first applied in 1867, was to last out the rest of the century despite the waves of words which buffeted it. It provided both a specific duty on carpets (so many cents a yard) to counterbalance wool duties and an ad valorem levy (a certain per cent on value) to furnish the manufacturer his margin of protection. The specific duty was a particularly happy inspiration since it resulted in increased protection as carpet prices declined.

The specific duty varied approximately with the amount of wool used in a given weave of carpeting. In the first tariff of 1867, to offset the duties of 3 cents a pound on cheap wool, two-ply ingrain was given a specific duty of 12 cents a yard, three-ply 17 cents, tapestry 28 cents, velvet 40 cents, brussels 44 cents and wilton 70 cents. The superimposed ad valorem rate was 35 per cent on all types.

Though the principle was established, the operation was not always smooth. After Bigelow's death in 1879, the carpet men under the leadership of John Houston of the Hartford Carpet Company founded their own organization to defend their interests more effectively against any movement to lower rates on carpets without corresponding adjustments in wool duties. In the first battle, in 1883, the association was not successful in maintaining the old relationships, but, as Elias Higgins prophesied, importations were few.[6] Indeed it was not one set of rates, or another, that was so harassing to the businessmen of the eighties; it was the continual possibility of change. Houston might protest the particular provisions of each proposal as a deathblow, but his main concern was "to be let alone." [7]

By 1890 it was apparent that the carpet manufacturers were not to be let alone. Under the highly protective McKinley bill, the increase in the tax on raw wool was not matched by compensatory duties, but Houston did obtain an increase in the ad valorem from 35 to 40 per cent. The Democratic free wool tariff of 1894 introduced minor alterations into the carpet schedule itself, but the election of the Republicans in 1896 brought the return of the previous order. With the issues settled temporarily in 1897, carpet manufacturers were allowed to forget the "barricades" for another dozen years.

Against a background of prosperity followed by a long depression, of expanding markets with declining prices, and of the substitution of American for foreign competition, the heads of the various carpet companies wrestled with problems arising not only from these general factors but also with those arising from internal conditions. The rest of this chapter and the three following will consider the courses taken in these respects by the predecessor concerns of the Bigelow-Sanford Carpet Company.

OWNERS AND ADMINISTRATORS AT LOWELL, 1852–1899

From 1852 to 1899 the Lowell Manufacturing Company grew mightily as its ingrains found their way into more and more homes in the expanding American market. Yet the story of these years reflects not merely a change in size. Old products were dropped, new were tried—and some were found wanting. Technological improvements continued, though on a modest scale as compared with the power-loom revolution. The Bigelow patents expired, opening the field to new entrepreneurs, and a great competitive struggle became the dominant note in the last twenty years of the century. Yet, while new firms arose on all sides to challenge the profits, they did not necessarily dim the prestige of the pioneer.

Directing the destinies of the Lowell Manufacturing Company were the descendants of the Bostonians who had created it. Children and grandchildren appeared on the ever-lengthening list of stockholders. From 550 owners of 2,900 shares in 1870, the list grew to over 800 in 1898. In the former year George Lyman's 80 shares topped the holdings; in the latter the largest individual owner was the estate of James Ayer with 51, followed by Arthur Lyman with 50. Ninety-eight per cent of the proprietors were New Englanders in 1898; of these, 41 per cent lived in the Lowell area and 35 per cent around Boston. This division into two large blocks, which is typical of the whole period, is significant because the Boston group controlled the management while the Lowell clique had to content itself with vigorous complaints. As mere stockholders the men of Lowell had little to do with the administration of the company, the idea of making the stockholders a responsible voting group being completely foreign to the group in power.[8] Still the owners made themselves heard in the years from 1858 to 1864 and from 1877 to 1882—in the later period with some effectiveness.

The board of directors, whose powers continued unabated, was as previously a nonoperating board except for the treasurer and the representative of the selling house. As the directors expressed it in 1879: [9]

The Directors have no compensation for their services except the honor of the official position and the consciousness of the faithful discharge of their duties, and they can not be expected to take any active personal management of the business of the Corporation, except in the general oversight thereof.

Financial matters attracted most of their attention, especially company indebtedness and depreciation of physical assets. For a period the directors allowed the treasurer to issue company notes to the extent he thought desirable, but as indebtedness increased they became more cautious. During the eighties and nineties the directors set a maximum on the amount of allowable indebtedness, a maximum which was raised several times.[10] Their depreciation policy at the end of the period as in the beginning consisted of writing off large sums at intervals, usually when earnings could stand such a reduction. At various times depreciation reserves appear temporarily and without apparent logic. In 1889 there was mention of allowing 5 per cent annual depreciation on machinery and buildings, but such a policy was not formalized.[11] At the end of the century the best that could be said of Lowell policy was that the directors recognized the existence of a depreciation problem; while there had been glimmerings of light, the glimmerings had flickered out and the management was no nearer a modern solution than it had been fifty years earlier.

Among the officers of the company the secretary was a minor functionary and the president remained merely the chairman of board meetings and a member of temporary investigating committees. Four men held the latter office in this period: Samuel Cabot from 1853 to 1860; William Amory, the long-time treasurer of Amoskeag, from 1861 to 1873; Daniel Richardson, a Lowell lawyer and only member of the board who lived in that area, from 1874 to 1890; and his brother, George F. Richardson, from 1890 to 1899.

In a company organized and operated like Lowell the caliber of the chief executive officer, the treasurer, was vital. To attract able men the

Ingrain Carpet; flat, non-pile fabric; principal type of carpeting made in 19th century

Brussels Rug; pile fabric; most popular quality carpet in 19th century; toward end of century rugs with mitred borders replaced wall-to-wall carpeting in more fashionable homes

Tapestry Rug; least expensive of pile fabrics; wider color and pattern range than ingrain; ranked second in volume between Civil War and World War I

Axminster Rug; medium-priced pile fabric; became popular after invention of axminster power loom by Alexander Smith and Halcym Skinner in 1874; most popular carpet in first half of 20th century

salary was raised from $5,000 to $6,000 in 1857, and to $10,000 in 1879. Five men of varying backgrounds served in the post: Israel Whitney, Charles L. Harding, David B. Jewett, Samuel Fay, and Arthur T. Lyman.

Whitney left at the end of 1863 with a farewell gift of a year's salary— an extravagance hardly justified, according to stockholder James C. Ayer, by his very ordinary fitness and skill.[12] His successor, Charles L. Harding, a former wool manufacturer, stayed but two years.[13] Jewett, a former dry-goods merchant, carried on until, plagued by poor health, he declined re-election in 1874.

Samuel Fay's election marked the elevation of an insider. Quite different was his training from that of the merchant aristocrat, Lyman; the owner-manufacturer, Harding; or the merchant, Jewett. A manufacturing man who had risen through the ranks, Fay's long service to the company in many capacities established his right to be bracketed with Arthur T. Lyman as one of the two most important men in this period of Lowell Manufacturing Company history.

Fay, a Massachusetts farm boy, had been recommended to Alexander Wright for the position of paymaster in 1846 by the management of the Lawrence Corporation. Advancing to the position of assistant superintendent, he had taken over as mill agent on Wright's death in 1852. Thus he brought to the position of treasurer in 1874, a diversified training in office and plant and he soon acquired a reputation as an excellent judge of wool and wool markets.[14] His weakness lay in broader financial problems, a weakness accentuated by his relationship with his directors. Cast in the role of a well-paid employee, he could perhaps not speak as plainly in the depression years or demand as much in funds for modernization as one of the Boston financial fraternity.

His successor certainly was a member of the "ruling" classes. Arthur Theodore Lyman, in addition to inheriting a wide range of industrial and financial interests, inherited from his father [15] a reserve and self-possession which gave him an air of complete serenity even amid the greatest business disorder. Born in 1832 Arthur Lyman was graduated, Phi Beta Kappa, from Harvard in 1853. Over the next dozen years he was a clerk in a countinghouse, a merchant in the India trade, treasurer of the Hamilton and Appleton mills, a member of J. W. Paige & Company, and treasurer of the Glendon Iron Works in Pennsylvania. The India trade he found unremunerative, the mills harassed by Civil War, the selling agency wracked by a fight with a client, and the iron works upset by a family quarrel.

After such a decade Lyman might well have been discouraged. "Gaining experience" can become a demoralizing process. Yet no one could rob him of the insight he had acquired, and with his natural intelligence and conscientiousness he was well trained for the position of treasurer of the Hadley Company, of Holyoke, to which he was elected in 1866. This gave him further preparation for taking over his father's manifold interests—slowly in the seventies and then completely in the eighties. Director of many companies, president of nine, his chief stewardships were the Pacific Mills, Lowell Machine Shop, and the Lowell Manufacturing Company.

To the Lowell Manufacturing Company he came as a director in 1878. Seeking an active role, he served on many committees and thus gained some inside knowledge of the carpet business to go along with the broad familiarity with administrative techniques and financial methods which he was to bring to the office of treasurer in 1881.

Though the treasurer carried the over-all responsibilities of innovating, planning, and supervising, he directly managed only the purchasing and financing. Of the other functions, manufacturing, except during the Fay and perhaps the Harding periods, was the province of the superintendent; marketing was left to an outside agent, and labor relations, as we know them today, hardly existed.

Over long periods—the Whitney and Lyman administrations—the superintendent was the top full-time employee. Andrew Freeman Swapp, a Scot who had had training both as a machinist and a dyer before he started up the managerial ladder, was superintendent under Fay. In 1879 Swapp had come under fire of the stockholders for being behind the times, but Fay had backed him to the limit and Lyman retained him in his position.

Upon Swapp's death in 1883, Lyman went outside the company for a successor, hiring Alvin S. Lyon for three years at $7,000 a year.[16] Lyon, another Massachusetts farm boy, had started as a wool sorter in a Lawrence factory. After spending some time as a weaver, carder, and spinner at various plants, he had become overseer of several quilt and weaving departments and finally a superintendent. When he left the Lowell company after twenty-three years, it was to assume the management of the big Wood Worsted Mills, of the American Woolen Company, a position commensurate with his reputation as a top mechanical man and manager.[17]

Occasionally Swapp or Lyon might acquire staff assistance, such as a chemist or an engineer, but the addition of an accountant for an annual audit in 1878 was for the succor of the stockholders' committee.[18] Carrying most of the detailed administrative burden, responsible for the important manufacturing operations, taking care of routine purchases, the superintendent found his main support in the line foremen.

As years passed the Scottish predominance in the foreman group gave way to English and Yankee. "A Copy of Rules . . . to be Observed by the Foreman and Section Overseers of the Carpet Weaving and Rug Room," dated September 28, 1854, sheds light on their duties: [19]

The Foreman is to have general charge. . . . He is to see that no incompetent persons are employed, that the work is done in a proper and economical manner and is to give such directions to the help from time to time as circumstances may require. (All his orders are to be given through the Section Overseers. . . .)

The Section Overseers are to observe the directions of the Foreman. They are not to employ or discharge help without the direction or approval of the Foreman. . . . Any one discharged by a Section Overseer is not to be employed in another section of the room except by the permission of the Superintendent. The time of the help to be kept correctly and reported to the Foreman once each week.

This then was the structure of the manufacturing organism; these the men. So important are men in the history of the company that the half-century after the death of Alexander Wright can be divided into the Whitney-Harding Regimes, the Jewett-Fay Stewardships, and the Lyman Era. The first was a period of general prosperity, briefly interrupted by war; the second a time of instability and deep depression; and the third an age of profitless expansion under the goad of heavy competition.

THE WHITNEY–HARDING REGIMES, 1852–1865

The years when Whitney and Harding held the office of treasurer coincided with the Golden Age of the Lowell Manufacturing Company. Standing pre-eminent in the industry, the company reaped the rewards in reputation and in profits of the hours and money invested in the forties. Yet it was not a period without challenges. Five special problems arose: marketing, the stockholder rebellion, the Hartford lawsuit, product determination, and Civil War operations.

Well-meaning, but not necessarily perceptive directors, might have attributed difficulties in marketing and stockholder relations to the ambitions of the irrepressible James C. Ayer. A patent-medicine manufacturer in Lowell, Ayer was a large minority stockholder in most of the Lowell corporations. Since his own success was based on colorful advertising and aggressive marketing, the sales organizations and techniques of the textile concerns were anachronisms to him.

A. & A. Lawrence & Company was still the selling agent, the New York partner handling most of the carpet business. In addition to the regular 2 per cent commission paid by the Lowell company to the selling house, Lowell made special payments for the work of the selling agent's designing department, for special advertising, and for out-of-the-ordinary marketing procedures, such as auctions.[20] It also carried its own Guaranty Reserve to take care of any credit risks the selling house might incur.

As is natural in many cases where there is not complete identification of interest, there was friction. Two sharp panics brought matters to a boiling point. After the panic of 1854, the Lawrence house had resorted to an auction to dispose of 2,200 rolls of ingrain, resulting not only in additional selling expense to Lowell but also in the demoralization of the markets for ingrain.[21] These auctions did, however, net a profit for the Lawrences, an outcome which did not set well with some stockholders. Their annoyance was magnified when, following the panic of 1857, the carpet company lost money and was forced to pass the first dividend in 1858 and limit the second dividend to 3 per cent. As the discontented reviewed the situation, the profits which the sales agents were making on Lowell goods were an obvious point of attack.

In 1856 a directors' committee of Samuel Cabot, Whitney, and George Lyman had unsuccessfully taken up the matter of commissions. Two years later Ayer made a more drastic proposal: that the company handle its own marketing. After this suggestion had spent a year "under advisement" Ayer garnered enough support to force the appointment of a stockholders' committee of himself, Peter Lawson, and Horace J. Adams to investigate the marketing setup.

Prodded by this turn of events, the directors' committee and A. & A. Lawrence reached a new agreement as of March 1, 1859. The commission on carpets and woolens was dropped from 2 to 1½ per cent, while that on cotton, by then a minor portion of the business, was raised from 1 to 1¼ per cent.

Claiming this as a victory, the Ayer stockholder committee, nonetheless, recommended direct selling to wholesalers. A. & A. Lawrence it held, "without any risk, . . . or even any considerable investment of capital," averaged $24,000 a year from commissions and in addition the Lowell company had to foot a bill for expenses averaging $14,000 a year. All told, for over seven and a half years the selling expenses had been $287,091 on a gross of $10,373,449—that is, 2.77 per cent. A good agent and a house in a better location in New York would cost $10,400 a year. The Boston agency could be closed and the warehouse, worth $27,000, sold. Since there were few carpet wholesalers, contacts would not be difficult and credit risks minimal. The whole could be supervised by the treasurer, who was more than adequately reimbursed.[22]

Despite this cogent presentation the Ayer Committee undoubtedly underestimated the difficulties of selling. It required an amount of time and a specialization of knowledge and contacts which an all-purpose executive like the treasurer did not have. Location of the treasurer's office in Boston, while the carpet market was in New York, would have made the task more difficult still. Furthermore, as the market spread westward the problems of contacts and credit risks were likely to increase even with improved technical and business methods. In addition to administrative difficulties there was a financial question. To do its own marketing the Lowell company would have had to acquire additional working capital. The time was near at hand when commercial banks could provide money for current operations, but, for the present, the financial assistance of the selling agent was important.

The pigeonholing of his report further convinced Ayer of the unholy alliance of the inner clique, and for the next five years he attacked the few who perpetuated themselves in office as men who controlled great properties in defiance of their owners. Behind his demands for procedural reforms was the fundamental constitutional question of control by the stockholders. Specifically Ayer objected to holding annual meetings in Boston before the morning train from Lowell arrived and in rooms too small to accommodate latecomers; to calling the meetings of several corporations simultaneously to give the proxy-backed officers the advantage over the independent dissidents; and to the failure to give addresses on stockholder lists.[23] His complaints went unheeded. His efforts to have annual meetings held in Lowell, to appoint nominating committees from the floor, and to investigate the proxy system, failed.[24] When he attempted to procure compliance with a new state law requiring corporations to divide their stock into $100 shares and limiting an officer to 20 proxy votes,[25] he was overruled on the grounds that the Lowell shares with a par value of $690 could not be so divided. Only in the minor matter of payment of train fares to meetings, of stockholders who resided out of Boston, did he win a victory.[26]

Another struggle of the period, though one in which Ayer was not involved, was with the Hartford Carpet Company over the renewal of Erastus Bigelow's ingrain patents. The Hartford company, which had bought and put into operation the Tariffville plant on the assumption that the days of royalty payments were about over, objected, and successfully, to the renewal by Lowell in 1860 of the key 1846 patent. Immediately, Hartford stopped remitting to Lowell, thereby precipitating a long legal struggle. The Lowell company, having procured Bigelow's co-operation by a laudatory resolution and $5,000, sued the Hartford company early in 1861 on the basis that the looms in use contained devices patented in 1849. When a court decision in 1864 supported the Hartford contention that the license granted to it by Lowell in 1847 did not require any payment on patents obtained by Lowell after that date, the Lowell management planned to appeal, but eventually the matter was quietly dropped.[27]

Though the construction program of the late forties and early fifties had settled the main product policies, Whitney and Harding continually reassessed the decisions in the light of current events. Despite the troubled political waters in 1860, Whitney suggested an increase in carpet capacity of 240,000 yards a year, a project costing $120,000. By the end of the year most of the necessary construction was completed, but the 43 improved Murkland ingrain looms to which Lowell had patent rights, were not ready for operation before the outbreak of war temporarily disrupted company plans.

On the cotton side of the business, the treasurer was ordered to sell the pantaloon looms in 1859. In 1860 Whitney reported that "the demand for Osnaburgs had for some time been falling off and in the opinion of the Selling agents it was desirable to reduce the quantity and to substitute a shirting." [28] This project was authorized but it was the last serious consideration given to a cotton line. Under the pressure of the wartime cotton famine, the management in 1863 converted the cotton mill into a worsted mill for the manufacture of army blankets, serges, and lastings at a cost between $100,000 and $125,000. [29]

The war, which disrupted the cotton business, did not leave the carpet manufacturer untouched. Even before Lincoln's inauguration, the directors voted "to reduce the production of Carpeting one third or one half." In August, 1861, the last loom was stilled. With the general revival in the fall, the directors authorized Whitney to start up the cotton and carpet mills, [30] but it was the summer of 1862 before the concern was doing the usual amount of business. [31] Though there were spasmodic interruptions thereafter, the worst was over.

Meantime costs had been rising. The greatest jump in wool costs came in 1864. Wage rates rose after 1862, and especially after 1863. By 1865 workers were receiving about $3.00 more per week than they had been three years earlier. Since the price of room and board went up only from $1.75 to $2.25, the Lowell employee was probably as well, if not better, off during the later years of the war, when employment was steady, than he had been in the fifties. [32]

Carpet prices had gone up earlier than costs, but they had begun to decline by 1865. In 1865 the increase in volume offset the price drop, however. Sales, which were 1,300,000 yards in 1863 and 1,200,000 yards in 1864, rose to 1,600,000 yards in the next year. Corresponding dollar figures were $1,500,000, $1,900,000, and $2,600,000. [33]

Despite the panics of 1854 and 1857 and the wartime upheavals, the Whitney-Harding years were profitable for the Lowell Manufacturing Company. Profits averaged $200,000 from 1853 to 1860, easily supporting an 8 per cent dividend rate. As a result the net working capital rose by $650,000 and the liquidity ratios, which were adequate in all years, pyramided in 1859 and 1860.

On the whole the management pursued a cautious financial policy during the first years of the war. Cash balances were high, some of the spare funds being put into government bonds and some loaned to A. & A. Lawrence. Payables were carried at moderate amounts or cleared off the books at the time statements were made up. Dividends amounted to 12 per cent during the war years, an enviable record amid the general distress of textile companies. As a result Lowell's stock, which in the fifties had been selling for as much as 30 per cent below par of $690, climbed steadily to a peak of $1,310 in 1864. With reserves high and with an adequate liquid position, Whitney and Harding left the company in a sound financial condition to face the problems of a postwar return to "normalcy."

THE JEWETT–FAY ERA, 1865–1880

The expiration of the Bigelow patents inaugurated a period of ruthless competition from young and aggressive firms. While Lowell maintained a reputation "unsurpassed, by any in the world, [for] . . . excellence of fabrics," [34] the additional capacity in ingrains, the growing popularity of other fabrics, the flood of importations which reached 4,700,000 yards by 1872,[35] provided a challenging background for the activities of the Lowell management. In addition, general economic conditions taxed the abilities of the executives. The mild postwar boom was but a prelude to unsettled years when instability was compounded by the vicissitudes of a currency severed from gold. Then came the major postwar depression.

After three extremely profitable years from 1866 to 1868, profits began to drop sharply under the impact of declining prices. In terms of the paper currency in which the major part of the domestic business of the day was conducted, the price of superfine two-ply ingrain was $1.08 in 1870, 27 per cent below 1865. Five years later, at the beginning of 1876, with, according to a current comment "the growth of carpet manufacture . . . progressing at a greater rate than any period in the past," [36] the price had slid another 24 per cent downward to 82 cents. As conditions did not improve measurably over the next two years, the directors could but conclude: [37]

With a falling market and great failures to an unprecedented extent among those who are also engaged in trade, it seems to us a subject of congratulation that our Treasurer has been able to manufacture and our selling agents to dispose of our goods, so that we have our capital unimpaired and some surplus and have with few exceptions returned to our stockholders every six months some profit on their investment.

It was against this background that Treasurers David Jewett and Samuel Fay sought the answers to their company's problems. These problems fell principally in five areas: products, marketing, costs, stockholder relations, and finance.

The decisions on products made during these years had two aspects: the determination of what should be made and how much. At the end of the war the capacity of the ingrain mill was about 1,800,000 yards a year, or roughly 10 per cent of the total domestic output on 5 per cent of the country's looms. Production ran about 1,500,000 yards. In addition, the company was manufacturing some minor articles of a by-product nature, such as poplins, serges, and lastings.

None such as these could fill the sales void created by the abandonment of the osnaburg line, which in 1860 had accounted for from one-fourth to one-third of the total fixed investment. While an increase in ingrain capacity was a possible answer, it did not provide for spreading risks. Trends in the carpet market also militated against this solution. Domestic production of ingrain was already up by more than 4,000,000 yards in the decade and the effect of more mills and more efficient machinery was just beginning to be felt. Brussels and tapestry, on both of which Bigelow loom patents were expiring, presented much more favorable prospects, since of the 1,500,000 yards of the former and of the 3,000,000 yards of the latter annually consumed in this country, two-thirds was being imported. To satisfy a rapidly expanding market there were but two important domestic makers of tapestry—the Higgins firm in New York and the small Roxbury Carpet Company in Boston—while Bigelow was the only sizable producer of brussels.

Three considerations pointed to the selection of brussels rather than tapestry: quality, equipment, and process. Primarily the Lowell reputation was based on high-quality goods. With a choice between a better grade, conservative fabric and a cheaper, flashier one, the inclination, apart from practical considerations, would be to take the former. And the existence of certain marketing contacts would point the same way. As for equipment, since the firm had acquired worsted spinning machinery during the war, brussels merely required new looms while tapestry would also demand an investment in drums for dyeing. Dyeing for tapestry was a tricky operation which would involve training additional labor in new skills. Furthermore, largely because of this dyeing process, tapestry cost more for labor per yard,[38] and lower labor costs had always been a prime Lowell objective.

After some such considerations the directors voted in March, 1869, to proceed with the establishment of the brussels line, thus leading the movement which over the next five years was to bring the total of brussels power looms in this country to 220 and the number of manufacturers to nine. This was a decision of great moment, for the time would come when the Lowell company would be grateful that it had not continued to place all reliance on its ingrain products.

To procure its brussels looms, Lowell had sought a foreign supplier. The Clinton Company had closed during the Civil War and no other American textile-machinery manufacturer had yet included carpet looms, let alone brussels, in his regular line. Moreover, little worsted equipment was made in this country since the demand for it was very small. Rather than build the unfamiliar looms in the company machine shop, Jewett had decided to buy from William Smith & Brothers of Manchester, England, through the agency of Thomas Porter. In one of the orders placed with Smith & Brothers five looms cost £382/10.[39] Of the preparatory machinery, the combs, gills, and drawing and roving frames were also of foreign make.

With the completion of the brussels program in the early seventies, the Lowell factory had 290 carpet looms with a capacity of 2,000,000 yards a year.[40] The Lowell reputation in brussels soon matched that of its ingrain. Of its display at the Centennial Exposition in 1876 the Awards Committee wrote, "An imposing exhibit of brussels, . . . and two-and three-ply ingrain, all of the best fabrication; the designs original and tasteful, and the colors clear and bright; the material and texture indicating excellent wearing qualities." [41] In winning such renown the Lowell concern was helping not just itself. By disproving the almost universal belief in the superiority of British manufactures, it aided the whole domestic industry.

In the same year that the management reaped such praise from impartial judges, it received considerable criticism of products as well as of other matters from its presumed lord and master, the common stockholder. Spurred by this censure the directors considered and vetoed the idea of introducing tapestry into the line, and also the proposal to add more brussels looms, the latter suggestion being rejected because space was not available.[42]

By the end of the decade, the directors' inclination to sit tight, as they had done when the depression first struck, was shattered. Further criticism by the stockholders and the accession of the energetic Arthur Lyman to the board contributed to the acceptance in 1879 of Fay's project for a new brussels mill with twenty additional looms, to cost $100,000. In contrast to a decade earlier the corporation made its own looms, but much of the preparatory machinery came from Prince, Smith & Son and Hall & Stells in Great Britain. At this time no serious consideration seems to have been given to any other line and the Lowell company became more firmly committed as a brussels and ingrain producer.

In contrast to the prewar period there was little stockholder criticism of marketing operations in the years from 1865 to 1880. A. & A. Lawrence retired at the end of the war to be succeeded by George C. Richardson—no relation of Daniel—who had been in the dry-goods business in Boston since 1835 and who already had a dozen important accounts. Richardson took the agency "on the same terms and conditions [as Lawrence] except that an increase of 1 per cent commission on sales of dress goods was agreed upon." [43] In 1871 the Lowell firm agreed to raise the commission on sales of carpeting to 1¾ per cent. The lean years of the mid-seventies led to attempts to reduce the commission in 1876 and again in 1878, but despite the failure to obtain concessions, there was little of the rancor which had characterized many of the written and verbal exchanges with the Lawrences.

Although the marketing organization remained the same, new customers appeared and more aggressive techniques were adopted. The new techniques included the traveling salesman, the branding of products, and a new outlet, the department store.

The wholesalers-retailers, such as John H. Pray of Boston and Arnold, Constable of New York were still important. Much of their business was done on a contract basis and Lowell filled their orders in sequence; thus when a premium grade of ingrain was introduced in 1877, Hemphill, Hamlin & Company of Philadelphia effectively monopolized the new fabric by putting in such a large order that the allotted capacity was taken for the season.[44] Yet while contract work was the desideratum, the management realized that it would not support capacity operation and increased efforts were made to find other customers. The old instrumentality of the auction was not important in these years except for cheap Philadelphia ingrains.[45] Because such a procedure incurred the ill will of the regular distributors,[46] Richardson preferred to dispose of excess goods through large job-lot sales.

A more important marketing tool was the drummer, the traveling salesman. To reach the growing Middle Western market, men were sent out twice a year by the selling firm with trunks full of samples. The system was well enough established by the late seventies to resist the attacks of those who called it costly and wasteful and conducive to sharp practices.[47]

Supplementing the work of the drummer in pushing the product was the famous Lowell trade-mark, the hollow stick, adopted by the concern in 1871. Unlike modern trade-marks this early identification was not an insignia attached to the carpet itself. It was a uniquely fashioned stick around which carpets were rolled before they were sent to wholesalers. Still, the introduction of such an identifying device, a step in which the Lowell management was one of the pioneers, was a definite advance in marketing methods.

While innovations were increasing the costs of marketing, improved processes and equipment and larger output were lowering manufacturing costs. Still the inefficient use of labor was one of the major complaints of the stockholders at the end of the seventies. How much this assertion of owner-interest accomplished is doubtful, but at least the complaints obtained a more respectful hearing than earlier. Two Lowellites, Peter Lawson, the former company designer, and Dr. Gilman Kimball, led the double-pronged movement by the stockholders for greater participation in management and greater manufacturing efficiency.

At the annual meeting in 1876 Lawson succeeded in having a committee appointed by the chair to look into all the affairs of the concern, the main result of which was the overhauling of the designing department in New York. Such limited action did not satisfy the minority. Two years later the directors, to head off another stockholder investigation, appointed a committee to inquire into the efficiency of Andrew F. Swapp, the superintendent. Early in May, 1878, the committee recommended Swapp's removal, but upon learning of Fay's opposition, the directors left the matter to his "careful consideration." Dissatisfied, Kimball immediately returned to the attack, questioning, in a letter to the directors the efficiency of the machinery. The latter invited him to their next meeting and, after further consideration of his charges, ordered the committee to resume investigation.[48]

This time the committee engaged the services of three outside experts, including John Houston of the Hartford Carpet Company. In a letter to Fay, assuring him of their confidence, members of the committee outlined the task of the experts: [49]

The substantial points . . . are, that there is a superfluity of labor employed, a generally inefficient operation of the existing machinery, and that the machines are in several departments, if not in all, antiquated and extravagantly costly to use.

To settle the question of the correctness of these very broad charges no minute investigation can be needed. . . . Of course there may be a question as to the relative value of some special machines, but there can be no difficulty in deciding whether the machines in use are approved machines . . . or not. . . .

Special objection has been made to the wool washing process as carried on in the Lowell Co. While it may fairly be said that starting anew, with limited space, the present arrangement would not be reproduced, there are considerations which may make a change unwise.

On December 14, the three outsiders after a cursory check declared that the equipment was standard and the cost per pound of carpet was as low as or lower than any with which they were acquainted. Fortified by this justification the directors made an unusually long report to the stockholders, defending themselves and their management and stressing the general economic malaise. Further complaints, warned the directors, would just continue "to operate injuriously upon the market value of the stock." [50]

This outburst of stockholder antagonism had been precipitated by a reverse in company fortunes. The first full year of peace, 1866, had been probably the most profitable of the century, as earnings reached a half million, even after a depreciation write-off of $62,000. For the whole period from 1866 to 1871 profits had averaged $310,000—a 15 per cent return on capital. But at the same time dividends had averaged $300,000. Consequently, the company had paid out nearly all its earnings in this period of handsome profits.

Following 1871 came five years of living off the fat of earlier gains. In

1872 profits dropped below $100,000 for the first time since 1861. Competition from imports was at a peak, 50 per cent consisting of tapestry, which bore heavily on the three-ply ingrain. Furthermore, domestic production was expanding rapidly. Under these pressures prices declined, while profit margins were further cut by a rise in wool prices.[51] To finish the brussels construction program the treasurer was forced to borrow large sums in 1872. Early the next year more money was needed when many customers asked for extended credits. Then in the fall came the major business crash, and the carpet mill went on three-quarters' time.[52] Under the impact of such events the firm lost in the neighborhood of $200,000 in 1873 and the value of its stock dropped below par. Still a 7 per cent dividend was paid, making a total drain on reserves of almost $350,000.

The drain continued as the company paid out more than it earned in 1874 and 1875. When the concern suffered another loss in 1876 the surplus sank to a scant $6,000. In such a situation it is not surprising that the directors passed the dividends at the end of 1876 and the first half of 1877. Over the next three years modest earnings allowed the payment of dividends averaging 4 per cent and the restoration of the surplus to $136,000. Finally in 1880 there was a brief return to the halcyon days of the sixties as the company earned over $400,000 even after a write-off of $119,000.

Despite this large profit and general build-up after 1876, the entire period from 1872 to 1880 saw $200,000 more paid out than earned. The average profit for those years was $98,000—5 per cent on capital—while dividends ran at $120,000 a year, or 6 per cent.

THE LYMAN PERIOD: PRODUCTION, 1881–1899

Arthur T. Lyman succeeded to the office of treasurer in 1881, but his period might almost be said to have begun with his accession to the board in 1878. Immediately he plunged into the work of the investigating committee, and from this review he became convinced of the necessity of doing something more than merely preserving the status quo. As a result of his vitalizing influence and constructive proposals, the period of the late seventies and early eighties was to witness the greatest activity in company affairs since the forties. Close scrutiny of all phases of operations continued even after this first burst as Lyman strove to keep his company abreast of developments in the rapidly changing business world. Though his new policies especially stressed efficient production, no function was neglected and a consideration of them individually is in order.

The first product decision of Lyman's term of office came in 1882. In a succinct statement to the board he summarized both the nature of the problem and, as the industrialists of the eighties saw it, the nature of the solution; Lyman's approach was to increase the production of existing lines of goods; diversification with an intent to halt the inroads of low-priced pile carpetings was not in his thinking. "It seems to me that the permanent interests of the mill will be favored by an increase of product which should put it on a fairer basis of comparison or competition with mills that have a much larger output compared to their capital." [53] In line with this object Lyman abandoned the manufacture of lastings to make room for spinning equipment and constructed a new building for 60 more brussels looms.

Next, Lyman turned to the introduction of a line of fine wilton rugs for distribution by Arnold, Constable & Company. This firm had urged Lowell to meet the demand resulting from improved hardwood floors in fine homes and apartment houses.[54] With the new floors there was no necessity of wall-to-wall carpeting to cover unsightly boards. After two years of experimentation, Lowell "Daghestan rugs" were offered to the public in 1887 with what a trade paper called "notable success." [55]

A third important product decision came in 1886 when Lyman decided to expand appreciably the ingrain capacity, making Lowell the largest ingrain mill in the world. In 1892 this capacity was further extended by the replacement of old Bigelow looms with modern looms which could produce 25 per cent more yardage. The new looms were purchased from the Crompton Loom Works of Worcester. Both these moves contributed to the increasing flood of ingrain reaching the market, forcing prices ever further downward. To get a premium-grade ingrain with an exotic brand name became the fad, and Lowell negotiated with Henry Hardwick, the ingrain inventor employed by the Hartford company, for rights to use some fancy weaves. On February 21, 1893, Hardwick reported to John Houston, president of the Hartford firm: [56]

My idea in regard to Licensing . . . would be 1¢ per sq. yd., 2¢ if we could get it. . . . They must do something to get ahead, and perhaps they might be tempted to infringe something and the way matters stand now it will be hard to do anything without infringing our rights in some way. Had we better be careful not to put them at bay and thus spend money instead of earning it.

Evidently the first overtures were successful because Crompton in March was fitting up some looms for Lowell with Hardwick attachments.[57] Whether final agreement was reached is not clear. Probably not. Panic was upon the country and "the outlook for business had made Mr. Lyman so blue he disliked very much to part with so much money." [58] Not until 1895 did Lowell market a branded premium-grade ingrain, and then in typically Boston fashion it was called "Middlesex."

In that year, 1895, Lyman undertook a thorough review of the product position of his company. What he discovered was not encouraging. As western farmers followed city folk in buying better grades of carpet, ingrain, which was the very backbone of the Lowell company's business, was threatened. True, with better days toward the end of the nineties, ingrain sales surged again, but the statement of one writer concerning ingrains that "nothing produced . . . can ever hope effectively to take their place," [59] belongs in the category of famous last words. Whether Lyman fully recognized the trend is doubtful. He had, after all, increased his ingrain capacity in 1892. But the panic of 1893 may have given him pause as well as the blues.

While the fate of ingrain was beclouded, the consumption of brussels had entered into a rapid decline. Its market had never approached ingrain in size, being limited to the upper-middle class—a class which before the turn of the century was moving into cut-pile fabrics: wiltons, axminsters, and orientals. Meanwhile the brussels looms in use had jumped from 590 in 1880 to 1,225 in 1888.[60] Clearly, the industry had excess capacity on two scores and, despite periodic pleas for parallel policies by first one industry leader and then another, the problem knew but one answer. The year 1890 was "memorable." After the greatest convulsion in the brussels trade since the founding of the industry,[61] two of the seven large producers went under, providing a temporary breather for the survivors. But the shrinking market soon revived the menace of overcapacity.

The introduction of a slightly less expensive grade of brussels under the trade name of "Middlesex" and the adaptation of some of the brussels looms to wilton production did not provide an adequate solution. The former could make little headway in the lower-middle-class market against entrenched tapestries, and while the output of the latter quadrupled during the nineties, the level was not yet high enough to absorb yardage losses in brussels. Naturally wilton prices dropped under the onrush, the severest drop coming in 1895.

The two other fabrics which were rapidly becoming popular were smyrna and axminster. The former, an inexpensive reversible tufted fabric, was hardly the quality pile that would appeal to Lowell.[62] Axminster, on the other hand, had almost infinite pattern and color range. High-pile, it was less expensive than wilton, and therefore appealed to a broader public. Though it required new looms, process changes were fairly simple. Furthermore, Lowell's two chief rivals—Bigelow and Hartford—had long been in the axminster field. In the summer of 1895 Lyman ordered 50 axminster looms from Crompton, and in July, 1896, the carpet trade journal reported: "The appearance of axminster on the Lowell price list marks an epoch in the company's history. . . . It is wilton, magnified, and expanded into a cloth of illimitable beauty." [63]

At first the Lowell product was too heavy for practical use,[64] but Lyman and the sales agent soon arrived at a more marketable commodity. Yet, production of axminsters was not on a large scale, and at the end of the Lyman regime the firm was still primarily an ingrain and brussels producer. In summary it might be said that Lyman's efforts, product-wise, had been directed toward cultivating more intensely the old stand-bys rather than spreading efforts over new lines.

Lyman made no great innovations in procurement methods. As before, the superintendent made the minor day-to-day purchases, while the treasurer was responsible for the important wool and dye requirements. Though the dyes did not approach wool in amount or value, their selection demanded much care for two reasons. First, whether justified or not, most of the complaints about American-made carpeting after 1850 were based on the dyes.[65] Secondly, the development of synthetic dyes took place rapidly after 1870 and especially after 1885. While these dyes were immediately adopted by some who wanted brilliance and novelty,[66] their tendency to fade rapidly gave pause to the more conservative manufacturers. As their quality improved, the synthetics brought an endless multiplication of shades, many of great delicacy, marvelous variety and picturesqueness [67]—thus making possible the fad of the late eighties and early nineties for pastels and delicate shadings. Eventually synthetic dyes simplified procedures and reduced the training period for dyers; [68] immediately, however, they required much painstaking experimentation.[69]

In the purchasing of the other major ingredient, wool, the treasurer continued to buy from importers and through agents. Auctions were rarely used. Since wool was the most speculative element as well as the greatest single item in the cost of producing carpets, with no market mechanisms for hedging, opportune procurement could mean the difference between a profit and a loss.

The second major cost in producing carpets was labor. While labor relations received scant attention in comparison with that received in either the pre-Civil War or post-World War I eras, Lyman's attitude on the whole was conciliatory. The directors' committee, of which he was a member, wrote in 1879: "We have kept our mills in operation thus still keeping together our experienced and skilled help. . . . Our help have been contented that we have been able to do as well by them as we have done." [70] In 1885 Lyman in his annual report stated, "I am sorry to say that the recent sharp declines in the prices of carpets have made it necessary to give notice of a reduction of wages," and then reiterated "how helpless manufacturers are in this matter of a reduction of wages in the face of the crushing fall in prices."

At the same time the company became less paternalistic. By the early eighties the character of the famed Lowell boardinghouse had changed considerably. As the Yankee farm girl was supplanted by the immigrant, the immediate advantage of the houses to the company declined. As the immigrant group became ever more varied, the feasibility of all living together decreased and the new groups took less kindly to the rules and to restrictions on meals.[71] As a result, when a block of tenements was torn down in 1882 to make room for the new brussels mill, Lyman decided not to replace the housing. While later there were some complaints from the workers that because of the lack of company housing they had to pay high prices on the "street," [72] a union leader, familiar with other carpet centers, stressed the low cost of favorable living conditions in Lowell in this period.[73]

He was equally emphatic on the merits of Lowell's working conditions. The new buildings of the eighties provided more space, light, and ventilation.[74] In the late eighties, also, the 1½-hour early closing on Saturday initiated in 1864 was extended to free the whole afternoon.[75] By this time, hours, which had been set by the agents at 11 a day in 1853, had been reduced by law to 60 a week in 1874. A further reduction to 58 came in 1892.

Though the workers always had the advantage of being paid in cash, they were paid but once a month until 1884. Then, despite the increased clerical work, the interval was reduced to a fortnight. Finally in November, 1885, weekly disbursements were instituted.

These steps were taken at a time when there was considerable agitation over wage rates. Though the employees had suffered several cuts in the seventies, their living standards had probably improved [76] and, in contrast to the turbulence of this period in the Philadelphia area where wage rates were higher, Lowell merely experienced a walkout by 11 warpers in 1878. They were immediately discharged and their positions filled without incident.[77]

The first major labor trouble in the history of the Lowell Manufacturing Company came in the mid-eighties when workers all over the country were afire with a newly acquired sense of importance. The brussels weavers of Philadelphia, a comparatively homogeneous group of Scottish and English, strong in union traditions, with above average economic strength and interest-consciousness, led the way to rebellion among the carpet workers. Their long strike from May to September, 1884, against a wage cut was no sooner lost than the ingrain weavers went out in protest against a rate reduction from 6 to 5 cents a yard. After the manufacturers had tried unsuccessfully to recruit replacements in Lowell and elsewhere, the matter was compromised in April, 1885, at 5½ cents.[78] Only a short strike by the same ingrain weavers in 1888 marred labor relations in Philadelphia for the rest of the decade.[79]

While the Philadelphia manufacturers were having their troubles, there was labor unrest elsewhere. The Higgins mill in New York had repeated difficulties, complicated by a jurisdictional dispute. A few miles to the north at Yonkers, the employees of Alexander Smith were out on one strike or another for the better part of the time from December, 1884, to July, 1885. Closer to Lowell, 600 operatives of the Roxbury company walked out in January, 1885.[80]

With the possible exception of the one at Roxbury, all the previous upheavals were directly connected with the Knights of Labor. The interruption at Lowell was not—though obviously it was influenced by the Knights. The Lowell workers had accepted a 10 per cent cut in February, 1884, without complaint. Despite Lyman's profession of helplessness and hope that a reduction would keep the mills in operation,[81] the employees were "uneasy" when the next 10 per cent reduction was posted in February, 1885. Winders, brussels weavers, and finally ingrain weavers walked out, the last proving the weakest link. Gradually they drifted back and after a week they voted to return. Such a defection caused a momentary reconsideration by the brussels group, but they hung on for two weeks more.

Though the strike was lost, tempers were not. Lyon, the superintendent, had been courteous and conciliatory throughout, the workers well behaved. No attempt was made to bring in outsiders or to expel the leaders.[82] In fulfillment of the promise to raise wages as soon as business permitted, the restoration was ordered on April 23.[83]

With the restoration came nine years of labor peace. The panic of 1893, with losses to the company and reduced earnings to the employees, created another impasse. After shutdowns throughout the summer and fall, the treasurer made some recommendations in a directors' meeting at the end of December, and according to the minutes,[84]

it was voted that in the opinion of the Directors, it is advisable to start up the Mills for a two weeks run, and that if at the end of that time the prospects of business should in the judgment of the Treasurer warrant a continuance of manufacture, and the work people can be engaged to go on at reduced wages, the Mills be run for a longer period.

The attitude of the workers was indeed crucial. They returned to work on December 26, and in January came the wage cut of 17 per cent. Equally disturbing to the operatives was the short working time. By March the mills were running only 37½ hours a week instead of 58,[85] and yet the new fast looms maintained the former output.[86]

On May 1, after hours had dropped to 30, a delegation of "lady" ingrain weavers waited on Lyon "to ask that the machinery in their department be run on full time" so they could make better pay, or that "pay be raised, or that a complete shut-down be made." Lyon maintained that trade was too bad to accede to the first two suggestions. The women were politely unimpressed, pointing to the fact that they received about $4.00 a piece (web) while Lowell's competitors paid $5.17.[87] Not only was the ensuing strike unusual in its instigation by women, but it also was the only significant disturbance in the carpet industry during that year and indeed it was the only important agitation in Lowell.

Other carpet employees soon joined the women, but their adherence brought matters no nearer a settlement. Only with the seasonal revival of business in July could the company offer the necessary full time.

THE LYMAN PERIOD: MARKETING AND FINANCE, 1881–1899

The failure of wool prices and labor costs to keep pace over much of the period with the decline in carpet prices gave impetus to the cost-conscious executive's drive for more efficient manufacturing methods. New buildings and new machinery played their part in reducing expenses and Lyman stressed the rearrangement of processes to insure a systematic flow of goods.

Unit costs were of course also reduced by the 80 per cent increase in Lowell's productive capacity during the eighties. The plant could turn out 3,600,000 yards of carpeting a year—35 per cent of it brussels—representing about 8 per cent of the ingrain and brussels output of the country. However, a similar great expansion by almost everyone in the business resulted in the large output which contributed greatly to the profitless prosperity of the eighties—profitless to the owner, that is, though most advantageous to the consumer.

In addition to price wars, the competitive battle was waged with increasing vehemence in the field of style. Under economic pressures style cycles shortened, the number of patterns in a line doubled and trebled, and offerings of new styles were presented twice a year. As the items in each offering passed rapidly into oblivion the wholesaler and retailer and even the manufacturer felt impelled to dump old stock, whatever the loss. Thus the end of each season was likely to see a precipitous drop in prices.[88] One observer commented in 1890: "It [is] impossible to determine from one season to another what freak or fluctuation in the popular taste will next dominate the market. In this state of facts the designing department becomes the real key to the success of the mill." [89]

The Lowell firm was always style conscious, if not a leader in style extremes. Large customers, such as John H. Pray, might provide their own patterns or at least make suggestions, but Lowell from the first days of Peter Lawson had had its own designers. At first they were inclined to be mere copyists. Then in the fifties came the introduction of original and more artistic fashions—a lead quickly followed by the rival Hartford company.[90] Simultaneously the main part of the designing department was shifted from the mill to New York. In 1876 the designing staff consisted of six Scots. The facilities were further expanded at the end of 1882 and by the mid-eighties there were about eight regular stylists. Undoubtedly some of these were American, but the majority were still foreign-born.

While each designer expressed his own personality, he was dominated by prevailing trends. In the fifties Lawson's designs were asymmetrical and Elemir Ney's symmetrical, but both were composed of flowers, fruits, and sweeping foliage. Dark colors, reds and greens, predominated.[91]

A few years later arabesques, Etruscan patterns, and small geometric figures were the rage.[92] One creation, a large red medallion surrounded by huge figures in red and green on a black background, achieved a popularity which lasted over twenty years.

The Gilded Age of the seventies brought on spirals, flowers, ferns, geometrical designs within geometrical designs, and all with a bigness, a vividness, that was overpowering. While such modes were pre-eminent in tapestries, they soon spread to other cheaper fabrics. The special ingrain created by Lowell for the Centennial Exhibition—Chimerique by Guiraud—was a fanciful concoction of monstrous figures emblematic of the seven deadly sins, all encompassed by bold scrolls.[93] In its better-grade fabrics, brussels and wilton, the firm was more conservative. Here, catering to a taste influenced by Persian carpets imported by such houses as W. & J. Sloane and John H. Pray,[94] Lowell brought out Persian, Japanese, Pompeian, and medieval motifs in the mid-seventies. Even here caution was necessary. One experiment to improve public taste was a failure and the carpet trade journal warned against high art in brussels—too high for anyone but the managers to appreciate.[95]

By the end of the seventies the conglomeration of blacks, scarlets, and dark greens was being displaced by lighter background hues, such as tans and olives. Flowers there were in profusion, but they were more likely to be spaced in separate clusters. A sudden passion for borders was another feature of the decade.

As the eighties drew to a close, the light backgrounds continued but in pastel shades. Daintiness, choice small effects, became the keynote.[96] But no sooner was this style hailed as an advance than taste changed. Sharp outlines were demanded. The ensuing switch from extremely light to extremely dark carpets was so rapid in 1897 and 1898 that many a room became a nightmare or a decorator's bonanza.[97] The great popularity of orientals influenced the domestic artists throughout the nineties, but the range for better fabrics included every phase of decorative art—antique, oriental, Empire, Louis XIV, Colonial, Indian.[98]

The increased importance of styles gave rise to a new merchandizing tool: the "showing," or formal presentation of lines, which started about 1890. Otherwise the marketing techniques remained the same as in previous decades; yet the competitive pressures of the eighties so intensified their use that they often seem to be new phenomena. Only in advertising was the advance slight. Trade-marks became more important. Most manufacturers had concocted some form of identification by the mid-eighties, several cases were fought over Lowell's famed hollow roller stick which had been registered in 1871, and Lowell added several more brand names in the nineties. Despite these indications that the company recognized the importance of establishing brand preference, the effort was directed only toward wholesalers and retailers and not toward the ultimate consumer.

These developments, plus the general changes in American economic life, altered the methods and functions of the selling house. In order to save the commission, to gain efficiency through integration, and to sell more aggressively, many carpet firms were taking over the selling task themselves. Not only was the selling agent's performance suspect and his profits coveted; his *raison d'etre* in many instances had ceased to exist. First of all familiarity with distributors was common property after fifty years in a business. Better communications facilitated the establishment of sales headquarters in New York which could be closely controlled by the home office in Boston. Better communications and improved manufacturing methods permitted selling from samples. More intensive soliciting of customers sent salesmen into byways of the land—to a large extent superseding the annual visits to New York by many country merchants. The agent with many accounts had lost his magnet value and a roving sales force could be directed by the manufacturer—who was already bearing the cost.

Furthermore, the development of credit-rating agencies had made credit information generally available, and in the hurly-burly of competition the manufacturing company was often more willing to take a risk to clinch a sale than the agent would have been. Finally, the strongest link in the agent's chain of usefulness—financial support—was no longer necessary; company reserves and improved banking facilities rendered this nugatory.

Despite these conditions—and while other concerns were setting up their own sales departments—Lowell continued with agents; Smith, Hogg, & Gardner succeeded Richardson on the latter's retirement in 1885. Relationships changed, however. Arnold, Constable received exclusive distributing rights for the new Daghestan rugs, while large dealers, such as Arnold, Constable, Sloane, and H. B. Claflin, all advertised Lowell goods at the same list price as the agent. More and more the Lowell firm had to pay for the necessary, and expanding, marketing services. The agreement in 1886 with the new selling agents, Smith, Hogg & Gardner, illustrates this development: [99]

The carpets, or yarns . . . are all to be sold by you and a commission of 1½ per cent is to be allowed on the net sales of yarns, and of 2½ per cent on the net sales of carpets. These commissions are to cover all expenses or charges for commission, handling, labor, truckage, postage, telegrams, rents, storage, and all incidental expenses after delivery by freight lines, excepting the expense of salesmen in travelling, rent of office . . . for designers, special advertising, ordered or authorized by the Treasurer and . . . costs actually paid for collecting checks or notes.

The big expense was the road salesman. As competition increased, his tempo whirled ever faster. Originally the salesmen went out to take orders from the wholesalers early in the spring and again early in the fall. Gradually the "fall" departure date was pushed back through the summer until in 1882 most salesmen went West before the middle of June. Because of the Christmas rush, the majority waited until after the first of the year before departing for the "spring" tour. Then too, the volume of consumer buying was not as heavy in the spring as in the fall. Originally quite the contrary had been true, but late in the century with more people vacationing in the summer, redecoration was left to the autumn.[100]

While the Lowell sales agent organized a traveling staff, he did not participate in the revival of the auction system. Stephen Sanford & Son started the process with auctions in 1880 and 1881, and Alexander Smith followed with one in 1886. But it was the big Smith auctions of the nineties which shook the industry. On four days in November, 1891, W. & J. Sloane, the agent for Alexander Smith, disposed of $2,500,000 worth of goods, a volume which sent prices reeling. Lowell immediately cut prices by 5 and 10 cents a yard.

It was not merely a matter of volume or price level which disrupted the market and left the manufacturer and merchant groping. It was the unexpected change in the marketing philosophy that troubled carpet men. Previous auctions had been a device to clean out old patterns. The new policy adopted by Alexander Smith, was to operate at full capacity, depression or no, and then dispose of the surplus by auction. Gloomily John Wood, of the Higgins company, commented:[101]

There is no way of accounting for the action of Alexander Smith and Sons. With the market glutted in goods, a condition of things for which they are mainly responsible, they are running full force on new goods at prices which are below the cost of production. It seems to me that a conservative management would require a limitation of production.

A second huge Smith auction followed in 1892, and a third, the most disastrous of all, in 1898. With forced sales on a dead market, bids were low and deals were consummated at 10 to 20 per cent below wholesale.[102] More than a year later the *American Wool and Cotton Reporter* still remembered the occasion with pain, "It will . . . take considerable advance on all lines of carpets to bring them up even to what was the natural price before the 'auction slaughter' of May and June, 1898." [103] The ingrain market received a body blow as the disastrously low prices of the Smith tapestries enticed many customers in the rural areas. With improving economic conditions after 1900 their defection was permanent.

While Lyman and the sales agent ignored the auction as a marketing device, they assumed leadership in the establishment of price-maintenance contracts. Welcomed by large dealers, the first price agreement, instituted in 1883, provided that the dealer would not sell ingrain for less than list. To prevent clandestine concessions, his terms of sale were spelled out. Dealer sales made before September 1 (or March 1) could be dated as of

TABLE 7

LOWELL MANUFACTURING COMPANY

Prices for Various Fabrics, Selected Years   1882 to 1895

(Per Yard)

	1882	1885	1890	1895	Per Cent of Decline from 1890 to 1895
Wilton, five-frame	$2.35	$2.05	$2.10	$1.75	16
Brussels, five-frame	1.40	1.20	1.20	.975	18
Ingrain, Superfine three-ply	1.10	.825	.75	.675	10
Ingrain, Extra Superfine two-ply	.85	.65	.575	.475	17

Source: Price lists in *The Philadelphia Carpet Trade* and *The American Carpet and Upholstery Trade.*

that time; for the rest, credit was to be limited to four months with no discounts to exceed 3 per cent, 30 days, or 4 per cent, 10 days. Enforcement provisions included forfeiture of discounts and loss of the account.[104] Later an additional clause allowed a rebate of 2½ cents a yard on a sale of 25 pieces or more.[105] Lowell's own terms—or more accurately those of its agent—to the dealers were two months or 2 per cent for cash in 10 days, until 1887 when they became 30 days less 2 per cent. After 1886 the firm released dealers from price maintenance late each season. This concession to end-of-season price-cutting may have undermined the effectiveness of the agreements, for by the nineties nothing was heard of them.

While the Lowell scheme may have contributed to price stability within a season, it could not deter the annual downward trend. Lyman reported that at the end of 1884 prices were about 25 per cent below those of four years earlier (see Table 7). The almost continuous downward drive of the carpet prices after 1884 aroused even Smith, Hogg & Gardner from their lethargy of usually "permitting the merits of the Lowell Company's fabrics to speak for themselves," [106] and caused the Carpet Manufacturers Association to make futile efforts to establish price agreements. Volume reached new heights; inferior goods undermined those of reputable companies.[107]

Among the changes in financing from the prewar days are two negative aspects and one positive. First, while financial support had been a prime function of A. & A. Lawrence, the contract with Smith, Hogg, & Gardner carried no stipulations on the matter. Secondly, little was done in the way of permanent financing since no new capital was added and few profits were available. Finally banks, commercial and private, had assumed much of the burden of supplying funds for current operations. After a lapse following the Civil War, loans from the Massachusetts Hospital Life Insurance Company were resumed on a large scale in 1881 and 1882. The immediate occasion for the renewal was the expansion program of those years but after 1884 loans of from $50,000 to $250,000 were an integral part of Lowell's medium-term borrowing program.[108]

For the purpose of obtaining loans Lyman had the authority to issue notes of the firm up to $1,000,000. During the eighties this limit was raised to $1,500,000 and in the nineties to $1,800,000. In the latter decade F. S. Moseley was the largest customer for these notes, discounting paper worth between $50,000 and $125,000 for three to four months' duration at 2½ to 4 per cent interest. Other discounters included, in New York, the United States Trust Company and the Fourth National Bank of New York; in the Boston area, the National Bank of the Commonwealth, the Provident Institution for Savings, Suffolk Savings Bank, Harvard College, and the Lowell Machine Shop, to mention but a few. At various times the mills in Lowell also discounted one or another's notes.[109]

Inventories were the most important single factor behind the greater investment of the eighties. Increased capacity required larger reserves; increased style diversification demanded more varieties. Driven by such pressures, inventories rose from a postwar average of $800,000 to equal the Civil War peak of $1,300,000 by the end of the eighties.

Lyman apparently experienced no difficulty in borrowing. On the whole his financial policies were conservative. Though the concern suffered losses of $48,000 and $36,000 in 1881 and 1888, respectively, he managed to add a few dollars to his surplus in the years from 1880 to 1892. To accomplish this, dividend payments were twice passed and the annual average for the period was but 4 per cent, or $86,000. With earnings averaging only $88,000, the expanded capacity had to be financed by borrowing.

The financial gains of the early Lyman era, such as they were, were quickly wiped out by the losses following the panic of 1893. After deficits of $20,000 in 1893 and $40,000 in 1894, semiannual dividends were passed three times in succession, and in 1897, after a poor year, another dividend was passed. Despite these precautions over the whole depression span from 1892 to 1898, dividend payments, averaging $56,000 annually, exceeded the average earnings of $42,000. This excess, and a modest addition to plant and equipment, came at the expense of the working capital.

Stock prices naturally were affected by these variations in earning power. In the good year, 1880, the market price surged to $1,000. In 1884 a low of $551 was quoted. For most of the time in the eighties the price range ran from $575 to $725—a symbol of peaceful days compared with what was to come.[110] After 1893 the quotation never rose above $587.

AN APPRAISAL

Though the Lowell Manufacturing Company's financial position appeared less favorable in 1898 than in 1880, the company's performance has to be judged against its background. Amid the economic vicissitudes of the eighties and nineties, Lyman's record was a creditable one. Financially Lyman had preserved the company's excellent credit rating. He had dealt with his working men and women in a difficult period without leaving a heritage of rancor. He had improved his equipment and buildings and cut costs. Finally he had broadened the product base by strengthening the production of wilton and going into axminster.

In their search for new products, Lyman and his predecessors were typical of the businessmen of the last half of the nineteenth century. Those firms which could not, or would not, develop new lines died. Because toward the end of the century Lowell was slow in getting into axminster and into seamless rugs, both of which became dominant features for a long period in the future, the company's previous adaptability is often overlooked. Lowell was one of the first to go into brussels on a sizable scale after the expiration of the brussels patents. By doing this Lowell benefited from the windfall of the expanding market. Tapestry might have brought greater gains, but that is questionable, and Jewett had sound reasons for making his decision not to enter tapestry production. Likewise the increase in capacity in the late seventies and early eighties seems to have come at a time when the demand was growing rapidly. Unfortunately, however, other manufacturers were also expanding. The creation of excessive capacity was accentuated by rapid changes in public taste and by the almost immediate appearance of competing carpet weaves. The allotted time-span of brussels' quantitative importance proved to be but twenty years. This relatively short period of large-scale demand upset the calculations of 1869 and 1882, leaving Lowell with a heavy fixed investment which denied it a certain flexibility—especially in money-scarce times. It seems that Lyman should not have invested in new ingrain looms in 1892, but the alternative might well have meant the abandonment of ingrain. And, after all, ingrain still accounted for more yardage than all the rest put together. Significantly, no other major producer dropped ingrain during these years.

Overproduction was a concomitant as every company tried to meet its problems in the same way. Even when the necessity for limitation on output became obvious, it was done on a factory-by-factory basis rather than in conformity with any industry-wide scheme.

The same reluctance to co-operate was evident in relation to price agreements. As the nineties progressed Lowell played a lone hand. Perhaps this was because of her age-long role of price leader. Perhaps the range of her products made an agreement with any one segment of the industry impracticable. Whatever the reason, Lowell frequently distressed the industry by large price cuts and sales at the end of the season.

Apart from these sporadic flashes, Lowell's marketing methods were hardly aggressive. Indeed, marketing would seem to have been the firm's greatest weakness. Here was divided authority as in no other function, and the diffusion of responsibility almost certainly decreased the possibility of aggressive action. This is not to belittle completely Lowell's marketing efforts. The company through its selling agents seems to have adopted the use of salesmen at least as early as other companies. In 1898 its New York showroom followed the others uptown—to Herald Square. The Lowell company took an active part in exhibitions, and it was a leader in the adoption of trade-marks. Since the idea of a concerted direct appeal to the customer was twenty-five years in the future, Lowell's limited and colorless advertising program cannot be condemned by such standards. But the fact that advertising was not considered a necessity in the nineties seems to indicate a lack of awareness of selling as a major problem.

There is no question that Lowell had one of the "names" in the industry at the close of the period. However, the same dominance it had before the Civil War could hardly be expected. In ante-bellum days Lowell and a few companies were the sum total of the American carpet industry and ingrain was virtually the only product; by the end of the century many large units were turning out a wide variety of fabrics. Furthermore the dramatic days in ingrain manufacture belonged to the past. It was the man or the company making the newer and more exotic fabrics that caught the attention. The newcomers and the old-timers might bow with respect to the Lowell name—if they paused; but in an exhausting era of pushing for position and profit, who had time to pause?

Lowell was alive because it had not paused itself. Though it was not the innovator which it had been in the first period, we seriously becloud our judgment if we measure its activities only in terms of the originators. At all times its management had showed a willingness to move ahead, to spend money, to adopt other people's ideas. After three-score years and ten, after three decades of economic storm, the structure was intact. There was little in the record to suggest that it was to have no future as an independent unit.

Yet the factory, the raw materials, the working people, the salesmen, the financial resources, all these depended on a guiding hand. It was the failure to provide for management succession which was to doom the concern in spite of the otherwise adequate performance of its multiple functions. This episode is a striking example of the importance of the man with business and administrative aptitudes.

The problem of maintaining strong executive leadership was as critical as any. Often the task of providing the leader for the next generation is considered as the special concern of a partnership or a small family-owned enterprise. Certainly it was to be an issue sooner or later in the Higgins, Sanford, and Bigelow firms. It was to be equally a challenge to Lowell and Hartford.

Originally, of course, the owners provided the management. George Lyman was a large stockholder; and, though he held many other executive positions, the relatively small size of the unit and the concentration of the marketing function elsewhere enabled him to work on a part-time basis. His son Arthur operated in the same manner. But in many respects Arthur Lyman was a throwback to a bygone age. As a result of the dispersion of the stock an individual was rarely sufficiently interested to feel called upon to assume continuing responsibility. Sale of stock offered the easy way out if the situation looked bad. Secondly, an increasing unit size meant that supervision of a successful company was a full-time job. Thus, though Arthur Lyman had three sons, they could not assume active direction of their father's manifold interests at Lowell, at Holyoke, in Boston and elsewhere.

Where could the owners turn for the management they were themselves unable or unwilling to provide? To the organization? In the nineteenth century a business the size of the Lowell company had few executives. In the Lowell company the treasurer and the manufacturing man were the only important ones, thus limiting promotion from within to virtually one man—the factory agent. Samuel Fay came to the fore in this way. But if the factory agent did not have sufficient breadth of vision or the necessary connections, the owners had to find an outsider. In the forties they selected Israel Whitney, who in addition to his mercantile background had previously acted as the agent of Boston capitalists. Next came a manufacturer, temporarily at loose ends, and then another merchant.

But reliance on outside sources is never a secure basis for management succession, nor really any kind of a solution. Indeed, though Arthur Lyman faced many problems at the end of the 1890's—cost relationships, product-determination, marketing structure—none was so critical as the necessity of providing for his successor as chief executive of the Lowell Manufacturing Company.

CHAPTER 5

YEARS OF ADAPTATION:

The Hartford Carpet Company, 1854–1901

The careers of the Lowell Manufacturing Company and its oldest and closest rival, the Hartford Carpet Company, are parallel in many respects —and in none more than in the character of their stockholders and management. The Hartford owners were Connecticut versions of the Boston coterie. The 93 men who subscribed to the stock of the Hartford Carpet Company in December, 1853, and January, 1854, were capitalists with a wide variety of interests. With a hand in many of the projects which were creating a manufacturing and insurance center in Hartford, these men were too busy to give their carpet enterprise more than general policy attention. As a result, Hartford like Lowell laid itself open to difficulties of management succession.

REVIVAL: THE HARTFORD CARPET COMPANY

By the spring of 1853 it had become obvious to the trustees of the bondholders, Brown Brothers, that the old Thompsonville concern could not be reconstituted. Neither would the Lowell company consider joining them in a new venture, though it had agreed to transfer the important Bigelow loom contract to a successor.

It was left, therefore, to a new group, Hartford businessmen and professional men, headed by Timothy Mather Allyn, Edmund Grant Howe, and William R. Cone, to organize a new company to take over the plant at Thompsonville. Cone was one of Hartford's outstanding lawyers.[1] Allyn and Howe were both farm boys who had established themselves in the dry-goods business in Hartford about 1830. Allyn had invested his first profits in real estate but by the end of the forties was ready to put his funds into industrials. When his current trading partnership had become a creditor and then a stockholder of the bankrupt Thompsonville company, he had been elected treasurer of the stricken firm. Howe, after partnerships with Junius S. Morgan, Roland Mather, and Joseph Pratt, had served as founder, president, and director of several of Hartford's young insurance companies and banks. For a period he was a member of a New York banking house, Ketchem, Howe, & Company.[2]

Though these men did not have the resources of the Lowell capitalists, they had much the same motives in shifting their funds from the old mercantile pursuits to the new industrial enterprises. With no direct manufacturing experience they availed themselves of the know-how of Orrin Thompson who agreed to join with them and to serve as superintendent. His first assignment was to arrange for the purchase of the bonds at 50 cents on the dollar.[3] Next he assisted in getting a charter for the Hartford Carpet Company from the Connecticut legislature in May, 1853, a step which was necessary despite the state's General Incorporation Act because of the size of the capital involved. The summer was spent in arranging for the acquisition of the Thompsonville property and bonds. After a court decision supported the prior claim of the bondholders, the creditors had to be content with a token payment of $50, paid by Allyn in December, 1853.

Renewed efforts to interest the Lowell concern in the project proving futile,[4] Allyn, Cone, and Howe turned to their own community for financial support. On December 1, 1853, 35 men subscribed for the $200,000 (in $100 shares) required for organization, and soon after the New Year the company was formally called into existence with the election of seven directors. Operation was many steps removed from mere existence, however, and the next two months were busy ones. Cone and Allyn were paid $400,000, partly in stock and partly in cash for the property, the bonds, and the expenses incurred in obtaining a charter. Within a week a committee raised $300,000 in addition to the first subscription—the task being simplified by the hint that the valuation was fixed so low that stock dividends were a future certainty. Another committee was chosen to get the manufacturing under way, bylaws were adopted, and two $10 installments for March 1 and April 1 were called on the subscribed shares.

Finally at the end of February the full complement of officers was acquired. After much hesitation Howe accepted the office of treasurer and his partner, Roland Mather, the position of secretary. Allyn became president and general handyman. With the formal organization completed, Howe wrote modestly to Israel Whitney of his plans: "The incipient stages to get in running order have been taken, and goods will doubtless be turned out during the spring in small way. . . . I take hold of it with *everything* to learn about it, and may be glad in a Yankee way to ask you some questions."[5]

Since the new executives were strangers to the carpet business, they hastened to assemble a staff from the old Thompsonville firm. While many of the former employees had drifted away, some like John Houston remained to form the nucleus of the new force. Thompson who had asked for a salary of $2,500 and stock worth $5,000, accepted $2,000. For the $5,000 in stock he had to wait until 1860 when the directors voted him the sum in cash, with provisions to prevent attachment by his creditors.[6]

TABLE 8

HARTFORD CARPET COMPANY

Production and Sale of Carpeting   1854

(In Yards)

	Production	Sale
Ingrain		
Extra three-ply	71,325	42,337
Imperial three-ply	56,678	27,837
Superfine two-ply	241,793	150,632
Venetian		
Twilled	56,558	11,994
Plain	76,153	13,737
Brussels	3,593	596
Total	506,100	247,133

Source: Hartford Carpet Company, Directors' and Stockholders' minutes, Jan. 24, 1855.

By the spring of 1854 Howe considered his job done and on June 14 he was succeeded as treasurer by Roland Mather, who also continued as secretary. At that time Allyn officially became the general agent with a salary of $2,000 a year as against $1,000 for Mather.[7]

The selling function was handled by J. W. Paige & Company, an arrangement undoubtedly influenced by the fact that Henry G. Thompson, former sales agent for the Thompsonville firm and son of Orrin, was to be in charge of the account.

By October 1, 1854, the last of the ingrain power looms and all the brussels hand looms were in operation—just in time for a business recession. Production was cut in November and December, whether by agreement with the Lowell company is not clear.[8] In December, wages were reduced. Weavers suffered a reduction in pay of almost one-third.

Still, at the first annual meeting the management could report: "While the Fabrics we manufacture have yielded in price about 10%[,] wool the principal material from which the Carpets are made has had to submit to a still larger reduction leaving the balance somewhat in favor of the Company." [9] The company had made 506,100 yards of carpeting, valued at $367,071 (see Table 8). Of this it had sold 247,133 yards for $168,890, which had produced a profit of $42,202.[10]

Instead of paying out the earnings in cash, the management recommended an increase of $100,000 in capitalization, $40,000 of which would be a stock dividend. The $60,000 in new cash would increase the working capital of the concern—the original estimate of $300,000 having proved inadequate—thus reducing time-consuming, costly, and risky borrowing.

When the stockholders agreed to this assessment, Mather considered that his job of placing the company on a firm financial foundation was completed. Accordingly he declined re-election as treasurer and George Roberts was selected in his stead.

THE MANAGEMENT, 1855–1901

The retirement of Mather and the election of Roberts, coming at the conclusion of the first year of operation, marks the end of the organizing phase of the history of the Hartford Carpet Company. The path had been charted, the tools provided, the successful trial run had been made. Now the election of Roberts settled the question of management for the next twenty years.

Son of a prosperous East Hartford farmer, Roberts had been a banker, iron merchant, and wholesale grocer in both New York and Hartford. Retiring from the wholesale grocery business in 1853, he had both time and money to give to a new venture. Eminently practical, he could be counted on for sound, if not imaginative, administration.

The bylaws of the new company as usual recognized three groups: the stockholders, the directors, and the officers. The original bylaws had created four offices: those of president, secretary, treasurer, and agent. Though the presidency had the Orrin Thompson tradition of an active executive behind it, the company constitution delineated a Lowell-type official, an incumbent who did little more than preside over the meetings of the directors. In contrast to the Lowell company, however, the executive duties were not given to the treasurer who was a strictly financial official. Rather they were given to the "agent" who was considerably more than a mill superintendent. He handled purchasing, acted as general manager of the concern and drew drafts on the treasurer. Completing the group was the secretary, a minor record-keeping functionary.

The Hartford company had no need for so many executives. Under Roberts and later under Houston the three top offices—presidency, treasurership, and factory agency—were combined in one man, but a division of tasks in 1896, when Houston was ill, reveals that there had been changes in the duties of these offices. At that time the board defined the duties as follows: "The President to have charge of the buying of the Wool, Yarns and Coal. The Treasurer to have control of the finances of the Company, the selling of the goods, and the New York agency. The President and Treasurer to mutually decide as to wages, production of goods, purchase of new machinery, . . . additions to plants, etc." [11] While this listing was probably influenced by the capabilities of the individual men and the exigencies of the situation, the numerous activities of the president are in strong contrast to the duties performed by the Richardsons in the Lowell company. By the beginning of the twentieth century the president per se had assumed many functions and was well on the way to becoming the chief executive officer of the Hartford company.

The powers of the directors were much more extensive than those of their Lowell counterparts, since they elected all the officers and drew up the bylaws. In practice the Hartford directors contented themselves with a very general oversight of the company's business and, using few committees of investigation, they devoted even less time to the firm's affairs than did the members of the Lowell directorate. Throughout the period they continued to be selected from the Hartford business community, with little turnover in personnel. On a board of seven, only 18 names appear in forty-seven years, and of these John Houston and William Wetmore, the New York iron merchant who had been prominent in the last days of the old Thompsonville company, were the only ones who were not members of the group which was directing the business life of the rising city of Hartford.

Although in 1900 the members of the board held only 1,200 out of 15,000 shares, they were representative of their constituents who were primarily Hartford businessmen and their families. The total number of owners had grown from the original 35 subscribers in 1853 to over 550. When the firm got under way in 1854, 19 of these stockholders owned 57 per cent of the stock—the large holders being Allyn and Cone. The median investment was about $3,000 to $3,400. At the end of the century the median was about $1,000, with 58 stockholders controlling a majority of the stock. Francis Goodwin, a relative of J. P. Morgan, held the largest block, 569 shares. His brother, James, who was a director, owned another 471.

The Hartford stockholders did little more than elect the directors. They had no vote on the chief executive, no share in making the bylaws, and, after 1857, it took 20 owners holding 2,000 shares to call a stockholders' meeting for a stated purpose.[12] With little to do, stockholder interest lagged—and with it, attendance. Except for 1866, the shares voted at the annual meeting before 1880 averaged about 24 per cent of the total—after that about 16 per cent.

More important in the actual direction of the concern than the stockholders was an executive left unmentioned in the corporation constitution: the mill superintendent. Perhaps his importance was enhanced by the caliber of the men who held the position. The first was Orrin Thompson, the second, John L. Houston. As Thompson was the most important figure in Thompsonville's history in the first-half century, Houston was to be in the second. He succeeded Thompson as superintendent in 1861, and Roberts as chief executive in 1878. Houston's successor as superintendent in 1878 was his brother-in-law, Lyman Upson.

Following Houston's retirement in the mid-nineties, George Roberts, Jr., became the chief executive for the few remaining years of the firm's history. Perhaps because we know that the end is coming, the regime of the second Roberts takes on the coloration of mere waiting, marking time, an epilogue to the creative years of the company under George Roberts, Sr., from 1855 to 1878, and then under John L. Houston to 1894.

THE REGIME OF ROBERTS, SR., 1855–1878

The term of office of George Roberts, Sr., coincided with the prosperity of the fifties, the Civil War, the ensuing years of economic uncertainty, and finally the depression of the mid-seventies. Despite the shadows of the postwar years, Roberts' career ran its course under much more favorable circumstances than did that of his successor.

With the Thompsonville operation in order, the Hartford directors turned their attention in 1856 to the sister plant at Tariffville, which the Brown Brothers had not been able to unload. In view of the previous close connection of the two plants, this interest was natural. But there was a deeper motivation. The owners of the Hartford concern wanted to be sure that for the time being products from the Tariffville mill would not flood the market. As officially explained: "The Board were induced to become the purchasers of this property from the consideration that the present consumption of carpet would not warrant the putting in operation of so large an establishment." [13] The Lowell company, while declining to join immediately in the deal, offered to pay the Hartford company $6,000 annually for four years,[14]

provided that the mills . . . shall not be used for the manufacture of Carpets or Carpet yarns . . . and provided further that whensoever the said Hartford Carpet Company shall desire . . . to use the said mills, within the term . . . they shall be bound first to offer to the Lowell Manufacturing Company one undivided half of said purchased property.

This proposal, the Hartford directors rejected. Instead, they went forward alone, and on May 21, 1856, Hartford bought the property from the bondholders for $120,000, of which $20,000 was payable in cash and the rest in 6 per cent bonds due in five years. For security, a mortgage was given.

By 1859 the approaching expiration of the Bigelow patent, and generally better business, induced the directors to put the Tariffville plant into operation. This required additional capital, but, with good dividend payments assuring the favorable acceptance of a new issue, 63 shares were sold at market value and 3,312 were offered to stockholders at $85 a share. The first installment of payments for shares was not due until February 1, 1860, and then only 10 per cent was required monthly, but to encourage

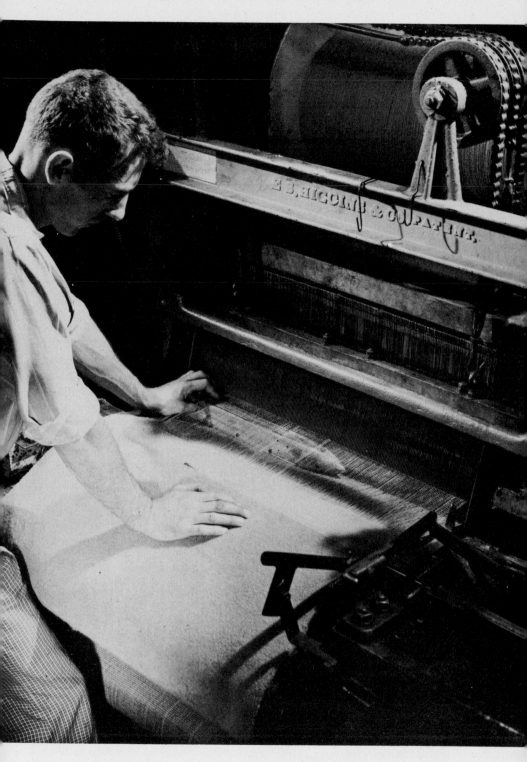

Narrow Loom; originally fabrics were woven in 27- or 36-inch widths and sewed together to make rugs or wall-to-wall coverings

Axminster Broad Loom; yarn is fed from individual tubes into loom and there cut and tied into fabric; rows of tubes with protruding ends are clearly visible

Wilton Broad Loom; note the jacquard attachment; cards with punched holes guide needles to select yarn, thereby producing pattern

early payments 6 per cent interest was paid.[15] With the financing arranged, repairs were completed and William Whitworth, who had been the yard contractor at Thompsonville for many years, was installed as superintendent.

In the same year, 1859, the Hartford company took an important step in the organization of its marketing. In January, Roberts was authorized to make an arrangement directly with Henry G. Thompson to sell the company's goods after the first of May.[16] Just why the change was made is not clear. Perhaps Hartford, like Lowell at this time, was experiencing dissatisfaction with the use of a large selling house as its marketing outlet. On the other hand, it may have been a mere shift in form, since Thompson had handled the account at Paige's. In choosing Thompson,[17] the Hartford company was selecting a man whose whole career was closely associated with the factory at Thompsonville; a man who, since he had no other large accounts, was more like a division head even though he was paid a 2½ per cent commission. One of Thompson's assistants, Reune Martin, became a partner in 1861 and took over the business in 1870; in 1901 Reune's sons were still vending "Hartfords."

The prosperous years before the Civil War gave the business a firm foundation. The panic of 1857, while producing "almost an entire stoppage of the sales of carpets" and resulting in inventory losses, represented but a temporary setback.[18] Sales reached almost 1,200,000 yards in 1859, though the value was but $775,000, compared with $849,000 received for 1,000,000 yards in 1856. Despite the lower unit return, the margin was favorable and profits reached a prewar high of $170,000. Indeed the owners of the Hartford company could congratulate themselves on their favorable position. With a reputation approaching that of the Lowell company, they had considerably more production capacity. The addition of Tariffville raised the possible output to 1,700,000 yards of ingrain, 500,000 yards of venetian, and 200,000 yards of brussels, a year. And it represented capacity obtained at bankruptcy rates. Hartford earnings were on a capitalization of $662,500 while those of Lowell were on $1,400,000 (if two-thirds of the total represented carpets). For a more detailed comparison see Table 9. For the six years from 1854 to 1859 Hartford averaged 12 per cent return on capitalization. Approximately 60 per cent of these earnings was paid out in cash dividends and 40 per cent retained in the business. By 1860 a purchaser of one share in 1854 would have received another half share as a stock dividend and from dividends amounting roughly to 8 per cent a year, $71.30 in cash.

After the largest cash dividend to date, in 1860, 22½ per cent, the management found itself short of cash. Additional inducements were offered for the speedier payment of stock installments, and the stockholders grudgingly voted a new 1,000-share issue, payable in May, 1861.[19]

By this time the political pall which had settled over the country with the 1860 election had been succeeded by violence. Waiting for the economic currents to pass by, the directors closed the mill, disposed of a large stock of carpets by a $70,000 sale to A. T. Stewart, sold a large supply of wool, and passed the July dividend. By November they cautiously started half the looms running during daylight, only.[20] This conservatism paid off. Carpet sales were off 3 per cent, but, with the sale of wool, over $100,000 was earned, the surplus was almost doubled, and a 6 per cent dividend was voted.

TABLE 9

HARTFORD CARPET COMPANY AND LOWELL MANUFACTURING COMPANY

Comparison of Profits   1854 to 1859

	Hartford	Lowell Total	Lowell Carpet	Lowell Carpet Minus Proportion of Interest and Rent [a]
1854	$ 42,000	$146,000	$145,000	$111,000
1855	99,000	98,000	77,000	58,000
1856	105,000	174,000	141,000	128,000
1857	55,000	31,000	38,000	24,000
1858	86,000	114,000	103,000	96,000
1859	170,000	257,000	219,000	214,000

[a] From the total profits of the cotton and carpet mills the company deducted an item entitled "Loss on Interest and Rent Accounts."

Source: "Statement of Case and Evidence," *Application of Erastus B. Bigelow to the Commissioner of Patents for an Extension of his Letters-Patent, for Improvements in the Power-Loom for Weaving Ingrain Carpets* (Boston, 1860), App., p. 50.

While the next three years were full of fluctuations and surprises, they were prosperous ones for the company. With the mills running full time, the volume of production and the yardage sold in 1863 was up 30 per cent over 1860. Dollar sales were up 130 per cent. In 1864 sales reached $2,184,-000. Though there is no record of manufacturing costs, the profit margin must have been widening, for earnings rose steadily to $415,000 in 1864. As at Lowell, a part of this represented inventory profits and, of course, all earnings were in terms of depreciated dollars. Though payments of 11 per cent in 1862, 12 per cent in 1863, and 16 per cent in 1864 were made to the proprietors and though two stock dividends transferred $230,000 to the capital stock account, the total balance in the surplus account grew from $77,000 in 1860 to $700,000 in 1864 and the cash on hand reached $357,000.

This financial cushion was doubly fortunate as a bulwark not only against a possible depression but also against a severe and unexpected financial loss. With such large liquid assets Roberts had been lending on call in the New York money market in order to realize some profit for the company from its excess resources. Over $700,000 was loaned to Morris, Ketchum & Sons, one of the honored banking houses in the city. Unfortunately Ketchum senior had gone into semiretirement and his son, energetic Edwin, was soon caught in the whirl of speculation. To cover his losses the younger Ketchum began to forge gold certificates. Suddenly on August 14, 1865, he absconded. When the news reached Hartford, the carpet corporation was not the only center of agitated activity,[21] but evidently it was one of the largest losers, for its representative, William Cone, presided at the meeting of the creditors. Though the balance sheet of the defunct banking house offered hope for a 60 per cent salvage, the Hartford company had lost $279,670.[22]

Such a catastrophe was bound to cause criticism. Led by David Clark, a large owner who had never participated in the management, the dissidents expressed their disapproval at the annual meeting of the company in January, 1866, with the following resolution:[23] "The Stockholders of the Co., were greatly surprised, to learn that the funds of the Co. to the amount of more than Seven hundred thousand Dollars, had been loaned by Geo. Roberts the President, Treasurer and Agent of this Co., to Morris Ketchum Co., Stock, Gold and money broker and gambler, without security. . . ." They also looked askance at the settlement, recommended that the top executive offices of the company should not all be held by one man, and opposed the increase in Roberts' salary from $5,000 to $7,500. Their opposition failed of its purpose. No condemnatory resolutions were adopted and Roberts received his raise and continued as president, agent, and treasurer. Perhaps a 15 per cent cash dividend, plus a stock dividend of one for eight helped to stifle the rebellion.

Any further dissatisfaction apparently was buried beneath the earnings of the most profitable year in the company's history. At $677,000 in 1866, they were one-third higher than any other previous or future year. On the capitalization of $1,500,000 this represented a return of 44 per cent. On the market $300 was the asking price per share—and transactions were few as owners clung to their investment.[24]

Yet another testing time was upon the firm. Fire was an ever-present hazard. In 1864 the brick spinning and carding mill at Thompsonville had gone up in flame so fast that many of the operatives on the second floor had been forced to jump.[25] Now in June, 1867, Tariffville was the victim. At 6:45 A.M. one morning, some foreign matter in the wool struck a spark in the steel picker. Rapidly the fire spread through the surrounding oil and lint; soon it enveloped the power loom shed and eight other major buildings and nine houses. By noon the fire engines—and the executives—arrived from Hartford to find the streets filled with men, women, and children, and the air resounding with the round tones of provincial English and the shrill accents of the Irish. Carpets, yarns, bobbins, furniture were heaped everywhere and over all was a black cloud of smoke.[26]

In Hartford the stock plummeted downward to $240, as the "city" estimated that the carpet corporation had but $332,000 in insurance to cover $1,000,000 in damage. Yet the decline in the price of stock stopped as a second evaluation revealed that business was good and that, with two shifts at Thompsonville, volume could be maintained. As rapidly as possible workers were removed to the Connecticut River town. Reversing the trend which had been taking the firm out of the home-owning business, the management rushed to construct new tenements. Not only did the operatives crowd into Thompsonville but the tradespeople followed.[27]

While the two-shift operation provided a temporary solution, new construction was essential. With no reason to perpetuate the reduced management efficiency which divided operation entailed, the management constructed a new mill of 100-loom capacity and subsidiary buildings in Thompsonville.[28] By the end of 1868 the fixed investment was larger than before the disaster. Much of this was due to higher replacement costs, but the new equipment was more efficient. Furthermore, with earnings exceeding $400,000 the reconstruction costs were covered at the same time that a 25 to 30 per cent dividend rate was maintained.

As soon as this program was completed, Roberts turned his attention to brussels. Hartford had always produced some brussels; first on hand looms, and after 1859 on 10 English-style Weild power looms. With imports of over 800,000 yards a year and with the end of the Bigelow patents, Roberts like Jewett at Lowell was interested in making a large-scale invasion of the brussels market. In 1869 he put up a new building to house 20 looms ordered from Manchester, England. By 1871 the factory was turning out 1,200 yards of brussels a day. In addition, the 247 ingrain looms could produce around 6,000 yards a day.

This new equipment stood the firm in good stead in the depression years after 1873. Though earnings declined, as prices dropped 30 to 40 per cent from 1871 to 1878, they still remained much higher than those of Lowell. Until the mid-seventies they were well over $300,000 except for 1873, and the surplus account reached an all-time high of $987,000 in 1875. Even in the later years of the decade profits were about $200,000, a 13 per cent return on capital.

In continuing to pay 20 per cent dividends, Roberts was guilty of the same deviation from high financial standards as Fay at Lowell, but he had a more profitable company, had much higher reserves, and made much smaller inroads on them. Roberts' record as a manager certainly compared favorably with that of the Lowell group. While the peak of the Lowell surplus came in 1868, that at Hartford came in 1875, and while Lowell suffered lean years and losses almost from the beginning of the seventies,

Hartford was not seriously hit until 1876, and indeed it might almost be said not until the mid-eighties. Undoubtedly the new buildings and equipment of 1868 gave Roberts a cost advantage—indeed the Tariffville fire may have been a blessing in disguise. Closer control of the marketing process may also have helped.

On March 26, 1878, Roberts died suddenly. On April 2, John L. Houston was elected president and agent at a salary of $6,000. For some reason the office of treasurer was not immediately filled, but at the annual meeting in 1879 Houston also assumed that responsibility with a stipend increased to $9,000.

THE HOUSTON REGIME, 1878–1894

In selecting John L. Houston as chief executive, the Hartford directors, like their Lowell counterparts four years earlier, were turning to a man who was well acquainted with efficient manufacturing techniques, who probably knew more about the concern than anyone else and who had constructed the efficient manufacturing base upon which profits had in large part depended. Born into the industry and into the Scottish aristocracy of the town, he derived great benefits from the loyalty of his workers, a loyalty which he reciprocated. They were his people, it was his company, his town.

In the old Thompsonville firm Houston had gone to work in his father's dyeing department in 1847 at the age of fourteen. Recognizing Houston's ability, Orrin Thompson had brought him into the main office, and upon reopening the plant under the name of the Hartford Carpet Company had made him assistant superintendent. Houston was then promoted to superintendent, a position which he held for seventeen years. He was a short, unpretentious-looking man with a naturally retiring disposition. His sound judgment, executive ability, and forceful speech placed him at the head of his peers in the industry.

Houston, like Fay of the Lowell company, was weak in dealing with his directors on financial matters, but he displayed much greater activity in his conduct of company affairs. Perhaps this was partly attributable to the fact that his period of leadership came in the frenzied eighties and nineties, not in the anesthetized seventies. Whatever the reason, until his health gave way in 1894, Houston continually sought out new ideas and new techniques at home and abroad. The product development and manufacturing process fields may have witnessed the greatest number of innovations, but other functions such as purchasing, labor relations, and marketing were not neglected.

For Houston the center was always Thompsonville. Assisting Houston in the conduct of the business were George Roberts, Jr., the secretary who ran the Hartford office, and Lyman Upson, Houston's brother-in-law.

Born in Westfield, Massachusetts, in 1841, Upson had come to Thompsonville in 1864 after a normal school training and a stint in the Army. Of
definite mechanical and organizing ability, he was personally stubborn
and tactless—traits which matched those of his Scottish workers. To these
he added an aloofness and a domineering and critical attitude which were
heartily resented.

Under Upson were two divisions, the mill office staff, consisting of the
paymaster and a clerk or two, and the factory personnel. The contract
system having been abandoned, the line supervisors were all directly under his authority. Most of them had come up through the mill. The overseers of the washing and spinning mills were of Irish and English descent;
those in weaving and dyeing, Scottish and English.

For specialized assistance the management employed outsiders. In
legal matters, the firm of Hungerford & Cone, which took care of the
patent and tax cases in the first years, was succeeded by a New York partnership, Witter & Kenyon. In 1890, twelve years after a similar move by
Lowell, the stockholder's auditing committee employed an expert accountant. Houston was a pioneer, however, in hiring a product development
man and an efficiency expert. In 1891 he enlisted the services of Harry
Hardwick, Philadelphia carpet man, to suggest improvements in the manufacturing system, as well as to introduce some new products.[29]

This step was a natural outcome of Houston's product awareness.
While Roberts' only innovations had been the introduction of mats in
1856—an experiment of minor importance and brief duration—and the expansion of the brussels division, Houston further increased brussels capacity, came out with a cheaper grade of brussels, introduced wilton, and
obtained the rights to utilize the moquette machinery of Alexander Smith
for a new type of axminster. All this Houston did within a year or two of
taking office.

The new medium-grade brussels, called "Enfield," was dropped from
the line after about a year, only to be revived in the mid-nineties under
the name of "Manchester." While Houston's brussels program did not
compare with those of Fay and Lyman, he did increase his capacity 25
per cent by adding 10 looms in 1879 and a few more in 1881.[30]

The move into wilton was a natural extension of brussels manufacture.
By January, 1879, the company was turning out 1,000 yards a month and
during the next twelve months produced 39 per cent of the domestic wilton output. Though the market was small, Houston had shown considerable foresight in obtaining so dominant a position.

Even more audacious was Houston's decision to go into moquette, a
form of axminster which used four shots of filling instead of three, thus
reducing considerably the amount of wool and giving the moquette a
distinguishing ribbed back.[31] In selecting moquette, Houston was not

making a routine decision. Only 76,000 yards of axminster had been imported in 1878; nor did domestic production of a couple of hundred thousand yards open wide vistas. It would be necessary to create a demand by offering a lower cost product. Lowell, at the same time, 1879, was putting all its money into brussels, but Houston evidently preferred to spread his risks. Tapestry or velvets were the other major possibilities, but moquette presented the same opportunity to use an unlimited number of colors, which, moreover, could be produced by the regular dyeing technique. Not only was this more economical, but the finished patterns had clear-cut lines rather than the fuzziness characteristic of tapestry and velvet.

Quite apart from manufacturing techniques was the competitive situation. With the expiration of the Bigelow patents, the tapestry field had been crowded with producers. The moquette power loom, on the other hand, had just been perfected; only its owner, Alexander Smith & Sons Carpet Company, was using it. Through its automatic processes it eliminated the prohibitive cost of tying-in knots by hand, thus gaining such a production advantage that no large-scale competition was likely to arise immediately.

Early in 1879 Houston entered negotiations with the Smiths. In a letter of March 1, Warren B. Smith, after promising to send samples, launched into a lengthy exposition of the advantages of axminster fabrics in general and of moquette in particular: [32]

> The fact that any kind of design, containing an unlimited number of colors, can be made from any kind of stock, either fine or coarse wool and with scarcely any waste of yarn, and a back or body composed principally of jute, the cheapest material that can be bought, must incline a practical manufacturer like yourself to believe . . . that Mr. Alexander Smith . . . was right . . . that it would, eventually, prove to be almost exclusively, the process for producing the carpets of the world.

As between axminster and moquette, best-quality axminster cost $1.16 a yard to make, moquette $.67. In addition, the surface of axminster was so uneven that six to eight ounces a yard were sheared off, while moquette lost only one-fourth of an ounce. Another advantage of moquette was the possibility of turning out a still cheaper grade running around 53 or 54 cents a yard by reducing the number of tufts to the inch. Because of the even distribution obtained with the new machine, the carpet would look as well as one with more tufts. The cheaper grade of moquette could pay a 20-cent-a-yard royalty and still sell for about $1.00 a yard, thus allowing the development of a large volume market.

Houston and his directors were convinced. Under a contract signed in April, 1879, the Hartford company paid $25,000 in cash and $25,000 in a twelve-month note for 50 looms. Over the next two years it had the option of adding 50 more on similar terms, but in no case was the Smith company to license any other manufacturer. In addition Hartford agreed to pay the 20-cent royalty per yard.

Evidently the initial public reception was favorable. The first moquette came off the looms in December, 1879; and in the first full year, 1880, some 59,000 yards were made. Production grew to 273,000 yards in 1882, selling at $1.55 a yard and a year later Houston ordered twelve more looms of a greatly improved variety. By 1887, Arnold, Constable reported 50 per cent more business than any past spring, but within a few years the cheaper moquette gave way to the better-grade axminster. Whether the moquette project had been a financial success is not clear. Prices had tumbled rapidly in the eighties on this fabric as on others, and some authorities implied that the royalty was too high to be carried by such low-priced material.[33]

However the profit and loss statement may have read on the moquette venture, Houston's ardor for new products was not dimmed. As soon as the Smith patents expired, he contracted for 60 of the new Crompton axminster looms at $2,000 apiece and a 5-cent royalty per yard.[34] Shortly thereafter he bought from the Englishman, William H. Smith, exclusive American rights to his Royal Princess Seamless Carpet Loom for the manufacture of a small seamless chenille rug. The firm agreed to buy four looms for £2,000, with Smith to supply a competent man to set them up and also to provide the chenille weft, chains, and filling for the first loom at cost.[35]

While Houston showed himself willing to move with the times into new fields, he did not neglect the old staple, ingrain. In 1893 he replaced many of his old ingrain looms with the more modern and efficient machines from the Knowles Loom Works in Worcester. Less popular lines—like Imperial three-ply in 1882—were dropped, while other items were taken up. In 1884 Houston was one of the first to manufacture ingrain art squares. More intensive was the effort to develop new weaves to compete with tapestries and other better fabrics. To supplement the Hartford company's own "Criterion" weave of 1887,[36] Houston bought a half-interest in Alfred Heald's "Bagdad" patent for $5,000 in 1890 and entered negotiations with Harry Hardwick who had invented some fancy ingrain weaves. The crucial decision was whether to buy Hardwick's "Agra" weave. Though Reune Martin, the sales agent, pointed out that any sizable output would cause such a price break as to wipe out the premium and though Upson, the factory superintendent, doubted the feasibility of paying any large sum for rights upon which he thought it virtually impossible to maintain a monopoly, Houston was loath to abandon the idea. He asked, "Is there any way in which we can come together on the basis of our getting assured value in hand at the time of making payment?" [37] Hardwick thereupon agreed to drop the demand for $50,000 in cash, and in the agreement signed January 2, 1891, Hartford contracted to pay $200 a loom and also pay for all new patents, which were to be assigned to it.

If Houston planned on profits from licensing the weaves to other manufacturers, he was due for disappointment. After several modifications of the agreement, the Hartford firm returned the ownership of all patents to Hardwick for $2,500. The Hardwick weaves which the company had produced had not been too successful. Two of them, "Bundhar" and "Kandahar," were soon dropped from the line. Indeed, the whole ingrain-weave project stands as probably Houston's biggest mistake—though one for which he should not be too strongly condemned in view of the fact that almost every other ingrain manufacturer assayed a similar venture.

An attempt to launch a higher grade of wilton was more successful. Two new grades, French and Saxony, came onto the market in 1893. French wilton was an all-worsted fabric with a fine, low pile, but one so thick and with so much sheen that it appeared like plush.[38] The even more famous Saxony, a luxurious high-pile construction, eventually became in future years the best-known and best-selling item in the entire Hartford line.

Houston's efforts to keep abreast of times by following product trends had left Hartford with probably the most extensive line of any manufacturer in this country: brussels, wilton, axminster, extra superfine two-ply, and three-ply ingrain, ingrain art squares, chenille, French and Saxony rugs and terry cloth—an output truly remarkable for variety, commented the carpet trade journal in 1896.[39]

Such additions were reflected in the increase in equipment. From about $250,000 before the war, the investment in plant and machinery had risen to $610,000 after the new mill was built in Thompsonville in 1868, at which figure it stood when Houston took over. By the end of 1894 it had reached $900,000. Since no new building program had been undertaken, this growth represented new machinery: looms, spinning mules to replace jacks, Noble combers from England, and larger-capacity washing machines, steam kettles, and drying machines.

Despite the fact that no important new construction was undertaken, the working conditions of the employees improved. Better ventilation was obtained by modifications in the old buildings, and beginning in 1884 the substitution of electricity for the fitful light of an open gas flame constituted a major advance.

While modern fringe benefits were undreamed of and safety precautions were in their infancy, the greatest divergence from our current operating practices and working conditions lay in hours and discipline. In the nineties the work week was 56 hours, with Saturday afternoon free.[40] As for discipline, much of the prewar informality, with interludes of fisticuffs, persisted. Though the management had had experience in handling factory labor, much of the labor itself was industrially uneducated, the Irish and French-Canadians providing much of the force. Workmen expected to be able to go home for a short visit, to go out for a drink, or to do a job outside for the foreman. Spare hands were available to take over if need be, but often the free time was the result of scheduling deficiencies, yarn breakage, or just a lag before finished work was passed by the overseer. Though there were shop-wide rules of most matters, the enforcement and the atmosphere depended on the personality of each overseer and the reaction of individuals to him. Most overseers were human, but William Martin, boss of brussels, an excellent production man and an able mechanic, left behind him a reputation for violence and favoritism.

The Irish and French-Canadians supplied most of the children in the mill, who were used for such jobs as doffing in the spinning mills or as creel boys for the brussels weavers. The Census of 1870 reported some 220 children out of a total of 1,138 operatives; the stricter legislation of 1895 was primarily responsible for the reduction to 40 or 50 by 1900. Women, who were concentrated in the preparatory processes and in ingrain and moquette weaving, accounted for about 50 per cent of the adults throughout the period.

Meanwhile the total working force grew from about 600 employees in 1860 to 1,800 in 1889. Then in the depression years of the nineties it declined sharply. According to a rough draft of a report sent to the Census Bureau in 1899 it varied from an average of 774 in January to 1,062 in December.

The more skilled employees, such as the brussels weavers, owned their own homes, but 245 families in 1899 were housed in company tenements. At that time six-room units rented for from $4.00 to $9.00 a month. Most tenants had truck gardens, and further savings were made by buying coal at wholesale prices from the company.[41]

Not only did the corporation supply the housing; it furnished most of the community facilities. Since the company undertook so many public functions, there is no question but what it dominated the political life of the town. Superintendent Upson annually took his stand at the ballot box to watch the pink and white slips go in. Rarely did the Democrats attain more than the automatic minority representation on town committees.

Along with its domination, management accepted its responsibilities as it saw them. Older employees were continued on the job as long as they wished—despite the production inefficiencies entailed.[42] As president, Houston especially concerned himself with providing regular employment for his men. When the wool house burned, he gave 22 workers tasks elsewhere. As layoffs became more frequent, Houston attempted to use his workers when jobs on roads or construction were available. Such work as there was in the hard years was carefully rotated among the weavers.[43]

Houston always remained accessible to his workers, for grievances, for problems, or just chit-chat.

The attitude of the operatives toward the company is hard to recreate. With the introduction of the power loom, union activity died out. Not until the company went into the production of brussels carpeting were skilled workers again needed. In 1881 these workers organized the Brussels Weavers Mutual Defense & Benefit Association with the motto, "The injury of one is the concern of all." [44] Though the association collected and disbursed small benefit funds, and arranged the usual number of excursions and parties, the primary interest was in wages.

In 1882, 97 brussels weavers petitioned for an increase. They cited the inevitable comparison with Philadelphia rates, quoted at 7 cents a yard. In addition, they said: [45]

It is a well known fact that the comparative freedom of the Hartford Carpet Company from heavy taxation and rents, with other singular advantages both local and financial enable the Corporation to pay the best wages going. . . . Taking into account the skill and ability employed in the direction and working management, it would be unjust to even suggest that the old established H.C.C. with all its well earned local and financial advantages to boot, failed to secure equal profits. . . .

We cannot leave the question without our emphatic protestations against strikes . . . believing that reason and good faith . . . is sufficient to accomplish all and more than ever combative associations or strikes did or ever will do.

Evidently this subtly worded plea failed of its end. Words never softened the irascible overseer, William Martin, and these undoubtedly infuriated him. On May 24 the brussels weavers asked Upson to dismiss Martin, complaining of "vulger abuse," "savage and brutal treatment," and "ignorant assumption of misspent power and tyrannical domination." It was said that "The blasphemy that characterizes his communications has made a proverb that where Bill Martin is there is neither God nor good." Specifically, the weavers charged that Martin had fired the union secretary, had refused to give passes for funerals or illness, had insisted that men buy tea from him, had rebuffed a man who wished to bring in his son, and had given his own son the best of creelers and service. He would not discuss poor yarn, and he had kept men waiting unduly before passing their work.[46]

With labor matters in such a state the directors ordered Reune Martin, the sales agent, "to Make all contracts for future delivery of our Goods as to relieve us from liability in case of Strikes or Accidents." [47] But Houston was successful in bringing peace. Overseer Martin remained; wages were advanced 5 per cent.

In contrast with all the other major carpet producers, this was the only disturbance of the decade in Thompsonville. While Philadelphia, New

York, Clinton, Amsterdam, and Lowell all had their walkouts during the
strike-filled eighties, Hartford experienced no interruptions.

Two other fields of management came directly under Houston's sway:
purchasing and manufacturing. No detailed judgment of Houston's ability
as a purchasing man is possible, but low manufacturing costs imply some
proficiency. Skillful purchasing is related not only to price but also to
quality. Though the Lowell sales agent, trying to explain a price differ-
ential, once accused Hartford of using shoddy, Houston was proud of the

TABLE 10

HARTFORD CARPET COMPANY

Production of Carpeting   1879, 1882, and 1899

(In Yards)

	1879	1882	1899
Wilton a	59,869	75,027	8,332
Brussels a	607,107	633,273	121,609
Three-ply ingrain b	257,123	331,205	32,485
Two-ply ingrain b	1,334,349	1,074,563	896,178
Moquette a	—	152,406	—
Axminster a	—	—	487,340
Ingrain rug b	—	—	97,642
Scotch chenille a	—	—	2,546

a Running yards.
b Square yards.

Source: Hartford Carpet Company, Production Book; Bigelow-Sanford Manuscript Collection.

quality of his materials and products. In 1892 Hardwick, the inventor,
complimented him on this, attributing "superior color effects . . . principally to the high order of the materials used." [48]

Continuous production figures for the whole Houston period have not
survived. The records for 1879 and 1882 and for the last year of the century are given in Table 10.

The gain from 1879 to 1882 is accounted for by the new brussels, wilton, and moquette looms. Thereafter though capacity must have continued
to increase as Houston acquired more efficient machinery, the volume actually turned out was another matter, dropping over 25 per cent by 1899.

While better machinery and better systems, such as the one Hardwick
introduced for spinning,[49] might cut labor and overhead costs, the mul-
tiplicity of products, of lines within products, and of designs within lines
worked against the reduction of expense. At various times Houston tried to
reduce the profusion of offerings, but competitive pressures soon forced
him to cover every demand possibility.

Hartford had followed Lowell closely in achieving pre-eminence in
designs. By the seventies the company had six designers, including Levi

Makin, who made a specialty of Masonic fraternity emblems. The George Washington carpet created for the Philadelphia Exhibition in 1876 belonged in the realm of misplaced originality since the public rejected the idea of walking on the father of their country, but a special Persian carpet received accolades for its "modest design, with rich effects, yet of neutral colors that would harmonize with almost any style of furnishing, . . . a decided departure from the old styles, for which it was necessary to select the furniture so as to avoid disagreeable contrasts with the carpet's gaudy pattern and colors." [50]

To design the new line of moquettes which called for a larger and more striking color range the management hired George Wright, who had acquired experience on Higgins' "taps." In addition Houston reached outside his own staff for ideas by making exchange agreements with British manufacturers.

Most of the stylists lived in the New York area and Reune Martin, the sales agent, was probably responsible for their work. Martin, who had taken full charge of the selling upon Henry G. Thompson's retirement in 1870, was assisted after 1886 by two of his sons. A few years later, following the admission of a third son into the business, the elder Martin surrendered active control.

The sales office was located downtown in New York on Worth Street. In 1884 the directors and Martin discussed the site of a proposed retail store in New York, but the whole project was dropped after a year of investigation by a committee.[51] That the possibility was even explored is interesting because none of the other large companies seems to have considered such a step.

In other marketing matters Martin was typical of the eighties. As an agent he worked on commission—2 per cent in 1870. He had a few other minor accounts; but his fortunes were much more closely tied to the Hartford company than were Richardson's or Smith's to Lowell. Though Martin did not sit on the board, Houston confessed that he would recommend no important product action to the directors without Martin's concurrence. Indeed, the whole arrangement suggests that Martin was considered as the operating head of a division, a position analagous to that of Upson.

Sometime in the late seventies or early eighties Martin, like his competitors, acquired a selling crew. Branch offices in a few main centers like Chicago were set up in the eighties, abandoned temporarily in the nineties, and then re-established before the end of the century.

Hartford advertising followed the same limited paths as that of Lowell: periodic exhibitions and matter-of-fact trade journal notices. Under the economic pressures of the mid-nineties, even this small expense was eliminated and the long-term familiarity of the wholesalers with Hartford was left to do the selling job.

The aggressive selling possibilities of the large-scale auction were also bypassed though the directors discussed the matter in 1884.[52] Like Lowell, Hartford sold its surplus in large job lots to wholesalers.[53] The terms of sale remained the same throughout the period: 60 days, 2 per cent off for cash in 10 days. This is in contrast with the terms of Lowell, which were changed to 30 days, less 2 per cent, in the mid-eighties. The only evidence on mark-up policies comes from a case for design infringement in 1879; according to a reckoning of loss inflicted, the cost of making and selling a brussels was $1.08 a yard while the selling price to the wholesaler was $1.75.[54]

TABLE 11

HARTFORD CARPET COMPANY

List Prices   1879 and 1894

(Per Yard)

	1879	*1894*	*Percentage Decline*
Ingrain			
Extra super two-ply	$ .85	$ .525	38
Three-ply	1.125	.725	35
Brussels	1.80	.975	45
Wilton	2.40 a	2.00	16

a 1881.

Source: Price lists in *The Philadelphia Carpet Trade,* and *The American Carpet and Upholstery Trade.*

This margin undoubtedly was squeezed by the declining prices of the next twenty years. On the whole, Hartford prices paralleled those of its competitors, though occasionally they were 5 cents below Lowell or Bigelow for a short interval. From the beginning of Houston's regime until his illness in 1894, the price decline ranged from 16 per cent for wiltons to 45 per cent for brussels, as is shown in Table 11.

This then is the background against which to view Houston's financial achievements, the yardstick of his business success. Since there were no new issues of capital stock after the Civil War, money for the additional equipment and expanded operations came from earnings and borrowing. It is questionable whether the selling agent ever provided much working capital. Suppliers furnished some, but apparently on a short-term basis. New York banks with which the concern had accounts, such as the Metropolitan or after 1884 the National Bank of Commerce, may have made loans to the company or discounted its notes, but a growing source of funds was nearer at hand. Roberts had discounted receivables with the Hartford insurance companies and Houston continued to utilize the same source of funds.

Whatever the volume of borrowing may have been during any year,

the final balances were always low. Before the Civil War, year-end obligations had run from $200,000 to $500,000. In twenty out of the thirty-five
years after the conflict, they were below $20,000, with a peak of $114,000
in 1891. This state of affairs is in striking contrast with the ever-growing
indebtedness of Lowell.

Alongside this conservatism on indebtedness and liquidity must be
placed the case of the declining surplus in judging Houston's financial
skill. In 1878, when Houston took over, the surplus and reserve accounts
totaled $858,000, slightly below the average for the seventies. Over the
next few years, the surplus grew, and it was 1884 before it dropped below
the 1878 total. Slowly during the rest of the decade it dwindled, and then
under the blows of the panic in 1893 it dropped to $582,000 in 1894 (see
Appendix 4).

Behind this decline lay the simple fact that Houston was paying out in
dividends more than he was earning. As a result, total assets declined over
$300,000. Profits had fluctuated between $200,000 and $250,000 from 1878
to 1884. Then by gradual stages they dropped to $45,000 in 1889. After
a slight recovery the corporation's earnings dropped again, this time to a
mere $27,000 in 1893. In 1894 Hartford suffered its only loss—$95,000.
Thus while earnings on stated capital had been about 15 per cent from
1878 to 1884, 6 per cent from 1885 to 1891, they were −1 per cent from 1892
to 1894. Meantime the dividend rate had been 16 per cent in the first
period, 11 per cent in the second, and 2 per cent in the last. In the last two
years, 1893 and 1894, however, Houston made no dividend disbursements.

The failure to take sufficiently drastic financial measures before the
years 1893 and 1894 is probably due to the fact that, as an outsider, Houston was reluctant to impose sacrifices upon the prominent Hartford families who were his stockholders. True, Roberts, himself a member of the
Hartford moneyed group, had maintained a 20 per cent dividend rate
even though in three years, 1873, 1876, and 1877, the company had not
earned these amounts. But it might be said that Roberts had failed to
realize immediately the fact that reduced profits were there to stay.
Houston could not plead such ignorance when year followed year of lowering profits. While he slashed his dividend payments, his actions were
never drastic enough. Only in two years out of seventeen, 1890 and 1891,
did his profits cover dividends.

Dividends in the eighties represented three to four times as much as
Lowell was returning to its stockholders. All told, to the $778 which a
purchaser of one $100 share in 1854 had received by 1878, Houston in the
next seventeen years added $366 more—an average return of $27 a year for
forty-one years. Houston could have followed Lyman's course of not living beyond his means and still could have paid three times as much as
his competitor. With conditions never so desperate as those which Fay

and Lyman faced, Houston succumbed to pressure to liquidate part of the investment. For Lyman it was essential to build up the financial cushion and this he did. That Houston was unable to present a sufficiently convincing case to persuade his board to husband company resources is the severest indictment of his leadership.

A second possible criticism of Houston's conduct of financial affairs is his policy of letting the total assets in the corporation shrink. In this procedure he was also at variance with the practice followed by Lyman, who was increasing Lowell's total assets by borrowing—at the expense, it is true, of a normal degree of liquidity.

Against these two complaints is Houston's record. He had only one losing year to four for Lyman. On a business capitalized at $1,500,000 he earned $2,400,000 over seventeen years; on $2,000,000 Lyman (and Fay) earned $1,500,000. While paying the stockholders three to four times as much as Lyman, he still maintained a surplus twice Lyman's. To what can this difference be attributed? The period of the Hartford company's overwhelming earning superiority lay before 1884 when its manufacturing plant was newer than Lowell's. While Houston had procured new machinery in the early eighties, he did not have the advantage of new construction. By the year 1884 most of the Lyman modernization program had been completed, and over the next ten years, his profits equaled Houston's. From 1890 to 1894 Lowell's profits were double Hartford's—a result perhaps of the continuing expenditures of the late eighties, a period during which Houston could not, or did not, get funds for capital investment from his directors. Though he received authorization to buy new ingrain and axminster looms in 1893 and 1894, his over-all program for improving plant efficiency was rejected.

Perhaps the antiquity of Hartford's plant and equipment is overemphasized; in 1900 one director complained, "those speaking disparagingly of the Hartford company's equipment are altogether misleading." But then came the faint praise: machinery "that will compare favorably," or conditions "no worse than most of the trade." [55] Generally it seems safe to say that Houston's and Hartford's forte, from the middle fifties to the middle eighties was in low-cost production. With Houston's great ability as a manufacturing man must be considered his skill in labor relations, his probable proficiency in purchasing, and his awareness of the importance of new methods and new products.

LAST YEARS OF THE HARTFORD CARPET COMPANY, 1895–1901

On election day, 1894, John L. Houston suffered a stroke from which he never fully recovered. Though he did not retire until three months before his death in 1898, the responsibility for management fell more and more on George Roberts, Jr. In 1895 Roberts had been elected assistant treasurer. In 1896 he had become treasurer and in 1898 president, as Houston resigned these offices in turn.

While the worst of the financial crisis was over by the time of Houston's semiretirement at the end of 1894, the program for the rest of the century was much in the nature of a holding operation. Sluggish business in most years, an acute depression in 1897,[56] in short, no material prosperity to fire the imagination of the management, or to loosen its purse strings, describe the situation at Hartford in the late 1890's.

Meanwhile the company lost one of its great assets, labor peace. Apparently the semiretirement of Houston removed the reluctance of the workers to give positive expression to their grievances. From 1890 on, wage cut had followed wage cut, until the weavers received only 4 cents a yard in 1894 as compared with 5⅜ cents in 1890. Shorter hours had further undermined the standard of living, while the papal encyclical, *Rerum Novarum*, reinforced by the efforts of priests, had encouraged such men as Frederick Furey, among the weavers, to take a more active part in the labor movement.

A rise of a few cents in the prices of some items in the line in the summer of 1895 inspired the workers with the hope of a wage boost, especially since weavers in Philadelphia successfully struck for a 10 per cent increase.[57] At the same time, the Hartford directors after two and a half years renewed dividend payments—proof positive to the workers that the financial position of the corporation was sufficiently strong to warrant a readjustment of their wage scale. In August, 132 brussels weavers petitioned Upson and the directors to restore rates to 5 cents a yard for brussels and 11½ cents a yard for wilton. They also asked that weavers who worked without creel boys should each receive a share of the boys' wages.[58]

Receiving nothing more than courtesy from Upson, the weavers left the plant on August 15. A week later the local newspaper reported: [59]

The conduct of the strikers . . . has been such as to win respect. . . . [They] prefer no work to work at wages below what other people pay. Had a single workman taken this position and retired, no one could have said it was not his privilege. The strike today differs only that every operative in the brussels department . . . left after considering the situation.

The paper was fair also to the company, saying that the Hartford company should know what it could pay. Prices, considering the relative cost of wool, had fallen even below what they were when the wage reductions had been made and the management had offered a quarter of a cent more to show its desire for reconciliation.

With the usual fall recovery in business, the Hartford company offered a general wage advance, irregular in amount, but aggregating 7½ per cent, to go into effect, September 9, 1895.[60] By October this concession, a decline in outdoor jobs, and a breaking point in grocer-extended credit had brought most of the brussels men back to their looms.

Though this crisis was over, continuing unsatisfactory conditions left the basic causes untouched. With little work, the existence of bad feeling was unavoidable. On December 18, 1898, the workers were informed of a general reduction in wages in these departments, varying in amount, but averaging 7½ per cent. While the rate was not cut again in 1899, the weekly take-home pay was hit in October when the management decided to take advantage of the shortening days to run nine hours instead of ten. A strike of the dyehouse workers resulted but was settled when the company granted a small wage increase "with the understanding that there be work for only such hours per week as best suits the convenience & economy of the work to be done." [61]

While labor commanded more attention than ever before, old areas of management also received consideration. Advertising was resumed temporarily in the carpet trade journal. More significant was the move by the Martins to Union Square in 1898. In making this shift uptown to the new Hartford building, the agents correctly analyzed location trends and their competitors soon followed.

Profits ran about $60,000 a year—compared with an average of about $80,000 at Lowell. After 1895 practically all earnings were promptly paid out in dividends—at a rate of about 4 per cent on stated capital. In 1900 an extra 2 per cent disposed of an income of $90,000. Thus the financial and physical condition of the company was in no better condition when the tide of prosperity began to flow in the fall of 1900 than it had been six years earlier. Indeed, a businessman such as Roberts, whose whole executive career had been a succession of false springs and deeper winters, probably considered the signs of better times unworthy of much attention.

Roberts' talents and his role from 1895 on, and especially after he assumed the presidency in 1898, are difficult to assess. Generally he seems to have continued in the paths trod by Houston. Like his directors, Roberts had many other business interests. From none of these men, perhaps more because of diffusion of energy than lack of ability, came the vitalizing spark, the aggressiveness, the freshness, needed to take advantage of the new century and the new possibilities. Again management seemed in default, more able to bear "patiently and manfully " [62] than to provide enterprising and inspiring leadership. To fill the void came an energetic group of men from the Higgins company, headed by the young and able Robert Perkins.

CHAPTER 6

YEARS OF ADAPTATION:

The New York Companies, 1854–1901

During the second half of the nineteenth century the small New York concerns of E. S. Higgins & Company and Stephen Sanford & Sons advanced to the first rank in the carpet industry. In both cases the achievement was primarily the work of one or two men. Stephen Sanford alone bore the major responsibilities—and produced the results—for his firm. Elias Higgins and his brother, Nathaniel, arrived at the decisions which made the Higgins company.

THE EXPANSION OF E. S. HIGGINS & COMPANY, 1856–1888

Of the two Higgins brothers who continued in the management of E. S. Higgins & Company, after the retirement of Alvin Higgins in 1856, Elias was the better known to the trade. As senior partner, as the marketing man, as the extrovert, he overshadowed, in the industry and the public mind, the quieter Nathaniel. But the latter, assuming the responsibility for the manufacturing end of the business, contributed greatly to the success of the firm. The spectacular growth of the partnership in the seventies and eighties was probably as much the result of the superior inventiveness of the mechanics, trained and directed by Nathaniel, as of the happy expansion of tapestry sales.

After twenty-six years of achievement this management team was disrupted by the death of Nathaniel in 1882, thus posing for the first time in concrete form the problem of second-generation leadership for the firm. Higgins, as Lowell and Hartford, was to have its management crisis—and one of much longer duration. Over the next seventeen years the crisis steadily deepened as first Nathaniel's son-in-law and then the son-in-law of Elias proved uninterested in carrying on the business. Finally in 1899 the situation grew acute when Eugene, the son and direct heir of Elias

Higgins, decided that he wanted nothing more to do with the manufacture of carpets.

Elias and Nathaniel Higgins built their carpet business on two fabrics: ingrain and tapestry. While they became more famous as leaders in the production of the latter, it was with ingrain that they had started as carpet manufacturers. By 1860 they had some 76 ingrain power looms of their own invention in operation [1] and from this line they must have drawn the bulk of the manufacturing profits of the ante-bellum years. By 1886 the total ingrain output had reached 991,000 yards, again due in part to 24 additional looms and in part to the installation of the more efficient Duckworth loom—the joint creation of William Murkland, formerly of Lowell, and John Duckworth.[2] By the mid-seventies this loom was producing 45 yards a day in comparison with the 25 yards of the old Bigelow loom, and modifications soon added another 10 yards to the daily output, giving it at one time a 20 per cent superiority over its nearest rival.[3] Whether because of this advantage or not, even the best Higgins ingrains usually sold at 2½ to 5 cents lower than Hartford's and Lowell's, and in addition the New York firm offered a wide range of cheaper varieties.

While the Higgins firm was always important in the ingrain market, it was for years, with one or two other manufacturers, dominant in the tapestry and velvet fields. In contrast with ingrain, tapestry and velvet could offer a high pile and a variety of colors. In relation to regular brussels and wilton, these two weaves not only enjoyed color superiority but had two further advantages: cheapness and economy of loom space. It was estimated that tapestry needed 9 ounces of worsted per running yard, velvet 13½, five-frame brussels 19 ounces, and five-frame wilton 30.[4] While labor costs were relatively high in the city of New York, the Higgins firm constantly dragged them downward by effecting machinery improvements. In the matter of space requirements three tapestry, or "tap," looms could occupy the area of one brussels, since one beam was substituted for the many frames holding 1,300 individual bobbins.[5]

The small original resources of Higgins, the need for the accumulation of know-how and for technical improvement, and the inadequacy of the demand delayed the great surge in tapestry production until after the Civil War. In ante-bellum days many a solid citizen quailed before the plethora of color in tapestry carpeting.[6] In the Gilded Age, however, color, ornateness, and extremism hardly appalled the *nouveau riche* or the middle-class neighbor trying to keep up with the Joneses. Increasing imports, over two million yards a year, plus the first reported American production of a million yards in 1869, attested to the growing popularity of tapestry and velvet.

To serve this market there were just two American manufacturers— Higgins and the Massachusetts firm, the Roxbury Carpet Company.[7] Both had been licensees under the Erastus Bigelow patents. As late as 1872 no new competitors had entered the field—though the Bigelow patents had expired several years previously. In the next year, however, five new producers began to compete for the market, and by 1879 the total number of tapestry or velvet looms had grown from 143 to over 600,[8] producing over seven million yards. Imports had dropped to 77,000 yards.

Higgins, with 138 looms, still headed the list of tapestry manufacturers in 1879. The company's first important step after the war had been the purchase in 1868 of the right to use the William Weild patents, which improved the Bigelow loom by giving more support to the wire over which the pile was looped, thus increasing the speed and the daily yardage from 23½ to from 30 to 40. To simplify this machine, John Duckworth and E. K. Davis (formerly of the Clinton Company and of Lowell but now head machinist at Higgins) introduced further modifications which raised production to 58 yards a day.

Meanwhile Davis and Nathaniel Higgins had held several meetings with an inventor, William Webster, who had his own ideas about improving the loom—and thus was laid the groundwork for what is the most famous suit in carpet-industry history. Upon receiving a patent in 1872, Webster sued the E. S. Higgins & Company for royalties, claiming that Davis had stolen his ideas. The first decision in 1879 declared the Webster patent null and void, thus accepting the contention of the Higgins firm that Webster had been unable to construct a practicable operating machine until he had seen the Davis-Duckworth loom at work. Webster immediately appealed and in 1882 the United States Supreme Court upheld the validity of his patent. Assuming that without the new loom Higgins would have had to use the old Bigelow machine and therefore could have turned out only 23½ yards a day instead of 58 on each of 61 looms, Webster demanded the profits on 4,145,872 yards for the eight years of infringement. At 36¾ cents a yard this would have amounted to $1,523,607.96. Higgins insisted that the comparison should be based not on the Bigelow loom but on the best of the other looms available in the early seventies. After seven years of wrangling, with several deaths among the people involved and several changes among officials, the Supreme Court upheld this interpretation,[9] and the Websters evidently admitted defeat.

By that time the mechanism was largely obsolete. As early as 1884 the Higgins company had a new loom which averaged 90 yards a day. It also made improvements in other equipment, and in the new building of 1881 replaced its old hand drums with power drums for dyeing.

Whatever the technical proficiency of E. S. Higgins & Company, the concern made no pretense of leadership in the field of design. Originality was not one of the demands made upon the staff of nine designers. The pattern book for 1879 contained a copy of the Bigelow Pagoda, an Arnold,

Constable Persian, and a Sanford combination of scarlet blocks, drab, and chintz. The next year copies of an Alexander Smith velvet, a Bigelow brussels, and a Roxbury olive drab were used. In 1881 a Lowell pattern composed of flowers and leaves, and a Hartford design of carnations, yellow and blue flowers, and a little architectural work furnished models.[10] Naturally adjustments in the patterns were made for color techniques of tapestries and velvets. Light hues had to be made more prominent because the dark had a tendency to overspread them.[11] Furthermore, the tastes of the clientele demanded ever bigger and better roses—until they reached cabbage-like proportions.[12]

TABLE 12

E. S. HIGGINS & COMPANY

Sales and Profits   1857 to 1864

Year	Sales	Profit	Year	Sales	Profit
1857	$ 895,000	$47,000	1861	$ 652,000	$31,000
1858	861,000	38,000	1862	no statement	
1859	1,000,000	59,000	1863	1,700,000	40,000
1860	1,000,000	50,000	1864	2,000,000	26,000

Source: A. & E. S. Higgins Company, Sales Book, *passim.*

Evidently Higgins' stylists were successful in their aim. According to the carpet trade journal in 1878, "one distinguishing feature of the productions of the firm . . . is their adaptation of styles for the masses rather than to exclusive fine tastes." [13]

Awareness of public taste and leadership in technical matters were not the only foundations upon which prosperous business was built. The Higgins firm was noted for its "incomparable methods of selling carpets." [14] Though its advertising was no more advanced than that of Lowell and Hartford, and though it did not use road salesmen until 1884, the concern's location in New York and its direct selling to wholesalers and large retailers like Marshall Field permitted efficient and aggressive merchandizing in terms of the marketing system before 1880.

Among the weapons in the arsenal of E. S. Higgins & Company were liberal credit terms—the four months' net, or 4 per cent discount for cash, being twice as good as the terms allowed by Lowell and Hartford. Promptness in delivery [15] and extensive use of brand names were other effective tools. Finally there were lower prices. While these perhaps can be attributed to lower manufacturing costs, two other factors are important: the saving of the commission and, judging from the figures of profits on sales during the fifties and the Civil War, the willingness of the Higgins brothers to take a small unit return. In the best of these years, 1859, they made $59,000 on sales of $1,000,000, compared with Hartford's $170,000 on

$775,000 (see Tables 9 and 12). The existence of a retail business and the purchase of carpeting from other manufacturers—in 1858 they took a thousand-piece job from Lowell—partially explains this low rate of return, but though retailing was discontinued and the need for outside suppliers abated, the philosophy of the small margin remained.

If location in one of the great marts of the world was an advantage to Higgins saleswise, it had both desirable and undesirable aspects in the field of labor. The continuing flood of immigrants furnished a ready supply to fill the 1,600 to 2,000 jobs of the eighties. Whether this was cheap labor is a question. In 1874 Elias Higgins claimed that he was paying wages from 15 to 20 per cent higher than other manufacturers.[16] In 1878, however, his rate for weavers was 3½ cents a yard on the new looms, and 4½ cents on the old, while Lowell and Hartford were paying 4 cents, and Philadelphia manufacturers 4½ to 6 cents.[17] In 1883 one group of workers charged that Higgins paid the lowest wages in the country while another denied this and pointed out that, even though rates were lower, the looms were faster.[18] Four years later the consensus was that Philadelphia, New York, and Worcester wages were on a par, the others somewhat lower.[19] Regardless of the actual rate, the continual labor bickering in the mid-eighties, much of which was directly attributable to the fact that the big city was a hotbed of union activity, must have been expensive.

The first recorded labor walkout at the Higgins company came in 1874 when the partners tried to reduce all wages above $40 a month by 15 per cent and those below by 10. When after six weeks the cut was limited to 5 per cent, the strikers returned. While there were sporadic difficulties over the next nine years, no major trouble occurred.

In 1883 the Higgins plant was organized by a machinist and labor leader named Thomas Morrison. Under Morrison the Higgins workers became Local Assembly Number 2,985 of the Knights of Labor. Morrison proclaimed that the new union was going to elevate labor, abolish the "base tyranny, which existed in the mill," and stop those who were doing none of the work from getting the largest wages, such as the bosses' friends and sons. The company itself soon provided another issue. On November 13, 1883, the management notified the tapestry weavers of an intended 10 per cent wage cut. Negotiations to head off a strike failed; and, when the tapestry weavers went out, Elias Higgins closed the whole mill.

The workers blamed the superintendent, Thomas Campbell, a former Lowell and Sanford employee.[20] They claimed that he still begrudged a wage advance given the year before. In the words of a sympathetic worker at Sanford's, "Winter is coming on and he thinks cold and want will force them [the operatives] to yield to his unjust and cruel demands." [21] However, with the inflow of spring orders the advantage shifted to the workers, and Elias Higgins, meeting with a committee of employees, agreed to submit the wage cut to arbitration. Each side selected one representative and these, a third. In addition to considering the wage reduction, they were to go over the whole payroll with a view to eliminating inequities. At the same time Campbell resigned as superintendent, though staying on as a wool buyer. What the final terms were is not known, but Morrison and his union turned their attention elsewhere.

In 1885, after there had been a bitter strike at Alexander Smith's, the Higgins concern quickly granted a 10 per cent increase. The next year Higgins suffered further labor trouble. This time the situation seems to have been largely beyond the company's control, though the changes in the factory's management may have been a contributing factor. With the retirement of superintendent Campbell, a Higgins nephew had taken over only to be succeeded, after his untimely death, by another nephew who also lived but a short time. This nephew was replaced by a grandnephew, Alvin Dyer Higgins.

A. D. Higgins, who was to become a leading architect of the merged Higgins and Hartford companies, was born in Charlestown, Maine, in 1850. He had entered the family business in 1867, but on the advice of his great-uncle, Nathaniel, had left temporarily to study the machinist trade in Kingston, New York, thus acquiring the valuable technical background which so many of the family had. Hard working, narrow in his interests, thorough rather than brilliant, "A. D." nevertheless showed an imaginative grasp of style trends. He has also been credited with instituting the regular employment of women in the offices of the company.[22] For eleven years prior to his appointment as factory manager in September, 1886, Alvin had gained experience in manufacturing and organizing methods as assistant superintendent.

A. D. Higgins' promotion came just at a time when Morrison was experiencing considerable internal trouble in his union, and strong-willed A. D. took a dim view of the shenanigans and maneuverings which had nothing to do with the business, yet hurt it. Morrison had run into difficulties with the District Assembly under which he served as an organizer for the Knights of Labor. Apparently he had failed to transfer properly his membership from the machinist to the carpet local. As a result he huffily created his own district assembly, Number 126. In this move he was assisted by a demand among some of the carpet workers for their own district group, free from the domination of 60,000 hod carriers, shoemakers, and the like.[23] But others in the Higgins employ preferred to remain loyal to old District Assembly 49. While the General Assembly hardly approved of such tactics, it accepted the inevitable.

Early in 1887 the pot began to boil. Higgins laid off some men. "Lack of work," A. D. said; "Discrimination against the union," said Morrison.

During the ensuing negotiations Morrison discovered that a 10 per cent wage cut was in the offing, and he immediately ordered a strike for January 24, 1887, demanding reinstatement of the men, a closed shop, and no wage cut.

Some of the carpet workers who had remained in District Assembly Number 49 appealed the strike order to the General Assembly of the Knights and the General Assembly countermanded the strike, pending further discussion. Came the day of the strike and some workers went out, some remained on the job. However, with the majority of the employees supporting Morrison, A. D. Higgins had to capitulate. He reinstated the strikers, instituted a closed shop, cut wages only 5 per cent instead of 10, agreed to participate in a joint grievance committee, and surrendered to seniority principles on layoffs.[24]

Morrison had two more objectives: the ejection of opposing unionists and the replacement of A. D. Higgins. Despite the insistence of Morrison, A. D. refused to fire workers who did not belong to the Morrison union. However, when the engineers and firemen who still belonged to District Assembly Number 49, joined in the general strike of coal handlers and Longshoremen in New York in February, 1887, Elias Higgins stepped in. Early in March all adherents of District Assembly Number 49 were fired. This brought a general boycott by the General Assembly of the Knights, but Elias Higgins refused to yield.[25] The recalcitrant Morrison and his union were read out of the national organization. But Morrison maintained control over most of the tapestry workers in the carpet industry.

With the elimination of the rival union, Morrison also accomplished the removal of A. D. Higgins. To replace the latter, Elias summoned back to the company his nephew, John Hamilton Higgins, who had served as head of the mills from 1861 until, in 1874, he had returned to Maine to enter the ministry. Undoubtedly John was a gentler, more sympathetic man than A. D. "His methods . . . were quiet, deliberate, well-planned," according to a historian of the family.[26] Aided by worsening economic conditions and a nationwide decline in labor movement enthusiasm, John Higgins reduced the union to quiescence. Late in 1887 the union accepted a 5 to 10 per cent cut,[27] but its refusal to accept a 12 per cent reduction the next year enabled the superintendent to bring in new workers.[28] Soon Morrison turned his attention elsewhere, and, after a stormy decade, ten years of labor peace came to the Higgins mill.

THE HIGGINS COMPANY UNDER NEW MANAGEMENT

The second superintendency of John Higgins marks the beginning of the actual shift of the responsibilities of top management from the founders to younger men. Nathaniel Higgins had died in 1882, both Elias Higgins, and his lieutenant-in-marketing, Benjamin Lynes, a former dry-goods merchant who had joined the Higgins firm after business troubles in 1857, suffered from poor health in the eighties. The ability of the older generation to provide adequate leadership was declining without any indication of executive skill or assumption of responsibility on the part of the second generation. Elias' only son, Eugene, who had graduated from Columbia in 1882, was devoting his efforts to yachting, swordplay, and beau brummelling. In this crisis top policy determination often seemed in default, charting no path for operating managers, mapping out no program to combat aggressive competitors.

It was during this hiatus that the Higgins firm yielded primacy as tapestry producer to Alexander Smith. During the eighties tapestry yardage in the country jumped from 7,000,000 to 15,000,000 yards and velvet from 45,000 to 1,800,000.[29] The Higgins concern's peak year was in 1886, when the output of 2,300,000 yards equaled roughly 13 per cent of the tapestry and velvet market. Yet already it had fallen behind in the race with Smith, and the efforts of other tapestry manufacturers permitted no relaxation. In addition to competition with its nearest rivals, Higgins' tapestry faced a war with ingrain in 1887. Brussels producers also were being forced down to the tapestry level, and rumors that tapestry would eliminate brussels alternated with reports that brussels was eradicating tapestry. A still more ominous threat for the future was the new low-low-priced, high-pile axminsters which could offer even better color than tapestry.

Tapestry prices were declining under the growing competition of the eighties and declining prices were cutting into dollar sales totals. Where $1,000,000 had been a good volume before the Civil War for Higgins, inflation lifted it slowly to $2,600,000 in 1865; ten years later it reached an all-time high of $3,300,000. After 1881 it did not go over $3,000,000, and from 1887 to 1889 the total did not reach $2,000,000. From 1886 to 1889 production of ingrain and tapestry was off 22 per cent, but sales value declined 32 per cent.

Thus John Higgins in again assuming the management of the plant for his ailing uncle, Elias, was taking on more than a routine responsibility. His associate in top management was George Squire, who was appointed a marketing chief upon the death of Benjamin Lynes in 1888.

After graduating from Sheffield Scientific School at Yale in 1866, Squire had gained a reputation as the most effective American salesman of the tapestries of the famous English reformer and manufacturer, John Bright.[30] He had been a Higgins salesman for two years after 1879 and then had headed the carpet department for two other concerns before Elias Higgins summoned him for the big job of guiding the Higgins interests. Squire's assistant in sales was Alvin Hamilton Higgins, perhaps the ablest and certainly the most personable of Elias' nephews (not to be confused with Alvin Dyer Higgins, who was a grandnephew).

John Higgins and George Squire had scarcely assumed their tasks when in 1889 the death of Elias Higgins threw the future of the firm into the realm of speculation. Elias' only son, Eugene, came home from Europe in 1889 more interested in spreading the art of swordplay than the market for carpets.[31] Nursing his indifference to carpet manufacture was his obsession with the value of the New York City land on which the carpet plant stood. For the moment, however, it was a poor time to put a carpet business on the market. Stock and know-how were worth little in the depressed and uncertain economic climate of those years.

For three years, while the estate was being settled, Squire and John Higgins, in spite of their anomalous position, injected new vigor into the concern. After overhauling the production system, Higgins went to work on wiltons, introducing modifications which enabled the mill to produce a much higher pile fabric.[32] With ingrains, the emphasis, as at Hartford, was on new weaves, as styles suggestive of moquettes, brussels and the popular French cretonnes were put on the market.[33] John Higgins continued the small brussels line and started the production of inexpensive axminster. With this addition, he had achieved a rounded production which enabled the Higgins salesmen to furnish a store with a complete line of carpets.

The inclusion of new items put a strain on old facilities, making it necessary to expand the plant. In 1891 a new four-story building for winding, setting, and printing was started as was another to house the new 700-horsepower engine.[34] All told, capacity was increased by one-third.[35] As production of the two staples, ingrain and tapestry, steadily advanced toward the 4,000,000-yard mark, sales volume climbed back to $2,600,000.[36]

Meanwhile two important management changes occurred. John Higgins retired and Alvin D. was put in charge of manufacturing for the second time. While Elias Higgins' estate was being settled his son-in-law withdrew from the business, leaving Eugene as the sole owner. Eugene retained title to the physical assets but he took in John D. Wood as the managing partner. A Yale alumnus and a member of the firm of Wood & Payson, the new partner was a wool merchant whose specialty had been carpet wools. Besides his own funds, Wood had those of his wife, a Colgate heiress.[37]

The search for new blood continued, and the significant acquisition of Robert Patterson Perkins was soon made. Perkins, one of the outstanding leaders and executives in the carpet industry after the turn of the century, was born in 1861, the son of a New York City merchant. Descended from a Massachusetts family, he had attended St. Paul's and Harvard, where he captained the crew in 1884. After a brief stay in the freight department of the Delaware, Lackawanna & Western Railroad and a tour of duty as a salesman for P. Lorillard & Company, he had become the Philadelphia agent for H. C. Thatcher & Company, importers of wool. Transferred to New York in 1889, he undoubtedly had occasion to come into close contact with the Higgins management.[38]

Perkins was a handsome man and charming in personality. The prototype of the aristocratic gentleman, he had the faculty of winning his point without throwing his weight around and the ability to get things done without displaying force.[39] By background and by personality, he was eminently suited to deal with the financial magnates who were to be so important in his company's future history.

Perkins' arrival coincided with the incorporation of the firm. On March 23, 1892, Eugene Higgins and 10 of his associates established the E. S. Higgins Carpet Company under the laws of New Jersey. Six of the group were operating men of the carpet company: Wood, Perkins, Squire, A. D. Higgins, Benjamin Firth, superintendent of the yarn mill, and Oren M. Beach, treasurer. Of the rest, one was a resident of New Jersey, a qualification necessary for incorporation in that state, two were lawyers, and a fourth was Stephen Lynes. A brother of Benjamin Lynes, Stephen had come to the Higgins company with experience as a dry-goods merchant and as bookkeeper of New York County during the days when the notorious "Boss" William M. Tweed ran New York. Despite this rather questionable connection Lynes must have served the Higginses, father and son, faithfully, for in 1892 he was manager of Eugene Higgins' private and real-estate interests.

To provide for the management of the concern in the almost perpetual absence of Eugene, and at the same time to protect his interests, the by-laws of the new corporation, in contrast to the simple and direct management techniques used by the founders, envisioned a complex organization with an elaborate system of checks and balances. The stockholders, that is to say Eugene Higgins, had rather more authority than was customary in incorporated businesses: the power to declare money available for dividends, to elect directors, and to approve by a four-fifths vote the sale or mortgage of any real or leasehold property of the company. The eleven directors (Higgins and the incorporators) were empowered to elect the officers from among their own number, vote dividends, borrow money, revise the bylaws, and set aside annually a sum sufficient for working capital, in addition to formulating policies and directing day-to-day operations through weekly meetings.[40]

The officers consisted of a president, vice-president, secretary, and general manager—all but the president removable by the board. The president, or his stand-in, the vice-president, was the real executive head. The treasurer was primarily a financial figure, handling funds and looking after the stock books. The secretary, a minor functionary, kept the minutes and audited vouchers and payrolls. The duties of the general manager were left undefined in the bylaws, the board determining the assignment according to the abilities of the incumbent.

Committees were provided to supervise the officers closely, each committee consisting of the interested officer and two or more other directors. Of primary importance was the executive committee of five, which, according to the bylaws, might "transact any business which they deem necessary to promote the welfare of the Company." The committee on management handled purchasing and manufacturing, the committee on accounts established accounting procedures and prepared monthly reports. Thus was reared the structure of group responsibility.

Putting flesh on the administrative skeleton, the directors elected Eugene Higgins president, with a salary of $25,000 a year. John D. Wood became vice-president at $15,000 plus 10 per cent of the net profits after the payment of the rent and dividends on preferred; Oren M. Beach became treasurer at $4,000; Perkins, secretary at $3,000; and Squire, general manager at $6,000. The membership of the standing committees was as follows: Wood, Perkins, Beach, Squire, and Lynes were assigned to the executive committee; Alvin Higgins, Firth, and Perkins to the management; and three nonoperating directors, John Duer, Lynes, and William Lawson, to the one on accounts.

With these preliminaries completed, Eugene Higgins formally turned over in March, 1892, to the E. S. Higgins Carpet Company the assets of the carpet business except for the Manhattan real estate. In return he received the 10,000 shares of preferred and 9,990 shares of common stock for which he had subscribed. The total capitalization was $2,000,000 and since the value of assets aside from real estate did not quite reach $2,000,-000, a debit balance in profit and loss was set up which was attributable to goodwill. The land upon which the factory buildings stood was leased from Eugene Higgins for a period of twenty-one years at $60,000 a year and the White Street store property was rented until 1897 at $18,000 a year.

Next in order of business came a review of all phases of administration. Several small construction projects were undertaken with a view to reducing manufacturing costs. More important, following in the footsteps of Houston at Hartford, the Higgins management went outside the firm to get an expert's appraisal of the business. In the summer of 1892 an expert on carpet mills was brought from England at a cost of $625 to make a thorough examination of the plant and manufacturing process.

Purchasing procedures remained untouched; in selling, the idea of using auctions was considered and rejected. However, to strengthen company facilities in the marketing area, the number of road salesmen was increased from five to nine and a Chicago office opened.

The new corporation got off to a slow start. While a steady sales volume was maintained throughout 1892, profits were not satisfactory. At the first annual meeting, a committee recommended a general reduction in expenses but, in the hope of improvement, delayed salary cuts. On the contrary, Robert Perkins' salary as secretary was doubled to $6,000—an indication of his growing importance in the affairs of the company. In January, 1893, only 1½ per cent—$15,000—of the required 7 per cent was paid on the preferred.

Yet, instead of the hoped-for improvements, a major depression was soon upon the country. Credit policies were tightened; efforts were made to obtain more business on the Pacific Coast; the mill was shut down for several months. With sales down 25 per cent and chances for profit-sharing very slight, Wood resigned in October, 1893. To replace Wood as vice-president Higgins selected James B. Fitzgerald, the former head of the carpet department at A. T. Stewart's and at W. & J. Sloane's.[41] While at Sloane's, Fitzgerald had concentrated on the development of Alexander Smith's tapestry and moquettes, and much of the latter's growth in the eighties was attributed to him.

Fitzgerald's first move was toward product simplification. The small brussels and wilton lines were dropped. To enable his salesmen to continue offering a full range of fabrics, he contracted with Whittall for its brussels,[42] and he arranged for the purchase of small quantities of cheap ingrains from Philadelphia houses.[43] Not even Fitzgerald's best efforts, however, could keep the looms throbbing in dolorous 1894. Employment was spotty throughout the spring, and in July the plant was completely shut down for two weeks.

As the management was prepared to resume operations it was halted by an abrupt cablegram from Paris. On July 11 Eugene wired: "Don't wish anything done about starting up mill until my return. Sail Lucania July fourteenth." Immediately the directors replied: "Unanimously advise you to rescind order to close mill." Before this judgment Eugene bowed—with a condition: "Don't want a lot of unsaleable goods piled up in times like these." [44] As ordered the managers took care, on opening the mill, to produce no more than they felt certain they could sell. The result of the year's activities was a loss of $36,000.

Continued depression, falling prices (see Table 13), and changes in fashion made 1895 nearly as bad a year as 1894. Although the Higgins production of ingrains and tapestry in 1895 reached an all-time high of 4,600,000 yards, profits amounted to only $42,000 and it was decided that there should be no dividend payments even though the corporation had sizable cash balances.

In 1896 general business jitters were aggravated by one of America's bitterest elections. With production down 17 per cent and with a loss of $49,000, Fitzgerald resigned as vice-president. To replace him Eugene Higgins this time promoted from within. Robert Perkins, beginning his long career as chief executive, was raised to the positions of vice-president and general manager, but at $10,000 a year instead of the $12,000 given Fitzgerald. The carpet trade journal hailed Perkins as "business man of culture" noted for his great thoroughness.[45] Squire took over his position as secretary and A. Hamilton Higgins became a director.[46] A year later, when Beach resigned as treasurer, Perkins took over his post and Alvin D. Higgins became general manager.[47]

In Perkins' first year at the helm, 1897, production increased slightly, and a profit of $45,000 was returned. Still no dividends were paid and

TABLE 13

E. S. HIGGINS CARPET COMPANY

Prices of Selected Products   1895 Compared with 1889

	Autumn, 1895 (Per Yard)	Change from 1889 (Per Cent)		Autumn, 1895 (Per Yard)	Change from 1889 (Per Cent)
Three-star tapestry	$.425	—15	Ten-wire tapestry	$.575	—14
Double-star tapestry	.50	—13	Wilton velvets	.475	—15
Single-star tapestry	.575	—14	Imperial velvets	.725	—21
			Three-ply ingrain	.60	—20

Source: Price lists in *The Philadelphia Carpet Trade* and *The American Carpet and Upholstery Trade.*

Eugene Higgins waived the payment of his salary. The following spring the inventory backlog was so large that wool purchases were temporarily stopped and Perkins considered participating with Alexander Smith in an auction.

To cut costs, the store and warehouse on White Street were given up. Instead a warehouse was built at the mill and a more desirable location for the sales headquarters was leased in the Hartford building. Perkins acquired some new ingrain looms and spinning equipment and the rights to a loom attachment which enabled the company to dispense with one girl for every four looms.[48] Though the introduction of this device was accompanied by a 15 per cent wage increase, the girls complained that the time lost by breaks would more than offset this and that they would become physical wrecks. The finishers also protested that the extra defects would decrease their earnings. Charges of poisonous dyes and unsanitary working conditions were thrown in with the complaints, for good measure. After an investigation, the State Board of Mediation and Arbitration ruled, as a face-saver, that the girls should not be compelled to work until proper tests were made as to safety and that those displaced should not be fired.[49]

Perkins' worries were not limited to conditions in the carpet business. For four or five years the management had expected hourly a cable from Eugene Higgins directing it to close shop.[50] In 1899 the moment arrived. Higgins had spent most of the nineties in Europe, fretting because he was branded as a wealthy carpet manufacturer instead of a gentleman millionaire. In addition to this "mental anguish," he had to endure the company's "non-support." With small profits alternating with losses, with no dividends and even no salary, an astute businessman as well as a society-oriented playboy might question the desirability of keeping his capital in such a line of endeavor—especially when the New York property was so valuable for other uses. The death of Stephen Lynes in June, 1899, was probably the final factor in Eugene's decision to sell. Lynes had been the guardian of Eugene's interests in New York and had managed all his personal affairs while the "carpet manufacturer" was abroad. With Lynes gone the headaches were certain to grow worse.

Upon receiving intelligence of Higgins' decision to dispose of the carpet business, Perkins turned to a Harvard friend, Neal Rantoul, of F. S. Moseley & Company, Boston. The step was a natural one. Earlier that year Rantoul had approached Perkins with an offer on behalf of Charles Ranlett Flint, the trust promotor, to purchase the Higgins business in conjunction with the formation of a carpet trust, but the project had fallen through.

Rantoul naturally was interested in what Perkins had to offer. Over-all commodity-price indices had been advancing for three years and carpet prices would undoubtedly soon follow the trend. As a first step Rantoul proposed to Kidder, Peabody that it join the Moseley Company in finding the capital to take over the going concern. Higgins' price was $1,000,-000 cash. When an expert estimated that the raw materials and finished inventory alone were worth more than that, the investment bankers jumped at the opportunity.[51]

On October 9, 1899, Eugene Higgins sold to the bankers all the materials and equipment of his New York carpet enterprise and the use of his name until January 1, 1901. The old lease of the buildings and land was canceled and a new five-year agreement was substituted.[52]

After making arrangements for the purchase of the property, the bankers spread ownership of the new assets among slightly more than a hundred people. Robert Perkins, with 187 shares of preferred and 3,290 of common, was the largest single owner. Kidder, Peabody had 251 shares of preferred and 2,263 of common, and F. S. Moseley owned 350 shares of preferred and 1,470 of common. Other investors included Hamilton Higgins, A. D. Higgins, and George Squire, of the management, J. P. Morgan, Frank G. Webster, S. Endicott Peabody, and Rantoul, of the banking fraternity, and the Sloanes and Frank S. Chick of John H. Pray among the marketing men.

The operating men—Perkins, Hamilton Higgins, A. D. Higgins, and Squire—remained directors. The new interests were represented by T. L. Manson, Jr., F. G. Webster, William Endicott, Jr., and Neal Rantoul. While the officers were carpet men—Perkins as president, Squire as secretary and treasurer, A. D. Higgins as general manager—the investment bankers assumed ultimate responsibility for guiding the destinies of this company.

The bankers' methods in this case were similar to those used in their other operations. Perkins was given a free rein, except for the existence of an executive committee composed of himself, A. D. Higgins, Squire, Rantoul, and Endicott. This committee made periodic re-examinations of policies rather than daily checks of operating details. All the other committees were dropped.

The first year of the new team, 1900, saw improving business conditions. Prices were 5 to 10 cents above 1898 lows, and Higgins' ingrain and tapestry output climbed to over 4,500,000 yards. Early in 1901 the carpet trade journal estimated that Higgins had made 14 per cent in 14 months, and this "amid conditions not wholly favorable to big profits." [53] In these circumstances the preferred dividends were paid from January 1, 1900; and, on the prompting of Webster, Rantoul and Endicott, a 6 per cent return was made on the common stock in January, 1901.[54]

However gratifying these results, they did not alleviate the need for major changes and decisions. The product situation was serious. Tapestry demand had been cut almost in half in ten years, and the ingrain market had long ceased to show any real vitality. But quite apart from the normal business considerations were the problems caused by the terms of agreement with Eugene Higgins. Within a little over a year a new name had to be found, within five a new home. The merger with the Hartford Carpet Company supplied the solution to both.

With this combination disappeared the enterprise created by Elias S. Higgins. It was a disappearance in name and in physical embodiment but not in spirit, for from the plant on 43rd Street came the managerial skill which was to guide the operations of the Hartford Carpet Corporation and Bigelow-Hartford. Even the great-grandchild, Bigelow-Sanford, was to derive part of its management from the Higgins-trained group until the close of World War II.

The success of the company's strong man, Elias Higgins, is difficult to appraise. Reputedly he was worth $30,000,000 at his death—but much of this was due to real-estate holdings. In the first years he and his brothers

had made small profits from which they had laboriously built up their resources. The post-1870 period saw the great expansion in capacity and
the first large returns from tapestry. Meanwhile, because of direct marketing and technical proficiency, costs were undoubtedly low. While such
vague statements leave the degree of profitability undetermined, none
can gainsay the fact that by the time of the founder's death, E. S. Higgins & Company was among the first ten American carpet companies in
size. Further expansion over the next few years may even have enabled it
to surpass Lowell and Hartford in output.

By the end of the nineties, however, the management could no longer
just tread the paths first laid out by Elias Higgins. Elias in selecting mid-
dle- and lower-grade ingrains had picked the great mid-century market. In
choosing tapestry he again showed his genius for product determination.
But one or two such decisions do not suffice for all time and in the grim
years of the late eighties and the nineties there was no one to plan for the
future. Elias was sick; Eugene was not interested. The assistants had not
the authority to make radical departures. They battled against the depression as best they could by the intensification of old procedures. Such
measures raised Higgins from a 14 per cent share of the tapestry market
to 23 per cent—but it was a share of a smaller market and perhaps the
increase merely meant other manufacturers were abandoning the field.
For a better future, energetic steps had to be taken. The departure of
Eugene Higgins removed one obstacle. There remained a key question:
would the new financial ownership give Perkins and his associates a free
hand to make the needed changes?

STEPHEN SANFORD & SONS

Like the Higgins company the firm of Stephen Sanford & Sons, at Amsterdam in upstate New York, came to the fore on the wave of the tapestry
demand in the years following the Civil War. Like the former, it was
privately owned and even more the creation of one man: Stephen Sanford. In the seventies his sons John and William were initiated into the
business—at about the same time they were entering New York society.
The nonfamily members of the organization were strictly lieutenants. Supervising every detail of his business, from procuring favorable freight
rates down to locking the windows at night, Stephen Sanford shrugged off
the competition of the big corporations: "It was never the great corporations that bothered me . . . they had heads of departments . . . with
large salaries, and not one in a dozen understood the business." [55] Another
of his maxims was that "wise men dip into the future," [56] and this he did as
rapidly as his means allowed.

In 1860 Stephen Sanford's small properties, rebuilt after the fire of
1854, represented an investment of $30,000, including a few Greene power

looms for ingrain. Sanford employed about ninety men and women who turned out about 180,000 yards of carpeting a year worth $130,000, a dollar volume approximately the same as ten years earlier. Though the outbreak of war was a blow, entailing heavy losses on his southern accounts, he had sufficient funds by the late sixties to rebuild, after another fire, on an even larger scale. At the same time he extended his contacts and experience by serving a term in Congress.

In 1870 on the eve of a period of rapid growth Sanford had an investment of $400,000, a working force of over 300, a total of 140 looms—only 39 of which were power-driven—and an output of 452,000 yards of ingrain worth $510,000. Then, with Bigelow's brussels and tapestry patents expiring, Sanford constructed a four-story building in 1871 and ordered both brussels and tapestry power looms, as modified by E. K. Davis of Higgins, from the Gilbert Loom Company of Worcester.[57] Of Sanford's brussels little is known, but he was prepared for the tapestry boom of the next few years. Through the panic of 1873, the factory ran full time. In 1875 two new buildings were added and the number of tapestry looms increased from 20 to 40.

Not satisfied, Sanford continued to add to his tapestry line and became the first in the country to manufacture tapestry mats. In 1879 he opened a new tapestry mill with a gala Thanksgiving party. Thirty new looms and drums were procured from the Gilbert Loom Company. Bowes Brothers of Liverpool, with funds provided by Brown Brothers & Company and Brown, Shipley & Company, purchased abroad for Sanford worsted machinery from Prince, Smith, & Sons, and Phelps, Taylor, & Wordsworth. Two American firms, Davis & Furber and M. A. Furbush & Company, provided cards and other items.[58] More unusual than tapestry expansion was the integration of processes by the addition of a cotton mill.

Sanford's customers by the end of the seventies included A. T. Stewart, Field, Leiter, John H. Pray, W. & J. Sloane, Jordan Marsh, and H. B. Claflin. Against accounts with Claflin, Sanford drew as much as $45,000 in advances. The marketing agent, W. & J. Shaw & Company of New York, also advanced money. For the agent's services Sanford paid the rent and 2½ per cent commission. Standard terms to the wholesalers were two months' credit, 2 per cent for cash; however, they were open to considerable manipulation, W. & J. Sloane getting an additional 5 per cent discount as well as 4 per cent for cash.[59]

Still Sanford was not satisfied with his marketing arrangements. In the fall of 1880 he electrified the trade with the largest auction to date—and in the spring of 1881 he demoralized it with a still larger one. Prices plunged downward; dealers with stocks on hand bewailed betrayal; but the carpet trade journal praised Sanford for his courage and realism.

No sooner was his old stock cleared out, than Sanford took over his own marketing. Over the next few years his aggressive measures, striking advertising, liberal terms, and prompt dispatch of goods weaned several important jobbers from established firms and intensified the price wars of the mid-eighties. On this struggle, Sanford commented, "Business is sordid, but there is pleasure in it when you win." Only in 1889 did he revert to the auction—disposing of back patterns to a total of 10,000 rolls.[60]

In addition to strife on the selling front, Sanford fought with his employees. Sanford was not without heart; the use of hand looms was continued until all the old weavers had died or retired, and he had a reputation for not shutting down operations. But he was paternalistic and dictatorial. In 1877 and 1885 he quickly won victories over striking workers; but in 1886, after the prolonged Smith strike had ended with a partial victory for the workers, Sanford immediately changed his tactics and granted an advance. A few years later came a long and decisive test of strength. When it was over most of the pioneer carpet weavers in Amsterdam had been replaced by Polish immigrants.[61]

The decade of the nineties saw a major decision of Sanford's career —the decision to go heavily into broadloom axminster. At the beginning of the decade he was a tapestry and velvet manufacturer—having dropped ingrain eight or nine years before. In 1879 he had shown some interest in axminsters, but, unable to produce a competing loom, he waited until the expiration of the patents. Late in 1892 Sanford put up an axminster mill and hired several inventors to perfect a loom.[62] It was over two years before he turned out the first items in the new line and then in 1898 he introduced the famous *Beauvais* axminster—"gotten up especially for the introduction of oriental effects." [63] He was to be the first in this country to use "broad looms." The advantage was obvious. By turning out wide carpetings, the cost and unsightliness of sewing together narrow strips could be avoided. Furthermore, large, seamless carpet "rugs" could be cut to standard room size and sold for immediate and easy installation. For the next twenty years Sanford was to be the leader in manufacturing seamless axminster. In 1913 he had 418 looms, of which 154 were wide.[64]

In the long career of Stephen Sanford—sixty-nine years—his truly remarkable ability to estimate product trends stands out. He was almost always in the position of enjoying first profits before the margin was driven down by competition. Second in importance was his marketing policy in the eighties: his handling of his own sales to wholesalers, when few other carpet manufacturers were so progressive, and his livelier advertising copy. These decisions on products and marketing combined with his administrative ability raised his firm from the ashes in 1854 to among the first five or six carpet concerns in the country by the time of his death in 1913.

CHAPTER 7

YEARS OF ADAPTATION:

The Bigelow Carpet Company, 1854–1899

The history of the Bigelow Carpet Company from 1854 to 1899 is a saga of two families: Bigelow and Fairbanks. From the Bigelows the firm received the principles and pioneering reputation of Erastus and the managerial abilities of Horatio and his sons. From the Fairbanks it acquired financial resources and executive leadership.

In 1854 four men owned the Bigelow stock: Stephen Fairbanks, Horatio and Erastus Bigelow, and Henry Kellogg. By the end of the century, the capitalization had increased from $160,000 to $1,000,000 and the number of owners to 77. The Fairbanks family, with 179 of the 1,000 shares, controlled the largest block and the Bigelows the next. Of the newcomers the most important were James Beal, president of the Second National Bank of Boston, A. S. Wheeler, the company counsel, and John and William Sloane, the New York carpet dealers who had bought into the company before 1870.

With the exception of the Bigelows they all had representatives on the board. In later years the Bigelows were absent from the directorate but this circumstance did not prevent them from playing an important role in the concern's management, for two sons of Horatio Bigelow occupied the position of agent for much of the period.

The history of these years can be divided roughly into the period from 1854 to 1873, when Horatio Bigelow and Charles A. Whiting successively held the position of treasurer, and from 1874 to 1899, when Charles F. Fairbanks assumed the chief managerial responsibility. Of Horatio Bigelow's managerial ability we have already spoken. Of Whiting little is known. Charles Francis Fairbanks, the son of Henry, was born in 1843. In the sixties he went to work for the carpet company as a clerk in the Boston office and in 1874 he became treasurer. In addition to serving in this capacity for the remainder of his life, he was treasurer of the Clinton Wire Cloth Company and vice-president of the Second National Bank of Boston. Judging from the history of the concern, he was a pillar of financial conservatism and a staunch defender of Erastus Bigelow's precept of quality leadership.

Erastus Bigelow was president of the corporation from the death of Stephen Fairbanks in 1866 until his own in 1879. Though never very active on an operating level, he defined the principles of operation and gave the company a prestige which has lasted until today. Through his inventions, through his writings on economic subjects, through his presidency of the National Association of Wool Manufacturers, and through his policy of advertising at exhibitions at home and abroad, he gave wide currency to the Bigelow name.

It was a name associated with quality and leadership. As the judges at the Philadelphia Centennial in 1876 stated concerning Bigelow carpets: "Much is expected of them because of the leading position they hold in the trade, and the most exacting will be satisfied both with the designs and the manner in which they are displayed . . . a brilliant display . . . in material, texture, design, and color, possessing all the elements of the highest manufacture." [1] Another critic wrote at the same time: "That the Bigelow Carpet Company holds first place among American Carpet-makers is no doubtful question." [2]

Mechanical proficiency, good materials, concentration on the better grades, and good design were the foundations of this reputation.[3] By 1881 the firm was paying $25,000 a year in salaries to its staff of designers, for while Bigelow was "intent upon the practical and useful" he also had the artist's eye for the beautiful in form and color [4]—combined with the educator's zeal. A contemporary comment said: "It seems to be the recognized province of the Bigelow Company to assume the role of public educators in the matter of taste in floor decorations. They have never pandered to what is considered vulgar taste, but have continually led in the direction of true art, not sparing either trouble or expense in securing superior designs." [5] In this tradition Erastus Bigelow's successors continued.

Particularly known for his refined judgment of art, his originality of conception and execution, and his commercial sensitivity was the head of the marketing department, William Burrage Kendall.[6] His career as salesmanager virtually covered the last half of the nineteenth century. The son of a Clinton doctor, he attended Groton before becoming a clerk in the Boston office of Henry P. Fairbanks at the time the latter was handling the sales of the carpet company. Upon the death of Henry Fairbanks, the directors decided to establish the main selling agency in New York with Kendall in charge. His forty years of service made him dean of carpet marketers. This long service together with a compelling personality and "the conceded pioneership and prestige of the Bigelow Company" [7] gave him leadership in his group. With the Sloanes, to whom he was warmly attached, he set the prices on brussels and wiltons.[8] He was equally congenial with Arnold, Constable's carpet man with whom he worked in arranging for the introduction of Bigelow axminsters. Price leader, style leader, respected authority on trade matters, financier, Brooklyn community leader, Kendall seems to have experienced a minimum of friction with his rivals, his customers, his staff, his treasurer, and his mill.

The agent completed the ranks of top management. Horatio Bigelow was agent from 1854 to 1864 when ill health forced his retirement. After a short interval his eldest son, Henry N. Bigelow, assumed the post. Henry was followed in 1882 by a younger brother, Charles B. Bigelow, who had worked in all parts of the mill from a position in the sorting room to purchasing agent and in addition had served as agent of the Clinton Wire Cloth mill. When Charles retired in 1898, the directors were forced to go outside the Bigelow family for his successor. Edward W. Burdett, the paymaster, who had frequently served as acting agent during Charles Bigelow's trips abroad, was selected.

While at Lowell the agent was also the superintendent; at Clinton the Bigelows were assisted in the management of the factory by the superintendent, who was usually a technical man with long experience in the plant. The first superintendent, William Eaton, was an associate of Horatio Bigelow's cotton mill days of the early thirties. His successor, John P. Buzzell, a Canadian, had started as a section hand in the Coach Lace Mill. When Buzzell retired in 1880, Junius Hayes, who had begun twenty years before as a helper in the spinning mill, was promoted from his position as spinning superintendent.

Under the plant superintendent were several ranks of supervision. Next to him were the spinning and weaving superintendents, most of whom were New Englanders. Under them were the department heads, whose numbers were continually being augmented as new departments were added, to some extent as the result of the division of labor but more often because of the assumption of new functions. The Scots still dominated the dyeing and coloring processes but native-born Americans had assumed responsibilities in the other departments. While small departments had but one overseer, most also had an assistant, known as a second hand. Around 1880 a third hand often was added, but his appearance was usually short-lived, perhaps due to the pressure of economy.

THE BIGELOW–WHITING ERA, 1854–1873

During the prosperous period from 1854 to 1873, when first Horatio Bigelow and then Charles Whiting filled the office of treasurer, the keynotes of company development were expanding capacity and integration of functions. In 1854, at the beginning of the era, the plant had only two operating units—for dyeing and for weaving—with a capacity of about 400,000 yards. By the end of the decade capacity had risen to over 600,000 yards, most of which growth was due to a 25 per cent increase in loom efficiency.[9]

Meanwhile the carpet company was taking on additional functions. In 1855 the management decided to establish an integrated production line. Prior to this time Bigelow had purchased worsted yarn from several of the small mills of the vicinity. As capacity expanded, quality control and regularity of supply pointed to the desirability of the concern's producing its own yarn. By the end of 1858 a small spinning mill was completed, and in the next year additional space was provided for the winding and the finishing departments. New departments meant increased power needs and in 1860 the management supplemented the water power with a new 120-horsepower Corliss & Nightingale steam engine.[10] A new dyehouse completed arrangements. Meanwhile the carpet company had acquired, in 1857, the machine shop of the Clinton Company and thenceforth handled its own repair and development work.[11] To finance this expansion and to provide working capital for the larger operation, the capitalization was raised from $160,000 to $300,000.

Like its competitors in the carpet business, the Bigelow company limped along during the first year and a half of the war, turning out a small line to keep its machinery fit and to retain a nucleus of skilled help. To supplement the limited carpet output, the mill obtained a contract for army blankets. After 1861 the output of carpets rose rapidly until by 1863 it was breaking all company records. For the rest of the war the firm maintained an average production of over 650,000 yards annually.

The expanding production was accompanied by greatly inflated costs. From 1854 to 1865 the costs of five-frame, three-fourths brussels, the biggest item in output, and five-frame, three-fourths wiltons were as shown in Table 14. After a general decline in the fifties, brussels costs shot up 171 per cent during the war, and wilton costs, because of the greater wool content, rose 200 per cent. The principal reason for the increase was the spiraling price of materials, especially wool (see Table 15).

A comparison of manufacturing costs with the prices charged by Bigelow to its jobbers is given in Table 16. From the figures it is apparent that wilton margins were more favorable than brussels early in the hostilities but less so after wool began to rise.

Though carpet prices started to rise with the outbreak of the war and reached their peak in 1864, wages dragged until 1863. Once started upward, however, wages continued to mount until 1866, after which the workers' gains were in large measure maintained until 1874.

TABLE 14

BIGELOW CARPET COMPANY

Average Costs of Manufacturing Brussels and Wilton Carpets

1854 to 1865

(Five-frame, Three-fourths Widths)

Year	Av. Cost of Manufacture Brussels Wilton (Per Yard)		Year	Av. Cost of Manufacture Brussels Wilton (Per Yard)	
1854 [a]	$1.32	$2.13	1860 [c]	$1.08	$1.56
1855 [a]	1.13	1.78	1861 [c]	1.43	2.08
1856 [b]	1.17	1.72	1862 [c]	.97	1.41
1857 [b]	1.30	1.96	1863 [c]	1.70	2.73
1858 [b]	1.10	1.67	1864 [c]	2.84	4.44
1859 [b]	1.14	1.73	1865 [d]	2.93	4.69

[a] For the five months ending December 31.
[b] For the five months ending November 30.
[c] For the six months ending November 30.
[d] For the six months ending May 31.

Source: Bigelow Carpet Company, Cost of Carpeting, 1850 to 1865.

TABLE 15

BIGELOW CARPET COMPANY

Changes in Costs of Carpets   1854 to 1860 and 1861 to 1865

	1854–1860 (Per Cent)	1861–1865 (Per Cent)
Labor	−25	+25
Miscellaneous expenses	+29	+113
Materials	−25	+218
Total changes in cost	−18	+175

Source: Bigelow Carpet Company, Cost of Carpeting, 1850 to 1865.

The Bigelow management was quick to take advantage of the change in the economic climate in the mid-war years, embarking on a program of expansion to meet the demand of the war-enriched middle classes. Late in 1863 the corporation had the opportunity to pick up most of the property of the Clinton Company for $45,000 [12] and thenceforth these buildings were used for the preparatory processes. But plans went beyond this chance acquisition. In March, 1864, the firm undertook a two-year building project which entailed an increase in capitalization, first to $500,000 and then to $800,000. The chief construction was a three-story mill on the site of the former coach-lace factory site.

With additional capacity and much new modern equipment, Bigelow faced the growing competition of post-patent years and the growing markets of the Gilded Age. In 1869 the American middle and upper classes were absorbing almost a million and a half yards of brussels—most of which were of foreign origin. The 605,000 yards of domestic production were largely from the Bigelow concern. In that year, while Bigelow was adding to its own capacity, Hartford and Lowell embarked on ambitious

TABLE 16

BIGELOW CARPET COMPANY

Costs and List Prices to Jobbers   1854 to 1865

(Five-frame, Three-fourths Widths)

	Brussels			Wilton		
Year	Av. Cost a (Per Yard)	Price (Per Yard)	Index of Cost-Price Relationship	Av. Cost a (Per Yard)	Price (Per Yard)	Index of Cost-Price Relationship
1854	$1.32	$1.26	104	—	—	—
1855	1.13	1.27	89	—	—	—
1856	1.17	1.35	87	—	—	—
1857	1.30	1.35	96	—	—	—
1858	1.10	1.27	87	—	—	—
1859	1.14	1.30	88	—	—	—
1860	1.08	1.20	90	$1.56	$1.80	87
1861	1.43	1.30	110	2.08	1.95	107
1862	.97	1.75	55	1.41	2.45	58
1863	1.70	2.15	79	2.73	3.00	91
1864	2.84	3.50	81	4.44	5.00	89
1865	2.93	2.50	117	4.69	4.00	117

a See Table 14.

Source: Bigelow Carpet Company, Cost of Carpeting, 1850 to 1865, *passim;* "Bigelow Prices for Forty Years," *The American Carpet and Upholstery Trade,* X (Feb. 1, 1892), 150.

brussels programs. The increased output undoubtedly contributed to the sharp decline in prices at the end of 1869, but despite the appearance of five or six other new competitors, the price level remained fairly stable throughout the rest of Whiting's regime.

PRODUCTION UNDER CHARLES F. FAIRBANKS, 1874–1899

In contrast to the general prosperity enjoyed by his predecessors, Charles F. Fairbanks, during his tenure as treasurer from 1874 to 1899, labored during unrelieved depression. Though the major postwar economic crisis had begun before Charles F. Fairbanks took office as treasurer in 1874, foreign carpet manufacturers had absorbed the first shock. In the fall when the payroll accounting system was reorganized from a daily to an hourly basis, some wage reductions were instituted, yet with prices holding fairly well, and a strong balance sheet, Fairbanks felt he could recommend extensive building plans for 1875. Capacity was almost doubled by the addition of a new building for 64 improved Bigelow looms, and two new spinning mills equipped with Noble combs.[13]

For the next ten years, while other companies added to brussels capacity and while such new fabrics as moquettes came on the market, Fairbanks undertook neither to expand nor to diversify his output. However, the wilton line, which had been started on a small scale before the Civil War, was given great impetus by the promotional efforts of W. & J. Sloane.[14]

In the mid-eighties, however, the treasurer at last took action both to strengthen his old line and to introduce new products. First he added fifty new brussels and wilton looms, bringing spinning and weaving capacity into better balance. In an effort to extend the market, cheaper "Lancaster" grades were offered in both fabrics—though unsuccessfully.

A more radical innovation was the departure into axminster. Prior to this time, with a strictly limited line of brussels and wilton plus a few by-products, like blankets and yarn, the firm had been highly specialized. Once Fairbanks determined to spread out, high-grade axminster was a logical choice to complement the other quality goods which the company distributed through its network of quality outlets. In this selection Fairbanks was encouraged by Arnold, Constable. Since the Alexander Smith patents were still in force, Bigelow bought the rights to a loom invented by Charles Skinner, the son of Smith's co-worker. The Skinner loom was similar to the Smith axminster loom but had a weaving mechanism which operated upside down from the original.[15]

Early in 1885, the Bigelow company began to pull down old buildings to make way for the new axminster mill. Two years later advance samples were submitted to the trade—for its paeans of praise. The favorable reception hastened the move by Smith from moquettes into the better-grade fabric, but in 1889 Bigelow's 72 looms represented about 75 per cent of the high-grade axminster capacity in the country. These axminster looms plus 202 brussels and wilton looms could turn out 2,000,000 yards of carpeting annually. Though Bigelow was smaller than Lowell, Hartford, and Higgins, it still had the largest brussels and wilton capacity in the world.[16]

Although during the nineties there were no major additions to capacity, product-wise there were two significant developments. First, the company tried to appeal to as many pocketbook levels as possible. The cheaper Lancaster brands were reintroduced in brussels and wilton. In the more expensive range Fairbanks and Kendall brought out Imperial brussels, wilton, and axminster, and a Saxony wilton. By 1899 the mill was turning out seven variations in widths and frames of regular brussels and four of Imperial brussels. In the wilton line there were seven regulars, two Saxonies, eight Lancasters, and one Imperial. One regular and two Imperial axminsters completed the carpet offerings.[17]

Perhaps the more significant product innovation was the appearance of Bigelow rugs in 1898. With the largest no more than 3 feet wide and 6 feet long,[18] these were a far cry from the broadloom of the future but the mere entry into the rug field was a step in the right direction. This line was made exclusively for Arnold, Constable, and that house did most of the promotional work.

Though the axminster mill was the major construction project after 1885, new machinery was acquired periodically and many of the other buildings were renovated in the eighties. Electric lights were installed, roofs were raised to improve ventilation, and window space was increased.

TABLE 17

BIGELOW CARPET COMPANY

Changes in the Component Costs of Brussels Carpeting   1860 to 1888

(Five-frame, Three-fourths Widths)

	Change: 1860 to 1888 (Per Cent)	Change: 1865 to 1888 (Per Cent)
Materials	—8	—70
Labor	+75	+40
Miscellaneous expenses	—40	—70
Total cost	—3	—64

Source: Bigelow Carpet Company, Cost of Carpeting, 1850–1865, *passim;* Bigelow Carpet Company, Cost of Carpeting, 1888, *passim.*

While these changes improved working conditions, the primary motivation was the reduction of costs through better working arrangements.[19]

Only one series of cost records survive for Fairbanks' period: those for 1888. During the eighties costs returned to their ante-bellum level. In 1860 the average cost for a six-month period of five-frame three-fourths brussels had been $1.08 a yard, the lowest in the prewar years. After the wartime peak of $2.93 in 1865 it had dropped to $1.10 in 1878 and $1.04 in 1888.

As before the war, materials were still by far the most important item in the cost of five-frame three-fourths brussels, but the proportion of the whole had declined from about 78 per cent to 67 per cent by 1888. The share of miscellaneous expenses had also dropped slightly to 13 per cent. Labor costs per yard, in contrast, had gained not only relatively but absolutely. Instead of a prewar 8 per cent, they now accounted for 20 per cent of the total and stood at 21 cents a yard as compared with 15 cents in 1865 and 12 cents in 1860. Wool was still the most important single ingredient, however, and the fall in carpet costs after the war as shown in Table 17 can be attributed primarily to the decline in the price of wool.

Labor relations in a small town like Clinton consisted of something more than wage rates and working conditions. Clinton was not a one-factory town; indeed, the Lancaster Mills employed more workers than the Bigelow company; but the importance of the Bigelows, the smallness of the community, the identification of carpet company management with that of the third largest plant, the Clinton Wire Cloth Company, combined to give the Bigelow firm a role in local affairs perhaps nearer to the Hartford company's position than the Lowell company's in their respective communities. Furthermore both Erastus and Horatio Bigelow were particularly interested in the community's educational and social undertakings.

As did its rivals, out of necessity, the Bigelow company provided some housing. At the time of the Civil War the company owned 18 brick tenements. When in the seventies the work force expanded from 200 to over a thousand, the holdings grew to over 30 houses which could accommodate 80 families.[20] While these buildings were twenty-five to fifty years old by the century's end, they had been built sturdily, and modern conveniences such as running water had been added in the eighties.[21] Still these facilities took care of only a small portion of the working force. Many of the others probably rented houses, but the local paper in 1888 reported that, "The men employed in our mills have enjoyed so much of personal success . . . that hundreds of them have bought land and erected neat houses." [22]

On the whole it was a satisfied and stable group of employees. Only one major labor disturbance occurred in the company's entire history. The protest in 1886 was not against a wage cut but against an insufficient advance in pay. The Scottish workers in the dyehouse wanted 15 cents an hour instead of the designated 14. After Charles Bigelow explained that Lowell was only paying 11 cents and most other competitors were equally low, he warned that if the workers went out their action would be considered "an absolute withdrawal from the employ of the company." [23] Nevertheless, the 77 men in the dyehouse voted to demand a further advance, basing their claim in part on the fact that an increase in the weight of dye packages from 80 to 120 pounds had caused damage to clothes and shoes. When they came to work the next day, they found no steam. The other departments ran for another week, but on April 5 the weaving mill was shut down.

Then came trouble. During the next week the management obtained the services of 15 local and 25 outside laborers. As the recruits were reporting to work on April 14, they were roughly handled by a crowd of about 1,500. It was obvious that the incident would be repeated, yet the town selectmen, three out of five of whom were members of the Knights of Labor, made no move to prevent it. By nightfall the next day some 3,000 people were on company property besieging the dyehouse. To avoid violence, Bigelow and Fairbanks decided to close down completely and to return the new employees to their homes.

Thus matters stood for three weeks. The Knights of Labor voted to support the dyers, though they had no formal connection with the dyers' union. Meanwhile the poll of public opinion had turned against the strikers. On May 7 a committee of workers informed Charles Bigelow that all the men were willing to return. While the agent was pleasant, he did not deviate from his role as the hirer of labor. He would consider individually each man who asked for a job as soon as repairs to the mills were completed. In the face of this intransigence, the dyers voted to dissolve their union and 66 of the 77 applied to Bigelow. Within the next few days Bigelow called for 15 of them, and 15 new men. A week later the dyehouse staff had grown to 60; only 25 of these were old-timers. A few new weavers were also necessary as some of the old ones refused to handle yarn dyed by the new men.[24] Thus ended the only strike in the history of the corporation.

MARKETING AND FINANCE, 1874–1899

At the close of the Civil War, Bigelow's average marketing cost per yard was 6 cents; two decades later it was 6.9 cents for five-frame three-fourths brussels and 11.4 cents for the same in wilton. The increase had been held to this moderate amount only by not using road salesmen, but in the fall of 1888 the company added traveling personnel to Kendall's staff,[25] bringing the Bigelow distribution system in line with the methods of other carpet manufacturers.

The Bigelow marketing organization was adapted to the Bigelow market. Much of the business was done on a contract basis with large hotels, steamships, theaters, and so forth. The demand for the rest was concentrated for the most part in the large cities of the eastern seaboard and the Middle West, and much of this was also made to order for such large houses as Sloane's and Arnold, Constable. In the eighties the on-order trade declined, and for this reason Bigelow's brussels was forced to compete with tapestry for the favor of the lower-middle-class customer wherever he might be. This shift required a wider contact with wholesalers and compelled Kendall to acquire traveling representatives. Still at the time of Kendall's death in 1898, only one man covered the entire area west of Pittsburgh.

Kendall's advertising remained dignified, if not much more. He laid considerable stress on the Bigelow name, its antecedents and its traditions; and he early recognized the importance of a trade-mark. His first one, patented in 1879, was merely a line of contrasting colors on the back of the carpet,[26] but in 1882 he progressed to having the word "Bigelow" woven in white in the back of each pattern.[27]

In the same year Kendall liberalized his credit terms, allowing 90 days instead of 60 and giving a 3 per cent discount instead of 2 per cent for cash within 10 days. The 3 per cent discount was extended to 30 days in 1895.

Because of its position as an industry leader, Bigelow occasionally was accused of price-cutting when it initiated a downward movement. Actually, in reductions, the company was more likely to follow than precede. It was in upward movements that Bigelow took the lead. Leading

TABLE **18**

BIGELOW CARPET COMPANY

Average Price of Bigelow Carpets   Selected Dates from 1864 to 1896

(Five-frame, Three-fourths Widths)

(Per Yard)

		Brussels		Wilton	
		Dollars in Currency	*Dollars in Gold*	*Dollars in Currency*	*Dollars in Gold*
July	1864	3.500	1.316	5.00	1.880
March	1865	2.500	1.426	3.75	2.139
January	1870	2.150	1.764	3.25	2.666
November	1876	1.750	1.595	2.85	2.597
December	1879	1.375	1.375	2.45	2.450
November	1885	1.125	1.125	2.00	2.000
May	1888	1.075	1.075	2.00	2.000
January	1896	.975	.975	1.75	1.750

Source: "Bigelow Prices for Forty Years," *The American Carpet and Upholstery Trade*, X (Feb., 1892), 150; Arthur H. Cole and Harold F. Williamson, *The American Carpet Manufacture* (Cambridge, 1941), 227.

upward, however, was an art little practiced in the Fairbanks regime. Bigelow prices had plunged in 1864 and 1865, but in the immediate postwar years there was only one sharp break in brussels and wilton, in 1869. Within two years after Fairbanks' accession to the office of treasurer, the company's prices broke again, and by December, 1879, brussels was selling 31 per cent lower than at the beginning of 1876; wilton, 18 per cent lower. A decade later brussels was off another 20 per cent and wilton, 18 per cent, the sharpest break coming in 1881. The early nineties brought little relief and in the last record of prices, as given by the management in January, 1896, brussels was 9 per cent below 1888 (see Table 18).

A comparison of the decline in brussels prices with the decline in costs in the years between 1865 and 1888 shows that 96 per cent of the fall in costs came before 1878, as against 67 per cent of the fall in prices. From 1878 to 1888, despite more efficient machinery, Fairbanks could not reduce brussels costs nearly so rapidly as prices were falling (see Table 19).

Just how stockholders fared under this adverse development is not clear since no dividend records survive. Though the concern's financial position fluctuated, its solvency was never remotely threatened and in 1898 the financial condition of the company was better by almost every conceivable test than it had been at the start of Fairbanks' stewardship in 1874. Most of this improvement occurred in the nineties.

From 1873 to 1889 the stated investment in plant and equipment increased by over $500,000. (Many of the charges were handled as current

TABLE 19

BIGELOW CARPET COMPANY

Changes in Costs and Prices of Brussels and Wilton Carpets   1860 to 1888

(Per Yard)

	1860 to 1888 (Per Cent)	1865 a to 1888 (Per Cent)	1865 to 1878 (Per Cent)	1878 to 1888 (Per Cent)
Brussels costs	—3	—64	—62	—5
Brussels prices	—10	—57	—38	—30
Wilton costs	+10	—63		
Wilton prices	+11	—46		

a In some respects the year 1865 is not a good one for measurement. Early in that year brussels costs exceeded brussels prices—$2.93 to $2.50. If the year 1864 is used, the decline to 1888 in costs is 63 per cent, in prices 69 per cent. Wilton figures are less subject to criticism, but for the over-all profitability of the company brussels is more significant.

Source: "Bigelow Prices for Forty Years," The American Carpet and Upholstery Trade, X (Feb., 1892), 150; Bigelow Carpet Company, Cost of Carpeting, 1850 to 1865; Bigelow Carpet Company, Cost of Carpeting, 1888; Dobson and Another v. Bigelow Carpet Company, 114 U.S. 439.

expenses and therefore did not appear on the balance sheet.) Funds for additions to capacity came from three sources: from $200,000 in new stock, from profits plowed back, and from greatly increased borrowing which reached a new high.

The decade of the nineties was a different story. Never reckless, Fairbanks concentrated even more on maintaining—and building—financial strength. With the fixed investment virtually stationary, the net working capital rose over $500,000 from profits returned to the business. The profits made it possible to eliminate short-term borrowing in the year-end balance statements (see Appendix 2). By 1898 Bigelow's surplus was at an all-time high, almost equal to its capital stock.

With its working capital and its surplus, Bigelow was financially the soundest of the Bigelow-Sanford predecessors at the turn of the century (see Table 20). Its outlook for the future was also good. The Bigelow name was still pre-eminent in brussels and wilton, and the company had been a leader in high-quality axminster. The plant had been modernized in the middle and late eighties. Though Kendall was dead and Charles

Bigelow had just retired (in 1898), and though Charles F. Fairbanks was getting along in years, there was no immediate management crisis. Henry Parker Fairbanks, the new director of marketing, was young and unproven but he had been trained under Kendall. Edward Burdett, the new manufacturing agent, was well tested; and Charles F. Fairbanks, instead of sloughing off responsibilities, was vigorously accepting even more.

TABLE **20**

BIGELOW CARPET COMPANY

Comparison of Selected Financial Figures, Lowell, Hartford, and Higgins 1897 to 1898

	Stated Capital	Surplus	Fixed Assets	Net Working Capital
Bigelow, 1898	$1,000,000	$915,000	$ 853,000	$1,000,000
Lowell, 1898	2,000,000	297,000	1,613,000	679,000
Hartford, 1898	1,500,000	618,000	904,000	1,200,000
Higgins, 1897	2,000,000	60,000	760,000	1,200,000

THE YEARS OF ADAPTATION: A REVIEW, 1855–1900

In reviewing the industry and the era as revealed by the experience of five companies, the factor of growth stands out. The individual companies greatly increased capacity, doubling and then tripling output. To this increase was added the production of the many new concerns which mushroomed as the various patents expired. More and more these newcomers made their bid from a position of technical equality with the old-time firms. Together, old and new, they drove the foreigner from the market by the mid-seventies.

Though this growth was predicated on demand, it resulted in a highly competitive market. The struggle for the consumer dollar was of an intensity and on a scale previously quite unknown. The market spread ever westward, but it was still primarily east of the Mississippi and north of the Mason-Dixon line. This factor, plus the overseas source of wool, kept the industry concentrated in the Northeast.

It was a market of many markets. In the beginning, ingrain was dominant. Pile weaves such as wilton, brussels, tapestry, and velvet, had been produced in such small quantities that they did not even appear in the census of 1860; axminster was nonexistent. By the end of the century ingrain was losing ground to pile fabrics of which 30,000,000 yards were placed on the market annually by domestic producers (see Chart III).

The growing popularity of pile weaves presented a crucial issue to the management of carpet companies in this country. Most companies had

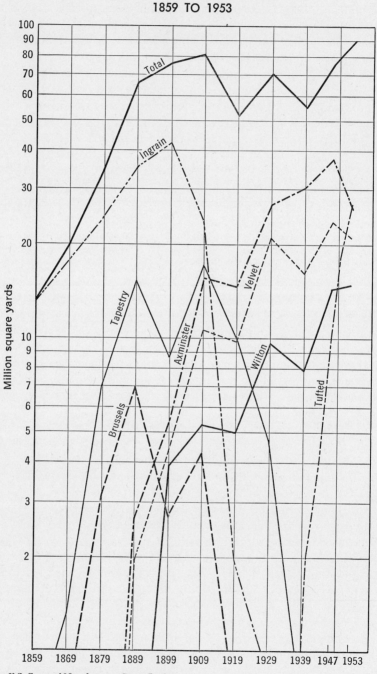

CHART **III**

CARPET PRODUCTION IN THE UNITED STATES
1859 TO 1953

Million square yards

Total

Ingrain

Tapestry

Axminster

Velvet

Wilton

Brussels

Tufted

100
90
80
70
60
50
40
30
20
10
9
8
7
6
5
4
3
2

1859 1869 1879 1889 1899 1909 1919 1929 1939 1947 1953

Source: U.S. Census of Manufactures; Carpet Institute.

confined their attention in the early years to one—or possibly two—fabrics. In the postwar period they could not ignore the new trends. The ingrain market might continue to be the big one; it was not necessarily the most profitable; and it was losing relative position. Immediately following the war the expiration of the Bigelow patents and the growth in affluence of both the lower- and upper-middle classes led the executives of Lowell and Hartford to introduce a brussels line and those at Sanford to go into tapestry. Meanwhile Bigelow expanded its brussels and Higgins its tapestry output. With markets still growing, with moquette possibilities limited by the unwillingness of the Smith company to license many competitors, and with no other startling new fabrics on the horizon, the decisions to produce more brussels and more tapestry were logical.

By the mid-eighties the saturation point of existing fabrics had been temporarily reached. Smyrna on the low end and axminster on the high were the coming products. The former was too cheap a fabric and too far-removed from current manufacturing procedures to appeal to the larger concerns in the industry, such as the five predecessors of the Bigelow-Sanford Carpet Company. All of these turned to the alternative, axminster, though in varying degrees. Houston of Hartford had made a start in the production of tufted pile carpeting through the adaptation of moquette in 1879, and in the nineties his company began to weave axminster; Fairbanks of Bigelow pioneered with better grades in 1887; Higgins came out with a cheaper gobelin axminster shortly thereafter; Lowell was slow, waiting until 1896; Sanford also delayed until after the expiration of the Smith patents, but then far surpassed the others in his scale of production.

Sanford likewise led the way in the other product innovation of the last few years of the nineteenth century: the broadloom rug. Such rugs as other manufacturers were producing late in the nineties were either of small size or seamed, but from 1896 on Sanford turned out an increasing number of the large seamless variety. In this instance, as in the development of a strong axminster line, Sanford had judged future trends correctly.

Perhaps the implied criticism of the others for their failure to rush into the new opportunities in the nineties is too severe. In the first place, all of them had a sizable investment in machines for other varieties. To introduce on a large scale a new product every twenty years required exceptional resources or a general and continuing prosperity, the latter of which was noticeable chiefly by its absence. Sanford, who made the shift to tapestry in the seventies and the shift to axminsters and rugs in the nineties, had two advantages: his original investment was not large and he had no stockholders to pay. True, Hartford and Lowell put money into new ingrain equipment on a replacement basis in this period, but would it have been wise to neglect the biggest market in the country? And to fill the gap in their business with any other item would have cost far more. Similar considerations apply to Higgins' tapestry expenditures.

In the nineties Lowell and Hartford did not provide the leadership they had theretofore displayed. The first profits often went to others. But it must be remembered that these predecessor companies were handicapped by a large fixed investment, were plagued by recurring business panics, and were in many cases faced with internal management complications. Under these circumstances they forged a modest but creditable record. In the continuing process of decision upon decision, they maintained a good average.

Yet the fact remains that the two great firms of the ante-bellum years—Lowell and Hartford—had been challenged by a number of upstarts. Higgins and Sanford had very small beginnings before the Civil War at a time when two New England firms were already comfortably established and prosperous. More notable still was the upsurge of the resourceful carpetmakers in Yonkers, New York: Alexander Smith & Sons. From modest beginnings in the 1840's that firm had shot forward as a large-scale tapestry producer after the expiration of the Bigelow patents—a success which it duplicated in moquette and axminster. By the late 1880's it had surpassed both Lowell and Hartford to become by all odds the largest carpet producer in the country.

The rise of aggressive younger firms had its effect on sales and profits. When the panic of 1873 first shocked old-line manufacturers, their reaction seems to have been to sit tight. Bolstered by business habits and reserves acquired during less demanding times, the established firms continued as before, planning to wait out the storm. As soon as conditions improved, with one accord they rushed to modernize in order to reduce costs. To do this, they introduced new and faster machinery. This meant more production. To reduce overhead unit costs, greater output was required. Thus new machinery and a desire to cut overhead led to a flood of carpeting.

By the end of the eighties it was evident to most manufacturers that the presumed cure had aggravated the disease. Efforts were still being made to economize on production costs by introducing better machinery and methods, but only at Lowell were these improvements on any considerable scale, and even then they did not compare with a decade earlier. Instead, schemes of production curtailment were rife and, though they never resulted in any specific industry-wide action, each factory pursued its own policy of shutdown and part time.

If low operating costs were so important, much more so was competent wool purchasing. A few cents in the cost of such an item could change the complexion of a balance sheet. Yet here we have scant information. The decline of wool prices had tapered off in the eighties. Improved marketing facilities may have enabled the buyers to get more nearly uniform and more satisfactory quality. Better methods of transportation and communication may have allowed better scheduling and reduced inventory charges. For the rest the mechanisms were the same. Importers, agents in producing countries, Liverpool auctions, all were used.

In marketing, too, there was little change in form. Only Sanford made any radical departure, dropping his agent to handle his own marketing. Higgins discontinued retailing but continued direct wholesaling. Bigelow used Kendall, perhaps as an agent but more as a division head. Hartford and Lowell stayed with the commission agent. Yet relationships were changing. Improved transportation and communication and more adequate commercial institutions eliminated the need for selling agents. They became mainly order-takers and design men, as financial responsibilities, selling costs, warehousing, and distribution were shifted to the manufacturer. It was only a matter of time before this vestigial remnant of the past would be cut completely from the new marketing structure.

Stiffer competition brought forth an emphasis on advertising, trademarks, and road salesmen. These innovations increased the expenses of the manufacturer—and at a time when prices were falling. However, with advertising restricted mainly to trade journals, which reduced the possibilities of developing consumer brand-consciousness, and with road coverage limited, the sales program had a long way to go before it approached modern thoroughness and importance. This stage of development was not unusual for the times, but the whole industry seemed apathetic compared with the more energetic industries of its own age.

Labor relations had two aspects, the friendly routine and the spectacular clash, and two phases, the thirty years of peace from roughly 1855 to 1885 and the fifteen years of sporadic turbulence to 1900. The power loom, with its actual or potential use of women, plus the general prosperity had inaugurated a quiet era in labor-management relations; depression pressures broke the calm.

While management had acquired the basic techniques of factory operations in earlier years, the ever-changing immigrant flow meant that the new labor with which it worked was still not acclimated to factory life. Irish and French-Canadian, Armenian and Polish, these had had no factory background. As a result, many of the strong-arm methods of discipline continued to be used.

Yet times were changing. In the postwar construction programs some attention was paid to light, ventilation, and the reduction of fire hazards. Furthermore, increased government interest expressed in new legislation on hours, child labor, and safety, affected business procedures and were to do so more in the future.

General attitudes and general conditions as much as any internal relationship between the carpet workers and their bosses caused the strikes of the eighties and nineties. A few good years interspersed among many bad produced the nationwide restlessness which encouraged wage demands by workers everywhere. In the carpet industry, contrary to the trend in raw materials and manufacturing, labor had become more expensive after the war. As a result, wage rates presented an obvious point of attack to cost-conscious executives.

Meanwhile the use of male weavers on the expanding brussels production brought a vocal element into the working force. It was this group which protested against Martin in Thompsonville and which led the Lowell strike in the eighties. At Bigelow, where there were no male weavers, it was the skilled male dye workers who struck. Neither the weavers nor the dyers had any direct connection with the Knights of Labor initially. But in New York, a center of the Knights' activities, virtually all the Higgins mill was unionized and all grades and both sexes participated in the struggles, compounded as they were by jurisdictional strife.

Only the Hartford management avoided an actual outbreak during the eighties, but in the nineties local conditions, personalities, and policies joined with economic doldrums to produce strikes there in 1895 and 1899. In contrast to the skilled male brussels weavers who participated in the first Hartford strike and the dyers who carried on the second, the leaders at Lowell in 1894 were the "lady" ingrain weavers. Only at Bigelow was there violence in either decade, yet the stresses and strains of economic adversity had made their mark on employer and employee, complicating greatly the task of human relations even in the limited fashion in which they were then understood.

In financial policies there were again many similarities among these companies—and many common pitfalls. None of the three corporations increased their capitalization after 1875. To finance the expansion and modernization programs of the eighties, Lowell resorted to borrowing, Hartford sacrificed its working capital, Bigelow plowed back its earnings.

Commercial banks and insurance companies replaced the sales agent as the chief source of outside funds. The role of the supplier was probably less important as the credit time was reduced, but the 60 days' credit on wool purchases was valuable. There is nothing to suggest that any of the concerns had difficulty in obtaining funds even when liquidity ratios were low—as they were at Bigelow and Lowell in the eighties.

Hartford's liquidity ratios never shared the weakness of the two Massachusetts companies, but Houston's dividend policy of the eighties drained the resources of Hartford, just as Fay's had reduced the reserves of Lowell in the seventies. Since both these men were employees representing owners, not really members of the controlling group, this relationship may have explained their reluctance to cut the outward flow. However, general conditions also may have influenced them. Roberts at Hartford, as well as Fay at Lowell, lived beyond his company's means when the depression first struck. That Houston continued to live off the accumulations of a more prosperous period while Lyman was more cautious, may have been due merely to the fact that Lowell's reserves had vanished while Houston had a more comfortable surplus. This was true even in the nineties, and so Lyman continued to husband his income, while the Hartford management distributed all the firm's earnings. What policy Fairbanks followed at Bigelow cannot be definitely stated since we have no records of earnings or dividends. The balances in profit and loss suggest that from 1883 to 1888 he may have been disbursing more than the earnings would warrant, but after that date his reserves rose steadily. The Higgins record covers such a short span that the only possible generalization is that Eugene Higgins made no effort to milk his company.

However much the criticism of excessive dividend payments, of declining reserves and working capital, and of inadequate ratios may be justified, the economic setting must always be recalled—twenty years of prosperity followed by twenty-five of depression. Indeed, to follow the managements through such contrasting business fortunes, to see the stresses which a long period of malaise, with only short periods of recuperation, create in even well-heeled and solidly established concerns, is one of the major interests of the period. To see smaller, newer firms seize on new products, push new methods, and aggressively carve their niche in the industry is another. Finally, to see the adjustment and adaptation of the older establishments to these new trends and to these new rivals is to witness a basic process of business life.

These ancestors of the present-day concern were constituted in a variety of legal forms. With two partnerships, which were primarily one-man concerns, with one corporation closely held and two widely held, they presented a broad range of organizational possibilities.

Compared with today, administration was simple. The complex committee arrangement at Higgins in the nineties was the result of a special situation and more a matter of form than reality. Otherwise, one or two executives generally supervised many now-separated functions. Size and complexity were increasing sufficiently to make management a full-time job by the end of the century, but they had not increased to the point of providing many full-time jobs for specialists. In short, the companies could not support an efficient division of labor at the top. While selecting and training executives was to be a major function of twentieth-century business, by the end of the nineteenth it was just coming to be recognized as a business problem. By the time there was an awareness of the problem, it had presented itself in crisis form to two of Bigelow-Sanford's predeces-

sors, Hartford and Lowell, and had figured in the ownership crisis of the
third, Higgins. As the owners sought men to run their companies, well
might they agree with Erastus Brigham Bigelow: [28]

The portion of the human race endowed with organizing and administrative
faculties . . . is not very large. . . . The demand for business talent is always
greater than the supply. One of the greatest difficulties experienced in forming
or in maintaining a business organization is in finding competent persons to take
charge of the various departments.

CHAPTER 8

THE RECONSTITUTED COMPANIES:

The Hartford Carpet Corporation, 1901–1914

The new century. The new prosperity. The "new look" in business organization. Mergers were the order of the day. In carpet manufacture two mergers marked the first steps toward formation of the present Bigelow-Sanford Carpet Company. From the Bigelow Carpet Company and the Lowell Manufacturing Company came the new Bigelow Carpet Company; from the Hartford Carpet Company and the E. S. Higgins Carpet Company, the new Hartford Carpet Corporation.

THE BIGELOW–LOWELL MERGER

The first proposal that a merger might provide a solution to carpet industry problems occurred in the late eighties, when it had become obvious that the fetish for more efficient mills had fed the ogre of overproduction. Paper resolutions on price maintenance had been tried and found wanting. Some action more binding than a gentleman's agreement was required— especially by the Philadelphians. Producers mainly of ingrains, the Philadelphians were in the midst of bitter competitive battles; as men of small resources they were least able to afford the debilitating struggle and least capable of shifting to other lines of output. In the fall of 1888 the ingrain manufacturers to the south of New York conferred with brussels manufacturers to the north, including Hartford and Lowell. Rumors of mergers became rife—until Arthur Lyman dismissed the possibility.[1] Lowell, said Lyman, would never enter the consolidation, and as everyone recognized, without Lowell the proposal was lost.

Efforts and rumors were renewed almost annually for the next five years. In February, 1892, Houston reported to the Hartford directorates: "an effort is being made to bring about a legal consolidation of the Carpet

Company and firms in New England and elsewhere, for the purpose of making the investment in the same more profitable than at present." In reply it was voted: "that the President and Mr. Goodwin . . . be a committee to attend meetings in furtherance of said object and represent the interests of the shareholders of the Company and they are hereby authorized in their discretion to consent to an appraisement of the assets of this Company." [2] This attempt proved as vain as its predecessors.

In the following year W. & J. Sloane submitted a proposal to the ingrain manufacturers probably for joint marketing—but again the hostility of the Lowell company killed the project. As the largest producer, Lowell's co-operation was essential and Lyman preferred to run the race on large volume and low manufacturing costs.[3] By that time it was clear that the dominant factors in the industry were not yet interested in amalgamation. Too many companies, too many products, too easy access for newcomers to the industry, all weighed against a successful venture. Furthermore, with most managements sunk in the gloom of their own financial predicaments from 1893 to 1898, the moment was not ripe for further endeavors in that line.

It took an outsider to initiate the next attempt, though the move was made more opportune by the disastrous effects of the Smith auctions in 1898. Charles Ranlett Flint was a professional promoter who earned the title, "Father of the American Trust," because of his work in the formation of such companies as United States Rubber, American Woolen, and International Business Machines.[4] In 1898 a dye salesman suggested to Flint that he investigate the consolidation possibilities in the carpet industry. Flint, a former partner of W. R. Grace and still a large importer of such Latin American products as wool, had his own connections in the industry. Obtaining financial backing in Boston and New York, he focused his attention on the makers of pile carpeting (in the terms of contemporary terminology, the producers of three-fourths goods). To have attempted a merger of ingrain producers would have involved too many companies. But a merger of pile-carpet manufacturers would include only a few companies and could concentrate on the weaves that were coming into demand.

On May 12, 1899, the *Lowell Daily Courier* asserted that Smith, Higgins, Sanford, Lowell, Roxbury, Bigelow, Hartford, and 75 per cent of the Philadelphia mills had agreed to join the new combination.[5] Robert Perkins of Higgins was enthusiastic. He said with certainty: "This is not a speculative venture, the mills will not be conveyed away for stock of problematical value." For further assurance to the public he reported: "It is not planned to reduce the wages. . . . There will be no exorbitant prices. . . . There will be no needless discharge of employees, but there will be a lopping off of certain burdens and expenditures that have for years sapped the foundations . . . and prevented the mills from obtaining fair returns. . . . The cost of distribution has been . . . far too great, and competition has been of a destructive character." [6]

Within a month Perkins had changed his mind. Flint asked Neal Rantoul of the Boston banking house of F. S. Moseley to talk to Perkins, but a conference at the Yale-Harvard boat races did nothing to overcome Perkins' sudden opposition.[7] Whether his reversal precipitated final defeat or just symptomatized a general feeling among the highly individualistic carpet company managers, the June 30 deadline passed with the options uncalled. With this was concluded the most ambitious trust effort in the industry's history.

Yet within a few months of the failure of Flint's effort, the first large merger occurred, the union of the Bigelow Carpet Company and the Lowell Manufacturing Company; and preliminaries leading to the second, the Hartford-Higgins consolidation, had taken place. Why had Arthur T. Lyman altered the position of opposition to mergers which he had maintained for over ten years? Management succession seems to have been the key factor in his about-face. As Lyman approached seventy, no budding executives within the Lowell company awaited his mantle. Quite apart from any desires he may have had to lighten his load, orderly progress in the future of the company demanded consideration of the question of his successor. Furthermore, Lyman could see other advances for his company in an alliance with Bigelow. Though he had done much to rebuild Lowell's finances, the surplus was still small, the dividends sporadic, and the indebtedness high. In addition to a more favorable balance sheet, Bigelow offered a direct marketing organization; and its strong brussels, wilton, and axminster lines bade fair to offset any decline in ingrains. Finally this amalgamation was no grandiose scheme as the others had been, but a conservative, workable proposition.

Originally a third party was interested in the transaction, M. J. Whittall, the owner of a small Worcester firm manufacturing brussels and wilton. To him, one of the coming men in the industry, merger offered the opportunity to secure greater resources and a larger field of activity than he could immediately hope to acquire from his own limited means.

The benefits to the Bigelow company of joining with Whittall and Lowell were less obvious, and perhaps for this reason the terms on which the merger was proposed were more favorable to the Clinton firm. However, there were other considerations. The Lowell factory had a cotton yarn department which could supply the Clinton plant. As the prospectus said, there were anticipated economies of size—especially in purchasing, designing, and marketing.[8] Then the unnecessary competition among certain jobbing houses handling goods made by all these mills could be eliminated.[9]

The first inkling of the impending change came on October 26, 1899, when Lyman called a meeting of Lowell directors for the thirtieth of the month. On November 10, the stockholders were informed of the details as follows: a new Massachusetts corporation with the same name as the old Bigelow company would purchase the assets of the Lowell company for $2,030,000. The new company would also buy the old Bigelow company's assets for $2,000,000, and those of the Whittall company for $540,-000. Payment was to be on the stock of the new concern, except for $70,000 in cash given to Whittall.

Specifically for each share of Lowell, par $690, the owner would receive seven shares of the new firm with a total par of $700. Lowell's $2,-030,000 share of the new capitalization was thus $30,000 in excess of its old. Since in 1898 its book value had stood at $2,297,000, this would seem to have been a conservative price. However, net working capital was merely $679,000, while $100,000 had been a good annual profit. Judging from this earning capacity the exchange value was generously computed.

Each shareholder of the old Bigelow company would get 20 shares of the new issue, which at $100 par represented a stated value of $2,000. Thus, in exchange for the $1,000 per share of the old Bigelow, the owner received not only a 100 per cent stock dividend, but also a more negotiable equity. The Clinton concern though capitalized at only a million dollars had a book value of $1,916,000. Under the merger, the Clinton stockholders would have about as large a share in the new company—$2,000,000 stated capital—as Lowell would have. For a smaller book value the Bigelow owners were receiving as much as Lowell. However, Bigelow had a net working capital of over a million dollars and this along with what doubtless had been a superior earning capacity warranted its equality in ownership rights with the larger Lowell firm.

The Lowell holders had approved the transaction and the Bigelow proprietors were about to do so when Matthew Whittall suddenly withdrew. For what reasons? Driving, domineering, pioneering, such a man would have had a difficult time working in harness with any other—especially if it were necessary to adapt his gait to that of the conservative, slow-moving Charles F. Fairbanks. Big as the new Bigelow was to be, it was probably not large enough for two such diverse top-flight executives.

If Whittall's withdrawal resulted in any indecision, it was momentary, for the Worcester mill was but a minor factor in the deal, and with an adjustment in capitalization to $4,030,000 the merger proceeded. At the organizing meeting on December 2, 1899, Charles F. Fairbanks, James Beal, Edward W. Hutchins, Alexander S. Wheeler, and John Sloane of the old Bigelow board were elected directors, along with Arthur Lyman and Jacob Rogers from Lowell. The bylaws were adopted and Fairbanks was elected treasurer. A few days later Lyman relinquished his cares as treasurer of the outgoing Lowell Manufacturing Company and assumed the less demanding post of the new Bigelow company presidency. On December 15 the new Bigelow Carpet Company, by filing papers with the secretary of state, formally began its active life.[10] The Bigelow property was transferred immediately; the Lowell, in March, 1900, by which time its securities, which had been worth but $540 a share in the stock market the previous September, had risen to $632. Organization expenses paid by the new firm had amounted to less than $10,000; $5,878 represented a legal bill of Hutchins & Wheeler and $2,500 the bite of the Internal Revenue Department.[11]

Thus was completed the first of the large-scale carpet mergers of this period. It was a conservative venture, internally arranged, based on an exchange of stock and resulting from a management problem pertaining to an individual firm. As interesting as what it was, is what it was not. It was not promoter-inspired, nor banker-managed. There were no commissions, no complicated capital structures, no "stock watering." Though it would be the largest producer of brussels, wiltons, and ingrains, and would make a respectable showing in the new axminster field, though in the field of brussels and wiltons at least it would reduce competition, it was not a trust within the monopolistic connotation of those days.[12] Finally the abortive aspect—the withdrawal of Whittall—is also instructive. Where important mergers have come about in the carpet industry, they have occurred only where one of the concerns does not include an active commanding personality.

THE HIGGINS–HARTFORD MERGER

Contrasted in many ways with the Bigelow-Lowell amalgamation was the merger of the E. S. Higgins Carpet Company and the Hartford Carpet Company under the aegis of the banking houses of Kidder, Peabody & Company and F. S. Moseley & Company, both of Boston. This outside sponsorship was natural since Hartford's meager resources precluded any extensive financing from that side, while in 1900 the two banking firms were the active owners of the Higgins concern. Because of the terms of the contract with Eugene Higgins, the financiers in that year were faced with the necessity of finding a new home, and, just as important, a new name for their business.

No location beyond a 250-mile radius of New York was considered in the search for new facilities; raw material and marketing considerations precluded other localities. The first public mention of Thompsonville as a possible site came on December 6, when the *Thompsonville Press* reported that Robert Perkins and A. D. Higgins of the Higgins concern were present at a meeting of the directors of the Hartford company. Action was not long delayed. The union had attractions for both companies. The advantages to the Higgins group were obvious. Though many of the Hartford company's buildings and much of its equipment was out of date, though its financial position was weak, though its location could not compare with certain other sites for direct waterborne delivery of wool, still it had a famous name, it had a much desired axminster line, it had people with skills, it had room for expansion, it was a going business, and it could be acquired through a stock transfer, thus requiring little cash.

For the Hartford owners the benefits were equally apparent. The Roberts family was ready to retire from business and none of the other owners could provide any budding carpet executives. With reserves at a low ebb, even a less tired management would have been hard put to find the means to modernize the equipment and to take the aggressive marketing action necessary to make the business once again a well-paying operation. With no management, and with little inclination to advance the needed funds, the stockholders were receptive to a proposal which would provide both. Since the largest proprietors, the Goodwins, were close relatives of J. P. Morgan, who held a large block of Higgins stock, the course of developments was perhaps preordained.

Though the Morgan firm acted as depository for the shares, leadership in the negotiations was taken by the Boston banking houses. On January 8, 1901, Kidder, Peabody made its proposition to the Hartford company. It planned to organize a new corporation capitalized at $5,000,000—$2,-000,000 in 7 per cent preferred and $3,000,000 in common—to take over the properties of the Higgins and Hartford firms. Hartford owners were given two alternatives: they could take $100 in cash for each share of their stock or they could trade 100 shares of the old stock for 67 shares of the common and 67 of the preferred of the new company. Since Hartford stock was selling at about 65, either proposition was generous. On the same day, Higgins holders were offered one share of new preferred for one of the old, and one and a half shares of new common for one share of old.

The merger was effected without any great difficulty. The bankers controlled the two-thirds majority needed to dissolve the old Higgins company. One Hartford proprietor, a Thompsonville resident insisted on asking questions as to the necessity of the merger and as to the standing of the Higgins concern,[13] but 14,600 of the 15,000 shares had been turned in by February 15, and of these the owners of only 1,600 requested cash payment.[14] On that very day the formal bid of purchase was made by Lawrence Ford, an employee of the Boston law firm of Gaston, Snow & Saltonstall, who evidently represented the Boston banking houses in the transaction.

While the old stockholders were formally registering their approval, Ford and Henry Skinner, a Hartford banker and local correspondent of

Kidder, Peabody, were chartering the Hartford Carpet Corporation. They and some of Skinner's employees were the first stockholders and directors of the new concern. As such their tasks were two in number. First they voted a 20 per cent assessment on the stock: $1,000,000. Next they voted to pay Ford for the Higgins and Hartford properties a total of $5,011,000, of which $1,994,000 was to be in preferred stock, $2,006,000 in common, and $1,011,000 in cash.[15] The preliminaries having been completed, the temporary officers and directors resigned. Robert Perkins became president, George Squire, treasurer, and Oren M. Beach, Jr., secretary. The next day, February 27, 1901, A. D. Higgins formally took over possession of the mill at Thompsonville.

Perkins declared that the $5,000,000 capitalization was based on a "conservative estimate of value and not inflated in the slightest degree." [16] "Informed" opinion of the time thought otherwise.[17] The preferred immediately sold for par but the common did not sell for more than 50 for many years. A look at the balance sheets shows that the Hartford concern on January 1, 1901, represented a book value of $2,148,000. For this the Hartford owners received securities with a par value of $2,010,000. On the other hand, the Higgins firm in 1898 had a book value of $2,012,350, which may have been slightly inflated to allow for goodwill. Since Moseley and Kidder, Peabody had found the inventories and machinery much undervalued, they had probably revised the balances upward—with a corresponding increase in the book value. As for earning power, Higgins' $200,-000 and Hartford's $60,000 provided, after paying the preferred dividend, only $120,000, or a 4 per cent return, for the common. "Informed" opinion estimated that the new firm would increase annual profits to a rate of about $300,000, which would have raised the return on common above 5 per cent.[18]

This inside estimate was based on the assumption that the Higgins earnings in 1900 were a normal average, not the isolated event that they appear in the history of the nineties. Whether they could be maintained, depended on the general economic conditions of the country. To make a success of this merger, greater prosperity than that of the previous decade was obviously an absolute necessity.

A CHANGING MARKET DEMAND AND SUPPLY

By the time of the Higgins-Hartford merger, the carpet industry was ready to enjoy the flood of prosperity which was to sweep the country for most of the next decade and a half. This was a prosperity which reached all classes and all sections of the country. The golden era of the farmer— the parity period so devoutly worshipped and actively sought—saw a spread of modern conveniences into the countryside. Roads, rural free delivery, telephones, mail-order houses, all brought the rural resident closer to the advanced stream of urban living. For the nation as a whole, one expert reported that realized national income per capita rose from $212 in 1900 to $319 in 1914,[19] while another states that the average real yearly income showed a gain of 5 per cent.[20]

That these more affluent Americans were interested in homes is proved by the great increase in housing construction and in home decorating magazines. Floor covering represented a long-recognized measure of comfort and well-being, and, as more people moved into the middle class, aspiration became reality. Later, other newly invented luxuries—such as the automobile—were to become seminecessities competing for the consumer dollar. But for the first decade of the twentieth century the home was the center of existence and carpet was a *sine qua non*.

The opportunity of supplying this demand went largely to the American manufacturer. While the efficiency of the American carpet industry was one bulwark against foreign competition, tariff protection was another defense. The tariffs of 1897 and 1909 retained the McKinley rates and imports averaged less than a million yards annually. The Underwood Tariff of 1913, which eliminated duties on imported wool, also brought lower protection, but its effect, other than psychological, was hardly felt before the war.

The output of the American carpet industry reached a peak in 1904. From 76,400,000 square yards in 1899 it rose to 82,600,000 in 1904, falling off slightly to 81,200,000 in 1909. By 1914 it had declined to the 1899 level of 66,000,000 square yards,[21] though the population had come to be about 50 per cent greater. Dollarwise the drop was much less. The $48,000,000 value of 1899 became $61,000,000 in 1904, $71,000,000 in 1909 and then $69,000,000 in 1914.[22] This relatively minor decline in the value of the industry output was due to two factors—rising prices and, more important, the slow but steady upgrading of the product.

The process of upgrading was the process of the substitution of tapestries and axminsters for ingrain, of wiltons and orientals for brussels. Substitution is perhaps too mild a word for the havoc wreaked on small ingrain producers and the adjustments forced on larger manufacturers as within fifteen years the ingrain volume dropped from 42,000,000 to 9,000,-000 yards. The farm market, the last stronghold of old ingrain, fell before the low prices and vivid varieties of tapestry spread before the farmers' eyes in mail-order catalogues. The expansion of velvets, described as "particularly adapted for the homes of people with moderate means who are seeking . . . a little more artistic refinement," [23] and of axminsters proceeded rapidly. Indeed, as the tapestry demand abated somewhat after 1909, axminster took over first place.

The market for brussels, which had shrunk considerably by 1899, expanded for a few years after the turn of the century, in line with the general trend toward better quality. No carpet wore better than brussels and it was the easiest to clean; [24] yet these advantages proved insufficient in the face of the growing demand for cut-pile fabrics. As brussels became less popular many manufacturers converted to wilton, touted as *"the* rug" for general use.[25] "The potent charm of the wilton rug," wrote a contemporary, "lies in the fact that it is possible to reproduce . . . by modern methods almost the exact counterpart of the priceless old rugs of the Far East." [26] With wear, they often looked better. While the yardage increased steadily, the fact remained that wilton was a high-priced product, the market for which offered no immediate possibilities for exploitation comparable to those for tapestries, velvets, or axminsters.

More revolutionary than the rise in popularity of axminster fabrics was the sudden demand for the rug, as opposed to carpeting. The term "rug" denoted a floor covering of definite size and shape which did not necessarily extend from wall to wall. Many were the causes of the demand for rugs: hardwood floors, health fads, and more adaptability to the never-ending city-to-city odyssey that comprised the life of ever more Americans. Oriental rugs set the example. Imports of these grew from less than $300,-000 in 1892 to $4,000,000 in 1907.[27]

In domestic products smyrnas and ingrain were the first carpet weaves to be produced on a large scale in the form of rugs. By 1901 all types of carpeting featured rugs on opening day.[28] By 1904 almost 20 per cent of the output was in rugs, seamed and seamless, with ingrain and smyrnas still dominating. Ten years later rugs accounted for 64 per cent of the production of the American industry.

By this time the seamless, or broadloom, rug was predominant. Following in the wake of Stephen Sanford, a few plants were making one-piece rugs in 1900.[29] Gradually others followed. Some might contend that "it is doubtful . . . if the average purchaser even notices the seam," [30] and that "large sized rugs made up from carpetings are fully supplying the needs of the present time." [31] Others saw the profit possibilities of the seamless products. On the eve of the first World War, seamless rugs exceeded both carpetings and seamed rugs, accounting for 34 per cent of the total industry output.

The scope of the change in styles was one reason for the decline in over-all yardage. Among carpeting, ingrain still held sway (with 34 per cent of the total), closely followed by velvets (28 per cent). In seamed rugs, axminster accounted for by far the largest share (46 per cent) with wilton a poor second (17 per cent). In broadlooms, tapestry was largest with 36 per cent of the total, followed by velvets with 23 per cent.[32] Thus, the cheapest fabric was still going into carpeting. The more expensive was going into seamed rugs. It was the lower middle-priced type of fabric—

tapestry and velvet—that was making headway in the new unseamed broadloom field.

Such changes in quality and in form placed a great premium on adaptability and financial resources—two attributes not possessed by the small Philadelphia ingrain manufacturer. For the large concerns with sizable ingrain lines—Hartford, Higgins and Lowell—the rapid decline of a staple product necessitated prompt action and expensive expansion in other fabrics. For the small undiversified firm it spelled disaster. The entire decline in the over-all carpet yardage from 1904 to 1914 fell on the Philadelphians. Their partial disappearance also accounted for the drop in the number of establishments. Corporations increased in number from 35 in 1899 to 60 in 1914, but the total number of firms fell from 133 to 97. Despite these fatalities—most of which occurred after 1909—the capital invested increased from $44,000,000 in 1899 to $85,000,000 in 1914. The average value of product per establishment almost doubled in that period, and by 1914 the 16 firms with annual sales of over $1,000,000 were doing 70 per cent of the business.[33]

While some firms were becoming but memories, new ones were coming to the fore. The popularity of tapestry and axminster and his own foresight in installing broad looms brought Stephen Sanford of Amsterdam nearer to the top. M. J. Whittall of Worcester, while not approaching Sanford in volume, was one of the pacemakers in the wilton industry and thus gained his niche among the leaders.[34]

Alexander Smith, with its large axminster and tapestry output, continued to be, as it had been since the late eighties, the colossus of the industry. Not only did this firm determine prices for its own products; it influenced all other types of carpeting which had to be keyed accordingly. Within this limit Bigelow (thanks to its merger with Lowell) and, to a lesser extent, Hartford, set the ingrain prices. Bigelow also dominated the brussels and wilton fields and was one of the first three or four in axminster production. While the Hartford company was not the leader in any one line, it was a rival for second honors in ingrains, brussels, and wilton and, especially, in tapestry and velvet. With a growing axminster production, it had the widest line of any concern in the industry.

OWNERSHIP AND ADMINISTRATION

The men who plotted the path of the new Hartford Carpet Corporation were by the very nature of events certain to come from the Higgins company. The Hartford owners had been searching for management. The Higgins group held the majority of the stock and held it in larger blocks. In contrast to Francis Goodwin's 750 shares, Perkins held over 6,000, Kidder, Peabody and partners around 5,000, the F. S. Moseley group 2,700, the Morgans 2,000, and Hamilton Higgins 1,300.

The directorate reflected these holdings. Representing F. S. Moseley was Neal Rantoul. From Kidder, Peabody came William Endicott, Jr., Frank G. Webster, and Robert Winsor. James T. Goodwin spoke for the Goodwin-Morgan family, A. Hamilton Higgins for himself. Charles W. Beach, Henry S. Robinson, and George Roberts came from the old Hartford group. Thomas L. Manson, a New York broker who assisted in the merger, Henry L. Skinner, and the four officers completed the list.[35] Roberts soon left. Due to death two vacancies occurred later: Charles W. Bosworth of Springfield, president of the Union Trust Company, succeeded Beach, but Hamilton Higgins' position was not filled.

The roll of the officers showed the same stability as that of the directors. Robert Perkins became president in 1901 at a salary of $18,000 a year. George Roberts was elected vice-president, signing a three-year contract at $8,000 a year. George Squire, who had started as treasurer in February, became the secretary in March, 1901, at $6,000. At that time George Perkins, Robert's brother, formerly representative of the company in Thompsonville, became treasurer at $4,500. Alvin D. Higgins was the agent at $12,000.[36] In the fall Roberts' contract was bought out and Higgins was elevated to the role of vice-president.

Though the executive personnel was thus set for the life of the Hartford Carpet Corporation, salaries were not. In 1907 Robert Perkins was raised to $22,000, Higgins to $15,000 and George Perkins to $6,000. Two years later a profit-sharing bonus was introduced. After deducting 7 per cent for the preferred dividends, 7 per cent for the common, and an amount equal to one-half that charged to additions to the plant, 10 per cent of the net earnings of the company was divided as follows:

> 5   per cent to Robert Perkins
> 2½ per cent to Alvin D. Higgins
> 2½ per cent to George Perkins

In 1912 a committee of the directors reassessed the plan. As a result Higgins was given a flat salary of $25,000 and George Perkins of $10,000, but the president continued with profit-sharing. He received a base salary of $22,000, and the entire 10 per cent net earnings, figured as above. In the event of small or no profits he was guaranteed a bonus of $3,000.[37] In granting this opportunity for profit-sharing, the directors were recognizing where the actual responsibilities for success lay.

Of the three groups who were given authority under the bylaws, the stockholders had the least to do, though they had slightly more power than the proprietors of the old Hartford. They elected the directors, approved the sale of property or amendments to the bylaws by a two-thirds majority of those voting, and removed officers or directors by a three-fourths vote. Though 50 per cent voted each year, it is doubtful that many were in attendance. The directors rarely appeared at the stockholders' meeting and the transaction of business was usually limited to the presentation of the balance sheet.

To the 13 directors was entrusted the management of the business, the election of officers, and the selection of the other agents and factors. Yet the nonoperating board members could not give day-by-day guidance and did not even attend the quarterly directors' meetings with any degree of regularity. From 1901 to 1914 there were 50 sessions with an average attendance of nine directors. The officers each attended 47 or more meetings. The Hartford-Springfield group of directors were present at from 30 to 40 each, while the bankers' records ranged from Winsor's six appearances to Endicott's 32. All their powers the directors could and did delegate to an executive committee of from three to five members— including Robert Perkins, A. D. Higgins, and T. L. Manson. On occasion a special committee of the directors examined a profit-sharing plan or scrutinized the valuations of the property, but the executive committee or perhaps the officers, in that capacity alone, arrived at most of the decisions. In 1909, when Perkins raised the problems of housing and loans at a directors' meeting, "it seemed unnecessary in the view of the Board to pass a formal resolution, . . . leaving the matter to be acted upon as in their [the executive officers'] judgment seemed best for the interest of the Company." [38]

According to the bylaws, as president of the company Perkins conducted the meetings of the directors and stockholders, appointed committees, and acted as the chief executive officer of the company. The vice-president was merely assigned a substitute's role, the secretary was just a secretary, and the treasurer handled the funds.

In addition to his over-all responsibilities of policy suggestion and management, Robert Perkins naturally handled purchasing. His primary concern was wool, the task of purchasing other articles having devolved on a lesser functionary. In 1910 the position of wool buyer was created, or formalized, but Perkins still dictated general policies as to prices, qualities, and timing of purchases. [39]

Manufacturing and personnel were the province of A. D. Higgins. Under him was an office manager and a plant manager. In the latter position Lyman Upson was replaced immediately by Thomas J. Firth, who had had the reputation of being one of the smartest of the young men in the Higgins mill. [40] Firth was supervising the new construction and orienting the Hartford workers to the Higgins system of doing things, when one Saturday noon in 1903 much to the surprise of everyone, after a brief argument with A. D. Higgins, he suddenly resigned. [41] His successor was William Lyford, who, coming from Higgins' home area in Maine, had joined the concern in the early nineties. Rugged in build, aggressive in character, brusque in manner, he was withal goodhearted.[42] Estimates as to his proficiency as a mill manager vary, but his position after 1910 as A. D.'s son-in-law may have colored judgments on both sides.

The selling function was brought directly into the company as it had been at Higgins. Reune Martin & Sons were dropped and Hamilton Higgins, assisted by George Squire, carried on. Following Hamilton Higgin's death in 1909, John F. Norman was promoted as sales manager. Norman, after a brief career with a Milwaukee store and with W. & J. Sloane, had become a member of the Higgins sales force operating out of Chicago in 1894. Just before the merger, he became manager of the Chicago office, and in 1903 he was brought to New York to take charge of the Hartford company's tapestry and velvet departments.[43] By 1909 his contributions, through original and aggressive marketing methods, had earned him a place on the bonus list.[44]

The final function, finance and accounting, was under the supervision of the treasurer, George Perkins, though he may have received more guidance than his fellow officers from the directors. How much direct assistance they may have given him in procuring operating funds and medium-term credit is not clear. On general accounting procedures, such as depreciation, the directors certainly made the basic decisions, although they followed no consistent rule.

In addition to advice from his directors, George Perkins sought recommendations from outside experts. In 1911, Gunn, Richards & Company examined the books of the company both in Thompsonville and New York. While the consulting firm suggested some slight changes, generally it found the Hartford method modern and efficient.[45] This system, as it appears from surviving factory records, was based on three accounts. First, for each department there was a record of its payroll and the sum of the materials received from and sent to every other department. Secondly, for each department there was a record of the materials—yarn, linen, jute— and labor. At the end of six months this amount was credited and transferred to the Cost Book. Thirdly, the Cost Book contained a summary of this second group of accounts, plus overhead, and a record of the carpeting produced. From these figures was derived a per yard cost for each type of carpeting.

In reviewing the management structure and methods, it is obvious that no great revolution had taken place. The stockholders were confirmed in their impotency and indifference. The directors, including the Boston bankers, left the task of providing a profit to the officers, particularly to Robert Perkins. Staff departments, such as personnel or advertising, were still things of the future. Yet there were changes. Where three executives had sufficed for the old Hartford company—Houston, Roberts and Upson—five were now necessary, partly because the selling function was now integrated but partly also because the unit was larger and management more complex. Methods of control had advanced, and the office force had grown from a half-dozen to a dozen and a half, not counting the clerks in individual manufacturing departments. Even in the six years from 1909 through 1914 all salaries grew from .054 per cent to .069 of the total payroll.[46] There is no concrete measure of how well the management performed its task, but in the press of the day Perkins and Higgins were effusively praised for their ability.[47]

EXPANSION OF PLANT AND LABOR FORCE

In the first years after the merger the executives faced the task of keeping two mills in profitable operation while at the same time they were virtually constructing a third. The new one was necessary not only because of the need to move out of the Higgins property in New York but also because of the need for modernization of the Thompsonville layout.[48] From the first news of merger in December, 1900, there had been rumors of the building plans. On March 7, 1901, only a week after the new group had assumed control, the *Thompsonville Press* could authoritatively announce that construction would be under way the following week. The long-heralded event did not come to pass without its bitter fruits. The first step involved tearing down the No. 2 ingrain mill with consequent unemployment for over 300, and subsequently old landmarks, such as the White Mill and all but a few of the Scotch cottages, disappeared. By May, 1901, the demolition had proceeded sufficiently to permit "the beginning" of the new tapestry mill, which was to extend for 900 feet along Pleasant Street. The other projects for the year included an ingrain extension, a finishing room, a worsted mill, a filling mill, a color house, a scouring mill and a dyehouse, for a total of almost 400,000 square feet. The whole program was expected to take well over two years. Actually with certain additions—the power plant and the designing department—it took almost four.[49]

As the buildings were completed, Higgins machinery was shipped from New York. Early in 1904 even the old bell was brought to Thompsonville. It was another year before the contractor left and the construction program of the Hartford company settled down to a normal one of repairs and periodic alterations to meet new demands.

New demands had been considered in the first program. The combined ingrain output of Higgins-Hartford had been slacked by abandoning the Higgins equipment. At the same time the axminster output had been increased. In 1908 the old Lozier Bicycle Works of Thompsonville was purchased for $13,000 for use as a rug finishing department. The following year saw the construction of a new $175,000 axminster mill for "consolidation" purposes. At the same time the ingrain department was finally shut down.

New demands involved decisions not merely on the volume of various fabrics, but also on the proportion of the fabric to be made in the 27-inch width as compared with that in wider dimensions. The issue of broad versus narrow looms was particularly important in tapestry and axminster. Rugs made on narrow looms and stitched together were a temporary solution only. But in 1906 the company reported only 25 broad looms as compared with 815 narrow.[50] Of the broad, 17 were ingrain and two were wilton. Three years later in 1909 Perkins brought up the necessity of installing wide tapestry looms and was authorized to purchase 20 looms at a total cost not to exceed $50,000.[51] In 1912 and 1913 these 20 were scrapped and 38 newer models were substituted. Compared with some 249 narrow "tap" looms, this was not a sizable proportion. However, the important fact is that all the new tapestry machines were broad. It was quite otherwise with axminster: 99 new looms were procured in 1906 and 1907 and 17 more in 1912—all narrow. Yet one of the big factors in the axminster market—Stephen Sanford & Sons—was basing its growth on the broad loom. The only surviving explanation of this blind spot in Hartford's policy is that Squire thought that broad looms were too expensive in relation to their output,[52] but this could hardly have been the whole story.

With 256 looms in 1914 the axminster division was second to the tapestry in size. There were 105 brussels and wilton and 12 Saxony looms; 60 ingrain looms were unused. If these last are omitted, Hartford had about 6 per cent of the looms of the country. It had 10 per cent of the tapestry and velvet looms, 9 per cent of the axminster, and 5 per cent of the brussels and wilton. In an industry with 97 firms, this was a creditable showing. Unfortunately, the strongest showing was in tapestry and velvet. The management could hardly be censured, however, for not foreseeing World War I and the consequent increase in labor cost which was to cut the ground out from under the tapestry demand.

If Perkins and Higgins failed to grasp fully the trend in looms, they were abreast of the times in power production. In 1899 there were only five electric motors with a total of 192 horsepower in the whole American carpet industry,[53] yet two years later A. D. Higgins planned his centralized electric power plant with a capacity of 4,000 horsepower.[54] Large motors were used in the preliminary processes where it was feasible to use a group drive, but individual drives were more economical for the operation of the looms.[55]

Along with changing the map of Thompsonville, the merger had repercussions in the field of employee relations. First came a certain amount of displacement. To quell misgivings Perkins assured the overseers that they would be retained.[56] Indeed in many departments—in so far as the companies were complementary—there were no duplications, yet almost immediately supervisory personnel began to leave. In all there were 13 changes in the top overseer group from 1901 to 1905. After this first shake-down, personnel changes proceeded on a routine basis. In the years before the first World War the rise of John Davidson as supervisor of the axmin-ster department is significant, and also the appointment of Frederick J. Furey, long a union leader, as a foreman in the winding department.[57]

Along with the supervisors from New York, not as replacements but as additions to the force, came about three hundred rank-and-file em-ployees—out of over two thousand. These had been wined and dined at the opening of the tapestry mill in 1903, promised a raise, and moved free of charge.[58] But many later returned to New York.

Following the merger the Thompsonville working force expanded steadily. In 1900 the roll had carried from 700 to 1,100 names. When the moving was completed in 1905, the plant had 2,000 workers. This number grew slowly to a peak of 2,900 in 1909 and 1910. Of these the tapestry department accounted for about 35 per cent, and axminster 20 per cent. Of the other big departments the worsted and brussels had about 10 per cent each, and the filling mill 6 per cent, a figure that was equaled by the rug department as it became more important.[59]

Not only did the merger affect the size of the Thompsonville work-ing force, it in some ways changed the character. In 1900 the group in Thompsonville was composed of descendants of the English, Irish, and Scottish and of French Canadians, the latter the least stable part of the staff since many returned to their farms when they had saved a sufficiency. The new elements which the Higgins group introduced were Armenian and Greek. Expanding employment opportunities soon attracted members of other new immigrant groups. Italians made their first appearance as strikebreakers in the dyehouse in 1902 and three Poles, hired in Chicopee for the same purpose, were the precursors of the several hundred who were in town by 1904.[60]

With so many newcomers, the company was forced to expand housing facilities. In 1902 the company laid out a completely new housing project in the North End. By 1904 it owned 102 houses consisting of about three hundred tenements, worth in total $172,000. More were added in 1905, 1906, and 1909.[61]

In taking care of the housing needs the company also led the way with a modern sewage system and new sidewalks. In addition to being the main support of the town it provided fire protection and playgrounds, and it gave land at nominal prices for schools and other public purposes. Yet the atmosphere had changed from the days of Upson, and Democrats actually were elected to competitive office.

The fact that the day of out-and-out domination had passed did not lessen the interest of the management in the employees' extra-curricular activities. Somewhat shorter hours in the age before there was a car in every garage or even a radio in every living room meant that most of the leisure time was taken up by social and athletic clubs, on one level, and by the saloon, on another. In addition to his desire to counteract the influence of the latter, Higgins wanted to provide a nucleus of activity under the company as opposed to union auspices and also was interested in doing something for all the new nationalities.

A. D. Higgins' first step as a newcomer to Thompsonville was to contribute $100 to the organization of a brussels baseball team under the management of the brussels overseer. Next he established the Higgins Lyceum, a club for women employees. Other clubs followed. The Polish Club had a room in the Lozier building, while for the Brussels Athletic Club Higgins provided a gymnasium and a reading room in 1910. When the original headquarters was torn down to make room for the storehouse, the company constructed a more commodious building—now a cafeteria— at a cost of $12,000. Another club was for the overseers. A golf club was open to employees and townspeople alike.

These activities undoubtedly contributed to the greater popularity of Higgins and the new company as compared with Upson and the old. More nearly fundamental was the increased prosperity resulting from higher wages and steadier employment. Economic well-being reduced the area of conflicts and improved dispositions which naturally affected the role of the unions.

While the dyers struck for higher wages both in 1901 and 1912—unsuccessfully—the most interesting conflict came in 1906 when Higgins tried to introduce new methods of training brussels weavers. Wishing to put 15 idle looms into operation and faced with a dearth of skilled weavers, he proposed a program for the rapid training of unskilled labor similar to ones he had installed in other departments without difficulty. To the brussels weavers, who had always introduced boys to the mysteries of the craft through a long apprenticeship—and thus controlled the labor supply—this was a clarion call to danger. However, with good feeling on both sides, after a three days' strike the men recognized their responsibility to supply an adequate number of competent weavers and specifically agreed to get 15 looms working within three months. In exchange the management abandoned its training plans.

Higgins' attitude toward labor organizations was paradoxical. His early experience in New York contained nothing which would lead him to look upon them with favor, and Frederick Furey, one of the leaders, felt that Higgins brought in overseers to combat unionism and used every device possible to undercut the unions. On the other hand, there was no general program of firing union leaders or adherents, and Furey admits to pleasant and co-operative relations. In 1908 the concern advertised in the official handbook of the United Textile Workers of America with "the compliments of a friend." Undoubtedly Higgins' main goal was to eliminate the unions' effectiveness—or power of interference—as far as possible without an outright challenge.

PURCHASING, PROCESSES, PRODUCTION

Purchasing and manufacturing processes did not change greatly in this period. Wool still was the predominant item in the $3,500,000 which Perkins and his assistants spent each year for raw materials. China had become the most important source of carpet wool in the first decade of the century, dominating the market for filling wools and for axminsters.[62] These along with Scotch and Donskoi wools were the main reliance of the Hartford plant.[63] Generally the management tried to keep at least a four months' supply on hand.[64] Some of this was bought abroad. The purchasing agent traveled extensively, and his son was resident in China for a period.[65] The Liverpool auctions, held six to eight times a year, were an important source, particularly for Indian and East Indian grades, while frequent recourse was had to American importers—Oelrichs & Company, J. B. Moore, Wood Brothers, and J. Kenworthy.

Rapid shifts in wool prices increased the speculative aspects of operations.[66] Events during 1913, when wars in the Middle and Far East sent prices soaring, illustrate the hazards. Perkins was complimented on his close analysis of the raw materials situation which enabled him to set his prices at a point which would both cover costs and at the same time enable him to get sufficient volume to keep his mills running, yet the Bigelow company, which slowed down, made much larger profits. No records of the prices paid by Hartford exist for the years before 1907. According to national estimates, the cost per pound rose from 21 to 33 cents, or by 53 per cent, between 1900 and 1905.[67] Company records indicate another advance of about 10 per cent between 1909 and 1912.

Production cost records survive from 1907 to 1912 and are summarized in Table 21. Late in 1907 the costs of all fabrics were at a peak in relation to the years that followed. After the panic plunge, they began to rise late in 1908 or early in 1909. Mid-1910 saw another downward turning point from which recovery did not set in until 1912.

Large-volume production placed the Hartford company at a distinct advantage in cost. While the joint Higgins-Hartford output had been 5,700,000 yards in 1899, the Thompsonville mill in 1909 was turning out 7,500,000 yards. Of the total yardage, tapestry accounted for from 50 to 62 per cent; axminster from 25 to 33; and brussels and wilton from 4 to 5 per cent each. Rug production grew from 33 per cent in 1907 to 57 per cent of the total in 1912. By that time about 60 per cent of the axminster, 85 per cent of the brussels and wilton, and 40 per cent of the tapestry were made into rugs. With the exception of some of the tapestry, all these were seamed.

Meanwhile the popularity of using brand names increased during this decade. Every new grade sported its own name. A linen-fringed, extra quality wilton rug introduced in 1912 was called Royal Iran. Kerman, a woolen-faced wilton, came in 1913. Among the axminsters, the standby—

TABLE 21

HARTFORD CARPET CORPORATION

Average Direct Production Costs, Selected Dates from 1907 to 1912

(Per Yard)

Date	Three-Star Tapestry	Two-Star Tapestry	Saxony	Wilton	Brussels	Axminster
December, 1907	$.39	$.48	$1.38	$1.52	$1.16	$.84
December, 1908			1.16	1.25		
June, 1909	.32	.37			.92	.64
May, 1910		.46	1.47		1.07	
July, 1910	.38					
February, 1911				1.49		.70
March, 1912	.33	.41	1.32	1.30	.96	.65
November, 1912	.37	.46	1.47	1.41	.98	.65

Source: Hartford Carpet Corporation, Transfer Report.

Bussorah—was joined by a lower-priced Vicanere in 1909, and by the Plaza in 1913. New brand names in the tapestry line included the Phoenix, a low-priced 7½-wire tapestry rug in 1908, and two seamless numbers, a Saranac in 1911 and Berkshire in 1914.[68]

The popularity of rugs not only brought a proliferation of types but a profusion of sizes within types. While 9 by 12 feet was the most popular, in 1908 Saxony was made in 19 regular sizes, plus any other desired.[69]

Moreover, the demand for a wide selection of patterns showed no sign of diminishing. In 1908 Saxony was offered in 45 designs and colorings. In addition to oriental, the French, American Colonial, and other period motifs were popular in the better-grade fabrics during this time. As decorators emphasized the background role of floor coverings and as simplicity began to be stressed in homes of better taste, two-toned effects gained a following.[70] Colors were soft and subdued—grays, gray-greens, mauve, tan.

While oriental patterns or those with small set figures or flowers appealed to the vanguard of American home decorators, the opposite attracted the average purchaser of tapestries and velvets. In these, the large bright-colored flowers of years gone by spread everywhere. Reds and greens were the favorites, but the majority of patterns managed to embrace four or more clashing hues within their confines. A fad of more recent origin was that of picture rugs. The spread of patterns depicting Little Bo-Peep, Mary Had a Little Lamb, and faithful dogs of various breeds was aided by the policy of some advertisers in using these rugs as premiums and also by their prominence in mail-order catalogues.

MARKETING AND FINANCE

The marketing organization was based on the Higgins system of direct selling to wholesalers. Headquarters were in the Hartford building in Union Square in New York until 1912 when they were moved uptown to Twenty-fifth Street and Madison Avenue. Boston, Philadelphia, and Chicago had branch offices in 1901. In 1906, a Marshall Field employee was hired to have charge of a San Francisco division.[71] The Philadelphia office was closed in 1913, but meanwhile new outlets had been opened in St. Louis, Kansas City, Denver, and Seattle.[72] The distribution of the growing salesforce is indicated in Table 22.

TABLE 22

HARTFORD CARPET CORPORATION

Distribution of Salesmen Outside the New York Office

1906, 1909, and 1912

	1906	1909	1912
Atlantic Seaboard	4	7	9
Middle West	3	3	7
South	1	1	1
West	1	1	4
Total	9	12	21

Source: *The American Carpet & Upholstery Journal*, XXIV (May, 1906), 84; XXVII (Nov., 1909), 104; XXX (Nov., 1912), 93.

Customers might be grouped roughly into five categories: contract purchasers, wholesalers, mail-order houses, large department stores, and retailers. The contract business was done with the government, hotels, theaters, steamship and railroad companies. Not only did contract sales offer production advantages, but they were important for prestige.

If the department store was an old but increasing menace, the mail-order company was a newer threat. It was in catering to this business that Norman first made his reputation. Sears, Roebuck and Montgomery, Ward dealt chiefly in the great carpet staples, that is, ingrain, tapestry, velvet, and latterly axminsters.

Both the large department store and the mail-order house presented the Hartford corporation with the opportunity of doing business on the same scale as the wholesaler, but the small retail merchant was a different proposition. When the carpet manufacturer acquired the facilities for dealing with him directly, the days of the wholesaler were numbered. Some of these facilities existed already in 1900, such as the credit-rating houses and an organized salesforce. Still, as long as the salesman was forced to rely on his trunk full of samples, freight charges precluded any town-to-town itinerary. Norman's introduction of colored plates of patterns revolutionized the whole marketing system by making it possible for a salesman to go from local dealer to local dealer. Temporarily the latter might cling to his old wholesaler, because of habit, time factors, freight charges, and inventory policies, but as the manufacturer provided equal services—and more—the old chain broke.

Among the services to the retailer which the manufacturer could perform better than the wholesaler was the extension of liberal credit and the carrying of larger inventories. Better times made it easier for manufacturers in general to fulfill these demands, and in particular the increased financial resources of the Hartford Carpet Corporation were important. The manufacturers also had to give discount and freight rates as favorable as those given by the wholesalers, and all this had to be done as tactfully as possible so as not to alienate those wholesalers who were still important.

Another factor in the growing importance of direct sales to retailers was the greater institutionalization of the formal spring and fall openings. Despite the increase in the salesforce, despite the uncertainties of the Smith auctions, despite the frequent delays in announcing prices, the bulk of the season's uncontracted production was disposed of at these openings, a great blessing in working out manufacturing schedules.[73] By attending these events early in May and November each year, the retailer with a minimum of effort and expense could plan for the year, or at least get the background to deal with the salesmen who arrived later.

With all these forces undermining his position, it is no wonder that the wholesaler was worried. The Hartford corporation was a leader in trying to give him a modicum of protection by refusing to do business with buying syndicates—small retailers who undertook co-operative purchasing.[74] Hartford also tried to avoid approaching retailers who bought its brands from local wholesalers. Finally the Hartford company did not undercut the wholesaler by establishing a cut-carpet department which made up individual wall-to-wall orders at the behest of the local merchant. Undoubtedly this was due primarily to the nature of its products. A cut-carpet department was a device useful in marketing expensive fabrics while the bulk of the Hartford output was in middle-class tapestry and axminster. The former was sufficiently inexpensive for the retailer to carry enough rolls to give his customers some selection, while axminster production was largely in rugs.

Despite these considerations of the wholesalers' position and despite the fact that it was to be another two decades before Hartford completely abandoned the wholesaler, there is no doubt of the general tenor of Norman's activities. Whether Hartford was one of the large manufacturers who, in the fall of 1913, decided to place the wholesalers and retailers on the same level as far as credit and dating were concerned is not clear,[75] but with Norman energetically pushing sales by every possible device, the role of the wholesaler was becoming ever more constricted.

Many of Norman's methods were common to the time but he showed unusual vigor in application. Emphasis was placed on helping the retailer move his goods. Salesmen gave him advice on the best methods of display, and the contract department was always ready to assist a dealer in trying to obtain a large order. Norman produced several booklets on the merits of his product, with sample advertisements and tips on how to sell it. He made catalogues and color plates available and closely coordinated company sales campaigns with the efforts of dealers in the area. Moreover, the general advertising campaign upon which he embarked aided the local distributor.

The turn of the century saw the rapid rise of the professional advertising agency.[76] While there is no record of Hartford's obtaining such services, and while there was no advertising department, no regular advertising budget, not even a continuing program, the Hartford management made great strides in putting its wares before the public. For the first time a real effort was made to establish the Hartford name before the ultimate consumer. Though the energy devoted to this endeavor might seem meager enough by present standards, the direct appeal to the householders was a highly significant innovation.

Basic to the success of any such scheme was the prompt registering of trade-marks on new products. Next came a resumption of trade-journal advertising and an improvement of copy. Usually less was crowded onto the page, the arrangement was such that points stood out, and efforts were made to present concisely a few significant claims.

Equally important was the wider utilization of magazines. During the first decade of the twentieth century periodicals devoted to homes and gardens increased rapidly. Perhaps the editors, in search of advertising, foisted themselves upon the manufacturers, but to Norman, who was making a vigorous effort to push his high-grade Saxony, the value of magazines with a circulation among the upper-middle classes was obvious. M. J. Whittall probably anticipated the Hartford corporation in the program of nationwide advertising via this medium since his advertising appeared in *House Beautiful* in October, 1909, and in *Country Life in*

America in November, 1909, and he is credited with even earlier displays. In February, 1910, the first advertisement of Hartford Saxony appeared in the former. Covering a half page was the picture of an Arab looking at a Saxony and reading copy to the effect that an oriental rug dealer was filled with wonder at the similarity to his product and with dismay at the low cost. Finally the address was listed simply as "A. B. Saxony, 41 Union Square, New York City." [77] The material was changed slightly each month and the mailing address was altered from A. B. to A. C. to A. D. etc.—thus enabling the management to tell by which copy the prospective customer had been attracted. Usually the advertisement was placed just for a few months in the fall and in the spring. *Country Life* also carried some Hartford advertisements but Norman does not seem to have followed Whittall into *Good Housekeeping*.

In 1911 Norman began to introduce slogans into his advertisements: "American Rugs for Private Houses and Public Places"; "Universally imitated but never equalled." He also began to stress the company's long years of experience. Meanwhile brochures poured forth unceasingly. A striking and artistic one of 1914 contained letters of approval from leading retailers.[78]

The fame of Hartford Saxony was spread not only by the printed word but by sidewalk tests and by exhibitions. In November, 1908, during the fall opening, the sales department launched an ambitious project by renting special quarters on Broadway. Buyers, hotel men, and decorators were sent special invitations in order to give them "an idea of the possibilities of the 'Hartford Saxony' rugs when assembled in their entirety." The general public was invited through notices in the newspapers [79] to view the $20,000 worth of rugs. So successful was the venture that the exhibit was taken on a national tour.[80]

Several years later this effort was surpassed. The rotunda of John Wanamaker's New York store was draped with Hartford Saxonies and the company and the store were complimented in a trade journal on the "largest and most attractive display ever made at any one time of any one kind of floor covering fabric and of one manufacturer's goods" and on "one of the best sales promotion ideas yet." [81] With all these devices it is little wonder that the carpet trade journal wrote in 1914, "all of a sudden, as it seemed, two or three years ago, the word 'Saxony' was found to be creeping all over the country." [82]

Meanwhile the other products of the company were not ignored, the Alaska-Yukon Pacific Exposition being the occasion for a special promotion of tapestries and velvets. An experienced tap weaver was sent with his loom to weave for the benefit of the public a special pattern based on a likeness of the Indian chief, Seattle.[83] In 1904 the company supplied all the rugs for the Connecticut Building at the World's Fair [84] and in

1911 it joined with Whittall and Bigelow in an exhibit at the Boston Chamber of Commerce Exposition.[85]

A final method of making known this Hartford product was the use of the new invention, motion pictures. In the fall of 1913 a movie crew spent several days in Thompsonville taking pictures of the process.[86]

In this, as in other advertising techniques, Hartford led the field— with the possible exception of the Whittall firm. While much of the groundwork was done before Norman's advent to the top position, efforts were intensified after his elevation, and his general reputation as a super-salesman confirms the important role attributed to him in the "marketing revolution."

Sales figures substantiate this claim. Despite generally declining prices after 1908, Hartford's sales held up well. In 1909 they totaled $5,900,000, in 1913, $6,500,000, with a five-year average of just over $6,000,000. There is no exact statement of the costs of selling but they seem to have risen proportionately from about $575,000 in 1910 to about $660,000 in 1913.[87] This included allowances and discounts, about which information is scarce.

Profit figures likewise are hard to discover but on a rough estimate they may have run around $500,000 a year from 1901 to 1908 and around $600,000 from 1909 to 1913, with wide fluctuations probable. Even admitting the inaccurate nature of these statistics, it is obvious that profits were much higher than the $240,000 to $300,000 anticipated by the promoters. Returns on capital averaged 12 per cent.

With such success there was no problem in meeting the preferred dividends. As a result, preferred sold below par for only one brief interval in 1908. By 1909 it had risen to 125 and thereafter did not vary greatly. Since the directors plowed the earnings back into the new plant, the first return on common was not voted until 1909, and the common stock which had started at 50 in 1901 sank as low as 15 in 1906. Only after the 2½ per cent dividend in 1909 did it begin to climb. Thereafter, with directors voting 6 per cent dividends in 1910 and 7 per cent in subsequent years, the market price leveled off at about 116 after January, 1911.

In 1914 on the eve of the merger with the Bigelow company, Hartford's preferred and common stocks were selling in the market for approximately the combined book value of the two issues: $6,900,000. Over the life of the Hartford Carpet Corporation the net working capital had increased some $600,000 and the fixed assets some $3,300,000. All of this increase came from profits. In addition, $3,635,000 were paid in dividends and $175,000 in bonuses. In general then the financial returns of the consolidation were adequate, though how much this was attributable to the merger cannot be determined, particularly in view of the highly dissimilar economic conditions of the decades before and after.

As important to the profitability and growth of the Hartford Carpet Corporation as the general prosperity of the early twentieth century was the strength of its management. The elimination of ingrain and expansion of axminster had accomplished construction of a new factory with its modern power plant, the adoption of good labor policies, the development of favorable manufacturing costs, and a strong marketing department. These were no small achievements for a little over a dozen years. The combination of Robert Perkins, A. D. Higgins, and the Boston bankers had worked more than adequately in its first trial.

CHAPTER 9

THE RECONSTITUTED COMPANIES:

Bigelow Carpet Company, 1899–1914

While the Higgins-Hartford merger resulted in the consolidation of manufacturing operations at Thompsonville, the Bigelow-Lowell merger created little change in plant or process. True, the existence of two plants, at Lowell and Clinton, introduced the Bigelow management to new problems in the area of co-ordination. But the Boston executives followed the course of minimum disruption. They made no effort to produce all brussels in one mill, all axminsters in the other. Each operation continued with its former superintendents and with individual policies.

OWNERSHIP AND ADMINISTRATION

Neither was there any great shift in ownership. The Fairbanks family controlled the largest number of shares of the new concern: 3,951, followed by the Bigelows with 3,396, the Sloanes with 2,160, the Beals with 2,300, and the Lymans with 950, a total of 12,757 out of 40,300 shares. A majority was concentrated in the hands of 57 people, each of whom owned 105 or more shares. The remainder was scattered among 772 individuals. Over 85 per cent of the proprietors were from New England, with Boston and its suburbs accounting for about 35 per cent and Lowell 25 per cent.

The board of directors reflected the predominating influence of Boston, with Jacob Rogers from Lowell and John Sloane from New York the only outsiders. Five of the seven: James H. Beal, Edward W. Hutchins, Charles F. Fairbanks, A. S. Wheeler, and John Sloane came from the old Bigelow group. Lyman and Rogers represented the Lowell Manufacturing Company. All told, the directors and their families accounted for 10,185 shares. Of the large interests, only the Bigelow family was not directly represented: its members were all retired from business pursuits.

This was primarily a nonoperating board: two were lawyers, two were bank presidents, one was a merchant. All had a multitude of outside interests, yet almost all had inside information about the carpet business or the company and with the exception of Wheeler and Sloane were diligent in their attendance at directors' meetings.

Bigelow stockholders had more authority than Hartford's, mainly because of historical antecedents. They elected the clerk and the treasurer as well as the directors, and they were represented on the auditing committee. Owners of one-fifth of the stock could call a meeting and any stockholder could request a report on the financial position of the firm. Amending the bylaws also fell into the province of the proprietors. Actually, however, they seemed to show the same lack of interest as their Hartford counterparts.

The directors elected the president, approved and removed employees, fixed salaries, and declared dividends. In general they had "all the powers in the management of the Company."

Of the officers the president was still mainly a chairman of meetings, the clerk a record-taker. In the treasurer was concentrated the executive power. Besides outlining his financial responsibilities, the bylaws said, "The Treasurer shall be the General Agent of the Company and shall superintend and regulate its affairs and make all necessary contracts relating thereto. He shall have power to make purchases and sales. . . . He shall appoint all Agents at the Mills. He may contract debts in behalf of the Company." For his services he received $20,000 at first and then, after 1906, $25,000.[1] In terms of functions Charles Fairbanks took upon himself the financing and the purchasing. Marketing was handled by his son, Henry, in New York. Manufacturing and labor relations were the direct province of each mill agent.

Both plants experienced considerable turnover in the position of mill agent from 1900 to 1914. Death, promotions, and offers from other concerns, all played a role in the rapid succession as in Lowell five men took the post of agent, in Clinton three. Alvin Lyon left Lowell in 1906 after twenty-three years' service in order to take over the direction of the gigantic Wood Worsted Mills of the American Woolen Company at Lawrence. This in itself bespeaks his ability as a factory manager. As his successor, Fairbanks selected his own thirty-year old son, William Kendall Fairbanks, who after attending Massachusetts Institute of Technology had entered the Lowell mill in 1900 as Lyon's assistant. Before he had much opportunity to make his mark, he was threatened with blindness and in 1911 died after an operation.

Thomas J. Firth, the former Higgins and Hartford superintendent, who had become superintendent of spinning at Clinton, followed Fairbanks. Upon his resignation in May, 1912, to accept a job in South America up stepped his assistant, Harold E. Wadely—a man whose previous experience pointed the way to a dynamic future. Born in Kidderminster, England, he had gone to Canada and the Brinton Carpet Company in 1905. After reorganizing the business of this concern, he had come to Bigelow in 1911. He was not slated to remain a mill agent long. In 1913 he was named manufacturing manager in charge of both the Lowell and Clinton plants, Thomas Collins succeeding him as agent. This newly created job portended greater co-ordination and greater executive specialization, but the Bigelow-Hartford merger in 1914 cut short Wadely's promising performance. Wadely subsequently joined and became president of the Firth Carpet Company.

At Clinton, Edward W. Burdett, though long in company service, had but recently undertaken the duties of agent at the time of the merger in 1899. Exemplifying fidelity, he even went to jail for his company. In 1901 the Clinton Gas Light Company got an injunction forbidding the carpet company to lay electric wires under the street between the weaving and spinning mill. When Burdett ignored the order, the company was fined $2,000, while Burdett was sentenced to jail for 20 days.[2]

It was almost a year after Burdett's death in 1907 before Paul T. Wise, an outsider, was appointed. Wise, like his contemporary, William Kendell Fairbanks, was a young man, not yet thirty. A graduate of Lowell Textile School he had held several supervisory jobs in the wool industry.[3] After four years he left in July, 1912, and Wilson S. Price, Wadely's assistant, was brought to Clinton from Lowell.

Amid all these changes no effort was made at salary stabilization. Lyon had received $8,000, while Burdett was getting $4,000 at first and later $5,000. Firth and Wadely both received $5,000 as agent, while William Fairbanks and Price got considerably less. After his promotion to general superintendent, Wadely was raised to $10,000 a year.

The marketing department saw fewer changes. Henry P. Fairbanks, who like Burdett had assumed his job just a short time before the Bigelow-Lowell merger, headed the division in New York at a salary of about $20,000.[4] In addition to being responsible for the selling, he also supervised the billing, shipping, and credit departments. For a time in 1907 he took over for his father. But he had trouble with his throat, and the generally precarious state of his health precluded aggressive activity for the present and the assumption of a greater load in the future.

MACHINES, MATERIAL, AND MEN

At Lowell and Clinton the new Bigelow company had a total fixed investment of $2,314,247 in 1899.[5] At the end of 1913 it had one of $2,-456,800, a deceptive figure in view of the great amount of construction that had been completed in the interim. This construction was not based on the necessity of creating a new plant as at Thompsonville. It was determined by considerations of obsolescence, process, capacity, and product. Among the major projects of the first few years were the construction of a four-story mill at Lowell to house rug-finishing facilities and the replacement of the 1828 spinning mill there.

Even the coming of less prosperous times did not deflect Fairbanks from his program for further improvements. His semiannual report in June, 1907, explains his plans in great detail: [6]

> It will be necessary to rebuild at Lowell our present wool house, also the dye house. Owing to the restricted territory . . . we decided to postpone the matter of the dyehouse until another year . . . [we plan] to construct a penstock in place of the open canal which supplies our water wheel and thereby recover the land now covered by the canal. . . .
> At Clinton we have commenced the foundation of the [axminster] mill. . . . Estimated cost . . . including sprinklers, heating, elevators, lighting, shafting, belting, etc. is $184,000. It is proposed in providing for additional power to look forward to centralization of our power plant, and we must look to an expenditure during the coming year or two, of at least $500,000 at Clinton, to which must be added the expenditure at Lowell of at least $300,000 more. This seems a large amount, but I am convinced that it is necessary to place the Company on a modern and economical basis and that it is warranted by our present financial condition, even in view of an anticipated falling off in general business.

Along with the construction programs came new machinery. At the time of the merger Lowell had a contract with Crompton & Knowles for 100 narrow axminster looms, 62 of which had already been installed. The cost of the outstanding 38 was $125,000, plus a royalty payment of from 1 to 4 cents a yard. Shortly thereafter, in 1901, Fairbanks decided to increase the axminster capacity at Clinton: [7]

> We have been largely oversold . . . so much so that last season we had no open line of our own. We have hesitated a long while about increasing this department, as it involved the erection of buildings and power plants. We have now decided to displace some thirty of our Brussels looms at Clinton and replace them with 20 Axminster Looms. This can be done we think, without any detriment to our Brussels Department.

These new axminsters, a modification of the Skinner loom used by the firm since the eighties, were made in the factory's own machine shop. When the new axminster mill was built in 1906, Fairbanks abandoned the Skinner pattern, turning to a Crompton & Knowles model capable of weaving 53 yards a day. Forty of these three-fourths looms cost $30,450 and eight four-fourths looms, $6,658.[8] The purchase of a few plush looms from the Worcester Loom Company in 1907 and 1910, and a few narrow brussels and wilton looms completed the weave-shed acquisitions during these years, but a great deal of new equipment was bought for the new dyehouses and spinning mill.[9] All told, for the buildings and machinery in major new projects Fairbanks spent $980,000 in Lowell and $340,000 in Clinton.

From his office in Boston Fairbanks bought wool for the carpet mills mainly from wool brokerage houses in New York, Glasgow, and Liverpool, brokerage fees amounting to ½ of 1 per cent and commission to 3 per cent.[10] The fluctuation of wool prices paid by Fairbanks between 1900 and 1914 appears in Table 23.

TABLE 23

BIGELOW CARPET COMPANY

Price of Wool, Selected Years from 1900 to 1914

(Annual Average Per Pound)

	1900	1907	1908	1909	1913	1914
China combing	$.15	—	$.24	$.18	$.3375	.18,
Scotch	.145	—	.24	.18	.25.	.1925
Donskoi	.21	$.335	—	.27	.3325	.26
China filling	—	—	.16	—	.23	.19

Source: Bigelow Carpet Company, Journal A, *passim;* Bigelow Carpet Company, Journal B, *passim.*

While purchasing was centralized, after the merger, labor policy remained primarily in the province of the local authorities. Indeed, with every foreman hiring, firing, disciplining and directing his own operatives, there was little uniformity in some important areas even within the local unit.

Differences between the city of Lowell and the town of Clinton as well as the previous history of the two plants further contributed to distinctiveness. In Lowell the factory was just one among many and, though a sizable establishment, it was of the second rank of Lowell corporations. In Clinton the carpet mill was the second largest among a few. In both Lowell and Clinton the management contributed to the hospital associations, but in Clinton it also provided a playground. While employee housing had long since been abandoned in Lowell, in Clinton the corporation still had sixty-five houses.[11] With many recreational facilities available in Lowell, the company was not called upon to assist such activities there; but in Clinton it contributed to a girls' club.

The character of the personnel was also quite different in Lowell from that in Clinton. At the turn of the century, of all the New England textile towns Lowell had the largest floating population.[12] French-Canadians, Italians, Poles, and Greeks all were drawn to the "textile city." This resulted in a much less stable, industrially less experienced and less mature working force than the one in the Clinton mill. Not that Clinton did not have some eastern and southern Europeans, but the descendants of the Scottish, Irish, English, and Germans continued to comprise 90 to 95 per cent of the workers.[13]

The Lowell mill had a much larger work force, employing over 2,000 as compared to Clinton's 1,300. These figures, however, are probably high for the number of those who worked with any degree of continuity. In the first year of the merged concerns, 1900, the Clinton factory was shut down for a considerable period in the spring because of high water and for from two to six weeks in the summer; at Lowell the ingrain employees bore the brunt of the year's unemployment. Overproduction bothered the Bigelow management in 1901 but by the end of the year Fairbanks could report, "The mills are well employed and the prospects for the coming six months are encouraging." This was to be the tenor of his pronouncements for the next few years. Not until December, 1903, did he report a change in the trend: "Our sales for the six months have kept up owing to the advance in prices; the volume shows some slight falling off. The prospects for the coming year are for decreased consumption. . . . We shall endeavor to produce as near as possible to the consumption and not accumulate." [14] His prophecy was fulfilled. Though the curtailment did not result in a shutdown, it did mean fewer workers.

The panic of 1907 brought more drastic action. In November both mills were closed for ten days, and when they resumed it was only on a four-day, 42-hour-week basis, instead of the allowed 56.[15] In the following spring there was another forced vacation for part of the plant at least. Thereafter, conditions were good until 1911, when short time plagued the workers for a good part of the fall.

At the beginning of 1912, hours were cut by state law to 54. The schedule in Clinton, which had run from 6:30 to 5:36 on five days with an hour for lunch and 6:30 to 12 on Saturday, was amended by dropping 24 minutes each day from Monday through Friday.[16] Few workers had to worry about overwork in the next few years, however, and by the spring of 1914 Lowell was limping along on three days a week; Clinton, four.[17]

In contrast to the absence of unions at Clinton, the Lowell mill had six: firemen, jack spinners, wool spinners, axminster weavers, ingrain loom fixers, and brussels carpet weavers were organized. However, the first challenge was made by an unorganized group. In January, 1900, the doffers and spinners asked for a 10 per cent advance based on a comparison with Philadelphia wages. Lyon rejected the contention. Conditions were different, he claimed; Lowell wages were as good as any paid in the Northern carpet mills, and the company had not followed the local cotton and woolen mills in cutting wages recently.[18] After a two-day strike the workers returned empty-handed.

The next trouble at Lowell concerned not wages but union working rules. On April 18, 1900, 300 women from the ingrain and axminster departments went out because Lyon would not fire a woman who exceeded the union's productivity norms. Dissension over religious differences added to the confusion. Though other groups joined the walkout, the factional split within the union and the particular issue made a successful strike unlikely. Lyon, though he had dealt with the union and, indeed, had hired its members exclusively, was of no mind to ease its difficulties. Within a week the strikers voted to rescind the rule limiting the amount of work, and the episode was over.[19]

This was the last disturbance of Lyon's regime, but the bad business conditions of the panic year, 1907, presented young William K. Fairbanks with an explosive situation. Every union except the loom fixers was reported to have grievances. On November 7, 1907, 240 brussels and wilton weavers, members of a union affiliated with the United Textile Workers of America, went out on strike because of the system of paying for the tying-in process. As it stood, the men were paid on the basis of the job taking a half hour—and it might vary from 10 minutes to 1½ hours.[20] At first the weavers went out alone, but gradually other groups joined in the action: the spinners because the foreman had fired a prominent union member, the machinists because they were ordered to fix a machine a scab spinner was using. By mid-January 2,500 were off the job. Meanwhile the executive committee of the national union had voted to assess its 18,000 members 3 cents a week for the support of the carpet men.

William Fairbanks shrugged off the episode with the comment that the strikers had bees in their bonnets. Business was bad; time was on his side—and he had plenty of it. By February all the strikes except that of the brussels weavers had collapsed. Thirty-eight of the brussels weavers had returned, but the majority were recalcitrant. Several large constituent unions of the United Textile Workers were grumbling about the continued financial drain, and the vague promises of aid from the Philadelphia carpet workers were cold comfort. Still they voted to continue the strike.[21]

In June the Bigelow treasurer reported to the directors that enough employees had returned to make mill operations normal.[22] With that remark labor strife at this plant passed into history. The factory remained at peace during the big cotton strikes in 1912, despite picket lines. At least one carpet union leader with wide experience had a soft spot for the old Lowell shop, "the most up-to-date plant in the carpet industry up to that time and the easiest for the employee." [23]

MARKETING AND FINANCE: 1900–1914

While there was no introduction of a new line, the old fabrics were made in still more varieties and grades. A listing of various brands or grades under the four main classes of products in 1900 ran as follows:

Wilton	*Brussels*	*Axminster*	*Ingrain*
Bigelow	Bigelow	Bigelow	Lowell Three-Ply
Saxony	Imperial	Imperial	Lowell Extra Super
Lancaster	Lowell	Middlesex	Two-Ply
Lowell	Middlesex	Arlington Rug	
Bagdad	Bagdad	Utopia Rug	
Daghestan	Ormond	Leamington Rug	

Over the next 10 years, as brand names became even more popular, the company added an Electra axminster rug. In the wilton field Kymric, Voiture, Merrimac, and Wellington were introduced in rapid succession. Later came a deep-pile wilton, the Balkan, and two wool wiltons, the Puritan and the Aberdeen. In addition the factory turned out plush for automobile and carriage upholstery.[24] But the sensation of the period was the Ardebil (wilton)—a copy of the $12,500 prayer rug which had been a wonder of the world for a decade.[25] Originally the name Ardebil was applied to a single pattern but eventually it was used as the brand name for a line.

On the designing of its own patterns Bigelow was spending from $50,-000 to $60,000 a year. Just before the war most of the patterns for the best grades were inspired by oriental rugs or Navajo Indian blankets though a few had flower motifs. Most of them had light backgrounds.

The peak production of the period was reached in 1902 with 6,690,977 yards as is shown in Table 24. Thereafter the total dropped; though axminster output expanded rapidly, it did not offset the decline in ingrain.

The marketing organization of the company at the turn of the century was based on the fact that contracts with large customers, such as hotels, steamship lines, the Pullman Company, clubs, and theaters, and the private brand and pattern orders of the exclusive stores comprised a large proportion of the firm's business.[26] The new consolidated concern dropped the Lowell sales agent, taking over the selling organization of the old Bigelow company, headed by Henry P. Fairbanks with C. P. Starr as general manager. The latter had started his career with A. T. Stewart, and then had served as western representative for Sloane before coming to Bigelow. Fairbanks never was in good health; by the turn of the century Starr was well along in years and not very aggressive. In 1914 it was noted, "The Whittall product has been something more than a runner-up for the Bigelow for the last few years and has grabbed a lot of business that used to be the sole property of the Lowell and Clinton corporation."[27]

To remedy this deplorable situation, to develop more aggressive marketing, A. V. Kline was brought in as sales manager in 1913. His twenty-eight years with Arnold, Constable, the last eight of which were spent as manager of the wholesale carpet department, had given him an excellent knowledge of distributors.[28] He also brought new men and new ideas.

A position as assistant sales manager was created and the department was split into contract, rug, and cut-carpet divisions.

Kline also changed distribution policies and techniques. Before Kline's time Bigelow had relied exclusively on wholesalers and contract orders. It had never sold at auction except in job lots of discontinued patterns; [29] it had relatively little mail-order business. It had refused to deal with buying syndicates [30] and had made no sales to retailers—except in so far as

TABLE 24

BIGELOW CARPET COMPANY

Production of Selected Types of Carpets at Clinton and Lowell Mills 1901 to 1913

(In Yards [a])

	Ingrain	Axminster	Brussels & Wilton	Total
1901	2,283,746	1,409,366	2,018,693	5,711,805
1902	2,330,643	1,898,035	2,462,299	6,690,977
1903	2,294,343	1,917,326	2,350,768	6,562,437
1904	1,810,404	1,491,945	2,225,287	5,327,636
1905	1,746,285	1,820,171	2,482,254	6,048,710
1906	940,533	2,022,374	2,614,475	5,577,382
1907	499,729	2,250,349	2,419,025	5,169,103
1908	550,416	2,085,747	1,870,398	4,506,561
1909	620,546	2,364,708	2,232,542	5,217,796
1910	550,123	2,582,982	2,357,165	5,490,270
1911	415,173	2,334,162	2,092,544	4,841,879
1912	179,777			
1913	242,270	2,478,172	1,473,930	4,094,372

[a] The records do not indicate whether these are square or running yards on the 27″ goods.

Source: Bigelow Carpet Company, Journal A, *passim;* Bigelow Carpet Company, Journal B, *passim.*

firms like Arnold, Constable and W. & J. Sloane were both wholesalers and retailers. Kline stopped selling only to wholesalers and sold to anyone who had good credit.[31] For the first time the company also actively sought small retail accounts. To do this a cut-carpet department was a necessity, since the small merchant could not afford to stock a wide variety or a great volume of the higher-priced fabrics made by Bigelow. Cut-carpet departments had been a factor in the trade for almost ten years. Their purpose was to perform at the factory a function which previously the retailer had had to perform for himself: the cutting of the carpeting to fit the size of the individual customer's room. With this system the customer ordered from sample, the retailer measured the room, and the factory undertook the tedious task of matching and sewing. The obvious advantages of such a procedure more than offset the increased prices resulting from handling many individual orders at the factory. Since most wholesalers were slow to offer such services, Bigelow took much business away from them even when the freight rates were slightly higher and time of delivery a few days longer.[32]

In his brief tenure Kline hardly had an opportunity to revamp the firm's advertising thoroughly. For advertising the Bigelow marketing men used five media: exhibitions, newspapers, catalogues, trade journals, and magazines with national circulation. In the first field the company limited itself to appearing in shows organized by other agencies: the Louisiana Purchase Exposition at St. Louis in 1906 and the Boston Chamber of Commerce Industrial & Educational Exposition, for example, in 1911. Bigelow's exhibit at the former on which well over $10,000 was spent, won the grand prize.[33] This inspired a brief newspaper campaign which was sufficiently successful to lead Fairbanks and Starr to undertake another in 1907.[34]

In 1904 the department put out a catalogue of 40 colored illustrations which received much favorable comment. The 1908 issue had 200 color plates. These advertising catalogues also presented a history of the company and industry and a list of hotels and clubs carpeted by Bigelow.[35]

The main reliance for most of the period was on trade-journal advertising, but in the spring of 1911 Bigelow's advertising in popular national magazines had its beginning. The copy carried a new trade-mark, a series of circles with the motto, "Carpets of Quality," and it contained slogans concentrating on one theme: "Your carpets like your glasses should be selected to suit you. Through one you see the world, through the other the world sees you." [36] Though this was a start, the reading matter was too long and the printing too small. The first advertisement under Kline did much to overcome these weaknesses; arrangement was striking, the message brief.

The increased amount of advertising enlarged the sales budget. The cost of marketing, including designing the carpets, rose from $92,000 in 1902 to $267,000 in 1912, and then fell off slightly in the poor year, 1913. In the latter year it was 4.5 per cent of sales as compared with 1.4 per cent in 1902. Meanwhile the level of sales had not altered materially as is shown in Table 25. The peak of $6,800,510 was reached in 1906. The average for the thirteen years was $6,050,000, the Clinton factory providing from 42 to 48 per cent of the total.

Though sales were higher in the earlier years, the financial returns to owners were greater in the latter, as in the first period Fairbanks was carefully building up the surplus of the new company by returning the large part of the earnings to the business. Total profits from 1900 to 1913 were over $7,300,000, not including the large sums for new buildings and machinery paid out as current expenses.

Net income varied from $248,000 in 1900, an unusually low year, to

$736,000 in 1913, an unusually high period, with the average $520,000. This income came from two sources: operation and interest. After 1905 the latter usually amounted to over $100,000, or 20 per cent of the total. In a poor year like 1912 it accounted for 33 per cent or $139,000 out of $415,000. The year 1913 was extraordinary. Interest earnings reached a peak of $146,000. More startling was the fact that with output down about 15 to 20 per cent and sales off 15 per cent, the company had the largest operating profit in its history, $589,000. Inventory profits may be the explanation.

TABLE 25

BIGELOW CARPET COMPANY

Sales   1901 to 1913

1901	$5,051,514.97	1908	$4,986,450.62
1902	6,204,367.06	1909 b	5,780,916.85
1903	6,445,126.54	1910	6,468,347.48
1904 a	6,918,387.04	1911	5,835,565.35
1905	6,444,120.56	1912	6,170,966.59
1906	6,800,510.75	1913	5,252,015.66
1907	6,345,439.50		

a Fifteen months. From 1901 to 1903 the sales years ran from November 1 to October 31. In 1904, the sales year was shifted to end on January 31, thus the period covered from November 1, 1903, to January 31, 1905.
b Eleven months. In 1909 the sales year was made to correspond with the calendar year.

Source: Bigelow Carpet Company, Journal A, *passim*; Bigelow Carpet Company, Journal B, *passim*.

In the early years before earnings built up a surplus, the company relied on outside financial aid. Though the 1899 merger itself had not involved any such assistance, as soon as it was completed, Fairbanks was authorized to borrow against a mortgage-bond issue of not more than $1,250,000.[37] The first of January, 1900, the company made an agreement for the mortgage with the Boston Safe Deposit & Trust Company. Actually only $750,000 worth of 4½ per cent bonds were issued, and instead of waiting for ten years Fairbanks began to retire them in July, 1902, completing the transaction six months later.[38]

Undoubtedly the firm did considerable short-term borrowing for current business in the first years, the Second National Bank of Boston being the source of some support. Whether such transactions continued is not apparent. As Fairbanks worked off the Lowell legacy of indebtedness, year-end payables declined from $685,000 in 1900 to $8,000 in 1913.

These resources were used to a decreasing degree to finance inventories and receivables. Since the fixed investment remained almost stationary, the additional funds went into cash and securities. Fairbanks started in 1899 with $115,000 in cash and ended in June, 1913, with $1,900,000, plus an additional $1,600,000 in bonds and loans on call.

F. S. Moseley & Company handled most of the carpet firm's outside investments. In 1904, $97,500 was put into New York Central bonds, $100,-

000 in American Telephone & Telegraph, and $50,000 in the Chicago, Rock Island & Pacific. By 1910 the surplus was going into loans to cities and industrials, the former receiving a total of $600,000. In addition Amoskeag, Blake Brothers, and Pacific Mills were using $100,000 each.[39] These investments, while safe, were not high income producers and they did not return as much as the money utilized in the carpet business.

Why was not more put into the manufacturing end? Of the possibilities for expanded production, ingrain was on the way out. The demand for brussels was declining nationally; wilton demand was increasing but it did not have a large-volume market. The volume markets were tapestry, velvet, and axminster. The first two required a new process and, with such giants as Alexander Smith, Hartford, and Sanford in the field, they offered no inducement for any new large-scale venture. For axminster, Fairbanks did build a new mill. It appears he might have done more, but perhaps that would have required entrance into a lower quality and more cut-throat market. The treasurer put out considerable sums in modernizing, which indicates that he was not averse to spending. The more probable explanation of his pyramiding reserves is that he believed in modest dividends and in high liquidity; moreover, there were no overwhelming opportunities which a conservatively oriented management could just not ignore. The failure to acquire broad axminster looms can possibly be explained on the grounds of the immediate competition to be met. The closest rivals of high-quality axminster rugs of the Bigelow company were brussels and wiltons. In these lines seamed rugs still dominated the output, since a satisfactory brussels broad loom had not yet been invented.

In summary, net working capital advanced from $1,800,000 in 1900 to $6,100,000 in 1913 and liquidity ratios spiraled. Cash and receivable balances rose by roughly $4,100,000 from 1900 to December, 1913, while bonds and debts were paid off to the extent of about $1,100,000. These funds were provided by the releasing of over $800,000 from inventories and by the addition of $4,400,000 from earnings (see Appendix 2). In addition some $3,000,000 was paid out to the owners. Fairbanks started with a $2.00 dividend in 1900. Thereafter he paid $5.00 a year until January, 1908, when he added another $1.00. The next year he raised the dividend to two regular payments of $3.00 and an extra of $2.00 or a total of $8.00.

These dividend payments were not much in excess of high-grade bond yields when considered in relation to the high market price of the security. The stock, which sold at 95 to 98 in 1900 and 1901, reached 120 in 1906. The panic year plunged the value downward—to 103 by mid-1908—despite the additional dividend. Thereafter the asking price rose until it reached 170 in 1912. Since the "informed opinion" was that the company had a bad year in 1913—despite record-making profits—the market value fell off to 145. At the latter figure, $8.00 a share was but a 5½ per cent return.

Despite these fluctuations, the stock was not actively bought and sold.

With its steady dividend, and with large liquid assets behind each share, Bigelow was eagerly sought—and held—as a sound investment. In 1901 only 384 shares were sold in 27 transactions with the largest a 56-share deal.

The owners thus registered their approval of Fairbanks' conduct of the business. On almost every phase of Fairbanks' administration diverse comment might be made. Thus he was wise in his modernization program and in his expansion of axminster, but he did not act on the trend toward seamless rugs, and Bigelow's increased axminster production did not keep pace with the national gain. With surplus funds it looks as if he might have done more. In effect he was gradually liquidating the business and holding the funds in reserve.

In marketing, Fairbanks had the funds to spend on advertising and on inventories, but he did not have an aggressive, pioneering organization. Only in 1913 did he take steps to rectify that condition. In mitigation it might be said that he produced on contract and for the upper-middle classes who would not scan the mail-order catalogues but who would go to a quality store like Arnold, Constable for furnishings and advice. But times were changing, and Whittall's success showed the rewards of a more dynamic approach.

There is no evidence on which to base a judgment on Fairbanks' efficiency as a purchasing man or on Bigelow's relative cost position. In labor matters Fairbanks was content to let the mill agents deal with the employees as in the past. There was no burst of paternalism as at Hartford. In Clinton all was quiet. At Lowell where conditions were very different, the company had more difficulty. Whether the trouble in 1907 and 1908 was handled wisely is questionable, but the incident had no sequel.

In financial matters the over-cautious and relatively unproductive use of excess funds might well be questioned. However, Fairbanks had created a highly liquid property. In place of the considerable indebtedness inherited from the Lowell Manufacturing Company, he had built up large surpluses, at the same time rebuilding his mills and paying adequate dividends. In an era when many corporations were running to bankers, he was one of the industrial capitalists who built up the internal financial strength of his concern. Having served his apprenticeship during the depression-ridden years of the last quarter of the nineteenth century, he built so that his company might survive any crisis, might take any emergency in stride, might have readily available the resources necessary to make any rapid adaptations. If he did not move as fast as more aggressive men in the industry, he provided the means for a successor so to do.

It was in the matter of succession that Fairbanks failed, as Lyman, Higgins, Houston had failed before him and as Sanford was to fail in the future. Of Fairbanks' three sons, one had died, one had been taken ill, and one had been slated to take over the Clinton Wire Cloth Mill. Among Fairbanks' directors there was not a single operating man—all of them had other interests with prior calls on their energies. Finally Fairbanks' assistants in the carpet business were few—and both his production manager, Wadeley, and his sales manager, Kline, had been connected with the firm but a short time.

Early in March, 1914, Fairbanks died. His son, Charles, not only declined the post of treasurer but was eager to sell the family holdings. With Thomas P. Beal, president of the Second National Bank of Boston, temporarily installed as treasurer,[40] a committee made up of Lyman, Beal, and Hutchins was appointed to work out the destinies of the two mills. As one of the committeemen, Arthur T. Lyman of the Lowell mill was faced with the irony of seeking, for the second time in fifteen years, a solution to the lack of management succession in his carpet enterprise.

Among those approached by the Bigelow committee were the banking house of Moseley and Kidder, Peabody. Both firms were old hands in the carpet business. Furthermore, Moseley, as counsel for the investment of Bigelow's surplus funds, had a close insight into the condition of the corporation. From this association and from the publicly known facts about the company's financial and physical status—the undervalued plant, the large surplus, the high liquidity—Moseley and Kidder, Peabody reached two conclusions.

First, they decided that the company had a surplus of funds; it was "overcapitalized" in the sense that it was not using its funds efficiently. Part of the capital on which it was paying a regular $8.00 dividend it was investing in ultra-conservative securities which were yielding 4 to 5 per cent. Two courses of action presented themselves: the carpet business could be expanded to use the funds and thus give a higher yield, or almost a quarter of Bigelow's capitalization could be drained off without affecting the company's operations in the slightest, though it would mean that for funds for future expansion and replacement and even for unusual current expenses the company would have to rely on bankers.

Secondly, Moseley and Kidder, Peabody saw that the steadiness of the return had practically put Bigelow stockholders in the preferred class with no risks. By converting a sizable proportion of the common into 6 per cent preferred, the bankers could free the remainder of the earnings for the common stockholders.

While these were the primary considerations, the bankers had to look beyond the immediate deal and provide for personnel to operate the valuable property. The solution to this problem was the Hartford management with which Kidder, Peabody and Moseley had such close connections.

From the Hartford point of view the proposed alliance with Bigelow had advantages of reputation, product line, marketing contacts, and labor. If time had tarnished Bigelow's pioneering spirit, it had not besmirched its name as a quality leader. Furthermore, its strong axminster and wilton line complemented Hartford's preponderance in tapestry and velvet. The Bigelow contract business and connections with better stores would help the promotion of Hartford Saxony, and competition would be reduced in this high-priced field. Finally since Clinton was the only factory in the country using women weavers on brussels and wiltons, it had favorable labor costs.[41]

Despite these benefits it is unlikely that Hartford would have initiated the project. On the whole, the merger of these two enterprises would seem to have been the result of the financiers' wish to grasp a profitable opportunity rather than a desire by the carpet-makers themselves to limit competition by absorbing a rival.

The first public indication that a major change was being contemplated for the old Bigelow enterprise came with the display of pronounced strength in the company's stock in early May. The *Boston News Bureau* explained the rise in value on the basis that, with the death of the conservative Fairbanks, investors were expecting larger dividends.[42] By the end of the month negotiations had progressed to the point where the bankers wanted a detailed survey of the plants by experts, and the secret could no longer be kept. As a countercheck two appraisals were made, one by Small, Nichols & Company, and the other by A. D. Higgins, Lyford, and other members of the Hartford management. Immediately the papers in Hartford, Springfield, and Boston, were full of the wildest rumors. They speculated on terms and quoted values with assurance. They moved mills in and out of towns with the greatest ease. They imagined that the talk of merger ranged beyond Hartford and Bigelow to include Smith and Whittall. In reply Beal was categoric. He had had no negotiations with Hartford—which in a strict sense was true—but he had had a tentative offer from quite another source.[43]

A few days later, on June 9, the formal offer was made by Kidder, Peabody and Moseley. Though there is no Bigelow balance sheet for the spring of 1914, judging from the previous ones, and from the eventual arrangements, the assets were probably roughly as follows:

Cash, securities and receivables	$5,368,100
Inventories	1,041,100
Plant and equipment	2,456,800
	$8,866,000

The bankers suggested to the directors that they vote the regular $3.00 dividend and an additional $50 one. After this was done, Moseley and Kidder, Peabody would buy the shares at $175 apiece. With the prospect

Amsterdam Plant; spread along bank of the Chuctenunda Creek from which original power was obtained

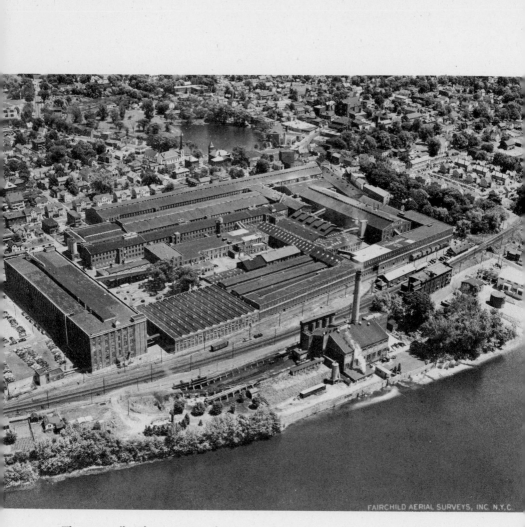

FAIRCHILD AERIAL SURVEYS, INC. N.Y.C.

Thompsonville Plant; power plant near Connecticut River; other buildings across railroad track arranged in compact order

of receiving $228 in cash for what a few months before had been worth in the market but $150, the directors heartily recommended the deal to the stockholders. At the same time the directors sent out a statement reassuring customers, salesmen, and employees that the sale of Bigelow's two mill properties would in no way change their operations as carpet producers. The new owners "will hope to retain the valuable services of the heads of the various departments, the superintendents and employees and to satisfy its many customers as in the past and in every way to maintain the Company's prestige in the trade." [44]

By July 22, 1914, more than the requisite number of stockholders had agreed to sell their shares to the bankers. At their final meeting on that date the old officers and directors formally transferred the stock, paid $15,019 to Hutchins & Wheeler for professional services, and $10,000 to Beal for his tour of duty, and then one by one resigned.[45]

The new owners, Kidder, Peabody and Moseley, now had a property with a book value roughly as follows:

	Value	Value per Share
Cash, securities, and receivables	$3,232,200	$ 80
Plant, equipment, and inventories	3,497,900	86
	$6,730,100	$166

They had paid $175 a share, however. The difference lay in undervalued inventories which Moseley and Kidder, Peabody now more than doubled to $2,750,000.

These calculations made, the bankers turned to a syndicate which they had organized early in June and of which they, themselves, were managers and participants. On July 22 the syndicate offered to buy the plant, equipment and inventories, and $250,000 in cash for $5,762,900, less a commission of $604,500. This would partially reimburse Kidder, Peabody and Moseley since it would provide the bankers with $143 a share minus the $15 commission or a net of $128.[46] At the same time it would leave them the undistributed cash, securities, and receivables: $2,982,200 or $74 a share. When the affairs were finally wound up, the bankers, who had paid $175 a share, had received $128 from the syndicate and had retained $74—or $202 a share. The gross profit was about $1,088,-100. But this figure was well above the net. Part of the figure represented a book profit which arose when Moseley and Kidder, Peabody, as members of the syndicate, had paid a paper figure to themselves as owners of the Bigelow assets.

The syndicate meanwhile had incorporated the Bigelow Carpet Corporation at an authorized $13,550,000, of which $5,500,000 was preferred and $8,050,000 common stock. Not all of this stock was immediately issued, however, much of it being held in reserve should the new company de-

cide to acquire the Hartford properties. The amount which was issued—
$3,000,000 in 6 per cent preferred and $3,550,000 in common—was sold, at
least in substantial part, to investors by the syndicate. Of the 35,500 common shares, 3,000 went to Kidder, Peabody for the $250,000 cash which
they had provided at the time of the sale of the property to the syndicate.
Exclusive of this payment for cash advanced, the syndicate had received
stock to the par value of $6,250,000 in return for a little over $5,100,000.
If the issues, when marketed to the public, sold at par this would represent
a 20 per cent profit, including commission.

The preferred stock was snatched up almost before it was issued,[47] and
the outlook for the common was good. The average profit for 1901 to
1912 was $520,000. If these earnings were to continue, the return on the
new common would be 9 per cent. The increase in operating efficiency,
which the promoters confidently expected to materialize, would bring
even greater returns. Before the common could be marketed, however,
World War I shut down the stock exchange.

This did not diminish the activity of the bankers. Perkins was elected
president and Alvin D. Higgins vice-president of the Bigelow Carpet Corporation. Though this move provided the concern with the needed management, it was a clumsy device and immediately plans for the final
merger were drawn. On August 4, Perkins briefed his Hartford directors,
according to the records: [48]

As far as he [Perkins] and the Hartford Company were concerned, there
was absolutely no agreement or commitment in any way regarding the possible
consolidation. . . . He further stated as an officer in the Hartford Company
and its largest stockholder that he believed it for the best interest of the Hartford Company to join the Bigelow Company in consolidation. He believed that
such a consolidation would lead to large economies in the distribution of goods
and the operations of the plants. He also stated that this consolidation if made,
would represent an output of between $12,000,000 and $13,000,000, that he
estimated that the Carpet industry of the Country was $70,000,000 to $75,000,-
000 per annum, and that there was one corporation [Alexander Smith presum-
ably] now in existence which sold as much, if not more. . . . He . . . stated
that more than ⅔ of the business of each company was supplemental to the
other, and in no sense competitive: that as to the competitive business, which
was less than ⅓, he did not consider the removal of such competition as existed,
as a factor of any considerable means in his conclusions, that the main advantages from a union of the two companies, would be the saving on overhead
charges. . . . The new Bigelow Corporation have $3,000,000 of net quick
assets, lands, building, machinery and water power assessed for $3,450,000
and valued by the Associated Mutual Companies at an excess of $4,900,000 not
including the water power, land and foundation, worth $600,000. . . . The
Hartford's quick assets . . . would be slightly less than $3,000,000 net. Their
plants had an appraisal value of about $4,000,000. Mr. Perkins stated, regard-
less of what past earnings of the Bigelow were, he was entirely satisfied that if
the Hartford and Bigelow combined, they could make more money, and more
money than if they were run as separate corporations.

The directors were convinced, and a month later, on September 10, the "Plan and Agreement" for the purchase and consolidation of Hartford and Bigelow was signed and sent out to Hartford owners.[49] A committee of three—Perkins, Bosworth, and Squire, representing certain large stockholders—was set up to carry out the scheme, and on October 13 it offered to purchase all the property and assets of the Hartford Carpet Corporation for 45,000 shares of the common stock of Bigelow Carpet Corporation and $2,000,000 in cash plus certain sums to take care of outstanding dividends. By these terms each holder of one share of Hartford common, currently selling for 116, would receive 1½ shares of Bigelow common. The Hartford preferred holders would take a loss since they received just $100 in cash when the market value was $120. However, since the preferred was callable at par, they had no recourse.

The stockholders—most of whose proxies were held by Perkins, Bosworth, Squire, and A. D. Higgins—accepted the proposal. The committee of three then sold the plant and assets of the Hartford Corporation to the Bigelow Carpet Corporation for 45,000 shares of common stock and 25,000 shares of preferred. With the completion of this transaction the name of the Bigelow Carpet Corporation was changed to Bigelow-Hartford Carpet Company.

Since the group behind the committee of three paid $2,000,000 in cash for Hartford preferred and received 25,000 shares of Bigelow preferred, which they were almost certain would market at full value, here was a chance for a profit of half a million—reduced of course by the amount of the original Hartford 7 per cent preferred they already held as investors. The amount of this reduction is impossible to determine; on the basis of the holdings in 1901, it would seem safe to conclude that the bankers and their close friends were rather small holders of the preferred and consequently stood to gain appreciably.

Thus the fourth important merger (including the Tariffville-Hartford) in the history of the present Bigelow-Sanford Carpet Company was completed. The new Bigelow-Hartford Carpet Company was the third largest concern incorporated in New England, following the American Woolen and Amoskeag in size.[50] Where in 1913 before the merger the total capitalization of Bigelow-Hartford had been $9,030,000, at the end of 1914 it was $13,550,000. Not only was the capitalization thus increased by $4,520,000 but around $5,000,000 in highly liquid assets had been drained off. Yet the underlying properties, especially those owned by Bigelow, had been so undervalued that $13,550,000 proved to be not excessive. With previous combined profits equal to $1,000,000, the common gave promise of earning about 9 per cent. Thus, though the amalgamation was the result of Bigelow's urgent need and the bankers' grasp of profit possibilities, the latter had created a company sound financially, and sound in management.

CHAPTER 10

THE BIGELOW–HARTFORD CARPET
COMPANY, 1914–1924

During the months while the Bigelow-Hartford Corporation was being formed, a great war had broken out in Europe and no man could calculate its effects on business in the United States and in the world. Early in the war wool prices began to rise and for the next several years they were to mount spectacularly. More critical still to the manufacture of carpets was the shortage of dyestuffs which occurred as foreign sources were cut off from American users.[1]

With these external problems to be faced by the new Bigelow-Hartford management there were also internal details of consolidation to be worked out: questions of inventory values, of personnel, and of plant and equipment. Since the Bigelow-Hartford directors and officers were drawn chiefly from the Hartford Carpet Corporation and the Boston banker groups, it is not remarkable that Hartford personnel should have been selected instead of those of the Bigelow company. Men naturally select as subordinates those individuals with whose ability they are already familiar. Especially important in this case, moreover, was the Bigelow company's lack of adequate managerial material, one of the reasons underlying its owners' willingness to sell their company.[2]

No effort seems to have been exerted to make clear to the employees just how the change in corporate organization would affect them. Yet probably, for the majority, no great alterations came immediately. The mills of the Bigelow Carpet Company at Lowell and Clinton and that of the Hartford corporation at Thompsonville continued to operate as business warranted, at least for the time being, so that any fears suffered by the mill operatives must have been quickly dissipated. While closing the Lowell mill was under discussion at the time of consolidation, no public mention of the question was made. It was not actually closed until

1916, so that a period of peace of mind was given to some, at least, of the Lowell operatives. But, elsewhere, reduction in the sales forces and office staffs followed consolidation; one of consolidation's traditional advantages is economy, including economy of personnel.

Reduction in the sales and office forces began as early as September, 1914. At that time John F. Norman assumed the duties of sales manager of the Bigelow company and continued to act in the same capacity for Hartford, until the merger should be completed. Henry P. Fairbanks, New York agent for Bigelow and a director of the Bigelow Carpet Corporation, resigned his agency in September and his directorship in January, 1915, thereby clearing the way for the new administration.[3] Six men were dropped from Bigelow's New York sales force, two from its Chicago staff, and two from its sales office in Boston. Nobody appears to have been dismissed from the Hartford organization.

Thus the two organizations were fused. From the Bigelow-Hartford Company's offices and salesrooms on the eighth and tenth floors of an office building at 25 Madison Avenue, New York, stretched out the lines of operation, into the district sales offices in Boston, Chicago, and San Francisco, marketing rugs and carpets to soften and brighten the floors of America. At the base of the pyramid, making the goods to sell, were the three mills at Thompsonville, Lowell, and Clinton.

One of the reasons given for the Bigelow-Hartford merger when it was announced in newspapers and trade publications was that, since the two companies had made different lines of rugs, their products henceforth would complement each other. This comment on the product lines was accurate only in a general way. The largest amount of Hartford output was in tapestries and velvets, which had not been made by the old Bigelow company; on the other hand, both companies had produced brussels and wilton floor coverings and the high-pile Hartford Saxony had been a wilton fabric that had been popular as a hotel carpeting. The question was one of emphasis: the Bigelow company had laid its stress on the more expensive types, brussels and wiltons, with 60 per cent of its looms devoted to those lines and the remainder to axminsters. Of the Hartford looms, 45 per cent had woven tapestry and velvet carpets and rugs in widths up to 12 feet; 37 per cent had made axminsters in widths up to nine feet; only the remaining 18 per cent had turned out wiltons in widths up to six feet.[4]

The three plants gave the consolidated company considerable weaving capacity. Thompsonville was by far the largest; its 125 wilton, 256 axminster, and 308 tapestry looms could weave 8,000,000 yards in a year. Next but much smaller in size was the Lowell mill; with 243 brussels and 155 axminster looms it was capable of producing 2,850,000 yards annually, and its various departments employed about 2,000 operatives when the mill was running full. Clinton was about the same size; it had a maximum labor group of about 1,600, it had 185 brussels and wilton and 134 axminster looms, and its yearly output could rise to 2,300,000 yards. All three plants had spinning equipment, dyehouses, railroad connections, and adequate sources of power.

The general superintendent of the three mills, Alvin D. Higgins, continued to live at Thompsonville where he had managed the plant for the Hartford company. His son-in-law, William E. Lyford, became superintendent of that plant, and John Davidson, manager of Thompsonville's axminster department before the amalgamation, was sent to Clinton to take charge of the mill there. There were clerical sections in the New York office for each plant; in that office, too, were the headquarters of Higgins' counterpart in sales, John F. Norman, who directed a group of 36 salesmen. Most of the company's products were sold through wholesalers.

In broad outline, this was the Bigelow-Hartford Carpet Company when the merger was an accomplished fact and combined operations were under way. After the inevitable arguments over property values had been settled, the asset valuation and liability to stockholders were satisfactorily resolved. At the end of 1914 the company's total assets amounted to $15,500,000. With a net working capital position of $6,110,000 and a ratio of current assets to current liabilities of 4.5 to 1, Bigelow-Hartford possessed adequate financial strength to begin its new corporate life.

PROGRESS AND PROSPERITY

The final months of 1914 were a confusing period for the floor-covering industry. Higher wool prices had led several manufacturers, Hartford among them, to raise the prices of their products in September in the first of what was to become a series of war-caused price increases. Then, in November, Alexander Smith & Sons held one of its plaguing auctions and sold $4,000,000 worth of carpets and rugs, much more than at any previous sale. But, while volume at the Smith auction was up, prices fell as the sale progressed. A looked-for improvement in the Christmas retail trade failed to materialize, and the year ended with buyers delaying to place orders.[5]

Some degree of comfort, some indication of stability was offered in the midst of uncertainty when Bigelow-Hartford reported a profit for the last quarter of 1914 of $312,000. Meeting in January, 1915, the directors decided that this profit was ample to permit payment of dividends on the preferred stock from its date of issue, at the prescribed rate of 6 per cent, and on the common from October 13, 1914, to January 1, 1915, at an annual rate of 5 per cent.[6]

The results of 1914's operations, even though these covered only a short period, seemed to show that the company was off to a good start. While the quarterly profit undoubtedly reflected the initial momentum given the new organization by its predecessors, it also derived from the positive steps taken after the merger. Sales Manager John F. Norman was a keen salesman, a domineering, pushing enthusiast who demanded results from the men under him—and seems to have obtained them.[7]

With a high level of sales in view steps were taken to expand production capacity. The mill at Thompsonville, probably because of its size, its relative modernity (80 per cent of its buildings had been erected since 1901), and its comparative proximity to New York, received attention first. In August, 1915, additions were begun: a new steam turbine was installed; looms were moved from Lowell bringing the number of wiltons up to 250; additional freight handling facilities, including a new depot, were erected in 1916; and a huge coal pocket was built in 1917.[8]

With the Lowell looms came many of the five hundred operators they required, and with both came rumors that Bigelow-Hartford intended to stop manufacturing in Lowell. These rumors the company at first denied.[9] In February, 1916, however, the directors took formal steps to sell the Lowell factory through an agent and, when the agent was unsuccessful, they advertised it for sale. "The move," said the company's announcement,[10] was "due to the desire to concentrate the respective mill equipment of the two former companies so as to obtain maximum output at highest efficiency."

Since Thompsonville and Clinton could be expanded and operated under existing supervisory forces, savings in overhead were obviously possible. A number of the looms remaining at Lowell were narrow and useless in view of the trend toward wider carpeting, so that there was little point in operating them if the other mills could satisfy demand. More than that, the Hartford management claimed to have found the Lowell plant to have been inefficient and poorly maintained.[11]

It was a pity, perhaps, to sever the eighty-nine-year connection between company and city but poor business to continue it. So the plant was closed, without much notice in the newspapers which at that time were preoccupied with war news, and without apparent regret on the part of city or workers. Fortunately for the last group, Lowell, an industrial center of more than 100,000 inhabitants, was busy with war production and the Bigelow-Hartford employees who did not move to continue their trade at Thompsonville or Clinton had no serious re-employment problem.

The Clinton mill also received attention. The directors approved the erection of a new building there in 1915, and John Davidson supervised its equipment while he made himself familiar with the plant of which he had so lately become superintendent. In the summer of 1917 the dyehouse was extensively repaired and enlarged.[12] The war led Bigelow-Hartford at the same time to convert some of the Clinton looms to the manufacture of cotton duck for the federal government.[13]

While these steps were being taken and before the United States entered the war, Bigelow-Hartford met strenuous marketing competition both of product and of price. To fight this the company turned to new product development and to changes in designs and colors to suit the changing demands of consumer taste. Old products were dropped, others reduced in output, and new ones added.

The desire to give customers what they wanted when they wanted it was, of course, the basic reason for the expansion of production facilities. Norman believed firmly in customer service and he took advantage of A. D. Higgins' work in manufacturing to increase the services offered by Bigelow. New emphasis was placed on both the cut-carpet and contract sales departments and the company announced that it was prepared to offer greater service in each.[14] By 1918 Bigelow claimed that it was operating the largest cut-carpet department in the world, shipping all such orders from the plant at Clinton.[15]

Both the Bigelow and the Hartford company had been active before the merger in the sale of contract goods to hotels, theaters, office buildings, ships—wherever handsome appearance and long-wearing quality were essential—and 1914 had been a record year for such sales.[16] These contracts were almost invariably obtained by co-operation with a dealer or a jobber who would know local construction matters and would submit bids for large carpeting contracts. Bigelow-Hartford's co-operation with its local supplier might take the form of assisting in the design of special merchandise, of providing technical information on the types of floor coverings best suited for the project, and of enabling the bidder to quote an attractively low price. For the latter reason, the contracts were not always highly profitable but they served to keep looms at work for long periods. The company's management, aware of the contribution to overhead and to steadier production made by contract business therefore actively encouraged it, and Bigelow-Hartford became the industry's leader in this field.

The list of contract customers throughout the war and into the early 1920's, when hotel building was reaching its height and the growing American love of luxury was demanding satisfaction, is a fascinating record of the country's social and commercial activity. The list included the Argentine battleship *Rivadavia,* the steamship *Leviathan,* the Hotel Statler in Buffalo, the Commodore Hotel in New York, the Los Angeles Biltmore, New York's Saks-Fifth Avenue Store and Capital Theatre, the Pullman Company, and many others. Almost alone among carpet companies, Bigelow was to be found exhibiting regularly at hotel shows and expositions.

But sales to domestic consumers accounted for by far the largest pro-

portion of the Bigelow-Hartford business. Here the fickle finger of fashion
pointed, now this way, now that, for style trends in the carpet industry
were no easier to develop, anticipate, or predict than those in home furnishings generally. Sometimes Bigelow continued to manufacture a weave
or a style long after it had passed its peak of popularity, at other times
the company attempted to influence demand by introducing and encouraging the sales of textures, designs, or colors different from those of
other companies. These were not always accepted by the buying public,
but "bloomers," as such mistakes were called by the industry, had to be
risked for the sake of leadership.

Certain aspects of popular taste in floor coverings were apparent at
the time of the Bigelow-Hartford merger and just after. Just as ingrain
had fallen from demand so the looped-pile fabrics which had succeeded it
in favor in their turn were displaced by axminsters, wiltons, and velvets.
There were also specialty products which rose and fell in popularity.

In addition to weave changes there had developed from 1899 a market
for seamless rugs woven on broad looms. Because a really satisfactory
wilton broad loom was not developed until the late 1920's, the production
of seamless rugs was confined to axminster and tapestry fabrics. Since the
old Bigelow company had devoted the bulk of its production to high-
quality brussels and wiltons, it is perhaps not surprising that its management did not make extensive purchases of broad looms for its rather small
axminster business. Most of the operations of the old Hartford company,
however, had been in the tapestry and axminster areas. Apparently the
Hartford management was not convinced that broad looms were a significant new development. From 1906 to 1913 the Hartford company had
bought 116 narrow axminster looms and only one broad axminster loom
and had made purchases of tapestry looms in which narrow looms also had
predominated. The total looms of the Bigelow-Hartford company in 1914,
excluding ingrain, were 1,406, of which only 46 or less than 5 per cent,
were broad looms.[17]

Until the war made itself felt, however, it is unlikely that the company
found itself at any serious disadvantage. The introduction of closed automobile bodies had created a new market for woven floor coverings which
could be met with 27-inch tapestry or velvet. Tapestry and velvet rugs,
moreover, were sold to consumers who could not afford more expensive
products and who would accept cheaper seamed rugs.[18] But unfortunately for Bigelow-Hartford, the rising cost of labor was soon to make
tapestry and velvet products, in which labor was the largest single component, too expensive in relation to their quality.

The new Bigelow-Hartford company had greater success with another
trend. The oriental rug had continued to be popular with those consumers
who could pay for it, and there were large groups of buyers who could

not afford the real oriental but who wished to obtain the next best thing. The Bigelow company had acquired a strong reputation among carpet buyers for the excellence of its oriental reproductions and Bigelow-Hartford continued to merit the reputation. Companies vied with each other over the design of more and more exotic patterns. One of those made by Bigelow-Hartford, its Ispahan Number 621, was sold in 1916 with a key from which purchasers could learn the meaning of the many Eastern symbols which adorned it.[19]

Such ventures into the realm of the exotic became less common as the war continued. The inevitable result of the shortage in materials and of higher costs was product simplification. Too much money was being tied up in a huge and diversified inventory. The increase in "bills payable" in Bigelow-Hartford's balance sheets during the war indicates that its finances were so strained by the high cost of materials that it was not paying its bills as promptly as before. Cutting inventories offered an opportunity to reduce indebtedness and any opportunity to do so was probably seized.

After an initially depressing effect on prices, the war brought about a sellers' market in which cost increases could be passed on to consumers without much adverse effect, at least in the short run. Price rises were generally announced when the spring and fall lines were introduced to the trade buyers but they were also made at such other times as circumstances warranted. Bigelow-Hartford, for instance, raised prices on January 13, 1916, and then sent them up again on January 27, the result of steeply soaring costs. Its competitors followed Bigelow's lead.

Price leadership, as in past years, was held by Alexander Smith & Sons and was established by that company's auctions. Never popular with other manufacturers and a source of irritation to wholesalers and retailers because of their uncertain time and frequency, these auctions were held throughout the war, except in 1918 when Smith was busy with military contracts. Much to the industry's surprise, in April, 1915, Stephen Sanford & Sons held the first auction it had had for years, at the same time as a Smith sale and as a move against it. Sanford's auction was not a success and was not repeated;[20] other companies left the field to Smith. After the lapse in 1918, Smith resumed its sales in the spring of 1919.[21]

Manufacturers, including Smith, either awaited the results of these auctions before announcing list prices or else adjusted previously announced lists in accordance with prices obtained at the sale. The auctions could not completely determine price structures since Smith lacked capacity to supply the entire demand, but they were a powerful barometer. In some years only one auction sale might be held; in others there might be several, as frequently as one month apart for three or four months.

Smith's ownership was so closely held that its management could keep its mills running at full capacity, knowing that the group of family shareholders could, at least temporarily, absorb any losses the company might suffer in the auctions. As far as that goes, Smith's profits can only be guessed at in view of the nature of its ownership group but the company was regarded as generally successful and as the largest carpet manufacturer in the country. The exact order of size before 1914 is uncertain but it seems likely to have been Smith, Bigelow-Hartford, and Sanford.

Smith was not always the leader in price changes. Bigelow-Hartford appears often to have been the between-auction pace-setter. In general, when one or another of the major manufacturers announced price changes, all of its competitors followed to some extent. In this period of a sellers' market, there were naturally no price wars.

Opening dates for trade showings were dependent on the Smith sales, and the lack of certainty as to when Smith intended to hold its auctions gave salesmen trouble in scheduling field trips. When the showing of fall goods in the spring of 1916 was delayed for this reason, Bigelow announced a definite date for its own display. The result, as reported in the *Carpet Journal*, was a successful showing in which all the mills participated and for which the company received praise from the industry. The Carpet Association of America, an organization of distributors, in 1917 asked store buyers to specify preferred opening dates, but there was no agreement among them. The Smith sales continued greatly to influence openings and prices for years, a situation about which the trade complained but over which it had no control.

Manufacturers could co-operate in other ways with greater success. In 1916, a committee of leading dyestuff users, including a representative of Bigelow-Hartford, met with the United States Department of State and the British and German ambassadors, to see whether safe conduct into the United States could be arranged for German dyes; it was moderately successful. Duties were placed on dyestuffs in the same year in order to encourage their manufacture in the United States,[22] the carpet industry having been loudly vocal in its urgings that this be done. In 1917 another committee, with John Norman and George Perkins as Bigelow representatives, went to Washington to urge that the 50 per cent ad valorem duty on certain seamless rugs be restored from the 20 per cent to which a recent court action had lowered it. The committee's recommendation was adopted.[23]

There were good reasons for mill managers to maintain close contact with the federal government, both as individuals and as a group. The American declaration of war in April, 1917, brought federal authorities into the market as exclusive purchasers of wool and other materials,[24] but this was not the major factor. Of greater significance, the government became, as it had shown signs of becoming even before war was declared, the mills' best customer.

America's entry into the war had a marked effect on Bigelow-Hartford's administration. President Perkins went on salaried leave of absence in November, 1917, as American Red Cross Commissioner to Italy; he was accompanied by Julius Roth, company purchasing agent. Perkins remained on active service until his return in January, 1919, with the exception of short visits to the United States. While he was away, active control of the company was exercised by the general sales manager, John F. Norman, who became a director, a member of the Executive Committee of the board (set up in 1916 to aid the president), and vice-president.[25]

Norman was the logical if not, indeed, the only man to run the company. A. D. Higgins, the general manufacturing superintendent, had died in November, 1916, and had been succeeded by his son-in-law, William E. Lyford, who had been manager of the Thompsonville mill. Not much more than one year later, Lyford was compelled by serious illness to retire; responsibility for the Clinton and Thompsonville plants was divided between the office and production managers in each mill in April, 1918.[26] The only other Bigelow-Hartford executive who was senior to Norman, Treasurer George Perkins, died in 1917 and was replaced by the company's cashier, Frank H. Deknatel. To have brought in an outsider when the president's absence was only a leave would have been inappropriate.

Norman promptly proceeded to seek government business for the Bigelow-Hartford mills, with some success. In May, 1918, the executive committee met to discuss a proposed contract for 20,000 blankets, which could be woven on carpet looms; but Bigelow lacked the necessary serging, fulling, and napping machinery to finish them properly. Since Norman intended to seek further contracts for blankets, the committee decided to purchase enough machinery to equip Thompsonville for this purpose and then, if additional contracts were actually forthcoming, expend not more than $25,000 on additional equipment.[27]

Before the Armistice on November 11, 1918, the company wove and finished 80,000 wool and wool-and-cotton blankets. In addition, its looms produced more than 400,000 yards of duck. Clinton executed many contracts for the spinning of worsted and woolen yarns, and Thompsonville spun large quantities of woolen yarn for the American Red Cross, to be used principally in sweaters. More than 4,000,000 pounds of yarn were made for use by other manufacturers, and about 100,000 pounds of raw wool were scoured for similar purposes.[28]

From 1915 onward, as American factories picked up momentum and employment increased, the carpet companies had difficulty keeping their workers from better paying jobs in other industries. Such a situation led inevitably to wage increases by the carpet-makers and to increased employee benefits. Smith, which had cut wages in 1913, restored the cut in August, 1915. Bigelow-Hartford also raised wages in November, 1915, from 6 to 10 per cent.[29] Such wage increases do not seem to have been the result of union pressures, for the only workers in the carpet industry who were unionized at that time were the jacquard or wilton weavers. Possibly competition for operatives was the basic reason: Thompsonville, for instance, is close to both Springfield, Massachusetts, and Hartford, Connecticut, and these cities offered lucrative employment in a number of factories. Bigelow granted five pay raises to Thompsonville employees between June, 1916, and June, 1918. In Clinton, a loom fixer who had received $20 weekly in 1913 saw his earnings go to $22 in 1916 and to $40 by 1919, while a spare hand with a weekly wage of $9.00 in 1913 was earning $13.50 by 1919, for the same or fewer hours worked.[30]

Much of the responsibility for employee relations rested on the individual mill superintendent and was to remain there for years, under systems not yet formalized by education or unionization. Wage increases were presumably determined by the factory superintendent in consultation with the president, for they were not recorded in the minutes of meetings of the executive committee or the board. The weakness or strength in this system, of course, was the mill superintendent, himself. In Clinton, labor relations were especially harmonious, an apparent reflection of an understanding local management.

During the war years the general trend for both sales and profits was upward. In 1915, the first full year of operations, Bigelow-Hartford's net sales amounted to $9,900,000. They rose substantially in 1916 to $12,000,-000; although that total was not reached again until 1919, the company earned better than 8 per cent on sales during the five years from 1914.

The available sales and profits figures do not differentiate between that portion of the company's business which arose from sales to civilian consumers and that which was obtained through government contracts, but some evidence indicates that Bigelow-Hartford found its defense work profitable. At the end of 1918 the company's record showed that Clinton had in that year made $371,700 from its military business, and Thompsonville's profit from government work was $444,600.[31] The total profit for that year, civilian business included, was $1,700,000.

These sales and profits figures are a record of encouraging progress. Dividend payments were maintained throughout the years and the rate paid on the common stock was increased, in February, 1917, from 5 per cent to equal the 6 per cent paid on the preferred.[32] There had been little change in the company's over-all balance sheet position, as a glance at Appendix 5 will indicate, but this fact also reflected new strength. Presi-

dent Perkins, addressing the annual meeting of shareholders in 1919, could
refer to 1918 as a good year, could boast that the company was free of
debt and possessed plenty of working capital, and, in a new-fields-to-
conquer mood, could announce that it was considering the export trade.[33]

RECONVERSION: CHANGES IN LEADERSHIP AND MARKET

The venture into export trade contemplated in 1919 was never taken,
perhaps because postwar America provided Bigelow-Hartford with problems enough at home. Reconversion to full consumer production was made
more difficult by the changes in the management group which had occurred during the war and by the change in Perkins himself. The president
returned from war service in 1919 with Italian government citations testi-
fying to the value of his Red Cross work but with sadly impaired health.
He had developed a severe illness in Italy from which he never fully recovered; he died five years later at the age of sixty-three. His friends felt
that his death was in large measure due to his war experiences.[34]

It is apparent, moreover, that Norman exerted greater influence on
Bigelow's affairs after Perkins returned from Europe than before the latter
went abroad, almost as much as when Perkins was away. Perhaps this was
due to Perkins' poor health, perhaps to his wish to devote some of his
time to outside interests, or perhaps it was due to the postwar period's
emphasis on successful salesmanship; certainly everyone agreed that Norman was a superlative salesman.

From 1920 to 1922, according to the minutes of the executive committee, Perkins and Norman seem to have shared responsibility almost
equally; from 1922 onward Perkins, with failing health, became less active.
He continued, however, to provide intimate contact with the other directors, particularly the Boston bankers Rantoul and Winsor, and his long
association, his strong financial interest in the company, and his high personal qualities made his existence important to Bigelow until his death
severed the connection in 1924.

Indication of Norman's considered value to the company at this time is
shown by the details of an arrangement for compensation entered into with
the two men by the directors in March, 1919.[35] Under the terms of the arrangement, Perkins was to receive an annual salary of $50,000 and also 2½
per cent of the net profits for the current year, the latter payable in common stock unless the stock sold above par, in which case the company had
the right to pay in cash. Norman received a salary of $45,000 and the same
percentage of net profits, but, in his case, the agreement was to be effective from July 1, 1918, to cover part of the period of Perkins' absence. As
his bonus for the latter part of 1918 Norman received 225 shares of Bigelow-Hartford common stock.

A committee of directors was to decide what the net profits were, and

the agreement was renegotiated each year. As time passed and Norman
succeeded Perkins as president, this head of a moderate-sized company
was placed, by reason of his bonus arrangement, on an income parity with
the chief executives of some of America's largest corporations. On the basis
of the published profits in 1920 of $2,200,000, Norman's share was about
$56,000 which, with his salary, brought his income to more than $100,000.
In a comparatively few years the anomaly of the situation became apparent, but in 1919, presumably, no one on the directorate could have
imagined the heights that Bigelow-Hartford's profits would reach.[36]
Profit-sharing as a means of executive incentive was comparatively new
and its various implications had not been thoroughly explored. Moreover,
with a day of superselling dawning after the calm night spent in a sellers' market, Norman's value to Bigelow was highly rated.

Under Norman's vigorous direction Bigelow lost no time and spared
no expense in reconverting and expanding. As quickly as possible the
looms that had been manufacturing duck were turned back to carpet
production and new equipment was added. The frequency of requests for
appropriations in the minutes of the board of directors gives some indication of the purposefulness with which the problem of modernized manufacture was faced.

Costs continued to rise. A series of government wool auctions, beginning in December, 1918, brought more carpet wool to market and temporarily reduced prices somewhat, but the trade felt that the government
wool authority was still holding prices too high. Wool remained scarce,
and jute, another essential carpet ingredient, went up in cost and down
in quality.[37]

There was, therefore, no alternative for the mills but to increase prices,
even in the face of consumer conviction that these must fall to what they
fondly thought of as normal. A continuing series of price boosts in 1919
helped to disabuse buyers of that notion. The Smith auction in March
drew the greatest crowds on record and brought high prices for the 40,000
bales that were sold, mostly to retailers.[38] Sales soared throughout the remainder of the year and into 1920, and prices kept on going up.

By October, 1920, when the spring styles for 1921 were shown, the
public's resistance had stiffened. Most of the major mills put price cuts
into effect and, when a buyers' strike was in full swing by December, there
were other reductions.[39] Whatever force the consumer movement possessed, however, had not been enough to keep Bigelow from a record-
breaking sales volume, for 1920, of almost $20,000,000.[40] Unfortunately,
the company's lack of yardage production figures prevents a comparison
with earlier years that might help to indicate to what extent inflation was
responsible for the increase.

The domestic carpet industry was aided in this period of rising prices by the shortage and high cost of imported floor coverings. European mills were prevented, by war damage and by the greater extent to which they had been converted to war production, from returning to peacetime operations as quickly as those in the United States; as late as March, 1920, they could offer only costly and unpopular fabrics. Bigelow-Hartford, capitalizing on European difficulties, had by December, 1918, developed a substitute for unavailable hand-tufted rugs from Austria, and stressed the sale of this new product to hotels where long-wearing qualities were important. Oriental rugs were plentiful but their prices soared so that many a prospective oriental rug buyer was forced to accept an American-made substitute.[41]

Among the company's competitors an interesting development was the introduction by Alexander Smith in February, 1919, of a line of tweeds for men's and women's wear and for hats and caps.[42] This new departure by a carpet manufacturer was probably the result of wartime planning for alternative products in case the carpet market slumped. It does not seem to have been especially successful and Bigelow, with Smith's other rivals, stuck to carpet-making.

Of rather greater competitive significance in the domestic carpet industry was the formation in September, 1920, of Mohawk Carpet Mills.[43] Mohawk was an amalgamation of McCleary, Wallin & Crouse and of Shuttleworth Brothers, two successful manufacturers whose mills were in Amsterdam, New York, where the firm of Stephen Sanford & Sons was also located. Recognized as capable and efficient weavers, Mohawk mills had a valuable selling agent in W. & J. Sloane, the large New York wholesale and retail house and once Bigelow-Hartford's major customer. The new company had a capitalization of $5,000,000, slightly more than one-third that of Bigelow-Hartford. Mohawk was to prove an aggressive entrant in the race for industry and market supremacy.

The Mohawk merger was effected just in time for a depression in the carpet industry. The year 1921 was a bad one for American industry in general and carpet manufacturers in particular. The fall in prices that had begun in 1920 continued until, on May 1, 1921, an axminster rug that had sold at retail one year earlier for $89.50 brought only $59.50. This was representative, for the Federal Reserve Bank of Philadelphia, comparing wholesale rug prices in 1914, 1919, 1920, and 1921, cited them for these years as $45.50, $117, $101, and $79.50 for a 9 by 12 wilton, and $18, $45, $46.25, and $33.50 for an axminster of the same size.[44]

For a man like Norman, to whom selling was the breath of life, whose nature resented obstacles, to whom, moreover, any reduction in Bigelow's profits meant a lowering of his own substantial income, the situation in early 1921, whether readjustment or panic, must have been nearly intolerable. By February, only about 25 per cent of the country's carpet looms were active.[45] Buyers were awaiting lower prices, and general industrial unemployment was reducing consumer purchasing power.

At the end of February a 25 per cent reduction in wages of wilton weavers was announced by companies making that material, Bigelow-Hartford among them.[46] The result was a strike by the employees affected. Although unaffected by the wage cut, the dyehouse employees, equally independent, followed the wilton workers out of sympathy.

With no wool in process through the dyeing department, the remainder of the Thompsonville mill was compelled to close. Norman promptly proposed the eviction of those strikers who lived in company houses. J. W. Pierce, the mill superintendent, further aggravated matters by urging the foremen to man the looms to keep the plant going. The foremen construed Pierce's request as an attempt to make them into strikebreakers and they joined the protesting weavers.[47]

In the face of general conditions there was no chance of victory for the strikers. Most of them capitulated at the end of a month and were back at work on April 18. The wilton weavers did not return until August, when they, like the other employees, accepted a 20 per cent reduction in wages. Even the foremen were compelled to take lower salaries.[48] Workers in other companies also gave in, and by the end of 1922 the Wilton Union had ceased to be a force in the industry.[49] Not until another depression affected the country did carpet weavers move once more toward unionism.[50]

The 1921 strike at Thompsonville should be examined against the background of Bigelow-Hartford's postwar labor policy. The company had done a great deal to improve the working and living conditions of its operatives. Houses had been purchased or built in Thompsonville and Clinton to provide low-cost housing in a time of shortage. Money had been allocated for recreational facilities, such as bowling alleys. The services of a woman had been obtained to work in the schools and among the families of the Thompsonville workers to, "if possible, improve the moral and physical conditions" in the town.[51] Since old residents of Thompsonville emphasize the ebullience of pay nights in a town where saloons outnumbered churches and where the population was a mixture of Scots, English, Irish, Italian, and Polish, someone was needed, even if no one is certain of the social worker's success. However, no formal policy of employee benefits existed. There are records of such cases as that of the widow of William Sayres who, in October, 1919, was awarded $30 monthly in recognition of her husband's long and faithful service,[52] but what was done for the employees was always at the management's discretion.

The company, which had awarded higher wages during the war, had thought in 1921 that it could rightfully withdraw them if it saw fit. The workers had thought otherwise. Surprisingly, however, no perceptible rancor had lingered among the workers as a result of the strike. Within Bigelow-Hartford the 1921 strike had receded well in the background and was almost forgotten at the end of a few months. By October new company houses were under construction, and in April, 1923, business had improved sufficiently to warrant a 10 per cent wage increase in both Clinton and Thompsonville mills.

Between the strike's end and the restoration of the wage cut was a period of intense activity on the part of the carpet industry. The biggest building boom the country had seen sent houses, office buildings, hotels, and theaters mushrooming all over America, and the floors of a pleasing number were covered with Bigelow's Austrian tufted rugs or its Hartford Saxony carpet, back on the market after a war-induced absence. The rush to building was not limited to immobile objects: ships needed carpeting, so did automobiles, and in March, 1922, almost all of Bigelow-Hartford's departments were working overtime on contracts for the Pullman Company.[53]

There were, to be sure, occasional clouds in the sky. Congress had failed in 1919 to repeal the war-imposed luxury tax on carpets and rugs, and late in 1921 the carpet manufacturers were protesting the possibility of an additional tax on their products.[54] Life was somewhat eased for them when, after considerable representation in Washington, the Tariff Act of 1922 made importation of carpet wool conditionally free. It had, however, to be stored in bond and its use in carpet manufacture proved in order to qualify it for duty exemption.[55]

The general selling pattern remained the same but there were refinements and evidences of change. Smith continued its auctions, and prices rose again in 1922 and 1923, to fall early in 1924 and then rise by the end of the year.[56] Advertising became more extensive, in an effort to focus consumer preference on a brand or a maker's name. Bigelow-Hartford in 1922 prepared a series of advertisements in various sizes which were made available to dealers without charge, each advertisement prominently displaying the company's name; the dealer, of course, paid the cost of insertion. Expenditures for advertising rose from $39,000 in 1921 to $157,400 in 1924.[57] Included were outlays for a large electric sign on a New York building and for a motion picture showing how Bigelow-Hartford products were made.[58] At the showing of goods for the fall trade, Bigelow-Hartford displayed 17 rugs, 11 plain carpets, and 14 pattern goods.[59]

Sold by the new methods or by older promotional devices, the significant thing is that the carpets were sold. One device was to put a rug down in front of a store so that passers-by could walk on it and judge its wearing qualities. This method was especially popular during World War I. It was much used by M. J. Whittall Associates, who claimed to have originated the idea.[60] At the end of some previously stated period, usually one week, the rug would be taken up from the sidewalk, washed, and displayed to show its condition, then sold to the highest bidder. It was an effective and simple way to draw attention to a rug's ability to stand abuse and was copied by makers of other types of floor covering, such as linoleum.

With sales climbing above the $20,000,000 mark in 1922 and 1923, small wonder that salesman Norman continued to urge the expansion of manufacturing facilities. From 1922 until he left the company a few years later, the board of directors authorized expenditures on Norman's recommendation of more than $5,000,000, even though the board members were not always able to examine some of the requests as closely as they would have liked.[61] That the directors had confidence in Norman, they themselves admitted. He was elected president of Bigelow-Hartford after Perkins' death on April 28, 1924, and his salary arrangement was renegotiated to give him $50,000 plus 12½ per cent of the company's net earnings after provision for dividends on the common stock.

Norman accepted the new arrangement with the pledge: [62]

As long as the management of this company remains in my hands, my aim will be to develop the operating efficiency of the two plants, improve the quality of our merchandise, and build up an organization to direct the affairs of the Company in a capable manner.

At this undertaking no one could cavil. Indeed, looking back, Norman could find much about the company's progress in which to take pride.

Corporatively speaking, there had been changes. In 1922 a stock dividend of 100 per cent increased the number of common shares to 161,000 and did away with the par value. In 1924 the capital expenditures of the past two years, over $3,500,000 to the end of January, made it imperative to bring the capital structure into line with the increased value of the company's assets. Accordingly, a further issue of 80,500 shares of common stock was voted by the shareholders, and this was also distributed as a stock dividend.[63]

On the board of directors who discussed and approved these changes were new faces. Thomas Beal, Thomas Manson, and Henry Skinner had died; Boston financial circles contributed Charles Francis Adams and Sewell H. Fessenden to the directorate; in New York Perkins' brother-in-law, W. K. Post, a lawyer, represented the Perkins family interest on the board and acted as general counsel for Bigelow-Hartford.

There had been a considerable increase in the value of buildings and machinery. At the end of 1914 these had a net value of $8,059,000; at the end of 1924 their value was $10,580,120. Production facilities had been greatly increased and in both plants some obsolete and narrow looms had been replaced by wide ones. Bigelow-Hartford enlarged its machine shops to provide the new maintenance skills and facilities required by the more complex equipment; like many of the other large carpet companies, it built more and more of its own machinery.[64]

Naturally enough, in view of Norman's special interest and of the trend of business, changes were made in the sales organization. In 1923 the company moved its New York offices into new and more impressive accommodations at 385 Madison Avenue where it leased the ninth and tenth floors of a large, modern building. In addition to the sales force that operated in New York, there were branch offices in Chicago, Boston, Philadelphia, Detroit, Atlanta, San Francisco, and Los Angeles—a considerable increase since 1914.[65]

Bigelow-Hartford ranked second or third in size in the American carpet industry at the end of its first decade. Because several of the major concerns were privately owned, detailed information about them was lacking, but the company could obtain enough data to indicate its comparative position. In 1923 Bigelow-Hartford's earnings before taxes had been $5,-300,000. Alexander Smith had earned $6,400,000, and Mohawk, youngest of the large manufacturers, had made $5,100,000. The next year saw Smith still in first place with earnings of $2,100,000; Mohawk had drawn abreast of Bigelow-Hartford with a gross profit of $1,870,000 (net profit not stated) against Bigelow-Hartford's net of $1,620,000.[66]

In 1914 the total value of America's production of carpets and rugs was $69,100,000; ten years later this figure had risen to $199,500,000. The average annual wage of workers in the industry was $470 in 1914, and by the end of another ten years was $1,378. Bigelow-Hartford's share of the industry's total in 1914 could not be measured, because of the company's short operating period in that year, and industry figures for 1915 are not available. By 1924, when census statistics again revealed the industry's sales, Bigelow's share was about 9.1 per cent. Its own position in 1924, compared with that in 1915, showed substantial growth, for 1925's sales were almost twice those of 1915. An exact comparison of wages for the company and the industry cannot be made, but in 1913 a loom fixer at the Clinton mill received a weekly wage of $20 and a brussels weaver earned $21.84; by 1923 their earnings had risen to $60.25 and $55 respectively.[67]

The transition from two independent companies to one larger combination had been effected smoothly and soundly. The new company had eliminated one factory and had made considerable additions to the other two. Unlike Alexander Smith & Sons and Stephen Sanford & Sons, its product line, thanks to the merger, had come to embrace the three major weaves: wiltons, axminsters, and velvets. This breadth of activity was to stand it in good stead in the years that lay ahead.

CHAPTER 11

CONTINUING GROWTH AND A NEW
MERGER, 1925–1929

The thread of continuity running through the Bigelow company's story under its various corporate names indicates that the effect of individuals has always been marked, for good or bad. This had been true in the company's early days but it reached a high point in 1924 with the election of John F. Norman to the presidency. It is true that Robert P. Perkins had not failed to make an impression on the organization of which he was for so long the head, but Perkins was comparatively inactive for some years before he died.

Perkins himself, apparently aware of his failure to impress his personality to a greater extent on his company, just before his death wrote to Robert Winsor of Kidder, Peabody & Company, saying, "I do think in the past I have been of some use to the Bigelow Company. Maybe I did not get as much out of it at the time as I might have if I had been a different sort of person." To this Winsor replied: [1]

I believe that you *laid the foundation and did a large part of the building up* of the Bigelow-Hartford Carpet Company, and that thus you are more—far more—responsible than anyone else for the present prosperity of that Company, and I know of nobody else who could have done what you did; so that, in my judgment, the stockholders owe a debt of gratitude to you which they can never possibly understand.

Whether or not Winsor wrote in this vein to console a man tired and in ill health, he seems to have been right in his last conclusion. Perkins is remembered for his gentlemanliness, his consideration for others, and his charm, but little stands out about his conduct of affairs. Little, that is, compared with Norman, for here the individual comes into his own. This flamboyant supersalesman was the personal antithesis of Perkins, the Harvard-educated, cultured aristocrat. Under any other circumstances the two men would probably never have met. However, when business conditions placed them in the same circle, their peculiar traits were complementary. Each appeared to recognize in the other qualities he himself lacked.

Perkins and Norman were also in marked physical contrast. The Boston man was tall, handsome, dignified. Whereas Perkins was slender, Norman was massive, heavy shouldered and thick necked, with a full face in which were small eyes, a broad nose, and lips that indicated a nature given to sensual living. Photographs seldom showed him smiling but his successful career as a salesman seems to indicate that he could be jovial with customers when the occasion demanded it. He could match drink for drink, smoking-car story with smoking-car story, in the salesman's tradition of the time.[2]

Norman was an executive at a time when marketing was looked upon as the most important function in business and salesmen were at a premium. Moreover, in those days the stress in selling was on sales, not on merchandising, on costs, or on efficiency. There was a belief that all a company needed to do was to get volume and everything else would follow. John Norman was pre-eminently a salesman, reared in the school of selling, and he was to behave as president of Bigelow-Hartford much as he had behaved as sales manager or, before that, as carpet drummer. The development of the co-ordination that he failed to give Bigelow awaited the pressures of another day.

JOHN F. NORMAN AS PRESIDENT

Under John F. Norman as president, the close ties of Bigelow-Hartford with Boston became more elastic. This was not surprising. Perkins had been not only the company's head but also the social equal and friend of the bankers who had ultimate control over the organization. Norman was the outlander, the professional executive in charge of one of the financiers' many interests and was valuable to them only as long as he did his job well. His strength lay in his ability as a salesman; he had an uncanny faculty for determining whether a design or color would sell. It was this ability that had led to his rise in the company; as long as Bigelow-Hartford continued to make sales, the Boston bankers allowed Norman a fairly free hand.

This also was characteristic of the times. Bigelow-Hartford was a fairly small company and had not passed the point where its chief executive could not make all the major decisions. The idea of "consultative management" lay fifteen to twenty years off for the company, and the practice of New England business had traditionally been for the senior manager to be allowed to run his organization without interference or contradiction.

It is not surprising, therefore, that the executive group which the new president gathered around him should have been described as able but

almost completely under Norman's thumb.[3] Its members included Harry V.
Campbell, who succeeded Norman as sales manager and later, in 1926,
became a vice-president;[4] James J. Delaney, Campbell's assistant and
Bigelow-Hartford's secretary after the death in 1925 of the veteran
George S. Squire; Philip F. O'Neil, purchasing agent and later assistant
sales manager; and F. W. Mortensen, for a short time in charge of contract sales.

The president apparently could not dominate two of his executives.
They were Frank H. Deknatel, the company's treasurer, and John Davidson, superintendent of the Clinton mill. Norman attempted to rid himself
of Deknatel, who was also a director and a member of the executive committee, but Norman's ignorance of corporate procedure kept him, according to Deknatel, from realizing that he, as president, had the power. He
also fought bitterly with Davidson but he needed too much the mill manager's manufacturing skills to be provoked quite to the point of dismissal.[5]

In spite of capricious conduct, Norman succeeded in giving the company a degree of manufacturing-marketing co-operation which it had not
always possessed. He was aware of his own lack of manufacturing knowledge and he took steps to overcome the deficiency. Monthly meetings
of executives were held in New York, and the superintendents of the
mills made the trip from Thompsonville and Clinton to attend them. The
product lines which the factories could make and the sales staffs could
sell were discussed and each group had to convince the president. If his
acute judgment approved a carpet, it went into production and into the
catalogue.[6]

But bringing manufacturing and marketing men into monthly association was not in itself enough to achieve true harmony. Like many another manufacturing company, Bigelow-Hartford had permitted its mill
superintendents a considerable degree of autonomy; indeed, this reflected
an organizational structure wherein all departments looked to the top
executive rather than function as part of an integrated whole. The
superintendents had allowed this self-government to extend downward.
Individual department heads bought supplies in large quantities without referring to purchasing authority, operating budgets were unknown,
looms were sometimes idle in one plant and working around the clock in
another, hiring was done by foremen with no attempt at centralization
and no one, regardless of rank or position, entered the mill premises unless the superintendent thought that he had a good reason to be there.[7]

Failure to have achieved internal co-ordination earlier is not remarkable. Those companies which had attained it to any marked degree were
mainly the very large ones, such as the major oil companies or those with
extended operating problems such as the railroads. The medium-sized
concern such as Bigelow-Hartford was slower to grasp the concept of

integrated management, perhaps because pressures toward that end had been lacking.

Bigelow-Hartford, moreover, was the union of several companies, and the merger of 1914 had occurred under circumstances not likely to bring the mills into harmony or to reduce them to subservience to distant New York. It was Norman's recognition of the unco-ordinated operation of the two mills that led him to appoint B. F. Connolly, in the fall of 1925, as plants manager of the company.[8]

The press announcement, which Norman presumably approved, stated that Connolly would direct the co-ordination of the activities of the company's factories and would establish closer relations between the operating departments and the executive offices in New York. By implication the statement indicated an awareness of a weakness and a desire to correct it.

Connolly succeeded in placing purchasing under a central authority and on a more economical footing but this was to be his only major accomplishment.[9] For some reason Connolly seems not to have received the support from Norman necessary to do his job successfully; promotions were made by Norman often without consultation with the plants manager and in other ways Connolly's authority was undercut. Within a year the plants manager was dismissed. Opinions are divided as to Connolly's capability but it seems fair to conclude that he was not given full opportunity to prove himself.[10]

Connolly's relations with the two mill superintendents most vividly pointed to the effect of Norman's failure to reinforce his attempts to obtain a cohesive manufacturing structure. Connolly to some extent had been responsible for the replacement of J. W. Pierce as superintendent at Thompsonville, apparently a commendable move since Pierce seems to have lost what limited usefulness he had possessed by his efforts to break the 1921 strike. Unfortunately his successor, William Pearsall, while more popular with the operatives, was qualified chiefly as a loom technician and could not adequately supervise the vast factory. His desire to be ingratiating led him to agree to some of Connolly's changes at Thompsonville, but he was said to have formed an alliance with his counterpart at Clinton which was intended to balk the manager of manufacturing wherever possible.[11]

John Davidson, the Clinton superintendent, did not bother to pretend any sort of co-operation with Connolly. He made it clear that he did not propose to accept either dictation or suggestion from the manufacturing manager, a whippersnapper with only 18 months of Bigelow-Hartford service at the time of his promotion over Davidson's head. Davidson refused to allow Connolly further into the plant property than the office and Norman took no action to improve Connolly's unenviable position.

Again it should be emphasized that Norman's unfamiliarity with production methods made him unwilling to antagonize Davidson too much lest that worthy take his talents elsewhere. The Clinton mill, fortunate in its access to a more ethnically homogeneous and less troublesome labor force than Thompsonville, seems up to that time to have been better managed than its Connecticut counterpart. Its products were known to be of high quality and its narrow looms were kept busy for long periods with large and profitable contracts for the Pullman Company.[12]

So Davidson and his Clinton mill continued on their way. The only time the Clinton superintendent co-operated with Thompsonville or with New York was at the monthly executive meetings, for whatever these accomplished. As long as the Clinton looms hummed happily along on full production this situation was not serious; but, when Davidson's resistance to change and modernization was itself combined with the falling sales of a depression, it was too late for co-ordination to correct the mistakes of the past.

Should Norman have insisted that Davidson fall into line? He had the power to compel that strong-minded Englishman to carry out orders that would have resulted in greater collaboration but there were obstacles in the way of his exercising that power. Deeply established New England textile tradition, Clinton's apparently efficient and profitable operation, the Boston financiers' reluctance to disturb a financially advantageous situation, Norman's eagerness to keep earnings high, and, finally, his lack of manufacturing ability, all helped to keep Davidson entrenched. Without an able man to place in absolute charge of production (a man whose ability or absoluteness would have been distasteful to the autocratic Norman), it was easier to ignore Clinton and make changes at Thompsonville.

PROBLEMS AND SOLUTIONS

The uncertain future of woolen floor covering sales made it even more unwise to upset a lucrative manufacturing applecart. John F. Norman took over as president in 1924 at a time when carpet sales were declining, gently at first, more rapidly later, with no year to equal 1923 for nearly a quarter century. Despite growing population and general prosperity in the years from 1924 to 1929, carpet sales seemed to have reached a ceiling.

One reason for this failure to advance was indirect competition. Much of the carpet industry's competition was in areas which might be regarded as normal, such as oriental rugs and hard- or smooth-surface floor coverings (the terms are synonymous)—linoleum and the like. After World War I, however, new sources of competitive difficulty appeared which were less obvious but significantly attractive to the consumers' dollar. Chief of these was the automobile. Cars were often carpeted but the amount each required hardly compared with the yardage a customer might have bought for his house had he not been so busy making payments for his vehicle. Installment buying was rising in popularity; whether it was hailed as a boon to industry or damned as an incentive to profligate extravagance, it was certainly a means of making widespread automobile ownership possible.

Hard on the wheels of the automobile in mass attraction was the radio. This new device was at first greeted by manufacturers of home furnishings as likely to get people out of their cars and back into their houses but it also proved a sales rival to carpeting. Guests were asked to strain their ears for distant stations received on some expensively cabineted superheterodyne (also paid for in installments) rather than to feast their eyes on new rugs. If the existence and growing strength of such competition meant that over-all sales of carpets and rugs could not be greatly increased from year to year (and the passing of time revealed this to be the case), then the business obtained by one company could be expanded only at the expense of other companies' sales.

One vital weakness of any carpet company's position at that time was the failure to develop strong brand preference among consumers. Retailers could easily divert sales from this company's products to that if they so desired, for buyers were generally inclined to accept the recommendation of a store in the absence of any marked familiarity with the makers of the merchandise shown.

The decline in sales in 1924 from the high mark of 1923 pointed up in the mind of the good salesman Norman the need for action to change this lack of consumer knowledge of carpet brands. An advertising agency, Erwin, Wasey & Company, was appointed to study and recommend what could be done. The most significant proposal advanced by the agency at the conclusion of its investigation was that Bigelow-Hartford begin to advertise its wares nationally; electric signs on New York buildings were all very well but they could not keep the company's name uppermost in the minds of the American carpet-buying public.

In 1923 Bigelow-Hartford had spent $107,000 on all its advertising (see Appendix 9); this amount was equal to four-tenths of one per cent of net sales. As a result of the advertising agency's recommendations, advertising allowances were sharply increased and in 1926 the company began to advertise in such widely circulated publications as *The Saturday Evening Post*.[13] In that year the company spent $257,000 on publicity, more than twice as much as in 1923 and equal to 1.3 per cent of net sales. More than one-half the advertising allowance was used for space in various consumer media.

Bigelow-Hartford was neither alone nor first among carpet manufacturers to use such media. Both its predecessor companies had been conspicuous advertisers; of their rivals, M. J. Whittall Associates seems to

have been the earliest company to advertise nationally, using women's
magazines as early as 1906 or 1907.[14] Mohawk Carpet Mills, which had
proved markedly aggressive since its founding in 1920, had become a
vigorous advertiser in a short time. In January, 1925, it outlined an extensive advertising program for the year. Each advertisement in consumer
publications was to feature the company's own name, together with that
of a particular rug.[15] In the next year Whittall began to use radio advertising on a fairly wide scale [16] and was followed into this medium by other
manufacturers of both hard and soft floor coverings.

Thus there was a much greater effort on the part of carpet and linoleum manufacturers to establish consumer preference for their products.
Bigelow-Hartford, in addition to using nationally circulated magazines,
continued to devote much of the efforts of A. N. Cook, its advertising manager, to the preparation of handsome, expensive booklets which helped
to make its name better known to the public. Cook wrote a short and
elaborately made-up history to commemorate Bigelow-Hartford's cen-
tenary in 1925; he spent several months in Florida on research into the
use of the company's products in hotels and large homes there which led
to another illuminated brochure; and he prepared the layout for the semiannual price lists which became noted for their appearance.[17]

Norman was well aware that advertising needed something about
which to talk and he was at least partly responsible for the introduction
in 1925 of a new rug. This rug, called the "Servian," was made with an entirely new weave on a specially designed loom; it had the appearance of
a handmade, high-grade oriental. Although the company sold the Servian
unwashed, washing with chemicals was later suggested to dealers as
likely to enhance the appearance of the product and make it more closely
resemble the new imported oriental.[18]

The importance of the Servian rug in Bigelow-Hartford's marketing
lay in its seamless construction. By 1925 most of the industry was convinced of the permanent popularity of carpets and rugs made in large
sizes without seams. A typical style pattern for the carpet industry had
shown itself again. A few years earlier a revival of the practice of carpeting floors from wall to wall in expensive homes had brought back a custom
out of favor since the turn of the century. As it frequently did, the new
taste moved from fashion leaders to fashion followers, downward into
less pretentious houses.[19] This descent was of obvious significance to
Bigelow-Hartford and its competitors, sorely hurt by the earlier shift in
carpet-buying habits which had led to reduced consumption.

The Servian rug was woven on a specially adapted axminster loom.
Thanks to the new product and to the increased use of sales aids, in the
middle of 1925 the company's axminster mills were running 24 hours
daily.[20] This may have been partly the result also of a spring strike in the

plant of a competitor, Stephen Sanford & Sons. The Sanford workers stayed away from their looms for several months and returned without their desired wage increases.[21] In the meantime, Sanford's customers turned to other suppliers, of which Bigelow-Hartford was an important one.

Bigelow, unlike Sanford but like the rest of the industry, had no strike at the time, in a measure no doubt owing to Norman's labor policies. Ever unpredictable and impulsively generous at times, Norman was eager to keep labor producing. The year 1925 brought employees a series of benefits which Norman at least approved if he did not originate. He was joined in his attitude by the executive committee,[22] but the president seemed eager to go further than his directors were prepared to follow.

A number of new company houses were built for the workers in Thompsonville and Clinton, and a grandiose scheme for employee housing was conceived by Norman, although it got no further than the architect's drawing board.[23] In New York, weekly sessions were held with the purpose of instructing office workers in the principles of carpet manufacture; departmental staffs met monthly, and a large banquet at the end of 1925 gave younger employees an opportunity to meet their superiors on an informal basis.[24]

At the close of 1925 Norman suggested to the executive committee that Bigelow-Hartford formulate and put into effect a definite pension policy, to care for employees with service periods of thirty-five years or more or who might be unable to work. Such programs existed in some companies, although they were not commonly found in the textile trades, other than for management personnel. Norman regarded pensions as a dramatic opportunity for Bigelow-Hartford to exhibit industry leadership.

This new pension plan was, however, too revolutionary for the company's directors. The executive committee, with Boston's Charles Francis Adams as spokesman, agreed only to consider and deal with each case annually, on its merits and without precedent. This is not altogether surprising. To the New England financiers conservative stability with substantial profits was the reason for a company's existence, a strong element of paternalism was traditionally present in the relations of textile companies with their workers, and there may have been doubt in the minds of the board members as to Bigelow-Hartford's ability to pay the long-run costs of such a pension scheme. So the issue of a formal pension program fell from view, to await the pressures of changed circumstances.

The directors did reach agreement on a scheme to make possible stock purchases by employees on a deferred payment basis, possibly because investigation showed this plan to have been successful in other companies. At first a thousand shares of Bigelow-Hartford common stock were set aside, and the amount was shortly thereafter increased to sixteen hundred. When, in later years, the price of the stock fell below that at which the employees had purchased it, the company came to their rescue and repurchased it at the original selling price.[25]

As a last gesture of goodwill for 1925, Bigelow-Hartford shared part of the year's profits with some of the employees. Sales had risen almost $4,000,000 over 1924, to a total, after discounts, of about $21,000,000, and earnings had proportionately risen. Norman received a bonus and salary for the year of more than $250,000, and office employees were paid a bonus of 5 per cent of their annual salaries, while heads of departments received 10 per cent.[26]

The year had been marked also by fairly stable prices at Alexander Smith & Sons' auctions and by rumored increases in the price of wool. One of the carpet wool's disadvantages as a raw material is its price sensitivity to conditions in any of the several countries whence it comes. Many of these countries suffered from political instability; in 1925, for example, internal strife in China threatened to cause the price to rise.[27]

The 1922 tariff, which had permitted, conditionally, free entry of carpet wools, had left restrictions as to type. The state of the wool market in 1925 led the manufacturers to seek transfer of certain other wools to the free list. This request by the manufacturers was refused, but Bigelow took the fight to the courts. The company waged a two-year battle and finally succeeded in obtaining a decision classing Buenos Aires sixes, a coarse wool, as carpet wool.[28] These tariff changes made customs interpretations somewhat more certain, and lower duties meant lower manufacturing costs; meanwhile prices were tending upward.

Bigelow, like its competitors, as far as is known, and like the textile industry generally, at this time had no formal research department. The company's engineers appear to have performed a variety of functions, ranging from equipment maintenance to equipment design, but there is no indication that serious consideration was given to a long-range research program. Those developments which took place in the carpet industry arose from haphazard tinkering or the sudden response to a need which might have existed for years.

Nevertheless, some technical progress was made and the machinery installed at Thompsonville in June, 1926, to increase seamless rug capacity, had been designed by company engineers. It had cost almost $250,000. By the end of the year, the manufacture of tapestry carpets, with its expensive drum-dyeing process, had been discontinued at Thompsonville, and the tapestry looms were being converted, for about $700 each, to weave a nine-foot carpet known as Brewster broadloom. Again, the conversion designing had been done by company engineers, who had also developed the fabric.

Brewster broadloom rapidly became a profitable item in the Bigelow-Hartford line. It was significant not only because it provided a means of converting obsolete tapestry looms at low cost to the manufacture of a salable fabric but also because it led to the introduction of raw stock dyeing. Raw stock dyeing was a mass-production method used when large quantities of a color were required; as the name implied, wool was dyed before being spun into yarn. Bigelow-Hartford was a very early user of the method and its adoption implied a willingness to seek technological change.[29]

The 1926 program still did not make Bigelow the equal of some major competitors in terms of wide looms. It is hard to explain why Norman was so slow in urging the adoption of wide looms. All the available evidence points to his considerable ability as a salesman and to his capacity for judging popular acceptance of designs and colors. Why, then, did he so underestimate the trend of consumer taste in seamless fabrics that Bigelow-Hartford was permitted to lag behind Sanford and Mohawk?

The best single explanation for Norman's attitude is probably the fact that a satisfactory wide wilton loom was not developed until the late 1920's. Bigelow-Hartford's leadership was in the wilton field, its contract sales being in narrow wiltons. While contract sales amounted to only about 10 per cent of the company's total sales, these were made in the highest quality grades and did much to earn Bigelow-Hartford's reputation for quality manufacturing.

THE FALL FROM GRACE OF JOHN F. NORMAN

When, in 1926, Norman requested additional funds for the purchase of wide looms, his directors were somewhat surprised. Because the need could be demonstrated, they gave grudging assent to his proposal, but they had been under the impression that the money they had voted from 1919 on had placed the company in a strong competitive manufacturing position. Sales in 1926, furthermore, showed signs of falling below the 1925 level, and it was hard for the directors to approve plant expenditures when sales and earnings were down.

Unfortunately for the company, Norman's apparent conversion to the idea of broad axminster looms came at a time when his directors had ceased to trust him, and they were therefore unwilling to go as far as they might otherwise have gone. The proposal confirmed to the board something about the company's position which the directors had come to suspect, that all was not right in Bigelow-Hartford's executive offices. Actually an awareness of this possibility had arisen in 1925.[30] Whether this came from the fact that Norman's arrogance had got the better of his common sense and had alienated some of Bigelow's large accounts is uncertain. What is certain is that by May or June of 1926, most members of the board agreed with Neal Rantoul and Robert Winsor that the situation needed correction.

While the directors had come to suspect that Norman's conduct both as an executive and as an individual would not stand careful scrutiny, they were in doubt as to how best to obtain positive proof. Frank Dekna-tel, a director and the company's treasurer, was asked if he would attempt to secure evidence as to Norman's malpractices but he declined. Although he knew that Norman had tried several times to get rid of him and he therefore had personal reasons as well as his interest in the company's welfare for wanting the president removed, Deknatel felt that the situation had to be corrected from the outside.[31] The board then looked for someone unconnected with Bigelow-Hartford to do the job.

The man selected was Louis K. Liggett. Winsor's firm, Kidder, Pea-body & Company, had been associated with Liggett in several corporate organizations, and Liggett had acquired a reputation for his work in this field, notably with Rexall Drug Stores.[32] He seemed capable of conducting the necessary investigation and of advancing solutions to correct a bad situation, if one was found to exist. The executive committee authorized Winsor to see whether Liggett would be willing to act. He was. In order that his examination of the company's affairs might create as little disturbance as possible, he was elected a member of the executive committee and he became a director, as soon as a board vacancy occurred.[33]

Liggett plunged into the task with the vigor that characterized all his activities. Eugene Ong, who had worked with him on some of the Kidder, Peabody projects, was commissioned to make a thorough study of Bigelow-Hartford's general operations; one of Liggett's accountants analyzed the company's record-keeping procedures; and the Barnes Textile Service, of Boston, surveyed the plants from a technical point of view. Ong also interviewed at length two former Bigelow-Hartford executives, B. F. Connolly and Julius Roth, manager of plants and purchasing agent, respectively. Both men were victims of Norman's anger and both were Bigelow-Hartford shareholders. Like Deknatel, they had strong motives for wishing to see Norman removed: revenge and concern for the company's prosperity. Even when their dislike of Norman had been fully discounted, they provided Ong with much useful evidence.[34]

Careful not to prejudice the investigator, Liggett gave Ong no inkling that the real reason was a checkup on Norman. He was simply directed to conduct an analysis such as he had carried through for Liggett on other occasions; in this way the president was kept from being suspicious and the results of the inquiry were objective. Inevitably, however, the root cause of the company's difficulties was seen to be Norman. The fact that Ong's conclusions, independently reached, supported those already held by others tended to make them more convincing.

The information which had reached the company's directors about their president had to do to a considerable extent with his personal habits. Norman, unknown to the board, had been indulging for years in high living of a type which had brought no credit to him or to his company.[35] His failures, human as some of them were, had not helped to make him an exemplary chief executive,[36] and he had been unable to keep his personal and his business lives separate.[37]

Within the company Norman's relations with subordinates had been particularly damaging. Men who disagreed with his policies, or whose continued presence might have proved embarrassing, were arbitrarily dismissed; others were harassed and humiliated until the impression grew in the minds of some of his associates that John Norman was mentally unbalanced. He seemed, as one man put it, obsessed with a desire to destroy anyone who had in any way helped him.[38]

It might seem odd that the effect of the president's actions on the company should not have come sooner to the attention of the directors, yet it is actually not too hard to explain. Norman had made considerable effort to be on good terms with Bigelow-Hartford's large customers and with his fellow board members, and he was for a time successful.[39] In addition, he had enjoyed complete freedom of business action only from the time of Perkins' death in 1924, although his personal foibles had been in evidence to his subordinates earlier. As long as Perkins occupied the presidential chair, whether or not he was active, his existence had a restraining effect on Norman. At first, when rumors of Norman's peculiarities penetrated to the heart of Boston financial circles, they were dismissed as preposterous. It was not until rumor had mounted on rumor and finally achieved the status of fact that the directors acted.

While Ong inevitably turned up confirmatory evidence about Norman's private affairs, the investigator concerned himself mainly with the president's conduct of Bigelow-Hartford affairs. Ong's major criticism was of Norman's failure to achieve proper correlation of manufacturing and marketing; the company had been run from the salesman's standpoint. Norman's failure to set up depreciation reserves to cover the obsolescence of narrow looms was among the incidents singled out for adverse comment. Another source of complaint was the special compensation arrangement, with its disparity to Bigelow-Hartford's size and earnings, its effect on the morale of other executives, and its tendency to encourage Norman to executive action that would redound primarily to his short-run benefit and the company's long-run disadvantage.[40] The accountants and the engineering consulting firm also reported adversely on Norman's management.

Robert P. Perkins; president of the merged companies, 1901 to 1924; friend of the Boston bankers who backed the mergers

John F. Norman; salesman-president, 1924 to 1927; pioneer in vigorous marketing methods; career cut short when directors promoted him to board chairman, later dismissed him

John A. Sweetser; personable president from 1927 to 1944; choice of Boston directors; died unexpectedly at age 54

James D. Wise; corporation lawyer; president since 1944; with advice from management consultants modernized company's administrative organization

They criticized particularly the company's control procedures and a number of its production methods and men.

All the investigating agencies submitted recommendations for correction of the deficiencies observed. While removal of Norman was, by inference or direct statement, the primary need, a number of other suggestions were supplied. Ong believed that a vice-president in charge of manufacturing was essential to obtain proper co-ordination. He felt also that employee relations required more attention, and he urged the installation of formal employee welfare departments, of employee insurance, and of a newspaper or magazine which would "communicate to employees Bigelow-Hartford's principles and policies and aid in the development of a spirit of pride and interest."

When, after several months of work, Liggett's investigation was complete, the only member of the Bigelow-Hartford directorate who wanted Norman to continue as president was John F. Norman himself. Yet his removal presented certain difficulties, as Rantoul and Winsor were both aware. If he was asked to leave, his going had to be effected in such a way as to preserve from further harm internal and external confidence in the company, and also to save the faces of Norman and the directors who had apparently tolerated or supported him. Moreover, Norman had to be neutralized lest he turn his undeniable ability against the company.

The decision finally reached was to promote the president into impotence. He was to become chairman of the board, an office unused since the early days of the Bigelow-Hartford merger, his salary of $50,000 was to be continued for one year as a trial, and his full time and efforts were to be given to Bigelow-Hartford. He was to preside at directors' meetings and to discharge such other duties as might be required of him but he was to have no authority. If he failed to live up to the agreement, the executive committee could terminate his appointment within the year.[41]

This arrangement, according to the company's legal advisor and director, W. K. Post, enabled John F. Norman to step aside with more grace and dignity than he had generally exhibited as president. There must have been tenseness and drama in the air at the directors' meeting on March 3, 1927, when the president vacated his office and assumed the board chairmanship. The face-saving announcement released to the press said that Norman had worked hard, well into middle age, and that he preferred to retire from active duty while keeping up his interest in the company in which most of his business life had been spent.[42] Editorial comment on the change was discreet. The new chairman was hailed by the press as a forceful leader and promoter of good practice, one who had given his best efforts toward stabilizing the textile industry.[43]

If Norman had been content to mend his ways, his future would have been secure. But, while he continued for a few months to perform the designated duties as chairman of the board, old habits were too hard to break. His behavior and attitude showed little improvement and the situation became intolerable. The executive committee urged that Norman go abroad to study European markets. During his absence the directors requested his resignation and abolished the post of chairman of the board.[44] His connection with Bigelow-Hartford was definitely ended. Norman left Bigelow-Hartford worth about $2,500,000, it has been estimated. He proceeded to open a sales agency of his own, and then to establish a plant in New Jersey, where he installed Austrian looms that would simulate the hand-tied knot of oriental rugs. The depression of 1929 killed that enterprise and he gradually lost his money, becoming reduced to living by borrowing from old associates and by peddling rugs. He died destitute in Chicago in 1939.

While the directors had debated what to do with Norman they had pondered a second vexing question—who was to succeed him as president. The elements that had involved L. K. Liggett in the situation worked also against promotion of someone within the company. Completion of the task of restoring Bigelow-Hartford's shattered morale had to be executed by an outsider. Someone was needed who was neither in Norman's circle nor in opposition, someone with textile experience if possible, but, above all, a man with personality and character and ability adequate to repair the damage Norman had done.

Since Winsor and Rantoul, the board members most concerned, had an extensive acquaintance among textile companies and in industry generally, obtaining a list of possible men was not too difficult. What was hard was selecting one who combined the greatest number of desired qualities. After the unfortunate experience with Norman, it was not surprising to see the Bostonians fall back upon a man with whose background and training they had more in common than they had had with the outgoing president.

In selecting John A. Sweetser to be the new president, the company swung back to the sort of person Robert Perkins had been. Sweetser, thirty-seven years old, son of a prominent Boston Back Bay physician, had a home in Brookline, was Harvard-educated, and had been a naval officer in World War I. He had had some years of experience as treasurer of various New England cotton textile mills, and he had a warm, pleasing personality. For the first few months of his presidency he was hampered by Norman's presence as chairman of the board, but when Norman resigned, Sweetser was left free to discharge his heavy new responsibilities.

COMPANY DEVELOPMENT UNDER JOHN A. SWEETSER

The immediate effect of Norman's replacement was one of relief, at least on the higher company levels. Sweetser was a new and unknown quantity to the employees, but he quickly dissipated any unpleasant uncertainties that may have existed. Eager to learn the mechanical (and the human) side of carpet manufacture, he spent much of his first year in the mills at Thompsonville and Clinton and soon became a familiar figure to the employees. He drove himself about in an old Ford station wagon and had a casual manner in contrast with that of his predecessor. His friendly approachability, genuinely sincere, made a deep and favorable impression; by those who worked for him he was called the "skipper."

The president was a busy man in that first year. In addition to the time he spent in the mills, he was in New York, attempting to do for morale there what he was doing in the plants, and he was also in Boston, establishing good relations with his directors. Throughout his tenure of office with Bigelow-Hartford, Sweetser continued to maintain his residence in Brookline. He went to Boston each week end and lunched on Saturdays with Neal Rantoul, keeping the director informed of the company's activities.

Bigelow-Hartford's internal affairs were not the only beneficiary of Sweetser's fence-mending. Norman's refusal to associate himself or the company with other carpet manufacturers had harmed the company in the past,[45] and Sweetser took immediate steps to alter that attitude. A simple beginning, but one that marked the commencement of more harmonious carpet industry relations, was the formation of the Carpet & Rug Traffic Association in May, 1927. Its object was to develop some community of action among its members on matters pertaining to transportation rates and traffic regulations. Most of the major manufacturers joined the association, and a Bigelow-Hartford man, A. M. Potter, was its vice-president.[46]

Sweetser wished to go further than this sort of specialized association. He believed that the carpet industry should organize in a group that would utilize paid staffs as officers functioning for the benefit of all members. The industry collectively could do for itself and its individual firms what no single concern could accomplish, regardless of size or capital resources, but Sweetser did not believe that activities of the industry organization should lead to the creation of agreements, control of prices, division of markets, restraint of trade, or curtailment of production. He joined and then shortly resigned from the Wilton Manufacturers Association because it seemed to be operating along these latter lines.[47]

In the president's mind was an organization that would accumulate knowledge and bring to the attention of the industry information of fundamental importance to every concern engaged in the manufacture of carpets and rugs.[48] Lack of available data had kept most carpet makers from realizing just what had happened to their industry through the years. American manufacturers had produced 83,000,000 square yards of woolen floor coverings in 1904 but had not matched that total again until 1923. The 1923 high mark was ephemeral and decline once more set in; in 1927 the industry's volume amounted to only 65,600,000 square yards. By way of unpleasant contrast, the makers of linoleum and asphalt base hard-surface floor covering had increased their output in the same period from 20,000,000 square yards in 1904 to 161,000,000 in 1927.[49]

Part of the carpet industry's loss to its hard-surface rival was owing, in Sweetser's opinion, to internal strain and to faulty realization of opportunity. Criticism had been leveled by the industry at such offsprings of the mechanical age as the automobile and the radio, which had siphoned off consumer expenditures that might otherwise have gone for carpeting. To the Bigelow-Hartford president, this was useless grumbling. The era of mechanization offered alternative opportunities to sell carpets and rugs, and he cited as an example the possibility of encouraging their sale, with draperies, as sound-proofing against the raucous noises that accompanied the new civilization. In this unrecognized area he estimated an annual potential market of 10,000,000 square yards might exist.

The result of Sweetser's efforts and arguments was the formation, in the summer of 1927, of the Institute of Carpet Manufacturers of America. The Carpet Institute was incorporated as a nonprofit organization in Delaware, with headquarters in Washington (these were later moved to New York), and the first president was Irving S. Paull, a former member of the Department of Commerce, whom Herbert Hoover had recommended for the post. A secretary with engineering and accounting experience was also employed. The Institute began with a membership representing 70 per cent of the carpet industry's volume; [50] although neither Alexander Smith nor Stephen Sanford were members at first, Sweetser was persuasive and they joined within a short time.[51]

Primarily the Carpet Institute was intended, as Sweetser had described it, to act as a clearing house for the collection and dissemination to members of information of value to the entire industry. Such information was obtained both from manufacturers and from such outside sources as government agencies. The Institute's Washington location and its president's association with government officials enabled it also to act as a listening post in the capital. It could keep its members informed about legislation that might be significant and it could see that the industry's views were presented promptly and effectively in appropriate legislative circles.

Partly because the textile industry felt depression in the 1920's sooner than did many other segments of the American economy, the struggle for shares of the existing market was bitter and strenuous. Sweetser recognized that good relations with fellow producers would not sell carpets. So, under his leadership, a program got under way to raise the confidence of wholesalers and retailers in the company's methods to the level enjoyed by its high-quality merchandise.

Sweetser attempted to institute changes in marketing methods that would generally strengthen and stabilize conditions. At its fall showing in 1927 Bigelow-Hartford announced that it would offer no goods in special sales during the season and that it would place its discontinued lines on sale only at each season's end.[52] The president hoped in this way to discourage off-price merchandise from finding its way into the hands of cut-rate retailers, whose sensational offers were harmful to the general trade.

The announcement was clearly intended to promote Bigelow-Hartford's standing with the better class of retailer, and it was accompanied and followed by other gestures in the same direction. From June, 1927, a small publication, *Bigelow-Hartford News,* was sent four times yearly to dealers as a medium through which the company could offer the best in quality and service.[53] In the following year the little paper invited Bigelow-Hartford customers who might be touring on vacation to visit the company's plants [54]—a forerunner of a later series of planned "open house."

Such moves helped to promote cordiality, but the practical steps taken to aid dealers in selling more carpets were of greater importance. The cut-carpet service was increased in scope in 1927 and again in 1928 so that stores could display samples of 15 Bigelow-Hartford qualities of plain and figured carpets, in 280 colorings. Retail carpet advertising was made easier through a company-prepared matrix series. Shops were urged to associate themselves with local showings of a motion picture in which all the rugs and carpets shown were Bigelow-Hartford products. Sales portfolios, display racks, and more handsome booklets provided point-of-sale merchandising assistance.

Increased advertising expenditures were made in the years from 1925 on, and for 1928 Bigelow-Hartford announced a campaign that would use color advertisements in nine national magazines reaching 4,300,000 readers.[55] Mohawk, however, remained ahead of Bigelow-Hartford; its 1928 advertising program called for advertisements in consumer magazines with a total readership of 10,000,000, and for a secondary series in fraternal, trade, and business publications, with an additional total circulation of about 2,000,000.[56]

Advertisements of both Bigelow and Mohawk showed a significant change in emphasis from rugs to seamless carpets and from figured designs to plain colors. The production of seamless carpets had stimulated the swing back to wall-to-wall carpeting; those customers who did not choose full carpeting would at least cover more of their floors than formerly. In the preference for plain colors Bigelow-Hartford was in a strong position. Its use of raw-stock dyeing permitted it to produce solid colors in large quantities; indeed, the company's early use of the raw-stock method may have started the trend toward plain-color fabrics.[57]

In efforts at market research the company analyzed the house plans of the *New York Herald-Tribune's* Home Service Institute from January, 1926, to June, 1927, and found a positive trend toward smaller rooms in new houses. The dining room was becoming smaller or disappearing altogether; bedrooms were diminishing in size because of higher building costs and changing family needs; as a result, only 75 of 341 rooms would accommodate 9 by 12 rugs.[58] The old standard size was no longer quite so standard. Moreover, apartment living was another change in American domestic habits and apartments generally contained rooms smaller than those in the average home.

About that time, too, interior decoration became something for the masses as well as the classes, and Bigelow worked with the trend. The growth in circulation of magazines edited primarily for women was partly responsible for a new awareness of decoration. The influence of high style from abroad, felt initially in the larger cities, was carried further afield by the mass circulation publications. The so-called "modernism," with an emphasis on cubes, angles, and violent colors, had its effect on carpet styles, and the company's first room-size rug designed in this eccentric manner was displayed in May, 1928. By then Bigelow-Hartford had a home decorating bureau in operation to answer queries from retailers and their salespeople on the many new designs and their proper settings.[59]

Rugs, if emphasized less in advertising, were still important. The trend toward smaller rooms was acknowledged later in 1928 when Bigelow-Hartford offered rugs in a 6.6 by 6.6 size designed for use in dinettes and other small rooms.[60] With the new sizes came lines designed to match furniture, draperies, and upholstery, products aimed at securing support from dealers. These ensemble styles, as they were termed, gave retailers an opportunity for larger unit sales, and they had definite appeal to manufacturers of other house furnishings, who might be expected to associate themselves with Bigelow-Hartford in joint sales promotion.

As the company's activity in the entire sales promotion field expanded, the staff for the function grew larger. The new position of sales promotion manager was given to A. N. Cook, the man who, as advertising manager, had prepared much of the company's literature. He was provided with trained assistance and was replaced as advertising manager by someone better qualified to deal with the broader advertising program.[61]

Two further steps were taken toward Sweetser's objective of better relations with the retail trade. To provide retailers with additional training in the effective selling of woven floor coverings, Bigelow-Hartford in 1928 offered a correspondence course in rug and carpet selling. More than 1,400 enrolled for the initial series at a cost to dealers of $10 each. The basis of the course, prepared for the company by an organization specializing in business training, was an extensive field survey of sales methods in the retail trade. This appeared to be so valuable that in 1929 Bigelow-Hartford took the further step of making the survey results available to store executives and merchandise managers.

A group of retail customers that assumed new importance in the 1920's and that became more and more significant to the carpet industry as time passed were the mail-order houses. Such concerns as Sears, Roebuck & Company and Montgomery Ward & Company recorded tremendous increases in sales (those of Sears went from $96,000,000 in 1914 to $347,000,-000 in 1928); [62] and their entry into retail store operation enabled them to reach a new class of customer.

The mail-order houses had for years sold rugs and carpets, generally under their own brand names, but from 1925 to 1930 their catalogues mentioned some manufacturers. Bigelow, Firth, Karagheusian, Mohawk, and Smith were named as makers of some patterns and qualities. The patterns supplied by the carpet companies to the mail-order firms were not those sold to regular distributors but were woven to special designs and specifications. Although makers' names disappeared from the catalogues and sales floors from 1930 onward, mail-order concerns absorbed more and more of the carpet industry's output.[63]

As indicated by the list of carpet companies in the mail-order catalogues, rivalry among the manufacturers was keen. The Smith auctions continued for a time but they lost much of their effect on the over-all price structure. After Smith's second 1927 auction, Sanford retaliated with drastic price cuts, below those reached in the auctions. The Smith company was besieged with demands from its jobbers to permit them to return auction goods. In 1928, when Mohawk began to handle its own selling functions, Smith employed Mohawk's abandoned sales agent, W. & J. Sloane, and thereafter held no more auctions.[64]

Following up its new marketing arrangement with still other changes, Mohawk converted its entire production to seamless rugs and carpets by mid-1929. At the same time it announced a new type of production control which, by careful scheduling of orders, would eliminate the necessity of selling discontinued or distress merchandise during its fall season. Smith, for its part, by deciding to market through a sales agent rather than through auctions, had removed much of the uncertainty which existed in each year's selling season but had done injury to itself. Before turning over its selling to the Sloanes, the Smith company had simply run its mill to its full extent and relied on auctions to move the merchandise; in March, 1929, for the first time in years, Smith's huge Yonkers plant was reported on short time as a result of overproduction.[65]

In 1929 the carpet industry was again agitated by the threat of changes in the tariff structure (culminating in the Hawley-Smoot Tariff Act of 1930). The demands of manufacturers and importers were still difficult to keep in balance. American cotton growers, for instance, wanted protection against imports of Indian jute but American carpet manufacturers did not wish to pay higher prices for their basic materials, of which jute was one. On the other hand, manufacturers were anxious to have barriers against foreign carpets kept high or made higher, a stand which made work for the Carpet Institute and for Sweetser, its chairman in 1929.

Two new products in 1929 were of particular interest. In March the company showed a rayon-surfaced rug in combination with cotton weft and cotton stuffer, foreshadowing extensive use of those fibers in later years. Of immediate sales value was a rug which had the sheen typical of synthetically dyed orientals. In 1929 American-made floor coverings which successfully imitated this sheen were rare. When Bigelow-Hartford's "Domestic Oriental" made its appearance in November, demand was so great that by the end of the year the company's two mills were falling behind in producing what the market would take.[66]

This particular problem of equating supply with demand was not peculiar to Bigelow-Hartford; other companies were reported in a similar situation. Sweetser had taken action soon after becoming president to improve the company's manufacturing position and his efforts had met with some success. In spite of his period of study in the mills or because of it, he had recognized that he was not qualified to direct the company's production facilities, and he employed outside consultants to help him. One of these was the Barnes Textile Service of Boston, one of the agencies enlisted in the Norman investigation.

The textile service's analyses led in 1928 to the institution of budget control in Bigelow-Hartford's factories as a means of controlling costs and measuring performances. Department heads and foremen were for the first time given a standard other than quality and output toward which to work, and their operations were assessed in relation to their adherence to budget allocations. Reinforcing this system, a point evaluation plan extended performance criteria to the operatives. Through succeeding years Barnes worked with Bigelow-Hartford personnel in the application of time study, work simplification, and productivity programs to the company's manufacturing.[67]

Sweetser also sought and obtained the board's permission to make large expenditures on plant equipment. In 1927 outlays for plant additions and machinery amounted to $1,136,000, and in 1928 an additional $307,000 was spent.[68] In that year Bigelow-Hartford engineers, working with the textile-machinery house of Crompton & Knowles, accomplished the notable feat of perfecting an 18-foot velvet loom adaptable to jacquard weaving. It was the first such loom to be produced in the industry and was to make possible the weaving of broadloom wiltons. Also in 1928, William Pearsall, superintendent of the Thompsonville plant, and John Davidson, of Clinton, were sent abroad to investigate foreign equipment that might give Bigelow-Hartford some technological advantage over its competitors.[69]

The European trip turned up nothing of value, and Pearsall left the company soon after. He was succeeded at Thompsonville by his assistant, Elliot I. Petersen, who had begun work in Bigelow-Hartford's New York offices as a designer's apprentice in 1915.[70] Pearsall had not been markedly effective and perhaps Sweetser should have replaced him sooner. It was characteristic of the president, however, that he moved slowly in such cases, that he gave those who were in positions of importance when he became president ample opportunity to prove themselves.[71]

Sweetser realized, perhaps because of the Pearsall episode, that a need existed in the company for over-all manufacturing supervision of a high standard. After World War I and the retirement of William Lyford as general manufacturing superintendent, there had been no central responsibility for co-ordination of mill activities. Norman appeared to have appreciated this deficiency when he made B. F. Connolly manager of plants, but his personality and Connolly's had combined to rob that move of success. Eugene Ong had recommended to Louis Liggett that the production function be headed by a vice-president with adequate authority to raise manufacturing to the level of marketing, but the new president had been too much occupied with the general and broad tasks facing him to solve the manufacturing problem immediately. Unfortunately there was no one within the company upon whom he could easily draw. By virtue of experience, John Davidson was the logical person but he had demonstrated that he was too much an individualist and too completely in the mold of the old New England textile mill manager to develop and apply company policy. Petersen had great promise but he was still young and inexperienced. Sweetser therefore turned to the consultants whom he had employed for help. One of these advisers was recruited for full-time service; in January, 1929, Richard G. Knowland was made assistant to the president for manufacturing.[72]

Knowland, a Bostonian like Sweetser, had received his degree in chemical engineering from Massachusetts Institute of Technology. He had worked in New England as a consultant in textile chemistry for some years and had done work for some of the cotton companies with which Sweetser had formerly been connected, as well as for Bigelow-Hartford after Sweetser had joined that company. Knowland's reputation as a textile manufacturing authority was high and he made sufficient impression in his new position to be elected a vice-president in 1930.[73]

Knowland's first responsibility was toward the mills and he speedily attempted to get them in line with the company's marketing operations. Thus, when the cost of goods sold in September, 1929, showed a considerable increase over the same month in the previous year, Knowland had so systematized returns that irregularities stood out. He informed the wool buyer and the two department heads involved of the disproportionate amount of wool in storage and goods in process and urged them to reduce inventories in line with the current rate of production.[74]

Some improvements were made in the physical setup of the mills but the new attitude that Knowland brought was more important. Davidson, approaching retirement, was still allowed to go his own way at Clinton but Petersen, a younger man, rose to the challenge offered him by new leadership and brought fresh energy to bear on Thompsonville. He began to submit annual reports to management, something that had never been done before. For 1929 he was able to report that the axminster looms in his mill had been speeded up by an average of 10 per cent, that the stores system had been reorganized, and that savings of $126,000 in operating costs over the previous year had been made. Petersen also noted that Thompsonville foremen had organized a craft club which met to hear speakers discuss significant developments in manufacturing and that employees were active in various athletic leagues. Such leagues, including baseball, softball, and bowling, became popular in both plant cities and helped to promote company loyalty.

Sweetser's general approach to his job seems to have brought an improvement in the attitude of Bigelow-Hartford's executive group. No longer did the vast gap exist between president and officers and department heads; even the difference in incomes that had been such a source of irritation to his subordinates during Norman's time was reduced. In March, 1928, the executive committee established a new compensation fund for management. This plan, providing bonuses to the officers and mill superintendents after allowance for dividends, made certain that no officer or executive would receive payments completely out of relation to the company's size.[75]

At the end of his first few years as president, Sweetser had thus accomplished much. He had attempted with some success to give the company better management, he had sought and obtained better coordination of its functions, he had seen to it that its factories were better equipped and that its marketing efforts were better planned and directed. In his efforts he had been supported by his board of directors and by the vast improvement in morale which he had effected among his subordinates. With these accomplishments behind him in 1929, some physical and some intangible, Sweetser turned his attention to what seemed to be a major problem in the company's future.

MERGER WITH STEPHEN SANFORD & SONS

The climax in Bigelow's adjustment of manufacture to the growing demand for broadloom carpeting came in 1929. It came, however, not through a large new installation of broad looms in existing plants but in merger with a carpet company already strong in broadloom carpet manufacture. This was a bold stroke—and, as it proved, a wise one—in acquiring manufacturing facilities commensurate with product demand in the changing market for carpets.

TABLE **26**

BIGELOW–HARTFORD AND STEPHEN SANFORD & SONS

Looms by Types and Widths   1929

	Narrow (*27" to 72"*)	*Wide* a (*Above 72"*)
Bigelow-Hartford		
Wilton	374	31
Axminster	358	120
Tapestry b	113	76
Total	845	227
Stephen Sanford & Sons		
Wilton	0	0
Axminster	211	217
Tapestry	90	129
Total	301	346

a At first all pile-weaving looms wider than 27 inches were considered broad looms. By 1929 the dividing point was 72 inches. Today the line is drawn at 9 feet.
b These were the tapestry looms that had been converted to Brewster broadloom.

Source: Bigelow-Sanford Carpet Company, Inc., Loom Inventories, 1927–1930, Manufacturing Department.

By 1929, Stephen Sanford & Sons, like Mohawk, was making seamless rugs exclusively. Bigelow-Hartford was still devoting only 21.6 per cent of its total looms to this type of production. While the company had thus increased its percentage of broad looms from 2.6 per cent in 1914, its increase had not been enough to catch up. The figures in Table 26 show that most of the added broad looms were devoted to axminster or tapestry; although a wide wilton loom had been built by 1927, the contract business was continuing to provide a profitable use for narrow wilton looms and therefore tended to discourage the expenditure of money on expensive broad looms.

Bigelow-Hartford's shortage of wide looms was not something that suddenly seemed acute in 1929. When the Barnes Textile Service had appraised the company's plants in 1926, its engineers pointed out that 500 of its narrow axminster looms were idle because of a lack of demand for their products while the few wide axminster looms that the company had were on 24-hour operation. While wide looms were added within the next few years, they were not acquired in sufficient numbers to come to grips with the issue. Sweetser and his colleagues, however, had the matter very much on their minds.

Two methods seemed to offer a chance of improvement in the company's position. One was the obvious plan of buying and installing broad looms to raise the total to a competitive level; the other was to buy another company already so equipped. The full realization of the first plan had the disadvantage of requiring space for the new looms, time for them to be manufactured and installed, and the disposal of old but still valuable machinery. Moreover, it would probably have been more difficult to convince the board of directors to authorize expenditures large enough for this purpose whereas, in the atmosphere of the 1920's, merger had a dramatic appeal. Not only looms would come from such a plan but other facilities, customers, and the prestige that seemed always to follow size.

Eugene Ong had advanced the possibility of a merger in 1926 as his solution of Bigelow's loom problem. He had recommended it for still another reason.[76] Growing competition from imported oriental rugs and from linoleum manufacturers worried him, and a merger of two or more companies could produce one with enough strength and power to assume carpet industry leadership and aid in overcoming such competition. This argument gained in cogency when price-cutting and other disturbing practices became common within the industry itself,[77] creating a situation that only a very effective company could overcome.

If wide looms were to be obtained and leadership made possible for Bigelow-Hartford by merger with some other company, that company had to be one of its large competitors. When Ong made his recommendation, two of these were possibilities, both because they were family-owned and could therefore be bargained with more easily than could a concern with many shareholders, and because they were stronger than Bigelow-Hartford in the broadloom field. These were Alexander Smith & Sons, whose huge mills at Yonkers made it the largest manufacturer of woven floor coverings in the United States, and Stephen Sanford & Sons, whose plant was at Amsterdam, near Schenectady. Both companies were old and well-established, and both made products that had high standing in the trade and with consumers.

The Sanford firm, smaller than Bigelow-Hartford, was not for sale when Sweetser became president. There did seem to be some possibility, however, of a merger with Alexander Smith. John R. Simpson, a lawyer with Wall Street affiliations, had become interested early in 1927 in the possibility of a combination of companies engaged in the manufacture of floor coverings. He had some knowledge of the circumstances that might make Bigelow-Hartford and Smith likely partners, and he initiated discussions between them.

The scope of the proposal was extended to include first W. & J. Sloane, Smith's wholesale selling agent, and then the Armstrong Cork Company, manufacturers of linoleum. Bigelow-Hartford's directors were reluctant to acquire a linoleum company with operations of a nature unfamiliar to them, but discussions about union of the other three concerns continued into 1928. Matters seemed about to culminate in a mutually satisfactory amalgamation when the Smith owners, for undisclosed reasons, suddenly refused to allow Bigelow-Hartford's production executives to inspect their plant. Sweetser and his associates would not go further without more knowledge of the Smith facilities; Smith stood firm and the Boston group thereupon withdrew from the merger plan.[78] Smith continued independent and Sloane remained as its sales agent.

For Bigelow-Hartford the idea of merger was not dead and the possibility of success in another direction appeared within the same year. When rumors of the Bigelow-Sloane-Smith deal circulated through the trade, John Sanford of Amsterdam, perhaps alarmed at what such a combination might do to the industry, had discussed the possibility of uniting his company with Mohawk Carpet Mills, also located in Amsterdam.[79] This plan, like the other, came to nothing, but the way was opened for sale of the Sanford company to Bigelow-Hartford.

John Sanford had entered the carpet business in the 1870's. Under the careful tutelage of his father, Stephen, he had progressed through each phase of the operations, but on the whole his father had given him little responsibility. His brother, William, having died in the 1890's, John had become the sole heir to the business. Upon the death of his father in 1913, John had incorporated the company immediately, but then had left the direction to the very able group of executives whom his father had trained. John's frequent and prolonged sojourns in Saratoga, Palm Beach, Paris, and Long Island precluded much active participation in the management of the concern, but he had kept well informed on the general pattern of its activities.[80] Indeed, John Sanford seems to have been genuinely attached to the family enterprise and during most of the twenties quickly had rebuffed any suggestion that he part with the business.

By 1929 his long-standing reluctance to dispose of the enterprise was changing. He may have been influenced (as Sweetser may have been) by the general trend toward mergers and larger business organizations in the 1920's. A more influential factor was the lack of interest of his son, Stephen (Laddie), in carpet manufacture; Sanford's two daughters were no more inclined toward trade, nor were their husbands. The Sanford executive group was not young and management succession was a clear problem. John Sanford himself had reached the point in life at which he wanted to make certain of his money and to slough off even the very general business responsibilities that he had assumed.

From Bigelow-Hartford's standpoint, sound reasons existed to consider the purchase of Sanford, perhaps better than those involved in the Smith discussions. Foremost was the modern Sanford plant, well equipped with desirable broad looms and manned by a usually stable and tractable labor force. Almost as important were the Sanford products that the enlarged company would sell; its Beauvais axminster line (still one of the best-known names in the carpet business) was generally regarded as the industry's leading line in the medium-priced range. Under Sanford management it had been produced to sell at prices that made it highly competitive.[81]

The two companies would complement each other as neatly as had the Bigelow and Hartford concerns in 1914. About 80 per cent of Sanford's production was made up of axminsters in the low- and medium-priced ranges and the remainder consisted of low-priced floor coverings that Bigelow-Hartford did not make. Bigelow-Hartford, on the other hand, wove axminsters that were higher in price than those of Sanford, and it went up the quality scale in other lines to produce most of the highest grades and types. Like many other carpet companies, it sold through wholesalers; Sanford, however, had been selling direct to retailers for many years. A combined organization could offer stores the choice of dealing directly with the maker or with wholesalers.[82]

These were among the practical considerations that appealed to Sweetser and his Boston directors. To Sanford something else was of significance, and this was Sweetser himself. In the Bigelow-Hartford president the carpet millionaire seemed to have found a veritable *beau ideal*, a man who combined charm and manner with ability and knowledge, exactly the person to assume responsibility for the fortunes of the company of which Sanford was so proud.

Sweetser and Sanford had met when the former attempted to persuade the Sanford company to join the Carpet Institute.[83] In this effort Sweetser had been successful; he was equally successful in arranging the merger of his company and Sanford's.

There was no difficulty this time in obtaining or giving information. Arguments over questions of valuation arose but the discussions were conducted on frank if firm lines. In charge of negotiations for Sanford was W. D. McGregor, a careful Scottish partner in that company's accounting firm. Sweetser acted for Bigelow-Hartford.

The basis for the sale agreement was the comparative size of the two companies and their earnings over a reasonably long period. Bigelow-Hartford was estimated to produce about 10 per cent of America's yardages of wool and worsted floor coverings while Sanford manufactured about 8 per cent; the higher price average of the Bigelow-Hartford grades meant that in dollar value its looms turned out about 12 per cent of the country's total, compared with Sanford's 7 per cent.[84] Earnings and net worth of the two companies are shown in Table 27.

In 1927 Bigelow-Hartford had increased its outstanding capital stock so that this consisted, at the time of the merger discussion, of 55,000 shares of preferred stock, $100 par, authorized and outstanding, and 241,500 authorized shares of no-par common stock, of which 240,085 shares were outstanding. The capitalization of Stephen Sanford & Sons

TABLE **27**

BIGELOW–HARTFORD AND STEPHEN SANFORD & SONS

Financial Comparison as of December 31, 1928

	Bigelow-Hartford	Stephen Sanford
Net worth a	$23,844,000	$22,519,000
Average net sales in previous 5 years	19,804,000	12,874,000
Average net earnings in previous 5 years	1,967,000	967,000
Percentage earnings on net sales	10.2%	7.5%
Percentage earnings on net worth	8.8%	4.3%
Net plant value	$11,185,000	$ 8,764,000

ª Manufacturing goods inventories adjusted to cost basis.

Source: Correspondence between John Sanford and John Sweetser (Secretary's office, Bigelow-Sanford).

was 187,200 shares, with a par value of $100. Neither company had bonded indebtedness.[85]

John Sanford's sale price was $20,000,000; he was willing to accept $16,000,000 in stock in the new corporation and to retain $4,000,000 in cash and securities of Stephen Sanford & Sons. Bigelow, for its part, declared that its stock was worth $150 per share and that its value should not be judged by current market price which was about $100 for the preferred and between $94 and $85 for the common in October, 1929. Sweetser held that Sanford should view Bigelow's value in terms of its earnings. At $150 per share, Bigelow-Hartford stock would be selling at about 15 times its 1928 earnings.

On this point no meeting of minds took place, for the Sanford men refused to consider the Bigelow-Hartford stock as worth more than $100.[86] Eventually the Sanford valuation of $100 per share was accepted and by Tuesday, October 29, 1929, "Black Tuesday" in Wall Street, the terms had been settled. Announcement of the merger was made, putting an end to the rumors circulated, some of which had said that Alexander Smith was to be included in the deal.[87]

At a special meeting on November 25, 1929, the Bigelow-Hartford stockholders ratified purchase of the assets and business of Stephen Sanford & Sons by their company. The Sanford shareholders received $5,000,000 in 6 per cent serial notes, 10 notes of $500,000 each, one of which was to mature each year over a 10-year period, with provision for anticipation of payments in whole or part. In addition, 85,000 shares of Bigelow-Hartford common stock were to be transferred to the Sanford owners, and the authorized common stock of the Bigelow-Hartford company was increased accordingly.

The new company was left with 55,000 preferred shares of $100 par and 326,500 shares of no-par common stock. This change and the change of the corporate name to Bigelow-Sanford Carpet Company, Incorporated, were duly noted by the Boston Stock Exchange, where Bigelow-Hartford's stock had been traded. The new capitalization meant that the Sanford holdings made up 26 per cent of the common stock total; next in consequence among the shareholders were F. S. Moseley & Company with 18,478 shares, and Kidder, Peabody & Company, whose investment amounted to 15,858 shares. The two investment houses thus had about 10 per cent of the common stock outstanding.

The number of directors was increased from eleven to fourteen, and John Sanford, Stephen (Laddie) Sanford, and Samuel Welldon (an official of the First National Bank of the City of New York, where for many years the Sanfords had done their banking) became members of the board. At the first directors' meeting of the new company, the office of chairman of the board was revived and John Sanford was elected to fill it.[88]

The executive staff of Bigelow-Sanford was much the same as that of Bigelow-Hartford. John Sanford had not told his executives of his intentions and they had not known of the sale negotiations; neither had he sought provision for their employment by the new company. They had been well paid through the years and he felt that they should have saved enough to retire.[89] There was some talk that they would have tried to buy the Sanford company themselves if they had had the chance but they had not.[90] Only C. H. Handerson, Sanford's vice-president and sales manager, and W. B. Cooper, manager of the Amsterdam plant, were employed by Bigelow-Sanford. Neither man remained long.

On lower personnel levels, the usual casualties of amalgamation were somewhat in evidence but do not seem to have been so numerous as in the 1914 merger. The Sanford offices in New York were closed and their functions assumed by Bigelow-Hartford's staff there, which probably meant some reduction of clerical workers; sixteen of the Sanford salesmen were reported to have been absorbed into the new company and those remaining were successful in securing new positions.[91] The wider product line offered to the trade and the feeling of business enthusiasm that continued for a time in spite of the stock market crash made serious work force reductions unnecessary, at least until the effects of the market slump were more severely felt.

Inevitably other adjustments to new conditions were required, part of the process of making two not altogether similar parts equal to the sum of their whole. Even before the sales arrangement had been ratified, Bigelow-Hartford had written one of its English wool brokers to say "we are not in a position to make you an offer [for wool] . . . due principally to our purchasing the Stephen Sanford & Sons Mill. . . . Our policy is to remain out of the market until we have completed the wool inventory at that mill. . . ." [92]

Settlement of the Sanford wool inventory value took until after the first of January, 1930. When it was completed, Bigelow-Hartford found that, after opinions of the two wool buyers had been reconciled, the value was less than the Sanford estimate, which had been based on prices prevailing as of June 30, 1929. Accordingly, a transfer of 11,650 shares of common stock was made to the company from the Sanford holdings. [93]

Although Sweetser announced that no changes in production or merchandising were contemplated by the new company, reduction of the number of Sanford lines was intended and was carried out. [94] Generally, though, Sweetser's policy of business as usual was followed, and Bigelow-Sanford walked softly until it could determine the best method to employ in this new area of expanded operation.

Typically, Sweetser tried to do for Sanford what he had done for Bigelow-Hartford when it was necessary to improve relations with competitors. Soon after the union, Sweetser was approached by A. W. Shuttleworth of Mohawk, who asked if Bigelow-Sanford would become represented on the directorate of the Amsterdam Chamber of Commerce; co-operation in the past from the Sanford mill superintendent had been poor. [95] Sweetser promised his support and urged the Amsterdam manager to do what he could to work with the city and with the Mohawk company. [96]

Looking at the figures for 1929, Sweetser could take comfort from the dollar signs of progress. He could also take satisfaction from the knowledge that he had restored the company's internal morale, that he had strengthened its manufacturing and sales organization, that he had regained for it the confidence of dealers and competitors, and that he had, through the Sanford merger, made his company the largest manufacturer of woven floor coverings in the United States.

CHAPTER 12

YEARS OF DEPRESSION AND RECOVERY, 1930–1936

THE DEPRESSION'S FIRST IMPACT

As the year 1930 advanced, factory chimneys across the country ceased to belch the smoke that meant good times. Grass grew between the rails of once-busy freight sidings, "For Sale" signs creaked on the fences of empty warehouses, manufacturers and retailers vainly tried every advertising trick to tempt the ever-diminishing consumer dollar. Where once queues of men had gathered to change shift, long rows formed outside employment offices, waiting desperately for jobs that never came. The gaunt hungry specter of depression was abroad in the land.

The depression hit Bigelow-Sanford as it hit many manufacturing firms —early and hard. In 1930 the company recorded a loss of $608,700, the first deficit year of Sweetser's management. Early in the year orders had flowed in at about the 1929 rate, and Sweetser, like many others, believed that the economic situation would remedy itself in short order. Wool had been bought in anticipation of continuing activity, and production had been scheduled at a high level of operation. With a production lead time extending over several months, carpet companies were forced to project their manufacturing plans well ahead. The result was a rapid accumulation of inventory. By the end of the year, sales had fallen so drastically that price cuts of 10 to 30 per cent were necessary and inventories had to be sharply written down in recognition of the new realities.

In May, 1930, Mohawk had passed a dividend, an action which decreased investor confidence in the carpet industry. Bigelow's common stock declined from 85 in December, 1929, to a new low of 59½. Sweetser, expressing an attitude held by other men in a position to be well informed about the condition of business, wrote John Sanford not to be alarmed at the stock's decline: "Personally I think it's cheap at this price and am contemplating buying some more myself." [1] By December, however, it had dropped to 32½, partly, at least, because of the decision not to pay the common stock dividend usually payable on November 1.

A fillip to the hopes of industrialists and merchants had come from the passing of the Hawley-Smoot Tariff Act, signed by President Hoover in June, 1930. This act, which the carpet manufacturers had joined to support, gave them what one of their number described as the best tariff they had ever had.[2] It continued to permit free importation of carpet wools, and it strengthened the position of the domestic manufacturer against the importation of finished carpets. Republicans, traditionally supporters of high tariffs, regarded the new act as a desirable step toward increased business. John Sanford was a firm believer in high tariffs and had taken a part in framing the McKinley Tariff Act a generation earlier. He was pleased with the new bill.

The directors had previously discussed the advisability of passing the August common stock dividend, but Sweetser felt that it should be paid and he was supported by Deknatel. While the dividend had not been earned, ample funds existed and the president still anticipated better business in the fall and in 1931.[3] Sanford did not share Sweetser's belief in the desirability of betting on future business; he recommended the payment of dividends only in accordance with earnings.[4] With the conservative soundness of that stand Sweetser did not quarrel; but Bigelow's new position of industry leadership imposed obligations, and failure to pay the dividend was likely to be construed as a sign of financial weakness. When, by the end of the summer season, matters had not improved, the president was willing to conform to the wishes of the board chairman.

Sanford's views might even have prevailed against payment of the August, 1930, dividend if there had not been changes on the board, changes that may have removed some degree of conservatism and that certainly robbed it of experience. In January Robert Winsor had died after a two-year illness, to be followed in March by Frank G. Webster. Both had been directors of Bigelow and its predecessor companies for many years, and both had provided a wide background of financial knowledge. The Kidder, Peabody connection was maintained by the election of Winsor's son-in-law, Walter Trumbull, Jr., and Kidder's New York resident partner, Charles S. Sargent, but these men had neither the interest nor the familiarity with Bigelow's business that the two veteran directors had had.

The dividend discussion did not mean that there was any significant dispute between Sweetser and Sanford. Relations continued harmonious. The older man deferred to the president as the operating executive in close touch with the situation, and Sweetser, for his part, drew on Sanford for astute advice and understanding of the difficulties with which he was faced—while he paid the respect due the company's major stockholder.

The industry was further demoralized early in 1931 when Alexander Smith appeared to be planning a return to its auction system. On January 29, 1931, the Smith management announced an auction of 45,000 bales, to be held on February 9. This announcement at a time when the industry was looking for stability made manufacturers and their customers disheartened. One man wrote a Bigelow executive that Philadelphia carpet circles were "sick over the auction," and that he had heard Mohawk was prepared to cut prices 25 per cent and was considering the appointment of John F. Norman as president.[5]

The effect of the auction was tempered somewhat by the realization that Smith merely intended to close out dropped patterns. Prices were from 10 to 29 per cent below list and the general feeling among Smith's rivals was that Smith had suffered more from the auction than had anyone else. No one was surprised when Smith cut its prices 10 per cent after the sale. Mohawk, then the small mills, then Bigelow, followed.[6]

Later in 1931 prices were cut again (in spite of guarantees to dealers), then raised, and cut again. Uncertainty was rife. A slight improvement in March permitted both Bigelow and Mohawk to operate their Amsterdam plants at near-capacity, but this proved temporary. October price-cuts sent Bigelow's sales in November and December below the million-dollar mark in each month.[7] Such a poor showing had not been in evidence in years, but a worse one was to be seen in 1932.

By dint of great effort and widespread economy, Bigelow emerged from 1931 with a profit of $414,000, somewhat better than Mohawk's net earnings of $311,000.[8] The normally optimistic Bigelow president was by this time convinced that the future was not promising.

In the meantime, friction had developed within the carpet industry. In April, Irving S. Paull resigned as president of the Carpet Institute in protest. A new president was elected, but Sweetser continued to serve as chairman of the Institute's board of directors.[9] Not much more than one year later Sweetser, too, decided to withdraw his company from the Institute. He took the attitude that Bigelow was bellwether to a flock in which some of the sheep were refusing to follow the leader, and he felt that his company would do better on its own.[10]

For Sweetser, who had had so much to do with the organization of the Institute, this was a remarkable about-face, but he was indignant over what he believed was the failure of his competitors to associate in the adoption of necessary sound, constructive policies. In view of the disharmony within the Institute, Sweetser's resignation would probably have meant its collapse. He was at length persuaded to continue Bigelow's membership, and the adoption in 1933 of the National Recovery Administration's carpet industry code brought some degree of stability to the Institute.

As Sweetser faced the problems of depression he expressed grave concern over his company's performance. Yet, in review, and in comparison with the experience of other manufacturing firms in the same period, the points which stand out in the Bigelow-Sanford performance are the company's limited deficit and its remarkably strong financial position throughout its years of travail. By the end of 1932, after an operating loss for that year of over a million dollars, and after the $5,000,000 debt owed John Sanford had been completely paid, there were still net current assets of over $10,000,000. This record of careful husbandry reflects the conservative influence of Boston bankers. Neal Rantoul and his associates must have sat down at Bigelow board meetings with a feeling that here at least their industrial investments were well protected.

MEETING THE CHALLENGE WITH NEW MARKETING METHODS

While Sweetser at first believed that the deterioration of the carpet market would not be of long duration, he soon recognized that forceful measures had to be taken. In the second half of 1930 he, accordingly, brought about changes in the marketing organization and initiated a series of new policies which were to be developed and implemented in the next few years.

Important shifts came in organization and executive personnel in the second half of 1930. To effect closer co-ordination between sales and manufacturing, R. G. Knowland, vice-president for manufacturing, was appointed general manager, to be responsible for both departments and to report directly to the president—the objective of this administrative innovation was not fully realized because antagonism within the executive group later compelled Knowland to relinquish his title of general manager and some of his functions.[11] What the president regarded as dead wood was pruned from the sales department itself. J. J. Delaney, secretary, was made general manager of sales. P. F. O'Neil was moved from purchasing to become assistant to H. V. Campbell, the marketing vice-president.

Three changes in marketing policy were especially significant. One was the institution of a new advertising program designed to obtain greater consumer recognition for Bigelow products. The second was the adoption of a policy of direct sales to retailers through company-owned warehouses, leading to the elimination of wholesalers and the careful selection of retailers. The third, more of long-run than of immediate value, was the development and sale of products new to the Bigelow line.

In April, 1931, the company's advertising agency was replaced by the firm of Newell-Emmett Company, which immediately set to work on an extensive survey of consumer taste to provide a basis for advertising recommendations. After eight months spent querying housewives in 21 large cities, Newell-Emmett felt that it could proffer an advertising program with some authority. In January, 1932, the results of its survey were given practical form in the most extensive advertising campaign in the carpet industry's history. Six leading magazines were the basic media, supplemented by publicity in trade publications, by a cut and matrix service for dealers, and by store-window and rug-department displays. The campaign, so the company's advertising manager asserted, was intended to reach every home in America that could afford a Bigelow rug or carpet. Advertising expenditures were increased from $442,000 in 1931 to $526,000 in 1932; of these amounts, $225,000 had been spent on consumer media in 1931 and $364,000 went for that expense in 1932. The total expenditures were 2.4 per cent of net sales in 1931, 4.7 per cent in 1932.

The significant feature of the new advertising was the way in which it sought to implant awareness of Bigelow's name in the minds of consumers. The agency's research had shown that only one-third of the women interviewed could name the make of one or more of their rugs, and 4 or 5 per cent thought that wilton and axminster were brand names. To correct this ignorance, Bigelow developed a name label which it fixed to all its products in such a way that the label could readily be seen by customers in a store and which it displayed prominently in its advertisements and sales promotion. The Sanford name was not used on the label although this did not mean a change in corporate title. A trade-mark was registered showing two hands tying a weaver's knot, with the legend underneath, "Woven by the Bigelow Weavers," and the trade-mark was printed in gold on royal blue satin.

The design carried an implication of craftsmanship, and this idea was stressed by the advertising copy. Since a workman is traditionally no better than the material with which he works, equal emphasis was placed on the high quality of the wool used by the Bigelow Weavers. "Lively wool" was the copy-writer's phrase, indicating that Bigelow avoided "kempy" wool in its products, wool that would not hold dye colors, that would break off and wear easily, that lacked resiliency underfoot. The argument was pointed up by drawings of gay, little sheep bounding over clouds on legs resembling coil springs, and the sheep became almost as much a part of the company's advertising as did the Bigelow Weavers' trade-mark.

Measurement of the effect of quality claims on consumers is difficult, and so is the judgment of quality by untrained purchasers. Bigelow regarded itself as the pioneer in the development of devices and methods of testing the qualities of its products, and it installed rigid inspection all the way through the manufacturing processes. Nevertheless, complaints did occur, and the company undertook to satisfy these and guarantee its merchandise. To help its sales force meet and satisfy customer complaints, a complaint manual was issued early in 1933. The manual listed the most frequent causes of complaints and suggested methods of dealing with them. As they came in from individual salesmen they were passed on to the mills and to the sales force in the field for preventive action.[12]

On the whole, Bigelow could honestly claim high quality for its floor coverings. In 1934 the company's manufacturing consultant, S. L. Duffett made a comparison of Bigelow rugs with those of its two largest competitors. Duffett found that the company's products were generally made of wools of higher grade and quality, were better finished, and were superior on most other counts.[13] Claims of high craftsmanship and excellence of materials were more than advertising jargon.

These themes continued to be stressed in advertising, but not at the expense of innovation. A new advertising manager, appointed in January, 1934,[14] sent around the country forty exhibits in which modern bedrooms were displayed with floors covered by specially designed contemporary rugs and carpets.[15] A planning service to assist retailers in better layouts of their carpet departments was established in 1935.[16] The 1936 advertising campaign used the radio, a decorator discussing rooms pictured in folios distributed to consumers and a contest encouraging listeners to design their own rooms.[17]

Direct distribution to retailers, the second of Bigelow's three major changes in this period, first began to take effect in 1931. There were many reasons for the changes. Several competitors had been shifting to direct selling in the belief that it would give better control of transactions at the point of sale. In Sweetser's view, advertising could overcome the important lack of consumer recognition but sales were made in stores, not on the pages of magazines, and Bigelow products could be sold aggressively only if the retailer had some direct incentive to do so. This incentive, Sweetser believed, could be provided only by direct contact between the carpet manufacturer and the carpet retailer; it could not effectively be achieved when a wholesaler stood between the two.

A more immediate influence on Sweetser's decision was the acquisition, at the time of the Sanford merger, of a distribution system already operating on a direct sales basis. Convinced that the Sanford system was an improvement over the old Bigelow-Hartford practice of selling through wholesalers, Sweetser determined to pattern his whole distribution system on the Sanford experience. In later years there arose some doubt as to whether the move toward standardized marketing was well conceived; partly it was thought that the lower-priced Sanford line did not lend itself to combined treatment with the higher-priced Bigelow-Hartford product, but more especially it was regarded as unwise to have tapped only one segment of the market when a combination of direct and indirect selling might have covered a larger range of consumer buying. Nevertheless, the considered judgment of the Sweetser management regarded the advantages of a single, direct system as outweighing the advantages of an overlapping marketing structure.

The shift to direct selling was accomplished slowly and with caution. Every effort was made to alienate as few wholesalers as possible. The shift had been made easier by the reduction in the number of wholesale outlets by turning certain territories over to exclusive distributorships in 1930, a move then effected to bring about more aggressive selling of Bigelow products. The Lack Carpet Company, for instance, had been given sole distribution rights for Bigelow-Sanford products in New York City; and the Warren-Allen Carpet Company had been awarded a similar commission for Cincinnati, Buffalo, Syracuse, and the entire New England area. These wholesalers had agreed to sell woolen floor coverings made only by Bigelow-Sanford in return for its promise not to sell through any other agency in their territories.[18]

As the depression deepened Bigelow's projected divorcement from its wholesalers received assistance from an unexpected quarter.[19] Many wholesalers, having anticipated an early end to the depression, had continued to order carpets and had found themselves faced with mounting inventories for which they could not pay. As financial attrition took place, Bigelow's wholesalers declined in number until by the end of 1931 only 12 remained.

Beginning in October, 1932, the company gradually replaced these remaining wholesalers with its own distributing organization.[20] The company announced that it would take over the functions of wholesalers only in cases of firms which were operating hazardously or which had gone out of business,[21] but the change ultimately went beyond those limits.

In Sweetser's view the direct sale of carpets on a large scale necessitated a national warehousing system. True, Sanford had used no warehouses; he had followed a policy of shipping directly from his mill to the retailer. But Sweetser believed that this informal system could not continue under the expanded conditions brought about by the merger. He felt that service would be an important ingredient of the new company's success. By establishing a warehouse in Minneapolis in 1932, he opened what was to become a number of centers from which rapid delivery of Bigelow carpets could be made.

Sweetser did not believe that any profit could be made from taking over the wholesaling and warehousing operation. He did hope that the main advantages of direct distribution—close contact with market conditions, control over product dissemination, and reduced credit losses— would justify the move. Animosity from wholesalers was anticipated; but, if the plan proved successful, it was hoped that the results would compensate for the loss of good will.

On entering the wholesaling business the company had to increase its New York office accommodation and ground-floor display space. In anticipation of this situation, the New York headquarters were moved in September, 1932, from 385 Madison Avenue to its present location at 140 Madison Avenue, where the ground floor, three upper floors, and an extensive basement were rented at a saving.

Most of the process of supplanting the wholesalers was accomplished by 1935. One large wholesale house, the Lack Carpet Company, continued to sell Bigelow products in New York City until December 1, 1939. Thereafter the company was selling direct to retailers everywhere.[22]

Having decided that its strength lay with the retailer, Bigelow sought his support by reducing the charge for its cut-carpet service. By this action Bigelow narrowed the difference in price between cut-carpets and full rolls and enabled retail stores to effect substantial inventory savings without sacrifice of the pattern and color assortments. Retailers were consequently placed on almost the same price basis as large-volume wholesalers, and the resultant hue-and-cry from the remaining wholesalers made Sweetser think that the policy would win retailer support.[23]

The National Association of Wholesale Floor Covering Distributors was loud in condemnation of the Bigelow-Sanford policy of wholesaler elimination, and it appealed to the National Recovery Administration for relief from the change in cut-order prices, a change which had been adopted by other manufacturers who were afraid that they would lose retailers to Bigelow if they did not make the same concession.[24] The wholesalers' association protested also to John Sanford, but he was equally certain that Bigelow's course was right and he left the matter entirely in Sweetser's hands. The NRA bureau refused to hold a hearing on the subject. There was nothing that the distributors could do, except to attempt to influence dealers away from the company.

However successful any such attempt might have been, by the end of 1936 Bigelow's 19 branches were supplying 9,514 retailers from their warehouses across the country. In that year those dealers accounted for a gross sales volume of $28,478,000, a 41 per cent increase in sales over the preceding year. Not all of the increase could be attributed to the new distribution system, but the company felt that the merit of its decision had been confirmed.[25]

The third and from a long-range standpoint perhaps the most significant of Bigelow's depression-born efforts to obtain greater sales was the development and introduction of new products; this was going on while the new advertising program and the change to direct distribution were being put into effect. Like the first two, the third step is difficult to evaluate in terms of influence on the company's growth, for the new products had to be considered over a fairly long period of time in terms of their success. Perhaps the most important point to be noted in connection with this step was the new attitude that it betokened. What was needed was a fresh approach to the entire question of how carpets should be made, what kind of carpets they should be, and whether, indeed, a carpet company to be successful over the long run should not make something else as well as carpets. The full realization of this philosophy in Bigelow-Sanford did not come for almost twenty years, but Sweetser's steps in the early 1930's started the company along the path.

While the carpet industry in the thirties was still in the era in which no fundamental research was being done, some opportunity for competitive superiority did seem to exist on the fringe of the carpet-making field. The desirability of eliminating expensive binding and seaming to prevent raveling of cut-carpet led Bigelow in 1934 to secure manufacturing and selling rights to a patented nonraveling process called "Lokweave." With this process a carpet would hold its edge after cutting without having to be seamed or bound, and the process made joining and repairing of the carpet much easier.

In July, 1934, the company began to sell 27 plain colors of this Lokweave carpeting under its license agreement. Manufacturing difficulties were overcome and the new product quickly became successful.[26] By 1936 a thermoplastic sealing tape had been developed which permitted quicker joining. While the output of 137,000 square yards of Lokweave in 1936 was small compared with the more than 2,000,000 square yards of velvet floor covering produced in the same period, it was a sign of progress.

Another improvement was the introduction of hard-twist carpeting, new-style products in which the yarns were twisted to provide greater wear resistance; the name "Twistweave" was registered with the patent office in 1936.[27] Like Lokweave, Twistweave goods were priced higher than conventional wiltons and velvets because of their special qualities. While, therefore, a consumer might be moved toward these fabrics by their particular virtues, that customer would generally be one who had anticipated buying a high-priced product. Twistweave and Lokweave provided dealers with sales arguments, but they did little to help them obtain volume sales, for customers who could afford the high end of the line were all too rare in those years.

The other extreme showed a greater number of householders whose tastes might incline toward woolen carpets and rugs but whose income made them buyers of linoleum or some other hard-surface floor covering. Carpet-makers could not compete effectively on a price basis with linoleum manufacturers, and price was the basis on which, in many instances, they were compelled to compete.

In its desire to develop or find some product that it could market in direct, or nearly direct, competition with linoleum, Bigelow looked far afield. Its investigators finally located a small bankrupt company which had been making a floor covering that seemed a possible solution to the problem. This was a felt rug, made with burlap backing, a jute interlayer, and a face composed of wool and hair, punched through to the back by a needling machine. Colors and designs were imprinted by huge cylinders; before printing, a heavy impregnation of a water-dispersed rubber solution was made on the back of the fabric, holding the face material in place and offering a degree of resiliency and some protection against slipping. The resulting felt rug had some resemblance to a conventional woolen, woven carpet, because of its face, but it could be made much more cheaply, thanks to the materials and to the needling process.

Bigelow's decision to buy the necessary machinery to make these rugs was based on its executives' conclusion that one hundred thousand 9 by 12 felt rugs could be sold annually for an average price of $5.90. In April, 1933, the equipment (worth, according to R. G. Knowland, $250,000) was purchased for $40,000 and moved to Amsterdam. Manufacture and sale of the felt rugs, first called "Fiburtex" and later "Marval" began soon thereafter. By 1936 the target had been overshot as the annual volume had passed $1,000,000.[28]

In March, 1936, in spite of the opposition of some of the senior executives,[29] Bigelow announced its entry into linoleum selling, to begin in the fall with a line of heavy-duty, felt-base yard goods and rugs, made for the company by Congoleum-Nairn, Incorporated. The new products were to be marketed through regular dealer outlets, and a special Felt Base Division was established within the marketing department. In November that division's manager also assumed responsibility for the sales of needled felt rugs, the Fiburtex-Marval line,[30] a logical step in view of the general price appeal of the two lines, and probably an economical one from the standpoint of staff and administration.

Whatever the long-run merits of Lokweave, Twistweave, and Marval, there seem to have been few in the sale of linoleum. Within a year and a half, the company experienced a gross loss of $228,000 on the linoleum operation. The failure of this venture was attributed by executives to the inability to obtain a product sufficiently outstanding to induce dealers to switch from their established sources of supply and to the public's lack of familiarity with the Bigelow label in the felt-base field. In addition, the company had been unable to obtain a full linoleum line and its dealers, with only 10 patterns to offer, were at a competitive disadvantage. Finally, the company had too few distribution points in relation to the large number possessed by the two major linoleum manufacturers: it had only 19 warehouses to their 120 and 80, respectively. It could not, therefore, provide such prompt service on shipments.[31]

In November, 1937, Bigelow announced that it would withdraw from the linoleum business in 1938. Its product line was assumed by a sales agent who planned to use it to round out his other merchandise.[32] The company's new sales division continued to sell Marval, and later other products were assigned to it.

The manufacture of the felt rug, Marval, of Lokweave, and of Twist-weave introduced new complexities into the company's production process. Bigelow workmen had to use such materials as rubber, pyroxylin, and thermoplastics and such methods as needling, cylinder engraving, and color printing, which were far removed from the traditional wool, jute, burlap, and cotton, and from spinning and weaving.

These changes necessarily required personnel with skills new to the company, and the beginning of the engineering revolution within Bigelow might almost be said to date from this period. Knowland had been quick to bring in a technical director; in 1935 a quality control department was installed under the technical director to aid the mills and the sales force in solving the problems posed by the more complex operations. The chemists and engineers who came in were regarded with suspicion at first by dyers, foremen, and operatives. Gradually they were able, by patient work, by tactful demonstration of results, and by understanding of the others' problems, to break down the opposition and to obtain acknowledgment that their presence and their ideas spelled progress.[33]

A significant new trend in customer tastes by the end of 1936 showed how fickle was the carpet market. In three years the output of Bigelow-Sanford's velvet weaves had doubled, whereas its axminster and wilton output had increased only about 30 per cent. The change was an indication that a new product was coming to the fore. These new velvets were not the old-style product which had been simply a cut-pile version of printed tapestry weaves (see Chart II, page 4). They were a more expensive product of a wilton type and were chiefly solid-color materials. Bigelow had itself led the way in establishing an earlier trend toward this new fabric when it had begun raw-stock dyeing at Thompsonville in 1926.

Whether new advertising programs, direct distribution, or new product lines were responsible, sales did improve considerably. After 1932, which later events showed was the company's low point, sales climbed upward through 1937. While profits did not approximate sales as closely as the shareholders might have wished, no losses were incurred from 1933 to 1937 and the objective of increasing volume, thereby keeping the mills fairly busy, was reached. Moreover, three quarterly dividends on the preferred stock which had been passed in 1933 were paid cumulatively in

November, and payments on common stock were resumed in 1935. In 1936 common stockholders received special dividends of $2.00 per share and were thus compensated to some extent for the lean years through which they had held the stock without return.

Reasons for the varied sales-profits relationship were several. A good part of Bigelow's 1933 profit, which was well over $1,000,000 and in marked contrast with the 1932 loss of $1,949,000, came from finished goods made from cheap wool and other raw materials and by labor whose wages had not yet been raised by NRA codes. In 1934 there was no longer the same spread between the cost of goods sold and the selling price; [34] both material and labor charges climbed higher in the next few years.

The new marketing system tended also to reduce profits for a time. Bigelow's general administrative and selling expense in 1934 showed an increase of about $416,000 over the previous year. Some of this difference was the effect of the change to direct distribution.[35] In spite of the increased expense, both Sanford and Sweetser remained convinced that direct distribution was a desirable policy. They believed that by personal relations with retailers the increase in annual sales volume would more than compensate for the added cost.

The NRA was a confusing element in the marketing situation from 1933 to 1935, although its effect cannot be accurately determined. Sweetser was initially an enthusiastic Roosevelt admirer (he later changed his views) and he worked with the Democratic administration through the Carpet Institute to help frame a code for the industry. He was convinced that desired stability could be obtained only through some sort of government action. When part of the action was the institution of a 40-hour week with a minimum weekly wage of $14, thereby raising manufacturing costs and lowering profit margins, it is not certain that he remained convinced.[36]

Whatever Sweetser's personal political views, Bigelow honored the carpet industry code. Other regulations included quality specifications and forbade selling at retail by manufacturers and wholesalers; some of the regulations imposed were condemned by various segments of the industry even before the code became effective on January 15, 1934. Its prohibition of quantity discounts remained the subject of opposition and was under attack when the NRA was outlawed in June, 1935.[37]

An evaluation of the company's performance during the depression is not easy in terms of what the rest of the industry was doing. Among competitors only Mohawk was issuing public figures in those years and even its figures were not so complete as those made public by Bigelow.[38] Nevertheless the Mohawk figures were closely watched by Bigelow executives —the more so when this considerably smaller company showed a marked disposition toward a better ratio of profits to sales than its larger rival (see

Table 28). The management believed that a substantial part of this difference in reported performance was due to variances in accounting methods. In general the executives believed that they had done as well as the other important firms in the industry.

TABLE **28**

BIGELOW–SANFORD AND MOHAWK CARPET MILLS

Comparison of Net Sales and Earnings   1932 to 1936

	1932	1933	1934	1935	1936
Net Sales					
Bigelow	$10,424,659	$12,569,746	$14,572,320	$19,662,134	$27,058,670
Mohawk	7,611,462	8,709,779	9,561,357	13,901,591	17,591,647
Net Profit					
Bigelow	1,948,737 a	1,140,680	173,023	416,260	1,672,206
Mohawk	1,087,799 a	348,372	73,568 a	633,190	1,261,505
Per Cent:					
Profits to					
Sales					
Bigelow	—	9.0	1.2	2.1	6.1
Mohawk	—	4.0	—	4.6	7.2

a Loss.

Source: Sales Department, Bigelow-Sanford.

MANUFACTURING DIFFICULTIES: SUPPLY, CO–ORDINATION, PRODUCTION

Side by side with the development of sales organization, policies, and volume in the depression went a development of manufacturing efficiency aimed at turning out products capable of competing in the market place in terms of price as well as quality. Such a development was difficult, for the problems of consolidation with Sanford were soon aggravated by those of the economic slump. In the wake of rigid economy, which seemed to offer a visible means of fighting reduced sales, came worker layoffs, the closing of the Clinton plant, disturbed employee relations, strike threats and strikes, and, eventually, unionism.

The immediate challenge to Bigelow's production executives in 1930 was the co-ordination of its new mill at Amsterdam with its existing facilities at Thompsonville and Clinton. Workers in the Amsterdam mill at first tended to resent the apparent subordination of the Sanford company in the new corporation and later they disliked the withdrawal of the Sanford name from the company's product lines. Executive personnel, too, presented difficulties. Cooper, the superintendent of Amsterdam, was cast in the same mold as Davidson of Clinton. Both were traditional individualists who resented any attempt by the New York office to make them conform to a general pattern. Indeed, the very mechanics of bringing the various units of the system into harmony were not clearly understood, and there remained a difference of opinion as to whether this harmony was ever achieved during Sweetser's presidency.

It is notable that while the merger with Sanford brought virtually no changes at the top executive level of the Bigelow-Hartford organization, it almost doubled the size of the operation for which the executives were responsible. It brought them responsibilities for a mill that equaled in size their largest existing unit, the mill at Thompsonville; it brought them a marketing system with which they had had no experience; it brought them a product line which was in various ways unfamiliar. It created, in short, a situation where a managerial force that was already harassed by depression worries was still further beset by the problems of an expanded organizational structure. Had the depression not occurred, some action might have been taken to adjust the top administration to its augmented responsibilities. As it was, the goal and the accomplishment were merely to bring certain parts of the new organization into co-ordination with the old without any change in the executive force.

Purchasing presented one area in which co-ordination was achieved. Wool buying was the most important aspect of this function, and steps were quickly taken to insure that Amsterdam, like Thompsonville and Clinton, obtained its needs through a central buyer. The wool buyer, the long-experienced W. J. Hines, had his office in Thompsonville, but the New York executives, Sweetser, the president, Deknatel, the treasurer, Knowland, the general manager, and P. F. O'Neil, the purchasing agent, all participated in the wool procurement operation.

The buyer sent periodic reports on the wool market to these officials and to the plant superintendents, using a wool symbol classification which had been introduced in November, 1930, to provide simplified coding of the commodity in production orders and buying estimates. At about the same time, mill consumption schedules were employed to guide the wool buyer. Each mill superintendent prepared a four-month forecast of needs; for Thompsonville, which changed its production runs more often, the interval was later changed to three months.[39]

Unfortunately, consumption forecasts and actual use were far apart during the first troubled years of the 1930's. This discrepancy called for changes in purchasing policy and in inventory accounting methods. The company had been charging wool in process out of inventory at cost, but much lower wool prices in 1930 made this practice unrealistic and helped to prevent pricing of finished goods in line with consumer market conditions. The value of wools on hand had to be written down to current market prices.[40]

Inventory losses were to occur again, despite care and study by company officials responsible for purchasing. Hines was not given a free hand although much reliance was placed on his knowledge of wools and of supply sources; in general he appears to have acted on instruction from, or in close consultation with, Deknatel and O'Neil. Deknatel, faced with the problem of financing purchases, had every reason to concern himself with the wool market, and O'Neil was interested in an effective procurement organization. Both men needed Hines' assistance. Carpet wool varied so greatly in quality, came from so many remote sources, and had so long a time in transit, that wise purchase placed a premium on experience and judgment. To make these qualities even more important, the price of wool was subject to wide and rapid fluctuations, changes that could easily mean the difference between profit and loss in a company's annual operations.

Carpet wool had no organized exchange in the United States (and still does not). Hedging was therefore impractical. Purchases through brokers were the usual means of obtaining the product whether from United States or foreign sources. Bigelow might buy in response to proffered prices and lots or it might have brokers bid to predetermined levels at auctions in Liverpool and elsewhere. Since credit reputation and reliability of quality and delivery were more important than ever with the increase in business failures from 1930, O'Neil had the company's credit manager check the financial standing of Bigelow's wool suppliers, and he had his department work out a method of checking samples against actual deliveries, to insure that quality was up to quoted specifications.[41]

Early in 1931 Bigelow sent its assistant wool buyer to China to investigate the possibility of savings through direct purchase, but the reduced consumption of American carpet mills and the existence of large wool stocks in the United States at the end of the year, with a resultant decline in the import price, made continuance of the company's old method of buying through brokers advantageous.[42]

Throughout the mills was felt a strong emphasis on economy, on cutting costs. O'Neil even went so far as to centralize the selling and disposition of waste from the three mills so that, as he wrote, "we are not selling from Thompsonville an item . . . that we might possibly, with a little urging, have used at Amsterdam and vice versa."[43] Indeed, what had been fit only for burning in 1929 might conceivably have utilization value in 1931 and 1932. Wherever possible, wage rates were adjusted downward and the efficiency of men and machines adjusted upward. At the end of 1931 in Thompsonville, for example, hardly an hourly rate remained that had been in force at the beginning of the year. Thompsonville's output was up to 3,256,000 square yards in 1931 from 2,669,000 in 1930, while its total payroll declined to $2,258,000 from $2,682,000 in the previous year. The 1932 decline in payroll, relative to output, was even greater.[44]

Fixed charges were more rigid. A severe drop came in both Bigelow's

Package Dyeing; used to dye small quantities of yarn replacing older skein-dyeing process; yarn wound on perforated stainless steel spindles is pressure dyed; eliminates a winding operation

and the industry's output from 1929 to 1932 followed by a partial recovery by 1936. Bigelow's decline was, however, greater than the industry's, its percentage of the industry production falling from 20.8 in 1929 to 17.8 in 1936.[45] One of the serious aspects of this drop was the fact that fixed charges continued and made up an increasingly larger portion of manufacturing costs. Insurance, maintenance, heat, light, depreciation—on three plants with a net value in 1930 of more than $16,000,000—were sizable items.

In July, 1932, Duffett of Barnes Textile Service reported on the possibilities of consolidating Bigelow-Sanford plants. As early as February, 1932, the executives and some of the directors had debated the advisability of closing the Clinton mill. Duffett recommended that this be done, and that Clinton's production be transferred to Amsterdam and Thompsonville. He estimated that such a move would effect savings of from $450,000 to $550,000 per year, the bulk to come from reduced labor charges but with substantial economies in overhead and supervisory costs. No economic reasons existed in his opinion for the continued operation of Clinton, particularly since minor machinery changes would provide the other two plants with a productive capacity greater than the 1929 sales of the Thompsonville, Amsterdam, and Clinton mills combined.[46]

Duffett made a supplementary report in November that reached a similar conclusion. In early December it was decided to close the Clinton mill. Public announcement was made on December 7, and the plant closed its doors finally in March, 1933. By that time only a few employees remained. When the mill's fire department disbanded on March 1, an eighty-four-year-old connection between company and town came to an end.

When the Bigelow-Hartford company had closed its mill in Lowell during World War I, that city's size and general preoccupation with war work had greatly lessened the impact of the move on both the workers and Lowell. The case was different with Clinton, a town of about 12,000 of which about 2,000 people were on the relief rolls in 1933. One by one, Clinton's few large employers had been forced to give up, and Bigelow was the last to go.

The desperate civic leaders had done everything in their power to keep the mill operating but to no avail. The mill had gone its traditional way too long; many of its looms were obsolete and its buildings were too poorly laid out to support new, heavy, and more efficient machinery. To have continued it in operation would have cost the company the advantages it had sought and obtained from the Sanford merger, and not even the Clinton mill's reputation for quality production and its capable labor force were strong enough reasons for continuance.[47]

Under the circumstances, however, it was perhaps inevitable that the reasons for the closing should be misunderstood or misinterpreted. Some

Clinton executives and other Bigelow personnel who had worked there remained unconvinced that their mill should have been closed, and some townspeople retained an attitude of hostility. It helped to place the blame on the executives at the top and many in Clinton became convinced that it was because the old Bigelow Carpet Company lacked representation on the Bigelow-Sanford directorate, that the mill in Clinton had been unfairly treated.[48]

The company set up a layoff payment scale on the basis of two weeks' wages for service of one to two years, four weeks' pay for those who had worked for two to 20 years, and 12 weeks' wages for those with longer service. A total of $110,910 was paid to the 998 eligible workers. The allowances were meager, particularly since many of those affected were too old to find new employment, and claims for better treatment were made by employees as late as 1937. In that year management made an inquiry into the financial condition of all former employees who had been with the company forty years or more in 1933 and found that 15 were in extreme difficulties. Pensions of from $10 to $50 per month were paid to them, depending on their relative needs. Most of them had been out of work since the plant had closed and they were pathetically grateful.[49]

J. M. Donnelly, who had succeeded John Davidson as manager at Clinton a year or two before the plant closed, was transferred to Thompsonville, where he became assistant manager. As quickly as possible, the factory buildings and the tenements in Clinton were sold, and by April, 1936, the company held no property there.

Because of the high quality of the materials woven at Clinton, Bigelow's sales department had quickly assured customers that Clinton's high-grade products would be duplicated by the company's other factories.[50] Since the Clinton looms had differed in some respects from those at Thompsonville and Amsterdam, it was necessary to transfer some of them, in spite of their age. The entire Thompsonville wilton department was rearranged, a complete worsted mill was installed, and 26 Clinton axminster and 24 velvet looms were put into operation there. Time would eventually demand their replacement, but they served immediate needs.[51]

When the Clinton mill was closed and its machinery was either disposed of or moved to Thompsonville, the directors agreed to management's request for permission to write off still other machinery and equipment in the Thompsonville mill up to $1,200,000 in book value. The board would not however, grant a number of requests which Petersen, the plant superintendent, submitted for the purchase of new equipment. In times when almost all companies were husbanding their cash, it was regarded as prudent management to forego equipment expenditures even when increased efficiency promised to return the investment within a short period.

Most of Thompsonville's equipment expenditures during the depression were for such items as new boiler systems, essential to keep the plants operating but not in themselves able to affect production significantly (see Table 29). For the remainder, new paint and thoughtful reorganization had to substitute for substantial equipment improvements.

By comparison with Mohawk, the only firm for which there are comparable figures, Bigelow's expenditures for new equipment during the depression were not unduly restricted. Yet the limit which these firms put on their capital outlay in the interest of liquidity was imposed at a cost which they would never be able to evaluate. For, in the very years when these

TABLE **29**

BIGELOW–SANFORD CARPET COMPANY

Expenditures for New Equipment   1930 to 1936

Year	Amsterdam	Clinton	Thompsonville	General	Total
1930	$ 37,130	$19,400	$376,341	—	$432,881
1931	89,230	43,157	98,351	$ 487	231,215
1932	18,909	48,392	46,103	1,260	114,664
1933	80,128	—	86,071	—	166,199
1934	356,702	—	284,860	—	641,562
1935	413,225	—	46,475	—	459,700
1936	350,500	—	232,050	—	582,550

Source: Manufacturing Department Reports, Bigelow-Sanford.

companies were failing to buy new looms, the demand for new types of carpeting was making existing equipment rapidly obsolete.

It was this type of shift in consumer demand that was so troublesome in the carpet industry. Some increase in velvet demand could be met by working existing equipment longer hours. But sooner or later a decision would have to be made regarding the purchase of new equipment. Would the shift to velvets continue or would demand decline before the new equipment had paid for itself? With capital expenditures carefully rationed, should the prudent manager invest his limited funds rather in the axminster line, since that line produced at least twice as much volume as the velvet line? Sometimes it seemed wiser to wait till the current market trend had clearly established itself as a long-range shift in basic consumer preferences.

EMPLOYEE RELATIONS IN DEPRESSION AND RECOVERY

For the company's other workers, closing the Clinton mill was a reminder of the grim insecurity of earning and jobs, raising the specter of fear in Amsterdam and Thompsonville households. During 1931 there had been sizable reductions in work forces, the dreaded layoffs which few manufacturers seemed able to avoid. These were intensified in 1932. The year began badly with a 10 per cent wage and salary cut, the first of several. Officers accepted two 10 per cent salary reductions so that all ranks were included, but few weavers would have admitted that Sweetser, whose annual salary fell from $75,000 to $60,750 in 1932, was as severely affected as they were. However, pay cuts at Alexander Smith and elsewhere showed Bigelow employees that they were not alone in their troubles.[52]

Some of the workers may have accepted the work cuts with the feeling that they were lucky to be employed at all but others took a different attitude. When, in March, 1932, the second pay slash brought the wages of weavers down to what was claimed to be the lowest level they had ever reached, a group of tapestry workers struck in protest. Their complaint had some reason. Low wages were bad enough but they were combined with the short work time induced by curtailed demand. Only about 100 operatives left their looms, however, with the remainder perhaps recalling the futility of such protests in the past. As it always had, Bigelow stood firm, protesting that it could not pay higher wages and still meet competition, and the strikers shortly thereafter returned to their jobs.[53]

In the background, a threat to both workers and towns, was the considered alternative of terminating or curtailing New England and New York operations in favor of a move to the low-cost sections of the South. A dispute with Amsterdam tax authorities in 1932 had led Duffett to report on southern opportunities and to recommend that Bigelow buy a mill in Decatur, Alabama.[54] The desired tax reduction was obtained and nothing came of the idea of moving south at that time.

As many as possible of the unemployed Clinton workers were placed at Thompsonville and Amsterdam. Not all the new employees were made welcome, however. Five Clinton women weavers were assigned to the Thompsonville wilton department, where no women had ever been employed. The operatives at Thompsonville rightly construed the innovation as an effort on the part of management to weaken their bargaining position. In addition, feeling developed among Thompsonville employees, many of whom were on part-time work or on relief, that Bigelow was trying to threaten the whole employment structure.[55] What had been done in part at least as a sincere effort to provide work for the unfortunate Clinton personnel boomeranged.

The introduction of the NRA production code in 1933 fortunately effected enough changes to take the workers' minds off the Clinton arrivals. The code brought a 40-hour work week and a minimum weekly wage of $14 as its major employment provisions for the carpet industry. Bigelow adjusted to the new requirements somewhat in advance of its rivals, and the problems of training new help, meeting production schedules, and suiting wage rates to minimum scales were solved without major upsets. Morale-boosting wage increases of from 5 to 7 per cent took effect in July, 1933, in both Bigelow plants and also in those of the Mohawk company. Other companies, in and out of the industry, were also restoring wage cuts. An additional 10 per cent increase in wages in April, 1934, by Bigelow and Mohawk was viewed as a check to disputes between carpet companies and their employees.[56]

Under the NRA's sympathetic attitude toward labor, the weavers at Thompsonville once more formed a union, at first a local of the American Federation of Labor's United Textile Workers but later an independent group. Original membership was reported in the vicinity of 2,600, an indication of strength perhaps to the company's surprise and, in some managerial areas, to its dislike.

After a series of bitter disputes and short strikes, the company's management recognized that improved market conditions, with a possible resultant labor shortage, and the growing strength of unions throughout the country made temporization and compromise advisable. Bigelow followed a policy of offering neither aid nor impediment to further union organization, much as it disliked the situation. When the NRA code was nullified in 1935, the carpet industry swung over to its own standard of fair competition, and wages and hours in effect under the code were continued.[57]

Reasons for the growth of unionism in the carpet industry are not hard to find. As Petersen wrote, summing up Thompsonville activity in 1932, "The hopelessness of the economic situation has had its effects on the morale of our employees and a great part of our effort has gone toward attempting to maintain morale so far as possible." [58] Layoffs, wage cuts, economy drives, Clinton's closing, these had done for Bigelow what not dissimilar events had done for so many other companies in so many other industries. Paternalism had gone with prosperity, and something had to be put in its place.

Recognition of this unpleasant truth was slow to reach other members of Bigelow management. Knowland, in his report on the manufacturing department for 1936, said: [59]

Employees are not union-minded. If let alone by outsiders, they are normally individualists and, if not abused, show definitely a conservative and doubtless sympathetic, though inarticulate loyalty to their company. They do not understand manufacturing problems, are not especially interested, and as a group comprehend nothing of the significance of political forces and events as the latter affect their own lives. Possibly the same description will serve for those who are now influencing the labor situation from the national and state capitals.

E. I. Petersen, superintendent at Thompsonville, took a more positive view. He urged his superiors to meet the personnel problems with which the company was faced as leaders, not as followers, to anticipate and not be compelled. He believed there was a need for some security plan to lessen the average workman's perpetual dread of unemployment, sickness, and old age. High-speed manufacturing methods and irregular production schedules imposed new strains on an already sorely tried work force, and Petersen recommended that the company lessen these by the adoption of group insurance and a pension plan.[60]

Unfortunately, Petersen's recommendations seem not to have received much consideration. It was ironic that Thompsonville, where the superintendent displayed so much understanding, should have been the scene of most of the company's labor troubles. In Amsterdam, where the superintendent exhibited less sensitivity and more autocracy, union organizers made little headway prior to the tremendous growth of the CIO in 1937. This was reflective more of the greater tradition of unionism in Thompsonville and of the more tractable ethnic background in Amsterdam than it was of the personalities and abilities of the two mill managers.

The conditions of work and the effectiveness of the workers were, however, given constructive attention. Under Knowland's stimulus, both superintendents placed emphasis on safety training and accident prevention, and in 1934 Thompsonville completed its first three-year period without a fatality. Safety training was a part of worker education. Another was the Bigelow School of Craftsmanship, a school for weavers started by Petersen in 1932 to train men for foreman positions. The school proved successful and won the co-operation of the Connecticut Board of Education. Graduates of the course formed a club which met regularly to keep its members informed on manufacturing developments. Other training courses were offered to help workers prepare for better jobs.

Each mill made changes in its employment department, not necessarily for similar reasons. Social Security laws required fuller record-keeping. But Petersen hoped to do more. He wanted hiring removed from the realm of the foreman's fancy and placed on the basis of skill, intelligence, and special aptitude. In 1936 he took a step toward his goal of economic peace of mind for the workers when he followed the example of some other industries and stimulated the organization of federal credit unions in his mill. These gave employees an opportunity to save and borrow on advantageous terms; the idea quickly spread to Amsterdam and to the New York offices.

Although in November, 1936, both mills received wage increases, the following spring saw the unions stronger than ever, and the Textile Workers Union (as it became), CIO, won recognition at Amsterdam.

The November wage increase had come as a surprise to the employees in that city and many had expressed appreciation to the company for it, but they still joined the union.[61]

W. B. Cooper, the Amsterdam superintendent, had associated himself with Petersen in that year in recommending that group insurance for company workers be established; he did so because he thought that the union would suffer. But, in the following year when group insurance and vacations with pay were granted, credit for these gains went, in the minds of the operatives, to union pressure.[62]

Bigelow's stated wage policy had been to approximate closely the carpet industry's average. As Appendix 12 shows, it followed that policy fairly well. Wages at Thompsonville were generally higher than were those at Amsterdam and they were also generally higher than the industry average. One reason for the difference between the weekly wage rates in the two Bigelow plants was the different nature of the operations. Thompsonville was the only plant which made wilton fabrics, and wilton weavers had higher wage rates than either axminster or velvet weavers.

ADMINISTRATIVE AND CORPORATE ADJUSTMENTS

As changes took place in the manufacturing and sales divisions of Bigelow-Sanford, so too they occurred in the company's over-all administrative and corporate structures. In the period from 1930 to 1936 these changes reflected chiefly two things: the nature of business conditions and the efforts of directors and management to sail before constantly shifting political winds.

The composition of the directorate and of the officer group remained, for the most part, constant. When in 1931 Kidder, Peabody & Company was forced into liquidation, its reorganization under new partners led to the resignation from Bigelow's board of Walter Trumbull and Charles Sargent. Almost 11,000 shares of common stock remained, however, under the control of Kidder Participations and Kidder, Peabody Acceptance Corporation, which became the Consolidated Investment Trust. Roger Amory, a Boston financier and professional trustee who had become president of those companies, sought board representation for his interests and was elected a Bigelow director in 1933. No other directoral changes took place in the early thirties.

Two new officers were added to the company. The host of new regulations and procedures which followed a changing legislative background brought additional work for already heavily burdened executives, and these new officers helped to lighten their tasks. In 1934, John J. Kenny, for some years personal secretary to Sweetser, became assistant secretary of the company, helping J. J. Delaney, who had taken over some of the sales direction in addition to his corporate duties. In 1936 an assistant treasurer was appointed; Mark Dunnell, the appointee, had been with the company six years.[63] The most significant change, already noted, was the appointment of R. G. Knowland, vice-president for manufacturing, as general manager, to report directly to the president and to be responsible for both sales and production.

The executive committee was composed of Sweetser, the president, Deknatel, the treasurer, and Neal Rantoul, Charles Francis Adams, Roger Amory, Louis Liggett, and Samuel Welldon of the board. Robert Winsor had been a member until his death. Relations between the directors as a board, the executive committee (which overlapped both board and executive group), and the company's executives remained much as they had been. Sweetser's principal dealings were with John Sanford and Neal Rantoul, his correspondence with the board chairman being less concerned with details of day-to-day activities than was that with the Boston financier. The president turned to both men for advice. Rantoul concerned himself especially with Bigelow's financial operations. He and Sweetser lunched or talked regularly each Saturday, when the president returned to his Brookline home for the weekend.[64]

Rantoul was in frequent association with the Boston men on Bigelow's board, Charles Francis Adams, Roger Amory, and Sewell Fessenden. Sweetser, in New York, saw Deknatel each working day and was easily able to consult or inform Liggett, Post, Welldon, and the other directors there. Formal directors' meetings were comparatively few. With the exception of 1932, when the directors met on six occasions, meetings were held five times each year.

Surprisingly, the executive committee met even less often: thrice in 1930, 1932, and 1933; twice in 1931 and 1934; four times in 1935; and six times in 1936. Perhaps the same communication system that made frequent formal board meetings unnecessary worked to permit the executive committee to function on a similar basis. Matters of significance, such as whether to pay dividends, were discussed by Sweetser and Deknatel, then by Sweetser with Rantoul, Sanford, or other interested directors (Welldon acted somewhat as a Sanford family representative), and then by the committee, with the final decision presented to the board for action.

John Sanford's conviction that dividends, even on preferred stock, should be paid only when they had been earned was not entirely shared by his associates on the Bigelow board. Preferred stock dividends were paid each year, but those on common were passed in several years. Sanford's stand was based on interest in the position of the common stockholders and in a belief that the company should pay its way. Other directors felt that the amount involved in preferred payments was relatively small and was generally justified by the company's liquid condition. Moreover, since these dividends were cumulative and had to be paid before the common owners could receive anything, it was better to maintain the preferred dividend record.

As long as Sanford could not swing the directors to his dividend policy, he recommended that the company buy and retire its own preferred stock whenever it could, thus increasing the equity of the common stockholders. With this idea Sweetser was in complete agreement, and he had taken the necessary steps even before Sanford made the suggestion.[65] The executive committee approved the purchase in January, 1932, of 158 shares of preferred stock at the low price of $50 per share, and additional purchases were made when the company could afford them and when the stock was available at a good price.

A feeling developed among the directors that it would be wise to broaden the market for Bigelow's stock and in 1931 the common was listed on the New York Stock Exchange while both common and preferred were continued on the Boston Exchange. Relisting took place in 1935 as a result of the Securities & Exchange Act of 1934.[66] The only change in capitalization occurred in 1936 when the preferred shares were reduced from 55,000 to 26,403, and the common from 326,000 shares to 313,609.

A chance to become substantially larger had been given to Bigelow a few years earlier. In 1933 two members of the investment firm of Hornblower & Weeks approached Sweetser and suggested an attempt to combine Bigelow-Sanford with Mohawk and Alexander Smith. Such a combination would have produced a concern so large as to arouse direct suspicions on the part of the Department of Justice, and Sweetser was wary. He did not think, in any event, that his company's shareholders would approve of the idea, and John Sanford concurred.[67] The proposal came to nothing and, with the development of stronger antagonism in Washington toward anything smacking of monopoly, the chance of such a merger grew less.

In spite of the difficulties under which it was laboring in the depression, Bigelow's financial position remained strong. When it needed to borrow money, its executives turned, naturally enough, to the financial interests represented on its directorate. Rantoul in Boston, through F. S. Moseley & Company, and Samuel Welldon in New York, through the First National Bank of the City of New York, could arrange for the company's money needs, but not on any preferential basis either way. Rantoul wrote to Sweetser in 1934: "When the time comes for you to borrow, I understand you will talk rates with me and then decide which way you want to play it." [68] He pointed out that his company's rate to another textile concern which had sought financing had been as low as that concern's own banks would have offered and possibly less.

The year 1936 ended with retail sales establishing new records for the year and not equaled since 1929,[69] and profits before taxes equal to those of 1929. Rugs and carpets were sharing in the holiday business as they never had before; what looked like permanent prosperity had returned to the country. The gadfly pricks of taxation and wage boosts could not greatly affect the optimism brought by the changed conditions. The gloom and despair of 1930 and 1932 had been dissipated by the sun of better times.

Like most other companies, Bigelow-Sanford had come through the period of depression to recovery with some gains and some losses. In the area of marketing, the significant move into direct distribution to retailers had been made; for the time being, the company considered that this had been a success. Bigelow had displayed leadership in the advertising program which had launched the Bigelow Weavers' name and symbol, and it had exhibited a flexible approach to the presentation of new products. Some of these, such as Lokweave and Marval, seemed to have established themselves; others, such as linoleum, had proved failures.

In manufacturing, the company's mills had been as well maintained as was possible within the funds available and improvements in the production facilities had been made. While Bigelow still suffered from a shortage of wide looms in some fabric areas, at least there was an awareness of what its needs were. Perhaps the most important thing the company had done was to stress technical improvement and research; what remained was to increase the emphasis on research, to work with the industry in the development of new techniques, new machines, new approaches to problems. If the industry preferred to remain behind, covered by a cloak of traditionalism, then the company had to move on alone. If the company did not move ahead, there was no guarantee that some other firm would not do so. Bigelow, itself, was evidence of the fact that carpet manufacture was no longer limited to time-honored textile operations.

CHAPTER 13

FROM RECESSION TO PROSPERITY, 1937–1941

For the carpet industry 1937 began with orders flowing in from dealers everywhere and with a general feeling of optimism in the air. The January showing of spring styles was reported the best in years, and a belief that good times were at hand again was as widespread as were the price increases most companies were putting into effect.[1] The price boost in June was, in fact, the sixth in about a year, reflective not only of higher costs but also of expanding markets.

Unfortunately for Bigelow and its competitors, as indeed for the American economy generally, prosperity proved once more a temporary blessing. The year that had started so well in the race for increased sales and profits ended an also-ran, limping across the finish line accompanied by price cuts born of desperation.[2] The following year was even less successful. For Bigelow the loss in 1938 was the second largest in its history to that date, with overbuying of raw materials and a decline in inventory values partly to blame; other companies had losses also. Only when the fear of war in Europe gave way to reality, when the slack in America's industrial potential was taken up by defense preparation, was the situation generally improved.

SHIFTS IN SALES EMPHASIS AND EFFECTIVENESS

In an attempt to increase sales of woven carpets, Bigelow and other large manufacturers intensified their efforts to gain more support from dealers. One means toward this end was a system of higher volume allowances which went into effect when sales began to fall at the end of 1937.

The allowance plan became effective in January, 1938. Under it, a dealer who bought $5,000 of merchandise during the year would receive a rebate of 2 per cent. Previously such a small dealer would have received no rebate whatsoever. The scale extended upward to provide an allowance of 7 per cent on annual purchases of $75,000 or over; this was an increase of 4 percentage points over the 1937 rate on similar purchases. Smith's plan was identical except that it paid the basic 2 per cent on an annual volume of $3,500; Mohawk provided for rebates of 1 per cent on yearly purchases of $2,000 up to a maximum 7 per cent on dealer volumes of $50,000 or more; plans of other companies were similar in principle.[3]

In December of 1939 these rebates (which had been modified somewhat in the interim) were eliminated altogether. In taking that action the various companies acted with a unanimity that must have puzzled their dealers. In explanation they said that the system did not meet the requirements of the Robinson-Patman Act as interpreted by the courts.[4] The move was made necessary, the manufacturers explained, by the Federal Trade Commission's insistence that such rebates did not accurately represent the savings which the carpet companies were achieving through volume sales.

The retailers nevertheless raised their voices in condemnation of the manufacturers. Dealers everywhere were incensed at the loss of what they had come to regard as a normal discount series, and they made their feelings known. Dealer associations urged members to buy as little carpeting as possible, and results of the January, 1940, showing gave some sign that this pressure was having an effect.

The effect of such pressure was a break in the manufacturers' united front. In February Bigelow and Whittall returned to volume rebates, although on a modified basis, and Smith, Masland, Mohawk, and Karagheusian acted hard on their heels. To comply with the FTC regulations Bigelow's new rebate system required dealers to sign blanket order contracts for from six to twelve months in advance to be eligible for discounts. The maximum allowance under the new plan, which was modified in March, was 5 per cent. The systems of other manufacturers were again very similar to that of Bigelow.[5] Some makers whose products were not so well-known as those of the major companies allowed discounts on smaller minimum volumes as a means of combating their better-known rivals, but the maximum allowance was much the same for all companies.

The dealers liked the rebate system and intended to have it continued. From the viewpoint of the individual manufacturer, no company could afford to deviate from the general pattern, either to reduce his discounts or increase them for fear of a consequential loss of dealers or retaliatory action by competitors. From the viewpoint of the industry, the system served to maintain equilibrium of manufacturer-retailer relationships but did not provide the needed dynamism to stimulate total purchases of woven floor coverings.

While the battle of volume discounts was being fought, new shifts were occurring in methods of distribution. In August, 1938, Alexander

Smith announced that it had decided to do its own selling and that it would also market the output of C. H. Masland & Sons and Masland Wilton Mills, associated companies which made floor coverings of types not produced by Smith.[6]

Smith's ten-year contract with its sales agent, W. & J. Sloane, had expired in 1938 and Smith then purchased Sloane's wholesale division. The entire organization of the Sloane division became part of the Smith company, and its personnel continued to sell not only Smith but Masland products as they had done before. Sales were made to approximately 43 wholesale distributors, who in turn sold to retailers. This ended another revival of rumors that Smith had planned to return to the auction system, a method nostalgically and forgetfully regarded by some of the carpet trade as having stabilized sales and encouraged incentive.

Mohawk Carpet Mills, which some years before had successfully wooed some Smith wholesalers away compelling the Yonkers concern to establish its own warehouses in various cities, was apparently quick to sense a change in the wind. About six months later it dismissed 37 out of a sales staff of 45, closed its New York sales headquarters and moved them to Amsterdam, and took on more wholesalers.[7] It did so because Smith's action to reduce the number of wholesalers through which its product was being marketed meant that good wholesalers were going begging. Mohawk was able to obtain distributors whose abilities were reinforced by their irritation at being dropped by the Smith organization. When Smith later followed Bigelow into direct selling, Mohawk continued to distribute through wholesalers.

Bigelow felt that its plan of direct, selective distribution answered its problems, and continued to use it. However, management did discover that it had excessive warehouse capacity (perhaps an indication of economic conditions), and a warehouse consolidation was begun. In 1937 the company had 22 warehouses; at the end of 1938 it had 19; and the number was cut in the following year to 12, where it remained fairly constant. Showrooms, less costly to maintain and with some direct sales value, were continued, and a new one was opened in New Orleans in September, 1940.[8]

Renewed emphasis on inexpensive merchandise by carpet manufacturers was another reaction to the decline in general business conditions. During 1937 and 1938 Bigelow placed considerable effort on the promotion of its inexpensive 9 by 12 Marval rug; a Marval rug could be sold by retailers for about $10.[9]

The sales of Marval did not immediately respond to the increased effort, however, as Table 30 illustrates. In 1937 sales dropped well below the million-dollar mark which they had reached in 1936, and they remained even lower in the next three years. In 1940 rayon was combined with jute to give the Marval fabric a softer surface and more lustrous and fresher appearance.[10] This better appearance, and the European war which made all-wool floor coverings more expensive and harder to buy, improved Marval sales. A study by S. L. Duffett in 1941 to determine whether the product should be continued led to the conclusion that, if Marval's selling price should be increased by at least 25 cents a rug and its manufacturing costs reduced a similar amount, the resulting profits would warrant its continuance.[11] Bigelow persisted with Marval and during the war years that line accounted for an average of about one-tenth of sales to civilian consumers.[12]

TABLE 30

BIGELOW–SANFORD CARPET COMPANY, INC.

Sales by Divisions   1937 to 1941 [a]

	1937	1938	1939	1940	1941
Contract	$ 4,273,151	$ 2,098,742	$ 3,829,507	$ 3,251,624	$ 4,838,818
Cut-carpet	7,666,054	9,274,534	11,334,419	12,682,053	15,958,327
Discontinued lines	1,798,336	2,093,695	588,960	2,367,202	1,301,313
Imperfect and mill ends	1,995,117	1,075,491	1,197,070	1,413,849	1,646,319
Lokweave	1,425,061	992,535	1,796,223	2,167,327	3,626,493
Marval	685,189	455,284	508,629	611,815	906,932
Mail order	2,189,453	215,716	1,242,603	1,271,685	2,584,676
Regular	12,012,733	6,331,331	6,919,768	6,494,459	10,354,380
Total sales	$32,045,094	$22,537,328	$27,417,179	$30,260,014	$41,217,258

[a] Total sales do not agree exactly with those used in published profit and loss statements, but the differences cannot be reconciled by Bigelow-Sanford's sales and accounting department. They are so slight that they do not greatly detract from the usefulness of the figures shown here.

Source: Delaney reports, Sales Department, Bigelow-Sanford.

After the sale of linoleum was discontinued in 1938, the company confined its product line to textile carpets and rugs, with one or two minor exceptions. Felt lining or underlay, used under carpeting to produce greater resiliency and longer wear, was manufactured with moderate success. Packaged stair treads, effectively using small carpet pieces, were sold under the Bigelow Weavers' trade-mark.[13] In 1938 the technical department developed a cleaning powder which could be applied and taken up dry, making the cleaning of wall-to-wall carpeting easier. Since Bigelow lacked adequate manufacturing and sales facilities for such an item, the Von Schrader Manufacturing Company of Racine, Wisconsin, was licensed in 1940 to make and sell it. The compound was distributed to carpet cleaning houses under the name "Dri-Sorb-Ene," and was later packaged and sold to householders with the new title, "Powderene." [14]

The substantial increase in sales of Bigelow's Lokweave, shown in

Table 30, reflected continued and intensified emphasis on products in which the company had patent protection or some other competitive advantage. In 1937 agreements were signed with two distributors, making them exclusive sales agents to market Lokweave to the automotive trade.[15] Since the fabric was made on nine-foot looms, an increase in its sales was of advantage to the production division.

Despite these smaller accomplishments Sweetser had been for some time dissatisfied with the general marketing progress. A sharp trend in consumer taste away from axminster rugs and carpets toward broadloom velvets was accentuating already maladjusted manufacturing facilities and was regarded by Sweetser as one of the reasons why sales from 1936 had not kept up with those of its competitors.[16] At length, after due deliberation, the president concluded that one of the needed steps was a shake-up of the sales department. Early in 1938 he sought and obtained the resignation of H. V. Campbell, vice-president in charge of sales, in whom he had lost confidence. J. J. Delaney succeeded Campbell as vice-president, and Delaney's positions of sales manager and corporate secretary were filled by P. F. O'Neil and J. J. Kenny, respectively.

Delaney's promotion had the effect of confining R. G. Knowland's activities almost entirely to manufacturing. Knowland, it will be recalled, had in 1930 been made general manager with authority over both production and sales. In this capacity he had to some extent assumed the burden of what should have been Campbell's responsibility. This situation had not been completely satisfactory to everyone in the executive group; with Campbell's departure and his replacement by a stronger man, the situation was more or less tacitly altered. Knowland remained the senior vice-president and continued to act as the chief manufacturing executive and special assistant to Sweetser; but the sales responsibility was removed from his jurisdiction and was placed squarely on Delaney.

Bigelow's advertising policy may have had some effect on the sales decline. Whether or not Campbell had failed to press for more aggressive advertising, the initiative taken in 1932 with the extensive "Bigelow Weavers" campaign had not been sustained. Neither was it to be recaptured under Delaney. Delaney's philosophy as sales vice-president was that advertising should be subordinated to sales promotion, that it could not be expected to do as much as forthright selling by the sales force.[17] In the five-year period from 1937 through 1941 annual advertising expenditures averaged about 1.5 per cent of net sales, of which consumer media expense accounted for about .7 of 1 per cent and sales promotion activities for the rest. Alexander Smith's annual expenditures, on the other hand, were larger than were those of Bigelow and equaled more than 2.5 per cent of the Smith company's net sales in each of the five years.[18]

Advertising managers came and went. There were three managers in the early 1930's; in 1940 a new manager succeeded to the post, and, not much more than one year later, he was transferred to the Middle West sales force. His successor remained about the same length of time before his entry into military service made necessary another appointment.[19]

The criteria applied to the selection of men for the position were a lengthy experience in the company and a good knowledge of its products, but no particular mastery of advertising practice. The advertising manager reported to the vice-president for sales, who could and did exert much influence on advertising programs.

Advertising campaigns might therefore be changed or modified to suit the ideas of the salespeople, who were not necessarily qualified to judge advertising strategy. No advertising practitioner could thus feel free to attempt a long-range program in the sure hope of carrying it through to completion. The basic ideas underlying the use of the Bigelow Weavers' trade-mark and the Lively Wool slogan as quality symbols had been to win and hold consumer recognition and acceptance, but their effectiveness depended on the general support of management. The pattern of advertising expenditures seems to indicate that this support was not given.

Long-term consumer acceptance of Bigelow products was dependent on two things: their style and their quality. In such goods as carpets where the initial investment is considerable, quality is of obvious significance in that long wear is involved. Style, expressed in color, design, and pattern, is equally important, for floor coverings determine the appearance of a room to a large extent. Advertising can attract attention to carpet styles through pictures and copy that are well presented but personal inspection by consumers and the advice of a trusted retailer are usually needed to complete the sale of style goods.

What advertising can do is to give the consumer assurance of qualities in carpets which one is unable to judge for oneself.[20] Bigelow executives were firmly convinced that their carpets and rugs possessed qualities of construction and material that made them generally superior to those produced in the same price range by other companies.[21] These qualities had given the goods a favorable reputation with dealers and with consumers, although they had been achieved only by extra costs, which meant that Bigelow prices usually fell in the upper brackets of their price ranges. More emphasis in aggressive advertising on the hidden qualities was one way to overcome resistance to the sometimes higher prices and thus develop sales for the regular lines.

PRODUCTION FACILITIES

Bigelow's manufacturing department, like its marketing counterpart, found the years following 1936 complicated by sudden shifts in general business conditions. In the spring of 1937 Knowland and the other manu-

Wilton Weaving; pile and backing yarns form "weave shed"; shuttle passes through shed forming weft; spare shuttle shown at left; carpet pile is formed over flat strips of steel, called "wires"

facturing executives had begun to plan, as was their custom, the needs for new equipment for the following year. Their conclusion was that $882,000 should be spent in 1938, a figure 25 per cent larger than the comparable figure for 1937. Hardly had agreement been reached when adverse business conditions forced the figure to be cut—first to $472,000 and then to $122,400. Conditions in 1938, a year in which only 11 workers were taken on at Thompsonville, did not warrant extensive equipment expenditures (see Table 31). For a time the plants reached an operating level even below the lowest attained when the 1932 depression was at its worst.[22]

TABLE 31

BIGELOW–SANFORD CARPET COMPANY, INC.

Expenditures for New Equipment   1937 to 1941

Year	Amsterdam	Thompsonville	General	Total
1937	$286,387	$372,813	$49,600	$708,800
1938	105,728	120,366	—	226,094
1939	238,047	318,379	—	556,426
1940	294,831	238,161	—	532,992
1941	259,900	230,268	—	490,168

Source: Manufacturing Department Reports, Bigelow-Sanford.

One effect of the economic situation was to attempt to increase manufacturing efficiency.[23] S. L. Duffett recommended as an economy move that the cotton-spinning mill at Amsterdam be closed and its machinery leased to a southern company. The cotton yarn used in rug and carpet backing could, he thought, be bought in the open market at considerable savings, including the wages of the 180 employees in the cotton-spinning plant. The company followed Duffett's advice and closed the mill in November, 1938. Along with the renewed emphasis on economy came an awareness of a need to study and appraise Bigelow's manufacturing costs, its materials qualities, and its selling prices. The major problem of how Bigelow qualities could be reconciled with noncompetitive costs and prices was, unfortunately, not solved for some time. There was, however, an appreciation on the part of the executive group of the issues raised by the increasing trend in consumer demand away from axminster rugs and toward broadloom axminster and velvet carpets and, later, toward broadloom wilton fabrics.

Bigelow's difficulties in 1938 were not simply the effect of changing consumer wishes; rather, they represented a combination of marketing and production weaknesses which had both long- and short-run implications and which were further complicated by the over-all industry situation—the failure of the carpet industry to do research to advance the art of carpet-making.

The situation that had developed in 1938 found the company with large numbers of the items in its lines in demand but not in production while other items were in production but not in demand. This failure to produce salable items was the result of a marketing department that had either been insensitive to changes in market demand or had been unsuccessful in getting the manufacturing department to translate these changes into production schedules. A part of the difficulty may be traced

TABLE 32

BIGELOW–SANFORD CARPET COMPANY, INC.

Sales of Axminster Rugs and Piece Goods   1935 to 1942

| | Woven Square Yards Sold | | | Percentage of Total Sales | | |
Year	Roll Goods	Rugs	Total Axminster	Roll Goods	Rugs	Total Axminster
1935	1,030,393	4,219,468	5,249,861	10.4	42.4	52.8
1936	1,466,452	5,517,945	6,984,397	10.6	39.7	50.5
1937	1,616,318	4,635,444	6,251,762	13.8	39.4	53.2
1938	2,758,479	1,790,846	4,549,325	32.2	20.9	53.1
1939	4,301,085	1,263,394	5,564,479	43.4	12.7	56.1
1940	4,680,047	1,137,659	5,817,706	47.1	11.5	58.6
1941	6,947,762	1,060,715	8,008,477	51.7	7.9	59.6
1942	5,448,183	435,065	5,881,248	51.9	4.1	56.0

Source: Delaney Reports, Current Book #1, Sales Department, Bigelow-Sanford.

to financial policy. As is indicated in Table 31, expenditures for new equipment during the late thirties were kept at conservative figures. But, then, conservative investment in fixed assets was a product of the times. In comparison with at least one competitor—Mohawk—Bigelow's performance showed up rather well. In the years 1937–1941, Bigelow, with 50 per cent larger sales volume than Mohawk, put 120 per cent more money into new equipment.

Intermingled with the maladjustment between demand and output was the other major issue involved: whether or not a more determined effort should have been made to keep abreast, if not ahead, of customers' wishes in the matter of loom widths. As year after year more broadloom carpets were sold, Bigelow's narrow loom equipment came to serve what was a rapidly declining market. The need to replace this narrow equipment was clear, but consumer tastes were shifting so rapidly that it was not easy to determine what new equipment should be bought. The dramatic shift from rugs to goods sold by the roll in the axminster field is shown in Table 32.

In March, 1939, Sweetser complained that the company was short of manufacturing facilities in the 12-foot and 15-foot widths but he was frightened by the amount of investment required if the deficiency was to be overcome.[24] He was equally afraid of a situation where much of the nine-foot equipment was standing idle while demands for still wider fabrics could not be met. At the same time he was under renewed pressure from Rantoul and the other Boston directors for caution and economy. Some additional machinery had been purchased with the return of better times and productivity per man hour increased from .98 yards in 1937 to 1.24 yards in 1941. But expenditures for new equipment in 1940 and in 1941 were kept well below the amounts sought by the manufacturing executives. Although returning profits reassured the directors, war clouds made them hesitant to tie up liquid funds in equipment that might soon be made unusable for wartime reasons.

At least one of Bigelow's competitors did strike out along lines that led away from conservatism in this period, however. In 1938 James Lees & Sons, of Pennsylvania, built and moved their operation to a large, one-story plant in Glasgow, Virginia.[25] This plant gave excellent materials handling and production scheduling; it could be heated at less expense than one in the North; it was built when building and machine costs were low, and it had some advantages in materials accessibility. Of equal importance was the fact that the Virginia highlands provided cheap, skillful, racially homogeneous labor. The result of this combination of elements was a series of profitable years for Lees, sometimes, as the future was to show, when Bigelow and some of the other larger companies were unable to make any money.

THE SEARCH FOR FREEDOM FROM WOOL'S DOMINANCE

While Bigelow could not make drastic expenditures on new equipment in the late thirties, it did explore other ways to improve its overall manufacturing position. One important area was action to minimize or eliminate the effects of wool price changes. Inventory losses from such fluctuations had been a major cause of the company's poor showing in 1938 and the uncertain tenor of wool prices made manufacturing costs subject to constant adjustment, with a corresponding effect on the price of finished goods. There seemed to be ways in which the situation could be improved: one was better control over inventories and the other was the development of some substitute for wool in carpet production.

Cotton appeared to be the only natural fiber that could conceivably replace or supplement wool. Some of the objections to wool applied to cotton: the price fluctuated with crop failures or successes and was beyond the control of the manufacturer, and supply could turn quickly short or long. Cotton lacked wool's properties and was subject to consumer resistance. While cotton rugs began to be sold for general use in the late 1930's, no carpet-maker appeared to regard the fiber as the answer to his materials problem.

Bigelow and other companies turned therefore to man-made substitutes for wool. In 1937 the research department investigated synthetic fibers made from lanatol and casein, those made directly from wood pulp, and the various types of rayon, including viscose, acetate, and cuprammonium.[26] Of these, cuprammonium rayon seemed most worthy of future study.

The problems facing the company in this development were numerous and they taxed the intelligence and ability of the engineers and technicians who had been added to the staff from the time of Knowland's appointment as head of manufacturing. Apart from the fact that rayon, in its early days as so-called "artificial silk," had earned itself a bad name, it lacked the properties needed for use in carpets. Rayon soiled easily, it was not resilient, and its dyeing and wearing qualities were uncertain. Furthermore, most machinery in use had been designed to spin and weave wool and was not adaptable to rayon processing.

On the other hand, rayon possessed many advantages, some of which awaited future development. The fiber could be made almost completely uniform, eliminating much of the waste of wool. Its price was independent of weather or political conditions in some far-away country. The hope existed among carpet men that the material could be endowed with qualities that would make it superior to wool as well as less expensive and in more certain supply. In time, it was assumed, these factors would eventually overcome objections to the material on the part of the buying public.

Since the large chemical companies seemed uninterested in working with Bigelow on carpet fiber, the company was compelled to look elsewhere. Knowland, a trained chemist and vitally concerned with the need to reduce manufacturing costs, was determined to do what he could to develop carpet rayons. He managed to form a connection with a small cuprammonium manufacturer, the New Process Company, which had a plant in New Jersey. Through joint efforts a machine for producing rayon staple was designed, developed, and erected at the New Process Company, and a pilot plant for actual manufacture of rayon was put into operation in 1937.

By the end of 1938, Bigelow's technical department believed that rayon could be blended with wool up to 50 per cent to produce a fabric apparently equal to standard wool-pile materials in wear, resistance to crushing and soiling, and appearance. Another year's work enabled the company to plan four lines using wool and rayon in equal amounts. Two of these were to be of plain colors and two of axminster construction and style. Gradually the synthetic fiber's ability to take dye colors had been increased, and it appeared that the color brilliance and fastness of wool could be approximated.

While Bigelow's research group had been trying to free the company from wool's dominance, other men had been seeking the same end. Raw materials scarcities in Italy and Germany had led to extensive synthetic textile investigation. How far this had gone with rayon was indicated in November, 1938, when the New York department store of John Wanamaker introduced an all-rayon oriental-reproduction rug made in Italy. The new product was reported to have created a sensation in the carpet trade.[27]

Even stronger incentive for progress in the development of synthetic fibers was provided by the outbreak of the European war in 1939. As foreign wools were embargoed by some countries, as shipping became unsafe, as prices went up and supplies went down, synthetics seemed to represent salvation to the carpet industry. Interest heightened, and in November a subcommittee on pile floor-covering materials was formed under the American Society for Testing Materials to discuss the use of rayon. Bigelow's new technical director, Neal Dow, was the subcommittee's chairman, and lack of resiliency in rayon was named as the major problem facing the group's investigation.[28]

The first wool-rayon carpeting, a 4⅜-row axminster rug, was shown at the June, 1940, opening. The Firth Carpet Company had shown a blended rug made with equal quantities of wool and rayon a few months earlier, and it followed this product with a second rug improved in material and construction.[29] Shortly after the June opening, Bigelow introduced rayon into the face of its Marval felt rugs.

Public acceptance of rayon in carpets was jeopardized almost at once by quality-cutting abuses. Rayon waste was about one half as expensive as rayon staple, and it was only about one half as good. Bigelow believed the waste was completely unacceptable for use in carpets but some companies began to use it. Delaney urged the adoption of minimum standards by manufacturers to forestall action by Better Business Bureaus or by consumer groups, and his company made its own position clear.[30]

Several improvements were made in rayon. The large chemical companies had finally become interested in the possibilities of the synthetics for carpet manufacture, and Bigelow worked with the American Viscose Corporation and DuPont in overcoming fiber deficiencies. The company's own mechanical development department, one of the numerous technical groups which had followed the formal recognition of the importance of engineers within the organization, made a satisfactory copy of the Italian oriental rug, using viscose rayon of American manufacture. The department also progressed toward solution of the important question of fire-

proofing rayon, in anticipation of an all-rayon product. The American
Viscose Corporation made a significant fiber change which provided
greatly increased soil resistance, thus in part solving the problem coming from the fact that rayon carpeting had been found to soil easily in
actual use.

At the end of 1941, then, rayon was proving itself in actual use as
carpet material but it had not demonstrated equality with wool in every
respect and it was still under consumer suspicion. By that time, however,
American participation in the war made its use no longer a matter of
option. The general shortage of soft-surface floor coverings was such that
a buyer who objected to rayon had little opportunity to select an alternative.

Bigelow, the industry, and the chemical companies continued work on
synthetics but there were so many other war-occasioned problems that
this one lapsed somewhat into the background. The company's attitude,
or that of Knowland, its prime mover in the search for synthetics, was
that it would have to continue its work without much outside assistance.
As Knowland wrote: [31]

I am more than ever convinced that most of the developments in the use of
carpet rayons are likely to come from the activity of the carpet manufacturer
himself, and not from that of the rayon manufacturer. The rayon manufacturer
quite evidently is an animal of great technical skill and little imagination. If we
had relied on them . . . to make carpet type rayons available, I question that
they would ever have been developed.

And he cautioned the company of the need for secrecy "so that no leaks
whatever occur to give outsiders an inkling re our activities re substitute
fibers."

Meanwhile, Bigelow had taken other steps to lessen the importance
of wool, or, at least, to control somewhat its effects on profits. The erratic
movements of wool prices had meant that purchases in the years 1930
to 1939 were made at prices ranging from 12 cents per pound in 1932
to 43 cents per pound in 1937. The question of how to deal with this inventory problem received much attention from the company's board,
officers, and auditors throughout 1938.[32]

To serve its retailers, Bigelow had to carry at all times a large inventory of raw materials, work in process, and finished rugs and carpets.
While the inventories expressed in dollars fluctuated from year to year,
the quantities remained more constant. In the past, the company had
followed the accounting method in most general use, "first in, first out,"
or FIFO, by which products were deemed to have been made from the
oldest raw materials on hand. Under this method, during a period of rising
prices the book profits shown were greater than the profits that could
be realized on a replacement basis (since, as materials were used, they

had to be replaced at higher prices). Later, when prices declined, the book profits made on a rising market were often offset by book losses. The FIFO method of valuing inventories in effect, wrote up the profits during a period of rising prices and wrote them down during a period of falling prices, even though the inventory quantities themselves remained virtually constant.

In March, 1938, Bigelow's auditors, Scovell, Wellington & Company recommended study of the LIFO method, "last in, first out." Under this system the raw material contents of goods sold were costed on the basis of raw materials last received, and therefore such material costs of sales corresponded more closely with current selling prices.

While some doubt was felt at first as to whether the LIFO method could be readily adapted to Bigelow's accounting procedures, recognition of LIFO's advantages eventually overcame those objections. When the Revenue Act of 1939 approved the LIFO method for federal tax purposes, the change-over was made. LIFO was introduced as of January 1, 1939, and Sweetser, in his semiannual report to shareholders, illustrated its workings.

In its adoption of LIFO, Bigelow was accompanied by most of its competitors and the system became almost industry-wide. Indeed, LIFO become comparatively general in American industry at the time, to meet a common problem. Only Alexander Smith among the large carpet companies held out against it, but in 1950 Smith finally changed to the LIFO system. In the intervening years LIFO had proved a valuable barometer to managements, indicating better than previous inventory control systems what the true state of profits was.

The policy of maintaining high quality came under scrutiny at this time. Knowland believed that the company, by paying a premium of 2 cents a pound over the average wool price for the industry, as it had for years, had inevitably put its manufacturing costs out of line with those of its competitors. S. L. Duffett agreed that quality was too high. He concluded in a 1940 report that quality standards, at least in the low-priced end of the line, should have been eased to compare with those of Smith or Mohawk.

Duffett's recommendations to cheapen the line were not directly followed, however. Sweetser had no intention of earning a bad reputation to carry over into the peace. Quality had steadily improved during his presidency—wear tests in 1940 indicated that the products manufactured in that year would wear about 25 per cent longer than those made in 1929 —and he hoped to continue quality improvement.

Naturally the question was raised whether consumers would pay a premium price for quality that they could not easily see for themselves. As Appendix 13 shows, the company's share of the carpet industry's total sales fell during 1939 and 1940, and this led to considerable executive preoccupation with Bigelow's manufacturing position in relation to the rest of the industry and especially to Mohawk. What was sought again, as it had been before, was a way in which the quality could be maintained and the production cost lowered.

Sweetser felt that Mohawk had made a relatively better showing than had Bigelow in 1939 and 1940 but he found it difficult to determine the reasons for the difference.[33] Indeed, on many counts Bigelow's production department could demonstrate clear superiority to its rival. Nevertheless, the president urged his executives to do what they could to bring the company's performance to the point where its ratio of profits to sales would at least equal the Amsterdam company's. This was one reason for the widely felt emphasis on economy.

RELATIONS WITH WORKERS: CONTINUED BUT EASING STRAIN

If the manufacturing department had had to contend only with materials and machines during the years from 1937 to 1941, its job would have been difficult enough. Unfortunately for those responsible for Bigelow's production, labor, the third element involved, proved equally complicated. The uneasy peace between company and employees at the end of 1936 was maintained for about a year only by concessions long resisted; the peace gave way to a bitter strike and intensified union organization.

In the spring of 1937, Bigelow signed its first agreement with the Textile Workers Organizing Committee, CIO, giving recognition to that union as bargaining agent for workers in the company's Amsterdam plant. In Thompsonville a different union was recognized: the United Textile Workers Union, an independent organization which was at the time debating affiliation with AFL or CIO. During the same period other carpet companies signed collective bargaining contracts with their employees.[34]

By September, 1937, the Thompsonville employees had decided to continue independently as the United Textile Workers. By November falling sales had resulted in layoffs of about 2,000 workers in the two plants and the company had refused new demands from the two unions. Knowland and the plant superintendents were inclined to believe that neither union any longer represented a majority of the workers, and Knowland did not anticipate that labor problems would be of major concern in 1938.[35]

Both Bigelow mill superintendents were aware of the need for sympathy and understanding at a time when many men and women were unable to find jobs. At Amsterdam, Wellesley B. Cooper, the autocratic superintendent whom Bigelow had inherited from the Sanford company, had been replaced in March by James M. Donnelly, assistant superintendent at Thompsonville.[36] Donnelly, like Petersen, under whom he had worked at Thompsonville, was quick to seek better communication with his personnel. He instituted regular weekly meetings with department heads, dinner sessions with foremen, a class in foremanship, and training classes along the line of the weavers' school at Thompsonville. Gradually he obtained much greater co-operation in the plant.

Unfortunately sales did not improve in 1938 but fell lower. Layoffs continued, and bitterness grew. Bigelow was accused by labor leaders of deliberately causing the layoffs to embarrass the federal government in its recovery attempts.[37] When in May the company's administration felt that a 10 per cent wage cut was necessary to aid in correcting the severe losses that had been incurred, labor leaders felt otherwise. The unions at Amsterdam and Thompsonville joined forces against the proposed wage cut, and on May 11 called strikes at both plants.

The company refused to arbitrate, on the grounds that an arbitrator might order a wage increase that could not be met; it was convinced that the time was at hand for management to take a strong stand against further encroachment on its prerogatives.[38] The union, flushed with CIO successes in other industries, stood firm through May and well into June. Pickets surrounded both plants but there was no violence.

Neither side wished the company's plants to remain closed but neither was willing to appear soft or compromising. At last a face-saving solution to the stalemate was hit upon when representatives of company and union asked New York's Governor Herbert Lehman to intercede. Lehman proposed that the issues be submitted to an arbitrator and this time the company agreed. The men went back to work on June 27 pending the arbitrator's decision, with the Thompsonville union entering the CIO. The Amsterdam union was already affiliated with the CIO.[39]

There was troubled peace during the arbitration period, with sit-down strikes and walkouts in both mills. On October 4 the arbitrator's decision was announced. He concluded that Bigelow's wages had generally equaled those prevalent in the carpet industry, but that the severe losses it had sustained in late 1937 and early 1938 had affected its ability to pay. The arbitrator recommended that one half of the 10 per cent reduction be restored to the employees, and that the payment be retroactive to the date when the cut was made.[40] The decision was accepted by both sides without further protest, and checks for back pay went to the workers in about two weeks. The outcome of the Bigelow case led to similar settlements in other carpet industry labor disputes at that time.[41]

Although the company found, when it signed a new contract on August 1, 1938, that it could avoid both the closed shop and preferential hiring agreements sought by the union, it was still not free from labor difficulties.

For the remainder of the year there were strikes in different departments, their causes ranging from the company's action in laying off for a week a Thompsonville worker who had collected union dues on company time, to the objection of Amsterdam employees to working with nonunion members. The union attempted to prevent closing of the Amsterdam cotton mill and invoked the aid of Governor Lehman but no walkout was called. The company was able to prove that its case had merits and that its action was not intended to be a threat to unionization.[42]

In the next year, company and union had become more used to each other, and no stoppages took place. Labor leaders continued to press for the closed shop and for wage check-offs; company executives continued to refuse both. A wage increase of from 2 to 15 per cent, depending on the job, was made when the contract was renegotiated in the middle of summer, and was promptly passed on to consumers in the form of upward price revisions. The Alexander Smith workers, who had chosen the CIO over their company union in May, also signed a contract providing for a wage increase, and Smith likewise raised its prices.

The rising tide of business from the end of 1939 enabled the Bigelow company to recall employees who had been laid off and to increase working hours for others. But, at the same time, workers began to drift away to industries more fully engaged than Bigelow in defense manufacture, where wages were higher. Thompsonville had suffered in World War I from proximity to Springfield and Hartford, with their arsenals and war plants; the situation in 1940 and thereafter paralleled the hectic days of 1917. Amsterdam was close enough to Schenectady, Albany, and Troy for carpet workers to seek better paying jobs in those centers. To combat higher wages, Bigelow and its rivals were compelled to raise their own. When, on August 9, 1941, workers in both plants received an increase of 3½ cents per hour, the new adjustment made a total wage boost of 12 per cent granted in 10 months.[43]

Furthermore, the armed forces were beginning to claim their share of available manpower, through the draft or through voluntary enlistment. In November, 1940, Bigelow announced its policy concerning those who left to enter the service. They were to be given leaves of absence and seniority accumulation during their absence, two full weeks' pay when they were called or reported for duty, vacation pay, and payment of their group insurance premiums for one year.[44]

The unanimity of contract bargaining obviously could not keep companies from acting separately in their day-to-day relations with labor. Flexibility in the field of management-labor relations was essential if the carpet industry was to continue dynamic. In Bigelow's case, the increase in productivity per man hour (shown in Appendix 12) was the result in large measure of improved equipment and of more efficient use of existing machinery. At the same time, the company's failure to keep pace with other segments of the industry was reflected in lower average weekly earnings and in lower average hours worked by its employees. Since increased productivity without increased costs could be obtained only through union co-operation, the company had to maintain open-mindedness in its dealings with organized labor.

Thus Bigelow joined with the union to study the problem of what to do with workers who had been displaced from their jobs by technological improvements. Since the company was using old equipment which it hoped to replace as quickly as it could, and since events had borne forcibly home to it that men could not be discarded whenever management seemed to feel they should be, the issue was of more than technical concern. The result of the study, which lasted for slightly more than one year, was the provision of severance pay for such displaced employees. The benefits provided for thirteen weeks' pay for workers with twenty-five years of continuous service, down to two weeks' pay for those with two years' service. This agreement became an amendment to the company-union contract of October 1, 1940.[45]

But what of the salaried employees in this period of adjustment and improvement for hourly workers; how did they fare with no union to plead their case? The senior executives had profited in mid-1939 when Sweetser recommended a restoration of the management bonus system which had been rescinded in 1936; thereafter bonuses were considered at the end of each year and awarded in recognition of effort. The rank-and-file salaried employees, however, found themselves clinging to the coattails of organized labor in so far as increased earnings were concerned. Some evidence existed, nevertheless, that the company's management and its directors were beginning to realize the need to bind salaried employees more strongly to the organization. Furthermore, a new tax ruling made it easier for companies to meet the initial cost of setting up a pension program.

Under the new plan all Bigelow employees with salaries of more than $3,000 annually were eligible for a pension. The plan became effective January 1, 1941, and replaced the old system whereby individuals were considered for pensions by the board of directors, a system which the company had come to find was full of inequities. The new plan provided a retirement income at the age of sixty-five to amount, with social security benefits, to approximately 35 per cent of the average income earned. Participation was on a contributory basis and the company was to bear the expense of "dating back" those employees over 40 at the time when the plan began. The highest income that would permit participation was $36,000, so that the president was eligible only to that amount of his salary.[46]

Steps were also taken to win back some of the worker friendliness toward the company that had been lost during the period when the union was actively organizing and when the strike was in progress. Bigelow's management felt certain that the attitudes expressed in the 1938 strike had not always been typical of the employees but rather had been those of determined and skillful labor organizers. There was some sensitivity and hurt shown by executives over the way the generally good relations of the past fifteen years had been so quickly overthrown. Both plant managers were convinced that the difficulty experienced in making management ideas known and understood had to be overcome.

With this aim in mind, Donnelly in Amsterdam investigated the desire on the part of employees for a plant or company newspaper. He found a real wish to have such a publication, and one was established under the auspices of the Amsterdam personnel department. In due course the paper was expanded to include Thompsonville and the New York office, to become, as Eugene Ong had recommended fifteen years before, a medium through which information could be passed on from the administrative office to the workers, and through which employees could obtain news of each other's activities on a company-wide basis.

How successful the newspaper was as a communication vehicle could not be calculated, nor could the success of an employee radio program in Thompsonville be readily determined. What was significant was the indication that the company recognized the existence of a need and tried to meet it. Perhaps in time both management and labor could be led to realize the fundamental similarity of their interests and their objectives.

PUBLIC AND GOVERNMENT RELATIONS

When Bigelow's manufacturing executives in 1938 discovered how difficult it was to make company policies known, understood, and believed by employees, they learned also that it was equally difficult to make their side of the strike issues comprehensible to the general public. Bigelow had made little formal effort to obtain good public relations other than to make and sell the best products it could.

Knowland urged at the end of 1938 that the management do as it had often spoken of doing and make some systematic public relations effort. His recommendation that a suitable man be given such responsibility under the manufacturing department's supervision was not followed, but plant managers did attempt to obtain better integration of the company into their respective communities. Contributions to local charities, membership in service organizations, tours of the mills by town residents and by outside visitors, were among the means adopted toward this end.[47]

Neither these excellent beginnings nor Knowland's recommendation went far enough. What was needed, it soon transpired, was a qualified public relations man, responsible to the president, who would concern himself with Bigelow's relations with the public in every area. Not the least important of such areas was that of government relations. The depression and the New Deal had spawned questions on wages, hours, prices, social security, unemployment insurance, and a host of other items with which businessmen had formerly involved themselves only as they saw fit.

The Carpet Institute, to some extent, acted as a public relations agency for the industry, particularly in dealings with the federal government. The Institute had proved successful in keeping tariff protection for carpetmakers and it had worked also to maintain a supply of free raw materials. It operated a publicity department which distributed news on industry developments and worked with member companies in the origin and employment of promotional ideas aimed at increasing sales for the industry as a whole.

Unfortunately, relations between the carpet industry and various sections of the government had not always been harmonious—and in 1940 these relations took a sudden turn for the worse. To its surprise and discomfort, Bigelow found itself named as a defendant in two government legal actions. If any consolation was to be derived from the unpleasant situation, the company could only find it in knowing that it had companions.

In the first action, the Federal Trade Commission accused several manufacturers and retailers of misleading the public in their advertising. The defendants had been advertising that some of their products were true copies of oriental rugs and the government agency maintained that this was not the case. The result of the situation was that Bigelow and the other defendants agreed to a cease and desist order and abandoned the practices of which the government agency had complained. Labels were altered to read "Woven on Power Looms in U.S.A.," and the criticized advertising was changed.[48] Since Bigelow had practically ceased to make rugs of the oriental type, in compliance with strong trends in taste toward broadloom and solid color fabrics, the only effect on the company was whatever damage may have resulted from the unpleasant publicity attached to the episode.

The company had more serious possible consequences to worry about in the second government action. This was an inquiry into possible violations of antitrust law directed against the Carpet Institute, Bigelow, Smith, Mohawk, Karagheusian, Firth, and others. Apart from the fact that "trust busting" was much in the minds of Attorney-General Thurman Arnold and the Department of Justice at that time, the underlying reason for the investigation appeared to be the resentment stirred up among retailers by the carpet industry's attempt to abolish volume rebates in

December, 1939. The reason given for this abolition, paradoxically, had
been that the industry wished to conform, in the matter of rebates, to
the interpretation put on certain aspects of the Robinson-Patman Act.
But, in conforming, the industry had acted so in unison that the Justice
Department, on having the matter called to its attention, believed that
a governmental inquiry was warranted.[49]

In February, 1940, subpoenas were issued against the various companies and the Institute, demanding the presence of their representatives
and records before a New York Grand Jury in March.[50] No Grand Jury
inquiry was held but the government's investigation, which lasted until
the end of 1940, sought evidence of price-fixing and other collusive
practices on the part of the manufacturers. The Carpet Institute, for its
part, was said to have issued letters and reports intended to help its
members carry out their conspiracy to fix prices and establish quotas to
reduce competition.[51]

While some Bigelow executives later admitted that there was some
truth to the charges leveled against the companies, they insisted that
the Institute had not been involved in whatever collusion existed.[52] In so
far as the companies were accused of having set up mutually determined
sales quotas or fixed prices in concert, those accusations appeared without
foundation. While one company might notify its competitors of its intention to raise or lower prices, Bigelow's brief to the Department of
Justice showed that other manufacturers did not always follow suit. From
September 11 to November 1, 1939, 28 price increases were made by 14
companies and these increases followed an irregular line and were not all
uniform, singly or in total. When Smith's increase proved smaller than
Bigelow's or Mohawk's, the Smith company was quick to urge its sales
force to capitalize on the difference.

Bigelow's brief also contained quotations from letters written by its
field salesmen that indicated the reality of competition, at least on the
actual selling level. These quotations demonstrated that throughout 1939
competitive activity by various members of the industry included:

(1) the continuous introduction of competitive variations in weaves,
    designs, and textures;
(2) the offering of special patterns and special deals to particular
    customers for the purpose of obtaining orders;
(3) competitive emphasis upon service;
(4) repeated price-cutting through various devices; and
(5) competition to the extent of being unfair, as in the piracy of com-
    petitive designs.

The issues raised by the government never came to formal trial. In
February, 1941, the companies involved agreed at a meeting with repre-

sentatives of the Antitrust Division of the Department of Justice to a consent decree prohibiting in the future the practices raised by the charge.

Adverse publicity for the carpet companies as a result of the consent decree was reduced by the pressure on news columns for space for war news. Then, too, by the time the decree was signed, Bigelow was too deeply involved in war work to worry much about the case. The government was itself fast becoming the company's most important customer.

These new government relations also brought increasing complications in the form of a horde of new regulations that poured out of the various governmental bureaus in Washington. New agencies came into existence and added to the confusion. One of the most important, to the carpet industry, was the Office of Price Administration. As early as July, 1941, the government price administrator was urging manufacturers to defer price advances to help resist inflation. The manufacturers, who were faced with higher costs themselves and were considering another general increase in August or September over one made in April, for their part urged the price controller to verify their need for price rises.[53] From that point onward, keeping costs and prices in balance was a job for the most skillful juggler.

The period ended without formal progress in public relations, at least in so far as an organization for Bigelow was concerned. Yet some gains had been made, some awareness developed of what was involved in good relations. Getting a favorable newspaper reaction was important, but recognized as more important was a standard of conduct in relations with the general public, with consumers, with retailers, and with employees that would make the favorable reaction follow logically. The company persevered toward attainment of the standard.

BIGELOW ON THE THRESHOLD OF WAR

The executive group remained largely unaltered throughout the period from 1937 to 1941 but there were changes in the directorate on the eve of war. In September, 1939, John Sanford died at Saratoga Springs where he had gone for the races. He was eighty-eight years of age, and his participation in Bigelow's affairs had greatly diminished in his declining years, although he had presided at a directors' meeting as recently as March of that year. With his death the office of board chairman lapsed. His son, Stephen, continued as a Bigelow director but he had never been actively identified with the company that bore his name. Connections between the Sanford family and the city of Amsterdam became limited largely to Stephen Sanford's ownership of a horse-breeding farm there.

In 1939 James D. Wise was elected to the board. Wise had become associated with Bigelow when his law firm, Wright, Gordon, Zachry, &

Parlin, had replaced that of Kinsolving Post, another company director, as legal counsel. The Post firm had become too small and specialized to handle the numerous and complicated legal matters with which the company now had to cope, while Wise's group was broadly acquainted with new developments in corporate law.

Wise had been helpful to Bigelow in the strike negotiations in 1938 and he did much work for the company in the antitrust and Federal Trade Commission difficulties in 1940. He gained intimate knowledge of Bigelow's affairs and of the carpet business from this work, and Sweetser recommended his election to the executive committee in 1940.[54] After 1938 the committee, at the management's request, had been meeting monthly rather than irregularly as theretofore. Its membership consisted of Charles Francis Adams, Roger Amory, Louis Liggett, Neal Rantoul, Sweetser, Samuel Welldon, and Frank Deknatel. New strength and vigor were added with the election of Wise.

The only other change in the membership of the board during the years 1937–1941 was effected by the death in August, 1941, of William Endicott. A representative of the Kidder, Peabody interests, Endicott had been a director since 1899. His place on the directorate was not immediately filled.

The pressures of government took some of the executives away from time to time and, in some cases, for the duration of the war. Wise spent a period in Washington late in 1940 in the office of the Under-Secretary of the Navy, and Knowland went on a three-month leave of absence in May, 1941, to work in the office of Production Management.[55] Such moves were sometimes advantageous to the company, for much helpful information could be gleaned by a man on the spot in Washington.

As the tide of defense preparation swelled, as more and more Americans became convinced that their country's formal participation in the war was a matter only of time, Bigelow found itself faced, on the one hand, with the intricacies of making and selling consumer goods in spite of material, labor, and equipment scarcities and, on the other, with the prospect of entering the new field of military supply manufacturing. Not only in production but in sales, the techniques of doing business with the government differed sharply from those to which the company was accustomed.

The rise in war-induced consumer demand, which reached a high point in 1941, put a heavy strain on management. Despite strong efforts of the manufacturing department, Bigelow looms fell far behind demand, while head-office files filled rapidly with angry letters from the field force of the sales department protesting six-month delivery dates. The manufacturing department was handicapped by shortages in both labor and materials. As has been noted, rayon was substituted for a part of the wool in some lines; jute shortages brought the use of cotton as a substitute, but a shortage in cotton was also threatened. To cope with these problems a substitute-materials unit was established in the technical department.

By the end of 1941 the situation with regard to consumer products appeared to indicate a further deterioration. Wool had been declared an essential commodity and so had other materials. Knowland's experience in Washington had led him to believe that the dislocation of consumer industry would be enormous, and that the carpet industry, in so far as consumer goods were concerned, might soon find itself out of business.[56] Sweetser took this view seriously; moreover, his intense patriotism made him feel that Bigelow's duty lay along the path of heavy war production.[57] More practical reasons were that the Thompsonville plant burned fuel oil, and the fast-approaching oil shortage made denial of oil by rationing authorities likely if the plant did not obtain war contracts.[58] Finally, by attracting war business, the company hoped to retain its skilled workers. The effect of all these considerations was the decision by Sweetser, supported by the executive committee, to commit Bigelow as wholeheartedly as possible to defense manufacturing.

The company had engaged in tentative preparations for defense work a year or so earlier. In 1940 Petersen had set up a defense training program in Thompsonville, the first of its kind, so far as he knew, in the industry. E. Wadsworth Stone, Bigelow's research and consulting engineer, surveyed the machine shops at Thompsonville and Amsterdam early in 1941 to determine what facilities could be given over to military production. By the end of 1941 such widely varied items as shell gauging and weighing machines, shaping and milling machine parts, bucket cutting machines, torpedo turbine bucket wheels, and miscellaneous torpedo parts had been produced in the company's two machine shops.[59] To utilize its looms for defense, the company quickly turned to blankets and cotton duck, as the Bigelow-Hartford company had done in World War I.

Having taken the initiative in the industry in so far as conversion to war work was concerned, Bigelow kept well ahead of its competitors. The company continued to manufacture consumer goods to some extent but, unhappily for its postwar competitive position, other manufacturers converted less wholeheartedly to defense production, managing thereby to retain their markets and keep themselves advantageously situated for reconversion to peacetime needs. A less idealistic man than Sweetser might have played the game more to the long-range advantage of his own company. But Sweetser, being the man he was, would have insisted on wholehearted participation in the war effort even had he known in advance what afterward proved to be the case: that his actions would one day seriously weaken the competitive position of his company in its struggles to capture its share of the postwar carpet market.

COMPANY AND COMPETITORS IN 1941: A COMPARISON

Like 1936, the year 1941 ended on a note of prosperity, but this time the prosperity was to be of longer duration. Whether working on civilian or military goods, the mills seemed assured of all the business they could handle. Bigelow, furthermore, appeared in 1941 well equipped to stand whatever strains were involved. The loss of 1938 had been offset in the series of successful years that followed. The year 1939 was the best since 1928 and although all earnings had been slightly lower in 1940 and 1941, this decline had been the effect of increased taxes and not of lowered sales, for the company had continued to expand the market for its product.

Bigelow's capital structure had steadily been strengthened after the 1938 difficulty and the adoption of the LIFO method had made its inventory valuation more realistic. Inventories themselves had been increased in 1941 over 1940 in line with Knowland's policy of reinforcing the company's raw materials position. Additional borrowings had been necessary but were justified by rising costs; working capital had been obtained without an increase in capitalization and the current ratio continued strong.

While the Bigelow-Sanford directors and executives could take pride in their company's strength and in its survival of depression, recession, and military preparation, their pride was tempered by contemplation of the records of Bigelow's competitors. Four other companies, Smith, Mohawk, Lees, and Firth, accounted with Bigelow for more than 60 per cent of the industry's sales in each of the three years from 1939 through 1941. A comparison of the company's performance with its four major competitors presents some interesting information.[60] Appendix 11 compares the sales and net income of five carpet companies beginning 1939; a sixth important concern, A. & M. Karagheusian, did not divulge information on its sales and income.

While Bigelow was able to improve its sales materially between 1939 and 1941, it was equaled in terms of percentage increases by Smith and was surpassed by Mohawk and Lees (see Appendix 11). Only Firth showed a smaller gain. Similarly, while its net income fell in 1940 and 1941—although it continued to make profits—Smith, Mohawk, and Lees were able to maintain their profit levels or advance slightly. Again only Firth made a poorer showing.

A comparison of the performance of the three largest companies in the industry is significant. Using 1936 as the base year, Smith's 1941 sales were 94 per cent over the base; those of Mohawk had increased by 72 per cent; the carpet industry as a whole had increased its sales by 62 per cent; but Bigelow's improvement over 1936 was only 45 per cent.[61] Profits showed a similar trend. For the six years from 1936 to 1941, Bigelow averaged $28,000,000 of sales annually, on which it earned an average of 7.2 per cent. Smith averaged $21,700,000 of sales, with an average return of 12.6 per cent. Mohawk, with average sales of $18,800,000, earned an average of 11.6 per cent.

What were the reasons for Bigelow's apparent loss of standing? Lees' new factory in Virginia must certainly have been one cause of that company's success; another may have been its spinning operation, making yarn for sale to other companies. Mohawk's apparently more efficient manufacturing techniques may have explained its relatively better performance.

Perhaps there was no cause for the company to be greatly concerned so long as it continued to be reasonably profitable, to turn out products that were recognized for their quality, and to provide fair terms of employment for its labor and fair returns for its shareholders. Certainly Bigelow had survived the years of depression and recession and had, indeed, benefited from them or from the stimulus they provided. Its work in synthetic fibers was calculated to be of far-reaching importance, and its new attitude of initiative and receptivity to change had enabled it to lead the field in war conversion.

On the other hand, Bigelow could not afford to stand still. It had a position of leadership to maintain, leadership that should have extended to all phases of its operations. With war all around it, perhaps not much could be done immediately to improve matters. Sweetser was aware, however, of the need for more positive action to remedy the situation. By gradual change, the Bigelow president was to try to regain the ground his company seemed to have lost.

CHAPTER 14

WARTIME OPERATIONS, 1942–1945

THE VICTORY PROGRAM AND ITS ACCOMPLISHMENTS

Within a few weeks of the attack on Pearl Harbor, Bigelow had created a War Sales Division to solicit orders for military goods. A group of 35 experienced salesmen was brought together, given special training at Amsterdam and Thompsonville, and then despatched to government and industrial centers to find products that could be made in the company's textile mills and machine shops.[1] As this field force remitted information about military requirements, Bigelow's technical facilities went promptly to work to determine what products the company could make. Some of the ideas and orders submitted proved readily feasible; others required experimentation and development before they could be transmuted into manufacture; and some were beyond Bigelow's capacity. As the war went on, the company gained skill both in negotiating with government agencies and in meeting their requirements, and the list of items that it could make successfully steadily grew.

The "Victory Program," as company records called it, evolved in three operational areas. These were the machine shop division at Thompsonville and Amsterdam, the welding division (which operated only at the Connecticut plant, using welding equipment bought for the purpose of war manufacture), and the textile division, which was active at both mills. The textile division was naturally the largest; it was broken down into three sections: blankets and cloth; duck; and sundries.[2]

The major production problem was the adaptation of carpet looms to blanket yarn, with a tensile strength of perhaps $\frac{1}{16}$ to $\frac{1}{20}$ that of carpet yarn.[3] Many experiments in spinning and twisting the weaker yarn were required, but Bigelow's foresight in investigating blanket weaving before the United States was actually at war gave it a distinct competitive advantage. Its research in 1941 led to the significant discovery that army blankets could be woven on axminster looms and the success of an experimental lot led the company to seek orders. An initial order for 50,000 blankets made from domestic wool placed Bigelow as the first of the wool-pile carpet companies to engage its looms on war work. With some difficulty the Quartermaster Corps was made to see that the axminster blanket was superior to that called for by military specifications and a program of blanket manufacture on Bigelow's numerous axminster looms was well under way by early 1942.[4]

The carpet industry realized quickly that defense production was not a matter for one, two, or several of the large companies but for the industry as a whole. Under the leadership of the Carpet Institute, manufacturers agreed to exchange all the technical information that could be obtained on loom conversion and on the manufacture of war products. Bigelow, because of its early lead in blanket weaving, was selected as the industry's guide in that field. In March, 1942, 30 technicians from various companies met at Amsterdam to investigate and observe the procedures of the blanket department which, with its Thompsonville counterpart, was busy on an order for 200,000 blankets.[5] For the duration of hostilities the wool carpet-makers shared information to the greatest extent possible.

The order for 200,000 blankets soon paled into insignificance beside others for more than one million. Statistics of the Victory Program verged on the astronomical. More than one half of the total of blankets and cloth made by the entire carpet and rug industry was woven on the looms of Amsterdam and Thompsonville, $56,500,000 worth. Bigelow manufactured more than one quarter of all the war materials turned out by its industry, and it was the largest single maker of blanketing for the armed forces, regardless of industry, in the United States.[6] The Amsterdam looms wove over 5,200,000 blankets or their equivalent in blanket cloth, while those at Thompsonville manufactured one blanket for every third man in military service, or over 18 million square yards.[7]

As soon as blanket production was started, the company undertook the weaving of cotton duck. Working with the Quartermaster Corps, as it had on blankets, Bigelow-Sanford developed a 48-ounce duck that could be woven on carpet looms. Regular duck manufacturers were at first able to underbid the company but by the end of 1941, the growing need for duck made the market more favorable to the carpet manufacturers. By converting old looms and by purchasing new, Thompsonville was able to produce sufficient duck on 123 tapestry and 37 jacquard looms, between March, 1942, and September, 1945, to have made a pathway one yard wide from San Francisco to Hiroshima. At Amsterdam, 106 looms were used for duck, and 8,100,000 yards were woven. Moreover, a necessary reduction in vital manpower was obtained by assigning one weaver to two duck looms, as opposed to one weaver per machine in carpet weaving.

Other war products included army squad tents, tire sandals to restore old tires to use, rayon fabric for tires, and camouflage netting. Both plants treated hundreds of thousands of yards of nylon and rayon with rubber to line self-sealing gasoline tanks and heavy-duty tires.

In the machine shops were produced parts for submarines, gun mounts, navy planes, radar equipment, and—although no employee knew their purpose—components for the atomic bomb plant at Oak Ridge, Tennessee. Bigelow's contribution to Oak Ridge was made under subcontract from another manufacturer. Indeed, most of the output of the machine shop and welding divisions and some of the work of the textile division were under such contracts.

TABLE **33**

BIGELOW–SANFORD CARPET COMPANY

Military and Civilian Sales and Profits   1942 to 1945

Year	Total Sales	Military Sales	Per Cent of Total	Civilian Sales	Per Cent of Total	Net Income After Taxes
1942	$41,511,394	$10,773,945	25.9	$30,737,449	74.1	$1,261,552
1943	37,667,636	27,019,570	71.7	10,648,066	28.3	287,571
1944	39,417,660	27,593,459	70.0	11,824,201	30.0	1,025,750
1945	34,679,455	21,185,044	61.0	13,494,411	39.0	890,677

Source: Annual Reports, Bigelow-Sanford.

Table 33 illustrates the way in which major emphasis shifted from civilian to military production. In 1942 the manufacture of consumer goods was, in terms of sales, about three times as great as was defense production. By 1943 the picture had changed dramatically, and not until 1945, only partially a war year, did civilian output again approach that for war.

Successful though Bigelow was in manufacturing for war, military work was not as profitable as the company may have hoped, as the drop in net income in 1943 from that in 1942 indicates. A variety of factors underlay this situation: rising costs which could not be calculated in advance, profit margins cut to obtain contracts, and, sometimes, lack of the necessary "know-how" to make government contracting profitable.

Blankets, of which Bigelow made so many, provide an example of the effect of lack of experience. In its early contracts the company sold blankets to the government for about $6.85 each, having calculated that the unit profit would be about 58 cents. With so small a profit margin and with wool costing about $1.00 per pound, strict adherence to weight specifications was required if the estimated profit was not to turn into a loss. Yet

Bigelow personnel were used to making carpets, with a high unit profit and with less attention paid to weight than to such things as pile and pattern regularity. The first blanket runs therefore resulted in some that were overweight and some that were underweight; tough army inspectors were quick to accept the heavy ones and reject the light, with an inevitably bad effect on profits from the contract. Correction was effected by a new system of quality control which, as new methods often are, was initially resisted by department overseers.[8]

Toward the end of 1944 defense authorities, realizing that a slowdown in the war machine was at hand, issued instructions regarding the ultimate termination of government contracts. From November, 1944, representatives of government and industry worked out the details of termination procedures.

Actual cancellation of Bigelow's contracts did not begin, however, until about the middle of August, 1945. By October the company was advertising contract termination inventories for sale, materials including wool, dyestuffs, paper, baling boards, soap, and thread.[9] By December, 1945, inventories relating to war production had been cut to $14,950, compared with about $2,600,000 at the end of 1944.[10] The Victory Program had become a name in the record and a memory in the mind.

LABOR PROBLEMS OF THE VICTORY PROGRAM

Throughout the war years general labor was both uncertain and expensive. In 1942 there were 1,503 hirings and 1,884 terminations at Thompsonville because of the tendency of new employees to "shop around" for the easiest and best-paying jobs they could find.[11] A similar situation prevailed at Amsterdam and both mills continued to experience labor turnover as jobs remained plentiful and workers comparatively few.

The employees recruited were relatively inexperienced. Where possible, women were used to replace men called into the services, and, being unskilled, they required instruction. Since the problem was common to most companies, the War Manpower Commission instituted a Training Within Industry program which, by reducing jobs to their simplest components (among other things), did much to shorten the time required to fit new workers for their jobs. Bigelow had completed its cycle of the plan by the fall of 1944; by that time the entire factory's supervisory staff had finished the various courses of instruction and had done its share of training operatives.[12]

Older workers shared the desire of Bigelow's new recruits to make more money. Patriotic and other government pressures did much to prevent strikes for wage increases as well as for other demands but they could not completely eliminate the traditional militancy of the carpet worker. The spring of 1942 was disturbed by a strike vote in both Bigelow locals

over wage increases, and the company in May organized labor-management committees to seek industrial harmony, at the urgent request of the
War Production Board. The result was a government-approved increase
for weavers in April, followed by a 20 per cent increase in June, with additional compensation paid also to finishers.[13]

Aware that government labor agencies were anxious to prevent strikes
and would apply appropriate pressure, the Textile Workers Union next
sought, as a goal it had long tried to gain, maintenance of union membership. This was one of the terms in the 1943 contract the union presented
for signature in late 1942. Bigelow's executives were reluctant to comply
but they were anxious to keep their labor forces intact. A decision of the
War Labor Board in another case seemed to indicate that, if the matter
was brought before the Board, the company would lose.[14] Both maintenance of membership and the check-off, together with another pay increase, were therefore included in the 1943 contract.

Mohawk made similar concessions. Alexander Smith attempted to resist, but in March, 1943, it agreed to the maintenance of membership and
check-off clauses, while serving notice on its employees that it had done
so only as a "wartime measure." [15] Indeed, these problems and concessions
were characteristic of American manufacturing, generally, during the war
years.

Labor disputes in 1943 were minor but wage increases continued to be
made. A comparison of average hourly earnings, including overtime, in
various companies at the end of the year indicated that Bigelow workers
were receiving an average of slightly better than 92 cents per hour, more
than the average of either Smith, Mohawk, or the Bureau of Labor Statistics compilation of earnings in 25 industries.

In May, 1944, a union request for 65 cents per hour as a minimum wage
for Bigelow machine operators and for a union shop in departments
where 80 per cent of the employees were union members was denied by
the War Labor Board. The Board ordered a minimum rate of 55 cents and
did not grant the union shop request. No strike followed the union's failure
to have its own way, but a vague arbitration award on another issue and
another unpalatable Board decision led to short strikes in two Thompsonville departments, both of which were settled without prolonged bitterness.[16]

Unquestionably the labor front showed more activity as the war displayed signs of coming to an end. In June, 1944, the office workers in
Thompsonville met to discuss union organization. In the struggle to secure
employees (and office workers were as hard to get as production personnel), Bigelow had been forced to offer rates competitive with those available elsewhere. The result was an anomalous situation in which some
senior office employees were receiving lower salaries than their juniors for

identical duties. The annoyance thus engendered provided fertile ground for union organizers; so did the lack of adequate grievance procedures for white-collar employees; and so did that group's realization that its gains had not matched those of hourly workers.

By September the National Labor Relations Board had agreed to hold what was to be the first election dealing with office workers in a New England industrial concern. With a vote of 82 to 39 the Thompsonville workers chose to become a local of the United Office & Professional Workers of America, a CIO affiliate. Contract discussions began in October, and in January announcement was made of wage increases running from $1.00 to $6.00 weekly, retroactive to December 1, and of contract provisions guaranteeing union security, seniority rights in promotions, vacations, sick leave, and arbitration of disputes.[17]

The war had emphasized what Bigelow executives had realized before it started: the arbitrary system of hiring and firing that had prevailed in the plants was a thing of the past. Personnel duties could not be left to untrained individuals, however sincere and well-meaning these individuals might be, and 500 hours of production executive time spent yearly on union meetings over grievances were wasteful. A first step toward the improvement of the personnel organization was the engagement of a director of industrial relations in mid-1944.

The organization as a whole was able to take satisfaction in the recognition it received for its wartime output. Thompsonville workers had much pride in seeing the first of Bigelow's Army and Navy "E" pennants fluttering from the mill flagstaff in December, 1943, and Amsterdam followed shortly with an "E" award of its own.

CONSUMER SALES ACTIVITIES IN WARTIME

Beginning in 1942 Bigelow's sales staffs were reduced as much as possible. By April of 1943 the field sales force had been cut from 146 to 46. It was possible to make this abrupt reduction only because there was so little for the salesmen to sell. By the time the war was in full swing, the company was marketing less than a third of the carpeting it had sold during the best peacetime years. Because of increased manufacturing costs and because of shortages of wool, Bigelow, by April, 1943, had reduced its entire list to a single regular line in each of the three major weaves of carpeting, all three being wool-rayon blends.

The Marval rug, its name changed to Marvin, still remained in production and for good reason. It was being made of punched felt with a rayon face, which meant that it could be sold without regard to dealer quotas, since it contained no wool.[18] Marvin was also sold under different names to mail-order houses. As Table 34 illustrates, its sales grew considerably during the war years.

Cotton rugs offered the company a second important supplement to its war-reduced wool products. These rugs had enjoyed increasing popularity for some years before the war, first for bathroom use and then as occasional rugs in other rooms. Bigelow had not followed the earlier example of some other companies in entering the small cotton rug field as manufacturers and its war work prevented use of its own manufacturing facilities to do so in 1942. Delaney, the company's sales vice-president, began negotiations, therefore, to obtain these rugs from outside suppliers, and by April, 1942, had secured representation for several lines; announcement of Bigelow's new venture into the marketing of cotton rugs was made in May.[19] Because of their low price, both rayon and cotton rugs proved

TABLE 34

BIGELOW–SANFORD CARPET COMPANY

Value of Shipments by Products   1942 to 1945

Year	Axminster	Wilton	Velvet	Marvin	Cotton	Total
1942	$18,124,783	$3,883,415	$8,137,637	$1,167,335	$105,924	$31,419,044
1943	5,561,931	2,039,303	1,636,382	1,230,950	253,822	10,722,240
1944	4,940,133	2,387,391	2,438,761	1,925,652	250,113	11,942,050
1945	6,340,358	2,436,668	3,177,169	1,520,764	243,065	13,818,024

Source: Secretary's Department, Bigelow-Sanford.

popular with migratory defense workers who, on setting up temporary homes, did not wish to invest much money in floor coverings.

As not only wool but other raw materials became difficult or impossible to obtain, the company had to allot its wool-rayon carpets to dealers on a quota basis. Beginning January 1, 1942, Bigelow permitted dealers to order 30 per cent of their 1941 average quarterly dollar billings. If the company could not make delivery within the immediate quarter, it shipped later and charged the shipment against the quarter when the order was placed. Quotas rose and fell irregularly, once going as low as 7.5 per cent of 1941 average billings, and the system had to be continued well into the postwar period.[20]

Yet, in spite of substitute materials to take the place of wool-rayon carpet shortages, and despite the company's best efforts to treat its retail dealers equitably, the quota system failed to prevent a deterioration in dealer relationships, for it was difficult to convince the customers that they were being fairly treated. When the 1944 sales of $39,417,000 were divided into war and civilian production, the fact that civilian goods made up 29 per cent of the total led to numerous inquiries from retailers as to why their quota had not been 29 per cent during the year. They did not realize that quotas were set simply on the basis of wool-rayon rug and carpet production, while the total figure included Marvin, cotton rugs, and rug linings.[21] Making retailers understand the facts was a difficult job for salesmen.

Part of the friction between Bigelow and its retailers arose from the fact that the company was concentrating such a disproportionate amount of its efforts on war production. Other carpet companies, less fully engaged in war work, consequently stood in a better position to service their retailers. Whereas Bigelow ordinarily supplied carpet outlets with 18 to 20 per cent of the carpet yardage produced in this country, in 1943 it shipped only 10.9 per cent (see Appendix 14). This decline in relative position was certain to be felt by normal trade outlets; the decline was also certain to be felt by the company itself when it tried to regain its lost position after the war.

ADMINISTRATIVE PROBLEMS AND DEVELOPMENTS OF WARTIME

No doubt part of the company's failure to maintain its wartime market position in consumers goods may be traced to the state of health of John Sweetser. While his friends did not know it until after his death, Sweetser's physical condition had declined almost from the date of the Sanford merger.[22] This fact provides an explanation of some of the company's difficulties during the closing years of Sweetser's administration. During much of the time the president was simply incapable of putting forth the energy required to cope with his many dilemmas.

Two situations in the middle of 1942, within a month of each other, illustrate the clashes between Sweetser and Knowland that had occurred sporadically even before the war and that happened with mounting frequency during it.[23] The first was the failure of machine shop defense production to rise to the level Sweetser had expected; the second was the inability of the mills to maintain duck deliveries on schedule. To the first criticism Knowland replied that the expected machine shop volume had been only an estimate and that the shops had been handicapped by a labor shortage which his executives were trying to overcome with an apprentice training program. He defended the duck delivery failures by pointing up a more serious flaw in organization: the lack of co-ordination of departments which had existed since John Norman's time as president. Orders for duck had been accepted by the sales department without consulting any production executive, and Knowland asked that "in the future . . . we [the production group] be given the privilege of making some sort of statement as to what we believe the capacity of the plants to be prior to placing orders for materials." This lack of co-ordination may not have been so serious in the depression years of the thirties, when the volume problem lay in sales rather than in production, but now the situation was the reverse.

In so far as Bigelow's capacity was concerned, the plants, especially its machine shops, were prevented from converting to certain products because the company's charter permitted it to operate only within the general textile field. Knowland believed that his department, under a broader charter, could have made war materials in large volume; but, he felt that, if operations were to be confined to the narrow base permitted, the company might not be able to keep busy. He, therefore, urged the president in July, 1942, to discuss a broader charter with the executive committee. This change was found not to be feasible, however. A revision of corporate powers would have given the stockholders the right to an appraisal of their stock, and the management did not wish to run the risk that a substantial number of stockholders might exercise their privilege to withdraw from the company rather than to venture with it into nontextile fields.

As for internal co-ordination, Sweetser recognized that manufacturing was not the only company activity that was suffering from inadequate knowledge of what others were doing, and he responded to the pressures from Knowland and from the directors toward better administrative balance. In 1943 he organized an Operations Committee, its membership to be made up of the various department heads and its purposes to ensure consultation and to avoid misunderstanding.[24]

One of the areas in which the new committee was to work was postwar planning; the president urged members to keep in mind the need for additional executive help after the war. Such a need had been emphasized by his belief, in which Knowland shared, that one of the manufacturing department's difficulties had been insufficient management personnel. At last, a situation which had been made almost inevitable by the Sanford merger of 1929 had come to pass with the return to capacity operations in the 1940's. Where Bigelow-Sanford's post-merger executive force had been able to get along unexpanded during the depression's below-capacity operations, it no longer safely could attempt to do so. Only Knowland and E. Wadsworth Stone, Bigelow's research and consulting engineer, had much knowledge of machine shop work, for instance, and the two mill superintendents were feeling a serious lack of competent assistance. Unfortunately, the earlier failure to recognize this deficiency had carried Bigelow into mid-1943, by which time capable production administrators were almost impossible to obtain in the competitive wartime labor market.

There was agreement between Sweetser and Knowland over some of the problems and the ways to solve them. During Sweetser's three-month absence while ill during the fall of 1943, the production vice-president co-operated at Sweetser's request with J. D. Wise, temporary chairman of the executive committee, and with Treasurer F. H. Deknatel, who had been promoted to first vice-president over Knowland's head. But, when Sweetser returned, trouble flared up again. Because of a misunderstanding, which at the time loomed large but which might easily have been cleared up by straightforward and unemotional discussion, Sweetser, then obviously a sick and sensitive man, summarily dismissed Knowland shortly before Christmas, 1943.[25]

Knowland was paid a substantial fee to act as consultant to Bigelow for one year but this arrangement was a face-saving form of severance pay; strained feelings on both sides kept him from doing much consulting. His position as vice-president for manufacturing was not immediately filled. Sweetser himself handled the major production issues for several months, with some assistance from Deknatel.[26]

The comparative lack of friction between Sweetser and his other associates in the executive group did not mean that the president was convinced that the company's other, nonmanufacturing departments were operating effectively. On the contrary, he had come to comprehend that the sales organization also stood in need of change, and that the war offered an opportunity to make this change during a period when the sales department was more or less marking time. Since he began his reorganization while Knowland was still with the company and because he anticipated some resistance from J. J. Delaney, the vice-president for sales, and from other members of the marketing department, the president turned to an outside authority for advice, a not unusual procedure in business in such situations.

A Boston man in what was to some extent a Boston company, Sweetser went to the Graduate School of Business Administration of Harvard University for the advice of Professor Melvin T. Copeland. The president and Copeland had their first meeting in July, 1942, after which they were in frequent consultation. From Copeland, Sweetser obtained not only help on specific problems but assistance on all phases of Bigelow's marketing operations.[27]

Delaney had directed his department more or less autonomously, with each subordinate directly responsible to him. Copeland did not feel that all the sales functions should be organized in this way and Sweetser came to agree with him. Delaney was persuaded to limit his responsibility to sales only; merchandising decisions were put under the operations committee, the head of styling was to report directly to the president, and a search was begun in January, 1943, for an advertising manager who would be qualified to direct an intensive program of market research.[28]

The sales organization was streamlined; while at the end of 1944 it may not have approached the functional breakdown upon which Sweetser and Copeland had agreed, it seemed to promise fairly strong aid to reconversion. Under Delaney, as vice-president in charge of sales, were P. F. O'Neil as sales manager and an assistant sales manager. Under these men were, in the New York offices, the field office supervisor, the Lokweave service manager, the contract service manager, the special products division, the styling director, the training director, and the field warehouse supervisor. The last of these, although a member of the headquarters staff, had more direct field responsibilities than his New York associates, working closely with the division managers. The sales managers in New York had supervision of the three sales divisions, the Eastern, Central, and Western. Under the various division managers were the branch managers, with salesmen and warehouse crews reporting to them.[29]

The man named to the new position of director of advertising, sales promotion, and market research was B. K. MacLaury, an outsider, whose background included broad experience in the three areas over which he was to have responsibility. MacLaury was instructed to report directly to the president, a situation not wholly to Delaney's liking; he had some reservations about Copeland's views, and in the next two years there were attempts on his part and on the part of other sales executives to control advertising policy and execution, as they had in the past.[30]

A small staff to aid the advertising director, MacLaury, in market research was acquired and a planning service consultant was retained in December, 1944. The latter's function was to work with stores in the development and layout of their floor coverings departments. Bigelow had pioneered in this field eleven years before and the company expected that extensive modernization would take place in the immediate postwar period. Services of the consultant were to be offered to stores without charge, as part of an effort to regain dealer goodwill.[31]

Two other new positions reflected Sweetser's efforts to broaden the administrative base upon which the company stood. In 1944 Mark Dunnell, Bigelow's assistant treasurer, became controller, freeing Deknatel for broader responsibility as first vice-president and treasurer and laying the groundwork for more use of accounting methods as management aids. It was in that year also that the president established the post of director of industrial relations. H. S. Hall, a man who was described as "a combination of pugilist and Phi Beta Kappa," [32] was recruited from the aircraft industry to take the job.[33]

Sweetser's strengthening process extended even to the board of directors. Early in 1943 Sewall Fessenden died at the age of seventy-nine, after twenty years of continuous service as a representative of F. S. Moseley & Company on the Bigelow directorate. Fessenden was not replaced by another member of the financial house but by E. Kent Swift, then president of the Whitin Machine Works.[34] This election had sound implications for the future, for Bigelow had bought much of Whitin's textile machinery; engineers of the two companies had worked together on development of machines for special purposes. In the postwar period, speedy reconversion and replacement of obsolete equipment would be important but new machinery might be hard to obtain by those companies lacking influence with manufacturers.

The board's executive committee had been reduced in size to five just before Fessenden's death. The five members were Charles Francis Adams, Neal Rantoul, Sweetser, Samuel Welldon, and Wise.[35] Roger Amory, of Boston, and Deknatel were no longer members because of other activities. Louis K. Liggett, whose keen business sense had meant much to the company, had been removed by ill health from participation in the committee's concerns earlier. He resigned from the board itself in 1944 and died in 1946. In the opinion of R. G. Knowland, whose Bigelow association extended over fifteen years, Liggett and Neal Rantoul were the company's most effective directors. After Liggett's death the directorate consisted of nine members, and it remained at nine for some time.

PLANS FOR RECONVERSION

From late in 1942 much of the thinking of the executives, particularly those concerned with sales, had to do with strengthening Bigelow's position against the era of hard competition envisaged in the future. Some of the plans developed were tangible and practical, easy to make and follow. Thus Delaney, in a letter describing Mohawk's annual school for salesmen, wrote: "At our next Operation Committee meeting I hope to have some suggestions worked out about a training program that we might consider in our Post-war program for our own sales organization as well as for the sales personnel of our outlets." [36]

Less easy to determine was the proper course to pursue toward a successful sales policy when full civilian production had again become a reality. If advantage was to be taken of the breathing space provided by the war, definite decisions were required on a number of issues.

To this end were held frequent conferences of the senior sales personnel, the new advertising director, the treasurer, and, sometimes, of President Sweetser and Dr. Copeland. The Harvard Business School professor had concluded that one of the contemplated plans for marketing, the opening of company operated retail stores was unsound, although this plan had in its favor the elimination of the possibility of customers being sold anything but Bigelow merchandise. Copeland also had constructive suggestions to offer along other lines.

On one point there was general agreement. Whatever the company did should be directed toward obtaining greater recognition of its name and acceptance for its products. Since company-operated stores were ruled out, advertising and direct selling were to be pointed toward making the carpet-buying public insist on Bigelow floor coverings only.

Adoption of the Bigelow Weavers' label in 1932 and simultaneous promotion of the Bigelow name had been quickly copied by most manufacturers, illustrating the fact that competition constantly drives business to new endeavor. In 1940 the company had taken a further step toward consumer recognition with the advertising campaign built around the long-popular Beauvais axminster, a program well received by salespeople and dealers alike. In 1941 the advertising appropriation had been divided between Beauvais and another product, and again senior sales division executives had regarded the results as good.[37]

The success of the 1940 and 1941 programs led P. F. O'Neil and other members of the sales department to urge that Beauvais be used as the identifying name for the outstanding grade in each weave and fabric. This stand was opposed by Copeland and MacLaury, who maintained that the Bigelow name should be promoted.[38] They believed that dealers, retail salesmen, and consumers alike would find it difficult to understand why axminster, velvet, wilton, and Lokweave fabrics should be referred to under the same name. The Beauvais name had been exclusively an axminster title for many years—since the time before the merger when it was the chief product of the Sanford company. Dispute over the issue continued into 1945 and ended with rejection of the O'Neil plan.[39]

Another question raised and thoroughly investigated was that of participation in the sale of low-end goods. Copeland felt that the company's postwar field of concentration should be on better merchandise, high-quality products that were more profitable to make and sell.[40] If, however, the management felt it desirable to continue low-end production, then the consultant recommended that its styling should be distinctively different from that of the better qualities. If low-end goods were made for mail-order houses, those organizations should not be given a competitive advantage by high-style effects comparable to those of the better grades unless low-end merchandise sold to other outlets was equally well styled. Like the broadened Beauvais idea, the low-end question was debated for some time. The final decision to continue low-end manufacture included a plan to distinguish the merchandise from the better quality items with a different brand name, perhaps a revival of the Sanford line or even a division of the lines into three price and quality classes.

Consideration was given to Bigelow's distribution system. Sweetser was anxious to work out some lasting and satisfactory relationship with dealers, one that would make the company less vulnerable to price-cutting.[41] Among various proposals to win dealer support was retail price-fixing, which was not adopted, and more profit for the larger retailers who ran their own cut-roll departments, which was.[42]

A more important line of investigation was a continuation of Copeland's inquiry into the existing dealer setup. Surveys of the dealer organization were conducted, to find out not only how much each dealer sold but what sort of dealer he was—in other words, did he also sell furniture, was he a department store owner, an interior decorator, or a seller of carpets only? Information of this type seemed important if the right sales program was to be developed.

The various studies indicated among other things that furniture stores made up 70 per cent of the Bigelow dealer total and that stores selling better grades of its rugs and carpets as the major part of the line they handled provided 29 per cent of the 1941 volume, although they represented only 9 per cent of the total number of outlets.[43] Sound policy warranted cultivation of those stores and others which might become like them. Furthermore, it appeared that 80 per cent of the rugs and carpets that Bigelow sold direct to retailers in 1941 had been bought by 18 per cent of the stores. As a result of the realization that less than one-fifth of its retailers sold almost four-fifths of its goods, the company decided to pursue a policy of selective distribution which would eliminate dealers with limited dollar volume or little potential for growth.

Such a policy, if successful, would help Bigelow to obtain independence from mail-order houses and eliminate special concessions to large-volume buyers. Dr. Copeland believed that the company should seek such independence but Sweetser did not share his views. The mail-order houses had provided Bigelow looms with a useful cushion against idle capacity, mail-order selling could be done with comparatively small cost in relation to the size of the orders, and the company continued to do such business. It also continued to offer quantity discounts to large-volume purchasers.[44]

The basic thinking behind the flexible marketing plans was to emphasize the Bigelow name and to obtain its greater recognition by consumers, to have in mind the desirability of separating high-end from low-end business, and to maintain a protective bulwark of large-volume accounts. The success of the plans depended on the manufacturing department's progress toward efficiency. Sweetser's aim was to have his company exceed the high level of sales volume attained in wartime even including that proportion made up of war items. This could be done in peacetime at a worth-while profit rate only if the manufacturing processes were adapted to new conditions and requirements.

The executive committee also made plans to place postwar manufacturing on a regular two-shift basis. The cost of adding to or replacing equipment to handle such activity was estimated to be about two million dollars. Tentative orders were placed in mid-1943 for fifteen 16/4 axminster looms and ring-spinning frames, subject to acceptance by Bigelow and the machinery manufacturer of final prices and delivery dates. The entire new machinery program was to be reviewed by a southern engineering firm hired as consultants. The main reason for placing the order was to insure the earliest possible delivery of equipment after needs had been determined.

ANOTHER MANAGEMENT CRISIS

Whatever other plans Sweetser may have had, they were never put into effect. To the shock and dismay of his co-workers at Bigelow's Manhattan headquarters, word came that he had died suddenly and without warning on August 18, 1944, at his summer home near Woodstock, Vermont, where he had gone for a brief summer vacation. He had had a major operation in 1943 and had been absent from the office for a long convalescence. On his return to the office, however, the conduct of his affairs had seemed to indicate a renewal of his old vigor.

The suddenness of Sweetser's death made the problem of replacing him especially difficult. Like many comparatively young men in business, Sweetser, who was only fifty-four when he died, had given little thought to training anyone as a successor. There was some feeling that at one time he might have intended Knowland to follow him as president, but Knowland's fall from favor put an end to that plan if it had existed.

Actually Sweetser had given little attention to executive development as a managerial problem. He had given men authority to carry out their work and had expected them to deliver. When they had not, he had removed them from office, though he had always been slow to take this step and sometimes had left to others the distasteful task of informing the offending executive. For all his kindness and good intentions he had not, however, forced his executives (or made it possible for them) to familiarize themselves with the operations of other departments beyond their own. As a result he, and he alone, had known enough about the company's activities to co-ordinate them.

There was no one among the younger executives who might remotely have been considered a candidate for the vacated presidency. The marketing department, after Campbell's departure, had been split into several subdepartments with a specialist in charge of each. And in production, after Knowland's departure, no successor had even been appointed.

Under these circumstances the board of directors had no choice but to go outside the company for a replacement. On the board were still a number of influential men whose connections in management circles were many and whose services the company had relied on in the twenties when it had been necessary to find a successor to Norman. In addition, specialized management placement firms had come into existence in the intervening years and were prepared to secure for companies like Bigelow the executive talent needed when such companies were unprepared to handle management succession from within.

No thought was given to merging with a competitor—a solution which had been repeatedly used when similar management crises had occurred in the company's earlier history. Mergers had been the recourse of closely held companies when ownership had failed to perpetuate itself in the management function. With securities that could not command a general market, the owners often had found a merger the easiest way to liquidate their investment. Now that ownership and management were separated, a breakdown in management succession could occur without involving a change in ownership. This continuity of ownership, despite a void in the organization's top executive posts, clearly distinguished the modern, publicly owned Bigelow enterprise from its privately owned predecessor companies and indicated a stability that the old institutions had not possessed.

CHAPTER 15

ADMINISTRATIVE REORGANIZATION
AND POSTWAR ADJUSTMENT, 1945–1949

When, after Sweetser's death, the directors realized that no one in the management group possessed adequate experience, ability, or breadth of vision to become president, some of the board members tried to persuade one of their number, James D. Wise, to accept the post. In many ways Wise had become the company's most active director. Not only had he served the firm in a legal capacity for many years, but in 1943, during Sweetser's forced absence, he had acted as the chief executive officer. At about that time Sweetser, influenced in his thinking by the state of his health, had urged Wise to accept either the presidency or the chairmanship of the board. But Wise had declined. Again, in 1944, on Sweetser's death, Wise declined the proffered post. As a member of a highly successful firm of corporation lawyers he was not eager to leave the excitement and challenge of law practice to assume the uncertain responsibilities of carpet manufacturing. He did, however, consent to serve as chairman of the committee of directors appointed to seek a new president.[1]

Because of the extensive acquaintance of Bigelow's directors in the financial and industrial world, the company's need for a president was widely circulated. Agencies dealing in executive placement were consulted and so were a variety of unofficial sources of information. The task proved unusually difficult, however, because of the war. Many of the country's most able businessmen were in government service, while in industry a jealous guard was kept over the men already in executive positions.

After three months had passed and no one suitable had been found, the need for a chief executive became acute. The Victory Program was drawing to an end and someone had to be ready to make plans for reconversion. Aware of the heavy price the company was paying for lack of leadership and increasingly interested in the problems the company faced, Wise reconsidered his earlier decision and accepted the offer of the board.

He became president on November 9, 1944, taking formal office on December 1.[2]

Just as John A. Sweetser's background had differed widely from that of his predecessor, Norman, so Wise's background and training differed from that of the Harvard-educated Bostonian, Sweetser. Bigelow's new president, born at Greencastle, Indiana, educated at Leland Stanford University and Columbia University Law School, had begun the practice of law in New York City with, as he put it, no friends east of the Rocky Mountains except his Columbia classmates. His reversal of Horace Greeley's famed adjuration had been a successful one. His law work had proved profitable, and he had represented for his firm an impressive number of large corporations as clients.

The new chief executive was fully aware of the problems which lay before him. Since 1932, when his firm had become Bigelow's legal counsel, he had followed the company's course of action, and in later years had seen developing the administrative crisis in which Sweetser was becoming embroiled. He knew, moreover, that for all Sweetser's unpredictability in the closing years of his life, "the skipper" had held the unswerving loyalty of his devoted staff. Stepping into Sweetser's place, bringing to bear the lawyer's coldly analytical judgment where once the gentleness of an idealist had prevailed, forcing through unpleasant reorganizational changes— no one was better aware of the difficulties of these tasks than Wise.

One of Wise's first acts was to fill the post left vacant more than a year earlier by the dismissal of R. G. Knowland. As his choice for the production vice-presidency, Wise singled out the superintendent of the mill at Thompsonville, Elliott I. Petersen. The promotion took place February 14, 1945.[3] No position that Wise was to fill was to meet more general approval than the promotion of the Thompsonville plant executive. A Bigelow employee since 1915, Petersen had risen from the ranks and had made a mark for himself not only as a leader of men but as one who understood something of the workers' inner drives and compulsions.

To succeed Petersen at Thompsonville the company named as superintendent, James Jackson, a man who had worked for the company since 1920. Since most of Jackson's experience had been gained in the office side of mill operations, the company gave him as an assistant a veteran weaver by the name of William Fuge.[4]

Within a few months Wise had taken another significant step in his program of re-equipping the company with executive talent. Aware of his own limited experience as an administrator and desiring professional advice, he employed, in mid-1945, a firm of management consultants—Booz, Allen & Hamilton—a firm with whose work he already had some familiarity. The consultants were to investigate and analyze the management problems and were to recommend steps to improve over-all operations.

They estimated that their assignment would be completed within a few months. In actual fact it took much longer. It was easy, even for experienced specialists, to underestimate the task which lay ahead.

A first glance at the income and balance sheet statements showed the consultants that financially the company had come through the war years in a strong condition (e.g., a current ratio of 6.6 in 1945 as against 3.5 in 1941); but the gentle, yet clearly perceptible, decline in the company's position relative to its leading competitors had continued. For the four years from 1941 Bigelow's sales had averaged $38,000,000 annually, Smith's $33,000,000 and Mohawk's $31,000,000, so that Bigelow had at least retained its over-all sales leadership. But, while Bigelow had averaged 4.6 per cent profit on sales, Smith had made 5.9 per cent, and Mohawk 10.9 per cent. Moreover, while the Bigelow sales average had been a 36 per cent increase over that for the previous six years, Smith's had been 54 per cent and Mohawk's 67 per cent. Both of Bigelow's rivals had had a wartime sales average that was better than their 1941 showing, while the company's own $38,000,000 average had just about equaled its 1941 sales.

At the end of 1945 the company had a net worth of $26,321,000; Smith had a net worth of $23,200,000 (not including $4,300,000 invested in the stock of the hard-surface manufacturing concern, Sloane-Blabon, products of which were sold by Smith); Mohawk had $19,900,000 of net worth. Mohawk had kept $3,000,000 of its decade's earnings in its business; Bigelow had retained $2,900,000; and Smith had kept $7,800,000.

Smith, largely a family-owned concern, had earned $15,000,000 in the ten years from 1936, and had paid out only 48 per cent of its earnings in dividends; as a private company it was perhaps serving its stockholders best in that way. Bigelow and Mohawk, on the other hand, had disbursed more of their earnings as dividends; Bigelow had paid out 77 per cent and Mohawk 72 per cent. During the period Mohawk had made $11,500,000 against Bigelow's $11,000,000 and this in spite of having been only two-thirds the size of Bigelow when the decade began.

However, one bit of information gave Wise and the consultants quiet confidence that Bigelow could, if properly directed, regain its lost position. A consumer survey in 1944 had shown that 20 per cent of the people interviewed knew the Bigelow name without suggestion from the interviewer, 9 per cent knew the Olson Rug Company in Chicago (a concern that sold new rugs in partial exchange for old material sent in by customers), and 7 per cent knew the Smith name. Here was an important fact. The survey seemed to prove that Bigelow's efforts in the past had stood it in good stead, that the quality of its merchandise over so many years had not gone unrecognized, and that the efforts of its sales force and its advertising to keep its name in the forefront had not been in vain. If a period of hard selling should develop, this was likely to give the company strength.

ADMINISTRATIVE REORGANIZATION

The work of Booz, Allen & Hamilton was subdivided into a series of studies from which resulted a number of reports.[5] These reports took a generally similar form, usually beginning by tracing the historical development within the company of the department or function under study. Then followed an appraisal of Bigelow's standing at the time of analysis, and in turn a recommended plan of organization, an estimate of the personnel required, and a statement of the estimated benefits that would follow.

CHART **IV**

BIGELOW–SANFORD CARPET COMPANY

Senior Administrative Group, 1945

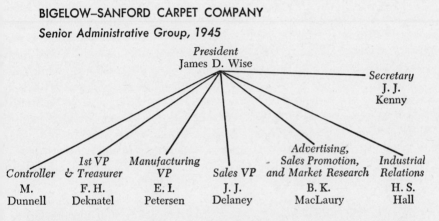

President
James D. Wise

Secretary
J. J.
Kenny

Controller	1st VP & Treasurer	Manufacturing VP	Sales VP	Advertising, Sales Promotion, and Market Research	Industrial Relations
M. Dunnell	F. H. Deknatel	E. I. Petersen	J. J. Delaney	B. K. MacLaury	H. S. Hall

The first study was an analysis of top management and its financial functions. In its broad outline the report dealt with the organization and responsibilities of the company's top echelon. As of October, 1945, when this first report was submitted, the senior executives occupied the positions shown in Chart IV. All of them were men who had worked under Sweetser in one capacity or another. All except MacLaury and Hall had been with the company for a number of years. Treasurer Deknatel had acted as executive vice-president after Knowland's departure—in addition to his duties as treasurer. Each of the other department heads had run his department more or less autonomously. All lines of authority ran directly to the president.[6]

This organization was larger than that in existence at the beginning of World War II. It reflected John Sweetser's recognition, not long before his death, that Bigelow required more management than it had had in order to cope with the problems both of the war and of the peace. Sweetser had died before he could add or develop all the functions that were desirable. Wise employed the management consultants to analyze and point up what else the company needed for sound administration.

Of the changes made as a result of the first Booz report, the most important was the addition of two top administrative posts: director of products and director of purchasing. The products director was to concentrate full attention on design and styling, with quality and price kept always in mind. These functions had formerly been handled by many people with inadequate communication among them. The Booz consultants argued that appearance and price were what influenced the consumer in the retail store and in their view these matters should be given the special attention of a man well up in the organization. For the post they advised the company to hire someone with experience in merchandising.

The move to establish a director of purchasing arose from a condition within the company which the Booz report termed "extremely unsatisfactory." This unsatisfactory condition was a result both of a lack of appreciation of the full significance of purchasing by management and of a substantial decentralization in its administration. Purchasing had for many years been recognized by the company as an important key to profits. In fact all the top executives had taken an interest in wool purchasing, though technically the responsibility rested with F. H. Deknatel, the treasurer, since wool purchases tied up such an important share of the company's liquid funds. But the purchase of requirements other than wool had not had such focused attention. A general purchasing agent reporting to the treasurer, placed orders through his department for materials other than wool, such as cotton and jute yarns, but did little more than process the orders for equipment and supplies, the purchase of which was often arranged for by other departments in the company. The Booz report regarded this arrangement as unsound and advocated that the purchasing job be assigned to a specialist trained in modern purchasing methods. Such a man would be given general cognizance of all matters relating to the purchasing function, from the initial decision to make or buy to the final observation of the material as it was being used; moreover, he would have specific responsibility for each of the actual steps in making a purchase, from the search for a supplier to the final commitment and follow-up. All materials and equipment, not just wool alone, were to come under the new setup; it was believed that real savings both in price and in smoothness of operation could be attained in jute, cotton, and a large number of other items. It was recognized that this centralization of the purchase authority would be a radical innovation and would disrupt many accepted methods of operation as established within the company, but the Booz consultants felt that the existing system of purchasing had led to what was in essence a speculative investment in inventories and they believed that only by close co-ordination could the company exercise a firm control over its costs.

At the end of 1945, after fifty-two years of service, Deknatel retired from the company, his departure already delayed a year at the special request of the board of directors. Into his place stepped Mark Dunnell, the controller, and to take Dunnell's post, the company hired R. F. Bender, who had previously been with the John B. Stetson Company, hat manufacturers. The newly created office of director of purchasing was assumed by F. Albert Hayes, a past president of the National Association of Purchasing Agents, and for many years associated with the textile and leather industries, as well as in the government service in both world wars. G. C. Denebrink, who was brought in from the Armstrong Cork

CHART **V**

BIGELOW–SANFORD CARPET COMPANY

Senior Administrative Group, 1946

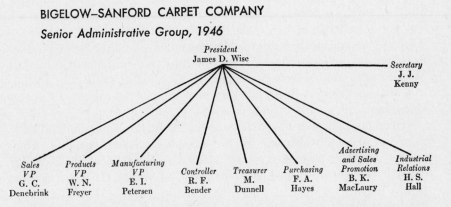

President
James D. Wise

Secretary
J. J.
Kenny

| *Sales*
VP
G. C.
Denebrink | *Products*
VP
W. N.
Freyer | *Manufacturing*
VP
E. I.
Petersen | *Controller*
R. F.
Bender | *Treasurer*
M.
Dunnell | *Purchasing*
F. A.
Hayes | *Advertising*
and Sales
Promotion
B. K.
MacLaury | *Industrial*
Relations
H. S.
Hall |

Company, soon replaced J. J. Delaney, who had disagreed with some of the changes made and had resigned. The new product division was headed by W. N. Freyer who was brought to the company from Montgomery Ward & Company. These men (see Chart V) were obviously chosen, not because of familiarity with the carpet business but because of their capacities as executives.

For a period of time it was thought best that each of the eight department heads continue to report directly to Wise. Both Wise and the analysts recognized, however, that this span of executive control was too wide for lasting effectiveness, but it was thought that the device would serve to acquaint the president quickly with the operating functions of his organization.[7]

By the second quarter of 1946 Bigelow had "bought," as Wise put it, "a modern management set-up" from Booz, Allen & Hamilton.[8] Quite literally this had been the case. In obtaining the kind of executive team he believed the company required, Wise had had to offer salaries that were closer to prevailing levels for similar management assignments than the company had been paying in the past. With a mandate from the directors to correct management deficiencies, Wise had been realist enough to recognize that he could not achieve his objective without meeting the market price. Furthermore he had almost completely re-manned his senior staff. All but Kenny were new to their jobs within a year and a half (although MacLaury and Hall were carry-overs from the last months of the Sweetser administration). More importantly, six of the eight were new to Bigelow—and indeed to the carpet industry itself. With a president who was himself a newcomer, and with an executive corps of widely varied backgrounds, a change of pace for the old Bigelow-Sanford Carpet Company was inevitable.

Within the top group over the next several years there was considerable experimentation with lines of authority and groupings of responsibility. Many arrangements were tried and abandoned. One which stuck was the bringing in of J. A. Donaldson in 1949 from Butler Brothers—a wholesale and department-store-management firm—and the placing of him in charge of the entire financial end of the business. Shortly thereafter Mark Dunnell retired as treasurer and R. F. Bender left the post of controller. Both vacancies were filled by men brought into the company by Donaldson.

To no one's surprise the changes instituted by the Wise administration were not wholly welcomed by the company's lower echelons. They were so rapid, so sweeping, to the personnel so unfathomable that they created widespread misgivings and even resentments. As one executive put it, Bigelow, under the pressure of circumstances, found itself having to push through, administratively, in two years what under more normal conditions would have taken at least ten.[9] One of the sources of concern was the mere presence of the Booz, Allen & Hamilton investigators. In the course of their work these men visited both of the plants and spent much time in them. They accompanied field salesmen on their rounds and spent many hours talking with personnel on all levels. Unfortunately for employee morale, a lack of understanding as to what the consultants were doing permeated the Bigelow organization with a resulting development of suspicion and uneasiness, the revival of old fears about "efficiency experts," and the apprehension that heads would speedily roll.

As the Booz group submitted report after report many changes were, in fact, made in the lower administrative levels. An illustration of the scope of these changes in the ranks of middle management is given in the following paragraph.[10]

In January, 1946, a Bigelow man was named sales analysis and control manager and in February another company man succeeded the technical director, who had resigned. In May an outsider was appointed as organization and procedures manager. In July the positions of cost engineering and procedures manager and quality control director were filled from within the ranks and a major change brought S. L. Duffett, the veteran textile engineering consultant, to Amsterdam to replace James M. Donnelly as plant manager when the latter retired after 38 years of service. (Duffett was to return to consulting in 1950, after which Amsterdam was managed by Spencer Garrity, a promotion from within.) Later in July of 1946 the new positions of internal auditor, sales training manager, and market research manager, were created and manned with men from outside the company; three other new jobs, assistant sales manager in charge of special accounts and quality control managers at Amsterdam and Thompsonville, were filled by Bigelow men. A wage and salary administrator, an assistant manpower manager, a purchasing assistant for wool, and a production control superintendent at Amsterdam were named toward the end of the year. Two of these latter appointees were Bigelow employees and the others were new.

A numerical expression of the significant alterations and additions among the middle management group shows that in 1948, which the company regarded as the year in which the organization reached its peak, there were 79 middle management positions, compared with 44 in 1945. The 35 new jobs fell roughly into the following categories: sales 6; manufacturing 12; personnel 5; advertising and sales promotion 6; controller 3; products 3. The additions had been filled in the proportions of about one-third from within the company and two-thirds from without.[11]

The recital of the various management changes serves to emphasize two significant points. First and more important, Bigelow was developing a modern line-and-staff administrative structure, a structure which, while it added overhead, was expected to increase management effectiveness so much that it would more than carry its own weight.

Secondly, the company was going outside its own ranks to fill many of the positions that accompanied the reorganization. Neither Wise, nor the management consultants, nor Bigelow executives generally were happy about this situation. They believed that no appointment of an outsider had been made until the ranks had been searched for someone who could do the job, but they felt that Bigelow could not continue to go outside the company to fill supervisory positions without a lasting ill effect on efficiency and morale. No alternative had been possible in the early years because of the preceding management's failure to develop adequate management skills among the employees, but it was desirable to begin quickly to bring men along for promotion to more responsible positions.

While only one senior executive resigned in direct protest against the changes, a number of departures on lower levels resulted from dissatisfaction with the way in which the changes were made. Some old-line personnel were dismissed because they failed to measure up to the new requirements, others left for better positions elsewhere, still others resigned to avoid dismissal, and a few were released as a result of economy programs. Some of the younger executives who had joined Bigelow after 1945 sought new jobs because reality had not lived up to their expectations. There was considerable muttering among those who felt overlooked or who resented the entire situation but did not dislike it enough to leave.[12] Generally there was a human reluctance to recognize that bad feeling or uncertainty was inevitable in so rapid a change as was being made.

Wise believed that men should be given sufficient training in general management techniques and sufficient experience of an executive nature so that they would be at least partially trained and qualified for promotion before vacancies occurred. Accordingly he established a number of programs to accomplish this end. These programs included sending two men to each thirteen-week session of the Harvard Business School's Advanced Management Program until economic conditions and internal needs in 1952 brought a suspension of this practice.

Of more general application within the company was an eleven-month management training course which was instituted in July, 1947. The first group of nine trainees, all war veterans, were recent college graduates, two with part-time Bigelow experience. Composition of later groups included both new university graduates and promising full-time company men. All received intensive instruction in Bigelow's operations. Their training began with a session in New York which brought them into contact with the executive officers from Wise down and ranged through actual machine operation to work in the sales field and warehouse.

Other management training plans included special conferences of men in various divisions, research engineers gathering for two-day seminars annually, and salesmen and sales engineers meeting to work out promotional plans. In October, 1946, a production management conference was held at a hotel in the Berkshire Hills, with foremen and plant supervisors participating, and Wise, Petersen, and other executives in attendance as speakers and observers. These Berkshire Conferences, aimed fundamentally at improving operations, became yearly events. Each conference had a basic theme such as "Leadership Wins" in 1946 and "Cost Reduction" in 1947. Special issues of a newspaper styled and sized like the *Bigelow Weaver*, called the *Berkshire Conference Reporter*, provided a record of the nature and results of the meetings.

Bigelow's management made several attempts to measure the impact of the administrative adjustments on those involved and on the company generally. In August, 1948, Opinion Research Corporation was employed to conduct a survey of attitudes among the Bigelow supervisory personnel.

The research group found that the members of the supervisory organization were a loyal and satisfied group. There were exceptions, and the survey pointed up several areas which might merit management's attention: [13]

1. On issue after issue, younger supervisors and those with less supervisory service were more critical than older or more experienced supervisors.
2. Substantial minorities, approximately four in ten, were not convinced that they were part of management.
3. Roughly two out of ten in the plants felt that their pay was unfair. Employees in the New York office were more critical than those in the plants.
4. Some feeling existed that the door to advancement was not as open as it should be. The main charge was that the company did not promote enough from the ranks—it brought in too many outsiders for the better jobs.
5. Union relationships at Thompsonville and in the New York office irritated some supervisors. In Thompsonville the company was considered to be soft in its union dealings; in New York, the union, by insistence on the seniority principle, interfered with promotions on merit.
6. Supervisors in the New York area were not being reached effectively by the company's communication media.

There is no measure against which to evaluate these findings; obviously they should to some degree be regarded as of common occurrence in business.

For these problem areas the research corporation suggested that management could review and correct situations where employee criticism seemed justified or it could explain its policies and operations, and the reasons therefor, where criticism was based on misinformation or lack of information. Some steps were taken by Bigelow's management along the lines suggested.

Where complaints seemed valid, correction was discreetly made. For example, if a man was not promoted when he might have had some expectation of it, he was given an explanation of the company's action or lack of action. Unfortunately for the success of such corrective measures, human nature frequently failed to be satisfied by the rational explanation. It was useless to tell a man who had worked ten or twenty years for Bigelow that his knowledge of the company and of the carpet business did not qualify him for a better job when it was filled by an outsider who could not tell an axminster from an Indian drugget. It was equally useless, in terms of employee understanding, to take a part of one official's supervisory responsibility from him and give it to another or to remove him from membership in a committee unless he could sincerely believe that his own interests were as well looked after as were those of the other men. When provided with such a monumental task of reorganization, Wise and his advisers had little alternative but to make changes in clean fashion and in so doing injure a few people's feelings.

From, or perhaps with, the many administrative changes that took place in the Bigelow organization evolved something that president Wise termed "consultative management." Consultative management aimed at replacing the old, semiautocratic system wherein policies and decisions were made by one or a few men and those charged with carrying them out were often completely in the dark as to the thinking that had led to the decisions or policies and, on occasion, knew that they could not be successfully executed. The new method substituted for this centralization of authority an organization made up of men who had specific responsibilities delegated to them, who worked closely with others in related areas, and who communicated with and were communicated with by other management people, vertically and horizontally. Consultative management attempted to utilize all the skills and abilities of the company's personnel, to replace individuals by a co-ordinated team.

Since the president was most anxious to insure the development of the management team, much of his personal effort at communication was directed toward that group. A mimeographed Management Newsletter became a frequent item over the president's signature; this was devoted to new information of general interest to executives. Contents of the issue of March 29, 1949, for instance, consisted of short articles on production change-overs, election of new directors, product testing, and general company philosophy. Executives kept other executives informed through a bulletin called Management Information. Quarterly financial statements were accompanied by Wise's detailed comments on the company's position, and the annual report of earnings and capital position received particular analysis and supplementation.

Consultative management almost automatically required increased use of committees. A company pronouncement on committees set forth that such groups were advisory except where specifically defined. Their purpose was to assist the responsible officers and employees to discharge their responsibilities, and this they did by helping the officers and employees to co-ordinate the various activities falling within the scope of the committee. They did not relieve any individual of responsibility nor were they intended to hinder prompt decision. A memorandum written at a later date summarized the philosophy of consultative management in these words: [14]

There are few decisions which do not impinge upon many others in the Company. Efficient operation requires that those most concerned should be consulted and informed about these decisions. . . . Those who exercise good judgment in this respect (consulting neither too much nor too little), are usually good managers. The existence of these committees should serve to assist all of us in this regard.

As he developed a new administrative structure for Bigelow, Wise also evolved a set of objectives for the company. Attainment of these objectives could be accomplished, in the opinion of the president, only through proper management practices. The objectives varied slightly from time to time as they appeared in speeches by Bigelow executives and in company publications but the basic thought remained the same. As they were set forth in 1948 the objectives were: [15]

1. To contribute to the public welfare by supplying constantly better carpets at lower cost, through continuously improving methods of production and distribution, at a fair profit to Bigelow.
2. To provide the greatest satisfaction possible to our employees within our competitive society through proper personnel practices.
3. To be a good citizen within our plant communities and nationally through proper public relations practices.
4. Through all the above to maintain and increase belief in our American society on the part of our customers, our stockholders, and the public.

MARKETING STRESSES AND STRAINS

There is no ideal time for a management reshuffle such as occurred at Bigelow beginning in 1945; but there could hardly have been a more difficult time than the years following the war. Even without any shifts in management personnel the organization would have been twisted and wrenched by the strain of reconversion to all-out production under the severest kinds of pressure from market demand. The accumulated desire of consumers to replace their old carpets or to build new houses and outfit them with floor coverings was insistent and created recurrent crises within the Bigelow organization as year after year the ability to sell outran the ability to produce.

There was, however, one aspect of the postwar boom for which the new administration could be grateful. Market demand was so great and sales came so easily that profits (after the removal of OPA price ceilings in 1946) were a continuing source of reassurance to the executive force and a screen behind which the new management was given time to work out its administrative Charley horses.

The sales division in particular felt considerable strain from the administrative changes. Many new positions were created at the suggestion of the consultants and the sales organization had to accustom itself to working under the new arrangement; the list for one year alone included the positions of sales analysis and control manager, sales personnel manager, and industrial sales manager.

The sales division was also placed in a state of chronic tension by the inability of the manufacturing division to meet its production schedules. Beginning in 1945 the company realized the heavy price that it was having to pay competitively for its extensive engagement in war work. Looms had to be reconverted. Workers had to be retrained. Warehouses had to be refilled. By the end of 1945 the company had been able to produce only 69 per cent of what it had set as its goal for the year.

Another complaint frequently voiced by the salesmen was against the somewhat lower quality of Bigelow products compared with prewar standards. Like many companies after the war, not simply in the carpet industry but throughout the country, inexperienced labor and imperfect raw materials made it difficult for Bigelow to regain the standards of performance it had enjoyed before the war. Gradually, through better training and tighter administration, the company improved its output, but as late as 1951 Wise was warning his management group: "We still have a major quality problem, which is all the more serious because Bigelow has always had the reputation of top quality in the carpet industry. . . . Quality is our first goal for 1952." [16]

The warehouses, which had been closed during the war, were put back into use as quickly as possible. Before the war these warehouses had had a record of good delivery service, but the desire to render service had so dominated the company's policy that serious maladjustments had resulted. To keep goods immediately on hand, large inventories had been maintained, subjecting the company to the risk of inventory losses in the event of price declines and style obsolescence. Furthermore, these large inventories had needlessly tied up valuable working capital. Wise came to feel that the interrelated aspects of the warehousing problem should be looked on as a whole and that delivery service, while it should not be ignored, should be considered in balance with other company policies. As a first step, taken somewhat before the full nature of the warehousing-inventory problem had clarified itself, the company established a regional system of distribution.

Development of a true regional plan took longer and went beyond the ideas of the management consultants. Bigelow executives wanted the regional managers to have something to manage and intended that each manager should control a major warehouse. In this respect company opinion was at variance with the expressed views of the consultants and in the end the company had its way over what it regarded as the more-or-less academic approach of the management specialists.

Under the company's system, responsibility was further decentralized so that the managers would have definite operating authority within their districts. Furthermore, it was expected that, as regional managers, men would receive training that would prepare them for other executive positions.

The regional warehouse and manager system was intended partly as a means of improving defects that had shown up in the way the company

Wool Sampling; cores taken from bales for testing in quality-control laboratory; note world-wide sources of supply

Chicago Carpet Market; buyers for retail stores gather twice yearly at Merchandise Mart; similar but smaller markets held in New York, San Francisco, Boston, and High Point, North Carolina administered its policy of direct sales to retailers. The direct sales policy had been adopted in the early thirties, following the merger with Sanford, in the hope that the company would be able by this means to put a finger on the pulse of the market. In operation, however, direct selling had been a disappointment. In the years when the company had sold through wholesalers, the warehouses had been stocked by independent businessmen who had made or lost money on their ability to judge market trends. In 1929–1930 it so happened that the judgment of these independent wholesalers had been almost universally wrong, and the Bigelow management had thought it could do better. But in place of the wholesalers who owned their own businesses the company had substituted its own warehouse managers who had regarded themselves merely as employees hired to do a routine job and whose errors in judgment had had no direct effect on their income. As a result the manufacturing end of the business had been even less informed about subtle changes in consumer preferences than under wholesaler distribution. With its new plan the company hoped that the regional managers would assume some of the responsibility of wholesalers, and it intended to judge their performance in accordance with the results achieved. Ideally each manager would keep in his warehouse enough stock to permit quick deliveries but not so much as to create dead inventory.

While the company was reorganizing its regional sales organization, it also was putting into effect the policy of selective distribution recommended during the war by Professor Copeland. Although Lees had been following a sales policy which in effect meant distribution through selected outlets, no large carpet company had ever made the switch from extensive to intensive marketing of its output. The result of Bigelow's action was an outbreak of adverse comment in the trade press not unlike that which had been heaped on the company when it had cut itself loose from wholesalers in the early thirties.

The number of retailers to whom the company sold was drastically cut in 1945 from about 10,000 to approximately 5,000. As a rule of thumb the company decided to sell to no outlet which handled less than $5,000 worth of its goods a year. Then after the initial, freehand reduction, the remaining retailers were carefully studied with a view to trimming the list still further.[17] By the end of 1948 the company had cut back its dealerships to about 3,500. Despite this sharp reduction in the number of stores where consumers could find Bigelow products on sale, the company anticipated that the new policy would be a success, for it was a more economical method of distributing rugs and carpets and created better relations with the principal consumer outlets.

A part of the new policy toward retailers was a careful effort to win loyalty to the Bigelow product and to repair whatever damage had occurred in retailer relations during the war. Consequently a large portion of the time and budget of the advertising and sales promotion division was devoted to "dealer services" of one kind or another. A series of institutes was inaugurated to show the retailer how he could improve his sales and increase his profits; among these were the Carpet Selling Institute, the Carpet Cleaning Institute, the Home Decorating Service, and the Store Planning Service. In a period when the company already had more sales than it could handle, the course of wisdom seemed to be to cultivate the retailer in the hope of retaining his goodwill when times grew hard.

MANUFACTURING IMPROVEMENT AND ITS DIFFICULTIES

Unlike the 1930's when the Bigelow directors had allocated funds sparingly to plant improvement, the postwar period saw a willingness to spend whatever was required to modernize facilities. The initial aim was to bring equipment up-to-date without adding in any substantial way to over-all capacity. The only important expansion program in the immediate postwar years was in the manufacture of the felt rug, Marvin, which in 1947 was redesigned as an all-wool product and renamed Glamorug.

Unfortunately the modernization program encountered delay after delay. The country's loom and spinning machinery manufacturers were so inundated by postwar orders that they were literally running as much as two years behind normal deliveries. As late as 1949 the lack of 12- and 15-foot velvet looms was causing the company to lose sales it might have made. Consequently the Bigelow company's own machine shop bore much of the brunt of the drive to re-equip the plants at Thompsonville and Amsterdam. The increasing popularity of lighter carpet colors led to a modernization of scouring and dyeing equipment; new carding machines were installed to yield higher output; a pilot plant was established to carry on experimental processing; and a modern electrical system was installed.

To an overworked manufacturing department these changes were not always greeted with enthusiasm. Every new installation meant "down time" for an old piece of equipment, and, in a period when there were worries enough in the mere process of getting out production, the problems of updating old equipment were far from welcome.

Another difficulty which beset the manufacturing department in the early postwar years was a serious shortage of skills among its employees. By the end of 1946 the prewar School of Craftsmanship had been revived to train new workers in the art of carpet-making and a series of courses had been inaugurated for the benefit of workers at all levels.

An effort to draw the supervisory force into the total executive operation was the formation of two "boards," as the company called them, in

November, 1948. These boards were designed to give the foremen and higher supervisors at Thompsonville and Amsterdam a definite voice in the formulation of practices and policies. Each board had an assembly, made up of 10 overseers and foremen, and a council, with a membership of five superintendents. Ideas or suggestions unanimously emanating from the assembly were passed on to the council; if that body also gave unanimous assent, they were presented to the plant manager. If he rejected the suggestion, he was required to give his reasons in writing to the assembly chairman and to the vice-president for manufacturing. Assembly and council met twice monthly; once a year they held a combined meeting with senior officials.[18]

One of the bedevilments of the postwar period was a shortage of yarn. The company had been buying some of its yarn from outside sources, but had found great difficulty in locating and then educating such sources to produce carpet yarn of satisfactory quality. The inability of the Bigelow mills to produce the needed yarn was due not so much to a shortage of equipment as it was to a difficulty in securing labor, especially to man the third shift. Good jobs were plentiful in the areas surrounding both northern plants, and this competition made it impossible to fully man the equipment which Bigelow had available.

In February, 1947, therefore, the company decided to purchase Bristol Mills, Inc., a small wool-yarn company in Bristol, Virginia. The Bristol company was bought for about $400,000 and incorporated under the laws of Virginia. Some equipment was added from the Northern mills and with a work force of about 75 the Virginia enterprise was operated as a department within the Bigelow organization.[19] For nearly three years, this subsidiary provided a much-needed addition and the difference in cost between the purchase of commission spun yarn and the Bristol yarn in a relatively short space of time more than repaid the initial investment and permitted Bigelow to cease the purchase of outside yarn.

A constant and, on the whole, successful effort was made to keep the mounting postwar costs from getting out of hand. The new dyeing equipment at Amsterdam, for instance, permitted a reduction of the dyehouse force from about 90 to 15 men. Experience showed that not all the jobs created in the new administrative organization were necessary and a saving was effected by abolishing some of them. Much of such saving was made in the manufacturing department; in 1949, for example, the manufacturing vice-president's staff was reduced from 85 to 59, with several of the new middle management positions among those eliminated. A simplified product line helped to reduce costs and maximize output by cutting the number of items produced from nine hundred (as of 1941) to approximately two hundred. Perhaps the best statistical indication of the success of cost-cutting efforts was the remarkable rise in man-hour productivity. Between 1946 and 1950, this index of efficiency increased by nearly 30 per cent.

By the end of 1949 the delivery of on-order machinery was proceeding at a satisfactory rate and the manufacturing department could feel that it was at last making real strides toward the solution of some of its most pressing production problems. By that time the company which, in 1945 had had a net investment in fixed assets of $6,567,000, had spent since the end of the war nearly $10,000,000 on improving and replacing its plant and equipment. (Some of this expenditure was charged as current operating cost, a fact which was later criticized by the Bureau of Internal Revenue, causing the company to revise its fixed assets upward as of 1949.)

Still aggravating the equipment problem was the continued shift in consumer tastes even during the period when machinery was on order and awaiting delivery. In the year 1939, for instance, total industry axminster production had been 31,400,000 yards; by 1949 the production was 47,000,000 yards, an increase of 15,600,000 yards or about 50 per cent. In wiltons a 1939 output of 12,800,000 yards had increased in 1949 by 8,400,-000 yards or 66 per cent. In velvet a 1939 output of 7,400,000 yards had increased in 1949 by 7,900,000 yards or over 100 per cent.

At first glance it might appear that a manufacturer would be glad to have a concentration of machinery in his axminster line where, even though the percentage increase had not been so great, the actual yardage increase had been almost the equivalent of the combined growth in the other two lines. But this was not the case. A manufacturer like Bigelow, with ample axminster capacity, could easily meet the 50 per cent increased demand for that weave. But with limited wilton capacity some of the 66 per cent increase in demand might very likely go to competitors. A rough indication of the extent by which Bigelow's productive facilities were still out of line with consumer demand is provided by the fact that its plants in 1948 turned out 24 per cent of the industry's total production of axminsters (the weave which was showing the slowest growth), whereas they produced only 10.9 per cent of the industry's total yardage of wilton. In velvet production the company was better situated, with 22 per cent of the total industry output.

One of the problems which the management consultants attacked but failed to solve was the long "lead time" involved in carpet manufacture. When a customer entered a retail store and ordered a rug or carpet which the store did not have in stock, the speed with which the buyer received delivery was quite unpredictable. If the item was "in stock" in one of the regional warehouses, delivery might be made within as short a time as a day. If, however, the item was not in stock (as was often the case with regard to popular items during the postwar period), then as much as three months might be required for the order to be forwarded to New

York, scheduled into production, produced, and finally shipped. Booz, Allen, & Hamilton suggested several methods by which this long lead time could be reduced, but after reviewing them the company rejected each and all—perhaps, as one man explained, because they were the proposals of men who, not being trained textile engineers, did not realize the incidental impracticabilities of what they recommended.

POSTWAR EMPLOYEE AND COMMUNITY RELATIONS

Among the many innovations of the James D. Wise administration was a completely new employee relations program. In a formal sense Bigelow had never before had any special program for its workers. A. D. Higgins, when he had been plant superintendent at Thompsonville in the first decades of the new century, had conducted his own personal employee relations activities, and his successors, notably Petersen, had given special consideration to employee problems as part of their work as chiefs of manufacturing. But a formal organization with a specialist in charge had not been instituted until 1944 when H. S. Hall had been hired as industrial relations manager a few months before Wise became president.

With the end of the war Hall and his new staff were faced with a problem of unexpected dimensions, a problem which they had to organize themselves hastily to meet, for the company was suddenly faced with the most severe labor shortage in its history. Wartime workers, especially women, who had looked on their jobs as temporary expedients, left in large numbers. Former employees who had been expected to return after release from military service, chose instead to enjoy extended vacations before taking up the routine of civilian life. And all the while the demand for carpeting was mounting.

An aggressive recruiting campaign was therefore begun in which the company stressed the idea that Bigelow was a good place to work. In the early autumn of 1945 an advertising program built around this theme was initiated in local newspapers and on radio stations in the plant communities. Through a new employee publication, *The Bigelow Weaver*, and in other ways, workers were told that each one who brought in a new employee would receive $5.00 if the recruit stayed at work for 30 days. A 90-day stay would increase the bonus to $10, and a grand prize of $100 was set aside for the person with the largest bonus when the campaign ended in the following February.[20]

New employees seemed likely to come largely from war industries and the armed forces. Each source was therefore approached. Bigelow sponsored tours and exhibits to arouse interest among other manufacturers and the public. Veterans who had worked for the company were placed in their old or better jobs; 97 of the 1,654 service employees had returned by October, 1945, and more than 516 were back at work by the following

March. To make use of other veterans and men without carpet-making experience, a training director was engaged to develop proficiency, and a retraining program offered instruction for out-of-touch company veterans and for newcomers, with special attention paid to disabled men from the services. The United States Employment Service was approached with a proposal that it assist in bringing in people from the other states and from Canada, and figures were quoted to show that Bigelow workers enjoyed the highest hourly and weekly earnings in the entire textile industry—an inducement that was somewhat counteracted by higher wages in some other industries.

In the company's postwar planning it estimated that it would require a work force of about 6,400 employees (in early 1941 the employees had numbered less than 6,000). This estimate quickly proved far short of what was actually the need. The labor shortage did not finally run its course until the middle of 1948, by which time the company was employing over 9,000 people.

To reduce the danger of strikes by its employees, as well as to help obtain new workers, Bigelow intensified its war-born program of increased wages, benefits, and improved working conditions. When contract negotiations with the labor union began in the late summer of 1945, the company's guiding principles, during the month or so that these negotiations covered, were to insure itself against strikes and to get conditions at the plants settled so that the recruiting program could go forward smoothly. The result was an October agreement, giving workers in each mill an increase of 10 cents per hour, six annual holidays with pay, a minimum hourly rate of 70 cents, and the right to vote on the question of union shops.[21] The following month, when a vote was held to determine the issue of the union shop, a majority of the workers in both mills registered their approval; thereafter all production workers were required to join the union within six weeks after employment.

From the company's experience with labor negotiations at the end of the war there evolved a bargaining pattern to be followed in the future. The annual contract was discussed between representatives of the Textile Workers Union of America, CIO, on the one hand and representatives of Bigelow, Smith, Karagheusian, and sometimes one or two additional companies on the other. Mohawk bargained separately, generally after the other companies had reached agreement, but its terms were usually similar.

The general policy of the Bigelow management with regard to labor unions was to do everything possible to keep production flowing and to do nothing that might be construed as an attempt to influence employee decisions about unionization. The production workers at Thompsonville and Amsterdam were members of the Textile Workers Union of America,

CIO, and the office workers in Thompsonville, after joining the United Office & Professional Workers of America, a CIO affiliate, in 1949 also joined the Textile Workers Union of America, CIO. New York office employees in 1946 selected the Office Employees International Union, AFL, to represent them in their dealings with management. The only other segments of the Bigelow organization to elect union representation were some warehouses, where staffs formed locals of the International Brotherhood of Teamsters, Chauffeurs, Warehousemen & Helpers, AFL, and some other AFL unions.

Except for occasional wildcat walkouts, the company went throughout the immediate postwar period without a strike or any serious labor disturbance. Negotiations continued to be conducted on a joint basis with only Mohawk, among the major companies, bargaining alone. The only really serious dispute occurred in 1949 when the unions turned from wages to pensions as their bargaining subject. In an industry as old as carpet manufacturing, the number of long-term employees in relation to the total work force made any pension plan an expensive concession and one which the carpet companies were willing to make only after careful consideration. At the end of 1949, for instance, the Bigelow company had nearly 1,000 workers who had been in its employ more than 25 years.

Before a pension arrangement was finally entered into by Bigelow it was submitted to the stockholders for approval. The final agreement called for noncontributory pensions of $100 monthly, including social security, at age 65 and after 30 years of service, proportionate amounts being payable for shorter periods of employment. If both company and union agreed, and if workers so desired, in some cases they were to be permitted to work until the age of 68 and in others until 72. The pension agreement was to run for five years from January 1, 1951.

While the future of mass pensions remained uncertain in so far as actuarial soundness and the ability of later generations to pay them was concerned, the move was significant. For Bigelow it marked a reversal of an earlier attitude on the part of the company's directorate. John Norman, it will be recalled, in 1925 had attempted to set up a pension system which would be clearly understood by all. His proposal had been rejected in favor of a plan which kept retirement allowances on an arbitrary basis, completely at the discretion of the board. Then in 1941 had come a plan which provided for employees with salaries in excess of $3,000 annually. This, in its turn, had given way to acknowledgment of the right of workers to be looked after when they were too old to work.

A concomitant of the employee relations program in the postwar years was a greater emphasis on community relations. To provide a better tone, the word "mill" was replaced by "plant" in all official company usage, thereby helping to eliminate such words of unpleasant connotations as

"mill hand" and "mill town." In due course, too, the title of "superintendent" was changed to "manager" for those in charge of the company's plants.
Beginning as early as 1943 the company followed a policy of selling its
tenements and other nonproduction property in Amsterdam and Thompsonville. The housing shortage in both towns made it possible to sell the
buildings for more than book value. Moreover, the company gained from
no longer being landlord to its employees; if a depression should occur,
it would not again be in the position of having to try to collect rents from
hard-pressed workers. Liquidation of the property also freed plant officials from responsibility for the supervision.

Contributions were made to charitable organizations in both Thompsonville and Amsterdam, a company trust being set up for their administration. Amsterdam received a park site in 1947 and a generous donation
toward a new town hospital a few years later. Both the Amsterdam and
the Thompsonville plant were opened to visitors in September, 1947,
in the first community-wide "Open Houses" ever held by the company, and
the Bigelow 125th Anniversary Celebration in 1950 made factory visits
gala occasions for the plant localities. In both towns the president discussed company policies and plans with community leaders, hopeful that
mutual understanding of problems would develop.[22] The Wise administration believed that the tremendous amounts of money being spent on plant
modernization made sound community relations particularly important.

FINANCIAL RESULTS

The postwar program had obviously been expensive, too expensive to
be financed in the old-fashioned way. Not since the turn of the century
had the Bigelow-Sanford company (or any of its predecessors) raised
long-term capital from any source outside its own treasury. It had borrowed from commercial banks and had obtained funds by the sale of
short-term paper for the purpose of financing peaks of inventories or receivables, but it had relied on reinvested earnings for its fixed capital
investments. Even the purchase of Stephen Sanford & Sons had been accomplished without resort to the sale of additional securities.

The Sanford purchase had, however, drained the company of $5,000,-
000 which might otherwise have remained in the treasury as liquid capital. This drain had not been important during the thirties when the company was not using its full resources anyway, or in the forties when its
business with the government placed limited demands on its working
capital. At the end of the war, however, the company foresaw that high-
level operations, refilled warehouses, and deferred repairs and modernization would put heavy strain on the company's liquid position. In the 17
years from 1929 to the end of 1946, Bigelow had been able to replace none
of its depleted liquid assets; in those years the company had earned $11,-

900,000 after taxes and had paid out in preferred and common dividends $12,073,000.[23] It was decided, therefore, to borrow enough money to replace the amount spent a decade and a half earlier in acquiring the Sanford property.

In July, 1946, a long-term loan of $5,000,000, carrying interest at 2.8 per cent and scheduled to mature in 1966, was obtained. Lenders were the Prudential Insurance Company of America, The First National Bank of the City of New York, and the Bankers Trust Company. In February, 1947, the number of directors was increased from nine to ten and Carrol M. Shanks, president of Prudential, was elected.

This $5,000,000 loan proved to be less than enough to meet the plant modernization needs as seen by the Wise administration. Fortunately, however, the company made substantial profits during those years—$15,-048,000 after taxes but before provisions for depreciation—and paid out in common and preferred dividends only $5,653,000. All these incoming funds were required to finance working capital needs as business expanded and prices rose with the postwar inflation. In the four postwar years the investment in inventories and accounts receivable rose by $12,-783,000. Therefore like many other prosperous and financially sound companies in the late 1940's, Bigelow's expansion was outrunning its capacity to finance itself out of earnings and it was forced to negotiate an additional $2,000,000 of short-term loans from the banks.

As it became evident that Bigelow might sometime in the future wish to tap the capital markets for additional long-term capital, Wise considered the desirability of bringing the company's securities to the attention of the investing public. Bigelow-Sanford stock was not actively traded on the New York or Boston exchanges and Wise knew that he could not obtain the interest he wanted unless more shares were available to the public. Accordingly, the executive committee recommended that the existing common shares be split two for one. The stockholders approved such a split in March, 1948, and Bigelow-Sanford's authorized common stock was thereby increased from 313,609 to 627,218 shares.

During the postwar years the Bigelow directorate had changed along with the rest of the company. In 1947 Carrol Shanks, as has been noted, became a director; in 1949 Thomas S. Nichols, chairman of the board and president of Mathieson Chemical Company, and Robert G. Page, president of Phelps Dodge Corporation, were elected; in 1951 Hardwick Stires, a partner in the investment firm of Scudder, Stevens & Clark, joined the board. Stires had succeeded Roger Amory, who had resigned because of age and health. Another director, Charles Francis Adams, in 1951 announced his desire to leave the board for the same reasons as Amory. The four new directors brought a new breadth of experience and association to the Bigelow directorate, in line with the president's broader philosophy.

A REVIEW OF CARPET TRENDS

By 1949 it seemed clear that the postwar boom had run its course. The company's sales, which had risen from $39,733,000 in 1946 to $83,591,000 in 1948, fell in 1949 to $67,377,000, and for the first time since reconversion some looms stood idle for lack of orders. In April of 1949 Alexander Smith announced a price cut, and within short order the rest of the industry felt obliged to follow. It was the first serious drop in carpet prices since the late thirties.

With the return to a buyers' market certain facts emerged for Bigelow's consideration. The company had succeeded in raising its share of the industry's business from a wartime low of 12.4 per cent to the prewar level of about 19 per cent, but it had still not recaptured the 21.3 per cent of the business that it had held in the middle thirties and that it had set as its postwar sales goal (see Appendix 13).

For the industry as a whole the end of the boom also brought a sobering realization. Although total industry sales at the peak of the boom had risen to $430,000,000, a figure 2¼ times the previous peak of $192,000,000 reached in 1923, the physical output of carpets had not greatly increased. In 1923 the combined output of 70-odd carpet factories had been 83,186,-000 square yards of woven floor coverings; in 1948 approximately 95 companies had turned out 89,640,000 square yards. These record figures had been nearly matched as far back as 1904 when the industry had produced 82,671,000 square yards of carpeting. Although dollar volume had increased enormously, physical capacity had remained fairly constant for approximately a half century.

It is easy to understand why the carpet companies had been slow to conclude that they were no longer in a growing industry. The twenties had been highly profitable and sales had held at a high level; no one had questioned the industry's basic soundness. The thirties had been hard, of course, but the thirties had been hard for everyone. Then came the forties and war, during which an artificial situation had prevailed. With the war over, there occurred a demand for carpets which taxed the industry's capacity. Expansion had been impracticable and the equipment ceiling had kept production from outdistancing previous records. As year after year went by, there developed among carpet men an almost unconscious sentiment that soon these abnormal conditions must end. Meanwhile, however, ingenious minds had been at work to find substitutes for the carpet-makers' hard-to-get and expensive floor coverings. Among these were asphalt tile, cork flooring, flagstone, and cotton tufted rugs. As a result new buying preferences had been forming and were likely to prove difficult to remove.

Concurrently the competition which had begun in the early twenties had intensified: not the competition of other carpet companies—the relative standing of the leading firms in 1949 had not altered appreciably from the relative standing before the war—but the competition of other goods and services. Whereas in the twenties the consumer had had to choose between carpets and such items as radios, automobiles, or refrigerators, by the late 1940's the choice had become many times more difficult to make, even though the consumer had more dollars to spend.

In view of the country's rapidly expanding population, the carpet industry's failure to increase its physical output had meant a steadily declining per family purchase of woven floor coverings. In 1900 carpet consumption had been more than four square yards per family per year; by 1948 it was less than half that amount. In contrast, the per family consumption of hard-surface floor covering had rapidly increased, with a growth trend that had become especially marked in the postwar years (see Appendix 15).[24]

Makers of soft- and hard-surface floor coverings were inclined to insist that they were not in competition with each other, but some evidence showed to the contrary. Linoleum, asphalt tile, and felt-base hard surface had moved out of the kitchen, first into bathrooms, then into halls, and even into other rooms. So-called ranch houses and other small, functional houses which were made popular by changing economic and social conditions in the postwar period seemed suited to less formal floors; hard-surface products were desirable for use over concrete slab, basementless construction, and with some kinds of radiant heating. More and more it became fashionable to use linoleum or asphalt tile in living rooms, with perhaps a scatter rug or a small oriental or two to point up decorative features.

It might be safe to generalize that most consumers preferred soft-surface to hard-surface floor coverings for feel, appearance, warmth, and pride of ownership. The carpet companies believed also that their product had a natural advantage in that it brought quiet and restfulness to a society that needed in the home a retreat from the strident noises of the world outside.

However, there was evidence that the advantages of carpeting were not strong enough to overcome a rising price barrier. Consumers were also inevitably if unconsciously affected by the difference in production times. Asphalt or rubber tile could be made from raw materials in 27 minutes while wool or rayon carpets took several weeks. The hard-surface dealer could stock a greater variety of product with less money tied up in inventory and he could generally be more certain of filling special orders in a definite time since the lead time on hard-surface coverings was so much less than on soft.

Another form of nonwoven floor coverings which had forced itself on the major carpet companies' attention in the postwar years was tufted cotton. As Appendix 15 shows, postwar sales of tufted cotton products in the form of bathmats, scatter rugs, and carpets had shown a rise over 1939 even more spectacular than that for hard-surface goods. In 1939 about 1,200,000 square yards of tufted cotton floor coverings had been sold with a dollar value of $1,838,000; in 1948 the tufted cotton yardage amounted to about 18,400,000 square yards.

What were the reasons for the carpet industry's failure to exhibit growth in the years from 1900? J. D. Wise was fond of comparing carpet manufacturing with that of automobiles. He once said that in 1949 a 9 by 12 Beauvais axminster sold at about 74 per cent above the 1920–1929 average price; a Chevrolet motor car also sold at about 74 per cent above the 1920–1929 average price, but the 1949 automobile was vastly improved over the earlier model while the carpet was basically the same.[25]

One of the handicaps under which the carpet industry had labored was a lack of incentive on the part of its machinery suppliers to provide it with ever more efficient machines. In 1949, according to Bigelow's president, the carpet industry accounted for only about 4 per cent of the total market for textile machinery in this country. Since the demand for carpet equipment was limited, the machinery makers felt reluctant to risk their capital on heavy developmental costs. Consequently comparatively little money had found its way into research on carpet-making equipment.

As a further handicap, carpetings had come to be, in part at least, style items. Being subject to the vagaries of popular taste one could hardly expect them to retain their position unchallenged by such new flooring styles as cotton tufted rugs. The very element which had given the industry a rising level of dollar volume in the face of an unexpanded capacity—the constant upgrading of consumer tastes from ingrains to axminsters to wiltons—had tended to raise carpetings out of the class of a standard home furnishing and into the class of a luxury style good.

By the close of the forties, therefore, the carpet companies faced one or another of three difficult and unpleasant alternatives. If they were to continue to grow either they would have to fight each other for a market which seemed unlikely to expand appreciably in the foreseeable future, or they would have to grow by diversifying into new lines where they could use their skills, their market structures, or their equipment. The third alternative was to content themselves with their existing share of the market, emphasizing low costs and efficient operation. Of the three, only the second, diversification of product, held the promise of a healthy future.

CHAPTER 16

PROGRESS UNDER ADVERSITY: 1950–1953

Early in 1950 one might have predicted that Bigelow, having survived the disruption caused by its management reorganization, was ready and equipped to meet the problems of a normal peacetime economy. There was still some friction within the organization, but no more than one might expect to find in any organization headed by a group of able and ambitious men who found it difficult to suppress their personalities and ambitions in the anonymity of a fully co-ordinated team. Time seemed all that was required to bring the administrative machine into smoothly operating efficiency.

But time was not to be granted. Once again the company fell victim to the strains of superabundant prosperity. The outbreak of war in Korea in June of 1950 led the carpet dealers of the nation to undertake a frantic rebuilding of their inventories. Previous experience had taught them that wars brought a reduction of carpet supplies and at the same time a heightened demand. For once the dealers were not to be caught. This time they ordered well in excess of current sales. Toward the end of 1950 Bigelow was receiving each day so many orders for carpets that the volume of sales, had deliveries been possible, would have been at the annual rate of about $200,000,000. Unable to fill more than a portion of these orders, the company placed its dealers on a rationing system similar to that which had prevailed during World War II.

Meanwhile the price of carpet wool, stimulated by a double impulse, was rising rapidly higher. Already high at the time of the Korean outbreak, wool prices climbed steeply with the threat of a short supply in a war-torn world and the promise of heavy consumer demands for carpets. Anticipating a busy season the company placed orders for large quantities of wool from New Zealand.

With the November reversal in the Korean war, following the entrance of the Chinese into the conflict, consumer purchases of carpets sky-rocketed. For a time the dealers seemed justified in their policy of carry-ing heavy carpet stocks, and volume-conscious executives at Bigelow's office strove to maintain or if possible advance the company's sales posi-tion in relation to the industry as a whole. Recognizing the seriousness of the wool situation, F. Albert Hayes, vice-president for purchasing, pre-pared for a trip around the world in continuance of the policy, established in 1946, of visiting foreign sources of supply. Because of the long lead time involved in the manufacture of carpet and the distant locations of prime sources of carpet wool, it was necessary to insure a large and de-pendable supply of wool.

By the end of 1950 the inflated demand had caused the company to bill $106,500,000 of gross sales before cash and volume discounts, making Bigelow the first American carpet company to obtain more than $100,000,-000 in gross sales of woven floor coverings made by itself. The year 1950 also witnessed a record net profit of $12,054,000 before taxes and $5,854,-000 after. It was fitting that these new records should have occurred in Bigelow's 125th year; the company in its advertisements took sentimental pride in its outstanding achievements and long life, longest of all American carpet manufacturers.

The year 1951 began in equally vigorous fashion with heavy advance buying at January markets and with a continuance of the courtship lav-ished by the company on its retailers. The wool situation, however, created a deep concern. With the mills operating at capacity, the company's wool needs were very substantial. While provision had been made to meet these needs by commitments made during the last quarter of 1950, the large purchases of wool in New Zealand (at prices which, by comparison with the prices of January, 1951, seemed very favorable) were being held from shipment by a waterfront strike in New Zealand which dragged on for months and showed no signs of ending. The company was left with no alternative but to obtain its supplies in the current market at prices far above those prevalent in the last quarter of 1950 (see Chart VI). By February 15, 1951, a typical blend of wool, for instance, was commanding $2.35 per pound whereas in January the price had been $1.65 and six months earlier less than a dollar. For a time the company bought at these disastrously high figures in an effort to keep the mills in steady operation. But, as Wise explained the situation, Bigelow's finished carpet prices were based on wool costs of approximately $1.40 per pound, and the company could obviously not continue to pay $2.00 per pound and more. Both Alex-ander Smith and Bigelow announced that they were suspending all pur-chase of raw wool for an indefinite period.

A somewhat similar situation existed for carpet rayon. Its availability both in quality and quantity from domestic producers was decidedly limited. The company had therefore made contracts with foreign rayon producers, but these sources claimed that conditions over which they had no control made it impossible for them to make delivery at the contracted prices and so new arrangements at substantial premiums became necessary.

Sales for the first three months of 1951 were 33 per cent higher than for the same period in 1950 dollarwise, although yardage was down about 5 per cent. Profits were also a trifle lower, the result of increased emer-

CHART **VI**

INDEX OF CARPET, WOOL, AND RAYON PRICES, 1950 TO 1953

INDEX BASE: JANUARY, 1953

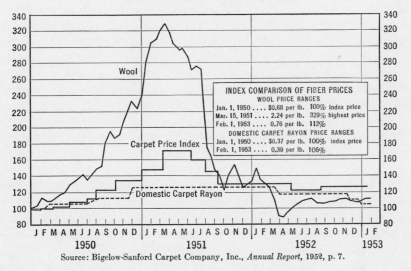

INDEX COMPARISON OF FIBER PRICES
WOOL PRICE RANGES
Jan. 1, 1950 .... $0.68 per lb.   100% index price
Mar. 15, 1951 .... 2.24 per lb.   329% highest price
Feb. 1, 1953 .... 0.76 per lb.   112%
DOMESTIC CARPET RAYON PRICE RANGES
Jan. 1, 1950 .... $0.37 per lb.   100% index price
Feb. 1, 1953 .... 0.39 per lb.   105%

Source: Bigelow-Sanford Carpet Company, Inc., *Annual Report*, 1952, p. 7.

gency taxes and continued advances in raw materials costs. Protesting against government refusal to permit compensatory price boosts, Smith withdrew its carpets from sale in February. In March, however, the Office of Price Stabilization permitted makers to put their prices up 15 per cent, and the manufacturers looked forward to continued high sales volumes.

But the 15 per cent price increase coupled with a consumer's strike which spread across the retail stores of America in the spring of 1951, brought an abrupt end to the industry's extravagant hopes. The enigmatic consumer flew in the face of all the portents and, with house and garage as full as was apparently desired, began to save money at an astonishing rate. Sales of consumer durables declined accordingly, and the carpet industry was surprised to find that its total sales for the second quarter of

1951 were 45 per cent below those for the first. Bigelow was no exception, and its second quarter showing was $15,277,000 compared with $22,323,-000 in the same period of the previous year. Its profits were also down. Retailers were so stocked with inventory that their orders from Bigelow fell below the rate at which sales were being made to consumers. As if to add irony, the wool which had been immobilized by the waterfront strike in New Zealand began to arrive—by that time high-priced and unwanted.

Production cutbacks were made in April, not only in Bigelow's plants but in those of some of its competitors, and layoffs inevitably followed. A four-day week was general by the end of May, and in June price reductions averaging 10 per cent on wool carpets were announced. These were followed by an average reduction of 8½ per cent on July 30 and by more on August 1. On August 29 some of the August 1 prices were revised upward to a level approximately 18½ per cent below prices prevailing earlier in the year, but hardly had this been done when a 10 per cent general reduction on the entire woven carpet price line was made known. The industry price structure was in a state of wavering disequilibrium. The advance buying which carpet dealers had engaged in during 1950 and early 1951 was to create an overinventoried condition throughout the country's carpet retail structure, and two years of painful price-cutting were to be required to work the inventory off.

Meanwhile the price of wool, which had begun to decline in March of 1951, had fallen precipitously in July, carrying with it a heavy inventory loss for those companies which, like Bigelow, had stocked themselves with high-priced raw materials. One result of the situation, which showed no improvement for the rest of the year, was the imposition of an austerity program throughout Bigelow. Orders were issued that employment was to be held to a minimum; advertising and sales promotion allowances were severely cut, and economy became the rule. In spite of everything, 1951's third quarter ended with a loss, although earnings from the previous six months permitted Bigelow to show a profit for the nine-month period.

The company was not so fortunate for the year as a whole. When its annual statement for 1951 was released, it recorded a loss of $2,303,000. This was another record of sorts, the largest loss the company had experienced in its 126 years. Of the figure, $1,592,000 was a year-end special provision for estimated losses on certain raw materials otherwise carried at values in excess of market under the LIFO system. (Wool used during the last three quarters of 1951 largely represented purchases that had been made during the months of advancing wool prices.) Exclusive of this special item, loss for the year was $711,000.

The early months of 1952 were a continuation of the unhappy condition in which the carpet industry had found itself at the close of 1951. As the months wore on, the raw materials situation improved somewhat, but conditions at the Amsterdam and Thompsonville plants concurrently grew worse. The Korean War was causing living costs to mount and was bringing economic stress to the many workers who had been put on a reduced work schedule. Frequent unauthorized work stoppages were occurring in both plants and discipline of union members for flagrant violations of well-understood rules was resulting in occasional slowdowns.

Moreover, friction had developed within the union itself. The Textile Workers Union of America, CIO—the union which represented the workers at both Amsterdam and Thompsonville—had fallen into internecine feuding due to the rivalry of two leaders, Emil Rieve and George Baldanzi. The feud had reached a boiling point after a coalition formed by Baldanzi had failed to win the leadership of the international union in April of that year. At Amsterdam a preponderance of workers favored Rieve, but at Thompsonville the workers and their union leaders sided with Baldanzi who led them out of the CIO and into the AFL.

Meanwhile an attempt was being made to negotiate a new carpet industry contract with the Textile Workers Union, since the existing contract was due to expire June 1. The union demanded a sharp increase in wages and the companies replied that the profitless state of the carpet industry prevented more than a very moderate advance. With the contending parties still far from agreement, the plants of Alexander Smith, A. & M. Karagheusian, Mohawk, and the Amsterdam plant of Bigelow went out on strike June 2. The strike was to last 11 weeks and was to be settled without major concessions on the part of the companies.

Throughout the strike, the Thompsonville labor force remained at work. This group, following the defection of George Baldanzi, had switched its allegiance to AFL and had instituted proceedings before the National Labor Relations Board in an effort to win certification away from Rieve's CIO as the legal bargaining representative for the Thompsonville plant. Certification proceedings dragged through the summer and still had not been concluded when the CIO ended its strike and signed a contract.

Bigelow was thereupon faced with a Hobson's choice. Either it could refuse to sign an agreement recognizing the Baldanzi group at Thompsonville, in which case the Thompsonville workers threatened to go out on strike; or it could recognize the Baldanzi followers (without waiting for the NLRB decision) in which case it would be accused of having taken the matter into its own hands and would run the chance of an almost certain renewal of the strike at Amsterdam where the Rieve followers believed their union to be the one with which the Thompsonville agreement should be signed.

The inevitable happened. Bigelow took a strictly neutral position and awaited the NLRB's pronouncement. The Thompsonville workers struck September 24 and remained out until October 27. Meanwhile, the NLRB had ruled that the two plants should be represented by a single union. A joint election therefore followed and, between the two mills, enough workers voted to remain with the CIO to make possible the defeat of the Baldanzi followers.

The strike had occurred at a time when the carpet industry as a whole was beginning to feel the need for a firmer stand against labor demands. In addition it had taken place at a period when the manufacturers were happy enough not to be manufacturing.

For Bigelow, however, the strike had darkened an already gloomy earnings picture. The 11-week period, when Thompsonville had been one of the industry's few big plants in operation, had been made less productive than might otherwise have been the case by reason of summer vacations, by the ordinary summer decline in carpet demand, and especially by the acute nature of the labor unrest. When, at last, the Thompsonville plant did shut down, the company suffered far more than it had gained from the previous period of operation. The seasonal pickup in carpet production, especially for the kind of carpets produced at Thompsonville, came just at the time when the Connecticut plant was on strike.

The two strikes contributed to a combined loss of $2,780,000 for the second and third quarters of 1952. Fortunately, however, the fourth quarter showed a substantial profit and confined the over-all loss for the year to $1,250,000. About the only consolation that could be taken from the deficits of 1951 and 1952 was that together they totaled less than the lush profits accumulated from the high sales of 1950.

In nearly all respects other than financial, 1952 was a favorable year. Physical volume, despite the strike, remained at approximately the same level as in 1951; consequently the entire decline of roughly 13 per cent in dollar sales volume between 1951 and 1952 could be traced to the demoralized price situation. By late in the year, however, the industry had worked off most of its excess inventory and prices grew more firm. By 1953 the company had regained its equilibrium and was again operating on a profitable basis.

A COMPARISON WITH COMPETITORS

Bigelow was not alone in its post-Korean travails. All companies in the industry were hard hit. But from company to company there was considerable variation in the degree to which the impact was felt.

Fortunately for an analysis of industry trends, more information is available for the years beginning 1946. That was the year, it will be recalled, when Bigelow felt the need for $5,000,000 additional capital. In the same year two of the other major companies, Alexander Smith and James Lees—companies which from their founding had been closely held family corporations—sought public financing and in so doing began to issue detailed financial statements. Only Karagheusian among the major American carpet producers continued to guard its financial data.

Judging from the statements put out by Bigelow's competitors, the performance of the carpet industry in the boom years, 1946–1948, and even into 1949 can best be summarized as consistent. The four top companies (not including Karagheusian) tended to hold their relative positions within the industry, and with respect to sales and profits all tended to move up and down together. Bigelow and Alexander Smith continued to spar for first place, leadership being a matter of definition, although Bigelow regarded itself as clearly the larger producer in the field of soft-surface floor coverings. Mohawk and Lees followed not far behind (see Appendix 11).

This pattern of consistency was to be destroyed, however, by the events which followed the Korean buying spree. The performance which filled the industry with surprise and admiration was that turned in by James Lees of Bridgeport, Pennsylvania. This company with its new plant, built in 1938 in Glasgow, Virginia—a plant which Bigelow's manufacturing head, E. I. Petersen, described as a money-maker after a visit in 1947 [1] —had demonstrated its ability to produce high profits even with a moderate level of sales. Its southern plant provided many advantages in materials handling, low-cost labor supply, accessibility to some raw materials, and to markets, although its production equipment, much of which had been moved south from Bridgeport, did not seem superior to Bigelow's.

Lees' move to Virginia had been a bold step; it had been taken in a year when many manufacturers were retrenching. Lees had not been unique among carpet companies in realizing the value of a move to the South and of a new mill; its uniqueness had come from taking action. Bigelow, for instance, had been handicapped not only by the reluctance of its directors to make heavy financial commitments in depression years but by heavy community commitments. Lees, a much smaller company than Bigelow in 1938, had been able to move part of its operations from one town to another without the effect on the forsaken town that a move by Bigelow from Thompsonville or Amsterdam would have had.

In the years 1950–1952, Lees spurted forward in relation to the rest of the industry. Like the others it suffered a decline in sales and profits, but even so its decline was more moderate than its competitors'. In the years 1950–1952 Lees led the field in terms of profits as a percentage of sales, and it showed signs of challenging Smith and Bigelow for their positions in regard to sales volume. The remarkable climb of the Lees organization from its position as a second-string producer in the late thirties to the most profitable company in the business in the early fifties was the subject of recurring comment throughout the carpet industry. The Lees management, still a closely knit unit despite the increasingly public nature of the company's ownership, was respected as a group of men who knew their business and tended strictly to it.

At Mohawk the post-Korean drop in sales was greater than at Lees and the decline in income was considerably sharper. But the Amsterdam company managed to break a little better than even in both 1951 and 1952, and its investment in a carpet mill in Mexico (to take advantage of the Mexican government's ban on rug and carpet importation) was regarded in the industry as moderately successful. The Mohawk managers at Amsterdam, still men of the same name as the founders, were considered to run a good, tight, sound business.

The company which suffered most during the years 1950–1952 was Alexander Smith. It had been the nation's leading carpet producer from late in the nineteenth century till the Bigelow-Sanford merger in 1929. It had gained its position on the basis of its skills and patent rights in the production of axminster fabrics. It had achieved, however, a certain diversity through its investment in the Sloane-Blabon Corporation, a producer of hard-surface floor coverings and through an agreement by which it distributed the wilton products of a moderate-sized carpet producer in Carlisle, Pennsylvania, C. H. Masland & Sons, another very closely held family concern.

Beginning in 1951 the Alexander Smith organization underwent a management shake-up that paralleled in many respects that which had occurred at Bigelow beginning in 1945. Because of the rather remarkable similarity between the Smith and Bigelow situations, a fairly detailed description of what took place at Smith seems appropriate.

The second oldest American carpet manufacturer like its older rival had failed to provide for management succession. Thus, for the second time a major carpet company had encountered trouble as it changed from an organization administered by heirs of the founders—a type of organization that had been common in the nineteenth century and that was still prevalent throughout the carpet industry—to one managed by professional executives who strove to provide their own management succession without regard to family ties or stock ownership.

To effect its management reorganization, Alexander Smith hired, as Bigelow had done five years earlier, the consulting firm of Booz, Allen & Hamilton. In April, 1951, a major corporate realignment consolidated the several operations of Alexander Smith & Sons Carpet Company and resulted in a change of name to Alexander Smith, Incorporated, as well as in a change of subsidiaries to operating divisions. New blood was injected into the top management group as a number of important personnel adjustments were made on the advice or suggestion of the consultants. On May 1 more reshuffling took place with the promotion of three men to new vice-presidential posts.

In both 1951 and 1952 the Smith company suffered losses. As at Bigelow reduced sales brought about layoffs and these, together with rising labor costs, led to unrest at Yonkers. William F. C. Ewing, president of Smith, met with union members of the Yonkers plant in an unusual move to ask them to help the company improve its competitive position. He denied that the company intended to leave Yonkers, as the rumors had it, although he admitted that the plant there was old and not completely up-to-date.[2]

Despite Ewing's protestations, rumors continued to fly. In March, 1952, Smith's president was forced to deny that mass firings had taken place on managerial levels, although, since the previous October, four vice-presidents, one executive vice-president, and some supervisors and rank-and-file workers had left. These departures, according to Ewing, were part of the normal adjustment to the company's considerable reorganization.[3]

To provide lower-cost facilities the Smith management entered into an agreement with the city of Greenville, Mississippi, whereunder the city built a plant, at a cost of more than $4,000,000, to be leased by Smith. The company also began a program to modernize its old Yonkers plant and eliminate superfluous land and buildings there.

Smith's difficulties received more public attention than had those of Bigelow, perhaps because its major administrative alterations happened to coincide with reduced manufacturing operations and consequent labor force reductions, and also because the location of the Yonkers plant in close proximity to New York meant that news found its way to the larger city more easily. Newspaper reports of Smith's troubles did not help the morale of its employees and neither did the company's unfortunate operating results in 1952. Smith's loss was $3,556,000, more than twice that of Bigelow.[4]

In April, 1953, Smith sold the Sloane-Blabon division to Congoleum-Nairn, Incorporated, hard-surface manufacturers, for about $10,000,000. Smith announced that it had done so to obtain funds for expansion and that it had decided that linoleum and carpet-making were incompatible. Alexander Smith had lost $6,600,000 on Sloane-Blabon since 1948, the last year the operation had shown a profit. The sale figure of $10,000,000 was well below the recorded value of $23,000,000, but the Smith management felt that it was better to take the immediate book loss in order to obtain cash to finance its long-range modernization program.

At about the same time Smith and Masland abrogated their sales agreement and went their separate ways. Masland hired G. C. Denebrink, who had recently left Bigelow where he had been head of the sales department, and put him in charge of developing a sales organization. (Because of the distribution agreement with Alexander Smith, Masland had not previously needed a marketing staff.) Smith thereupon set about meeting the serious situation presented by its lack of product balance and its heavy concentration on axminster weaves.

BIGELOW'S RECONSTITUTED MANAGEMENT

The ordeal through which the Bigelow management was forced to live in 1951–1952 was considerably less severe than Smith's. The earnings statements gave the appearance of a grave situation, but in many respects the company was healthier than in the period of postwar boom. In the earlier years, 1946–1949, the Bigelow organization had, under great strain, turned itself upside down in its efforts to remedy its management defects; but all the while its profitable operations had presented to the public a picture of serenity and prosperous success. In 1951–1952, on the other hand, the external evidence of profitless operations suggested weakness while actually the organization within was rapidly being pounded by adversity into a co-ordinated team bending its combined efforts to solve the company's long-range difficulties.

This new period of stress brought additional changes in executive personnel, though not so numerous as before. Some men who had initially joined the organization because of the liberal bonuses offered at Bigelow found themselves, during the years when no profits were earned, without bonus income and decided therefore to leave for greener pastures. Those who had joined the company to further their personal ambitions found themselves jousting with equally able men and decided to take their tilting matches elsewhere. Those who remained buckled down to the task of pulling the company out of the red.

In January, 1951, the top echelon of the company's organization was rearranged in line with the plan laid down by Wise and the management consultants in the first year of Wise's administration. To reduce the number reporting directly to the president, the office of executive vice-president was created and W. N. Freyer was named to the post. Freyer had already been serving for a year as special assistant to the president, his job of managing the products division having been filled by R. B. Freeman, a man who, like Donaldson, had worked for a time with Butler Brothers. The principal line functions in the company thereafter reported to Freyer, leaving certain of the staff functions to report directly to the president (see Chart VII).

One of these staff functions, public relations, had been established as a separate department only as recently as November of 1950. The man hired to handle the department was John Slaughter, formerly a partner of the public relations firm of Earl Newsom & Company. Slaughter was to remain only four months, however. Then the public relations post was taken by Peter Wright, one of the young men early added to the Wise team and therefore a person of experience within the organization. During

1951 H. S. Hall was lent to the federal government's Wage Stabilization Board and did not return to Bigelow. His place was filled in the spring of 1952 by Fletcher Waller, who had been with B. F. Goodrich Company and more recently had been Director of Organization and Personnel for the Atomic Energy Commission.[5] Another vice-presidency became vacant in early 1952 when G. C. Denebrink suddenly resigned the post for sales.

CHART VII

BIGELOW–SANFORD CARPET COMPANY

Senior Administrative Group, 1952

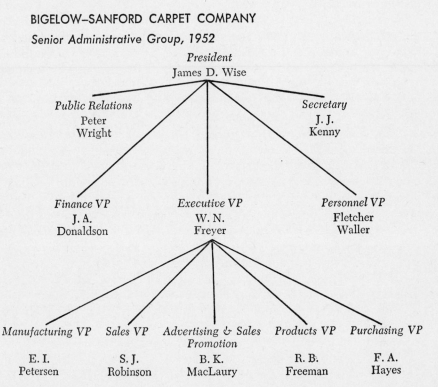

President
James D. Wise

Public Relations
Peter
Wright

Secretary
J. J.
Kenny

Finance VP
J. A.
Donaldson

Executive VP
W. N.
Freyer

Personnel VP
Fletcher
Waller

Manufacturing VP
E. I.
Petersen

Sales VP
S. J.
Robinson

*Advertising & Sales
Promotion*
B. K.
MacLaury

Products VP
R. B.
Freeman

Purchasing VP
F. A.
Hayes

Sumner Robinson succeeded Denebrink, and Robinson's job as general sales manager was filled by the promotion of Robert Howison from a regional sales managership. At the same time the new position of general marketing manager was established and the assistant general sales manager, Roland Brownlee, was appointed to it.[6] Early in 1953, when B. K. MacLaury suffered a fatal heart attack, R. R. Carlier was made director of advertising and sales promotion.

By the beginning of 1953 the new group was beginning to pull together as a team. For the first time consultative management was being practiced in spirit as well as in form. Previously executives had met and conferred, as the routine prescribed, but had returned to their offices only to take advantage of what they had learned in the group to further what they wanted to do as individuals. Under the pressure of profitless operations, however, a spirit of group responsibility developed, and consultation led to a mutual effort to advance the best interests of the whole.

NEW DEPARTURES

A part of the irony of Bigelow's unprofitable operations in 1951–1952 was the fact that the company had already undertaken strenuous measures to insure itself against precisely such a mischance. In the slacking-off period of the postwar boom, the executives had given broad study to the basic problems facing them and had initiated sweeping new policies to put the company on a footing of long-term soundness. These deliberations had had almost no opportunity to bear fruit when the rise and crash of the Korean consumers' market had occurred.

It would be impossible to encompass in short space the many new departures inaugurated by the Wise management after the immediate pressures of the postwar sales boom had subsided. A few of them, however, bear summarization.

In the field of management training the company had already accomplished much by 1949, although achievements in that field were, by the very nature of the problem, slow to bear fruit. In 1950 an industrial psychologist in Bigelow's own personnel administration conducted an opinion survey to determine what should be done to bring along supervisory personnel as first-line managers. The results of the survey tended to vary between Thompsonville and Amsterdam, but the general conclusion was that, while the top executives had improved their relations with their supervisory force, they had not succeeded in giving these men a sense of belonging to the managerial team.[7]

In 1951 the company decided to establish for its middle-management group a separate executive training program called an Institute of Industrial Management. There were actually two of these, one given at Amsterdam in co-operation with Cornell University and one at Thompsonville, where the University of Connecticut was the assisting educational group. These Institutes, the first of which was started in October, 1951, attempted to offer a selected group of management men the equivalent of a two-year university course in Industrial Management. Courses were given to the students in their plant communities. This was a pioneering venture in industrial education and, indeed, in co-operation between business and academic circles. Graduates of the first Institute in 1953 were convinced that the program had given them breadth of vision and had stimulated original thinking; specifically, it had helped them to develop insight into the various multiple departmental managements of Bigelow-Sanford.

The objectives of the Bigelow Institute of Industrial Management, applied with equal force to the company's other training media, are worth recording here. As set forth in the program for the final conference of the New York Institute, these objectives were:

1. To promote and foster self-development and self-improvement in the field of industrial management within the Bigelow management staff.
2. To provide an opportunity and means by which such development and improvement could be attained.
3. To develop in the Bigelow management staff a practical working knowledge of modern management techniques.
4. To develop and foster an understanding and analysis of the social and economic problems involved in the management of a manufacturing plant.
5. To develop a management staff which would be trained, objective, self-reliant and alert to the constantly changing industrial picture.

A second basic problem that was in the process of being solved when the Korean setback occurred was machinery imbalance. Much of the machinery was still perfectly usable, but the shifts in market demand had made it of marginal value. Professor Copeland, on being called in as a consultant during the war, had voiced the opinion that the company had subconsciously been influenced in its basic policy by the nature of its equipment problem. It seemed, he said, that the product line had been governed by the machinery, and therefore the company had fallen into the habit of making what it was equipped to make and then had tried to sell its output. To Copeland the reverse policy should prevail, especially in an industry as much affected by style considerations as the carpet industry had come to be. The market should be recognized as the dynamic element, he thought, and it should be the company's equipment policy to have on hand the balance of machines that would produce carpetings in line with consumer preferences. Wise concurred with this analysis and inaugurated vigorous measures to discover what machinery was no longer useful and what was needed in its place.

Of particular interest among the machinery changes was the company's effort to bring itself abreast of developments in demand for higher priced weaves and for broadloom products. Almost since the beginning of the carpet industry in America consumer preferences had been moving steadily upward from lower-priced to more expensive carpetings. After the 1890's the swing to broadloom products had also been persistent. It will be recalled that the New England predecessors of Bigelow had been the country's largest producers of ingrain, the cheapest of the old narrow-loom products; therefore the Bigelow company had had the farthest to travel of all the major twentieth-century companies in the race to keep up with market change. For the most part Bigelow and its predecessors had made successful adjustments, but their equipment had always tended to lag somewhat behind the needs of the times. As recently as the late 1940's the company had found itself having to convert some of its equipment in line with the still-continuing shift in demand, this time from 9-foot looms to looms of 15-foot widths.

There remained some demand for narrow-width carpetings, and some machinery was kept steadily busy with meeting this need. Stair treads and hotel hallways required narrow widths and large commercial installations, where the demand for durability necessitated weaves too heavy to be handled in broad strips, continued to make narrow weaving an important industry function. But large numbers of narrow looms, while still usable, were nevertheless not being fully operated. In 1948 and again in 1949 and 1950 the company investigated the possibility of selling the narrow looms abroad, to countries whose citizens were less anxious than Americans to cover their floors with broadloom carpets. Neither this plan nor the alternative one of entering into foreign manufacture with the narrow looms came to anything. Finally it was decided that the surplus narrow looms would have to be scrapped.

In redirecting its attention to the dynamics of its market, Bigelow was forced to make heavy expenditures at all levels—from an enormous silo-like structure at Amsterdam for the automatically controlled blending of wools to the small loom mechanisms that created sculptured effects in the weaving process. In its total postwar modernization program through 1952 the company spent approximately $20,000,000, a figure which would have been undreamed of in the years before the war, when an annual request for $750,000 in capital expenditures would probably have been pared to $500,000.

Third among the company's age-old problems was the proper adjustment of its distributing system. Wise had been deeply impressed by Copeland's insistence that the most valuable hidden asset a company could have was its system of distributing its goods. Bringing a fresh view to the problem, the president set about re-examining Bigelow's whole marketing structure.

The conclusion at which he arrived was that Bigelow had been over-emphasizing the desirability of finding a single best way to market its goods. For a short time in the early thirties it had used a double system; the Bigelow branch of the business had marketed through wholesalers and the Sanford branch direct to retailers; but soon it had decided that all sales should be direct, and the company had therefore set up its own regional warehouses to service its retail customers. Then, not wholly satisfied with this arrangement, Bigelow at the end of World War II had made two major adjustments. It had placed the warehouses in the hands of certain district managers and had drastically reduced the number of retailers to whom it sold its products.

Wise believed that this solution was suitable for a company with products which extended into the higher ranges of quality and price, but he had become convinced, from the inroads being made by lower-priced fabrics and hard surfaces, that more emphasis was needed in the popular price range. He believed his company was missing an important part of the market through its emphasis on quality products marketed through quality outlets.[8]

It was decided, therefore, after a period of experimentation, to market two distinct lines of products and through separate channels. The first was to be the Bigelow line with prices for its wool carpets ranging initially from $7.50 to $17 per square yard. This line was to carry all types of weave structures including tufted carpetings. Indeed a conscious effort was made to de-emphasize weave structures in advertising inasmuch as the structures themselves had undergone such radical changes in modern times that they no longer represented, as they once had, an easy key to carpet quality. The Bigelow line was to be sold as before, through direct sales to a moderately restricted number of outlets.

The Sanford name was to be used for the new, lower price line. This group offered rugs and carpets at prices ranging from about $2.95 to $11.50 per square yard. The line, with its own distinctive styling, was to be sold through wholesalers and with its own promotional efforts. The company felt that wholesalers were the best medium through which to contact the large number of outlets which typically carried low-priced products, and through wholesalers it hoped to reach a number of retail establishments which had not previously stocked Bigelow products under any name.

Meanwhile Bigelow's executives had been finding means of increasing the efficiency with which the company used its capital resources. Notable accomplishments had been effected in production lead time, in the purchasing operation, and in warehouse management. All of these problems had been wrestled with before, but never with success.

Production lead time had been running about fourteen weeks in postwar years and had been one of the soft spots that the Booz consultants had been unable to correct. The Wise management believed that the company was taking too long to make a carpet and that it would continue to be caught from time to time in situations like that which developed during the Korean War unless means could be found to adjust production more quickly to changing consumer demands. Vigorous efforts were made to solve the problem. Expediting the transmission of orders from the field to the plant was discovered to be one means of speeding up the process. Another important means was to keep on hand an inventory of pre-dyed yarn, ready for immediate use when an order arrived. Previously it had been thought impractical to dye yarn in advance because of the difficulty of matching colors, but it was found worth the effort because of the time it saved in the manufacturing process. As a result of these and other steps the lead time was decreased to six weeks and the capital tied up in goods in process was impressively reduced.

A similar reduction in raw materials inventory was effected by carefully controlled purchasing. When Hayes took over the work which the Booz report had termed "extremely unsatisfactory," he found that the raw wool on hand and on commitment equaled the demand of the next eight months. By September, 1949, the amount of wool on hand and committed had been reduced to a three months' supply. The Booz consultants re-evaluated the activities of purchasing and rated both wool and general purchasing performances as "sound and on the road to further improvement." While positions longer than three months might be assumed occasionally, the Bigelow management was firm in the belief that purchase for immediate use was the best long-range policy. Renewed efforts were made, however, to give the purchasing office timely information as to estimated future production levels and these efforts, in turn, were aided by the reduction in lead time.

In the warehouses, despite the best efforts of the regional managers, some lines had continued to accumulate dead inventory while others had recurrently run out of stock. In October, 1949, Wise determined to make another attempt to locate the nature and solution of the trouble. A task force, as he called it, produced a report which led to action in the following May. The group reported that in their opinion the difficulty arose from inadequate records too slowly reported. The many aspects of inventory and production planning were spread out among so many people and the departments were so far removed from each other physically that delay and waste effort were inevitable. The task force therefore recommended that departments be combined in the same physical area and that records be kept thereafter by machine.

Installing a new system and smoothing out its rough spots took more than a year. The system was therefore not in effect during the critical months when the Korean buying splurge unexpectedly burst upon the company. To aid the men who were responsible for the system's operation, Bigelow conducted experimental work with International Business Machines Corporation and with Bell Telephone Laboratories. Punched cards, key sorters, electronic calculators, and communication devices were put into use as fast as they could be adapted to Bigelow's needs, all with the aim of enabling the company to keep its delivery promises. By 1953 the new system was in full operation. Within 18 months the company had succeeded in cutting its inventory of idle warehouse stock by 25 per cent, with a concomitant freeing of working capital for use in more productive ways. At the same time the items which the warehouses had on hand for immediate delivery had increased from 75 per cent to 85 per cent of the total line of products, a figure in keeping with the best performance of the country's large-scale warehousers, such as Sears Roebuck & Company.

A DIVERSIFICATION PROGRAM

As a result of the soul-searching which Bigelow had engaged in once the postwar boom had subsided, there had come a double realization. First, the company had concluded that the co-ordinated management team it had developed was capable of handling, without further enlargement, at least a 25 per cent increase in operations over that made possible by its existing productive capacity. Secondly, the company's officers had decided that the wool carpet business was too narrow a specialty to provide balance or safeguards against trends over which they as managers could have no control. The natural outcome of these two conclusions was a determined effort to diversify the company's product line. The aim was to build volume, but the volume was to come not just from the increased sale of wool carpets but from the manufacture and sale of products which did not have the same demand characteristics as woven wool carpeting.

The first of the steps toward diversification was the acquisition of a company manufacturing cotton rugs. It will be recalled that Bigelow had sold cotton rugs made for it by various suppliers from 1942 to 1945 and had only discontinued their sale because of difficulties of supply. It was becoming increasingly apparent, however, that cotton floor coverings were enjoying a rapidly growing demand and presented a profitable opportunity. Undertaken simply as a means of broadening its product line, Bigelow's entry into the tufted process of carpet manufacture was to prove a fateful and fortunate move.

In November, 1950, Bigelow issued an announcement that it had purchased the Georgia Rug Mill, Incorporated. This was a small company with a factory at Summerville, Georgia, employing between 75 and 100 workers. The initial cost to Bigelow was 1,000 shares of its common stock at a price of $27.07 per share in exchange for all 300 shares of Georgia Rug Mill capital stock,[9] but the cost of modernizing and enlarging the Georgia mills' capacity required a much heavier investment.

The purchase of the Georgia Rug Mill marked the first entry of a major woven carpet producer into the manufacture of broadloom tufted cotton rugs.[10] The management of the Georgia company was retained and the productive capacity of the plant was greatly increased, giving Bigelow a leading position in this rapidly expanding branch of the floor-covering business. By October, 1952, tufted cotton carpet production was on a profitable basis. Most of the other large carpet companies announced that they would have tufted cotton carpeting in 1953.

The new year witnessed a phenomenal increase in the sale of tufted floor coverings (see Chart III), and Bigelow felt hard pressed to maintain its relative position in the market. True, it could thank its stars that its diversification program had put it in a position to benefit from this upsurge; nevertheless all was not what might have been wished. As the sales volume of tufted cotton soared, axminster sales declined. This rapid shift in market demand was to rack the industry—was once again to upset the delicate machinery balance that Bigelow had worked so hard to achieve in the postwar years, was to force, after all, the closing of Alexander Smith's ailing Yonkers plant (the plant which had been for three generations the axminster headquarters of the country), was to contribute to James Lees' decision to abandon its activities in the manufacture and sale of woolen carpet yarns, and was to close Bigelow's Amsterdam plant.

. It seemed possible that, if this development continued, the century-long trend in this country toward more expensive carpeting might be broken and the industry's threatened stagnation might be converted into a rough-and-tumble fight for markets. Indeed, if the 1953 production of tufted carpeting is added to that of woven floor coverings, the per family consumption of soft surface products is found not to be decreasing, as previously thought, but to have risen from 1.5 square yards per family to 1.9. The tufting process was impressively cheaper than weaving and could employ a wide variety of fibers in addition to cotton. The synthetic fibers, carpet rayon and nylon, found immediate consumer acceptance and soon challenged cotton as the principal material of tufted rugs and carpets. The rise of the tufting process was something the like of which the carpet industry had not seen since axminster leaped forward at the end of the last century to challenge ingrain as the carpet of widest popularity.

A second effort by Bigelow to break the tether that bound it to a sheep was the extended use of synthetic fibers in the manufacture of high-quality rugs and carpets. There were several reasons for this move. The company had itself undertaken considerable experimental work on carpet rayon, for the structure of this type of rayon differed markedly from the structure of clothing rayon. Wool, primary ingredient of the best woven floor coverings, had fluctuated in value too much, as the company had found out to its grief, to allow any stability in the carpet industry. Because of the large number of pounds of wool per unit of sale, carpet prices rose and fell with the movements of the wool market. Wise was anxious to minimize price fluctuations as much as he could.[11]

While synthetic carpets had acquired a bad name during World War II, the president felt that this had resulted from the poor quality of the synthetics used and that the bad reputation could be overcome by improvements in the basic fibers and by consumer education. Bigelow had investigated fibers of the hydrocarbon type (Orlon, Saran, Chemstrand, Dynel, and others) and from its investigations had come to the conclusion that the only source of inexpensive fiber for some time would be viscose rayon.

Like other fibers, viscose rayon was in short postwar supply, and the company's only quantity sources were in Italy and Germany. Its position was therefore vulnerable, as it was to learn when wool and foreign rayon prices went off on their Korean roller-coaster ride. Wise knew also that the carpet industry represented too small a proportion of the textile market for companies engaged in synthetics manufacture to be willing to devote much time or money to the development of artificial fibers for carpet use. He believed that Bigelow had to take most of the initiative itself, and in December, 1950, he recommended to his directors the purchase of an interest in the Hartford Rayon Corporation, which had a plant at Rocky Hill, Connecticut. Authorization was voted for the officers of Bigelow-Sanford to buy 238,991½ shares of Hartford common stock at $3⅛ per share, 16,050 shares of preferred stock at $5.00 per share, and $130,000 of outstanding notes. The net effect was to give Bigelow about 38 per cent of the rayon company's stock.[12]

The Hartford Rayon Corporation needed additional financing for future expansion and it needed new equipment to produce carpet rayon staple. These needs, together with the smaller concern's new relationship to Bigelow-Sanford, made the carpet company consider an increased Hartford investment. In March, 1951, the common stock of Hartford Rayon was enlarged from 660,000 shares to 1,000,000 shares and, by the expenditure of an additional $350,000, Bigelow obtained a majority interest. Wise, Freyer, Donaldson, and Freeman became Hartford directors and Wise was elected its president. As part of the offer to obtain majority interest, Bigelow had announced a proposed conversion and expansion of Hartford's facilities to produce 8,000,000 pounds of carpet rayon staple in place of the company's previous 5,000,000-pound capacity of continuous filament rayon.[13]

The extent of the Hartford Rayon modernization program, which was at first estimated to cost about $3,900,000, led Bigelow to secure full ownership of the Hartford company. By the end of October, 1951, this had been obtained. The Hartford preferred stock had been retired, and the outstanding Hartford common stock not already owned had been bought on the basis of one share of Bigelow for six shares of Hartford, the corporation becoming a wholly owned Bigelow subsidiary incorporated in Delaware. After acquiring full ownership, the Bigelow management drew plans to convert the remaining filament capacity to textile staple rayon.

The total capital expenditures to carry out the rayon program for 1951 and 1952 were estimated at $4,800,000.[14] Bigelow's 1951 plans called for carpet rayon to be used in 27 per cent of its estimated yardage; for the 1952 spring line the figure was raised to over 75 per cent. In 1952 over one-half of all soft-surface floor coverings sold in the United States contained surface fibers other than wool. The industry was no longer fully dependent upon a single surface fiber.

Another aspect of Bigelow's diversification program was a direct outgrowth of its work for the federal government during the Korean War. In World War II, it will be recalled, the company had been confined in its war work by the restrictions of its corporate charter. The Korean War brought to the fore once again the troublesome matter of the charter. This time Wise decided to take action, partly to enable the company to engage in profitable war work and partly with a view to future diversification into nontextile lines. Drawing on his knowledge of corporation law, Bigelow's president devised a means by which the company could be reincorporated.

The vehicle chosen for this reincorporation was the Bristol Mills of Virginia. This small subsidiary, purchased at the end of the war to produce carpet yarns for the plants at Amsterdam and Thompsonville, had been closed in the slump of 1949 but had been opened again during the boom of 1950.[15] With the reopening, a new subsidiary, Bristol Mills, Inc., had been formed in the state of Delaware. The proposal finally agreed upon in 1951 called for consolidation of Bigelow-Sanford and Bristol Mills in a new Delaware corporation to be known as Bigelow-Sanford Carpet Company, Inc. The most important result of the move was that the new company would use the broad charter of Bristol Mills and would be free to engage in more diversified activities, instead of being restricted to carpets and closely related products.

A proposal was made to stockholders, setting forth the aims of the plan. For the old noncallable preferred stock, which bore a rate of 6 per cent, a new 4½ per cent preferred was to be offered on a basis of one and one-half new shares for each old share; the 75 cents per share increase in the dividend rate was to compensate the holder for losing the noncall feature. Application was to be made to list the preferred on the New York Stock Exchange and also to sell 60,000 new shares of preferred, and it was hoped that the market for Bigelow's preferred would be thereby improved. The company also pointed out that new financing, if necessary, should be easier with the removal of the old, inflexible preferred stock.

Common stock in the new corporation was to be issued on the same basis: that is, one and one-half shares for each old share. The new stock would have a $5.00 par value but each share was to have assigned to it a capital of $25 as the old stock had had. The common stock was also to be listed on the New York Stock Exchange. The proposed consolidation was accepted by an adequate majority of Bigelow stockholders and became effective on June 20, 1951.

Corday Weave; textured effect created by profile wires or flat, steel strips over which carpet pile is formed

Cotton Tufting Machine; cotton is channeled from spools to loom through copper lined tubing; rapid action locks tufts which are then impregnated with rubberized compound; operates many times faster than conventional loom

A part of the recapitalization plan had been to retire the old issue of preferred stock, which amounted to only $2,640,300, and to put out in its stead a new and much larger preferred issue, the proceeds of which were to pay for the company's extensive program of diversification. Unfortunately for the prospect of obtaining new capital, the market for preferred stock appeared unfavorable and the prospective underwriters advised against trying to sell 60,000 new shares. The idea of a public sale of preferred stock was abandoned, but the exchange of new preferred for old was carried through. For those few common stockholders who had not assented to the merger, payment in cash was authorized.

While the aims of management had thus been partially met in that Bigelow had been freed of the restrictions of its charter and of its capitalization, the problem of financing remained unsolved. Again the company turned to outside sources for funds. In September, 1951, new long-term financing of $17,500,000 was obtained. Participating in the loan were the Prudential Insurance Company and five commercial banks. The loan called for equal repayments of one-half the principal sum before 1971 and repayment of the remainder at that time. Of the total amount $10,000,000 was to be added to working capital, $4,800,000 was to repay the existing long-term loan, and $2,500,000 was to be spent on the Hartford Rayon Corporation's plant.[16]

In the search for noncarpet diversification under its new charter, Wise formed a division, reporting to F. A. Hayes, vice-president for purchasing, known as the Defense Contracts Division. Hayes had had government procurement experience during World Wars I and II and was thought to be the person best fitted to obtain and supervise the defense contracts business. In addition to contracts for the manufacture of military blankets and duck, the company was successful in obtaining contracts for military tank parts and engineering. The textile products, on the whole, proved unprofitable because of the abrupt reduction or complete cessation of government needs prior to opportunity to amortize the expenditures required to convert looms and otherwise establish suitable facilities. However, the engineering and metal fabrication work proved to be reasonably profitable.

The first successful noncarpet product developed by the company's own research staff went on sale in December, 1952. This was a fiberglass mat for reinforced plastics. Production was carried on at Thompsonville. The near-range outlook was for a limited volume, but the long-range potential of laminated plastics appeared attractive since these plastics could be used for a wide variety of end uses including automobile bodies.

Nonwoven carpets of a different type from tufted cotton or felt seemed to offer still further chance for diversification, and Bigelow's expanded research department developed a method that appeared full of promise. Patents were obtained during 1952. The production method used high-frequency current to make wool, rayon, or cotton fibers adhere to the backing material. If successful the new method would prove to be an entirely new approach to carpet-making and the clearest possible indication of the fresh point of view with which the Bigelow organization was tackling its basic problems.

No company can branch into new fields without investing large sums of money and long hours of work in a research and developmental program. Bigelow's expensive but productive research department was one of the reasons why Wise believed that his administration could successfully carry an increased burden of a 25 per cent larger manufacturing organization without adding substantially to the company's overhead expense. In 1950, alone, the research staff under H. A. Reinhardt took out more patents than all the rest of the carpet industry combined.

By stated company policy these patents, instead of being used to protect the company's exclusive discoveries, were to be made available on a licensing basis to the rest of the industry. One of the first patents so licensed, and the one which proved most popular was that covering the "profile wire" principle. The "profile wire" was the means by which a textured effect could be achieved not in a separate shearing operation as formerly but in the weaving operation itself. This process, used in the company's Corday carpets proved so successful that all the major carpet companies secured licenses to use it. To extend the possibilities of the patent-licensing program, opportunities were explored abroad and an office was opened in Paris for a European representative. This change was a long-range program which envisioned the exportation of American carpet-making "know how" as well as patents.[17]

Although there had been no opposition of any consequence to the moves made by the president as part of his program of diversification, some of the directors later expressed concern over the amounts of money involved, particularly for Hartford Rayon.[18] Bigelow had been joined in this type of move by Mohawk, in the sense that Mohawk borrowed large sums to buy a rayon plant in Delaware in May, 1951.[19] Smith, Lees, and some other large carpet companies, on the other hand, believed that the best plan was to buy their synthetic fibers in the open market. The delays involved in getting Hartford Rayon into production led some of the board members to wonder whether Bigelow would have been wiser to have remained out of rayon manufacture.

The success or failure of the diversification program quite obviously lay in the future, but Wise and his executives were convinced that the program had been both sound and necessary, that Bigelow's position in the future would depend on its ability to move from the manufacture of woven carpet almost exclusively into the production of other products that would cushion it against a possible decline in carpet sales. How far it would go in this direction was uncertain, but the volume of potential sales for the immediate future was projected on the basis of two thirds of the total to come from sales of woven carpet and one third from nonwoven carpet and other products.

CONCLUSION

In many ways the nine years from 1945 to 1953 had been the most significant in Bigelow's history. In that short period Wise and his management group, so much of it new to Bigelow, had tried to remedy all the major defects that the company had accumulated since before the turn of the century. In their actions they had been bold, incisive, and far-ranging. Not all their remedies had been efficacious; mistakes had been made and had required correcting. Despite mistakes, however, progress had been achieved.

It was almost inevitable that this progress should have created friction. It was no easy task to convert a century-and-a-quarter-old textile company into a modern corporation in the span of nine years. Vested interests, traditional ways of doing things, long familiarity with rote operations all stood in the path of change. On the side of those administering the change were also obstacles. Although all were skilled in specialized executive functions, almost none had had the textile background that would have kept them from making technical errors in their new jobs. In addition they were men in a hurry.

In meeting their challenge these men had gone far toward resolving many of the company's basic and long-standing difficulties. First they had pondered what the difficulties were; then they had sought solution; and finally they had taken action to carry their solutions through to realization. In business, however, as in political life, problems are never really solved; they are merely coped with; for today's solution merely becomes one element in tomorrow's perplexity.

In the matter of management succession, this much at least had been achieved: not for the foreseeable future would the company again be thrown into turmoil by the sudden death of its chief executive. Within the organization there were men everywhere whose experience and education had been such that they could be called on to fill higher executive posts when vacancies occurred.

In respect to management succession Bigelow occupied what must have been one of the strongest positions in the industry. Other carpet companies may have had executives with longer experience in carpet-making and with those subtle insights into the eccentricities of the textile business which come only with experience. But in all those companies which had family managements there existed the latent possibility that what had happened several times to Bigelow, and had happened more recently to Smith, would someday happen to them. Entrenched in their businesses as they often are, family managers frequently, through pride and devotion, do not relinquish their duties till difficulties of crisis proportions have beset them. And often there is no one who can make them see their folly.

With regard to the balance of its productive equipment, lack of information makes it impossible to estimate what position Bigelow had come to occupy relative to its competitors. But in relation to its own history Bigelow was both better off and worse. By 1952 its wilton, velvet, and axminster capacity, and the ratio of its wide looms to its narrow, were probably better adjusted to market demand for those weaves and widths than at any other time in the century. But the rise of the tufting process would soon alter this balance and would leave the company with heavy excess capacity, particularly in its axminster lines. Machinery balance is one of those problems which is never solved but is merely adjusted to. Nevertheless, it was unlikely that the company would, for many years at least, again make the mistake of trying to sell only what it could produce.

The imponderable which the Wise management had found most difficult to cope with was the long-range trend of the industry. Perhaps it was enough that the company had become aware that in this area a problem existed. Perhaps the only suitable solution was diversification and in that direction the Wise administration had taken giant steps. Whether these innovations would be enough, time alone would tell. But there could hardly be any argument that the company, after nine years under the new regime, was at last equipped with a modern executive organization to meet and adjust to any future hardship which might come along.

APPENDICES

APPENDIX 1

LOWELL MANUFACTURING COMPANY Short Balance Sheets for Various Years, 1830 to 1898

	1830	1836	1842	1852 ᵃ	1860
Assets					
Cash	$ 522.25	$ 92.52	$ 63.44	$ 7,999.67	$ 3,143.92
Inventories	84,404.28	119,863.01	483,845.91	417,674.47	530,262.70
Receivables	55,648.01	272,943.92	45,200.59	730,169.01	618,949.50
Total Current Assets	140,574.54	392,899.45	529,109.94	1,155,843.15	1,152,356.12
Fixed Assets	258,634.11	271,972.88	305,125.60	1,448,161.71	1,306,166.82
Total Assets	$399,208.65	$664,772.33	$834,235.54	$2,604,004.86	$2,458,522.94
Liabilities					
Payables	$ 89,058.83	$106,788.85	$146,515.26	$ 658,161.77	$ 2,408.08
Surplus ᵇ	10,149.82	57,983.48	87,720.28	151,843.09	456,114.86
Capital Stock	300,000.00	500,000.00	600,000.00	1,794,000.00	2,000,000.00
Total Liabilities	$399,208.65	$664,772.33	$834,235.54	$2,604,004.86	$2,458,522.94

	1865	1871	1880	1892	1898
Assets					
Cash	$ 3,909.64	$ 30,367.58	$ 19,688.35	$ 51,784.40	$ 23,406.94
Inventories	1,135,457.93	823,555.13	484,053.22	476,920.92	313,619.34
Receivables	151,368.96	458,085.22	787,575.57	1,450,656.35	1,467,650.38
Total Current Assets	1,290,736.53	1,312,007.93	1,291,317.14	1,979,361.67	1,804,676.66
Fixed Assets	1,407,624.69	1,251,377.94	1,301,001.33	1,542,452.99	1,617,949.94
Total Assets	$2,698,361.22	$2,563,385.87	$2,592,318.47	$3,521,814.66	$3,422,626.60
Liabilities					
Payables	$ 166,698.60	$ 5,412.83	$ 237,523.68	$1,143,053.20	$1,125,437.63
Surplus ᵇ	531,662.62	557,973.04	354,794.79	378,761.46	297,188.97
Capital Stock	2,000,000.00	2,000,000.00	2,000,000.00	2,000,000.00	2,000,000.00
Total Liabilities	$2,698,361.22	$2,563,385.87	$2,592,318.47	$3,521,814.66	$3,422,626.60

ᵃ Profits are recorded for the years from 1844 to 1852 but these cannot be absolutely reconciled with the balance sheets. Since we have no way of knowing what adjustments were made, and since the profit figures exist for such a short period, the balance sheets are used as the basis of estimates.
ᵇ Including special reserves.

Source: Lowell Manufacturing Company, Directors' and Stockholders' minutes, *passim.*

APPENDIX 2

BIGELOW CARPET COMPANY Short Balance Sheets for Various Years, 1852 to 1913

	1852 ᵃ	1852 ᵇ	1869	1873	1889	1898	1900	1913
Assets								
Cash	$ 1,571.86	$ 4,383.15	—	—	—	—	$ 787,874.19 ᵈ	$4,898,482.80 ᵈ
Receivables	5,065.73	5,226.81	$ 981,053 ᶜ	$1,154,760 ᶜ	$ 307,602	$ 382,549	—	—
Inventories	74,761.94	95,848.73	—	—	1,137,982	697,769	2,139,979.52	1,292,721.60
Total Current Assets	81,399.53	105,458.69	981,053	1,154,760	1,445,584	1,080,318	2,927,853.71	6,191,204.40
Fixed Assets	109,653.96	114,114.93	334,987	334,000	874,542	853,268	2,467,901.73	2,456,800.38
Total Assets	$191,053.49	$219,573.62	$1,316,040	$1,488,760	$2,320,126	$1,933,586	$5,395,755.44	$8,648,004.78
Liabilities								
Payables	$109,501.82	$103,312.98	$ 327,308	$ 461,848	$ 877,261	$ 17,799	$1,110,008.61	$ 8,628.14
Surplus	21,551.67	4,260.64	188,732	226,902	442,865	915,787	255,746.83	4,609,376.64
Partner's Investment	60,000.00	112,000.00	—	—	—	—	—	—
Capital Stock	—	—	800,000	800,000	1,000,000	1,000,000	4,030,000.00	4,030,000.00
Total Liabilities	$191,053.49	$219,573.62	$1,316,040	$1,488,760	$2,320,126	$1,933,586	$5,395,755.44	$8,648,004.78

ᵃ January 1.
ᵇ July 1.
ᶜ For this year, in the report to the state, inventories and receivables were combined.
ᵈ Includes receivables.

Source: Bigelow Carpet Company, Cost Book, passim; *Abstract of the Attested Returns of Corporations, 1870* (Boston, 1871), p. 10; *Abstract of the Certificates of Corporations, 1874* (Boston, 1875), p. 28; *Abstract of the Certificates of Corporations Organized under the General Laws of Massachusetts during the Year, 1890* (Boston, 1891), pp. 64–65; *Abstract of the Certificates of Corporations Organized under the General Laws of Massachusetts during the Year, 1899* (Boston, 1900), pp. 92–93; Bigelow Carpet Company, Treasurer's Ledger, passim.

BIGELOW CARPET COMPANY *Average Costs Per Yard of Carpeting,*
1851 and 1854

	For the Six Months Ending July 1, 1851	For the Six Months Ending July 1, 1854
Labor Costs		
Coloring	02.033¢	02.409¢
Winding	01.785	02.045
Dressing	22.227	.292
Weaving	07.509	06.254
Trimming	01.747	.158
Harness mounting	.345	.222
Pattern drawer	.612	.578
Pattern cutter	.702	
Repairs machinery	.942	.658
Watchman and fireman	.862	.505
Engineer and fireman		.207
Overseer	.548	.318
Total	17.312¢	13.646¢
Material Costs		
Worsted yarns	53.717¢	69.557¢
Linen yarns	13.025	13.970
Cotton yarns		.209
Dyes	05.856	07.212
Fuel	02.275	02.312
Repairs		.900
Gas		.534
Burlap and twine		.384
Starch	.145	.160
Oil	.518	.216
Card paper	.430	.235
Total	75.966¢	95.689¢
General Costs		
Interest	03.537¢	06.255¢
Insurance	.548	.410
Taxes	.166	.481
Incidentals	02.074	01.198
Extra board		.052
Office		.534
Henry Kellogg, Sup.		.719
Transportation		.045
Total	06.325¢	09.694¢
Royalty	04.000¢	04.000¢
Commission	03.750	02.950
Total	107.353¢	125.979¢

Source: Bigelow Carpet Company, Cost of Carpeting, *passim.*

APPENDIX 4

HARTFORD CARPET COMPANY *Short Balance Sheets for Various Years,*
1867 to 1894

	1867	1878	1894
Assets			
Cash and Receivables	$1,152,758.92	$ 854,577.74	$ 360,994.93
Inventories	692,589.43	898,121.45	816,894.65
Total Current Assets	1,845,348.35	1,752,699.19	1,177,889.58
Fixed Assets	313,750.91	610,691.34	907,648.98
Total Assets	$2,159,099.26	$2,363,390.53	$2,085,538.56
Liabilities			
Payables	$ 18,178.40	$ 5,349.81	$ 3,606.12
Surplus	640,920.86	858,040.72	581,932.44
Capital Stock	1,500,000.00	1,500,000.00	1,500,000.00
Total Liabilities	$2,159,099.26	$2,363,390.53	$2,085,538.56

APPENDIX 5

BIGELOW–HARTFORD CARPET COMPANY Selected Balance Sheet Statistics, 1914 to 1928

(In Thousands of Dollars)

Year	Total Inventories	Total Current Assets	Total Current Liabilities	Net Current Assets	Plant and Equipment (Gross)	Total Depreciation Reserves	Net Plant and Equipment	Equity of Common Stockholder [a]	
								Amount of Equity	Equity Per Share
1914 [b]	$5,342	$ 7,483	$1,371	$ 6,112	$ na	$ na	$ 8,059	$ 8,682,000	$108
1915	5,480	8,512	2,141	6,371	8,288	294	7,994	8,864,000	108
1916	6,247	8,984	2,413	6,571	8,681	617	8,064	9,135,000	113
1917	6,574	10,679	3,944	6,735	8,849	924	7,925	9,160,000	114
1918	3,622	8,062	509	7,553	8,950	1,289	7,661	9,739,000	121
1919	5,325	9,875	1,022	8,853	9,121	1,659	7,462	10,854,000	135
1920	4,685	12,304	1,304	11,000	7,976	1,936	6,040	12,040,000	150
1921	4,759	12,077	1,512	10,565	8,232	2,198	6,034	12,565,000	156
1922	5,868	13,624	2,285	11,339	9,861	2,383	7,478	15,279,000	190
1923	6,013	14,728	2,318	12,410	12,025	2,689	9,336	18,409,000	228
1924	6,967	11,644	1,026	10,618	13,496	2,918	10,578	18,603,000	231
1925	6,295	11,945	1,137	10,808	14,240	3,336	10,904	19,118,000	238
1926	5,431	11,457	638	10,819	14,863	3,902	10,961	19,158,000	240
1927	6,406	12,045	1,210	10,835	15,953	4,479	11,474	19,676,000	246
1928	6,630	13,307	1,244	12,063	16,062	4,876	11,186	20,631,000	258

[a] Based on a single share of stock purchased in 1914. Bigelow-Hartford's original stock had a stated value of $50. In 1924 a 50 per cent stock dividend was made, but the value per share remained the same. In 1922 a two-for-one stock split reduced the value per share to $50. In 1924 a 50 per cent stock dividend was made, but the value per share remained the same. In the computation of the equity and earnings per share, compensation has been made for these changes.

[b] Not a full year's operation.

Source: Secretary's Department, Bigelow-Sanford.

APPENDIX 6

BIGELOW–SANFORD CARPET COMPANY *Selected Balance Sheet Statistics,*
1929 to 1953

| | | *(In Thousands of Dollars)* | | | |
Year	*Total Inventories*	*Total Cur- rent Assets*	*Total Current Liabilities*	*Net Current Assets*	*Plant and Equip- ment (Gross)*
1929	$15,299	$21,096	$ 2,749	$18,347	$29,785
1930	7,633	14,451	484	13,967	29,689
1931	7,054	12,132	398	11,734	29,597
1932	4,910	10,687	394	10,293	29,802
1933	8,009	12,178	635	11,543	27,627
1934	8,635	11,933	558	11,375	26,895
1935	11,296	15,011	3,003	12,008	27,664
1936	12,018	17,677	4,768	12,909	27,561
1937	13,482	18,323	6,197	12,126	28,138
1938	8,571	13,216	1,983	11,233	28,208
1939	11,373	17,044	3,807	. 13,237	28,218
1940	11,296	16,749	2,311	14,438	28,473
1941	14,828	21,780	6,221	15,559	28,826
1942	12,886	18,731	1,982	16,749	29,100
1943	11,657	19,490	2,229	17,261	29,159
1944	9,609	21,250	3,085	18,165	29,108
1945	13,762	21,200	3,171	18,029	29,011
1946	15,776	26,842	3,423	23,419	29,609
1947	17,065	30,612	5,755	24,857	31,029
1948	21,440	37,310	9,620	27,690	32,941
1949 b	21,434	33,490	6,672	26,818	35,889
1949	21,434	35,052	8,530	26,522	34,535
1950	22,852	39,532	11,957	27,575	37,338
1951	35,204	46,951	12,809	34,142	45,483
1952	24,595	39,483	10,681	28,802	47,277
1953	23,327	36,582	5,517	31,065	49,819

APPENDIX 6 Continued

BIGELOW–SANFORD CARPET COMPANY *Selected Balance Sheet Statistics, 1929 to 1953*

	(In Thousands of Dollars)		*Equity of Common Stockholder* [a]	
Total Deprecia-tion Reserves	*Net Plant and Equipment*	*Long-Term Notes Payable*	*Amount of Equity*	*Equity Per Share*
$12,752	$17,033	$ 4,500	$28,278,000	$320
13,302	16,387	3,000	24,819,000	237
13,818	15,779	—	25,069,000	239
14,658	15,144	—	23,052,000	221
16,025	11,602	—	20,894,000	200
15,453	11,442	—	20,553,000	203
16,576	11,088	—	20,772,000	205
16,805	10,756	—	21,345,000	210
17,377	10,761	—	20,652,000	204
18,055	10,153	—	19,081,000	188
18,395	9,823	—	20,711,000	204
18,927	9,546	—	21,686,000	215
19,600	9,226	—	22,464,000	222
20,176	8,924	—	23,267,000	230
20,957	8,202	—	23,800,000	235
21,694	7,414	—	23,795,000	223
22,444	6,567	—	23,681,000	224
22,997	6,612	5,000	24,138,000	225
23,671	7,358	5,000	26,614,000	258
24,093	8,848	5,000	30,051,000	290
24,896	10,993	5,000	31,106,000	300
15,845	18,690	5,000	37,572,000	361
16,995	20,343	4,820	41,415,000	399
21,265	24,218	17,350	37,049,000	336
19,760	27,517	17,000	35,359,000	320
21,713	28,106	16,000	38,680,000	350

[a] Based on a single share of stock in the predecessor company, Bigelow-Hartford, purchased in 1914. Bigelow-Sanford's stock in 1929 had a stated value of $50 per share. In 1948 a two-for-one stock split reduced the value per share to $25. In 1951 a 50 per cent stock dividend was made, but the value per share remained the same. In the computation of the equity and earnings per share, compensation has been made for these changes.
[b] Change in the series is basically due to revaluation of depreciation reserve for plant and equipment.

Source: Secretary's Department, Bigelow-Sanford.

APPENDIX 7

BIGELOW–HARTFORD CARPET COMPANY Annual Net Sales and Earnings, 1914 to 1928

Year	Net Sales	Net Profit Before Federal Income Tax	Provision for Federal Income Tax	Net Profit After Federal Income Tax	Per Share of Common Stock [a] Earnings	Per Share of Common Stock [a] Dividends
1914 [b]	$ 2,799,666	$ 311,667	$ —	$ 311,667	$ —	$ —
1915	9,983,871	874,217	—	874,217	6.76	3.60
1916	12,074,414	1,016,621	—	1,016,621	8.52	5.00
1917	10,380,228	840,635		840,635	6.36	6.00
1918	11,224,214	1,774,903	375,000	1,399,903	13.28	6.00
1919	13,872,512	2,588,935	500,000	2,088,935	21.84	8.00
1920	19,566,634	2,815,253	575,000	2,240,253	23.72	9.00
1921	14,032,285	2,024,716	416,144	1,608,572	16.40	10.00
1922	21,632,752	4,720,234	800,000	2,920,234 [c]	33.36	11.52
1923	25,528,290	5,278,997	725,000	4,553,997	53.92	16.00
1924	17,523,132	1,857,120	240,000	1,617,120	17.94	17.52
1925	20,563,808	2,473,672	350,000	2,123,672	24.36	18.00
1926	19,465,146	1,837,708	265,000	1,572,708	17.64	18.00
1927	19,440,622	2,481,874	345,000	2,136,874	24.66	18.00
1928	22,030,444	2,764,739	355,000	2,409,739	28.08	18.00

[a] See footnote a, Appendix 5.
[b] Not a full year's operations.
[c] After deducting $1,000,000 Reserve for Contingencies.

Source: Secretary's Department, Bigelow-Sanford.

APPENDIX 8

BIGELOW–SANFORD CARPET COMPANY *Annual Net Sales and Earnings,*
1929 to 1953

Year	Net Sales	Net Profit (Loss) Before Federal Income Tax	Provision for Federal Income Tax
1929	$23,964,903	$2,089,113	$ 235,000
1930	22,436,931	(608,702)	—
1931	17,067,778	413,724	—
1932	10,424,659	(1,948,737)	—
1933	12,569,746	1,140,680	—
1934	14,512,320	178,198	5,175
1935	19,662,134	493,860	77,600
1936	27,058,670	2,092,806	420,600
1937	29,309,102	682,613	120,000
1938	20,521,857	(1,491,032)	—
1939	25,038,397	2,670,344	490,000
1940	27,628,360	2,985,243	910,000
1941	39,251,161	5,124,304	3,080,000
1942	41,511,394	3,551,552	2,020,000
1943	37,667,636	437,572	(500,000)[b]
1944	39,417,661	1,827,751	802,000
1945	34,679,454	1,490,677	600,000 [d]
1946	39,222,359	2,238,095	990,000
1947	62,872,093	6,401,729	2,555,000
1948	85,205,160	8,966,584	3,770,000
1949 [c]	67,411,228	4,669,878	1,965,000
1949	67,411,228	5,298,239	2,025,000
1950	97,672,074	12,054,277	6,200,000
1951	77,503,171	(2,903,014)	(600,000)[b]
1952	67,272,765	(1,252,362)	—
1953	73,178,765	3,771,252	300,000

BIGELOW–SANFORD CARPET COMPANY *Annual Net Sales and Earnings, 1929 to 1953*

Net Profit (Loss) After Federal Income Tax	Per Share of Common Stock [a]	
	Earnings (Loss)	Dividends
$1,854,113	$16.17	$13.80
(608,702)	(7.37)	13.14
413,724	2.49	—
(1,948,737)	(20.10)	—
1,140,680	9.36	—
173,023	.15	3.00
416,260	2.46	—
1,672,206	14.46	9.00
562,613	3.84	10.50
(1,491,032)	(15.78)	—
2,180,344	19.36	3.00
2,075,243	18.36	9.00
2,044,304	18.06	12.00
1,261,553 [e]	10.56	6.00
937,572	7.44	6.00
1,025,751	8.46	6.00
890,677	7.14	6.00
1,248,095	10.62	6.00
3,846,729	35.82	12.00
5,196,584	48.66	16.20
2,704,878	24.60	14.40
3,273,239	20.04	9.60
5,854,277	54.96	12.00
(2,303,014)	(22.41)	14.40
(1,252,362)	(12.96)	2.25
3,471,252	29.88	—

[a] See footnote a, Appendix 6.
[b] Credit due to carry-back of unused excess profits credit.
[e] Change in the series is basically due to revaluation of depreciation reserve for plant and equipment.
[d] Includes Provision for Refund — Federal Excess Profits Taxes.
[e] After Provision for Postwar Expenses and Rehabilitation of Properties ($270,000).

Source: Secretary's Department, Bigelow-Sanford.

APPENDIX 9

BIGELOW–HARTFORD CARPET COMPANY Advertising Expenditures, 1923 to 1928

Year	Total Advertising Expense	Per Cent of Net Sales	Consumer Media Expenses	Per Cent of Total Adv. Exp.	Per Cent of Net Sales
1923	$106,502	.4	—	—	—
1924	157,409	.9	—	—	—
1925	166,234	.8	—	—	—
1926	256,564	1.3	$ 133,181	51.9	.7
1927	332,848	1.7	192,873	58.0	1.0
1928	264,952	1.2	112,905	42.6	.5

Source: Advertising Department, Bigelow-Sanford.

APPENDIX 10

BIGELOW–SANFORD CARPET COMPANY Advertising Expenditures, 1929 to 1952

Year	Total Advertising Expense	Per Cent of Net Sales	Consumer Media Expenses	Per Cent of Total Adv. Exp.	Per Cent of Net Sales
1929	$ 361,927	1.5	$ 190,174	52.5	.8
1930	396,910	1.7	171,373	43.2	.7
1931	442,204	2.4	225,049	50.9	1.2
1932	526,481	4.7	363,637	69.1	3.2
1933	405,786	3.0	307,912	75.9	2.3
1934	501,737	3.2	335,890	67.0	2.1
1935	469,125	2.2	309,278	65.9	1.4
1936	510,453	1.7	237,298	46.5	.8
1937	688,681	2.2	310,712	45.1	1.0
a	(341,675)	(1.0)			
1938	297,831	1.3	116,958	39.3	.5
1939	351,468	1.3	179,300	51.0	.7
1940	492,834	1.7	271,396	55.1	.9
1941	532,245	1.3	244,315	45.9	.6
1942	179,779	.4	122,058	67.9	.3
b		(.5)			(.4)
1943	197,026	.5	139,278	70.7	.4
b		(1.7)			(1.2)
1944	234,484	.6	140,155	59.8	.4
1945	344,167	.9	153,450	44.6	.4
1946	801,376	2.0	461,904	57.6	1.1
1947	1,212,116	1.9	674,280	55.6	1.0
1948	2,762,803	3.3	1,739,759	62.9	2.1
1949	2,777,671	4.1	1,660,988	59.7	2.4
1950	2,101,463	2.1	1,103,535	52.5	1.1
1951	2,369,185	3.0	1,284,144	54.2	1.6
1952	1,602,210	2.3	840,464	52.4	1.2

a Additional co-operative advertising expense.
b Excluding war work.

Source: Advertising Department, Bigelow-Sanford.

APPENDIX 11

Sales and Net Income of Selected Carpet Companies, 1939 to 1953

(In Thousands of Dollars)

Year	Bigelow Sales	Bigelow Net Income	Smith[a] Sales	Smith[a] Net Income	Mohawk Sales	Mohawk Net Income	Lees[b] Sales	Lees[b] Net Income	Firth Sales	Firth Net Income
1939	$25,038	$2,180	$21,810	$2,887	$17,430	$1,800	$14,792	$1,090	$ 7,633	$ 722
1940	27,628	2,075	23,629	2,652	17,630	1,580	16,836	707	8,172	594
1941	39,251	2,044	33,955	2,858	30,365	1,962	26,685	1,094	11,055	537
1942[c]	—	—	—	—	—	—	—	—	—	—
1943	—	—	—	—	—	—	—	—	—	—
1944	—	—	—	—	—	—	—	—	—	—
1945	—	—	—	—	—	—	—	—	—	—
1946	39,222	1,705 [e]	45,292	4,602	33,332	2,531	31,344	4,040	10,850	1,364
1947	62,872	4,553 [e]	63,161	5,561	46,879	2,734	40,259	4,220	14,652	1,500
1948	85,205	6,305 [e]	81,727	6,990	61,731	4,173	53,645	4,757	21,216	2,276
1949	67,411	3,273 [e]	70,196	1,479	56,854	3,157	48,062	3,444	16,045	1,143
1950	97,672	5,854	89,209	2,282	80,103	4,455	71,930	5,192	27,203	2,154
1951	77,503	2,303 [d]	82,501	1,907 [d]	69,594	1,349	65,517	2,620	19,608	338
1952	67,273	1,252 [d]	62,611	3,556 [d]	57,128	1,107	65,200	3,824	17,828	590
1953	73,179	3,471	46,039	3,155 [d]	61,425	1,403	60,293	3,175	16,384	303

[a] Includes soft-surface floor coverings, 1939–1941; after 1941 figures include hard-surface coverings.

[b] Lees' total includes sales of yarn.

[c] Breakdown of wartime sales of Bigelow's competitors not available.

[d] Deficit.

[e] These figures represent adjustments made retroactively in 1950. See Appendix 8 for preadjustment figures.

Source: Accounting Department and Secretary's Department, Bigelow-Sanford.

APPENDIX 12

BIGELOW–SANFORD CARPET COMPANY Employment and Wage Statistics, 1930 to 1941

	1930	1931	1932	1933	1934	1935	1936	1937	1938	1939	1940	1941
Average Number of Employees												
Amsterdam	2,205	2,070	1,585	2,284	2,944	3,127	3,393	3,439	2,898 a	2,789	2,576	2,878
Clinton	1,305	1,072	771	98	—	—	—	—	—	—	—	—
Thompsonville	2,701	2,350	1,875	2,320	2,490	2,928	3,016	3,078	2,451 a	2,505	2,396	2,630
Total	6,211	5,492	4,231	4,702	5,434	6,055	6,409	6,517	5,349	5,294	4,963	5,508
Average Annual Earnings per Employee												
Amsterdam	$ 825	$1,023	$ 722	$ 817	$ 815	$ 856	$ 981	$1,023	$ 862	$1,043	$1,117	$1,374
Thompsonville	1,035	997	770	858	994	1,059	1,143	1,197	994	1,169	1,147	1,627
Company Average	$ 930	$1,010	$ 746	$ 837	$ 904	$ 957	$1,062	$1,110	$ 928	$1,106	$1,132	$1,450
Average Weekly Earnings per Employee												
Amsterdam	$15.87	$19.68	$13.90	$15.73	$15.69	$17.75	$18.50	$19.65	$16.58	$20.06	$21.48	$26.43
Thompsonville	19.92	19.18	14.82	16.51	19.13	21.37	21.58	23.40	19.13	22.49	22.07	29.38
Company Average	$17.89	$19.43	$14.36	$16.12	$17.41	$18.94	$19.96	$21.23	$17.75	$21.21	$21.77	$27.84
Industry Average	—	—	—	$16.35	$17.41	$20.35	$20.50	$21.15	$19.91	$23.20	$23.48	$27.67
Average Hours Worked Weekly, per Employee												
Amsterdam	—	—	—	40.2	32.3	34.5	33.9	30.07	28.04	38.1	32.72	36.6
Thompsonville	—	—	—	37.9	35.5	38.2	35.9	33.97	29.10	33.2	31.33	37.8
Company Average	—	—	—	39.0	33.8	36.3	34.9	31.91	28.52	32.6	32.05	37.2
Industry Average	—	—	—	36.5	31.7	36.7	36.6	33.96	31.20	36.1	35.10	38.8
Hourly Production of Workers by Years (Average number of yards made per man hour)	—	—	—	—	—	—	—	.98	.92	1.03	1.02	1.24

a Omitting May and June (mills on strike).

Source: Manufacturing Department Reports, Bigelow-Sanford.

APPENDIX 13

BIGELOW–SANFORD CARPET COMPANY A Comparison with Total Carpet Industry Sales, 1934 to 1952

| Year | (In Thousands of Dollars) | | Bigelow's Percentage of Industry Sales |
	Bigelow Sales	Industry Sales	
1934 [a]	$14,500	$ 68,100	21.3
1935	19,700	92,600	21.3
1936	27,100	126,100	21.4
1937	29,300	138,700	21.1
1938	20,500	97,400	21.1
1939	25,000	135,100	18.5
1940	27,600	145,900	18.9
1941	39,300	205,000	19.2
1942	30,700 [b]	158,300	19.4
1943	10,600 [b]	82,800	12.4
1944	11,800 [b]	83,100	14.2
1945	13,500 [b]	79,300	17.0
1946	39,200	211,600	18.5
1947	62,900	324,300	19.4
1948	85,200	430,500	19.8
1949	67,400	362,900	18.6
1950	97,700	536,700	18.2
1951	77,500	429,800	18.0
1952	67,300	387,600	17.4

[a] Industry figures for previous years not available; figures do not include sa es of automobile carpets.
[b] Does not include wartime contracts.

Source: Sales Department Reports, Bigelow-Sanford; Carpet Institute.

APPENDIX 14

BIGELOW–SANFORD CARPET COMPANY Production of Principal Fabrics and Percentage of Industry Total, 1921 to 1945

(In Woven Square Yards)

Year	Bigelow Axminster [a]	Per Cent of Industry [b]	Bigelow Wilton [a]	Per Cent of Industry [b]	Bigelow Velvet [a]	Per Cent of Industry [b]	Bigelow Total [c]	Per Cent of Industry [c]
1921	5,200,742	—	946,035	—	3,189,702	—	9,936,803	—
1922	6,774,107	—	1,872,255	—	3,790,026	—	14,978,686	—
1923	7,432,913	—	1,803,928	—	6,332,324	—	15,335,383	—
1924	6,666,948	—	1,466,469	—	6,098,542	—	11,693,544	—
1925	7,059,820	—	1,522,120	—	3,560,127	—	11,565,515	—
1926	7,193,383	—	1,602,204	—	2,983,575	—	11,760,145	—
1927	7,298,968	—	1,404,878	—	2,964,558	—	11,808,706	—
1928	7,519,590	—	1,483,599	—	3,104,860	—	12,024,257	—
1929	9,191,030	—	1,542,058	—	3,021,068	—	14,504,828	—
1930	5,071,890	—	788,654	—	3,771,740	—	7,971,458	—
1931	5,693,047	—	719,756	—	2,110,914	—	8,150,536	—
1932	3,341,649	—	279,767	—	1,737,733	—	4,893,860	—
1933	5,188,902	—	601,255	—	1,272,444	—	7,296,830	—
1934	5,349,763	—	567,677	—	1,506,673	—	7,671,913	—
1935	5,717,182	—	768,912	—	1,754,473	—	9,369,118	—
1936	6,774,490	—	778,142	—	2,883,024	—	10,742,334	—
1937	6,386,625	22.2	881,500	13.0	3,165,512	18.4	10,433,637	19.8
1938	4,008,697	20.4	603,175	11.3	2,465,043	22.3	7,076,915	19.6
1939	6,333,216	20.1	797,269	8.6	2,816,450	22.9	9,946,935	18.8
1940	5,872,561	18.7	691,022	9.4	2,444,608	19.1	9,008,191	17.4
1941	8,341,414	21.9	842,601	8.1	3,221,463	20.6	12,405,478	19.1
1942	5,995,811	21.4	864,210	9.2	2,224,312	22.2	9,084,333	18.2
1943	2,010,846	11.7	466,560	8.5	490,618	12.8	2,968,024	10.9
1944	1,658,903	11.3	563,400	10.3	646,026	15.5	2,868,329	11.4
1945	2,196,157	16.2	578,524	12.3	801,089	20.5	3,575,770	15.6

[a] Figures for the years 1921–1928 apply to the Bigelow-Hartford Carpet Company.
[b] Industry figures for the years 1921–1936 not available.
[c] These figures include only production of axminster, wilton, and velvet weaves.

Source: Manufacturing Department Reports, Bigelow-Sanford; Carpet Institute.

APPENDIX 15

U. S. Production of Woven Soft-Surface, Hard-Surface [a] and Tufted Cotton Floor Coverings, 1939 to 1952

(In Thousands of Square Yards and Dollars)

Year	Woven Soft-Surface		Asphalt Tile		Linoleum		Felt Base		Tufted Cotton	
	Yards	Dollars	Yards	Dollars	Yards	Dollars	Yards	Dollars	Yards	Dollars
1939	62,350	$134,992	–	–	36,000	$29,400	164,200	$ 37,800	1,209	$ 1,838
1940	61,926	145,914	–	–	–	–	–	–	1,867	2,833
1941	75,709	205,022	8,424	–	57,000	–	205,000 b	–	2,059	3,394
1942	–	–	–	–	–	–	–	–	–	–
1943	–	–	–	–	–	–	–	–	–	–
1944	–	–	–	–	–	–	–	–	–	–
1945	–	–	–	–	–	–	–	–	–	–
1946	52,076	211,627	20,945	–	–	–	265,100	93,400	8,234	30,661
1947	69,200	324,273	–	–	63,100	67,700	280,000 b	100,000	17,439	39,238
1948	83,980	430,504	44,000	–	75,000 b	–	250,000	90,000	18,376	41,345
1949	68,815	362,879	50,000	$36,000	70,000	70,000	250,000	90,000	20,002	50,006
1950	85,721	536,696	61,600	–	70,000	75,000	264,000 b	–	29,035	72,586
1951	60,140	429,838	66,600 b	–	71,500 b	–	280,000	–	21,146 b	60,413 b
1952	62,000 b	388,085	–	–	70,000	–	280,000	–	25,734	73,000 b

[a] Excluding rubber tile, for which adequate figures are lacking.
[b] Estimated.

Source: Woven soft-surface figures from the Carpet Institute of America; hard-surface figures compiled by Bird & Son, East Walpole, Massachusetts, from U. S. Census and industry sources; tufted cotton figures from the Tufted Textile Manufacturers Association, Dalton, Georgia, and the Carpet Institute.

NOTES

CHAPTER 1: Pioneering an Industry: the Lowell Manufacturing Company, 1828–1852

1. *The Carpet Trade Review*, IV (May, 1877), 61.

2. *Village Register* (Dedham, Massachusetts), June 18, 1829, p. 3; Norfolk County, Massachusetts, Deeds, Vol. 83, p. 91.

3. *Boston Daily Advertiser*, Sept. 11, 1827, p. 3.

4. Norfolk Deeds, Vol. 82, p. 245.

5. L. Vernon Briggs, *History and Genealogy of the Cabot Family* (Boston, 1927), I, 279–80.

6. William R. Bagnall, "Sketches of Manufacturing Establishments in New York City, and of Textile Establishments in the Eastern States" (4 volumes of unpublished materials located in Baker Library), edited by Victor S. Clark (Washington, 1908), IV, 2549.

7. *Ibid.*, IV, 2540–2.

8. Lowell Manufacturing Company, Minutes of the Directors' and Stockholders' meeting, Feb. 22, 1828.

9. *Ibid.*, Directors' and Stockholders' minutes, Feb. 22, 1828; George Sweet Gibb, *The Saco-Lowell Shops: Textile Machinery Building in New England, 1813–1949* (Cambridge, 1950), p. 155.

10. Lowell Manufacturing Company, Directors' and Stockholders' minutes, Feb. 22, 1828.

11. *Ibid.*, Directors' and Stockholders' minutes, Apr. 17, 1828.

12. Middlesex County, Massachusetts, Deeds, Vol. 279, pp. 532–34.

13. Lowell Manufacturing Company, Directors' and Stockholders' minutes, Jan. 7, 1829.

14. Bagnall, *op. cit.*, IV, 2553.

15. Lowell Manufacturing Company, Directors' and Stockholders' minutes, Jan. 7, 1829.

16. Lowell Manufacturing Company, Directors' and Stockholders' minutes, Oct. 17, 1829, Nov. 21, 1829.

17. *Ibid.*, Apr. 8, 1831, May 30, 1831.

18. Thomas L. Wilson, *The Aristocracy of Boston* (Boston, 1838), p. 26; Bagnall, *op. cit.*, IV, 2567.

19. *Ibid.*, IV, 2577–80.

20. *Eighty Years' Progress of the United States* (New York, 1864), p. 306.

21. Arthur H. Cole and Harold F. Williamson, *The American Carpet Manufacture* (Cambridge, 1941), p. 28.

22. Edward H. Knight, *Knight's American Mechanical Dictionary* (New York, 1876), III, 2703.

23. Cornelia Bateman Faraday, *European and American Carpets and Rugs* (Grand Rapids, 1929), pp. 329, 338.

24. Joseph Gales and William Winston Seaton, *The Debates and Proceedings in the Congress of the United States, 1823–1824* (Washington, 1856), p. 743.

25. "Statement of Case and Evidence," *Application of Erastus B. Bigelow to the Commissioner of Patents for an Extension of His Letters-Patent, for Improvements in the Power-Loom for Weaving Ingrain Carpets* (Boston, 1860), p. 291.

26. Samuel Fay, "Carpet-Weaving and the Lowell Manufacturing Company," Old Residents Historical Association, Lowell, Massachusetts, *Contributions* (Lowell, 1873), I, 55.

27. Cole and Williamson, *op. cit.*, p. 49.

28. Middlesex Deeds, Vol. 327, p. 15.

29. Lowell Manufacturing Company, Directors' and Stockholders' minutes, July 23, 1831.

30. Victor Selden Clark, *History of Manufactures in the United States* (New York, 1929), I, 5.

31. Middlesex Deeds, Vol. 327, pp. 9–10.

32. Cole and Williamson, *op. cit.*, pp. 53, 75.

33. Bagnall, *op. cit.*, IV, 2563–4.

34. Nehemiah Cleaveland, *A Memoir of Erastus Brigham Bigelow* (Boston, 1860), pp. 13–14.

35. *Lowell Manufacturing Co. et al.* v. *Hartford Carpet Co.*, 15 U. S. 1021–4. Document printed in connection therewith. "Complainant's Bill," Circuit Court of the United States, District of Connecticut, *Lowell Manufacturing Company et al.* v. *the Hartford Carpet Company* (n.p., n.d.), pp. 11–15.

36. " Report from the Commissioner of Patents, Showing the Operation of the Patent Office during the Year 1842," 27 Cong., 3d Sess. (1842–1843), *House Executive Documents*, no. 109, p. 119.

37. Lowell Manufacturing Company, Directors' and Stockholders' minutes, June 24, 1842.

38. "Statement of Case and Evidence," *op cit.*, pp. 400–2.

39. *The Lowell Courier*, July 16, 1842, p. 2.

40. "Statement of Case and Evidence," *op. cit.*, p. 213, Appendix, pp. 38–44.

41. Bigelow-Sanford Carpet Company, Incorporated, Manuscript Collection, New York, New York.

42. *Lowell Manufacturing Company et al.* v. *the Hartford Carpet Company*, "Complainant's Bill," pp. 18–23.

43. Lowell Manufacturing Company, Directors' and Stockholders' minutes, Oct. 22, 1845.

44. Agreement between Erastus B. Bigelow of Boston and the Lowell Manufacturing Company, dated May 1, 1846.

45. Lowell Manufacturing Company, Directors' and Stockholders' minutes, Oct. 15, 1846.

46. United States Circuit Court, District of Connecticut, *Lowell Manufacturing Company and Erastus B. Bigelow* v. *the Hartford Carpet Company. In Equity. Testimony Referred to by Mr. O'Conor* (New York, 1863), p. 26; Lowell Manufacturing Company, Directors' and Stockholders' minutes, Oct. 15, 1846, Dec. 21, 1846.

47. Agreement between the Providence Machine Company and the Lowell Manufacturing Company, dated Mar. 4, 1847.

48. Contract between the Lowell Manufacturing Company and the Amoskeag Manufacturing Company, dated Mar. 10, 1847.

49. Alexander Wright to George W. Martin, Oct. 11, 1849.

50. Lowell Manufacturing Company, Directors' and Stockholders' minutes, Feb. 2, 1849.

51. *Ibid.*, Dec. 20, 1850.

52. Agreement between the Amoskeag Manufacturing Company and the Lowell Manufacturing Company, dated Feb. 1, 1851.

53. Lowell Manufacturing Company, Directors' and Stockholders' minutes, Oct. 22, 1845, Dec. 20, 1852.

54. "Manufacturers," Original Returns of the Assistant Marshals in Massachusetts, Seventh Census of the United States, I, 751, in the Massachusetts State Library, Boston.

55. John L. Hayes, *The Alleged Discrimination against the Wool-Growing Interests in the Recent Tariff Legislation* (Cambridge, 1883), p. 11.

56. J. T. Shaw, "The Wool Trade of the United States," 61 Cong., 1st Sess. (1909), *Senate Executive Document*, no. 70, pp. 28–30.

57. Lowell Manufacturing Company, Directors' and Stockholders' minutes, Mar. 13, 1846.

58. "Statement of Case and Evidence," *op. cit.*, p. 197.

59. "Manufactures," Seventh Census, *op. cit.*, I, 751; "Documents Relative to the Manufactures in the United States Collected and Transmitted to the House of Repre-

sentatives in Compliance with a Resolution of January 19, 1832," 22 Cong. 2d Sess. (1832–1833), *House Executive Documents*, no. 308, I, 338–40.

60. *Charters, Additional Acts, and Other Documents, Relating to the Proprietors of Locks and Canals on Merrimac River* (Cambridge, 1857), pp. 103–11.

61. *The Daily Courier* (Lowell, Massachusetts), Mar. 24, 1846, p. 2.

62. *The New England Offering*, I (Apr., 1848), 24.

63. *The Daily Courier*, Mar. 21, 1848, p. 2.

64. Elizur Wolcott to George W. Martin, Mar. 24, 1848.

65. "Statement of Case and Evidence," *op. cit.*, pp. 68–69, 207.

66. Timothy Pitkin, *A Statistical View of the Commerce of the United States of America* (New Haven, 1835), p. 529; Lowell Manufacturing Company, Directors' and Stockholders' minutes, Nov. 6, 1835; Erastus Brigham Bigelow, *The Tariff Question Considered in Regard to the Policy of England and the Interests of the United States* (Boston, 1862), p. 214.

67. "Documents Relative to the Manufactures in the United States," *op. cit.*, I, 339, 341.

68. Lowell Manufacturing Company, Directors' and Stockholders' minutes, Mar. 13, 1840.

69. "Statement of Case and Evidence," *op. cit.*, p. 261.

70. Bigelow, *op. cit.*, p. 214.

71. Lowell Manufacturing Company, Contract Book, *passim*.

72. J. D. Van Slyck, *New England Manufacturers and Manufactories* (Boston, 1879), I, 91.

73. "Statement of Case and Evidence," *op. cit.*, pp. 265–7, 285.

74. *Ibid.*, p. 221.

75. Alexander Wright to George W. Martin, Feb. 14, 1851.

76. "Statement of Case and Evidence," *op. cit.*, pp. 228–9.

77. Faraday, *op. cit.*, p. 329.

78. *Scientific American*, VII (Apr. 10, 1852), 235.

79. Chester Whitney Wright, *Wool-Growing and the Tariff* (Cambridge, 1910), p. 104.

80. *The Second Exhibition of the Massachusetts Charitable Mechanic Association* (Boston, 1839), p. 43.

81. "Statement of Case and Evidence," *op. cit.*, p. 262; Alexander Wright to George W. Martin, Apr. 23, 1850.

82. William H. Graham, *Statistics of the Woolen Manufactories in the United States* (New York, 1845), p. 117.

83. "Statement of Case and Evidence," *op. cit.*, pp. 98, 118–19, 236, 275, 282.

84. *Ibid.*, pp. 300–9.

85. *First Exhibition and Fair of the Massachusetts Charitable Mechanic Association* (Boston, 1837), p. 23.

86. *The Third Exhibition of the Massachusetts Charitable Mechanic Association* (Boston, 1841), p. 105.

87. "Documents Relative to the Manufactures in the United States," *op. cit.*, I, 338.

88. *Illustrated History of Lowell and Vicinity* (Lowell, 1897), p. 308. The figures for cotton cloth were:

1832	1,860,000 yards
1836	2,860,000 "
1846	4,940,000 "
1850	3,915,000 "

In 1850, 324,847 yards of linseys were also produced. By that date the value of carpeting exceeded that of the cloth.

89. Cole and Williamson, *op. cit.*, p. 249.

90. "Statement of Case and Evidence," *op. cit.*, p. 255.

91. Lowell Manufacturing Company, Directors' and Stockholders' minutes, Apr. 27, 1840.

92. *Ibid.*, Jan. 14, 1843.

93. Thomas G. Cary, *Profits on Manufactures at Lowell* (Boston, 1845), pp. 14–15.

94. Lowell Manufacturing Company, Directors' and Stockholders' minutes, Aug. 5, 1843.

95. *Ibid.*, Mar. 6, 1847, Apr. 19, 1849.

96. *Report of Mr. Sturgis's Committee to Twenty-Eight Manufacturing Companies* (Boston, 1852), pp. 6, 12.

97. Lowell Manufacturing Company, Directors' and Stockholders' minutes, July 15, 1848, Jan. 2, 1849.

98. Nathan Appleton, *Introduction of the Power Loom, and Origin of Lowell* (Lowell, 1858), p. 30.

99. Lowell Manufacturing Company, Directors' and Stockholders' minutes, Jan. 4, 1832, July 16, 1836.

100. *Ibid.*, Nov. 4, 1847.

101. *Ibid.*, Jan. 2, 1849.

102. *Ibid.*, Dec. 20, 1850.

103. Cf. N. S. B. Gras and H. M. Larson, *Casebook in American Business History* (New York, 1939), pp. 672, 703.

104. Joseph Gregory Martin, *Boston Stock Market* (Boston, 1886), p. 88.

CHAPTER 2: Pioneering an Industry: the Connecticut Companies, 1825–1854

1. Henry R. Stiles, *The History and Genealogies of Ancient Windsor, Connecticut* (Hartford, 1892), II, 225.

2. Charles W. Burpee, *A Century in Hartford* (Hartford, 1931), p. 41.

3. Simsbury, Connecticut, Deeds, Vol. 26, pp. 328–9; Vol. 29, p. 237.

4. *The Connecticut Courant* (Hartford, Connecticut), Apr. 19, 1825, p. 3.

5. *Resolves and Private Laws of the State of Connecticut, from the Year 1789 to the Year 1836* (Hartford, 1837), II, pp. 918–20.

6. Simsbury Deeds, Vol. 29, p. 271; Vol. 31, p. 313.

7. Clark, *History of Manufactures in the U. S.*, I, 466.

8. *Boston Daily Advertiser*, Dec. 5, 1826, p. 1.

9. *Ibid.*, Mar. 6, 1826, p. 3.

10. Simsbury Deeds, Vol. 30, p. 266; Vol. 32, p. 93.

11. "Documents Relative to the Manufactures in the United States," *House Executive Documents*, no. 308, I, 980, 1014.

12. *First Exhibition and Fair of the Massachusetts Charitable Mechanic Association*, p. 23.

13. Simsbury Deeds, Vol. 34, pp. 330, 350–62; Vol. 36, p. 30.

14. N. H. Eggleston, *A Discourse at the Funeral of Orrin Thompson* (Springfield, Massachusetts, 1873), p. 11.

15. Horace C. Brainard Manuscript Collection, Connecticut Historical Society, Hartford, Connecticut.

16. Eggleston, *op. cit.*, p. 22.

17. Brainard Manuscript Collection.

18. Thompsonville Carpet Manufacturing Company, Minutes of Directors' and Stockholders' meeting, Nov. 28, 1828.

19. John R. Commons, *A Documentary History of American Industrial Society* (Cleveland, 1910), IV, Supplement, 120–1.

20. Brainard Manuscript Collection.

21. Cole and Williamson, *The American Carpet Manufacture*, p. 30.

22. Thompsonville Carpet Manufacturing Company, Cost Book.

23. Brainard Manuscript Collection.

24. Thompsonville Manufacturing Company, Directors' and Stockholders' minutes, July 18, 1832.

25. Brainard Manuscript Collection.

26. James Wallace, for many years bookkeeper of the Thompsonville Carpet Manufacturing Company.

27. Brainard Manuscript Collection.

28. Thompsonville Manufacturing Company, Cost Book, *passim.*

29. Brainard Manuscript Collection.

30. *The Daily Republican* (Springfield, Massachusetts), Sept. 8, 1846, p. 2.

31. United States Circuit Court, District of Connecticut, *Lowell Manufacturing Company et al.* v. *the Hartford Carpet Company,* "Complainant's Bill," pp. 29–34.

32. *Ibid., Defendant's Answer,* pp. 45–49.

33. Thompsonville Carpet Manufacturing Company, Contract Book, pp. 21–22.

34. George W. Martin to Messrs. Thompson & Company, July 19, 1847.

35. Thompsonville Manufacturing Company, Contract Book, pp. 29, 33, 35.

36. E. Talbot to George W. Martin, Sept. 2, 1847.

37. James Miller to George W. Martin, Nov. 9, 1848.

38. Lowell Manufacturing Company, Contract Book, Alexander Wright to Orrin Thompson, Feb. 16, 1850.

39. *The Springfield Daily Union,* Apr. 12, 1873, p. 2.

40. Thompsonville Manufacturing Company, Directors' and Stockholders' minutes, July 17, 1830.

41. *Ibid.,* July 24, 1833.

42. Brainard Manuscript Collection.

43. Eggleston, *op. cit.,* p. 13.

44. Willard H. Furey Manuscript Collection, Thompsonville, Connecticut.

45. Commons, *op. cit.,* IV, Supplement, 52, 59.

46. *Ibid.,* IV, Supplement, 93–94.

47. *Ibid.,* IV, Supplement, 116.

48. *Ibid.,* IV, Supplement, 118.

49. Thompsonville Manufacturing Company, Directors' and Stockholders' minutes, July 24, 1833.

50. Commons, *op. cit.,* IV, Supplement, 25.

51. *Ibid.,* IV, Supplement, 57.

52. Thompsonville Manufacturing Company, Directors' and Stockholders' minutes, July 19, 1837; *Hartford Daily Courant,* Aug. 21, 1940, p. 2.

53. *Voice of Industry* (Lowell, Massachusetts), Sept. 11, 1846, p. 4.

54. *Ibid.*

55. *The Daily Republican,* Sept. 8, 1846, p. 2.

56. Lowell Manufacturing Company, Directors' and Stockholders' minutes, Oct. 15, 1846.

57. *The New York Journal of Commerce,* Sept. 18, 1846, p. 2.

58. "Statement of Case and Evidence," *Application of Erastus B. Bigelow,* p. 361.

59. George W. Martin to Orrin Thompson, May 1, 1847.

60. Brainard Manuscript Collection.

61. Description of working methods and conditions at Thompsonville in this period were written by a bookkeeper of the company named James Wallace and may be found in newspaper clippings for the years 1880 to 1885 in the Brainard Manuscript Collection.

62. Brainard Manuscript Collection.

63. Thompsonville Manufacturing Company, Contract Book, *passim.*

64. *Ibid.,* Cost Book, *passim.*

65. James Miller to George W. Martin, Nov. 9, 1848.

66. Commons, *op. cit.,* IV, Supplement, 58.

67. Thompson & Company to Thompsonville Carpet Manufacturing Company, Aug. 21, 1847.

68. "Statement of Case and Evidence," *op. cit.*, p. 364.

69. Thompsonville Manufacturing Company, Directors' and Stockholders' minutes, July 19, 1830, Sept. 6, 1830.

70. *Ibid.*, Sept. 1, 1836, Aug. 29, 1849, Apr. 22, 1852.

71. Thompsonville Manufacturing Company, Directors' and Stockholders' minutes, Aug. 20, 1851.

72. New York, New York, Conveyances, Vol. 589, p. 71.

73. Thompsonville Manufacturing Company, Directors' and Stockholders' minutes, Aug. 6, 1852.

74. *Lowell Manufacturing Company et al.* v. *the Hartford Carpet Company,* "Complainant's Bill," p. 41.

75. Lowell Manufacturing Company, Directors' and Stockholders' minutes, Jan. 29, 1853.

76. "Statement of Case and Evidence," *op. cit.*, p. 364.

CHAPTER 3: Pioneering an Industry: Three Younger Companies, 1837–1856

1. A. & E. S. Higgins, Sales Book, *passim.*

2. *The Carpet Trade,* VIII (Aug., 1877), 13.

3. New York, New York, Conveyances, Vol. 480, pp. 223–4; Vol. 493, pp. 370–1.

4. American Institute of the City of New York, *Eighth Annual Report* (Albany, 1850), p. 42.

5. James M. Donnelly Manuscript Collection, Amsterdam, New York.

6. B. R. Curtis, *In the Matter of the Application of Erastus B. Bigelow to the Commissioner of Patents for an Extension of his Letters-Patent, for Improvements in the Power-Loom for Weaving Ingrain Carpets* (Boston, 1860), p. 39.

7. Higgins, Sales Book, *passim.*

8. *History of Montgomery and Fulton Counties,* New York (New York, 1878), p. 91.

9. *Evening Recorder* (Amsterdam, New York), Centennial Number, Nov., 1910, p. 7.

10. *Ibid.*, Feb. 15, 1884, p. 3.

11. Montgomery County, New York, Deeds, Vol. 51, pp. 192–4.

12. *The American Carpet & Upholstery Journal,* XXXI (Philadelphia, Mar., 1913), 77.

13. W. Max Reid (The Hollander, Pseud.), Another Chapter on Amsterdam's Early History, "The Sanford Carpet Industry," p. 6, Article No. 14 of unbound typescript in the Montgomery County Department of History and Archives, Fonda, New York.

14. Henry Hall, *America's Successful Men of Affairs* (New York, 1896), II, 682.

15. Reid, *op. cit.*, p. 3.

16. Montgomery Deeds, Vol. 54, p. 352.

17. *Hunt's Merchants' Magazine and Commercial Review,* XXII (June, 1850), pp. 684–6.

18. *Evening Recorder,* Nov., 1910, p. 7.

19. Cole and Williamson, *The American Carpet Manufacture,* pp. 62, 65.

20. Donnelly Manuscript Collection, Erastus B. Bigelow to John L. Amory, July 11, 1848.

21. Worcester County, Massachusetts, Deeds, Vol. 452, p. 524.

22. Clinton Historical Society, *Historical Papers* (Clinton, Mass., n.d.), p. 60.

23. *The National Aegis* (Worcester, Massachusetts), July 11, 1849, p. 2.

24. *Ibid.*, Apr. 10, 1850, p. 3; *The Carpet Trade Review,* IV (June, 1877), 85.

25. Worcester Deeds, Vol. 465, pp. 433–4.

26. Donnelly Manuscript Collection.

27. *Ibid.*

28. Bigelow Carpet Company, Cost Book.

29. *Ibid., passim.*

30. *Hunt's Merchants' Magazine and Commercial Review,* XXVII (Nov., 1852), 642.

31. Bigelow Carpet Company, Contract Book, p. 9.

32. *Amer. Carp. Jour.,* XVI (May, 1898), 77.

33. *Ibid.*

34. Cleaveland, *Memoir of Erastus Bigelow,* pp. 10–11.

35. Bigelow Carpet Company, Cost Book, *passim.*

36. Andrew E. Ford, *History of the Origin of the Town of Clinton, Massachusetts, 1653–1865* (Clinton, 1896), p. 244.

37. Cole and Williamson, *op. cit.,* pp. 48–49.

38. *New York Daily Graphic,* Nov. 28, 1876. Quoted from Bigelow Carpet Company, *An Account of the Works of the Bigelow Carpet Company, and of its Exhibit at the Centennial Exhibition, Philadelphia* (Cambridge, 1876), p. 9.

39. Bigelow, *The Tariff Question,* p. 232.

CHAPTER 4: Years of Adaptation: the Lowell Manufacturing Company, 1852–1899

1. Robert F. Martin, *National Income in the United States, 1799–1938* (New York, 1939), p. 6; Willford Isbell King, *The Wealth and Income of the People of the United States* (New York, 1915), p. 48.

2. United States Department of Commerce, Bureau of the Census, *Urban Population in the United States from the First Census (1790) to the Fifteenth Census (1930),* (Washington, 1939), p. 3.

3. *The Philadelphia Carpet Trade,* VI (July, 1888), 578.

4. Wright, *Wool-Growing and the Tariff,* pp. 282–3.

5. Annual Report of the Hartford Carpet Company, 1858.

6. *The Carpet Trade and Review,* XIV (Mar. 15, 1883), 19.

7. *Bulletin of the National Association of Wool Manufacturers,* XIV (Mar., 1884), 65.

8. Norman Scott Brien Gras, *Business and Capitalism* (New York, 1939), p. 237.

9. Lowell Manufacturing Company, Minutes of the Directors' and Stockholders' meeting, Jan. 1, 1879.

10. *Ibid.,* Jan. 11, 1865, Feb. 9, 1881, Feb. 2, 1887, Feb. 17, 1893.

11. Lowell Manufacturing Company, Contract Book, p. 232.

12. James Cook Ayer, *Some of the Usages and Abuses in the Management of our Manufacturing Corporations* (Lowell, 1863), p. 8.

13. *Bulletin of the National Association of Wool Manufacturers,* XXI (June, 1891), 171–2.

14. Bagnall, "Sketches of Manufacturing Establishments," IV, 2587–9; Lowell Manufacturing Company, Directors' and Stockholders' minutes, Apr. 15, 1880.

15. Gibb, *The Saco-Lowell Shops,* pp. 232–3.

16. Lowell Manufacturing Company, Directors' and Stockholders' minutes, June 4, 1883.

17. James M. Donnelly Manuscript Collection, Amsterdam, New York.

18. Lowell Manufacturing Company, Directors' and Stockholders' minutes, Jan. 2, 1878, Nov. 9, 1878, Jan. 21, 1879.

19. Lowell Manufacturing Company, Contract Book, pp. 106, 110.

20. Lowell Manufacturing Company, Directors' and Stockholders' minutes, Jan. 10, 1855.

21. *The Carpet Trade and Review,* XIII (July 15, 1882), 31.

22. *Report of a Committee of the Stockholders of the Lowell Manufacturing Company, Presented at the Meeting of July, 1859* (Lowell, 1859), pp. 3–13.

23. Ayer, *op. cit.,* pp. 3, 4, 8, 22.

24. Lowell Manufacturing Company, Directors' and Stockholders' minutes, June 30, 1859, Jan. 4, 1860, Jan. 2, 1861, Jan. 1, 1862.

25. Ayer, *op. cit.*, p. 19.

26. Lowell Manufacturing Company, Directors' and Stockholders' minutes, Jan. 2, 1861, Jan. 6, 1864.

27. *Ibid.*, July 24, 1860, Sept. 27, 1864.

28. *Ibid.*, Mar. 16, 1860.

29. *Ibid.*, Mar. 11, 1863.

30. *Ibid.*, Feb. 13, 1861, Apr. 24, 1861, Aug. 16, 1861, Oct. 23, 1861.

31. *Saturday Courant* (Clinton, Massachusetts), Aug. 30, 1862, p. 2.

32. *Lowell Daily Courier*, Nov. 17, 1866, p. 2.

33. Lowell Manufacturing Company, Contract Book, pp. 162–3.

34. *The Awards and Claims of Exhibitors at the International Exhibition, 1876* (Boston, 1877), p. 368.

35. Cole and Williamson, *The American Carpet Manufacture*, p. 251.

36. *The Carpet Trade*, VII (Jan., 1876), 9–10.

37. Lowell Manufacturing Company, Directors' and Stockholders' minutes, Jan. 1, 1879.

38. *The Carpet Trade*, IX (Dec., 1878), 9.

39. Lowell Manufacturing Company, Contract Book, p. 187.

40. *American Textile Manufacturer*, I (Nov., 1873), 37.

41. *The Awards and Claims, op. cit.*, p. 24.

42. Lowell Manufacturing Company, Directors' and Stockholders' minutes, Apr. 8, 1876, June 3, 1876.

43. *Ibid.*, July 1, 1865, Jan. 4, 1871, June 3, 1876, Jan. 17, 1878.

44. *The Carpet Trade*, VIII (Oct., 1877), 14.

45. *Ibid.*, VIII (June, 1877), 13.

46. *United States Economist and Dry Goods Reporter* (New York), Jan. 4, 1873, p. 4; Apr. 26, 1873, p. 5.

47. *The Carpet Trade Review*, IV (Jan., 1877), 2.

48. Lowell Manufacturing Company, Directors' and Stockholders' minutes, Jan. 17, 1878, Mar. 2, 1878, May 6, 1878, June 4, 1878, July 31, 1878, Nov. 9, 1878.

49. *Ibid.*, Jan. 1, 1879.

50. *Ibid.*

51. *U. S. Economist*, Jan. 6, 1872, p. 6, Jan. 4, 1873, p. 4.

52. *American Textile Manufacturer*, I (Dec., 1873), 45.

53. Lowell Manufacturing Company, Directors' and Stockholders' minutes, Jan. 23, 1882.

54. *The Philadelphia Carpet Trade*, V (Sept., 1887), 735.

55. *Ibid.*, V (Sept., 1887), 741.

56. Henry Hardwick to John L. Houston, Feb. 21, 1893.

57. *Ibid.*, Mar. 15, 1893.

58. *Ibid.*, Nov. 29, 1893.

59. *Amer. Carp. Jour.*, XVI (Jan., 1898), 31.

60. *The Philadelphia Carpet Trade*, VI (Aug., 1888), 683.

61. *The American Carpet and Upholstery Trade*, IX (Jan., 1891), 33.

62. Cole and Williamson, *op. cit.*, pp. 122–4.

63. *The American Carpet and Upholstery Trade*, XIV (July, 1896), 32.

64. *Amer. Carp. Jour.*, XXVI (July, 1908), 56.

65. *The American Carpet and Upholstery Trade*, VIII (May, 1890), 461.

66. *Bulletin of the National Association of Wool Manufacturers*, X (Mar., 1880), 67–68.

67. United States Department of the Interior, Bureau of the Census, *Report on Manufacturing Industries in the United States at the Eleventh Census: 1890* (Washington, 1895), Part III, p. 40.

68. *Textile World and Industrial Record*, XXIX (Dec., 1900), 1037.

69. *The Philadelphia Carpet Trade*, IX (Oct., 1891), 884; IX (Nov., 1891), 976.

70. Lowell Manufacturing Company, Directors' and Stockholders' minutes, Jan. 1, 1879.

71. Henry Chamberlain Meserve, *Lowell—An Industrial Dream Come True* (Boston, 1923), p. 68.

72. *Lowell Daily Courier,* Feb. 7, 1885, p. 5.

73. Gladys L. Palmer, *Union Tactics and Economic Change* (Philadelphia, 1932), p. 144.

74. *The American Carpet and Upholstery Trade,* X (Sept., 1892), 862.

75. *U. S. Economist,* Oct. 21, 1871, p. 6; *The Philadelphia Carpet Trade,* V (June, 1887), 454.

76. "Wholesale Prices, Wages, and Transportation," 52 Cong., 2d Sess. (1892–1893), *Senate Reports,* No. 1394, Part I, pp. 9, 174.

77. *Lowell Daily Courier,* Apr. 29, 1878, p. 4.

78. *The Evening Recorder* (Amsterdam, New York), Apr. 1, 1885, p. 2.

79. *The Philadelphia Carpet Trade,* VI (Feb., 1888), 139.

80. *Lowell Daily Courier,* Jan. 27, 1885, p. 5.

81. Lowell Manufacturing Company, Directors' and Stockholders' minutes, Jan. 21, 1885.

82. Horace G. Wadlin, *Census of the Commonwealth of Massachusetts: 1895* (Boston, 1898), V, 26–29.

83. *Lowell Daily Courier,* Apr. 24, 1885, p. 8.

84. Lowell Manufacturing Company, Directors' and Stockholders' minutes, Dec. 20, 1893.

85. Massachusetts Department of Labor and Industries, *The Annual Statistics of Manufactures, 1894* (Boston, 1895), p. 275.

86. *Lowell Daily Courier,* May 3, 1894, p. 1.

87. *Ibid.,* May 2, 1894, p. 1; May 3, 1894, p. 1.

88. *The Philadelphia Carpet and Upholstery Trade,* VII (July, 1889), 630.

89. *Bulletin of the National Association of Wool Manufacturers,* XXV (Mar., 1895), 52.

90. *The Carpet Trade,* VII (Dec., 1875), 16.

91. *Godey's Lady's Book and Magazine,* L (Mar., 1855), 285–6.

92. Alexander Whytock, *Carpet Manufacture and Design* (Edinburgh, 1856), pp. 26–28.

93. *The Carpet Trade,* VII (June, 1876), 10.

94. *The Awards and Claims, op. cit.,* p. 362.

95. *The Carpet Trade,* VII (Nov., 1875), 7.

96. *The Philadelphia Carpet Trade,* VI (Dec., 1888), 1044.

97. *Amer. Carp. Jour.,* XVI (Sept., 1898), 46.

98. *The American Carpet and Upholstery Trade,* X (Aug., 1892), 775; XIII (June, 1895), 47.

99. Lowell Manufacturing Company, Directors' and Stockholders' minutes, Nov. 29, 1886.

100. *The Carpet Trade,* VII (May, 1889), 411.

101. *New York Times,* Dec. 11, 1891, p. 3.

102. *Ibid.,* May 7, 1898, p. 12; June 2, 1898, p. 9.

103. *American Wool and Cotton Reporter,* XIII (July 27, 1899), 859.

104. *Amer. Carp. Jour.,* XXVII (Jan., 1919), 32.

105. *The Philadelphia Carpet Trade,* V (July, 1887), 569.

106. *Ibid.,* V (Jan., 1887), 34.

107. *The Bigelow Magazine,* II (Sept.–Oct., 1950), 13.

108. The figures were procured from Loan Books of the Massachusetts Hospital Life Insurance Company by Professor Gerald T. White of San Francisco State College while he was Business History Fellow at the Harvard Graduate School of Business Administration. Some of the interest rates were, 1884, 4¾; 1886, 3⁹⁄₁₆; 1887, 5; 1888, 4¼; 1889, 4½; 1891, 5½; 1892, 4; 1893, 7; 1894, 3¾; 1895, 4; 1896, 5; 1897, 4; 1898, 3¾; 1899, 3½.

109. Lowell Manufacturing Company, New England Trust Company Bank Book, *passim.*

110. Joseph G. Martin, *Boston Stock Market*, p. 92.

CHAPTER 5: Years of Adaptation: the Hartford Carpet Company, 1854–1901

1. J. Hammond Trumbull, ed., *The Memorial History of Hartford County Connecticut, 1633–1884* (Boston, 1886), II, 130.

2. American Historical Society, *Encyclopedia of Connecticut Biography* (Boston, 1917), I, 175, 296–7.

3. Furey Manuscript Collection, Orrin Thompson to the Directors of the Hartford Carpet Company, Dec. 28, 1859.

4. *Lowell Manufacturing Company and Erastus B. Bigelow v. the Hartford Carpet Company, Testimony Referred to by Mr. O'Conor*, pp. 24–30.

5. *Lowell Manufacturing Company et al. v. the Hartford Carpet Company*, "Complainant's Bill," pp. 42–43.

6. Hartford Carpet Company, Minutes of the Directors' and Stockholders' meeting, June 25, 1860.

7. *Ibid.*, July 1, 1854.

8. Lowell Manufacturing Company, Minutes of the Directors' and Stockholders' meeting, Jan. 3, 1855.

9. Hartford Carpet Company, Directors' and Stockholders' minutes, Jan. 24, 1855.

10. *Ibid.*

11. *Ibid.*, June 29, 1896.

12. *Ibid.*, Feb. 1, 1854, Apr. 6, 1857.

13. Furey Manuscript Collection.

14. Lowell Manufacturing Company, Directors' and Stockholders' minutes, Mar. 19, 1856.

15. Hartford Carpet Company, Directors' and Stockholders' minutes, July 27, 1859.

16. *Ibid.*, Jan. 10, 1859.

17. *Ibid.*, Sept. 27, 1870.

18. Hartford Carpet Company, Annual Report, 1858.

19. Hartford Carpet Company, Directors' and Stockholders' minutes, Jan. 23, 1861.

20. Hartford Carpet Company, Annual Report, 1862.

21. *The Connecticut Courant* (Hartford, Connecticut), Aug. 19, 1865, p. 1; Mathew Hale Smith, *Twenty Years among the Bulls and Bears of Wall Street* (Hartford, 1870), p. 146.

22. *The Connecticut Courant*, Sept. 9, 1865, p. 2.

23. Hartford Carpet Company, Directors' and Stockholders' minutes, Jan. 24, 1866.

24. *The Connecticut Courant*, Jan. 5, 1867, p. 3; May 18, 1867, p. 3; June 1, 1867, p. 3.

25. *Ibid.*, Jan. 23, 1864, p. 2.

26. *Ibid.*, June 15, 1867, p. 3.

27. *Ibid.*, Feb. 15, 1868, p. 2.

28. Hartford Carpet Company, Directors' and Stockholders' minutes, Jan. 20, 1868. The Tariffville property had a varied career. In October, 1868, Roberts was authorized to sell it for not less than $50,000, but it was 1903 before it was finally disposed of—and for $30,000. *Ibid.*, Oct. 26, 1868, Feb. 24, 1873, Sept. 21, 1880, May 18, 1886; Simsbury Deeds, Vol. 48, pp. 274–5; Vol. 52, pp. 110–11; Vol. 56, pp. 256–7.

29. Agreement, Henry Hardwick with the Hartford Carpet Company, Jan. 2, 1891.

30. Hartford Carpet Company, Production Book, *passim.*

31. Cole and Williamson, *The American Carpet Manufacture*, p. 74.

32. Warren B. Smith to John L. Houston, Mar. 1, 1879.

33. Conversation, N. P. Norton with Frederick Furey, Overseer of Tapestry Weaving, Thompsonville, Connecticut, Oct. 11, 1951.

34. Contract with the Crompton Loom Works, Dec. 7, 1892.

35. W. H. Smith to the Hartford Carpet Company, Nov. 30, 1894.

36. *The Philadelphia Carpet Trade*, II (July, 1887), 569.

37. John L. Houston to Henry Hardwick, Nov. 24, 1890.

38. Conversation, Norton with Daniel Burgess, First Class Carpenter, Thompsonville, Connecticut, Nov. 26, 1951.

39. *The American Carpet and Upholstery Trade*, XIV (Jan., 1896), 51.

40. Conversation, Norton with Frederick Furey, Oct. 11, 1951; Thompsonville Carpet Manufacturing Company, Common Place Book, p. 128.

41. Hartford Carpet Company, Rent Roll, *passim.*

42. *Hartford Daily Courant*, June 4, 1879, p. 2.

43. Conversation, Norton with Samuel Gendron, Jacquard Weaver, Thompsonville, Connecticut, Oct. 27, 1950.

44. Conversation, Norton with Frederick Furey, Oct. 11, 1951.

45. Furey Manuscript Collection.

46. *Ibid.*

47. Hartford Carpet Company, Directors' and Stockholders' minutes, May 29, 1882.

48. Henry Hardwick to John L. Houston, May 9, 1892.

49. *Ibid.*, Nov. 1, 1890.

50. Furey Manuscript Collection.

51. Hartford Carpet Company, Directors' and Stockholders' minutes, May 5, 1884, Mar. 31, 1885.

52. Hartford Carpet Company, Directors' and Stockholders' minutes, Nov. 25, 1884.

53. *American Wool and Cotton Reporter*, XV (Feb. 14, 1901), 186.

54. *Dobson et al.* v. *Hartford Company*, 114 U. S. 439.

55. *The Hartford Courant*, Dec. 21, 1900, p. 3.

56. Cole and Williamson, *op. cit.*, p. 198.

57. *The American Carpet and Upholstery Trade*, XIII (Aug., 1895), 23.

58. Furey Manuscript Collection.

59. *The Thompsonville Press* (Enfield, Connecticut), Aug. 15, 1895, p. 2; Aug. 22, 1895, p. 2.

60. Thompsonville Carpet Manufacturing Company, Common Place Book, p. 117.

61. *Ibid.*, pp. 128, 131.

62. Hartford Carpet Company, Directors' and Stockholders' minutes, Apr. 18, 1898.

CHAPTER 6: Years of Adaptation: the New York Companies, 1854–1901

1. "Statement of Case and Evidence," *Application of Erastus B. Bigelow*, p. 331.

2. *The Philadelphia Carpet Trade*, V (May, 1887), 368–9.

3. *Ibid.*, V (Aug., 1887), 645.

4. *Wool and Manufactures of Wool* (Washington, 1912), p. 171.

5. Whytock, *Carpet Manufacture*, p. 19.

6. *Godey's Lady's Book and Magazine*, LII (Jan., 1856), 17.

7. *United States Economist and Dry Goods Reporter*, Feb. 8, 1873, p. 6.

8. *Scientific American*, XLII (Jan. 3, 1880), 10.

9. *Webster Loom Company* v. *Higgins et al.*, 39 F. 462.

10. E. S. Higgins Carpet Company, Tapestry Pattern Book, *passim.*

11. *The American Carpet and Upholstery Trade*, XII (Oct., 1894), 30.

12. Conversation, N. P. Norton with Leon Salley, Personnel Counselor, Thompsonville, Connecticut, Oct. 26, 1950.

13. *The Carpet Trade*, IX (Jan., 1878), 16.

14. *The American Carpet & Upholstery Journal*, XXXII (Philadelphia, Nov., 1914), 70.

15. *Ibid.*

16. *New York Times*, Dec. 5, 1874, p. 3.

17. *The Carpet Trade*, IX (Dec., 1878), 10.

18. *The Evening Recorder* (Amsterdam, New York), Nov. 27, 1883, p. 2; Nov. 30, 1883, p. 2.

19. *The Philadelphia Carpet Trade*, V (Sept., 1887), 753–4.

20. *The American Carpet and Upholstery Trade*, IX (Oct., 1891), 889.

21. *The Evening Recorder*, Nov. 27, 1883, p. 2.

22. Conversation, Norton with Leon Salley, Oct. 26, 1950.

23. Selig Perlman, *A History of Trade Unionism in the United States* (New York, 1922), p. 94; *Record of Proceedings of the General Assembly of the Knights of Labor of America, Eleventh Regular Session, Held at Minneapolis, Minnesota, Oct. 4 to 19, 1887* (n.p., 1887), "Statement of the General Executive Board in relation to the Difficulty with District Assembly No. 126," pp. 1463–7.

24. *Ibid.*, p. 1468.

25. *Ibid.*, p. 1474.

26. Katharine Elizabeth Higgins, *Richard Higgins, a Resident and Pioneer Settler at Plymouth and Eastham, Massachusetts* (Worcester, Massachusetts, 1918), p. 484.

27. *The Philadelphia Carpet Trade*, VII (Jan., 1888), 48d.

28. *New York Times*, Jan. 8, 1889, p. 8; Jan. 9, 1889, p. 5; Aug. 6, 1889, p. 8.

29. Cole and Williamson, *The American Carpet Manufacture*, p. 257.

30. *Amer. Carp. Jour.*, XXXII (Nov., 1914), 70.

31. *Ibid.*, XVI (July, 1898), 53.

32. *The Philadelphia Carpet Trade*, VII (May, 1889), 420.

33. *The Philadelphia Carpet and Upholstery Trade*, VIII (Jan., 1890), 35.

34. *The American Carpet and Upholstery Trade*, IX (July, 1891), 602.

35. *Ibid.*, IX (July, 1891), 601.

36. Furey Manuscript Collection, Contract between Higgins and the Fabric Measuring and Packaging Company.

37. *The American Carpet and Upholstery Trade*, VIII (Mar., 1890), 256; conversation, Norton with Julius Roth, former purchasing agent, Bigelow-Hartford Carpet Company, Oct. 10, 1951.

38. Class of 1884 of Harvard College, *Fiftieth Anniversary Report of the Secretary* (Cambridge, Massachusetts, n.d.), p. 6.

39. Conversation, Norton with F. H. Deknatel, Treasurer and Director of Bigelow-Sanford Carpet Company, Inc., Feb. 28, 1951.

40. E. S. Higgins Carpet Company, Minutes of the Directors' and Stockholders' meeting, Mar. 26, 1892.

41. *The Philadelphia Carpet Trade*, VI (Sept., 1888), 776.

42. *The American Carpet and Upholstery Trade*, XII (June, 1894), 46.

43. E. S. Higgins Carpet Company, Minutes of the Executive Committee meetings, Nov. 2, 4, 1892; Jan. 2, May 18, 1894.

44. E. S. Higgins Carpet Company, Directors' and Stockholders' minutes, July 11, 18, 1894.

45. *The American Carpet and Upholstery Trade*, XIV (Nov., 1896), 67.

46. E. S. Higgins Carpet Company, Directors' and Stockholders' minutes, Oct. 28, 1896.

47. *Ibid.*, Nov. 9, 1897.

48. *Ibid.*, Oct. 6, 13, Nov. 24, 1897; Feb. 23, 1898.

49. *New York Times*, Jan. 25, 1899, p. 4; Jan. 29, 1899, p. 5.

50. Conversation, Norton with Julius Roth, Oct. 10, 1951.

51. Conversation, Thomas R. Navin with Neal Rantoul, Nov. 13, 1950.

52. E. S. Higgins Carpet Company, Directors' and Stockholders' minutes, Oct. 9, 1899.

53. *Amer. Carp. Jour.*, XIX (Mar., 1901), 85.

54. E. S. Higgins Carpet Company, Directors' and Stockholders' minutes, Jan. 4, 1901.

55. *Amer. Carp. Jour.*, XXIV (June, 1906), 68.

56. *Ibid.*, XXVI (Feb., 1908), 105.

57. *U. S. Economist*, Oct. 27, 1871, p. 2.

58. Stephen Sanford, Letter Copy Book, 1879–1880, Vol. XXVI, *passim*.

59. *Ibid.*

60. *The Philadelphia Carpet Trade*, VI (July, 1888), 586; VIII (May, 1889), 418; *The American Carpet and Upholstery Trade*, XIII (May, 1894), 26–27.

61. Conversations, Norton with Fred Schofield, Weaver, Dec. 1, 1950, with James K. McKenney, Production Control Superintendent, Nov. 28, 1950; *Amer. Carp. Jour.*, XIV (Nov., 1896), 55.

62. *Ibid.*, XXVI (July, 1908), 56.

63. *Ibid.*, XVI (Jan., 1898), 31.

64. Letter, E. I. Petersen to John S. Ewing, Dec. 10, 1952.

CHAPTER 7: Years of Adaptation: the Bigelow Carpet Company, 1854–1899

1. Bigelow Carpet Company, *An Account of the Works of the Bigelow Carpet Company, and of its Exhibit at the Centennial Exhibition, Philadelphia* (Cambridge, 1876), pp. 6–7.

2. *The Carpet Trade*, VIII (Dec., 1876), 15.

3. *The Awards and Claims of Exhibitors at the International Exhibition, 1876*, p. 59; *The Philadelphia Carpet and Upholstery Trade*, VIII (Jan., 1890), 39.

4. *Bulletin of the National Association of Wool Manufacturers*, IX (Dec., 1879), 230.

5. Bigelow Carpet Company, *An Account of the Works*, pp. 7–8.

6. *The Philadelphia Carpet Trade*, VII (June, 1889), 524.

7. James M. Donnelly Manuscript Collection, Scrapbook.

8. *The American Carpet & Upholstery Journal*, XVI (Philadelphia, Mar., 1898), 47.

9. *Saturday Courant* (Clinton, Massachusetts), Nov. 14, 1857, p. 2.

10. *Ibid.*, May 19, 1860, p. 2.

11. Ford, *History of Clinton, Massachusetts*, pp. 245–8.

12. Worcester County, Massachusetts, Deeds, Vol. 674, pp. 171–3.

13. *Clinton Courant*, Mar. 27, 1875.

14. *Amer. Carp. Jour.*, XXVI (Mar., 1908), 53.

15. *The American Carpet and Upholstery Trade*, VIII (Aug., 1890), 755.

16. *Ibid.*; Clinton Board of Trade, *Clinton, Worcester County, Massachusetts* (Clinton, 1885), p. 16.

17. Bigelow Carpet Company, Analysis of Carpeting, 1894, *passim*.

18. *Amer. Carp. Jour.*, XVI (July, 1898), 79.

19. *Clinton Courant*, Aug. 30, 1884, p. 3; Apr. 18, 1885, p. 3; Mar. 27, 1886, p. 3.

20. Clinton, Massachusetts, *Assessment Record*, 1863; Clinton, Massachusetts, *Assessment Record, 1875; The American Carpet and Upholstery Trade*, VIII (Aug., 1890), 755.

21. *Clinton Courant*, Oct. 10, 1885, p. 3.

22. *Ibid.*, Dec. 29, 1888, p, 2.

23. James M. Donnelly Manuscript Collection, Scrapbook; *Clinton Courant*, Apr. 5, 1886, p. 3.

24. *Ibid.*, May 22, 1886, p. 3.

25. *The Philadelphia Carpet Trade*, VI (Oct., 1888), 884.

26. *Annual Report of the Commissioner of Patents for the year 1879* (Washington, 1880), p. 223.

27. *The Carpet Trade and Review*, XIII (Dec. 1, 1882), 20.
28. *Atlantic Monthly*, XVII (Oct., 1878), 485.

CHAPTER 8: The Reconstituted Companies: the Hartford Carpet Corporation, 1901–1914

1. *New York Times*, Nov. 22, 1888, p. 8; Nov. 24, 1888, p. 1.
2. Hartford Carpet Company, Minutes of the Directors' and Stockholders' meeting, Feb. 19, 1892.
3. *The American Carpet and Upholstery Trade*, XI (June, 1893), 43.
4. James Howard Bridge, *Millionaires and Grub Street* (New York, 1831), p. 278.
5. *Lowell Daily Courier*, May 12, 1899, p. 8.
6. *The American Carpet & Upholstery Journal*, XVII (Philadelphia, May, 1899), 65.
7. Conversation, Thomas R. Navin with Neal Rantoul, Nov. 13, 1950.
8. *Lowell Daily Courier*, Nov. 4, 1899, p. 5; *Boston Evening Transcript*, Nov. 27, 1899, p. 10.
9. *American Wool and Cotton Reporter*, XIII (Nov. 16, 1899), 1362.
10. Bigelow Carpet Company, Minutes of the Stockholders' meeting, Dec. 15, 1899; *Boston Evening Transcript*, Nov. 27, 1899, p. 10.
11. Bigelow Carpet Company, Ledger A, p. 109.
12. *Boston Evening Transcript*, Nov. 4, 1899, p. 15.
13. *The Hartford Courant*, Jan. 24, 1901, p. 5.
14. *Amer. Carp., Jour.*, XIX (Mar., 1901), 63.
15. Hartford Carpet Corporation, Minutes of the Stockholders' meetings, Feb. 25, 1901, Feb. 26, 1901.
16. *Amer. Carp. Jour.*, XIX (Feb., 1901), 50.
17. *Clinton Daily Item* (Clinton, Massachusetts), July 15, 1914, p. 1; *The Thompsonville Press* (Enfield, Connecticut), Aug. 6, 1914, p. 1.
18. *Boston News Bureau*, Jan. 11, 1901, p. 1.
19. Robert F. Martin, *National Income in the United States*, p. 106.
20. Paul H. Douglas, *Real Wages in the United States, 1890–1926* (New York, 1930), p. 587.
21. Cole and Williamson, *The American Carpet Manufacture*, p. 257.
22. United States Department of Commerce, Bureau of the Census, *Thirteenth Census of the United States Taken in the Year 1910* (Washington, 1913), VIII, 389; United States Department of Commerce, Bureau of the Census, *Census of Manufactures 1914* (Washington, 1919), II, 45.
23. *The House Beautiful*, XXVII (Jan., 1910), 39.
24. *Suburban Life*, IV (Feb., 1907), 68.
25. *Country Life in America*, XII (Oct., 1907), 698.
26. *The House Beautiful*, XXVII (Jan., 1910), 71.
27. *Amer. Carp. Jour.*, XXVI (Feb., 1908), 103.
28. *American Wool and Cotton Reporter*, XV (Nov. 21, 1901), 1487.
29. *Ibid.*, XIV (Oct. 11, 1900), 1194.
30. *Country Life in America*, XII (Oct., 1907), 667.
31. *Amer. Carp. Jour.*, XXI (Feb., 1903), Supplement.
32. *Census of Manufactures 1914*, II, 45.
33. *Ibid.*, II, 59–60.
34. *The House Beautiful*, XXVII (Feb., 1910), 72.
35. Hartford Carpet Corporation, Stockholders' minutes, Feb. 26, 1901, Mar. 3, 1902.
36. *Ibid.*, Minutes of the Directors' meeting, Mar. 21, 1901.
37. *Ibid.*, Jan. 30, 1907, July 28, 1909, Apr. 24, 1912.
38. *Ibid.*, Mar. 21, 1901, Jan. 27, 1909, Apr. 27, 1910.
39. Conversation, N. P. Norton with F. H. Deknatel, treasurer and director of the Bigelow-Sanford Carpet Company, Incorporated, Feb. 28, 1951.

40. Correspondence, Franklin A. Higgins with Leon F. Salley, Nov. 17, 1952.

41. *The Thompsonville Press*, Mar. 7, 1901, p. 2; Nov. 26, 1903, p. 2.

42. Willard H. Furey Manuscript Collection; conversations, Norton with F. H. Deknatel, Feb. 28, 1951, and with Samuel Gendron, Oct. 27, 1950.

43. *Amer. Carp. Jour.*, XXVII (Nov., 1910), 85; XLII (Aug., 1924), 91.

44. Hartford Carpet Corporation, Treasurer's Ledger, p. 3.

45. Hartford Carpet Corporation, Directors' minutes, Feb. 8, 1911.

46. Hartford Carpet Corporation, Treasurer's Ledger, p. 30.

47. *The Thompsonville Press*, June 4, 1914, p. 1.

48. *Amer. Carp. Jour.*, XIX (Feb., 1901), 50.

49. *The Thompsonville Press*, Mar. 7, 1901, p. 2; July 7, 1901, p. 2.

50. *Amer. Carp. Jour.*, XVII (Sept., 1899), 39; *Davison's Carpet Trade, 1906* (New York, 1905), p. 56.

51. Hartford Carpet Corporation, Directors' minutes, Jan. 27, 1909, Apr. 28, 1909.

52. Conversation, Norton with Julius Roth, former purchasing agent, Bigelow-Hartford Carpet Company, Oct. 29, 1952.

53. *Amer. Carp. Jour.*, XXXII (Dec., 1914), 48.

54. *The Thompsonville Press*, Mar. 14, 1901, p. 2; Mar. 6, 1902, p. 2.

55. Hartford Carpet Corporation, Machinery Book, *passim*.

56. *Amer. Carp. Jour.*, XIX (Apr., 1901), 50.

57. *The Thompsonville Press*, Apr. 24, 1913, p. 8.

58. Conversation, Norton with Rose McCormick, Tapestry Setter, Nov. 26, 1951.

59. Hartford Carpet Corporation, Mill Journal Transfers.

60. *The Thompsonville Press*, July 17, 1952, p. 1.

61. Hartford Carpet Corporation, Directors' minutes, Oct. 31, 1906, Jan. 27, 1909; *The Thompsonville Press*, Feb. 25, 1909, p. 2.

62. Wright, *Wool-Growing and the Tariff*, pp. 282–3; *Amer. Carp. Jour.*, XXXI (Jan., 1913), 52.

63. Hartford Carpet Corporation, Inventory Book, 1901–1908; *ibid.*, Inventory Book, 1908–1912; *ibid.*, Inventory Book, 1912–1915.

64. Conversation, Norton with F. H. Deknatel, Sept. 21, 1951.

65. Conversation, Norton with John Carey, July 31, 1952.

66. Gras and Larson, *Casebook in American Business History*, p. 727.

67. United States Department of Commerce, Bureau of the Census, *Manufactures 1905* (Washington, 1908), III, 98.

68. *Amer. Carp. Jour.*, XXIV (Jan., 1906), 93; XXVII (Nov., 1909), 70; XXIX (Oct., 1911), 85; XXX (May, 1912), 68; XXXI (Nov., 1913), 55.

69. *Ibid.*, XXVI (Aug., 1908), 59.

70. *Country Life in America*, XII (Oct., 1907), 698; XVIII (Oct., 1910), 663; *Suburban Life*, XV (Nov., 1912), 271, 285.

71. Hartford Carpet Corporation, Treasurer's Ledger, pp. 24, 33.

72. *The Hartford Courant*, June 2, 1914, p. 14.

73. Cole and Williamson, *op. cit.*, pp. 214–15.

74. *Amer. Carp. Jour.*, XXX (Oct., 1912), 56.

75. Bigelow-Sanford Manuscript Collection.

76. *Amer. Carp. Jour.*, XXV (Oct., 1907), 52.

77. *The House Beautiful*, IX (Feb., 1910), xxi.

78. *Amer. Carp. Jour.*, XXXII (Sept., 1914), 49.

79. *Ibid.*, XXVI (Nov., 1908), 67.

80. *Ibid.*, XXVII (Jan., 1909), 83.

81. *Ibid.*, XXXII (May, 1914), 85.

82. *Ibid.*, XXXII (Nov., 1914), 70.

83. *The Thompsonville Press*, Mar. 31, 1904, p. 2.

84. *Ibid.*, May 13, 1909, p. 2.

85. Bigelow Carpet Company, Journal A, p. 590.

86. *Amer. Carp. Jour.*, XXXI (Dec., 1913), 59.

87. Hartford Carpet Corporation, Treasurer's Ledger, pp. 34–35.

CHAPTER 9: The Reconstituted Companies: Bigelow Carpet Company, 1899–1914

1. Bigelow Carpet Company, Minutes of the Stockholders' meeting, Dec. 2, 1899; Minutes of the Directors' meeting, Dec. 13, 1906.
2. *Ibid.*, June 28, 1901.
3. *Clinton Daily Item* (Clinton, Massachusetts), Aug. 20, 1908, p. 1.
4. Bigelow Carpet Company, Cash Book, 1910–1913, pp. 19, 123, 461, 569.
5. Bigelow Carpet Company, Journal A, p. 1.
6. Bigelow Carpet Company, Treasurer's Reports, June 18, 1907.
7. *Ibid.*, June 28, 1901.
8. Lowell Manufacturing Company, Contract Book; *The American Carpet & Upholstery Journal*, XXV (Philadelphia, July, 1907), 56.
9. Bigelow Carpet Company, Journal A, pp. 507, 599; Bigelow Carpet Company, Ledger, pp. 14, 412; Bigelow Carpet Company, Journal B, p. 234.
10. Bigelow Carpet Company, Journal B, p. 166.
11. *Amer. Carp. Jour.*, XXXII (Aug., 1914), 52.
12. *American Wool and Cotton Reporter*, XIV (Jan. 25, 1900), 109.
13. Conversation, N. P. Norton with James M. Donnelly, Plant Superintendent, Amsterdam, Dec. 1, 1950.
14. Bigelow Carpet Company, Treasurer's Reports, Dec. 23, 1901, Dec. 23, 1903.
15. *Clinton Daily Item*, Nov. 21, 1907, p. 1; Bigelow Carpet Company, Treasurer's Reports, Dec. 12, 1907.
16. *Clinton Daily Item*, Dec. 27, 1909, p. 1; Dec. 2, 1911, p. 2.
17. *Lowell Courier-Citizen*, June 2, 1914, p. 2.
18. *Amer. Carp. Jour.*, XVIII (Feb., 1900), 52.
19. *Lowell Daily Courier*, Apr. 21, 1900, p. 1; Apr. 26, 1900, p. 1; Apr. 18, 1910, p. 1.
20. *Lowell Courier-Citizen*, Nov. 9, 1907, p. 1; Dec. 17, 1907, p. 1; conversation, Norton with Joseph Sullivan, Oct. 9, 1951.
21. *Lowell Courier-Citizen*, Dec. 18, 1907, p. 12; Mar. 24, 1908, p. 7; Mar. 30, 1908, p. 1; Apr. 3, 1908, p. 1; Jan. 9, 1909, p. 9; Jan. 14, 1909, p. 10.
22. Bigelow Carpet Company, Treasurer's Reports, June 16, 1908.
23. *Clinton Daily Item*, Mar. 28, 1912, p. 1.
24. Bigelow Carpet Company, Wage Book, *passim; Amer. Carp. Jour.*, XXIV (Jan., 1906), 93.
25. *The American Carpet and Upholstery Trade*, XIII (Sept., 1895), 34; *Amer. Carp. Jour.*, XXIV (Nov., 1906), 65.
26. Bigelow Carpet Company, Treasurer's Reports, Dec. 15, 1905.
27. *American Wool and Cotton Reporter*, XXVIII (July 30, 1914), 1015.
28. Conversation, Norton with Henry Ahrenhold, Jr., assistant to vice-president for sales, Oct. 29, 1952.
29. *Amer. Carp. Jour.*, XXVI (Aug., 1908), 85.
30. *Ibid.*, XXX (Nov., 1912), 67.
31. *American Wool and Cotton Reporter*, XXVIII (Apr. 30, 1914), 571.
32. *Amer. Carp. Jour.*, XXXI (Sept., 1913), 56.
33. Bigelow Carpet Company, Journal A, p. 590.
34. *Amer. Carp. Jour.*, XXV (Apr., 1907), 54.
35. *American Wool and Cotton Reporter*, XXII (Nov. 12, 1908), 1514.
36. *The House Beautiful*, XIII (Apr., 1911), xiii.
37. Bigelow Carpet Company, Stockholders' minutes, Dec. 30, 1899.
38. Bigelow Carpet Company, Directors' minutes, June 29, 1900, Dec. 23, 1901; June 19, 1902.
39. Bigelow Carpet Company, Ledger, pp. 32, 109.
40. *Clinton Daily Item*, Mar. 20, 1914, p. 1.
41. Conversation, Norton with F. H. Deknatel, Oct. 29, 1952.
42. *Boston News Bureau*, May 9, 1914, p. 3.

43. *The Hartford Courant,* May 30, 1914, p. 1; June 1, 1914, p. 1; June 2, 1914, p. 17; *Amer. Carp. Jour.,* XXXIII (June, 1914), 22; *American Wool and Cotton Reporter,* XXVIII (July 23, 1914), 964.

44. Bigelow Carpet Company, Directors' minutes, June 10, 1914.

45. *Ibid.,* July 22, 1914.

46. *Ibid.*

47. *Clinton Daily Item,* July 25, 1914, p. 1.

48. Hartford Carpet Corporation, Minutes of the Directors' meeting, Aug. 4, 1914.

49. *Boston News Bureau,* Sept. 14, 1914, p. 7; Hartford Carpet Corporation, Directors' minutes, Mar. 1, 1915.

50. James M. Donnelly Manuscript Collection.

CHAPTER 10: The Bigelow-Hartford Carpet Company, 1914–1924

1. Frequent references to high wool costs and dyestuff shortages are found in the floor-covering industry publications of the time.

2. Conversation, J. S. Ewing with F. H. Deknatel, Taconic, Connecticut, Sept. 21, 1951.

3. *The American Carpet & Upholstery Journal,* XXXII (Philadelphia, Oct., 1914), 67; The Bigelow-Hartford Carpet Company, Minutes of the Directors' meeting, Jan. 28, 1915.

4. These percentages are based on the loom figures given in the following paragraph. The loom figures, with the other mill information, are taken from two printed statements concerning the mills dated July 18, 1914, and Jan. 28, 1915 (F. S. Moseley & Co., Boston, Neal Rantoul's files), and from a letter to Ewing from E. I. Petersen, vice-president for production, Bigelow-Sanford Carpet Company, Inc., Dec. 10, 1952.

5. *Amer. Carp. Jour.,* XXXII (Sept.–Dec., 1914). Each issue of this magazine contained as its first feature a summary of the past month's activities in the industry and the final issue for the year summed up the highlights of the preceding 12 months.

6. Bigelow-Sanford, Accounting Dept., Financial Data Book; Bigelow-Hartford, Directors' minutes, Jan. 28, 1915.

7. A number of Norman's former associates and subordinates have been interviewed, and all are in agreement as to his ability as a salesman.

8. *Amer. Carp. Jour.,* XXXIII (Aug., 1915), 51; XXXIV (Mar., 1916), 64; XXXV (Sept., 1917), 40.

9. *Ibid.,* XXXIII (Dec., 1915), 36.

10. *Ibid.,* XXXV (Aug., 1917), 26.

11. Conversations, Ewing with John Davidson, former superintendent at Clinton, The Weirs, N. H., July 26, 1951; with Julius Roth, former purchasing agent, Bigelow-Hartford, New York, June 19, 1951. Roth made an inspection trip to Lowell soon after the merger and believed that his report (with which Deknatel was associated) led to the decision to close the Lowell mill.

12. Bigelow-Hartford, Directors' minutes, Apr. 21, July 28, Oct. 27, 1915; *Amer. Carp. Jour.,* XXXV (Aug., 1917), 28.

13. *Clinton Daily Item* (Clinton, Massachusetts), July 16, 1917, p. 1.

14. *Amer. Carp. Jour.,* XXXII (Nov., 1914), 18–19.

15. *Ibid.,* XXXVI (Sept., 1918), 45.

16. *Ibid.,* XXXII (Nov., 1914), 19. Such contracts were reported in the trade press and so were the shows and expositions at which Bigelow-Hartford displayed its wares. A partial list of the company's contracts is taken from the *Amer. Carp. Jour.,* XXXIII (Aug., 1915), 51; XXXIV (Mar., 1916), 64; XXXV (Nov., 1917), 32, 39; XLI (Dec., 1923), 46; XLII (Oct., 1924), 48. Conversations with Talbot Rantoul and Henry Ahrenhold, company employees who have been concerned with contract business, New York, Apr. 24 and June 21, 1951, were drawn upon for particulars of the way in which the business was sought and obtained.

17. Letter, E. I. Petersen to Ewing, Dec. 10, 1952.

18. Cole and Williamson, *The American Carpet Manufacture,* pp. 110–17.

19. *Amer. Carp. Jour.,* XXXIII (Nov., 1915), 45; XXXIV (Oct., 1916), 54, 59.

20. *Boston Transcript,* Apr. 11, Apr. 23, 1915; Bigelow-Sanford, Secretary's Dept., Report, Eugene Ong to Louis K. Liggett on the Bigelow-Hartford Carpet Company, Inc., Oct. 30, 1926.

21. *Amer. Carp. Jour.,* XXXIV (Nov., 1916), 26; XXXV (May, 1917), 36; *Boston Transcript,* Apr. 17, 1917, Mar. 26, 1919.

22. *Amer. Carp. Jour.,* XXXIV (Feb., 1916), 65; XXXIV (May, 1916), 28.

23. *Ibid.,* XXXV (Feb., 1917), 26.

24. *Ibid.,* XXXVI (Aug., 1918), 48.

25. *Ibid.,* XXXVI (Feb., 1918), 44.

26. Bigelow-Hartford, Minutes of the Executive Committee meeting, Nov. 14, 1916; Directors' minutes, Nov. 21, 1917, Apr. 24, 1918.

27. Bigelow-Hartford, Executive Committee minutes, May 14, 1918.

28. A. N. Cook, Bigelow-Hartford advertising manager, ed., *A Century of Rug and Carpet Making* (New York, 1925), pp. 56–57.

29. *Amer. Carp. Jour.,* XXXIII (Aug., 1915), 40; *Clinton Daily Item,* Nov. 29, 1915, p. 1.

30. *Amer. Carp. Jour.,* XXXVI (July, 1918), 42; Cole and Williamson, *op. cit.,* p. 175.

31. Bigelow-Sanford, Accounting Dept., Financial Records.

32. Bigelow-Hartford, Directors' minutes, Jan. 24, 1917.

33. *Amer. Carp. Jour.,* XXXVII (Apr., 1919), 36.

34. Julius Roth, who was Bigelow-Hartford's purchasing agent and who accompanied Perkins to Italy, said that Perkins never recovered from his Italian illness and that it was to some extent the result of his war work.

35. Bigelow-Hartford, Directors' minutes, Mar. 3, 1919.

36. Conversation, Ewing with Neal Rantoul, Aug. 27, 1951.

37. *Amer. Carp. Jour.,* XXXVI (Dec., 1918), 51; XXXVII (Jan., 1919), 58; XXXVII (Feb., 1919), 32, 38, 55; XXXVII (May, 1919), 54; XXXVIII (Jan., 1920), 47.

38. *Ibid.,* XXXVII (Apr., 1919), 28; XXXVII (June, 1919), 25; *Boston Transcript,* Mar. 26, 1919.

39. *Amer. Carp. Jour.,* XXXVIII (Oct.–Dec., 1920).

40. Bigelow-Sanford, Accounting Dept., Financial Trend Book.

41. *Amer. Carp. Jour.,* XXXVI (Dec., 1918), 51; XXXVIII (Jan., 1920), 25; XXXVIII (Mar., 1920), 33.

42. *Ibid.,* XXXVII (Feb., 1919), 52.

43. *Ibid.,* XXXVIII (Sept., 1920), 29.

44. *Ibid.,* XXXIX (June, 1921), 48; XL (Feb., 1922), 28.

45. *Ibid.,* XXXIX (Feb., 1921), 21.

46. *Ibid.,* XXXIX (May, 1921), 19; letter, Leon Salley (employee services supervisor, Bigelow-Sanford, Thompsonville), to Ewing, Aug. 8, 1951.

47. *Amer. Carp. Jour.,* XXXIX (May, 1921), 30; letter, Leon Salley to Ewing, Aug. 8, 1951; conversations, Ewing with Thomas Furey and Roland Leach, Bigelow employees who participated in the strike, Thompsonville, June 12, 1951.

48. *Ibid.*

49. Cole and Williamson, *op. cit.,* pp. 189–92.

50. *Ibid.,* p. 191.

51. Bigelow-Sanford Carpet Company, Inc., Minutes of the Executive Committee meeting, July 29, 1919.

52. *Ibid.,* Oct. 17, 1919.

53. *Amer. Carp. Jour.,* XXXIX (Oct., 1921), 45; XXXIX (Jan., 1921), 59; XL (Mar., 1922), 33.

54. *Ibid.,* XXXVII (Mar., 1919), 59; XXXIX (Oct., 1921), 45.

55. Bigelow-Sanford, Accounting Dept. files, American Express Co. to Messrs.

Despard & Co., insurance brokers, New York, Nov. 15, 1929; U. S. Tariff Act, 1922, par. 1101.

56. *Amer. Carp. Jour.*, various dates.

57. Bigelow-Sanford, Advertising and Sales Promotion Dept.

58. *Amer. Carp. Jour.*, XLII (Mar., 1924), 49; XLII (May, 1924), 43.

59. *Ibid.*, XLII (May, 1924), 49.

60. *Ibid.*, XLVII (May, 1929), 39.

61. F. S. Moseley & Co., Rantoul files, Neal Rantoul to John F. Norman, Jan. 25, 1924.

62. *Ibid.*, Norman to Robert Winsor, Mar. 28, 1924.

63. Bigelow-Hartford, Directors' minutes, Feb. 14, Mar. 6, 1922; Jan. 16, Mar. 3, 1924.

64. *Amer. Carp. Jour.*, XLI (Apr., 1923), 44.

65. Cook, *op. cit.*, p. 58.

66. F. S. Moseley & Co., Rantoul files, unsigned statement, Oct. 13, 1925.

67. Industry production and wage data from Institute of Carpet Manufacturers of America, Inc., New York; Bigelow-Hartford information from Bigelow-Sanford, Accounting Dept. records, and Cole and Williamson, *op. cit.*, p. 175.

CHAPTER 11: Continuing Growth and a New Merger, 1925–1929

1. F. S. Moseley & Co., Neal Rantoul's files, Robert Winsor to R. P. Perkins, Mar. 20, 1914.

2. There is considerable agreement on Norman's characteristics among his former associates with whom the author has talked. These include P. F. O'Neil (Mount Vernon, N. Y., June 19, 1951); Henry Ahrenhold (New York, June 21, 1951); Julius Roth (New York, June 19, 1951); John Davidson (The Weirs, N. H., July 26, 1951).

3. Conversation, J. S. Ewing with Henry Ahrenhold, June 21, 1951.

4. *The American Carpet & Upholstery Journal*, XLIII (Philadelphia, Mar., 1925), 63; XLIII (May, 1925), 37; XLIV (Aug., 1926), 34.

5. Conversations, Ewing with John Davidson, July 26, 1951, and with Julius Roth, June 19, 1951; F. S. Moseley & Co., Rantoul files, Report of Barnes Textile Service, Boston, Feb. 14, 1927; conversation, Ewing with J. D. Wise, New York, Sept. 17, 1951.

6. Conversations, Ewing with Henry Ahrenhold, June 21, 1951, and with P. F. O'Neil, June 19, 1951.

7. Conversations, Ewing with E. I. Petersen, New York, Mar. 13, 1951; E. Y. Bricker with Talbot Rantoul, New York. Apr. 24, 1951; Ewing with John Davidson, July 26, 1951.

8. *Amer. Carp. Jour.*, XLIII (Nov., 1925), 33.

9. Conversation, Ewing with P. F. O'Neil, June 19, 1951.

10. Interview, Eugene Ong with B. F. Connolly, New York, Dec. 1, 1926 (Bigelow-Sanford, Secretary's Dept., Report, Eugene Ong to L. K. Liggett, Oct. 30, 1926, p. 5); conversations, Ewing with F. H. Deknatel, Taconic, Conn., June 14, 1951, and with P. F. O'Neil, June 19, 1951.

11. Conversation, Ewing with James Jackson, Thompsonville, Mar. 28, 1951; Report, Barnes Textile Service, Feb. 14, 1927; interview, Eugene Ong with B. F. Connolly, Dec. 1, 1926; conversation, Ewing with P. F. O'Neil, June 19, 1951; conversation, E. Y. Bricker with E. I. Petersen, Dec. 12, 1951.

12. Conversations, Ewing with John Davidson, July 26, 1951, with P. F. O'Neil, June 19, 1951, and with E. I. Petersen, Mar. 13, 1951; Report, Barnes Textile Service, Feb. 14, 1927.

13. Report, Ong to Liggett, p. 13, exhibits 7 and 8.

14. *Amer. Carp. Jour.*, XLVII (May, 1929), 39.

15. *Ibid.*, XLIII (Jan., 1925), 39.

16. *Ibid.*, XLIV (Nov., 1926), 58.

17. Cook, *A Century of Rug and Carpet Making, passim; Amer. Carp. Jour.,* XLIII (Nov., 1925), 34; XLIV (Nov., 1926), 38.

18. *Ibid.,* XLIII (Oct., 1925), 49; XLIV (Apr., 1926), 43; Report, Ong to Liggett, p. 36.

19. *Amer. Carp. Jour.,* XLIV (Feb., 1926), 39.

20. *Ibid.,* XLIII (June, 1925), 40.

21. *Ibid.,* XLIII (June, 1925), 29.

22. F. S. Moseley & Co., Rantoul files, unsigned memorandum, "Stock to Employees, Bigelow-Hartford Carpet Co."

23. Conversation, Bricker with Talbot Rantoul, Apr. 24, 1951.

24. *Amer. Carp. Jour.,* XLIII (Nov., 1925), 40.

25. Bigelow-Hartford Carpet Company, Minutes of the Executive Committee meetings, Dec. 2, Dec. 16, 1925; F. S. Moseley & Co., Rantoul files, unsigned memorandum, "Stock to Employees, Bigelow-Hartford Carpet Co."

26. Bigelow-Hartford, Executive Committee minutes, Dec. 16, 1925.

27. *Amer. Carp. Jour.,* XLIII (July, 1925), 38.

28. *Ibid.,* XLIII (Apr., 1925), 42; XLIV (July, 1926), 40; XLV (May, 1927), 51.

29. *Ibid.,* XLIV (June, 1926), 32; Bigelow-Hartford, Executive Committee minutes, Sept. 17, Nov. 10, 1926; *Amer. Carp. Jour.,* XLV (Jan., 1927), 26; Report, Ong to Liggett, Oct. 30, 1926, p. 37; conversation, Ewing with E. I. Petersen, New York, Feb. 19, 1953.

30. Bigelow-Hartford Carpet Company, Minutes of the Directors' meeting, Oct. 5, 1927; Robert Winsor to Bigelow-Hartford Directors, Oct. 3, 1927.

31. Conversations, Ewing with F. H. Deknatel, June 14, 1951, and Sept. 21, 1952.

32. For some information on Liggett's methods and reputation, see Harold F. Williamson's article, "Management and Innovations: the Winchester Repeating Arms Company, A Case Study," *Bulletin of the Business Historical Society,* XXV (Mar., 1951), 1–14, and the same author's *Winchester: The Gun That Won the West* (Washington, 1952), *passim.*

33. Bigelow-Hartford, Executive Committee minutes, July 23, 1926; Bigelow-Hartford, Robert Winsor to Bigelow-Hartford Directors, Oct. 3, 1927.

34. This and subsequent information on Norman's faults comes from Eugene Ong's interviews with B. F. Connolly and Julius Roth (Bigelow-Sanford); conversations, Bricker with E. I. Petersen, Jan. 5, 1952, and with Eugene Ong, Jan. 9, 1952; Report, Ong to Liggett, Oct. 30, 1926.

35. Conversation, Ewing with Neal Rantoul, Boston, Aug. 27, 1951.

36. Conversations, Ewing with P. F. O'Neil, June 19, 1951, and with William Fuge, Thompsonville, June 13, 1951; Bigelow-Sanford, interview, Eugene Ong with Julius Roth, New York, Jan. 27, 1927.

37. Conversation, Ewing with Julius Roth, June 19, 1951.

38. Conversations, Ewing with F. H. Deknatel, June 14, 1951, and with Julius Roth, June 19, 1951.

39. Conversations, Ewing with Neal Rantoul, Aug. 27, 1951, and with J. J. Delaney, New York, Sept. 18, 1951.

40. Report, Ong to Liggett, Oct. 30, 1926.

41. Bigelow-Hartford, Directors' minutes, Mar. 7, 1927.

42. F. S. Moseley & Co., Rantoul files, W. K. Post to Neal Rantoul, Feb. 11, 1927.

43. *Amer. Carp. Jour.,* XLV (Apr., 1927), 34; *Sunday Union and Republican* (Springfield, Massachusetts), Mar. 12, 1927.

44. Bigelow-Hartford, Executive Committee minutes, Mar. 16, 1927; Directors' minutes, June 30, 1927; conversation, Ewing with Neal Rantoul, Aug. 27, 1951.

45. Conversation, Ewing with J. J. Delaney, Sept. 18, 1951; interviews, Eugene Ong with B. F. Connolly, Dec. 1, 1926, and with Julius Roth, Jan. 27, 1927.

46. *Amer. Carp. Jour.,* XLV (June, 1927), 37.

47. This and succeeding information on the Carpet Institute's formation from a letter, John A. Sweetser to C. H. Handerson, Stephen Sanford & Sons, Inc., Nov. 8, 1928 (Bigelow-Sanford, Sweetser-Sanford correspondence).

48. *Ibid.*

49. This and succeeding paragraph from the same letter, John A. Sweetser to C. H. Handerson.

50. *Amer. Carp. Jour.*, XLV (Aug., 1927), 46.

51. Bigelow-Sanford, J. A. Sweetser to C. H. Handerson, Nov. 8, 1928; Carpet Institute, membership records.

52. *Amer. Carp. Jour.*, XLVI (Jan., 1928), 42.

53. *Ibid.*, 50.

54. *Ibid.*, XLVI (July, 1928), 46.

55. *Ibid.*

56. *Ibid.*, XLVI (Feb., 1928), 59.

57. *Ibid.*, 46, 49, 59; conversations, Ewing with E. I. Petersen, Mar. 13, 1951, Feb. 19, 1953, and Bricker with E. I. Petersen, Dec. 12, 1951, Jan. 5, 1952.

58. *Amer. Carp. Jour.*, XLV (Aug., 1927), 68.

59. *Ibid.*, XLVI (Apr., May, June, 1928), various pages, for the information in this paragraph.

60. *Ibid.*, XLVI (Nov., 1928), 54.

61. *Ibid.*, XLVI (June, 1928), 37.

62. Boris Emmett and John E. Jeuck, *Catalogues and Counters, A History of Sears, Roebuck & Company* (Chicago, 1950), pp. 295, 653.

63. Conversation, Ewing with Henry Ahrenhold, June 21, 1951; Bigelow-Sanford, Sales Dept., sales records.

64. *Amer. Carp. Jour.*, XLVI (Nov., 1928), 40; XLVII (Oct., 1929), 3.

65. *Ibid.*, XLVII (Mar., 1929), 47; XLVII (July, 1929), 28.

66. *Ibid.*, XLVII (Mar., 1929), 30; XLVII (July, 1929), 27; XLVII (Oct., 1929), 39; XLVII (Nov., 1929), 30, 37.

67. Conversation, Ewing with William Fuge, June 13, 1951; Bigelow-Sanford, Thompsonville, Superintendent's files; conversations, Ewing with E. I. Petersen, Mar. 13, 1951, Feb. 19, 1953, and Bricker with E. I. Petersen, Dec. 12, 1951, Jan. 5, 1952.

68. Bigelow-Hartford, Annual Reports, 1927, 1928.

69. Bigelow-Sanford, Thompsonville, Superintendent's files, Pearsall Report, May 15, 1928; Bigelow-Hartford, Executive Committee minutes, Feb. 2, 1928.

70. Conversations, Ewing with William Fuge, June 13, 1951, and with James Jackson, Mar. 28, 1951; conversations, Ewing with E. I. Petersen, Mar. 13, 1951, Feb. 19, 1953, and Bricker with E. I. Petersen, Dec. 12, 1951, Jan. 5, 1952; Report, Barnes Textile Service, Feb. 14, 1927.

71. Conversations, Ewing with F. H. Deknatel, June 14, 1951, and with J. J. Delaney, Sept. 18, 1951.

72. *Amer. Carp. Jour.*, XLVII (Jan., 1929), 64.

73. Bigelow-Hartford, Directors' minutes, Nov. 25, 1929.

74. Bigelow-Sanford, Wool Buying Dept. files, memorandum, R. G. Knowland to W. J. Hines, E. I. Petersen, John Davidson, Oct. 25, 1929.

75. Bigelow-Hartford, Executive Committee minutes, Mar. 27, 1928.

76. Report, Ong to Liggett, Oct. 30, 1926, pp. 83–84.

77. Bigelow-Sanford, John A. Sweetser to C. H. Handerson, Nov. 8, 1928.

78. Information concerning the possible Smith merger is from the Bigelow-Hartford Directors' and Executive Committee meeting minutes, 1927–1928, and from a file of correspondence between John A. Sweetser and John R. Simpson (Bigelow-Sanford).

79. Conversation, Ewing with W. D. McGregor, late partner in the accounting firm of Arthur Young & Co., New York, May 8, 1951.

80. *Ibid.*; conversation, Ewing with Samuel Welldon, New York, May 7, 1951.

81. Conversations, Ewing with J. M. Donnelly and Spencer Garrity, former manager and manager, respectively, Amsterdam plant, Bigelow-Sanford, Amsterdam, Apr. 2–3, 1951.

82. Information in this paragraph from *Clinton Daily Item,* Nov. 4, 1929, and

some news release drafts (Bigelow-Sanford); loom data, from a letter, E. I. Petersen to Ewing, Feb. 18, 1953.

83. Conversation, Ewing with J. J. Kenny, June 21, 1951; Bigelow-Sanford, Sanford-Sweetser correspondence.

84. Bigelow-Sanford, Accounting Dept. files, F. H. Deknatel to U. S. Dept. of Justice, Mar. 5, 1930.

85. *Ibid.*

86. F. S. Moseley & Co., Rantoul files, summary of merger negotiations.

87. Conversation, Ewing with W. D. McGregor, May 8, 1951; *Springfield Republican*, Sept. 23, 1929.

88. Bigelow-Hartford, Directors' minutes, Nov. 25, 1929.

89. Conversation, Ewing with W. D. McGregor, May 8, 1951.

90. Conversation, H. M. Larson and N. P. Norton with John MacNee, Amsterdam, Nov. 29, 1950.

91. *Amer. Carp. Jour.*, XLVII (Dec., 1929), 39.

92. Bigelow-Sanford, Wool Buying Dept. files, Bigelow-Hartford to Edmund Buckley & Co., Nov. 15, 1929.

93. Conversation, Ewing with W. D. McGregor, May 8, 1951; Bigelow-Sanford, Wool Buying Dept. files, correspondence between F. H. Deknatel and W. J. Hines, Jan., 1930; Bigelow-Sanford, Directors' minutes, Jan. 7, 1930; Sanford-Sweetser correspondence, W. D. McGregor to John Sanford, Jan. 28, 1930.

94. *Amer. Carp. Jour.*, XLVII (Dec., 1929), 39.

95. Bigelow-Sanford, Accounting Dept., A. W. Shuttleworth to John A. Sweetser, Dec. 9, 1929.

96. *Ibid.*, John A. Sweetser to W. B. Cooper, Dec. 11, 1929.

CHAPTER 12: Years of Depression and Recovery, 1930–1936

1. Bigelow-Sanford Carpet Company, Inc., Sweetser-Sanford correspondence, John A. Sweetser to John Sanford, May 28, 1930.

2. Bigelow-Sanford, Wool Buying Dept. files, Joseph F. Lockett, Boston, to W. J. Hines, Thompsonville, June 21, 1930.

3. Sweetser-Sanford correspondence, John A. Sweetser to John Sanford, May 28, 1930.

4. *Ibid.*, John Sanford to John A. Sweetser, June 25, 1930.

5. Bigelow-Sanford, Wool Buying Dept. files, G. R. Griswold, Philadelphia, to W. J. Hines, Thompsonville, Feb. 6, 1931.

6. *The American Carpet & Upholstery Journal*, XLIX (Philadelphia, Mar., 1931), 16; Sweetser-Sanford correspondence, John A. Sweetser to John Sanford, Feb. 24, 1931.

7. *Amer. Carp. Jour.*, XLIX (Apr., 1931), 24; Bigelow-Sanford, Sales Dept., Delaney Reports; Sweetser-Sanford correspondence, John A. Sweetser to John Sanford, Jan. 20, 1932.

8. F. S. Moseley & Co., Neal Rantoul's files, correspondence; Sweetser-Sanford correspondence, John A. Sweetser to John Sanford, Feb. 26, 1932.

9. *Amer. Carp. Jour.*, XLIX (Apr., 1931), 23; XLIX (June, 1931), 12.

10. Sweetser-Sanford correspondence, John Sanford to John A. Sweetser, Oct. 7, 1932.

11. F. S. Moseley & Co., Neal Rantoul's files, John A. Sweetser to Neal Rantoul, Aug. 18, 1930; *Amer. Carp. Jour.*, XLVIII (Oct., 1930), 33; conversations, J. S. Ewing with F. H. Deknatel, Taconic, Conn., June 14, 1951, and with J. J. Delaney, New York, Sept. 18, 1951.

12. Bigelow-Sanford, Sales Dept., Complaint Manual, Jan. 28, 1933, and subsequent editions.

13. Bigelow-Sanford, Manufacturing Dept., S. L. Duffett Reports, 1934–1936, Report 5, June, 1934.

14. *Amer. Carp. Jour.*, LII (Jan., 1934), 11.

15. *Ibid.*, LII (May, 1934), 15.

16. *Ibid.*, LIII (Apr., 1935), 9.

17. *Ibid.*, LIV (Jan., 1936), 17; LIV (Feb., 1936), 4; LIV (Oct., 1936), 8.

18. *Ibid.*, XLVIII (Jan., 1930), 39; XLVIII (Nov., 1930), 56.

19. F. S. Moseley & Co., Rantoul files, information on dealings with wholesalers from unsigned memorandum, Oct. 17, 1932; Bigelow-Sanford Annual Report, 1931, President's Message.

20. Bigelow-Sanford, Minutes of the Executive Committee meeting, Oct. 20, 1932; Minutes of the Directors' meeting, Apr. 25, 1933.

21. *Amer. Carp. Jour.*, L (Nov., 1932), 17.

22. *Ibid.*, LIII (May, 1935), 13; LVII (Nov., 1939), 5.

23. *Ibid.*, LII (Mar., 1934), 11; Sweetser-Sanford correspondence, John A. Sweetser to John Sanford, Feb. 2, 1934.

24. *Ibid.*, John Sanford to John A. Sweetser, Feb. 9, 1934.

25. Bigelow-Sanford, Sales Dept., Delaney Reports.

26. *Amer. Carp. Jour.*, LII (June, 1934), 12; LII (July, 1934), 19; LIII (Nov., 1935), 4.

27. *Ibid.*, LIV (Nov., 1936), 4; Bigelow-Sanford, Manufacturing Dept. E. I. Petersen's reports on Thompsonville, 1935, 1936.

28. Bigelow-Sanford, Manufacturing Dept., S. L. Duffett Reports, 1932–1933, Report 11, Dec., 1932; conversation, Ewing with R. G. Knowland, New York, Dec. 19, 1951; *Amer. Carp. Jour.*, LI (May, 1933), 10; Bigelow-Sanford, Sales Dept., Delaney Reports, Current Book #1.

29. Conversation, Ewing with R. G. Knowland, Dec. 19, 1951.

30. *Amer. Carp. Jour.*, LIV (Mar., 1936), 4, 15; LIV (Nov., 1936), 11.

31. Conversation, Ewing with R. G. Knowland, Dec. 19, 1951; loss figure and reasons for failure from Wise memorandum to Department of Justice, 1940.

32. *Amer. Carp. Jour.*, LV (Dec., 1937), 6.

33. Conversation, Ewing with H. K. Reinhardt, Jr., manager, Technical Research Dept., Bigelow-Sanford, Thompsonville, June 14, 1951.

34. Sweetser-Sanford correspondence, John A. Sweetser to John Sanford, Jan. 30, 1935.

35. *Ibid.*, John Sanford to John A. Sweetser, Feb. 4, 1935.

36. *Ibid.*, especially letter of Feb. 4, 1935, cited above; *Amer. Carp. Jour.*, LI (Aug., 1933), 9.

37. *Ibid.*, LI (Aug., 1933), 9; LI (Oct., 1933), 19; LI (Nov., 1933), 13; LIII (June, 1935), 4.

38. *Ibid.*, LIII (Aug., 1935), 10; Sweetser-Sanford correspondence, John A. Sweetser to John Sanford, Feb. 26, 1932.

39. Bigelow-Sanford, Wool Buying Dept. files, F. H. Deknatel to P. F. O'Neil, Mar. 5, 1930; *ibid.*, general correspondence, 1930; *ibid.*, P. F. O'Neil to W. J. Hines, June 30, 1930.

40. *Ibid.*, F. H. Deknatel to W. J. Hines, July 18, 1930.

41. *Ibid.*, P. F. O'Neil to W. J. Hines, Apr. 27, May 14, 1931.

42. *Ibid.*, Apr., 27, 1931; *ibid.*, Bigelow-Sanford to Chandless & Co., Ltd., Tientsin, China, Nov. 13, 1931.

43. *Ibid.*, P. F. O'Neil to S. Arneson, Feb. 24, 1931.

44. Bigelow-Sanford, Manufacturing Dept., E. I. Petersen's reports on Thompsonville, 1931.

45. Bigelow-Sanford, Manufacturing Dept. Reports; Carpet Institute of America.

46. F. S. Moseley & Co., Rantoul files, John A. Sweetser to Neal Rantoul, Feb. 10, 1932; Bigelow-Sanford, Manufacturing Dept., S. L. Duffett Reports, 1932–1933, 1934–1936.

47. *Ibid.*; conversation, Ewing with R. G. Knowland, Dec. 19, 1951.

48. Various conversations, with company personnel formerly at the Clinton mill and with Clinton townspeople, led inescapably to these conclusions.

49. Bigelow-Sanford, Amsterdam, J. M. Donnelly's files; Bigelow-Sanford, New York, J. J. Kenny's files, correspondence, 1937, abandonment of Clinton.

50. *Ibid.*

51. Bigelow-Sanford, Manufacturing Dept., E. I. Petersen's reports on Thompsonville, 1933.

52. *Amer. Carp. Jour.,* L (Jan., 1932), 36; L (May, 1932), 19; F. S. Moseley & Co., Rantoul files, John A. Sweetser to Neal Rantoul, Oct. 23, 1934.

53. Thompsonville files, Clipping Book, 1930–1940, newspaper clippings, various dates.

54. Bigelow-Sanford, Manufacturing Dept., S. L. Duffett Reports, 1932–1933, 1934–1936; *Journal of Commerce* (New York), Sept. 26, Sept. 27, 1932.

55. *Springfield Daily News,* Mar. 10, 1933.

56. *Amer. Carp. Jour.,* LII (Apr., 1934), 13; *Springfield Evening Union,* Apr. 2, 1934; *Journal of Commerce,* Apr. 4, 1934.

57. Bigelow-Sanford Semiannual Report, June 30, 1935, President's Message.

58. Bigelow-Sanford, Manufacturing Dept., E. I. Petersen's reports on Thompsonville, 1932.

59. *Ibid.,* Knowland's summary, 1936.

60. *Ibid.,* Petersen's reports, 1933.

61. *Amer. Carp. Jour.,* LIV (Nov., 1936), 10; *Journal of Commerce,* Nov. 5, 1936; Amsterdam section of Manufacturing Department Annual Report, 1936.

62. *Journal of Commerce,* Mar. 21, July 15, 1937; Amsterdam Manufacturing Report, 1936.

63. Bigelow-Sanford, Annual Reports; F. S. Moseley & Co., Rantoul files, correspondence; *Amer. Carp. Jour.,* LIV (Nov., 1936), 17.

64. Conversation, Ewing with Neal Rantoul, Boston, Aug. 27, 1951; F. S. Moseley & Co., Rantoul files, correspondence.

65. Sweetser-Sanford correspondence, Jan., 1932.

66. Bigelow-Sanford, Directors' minutes, July 16, 1931, Jan. 10, 1932, May 8, 1935; F. S. Moseley & Co., Rantoul files, F. H. Deknatel to Neal Rantoul, May 1, 1935.

67. Sweetser-Sanford correspondence, John A. Sweetser to John Sanford, Mar. 22, 1933; *ibid.,* John Sanford to John A. Sweetser, Mar. 27, 1933.

68. F. S. Moseley & Co., Rantoul files, correspondence, Feb. 14, 1934.

69. *Amer. Carp. Jour.,* LIV (Dec., 1936), 5.

CHAPTER 13: From Recession to Prosperity, 1937–1941

1. *The American Carpet & Upholstery Journal,* LV (Philadelphia, Jan., 1937), 11; LV (Apr., 1937), 9; LV (June, 1937), 4.

2. *Ibid.,* LV (Dec., 1937), 17.

3. *Ibid.,* LVI (Jan., 1938), 5, 11.

4. *Ibid.,* LVII (Jan., 1939), 11; LVII (Dec., 1939), 10, 21; *New York Times,* Dec. 10, 1939.

5. *Ibid.,* Feb. 10, 1940; *Amer. Carp. Jour.,* LVIII (Feb., 1940), 4; LVIII (Mar., 1940), 4, 21.

6. *Ibid.,* LVI (Aug., 1938), 3–4; Harvard Business School files, Case BP 439, Alexander Smith & Sons Carpet Company, pp. 9–10.

7. *Amer. Carp. Jour.,* LVII (Jan., 1939), 5; conversation, J. S. Ewing with R. G. Knowland, New York, Apr. 15, 1952.

8. *Amer. Carp. Jour.,* LVII (Nov., 1939), 5; LVIII (Sept., 1940), 9; Bigelow-Sanford Annual Reports; *Journal of Commerce* (New York), June 15, 1939.

9. *Amer. Carp. Jour.,* LV (July, 1937), 11; LVI (Dec., 1938), 13; LVII (Aug., 1939), 15; LVIII (July, 1940), 15.

10. *Ibid.,* LVIII (July, 1940), 15.

11. Bigelow-Sanford Carpet Company, Inc., Manufacturing Dept., S. L. Duffett Reports, 1938–1942, Report #10, May, 1941.

12. Bigelow-Sanford, Sales Dept., Delaney Reports, Current Book #1.

13. *Amer. Carp. Jour.*, LVIII (Mar., 1940), 21.

14. Bigelow-Sanford, Manufacturing Dept. Reports, 1938; *Amer. Carp. Jour.*, LVIII (Dec., 1940), 19; Bigelow-Sanford, Sales Dept., J. J. Delaney's correspondence.

15. *Ibid.*, Jan.–Oct., 1937; Bigelow-Sanford, Manufacturing Dept. Report, 1939; Bigelow-Sanford, Sales Dept., Delaney's correspondence, J. J. Delaney to John A. Sweetser, Apr. 9, July 22, 1941.

16. Information on product sales and Campbell's dismissal, from: Bigelow-Sanford, Manufacturing Dept. Reports, 1937–1939; Bigelow-Sanford, Minutes of the Directors' meeting, Apr. 4, 1938; *Amer. Carp. Jour.*, LVI (Apr., 1938), 5; conversations, Ewing with J. J. Kenny and F. H. Deknatel, various dates; conversation, Ewing with P. F. O'Neil, New Rochelle, June 19, 1951.

17. Conversation, E. Y. Bricker with Talbot Rantoul, New York, Apr. 24, 1951; conversation, Ewing with J. J. Kenny, Apr. 16, 1952.

18. Bigelow advertising expenditures from figures compiled by the company's advertising dept.; Smith data from its 1946 prospectus for the sale of stock, filed with the Securities & Exchange Commission.

19. *Amer. Carp. Jour.*, LVIII (Jan., 1940), 12; LIX (Oct., 1941), 9.

20. For amplification of the use of advertising in such situations, see Neil H. Borden, *The Economic Effects of Advertising* (Chicago, 1942), p. 425.

21. Bigelow-Sanford, Manufacturing Dept. Report, 1937; Bigelow-Sanford, Executive files, Knowland correspondence, R. G. Knowland to John A. Sweetser.

22. Bigelow-Sanford, Manufacturing Dept. Report, 1937. Unless otherwise specified, information in this section has been taken from reports of the manufacturing department.

23. *Amer. Carp. Jour.*, LVI (May, 1938), 11; Bigelow-Sanford, Manufacturing Dept. Reports, especially E. I. Petersen's Thompsonville summary for 1938; *ibid.*, S. L. Duffett Reports, 1938–1942.

24. Sweetser-Sanford correspondence, John A. Sweetser to the Bigelow management group, Mar. 1, 1939; *ibid.*, John A. Sweetser to R. G. Knowland, Apr. 13, 1939; *ibid.*, Knowland correspondence, J. J. Kenny to R. G. Knowland, Apr. 27, 1939; Bigelow-Sanford, Minutes of the Executive Committee meeting, Apr., 25, 1939.

25. James Lees & Son, Bridgeport, Pennsylvania, Annual Reports.

26. Bigelow-Sanford, Manufacturing Dept. Report, 1937.

27. *Amer. Carp. Jour.*, LVI (Dec., 1938), 15.

28. *Ibid.*, LVII (Feb., 1939), 9; LVII (Nov., 1939), 10.

29. *Ibid.*, LVIII (June, 1940), 10; LVIII (July, 1940), 4–5.

30. Bigelow-Sanford, Sales Dept., Delaney Reports, Current Book #1, memorandum, Sept. 25, 1940, J. J. Delaney to John A. Sweetser, R. G. Knowland, etc.

31. Bigelow-Sanford, Knowland correspondence, R. G. Knowland to E. Wadsworth Stone, Aug. 7, 1941. Subsequent data from a letter, Dec. 2, 1941, R. G. Knowland to various executives; *ibid.*, Dec. 23, 1941; *Amer. Carp. Jour.*, LIX (Feb., 1941), 6; Bigelow-Sanford, Manufacturing Dept. Reports, 1941.

32. LIFO information from correspondence in the Rantoul files (F. S. Moseley & Co.); Bigelow-Sanford, Semiannual Report, June 30, 1939.

33. Bigelow-Sanford, Knowland correspondence, John A. Sweetser to R. G. Knowland, Feb. 7, 1941; *ibid.*, memorandum, Sept. 2, 1941; *ibid.*, memorandum, wage, comparison, Aug. 22, 1941; conversation, Ewing with R. G. Knowland, Apr. 15, 1952.

34. *Amer. Carp. Jour.*, LV (Apr., 1937), 11; LV (Aug., 1937), 11; *Journal of Commerce*, Apr. 1, 15, July 15, 1937; Bigelow-Sanford, Manufacturing Dept. Reports, 1937.

35. *Ibid.*

36. *Amer. Carp. Jour.*, LVI (Mar., 1938), 12; *Springfield Daily News*, Mar. 5, 1938; Bigelow-Sanford, Manufacturing Dept. Reports, 1938.

37. *Springfield Daily News*, Nov. 5, 6, 1937; *Hartford Times*, Nov. 30, 1937.

38. *Amer. Carp. Jour.*, LVI (May, 1938), 12; LVI (June, 1938), 1; *Journal of Commerce*, May 4, 11, 1938; Bigelow-Sanford, Directors' minutes, May 27, 1938; F. S. Moseley & Co., Rantoul files, correspondence, June, 1938; conversation, Ewing

with R. G. Knowland, New York, Dec. 17, 1951; Bigelow-Sanford, Manufacturing Dept. Reports, 1938.

39. Conversation, Ewing with R. G. Knowland, Dec. 17, 1951; *Springfield Union,* June 28, 1938; *Springfield Daily News,* June 28, 1938.

40. *Journal of Commerce,* Oct. 6, 1938; *The Thompsonville Press* (Enfield, Connecticut), Oct. 6, 1938; *Journal of Commerce,* Oct. 22, 1938.

41. *Springfield Union,* June 28, Aug. 3, 1938; *Journal of Commerce,* July 30, 1938; *Amer. Carp. Jour.,* LVI (Aug., 1938), 7; LVI (Sept., 1938), 11; LVI (Oct., 1938), 9, 10.

42. *Journal of Commerce,* Oct. 18, 26, 31, 1938.

43. *Amer. Carp. Jour.,* LIX (May, 1941), 9; LIX (Aug., 1941), 12.

44. *Ibid.,* LVIII (Nov., 1940), 4.

45. Bigelow-Sanford, Knowland correspondence, R. G. Knowland to Emil Rieve, Textile Workers Union of America, Sept. 6, 1939; *ibid.,* R. G. Knowland to Milton Rosenberg, TWUA, Feb. 19, 1941.

46. F. S. Moseley & Co., Rantoul files, J. D. Wise to Neal Rantoul, Dec. 6, 1940.

47. Bigelow-Sanford, Manufacturing Dept. Reports, 1938, 1939.

48. *Journal of Commerce,* Aug. 5, Sept. 13, 1940; *Amer. Carp. Jour.,* LVIII (June, 1940), 2; LVIII (Aug., 1940), 6; LVIII (Sept., 1940), 7–8; Bigelow-Sanford, Thompsonville, Plant Manager's files, E. W. Stone to Henry Ahrenhold, Jr., June 20, 1941; conversation, Ewing with J. D. Wise, New York, Apr. 15, 1952.

49. *Springfield Union,* Feb. 26, 1940; conversations, Ewing with R. G. Knowland, Dec. 17, 1951, Apr. 15, 1952, and with J. D. Wise, Apr. 15, 1952.

50. *Springfield Union,* Feb. 26, 1940; *Amer. Carp. Jour.,* LVIII (Apr., 1940), 4.

51. *Ibid.,* LIX (Feb., 1941), 13.

52. Conversations, Ewing with J. D. Wise, Apr. 15, 1952, with R. G. Knowland, Dec. 17, 1951, Apr. 15, 1952, and with J. J. Kenny, June 21, 1951, Apr. 16, 1952.

53. *Amer. Carp. Jour.,* LIX (July, 1941), 6.

54. F. S. Moseley & Co., Rantoul files, John A. Sweetser to Neal Rantoul, July 23, 1940.

55. *Ibid.,* J. D. Wise to Neal Rantoul, Dec. 6, 1940; Bigelow-Sanford, Directors' minutes, May 6, 1941.

56. Bigelow-Sanford, Knowland correspondence, Sweetser-Kenny-Knowland correspondence, May–July, 1941.

57. Conversation, Ewing with Samuel Welldon, May 8, 1951; conversation, Ewing with Talbot Rantoul, Apr. 24, 1951.

58. Conversation, Ewing with R. G. Knowland, Apr. 15, 1952.

59. Bigelow-Sanford, Thompsonville, Stone correspondence, letter and report, E. W. Stone to E. I. Petersen, Feb. 18, 1941; *ibid.,* Manufacturing Dept. Reports, 1940, 1941.

60. Competitive information from J. J. Kenny's files, Bigelow-Sanford, New York.

61. Bigelow-Sanford, J. D. Wise's files, Management Review, Nov., 1946, Supplement.

CHAPTER 14: Wartime Operations, 1942–1945

1. *The American Carpet & Upholstery Journal,* LX (Philadelphia, Jan., 1942), 4; *Journal of Commerce* (New York), Jan. 13, 1942.

2. Bigelow-Sanford, Thompsonville, Plant Manager's files, memorandum, Status of "Victory Program" as of December 30, 1944.

3. *The Bigelow Weaver,* Nov., 1945, p. 5.

4. *Ibid.,* Oct., 1945, p. 5.

5. *Amer. Carp. Jour.,* LX (Feb., 1942), 7; *New York Times,* Mar. 7, 1942; *Springfield Daily News,* Feb. 10, 1942.

6. Bigelow-Sanford Annual Report, 1945.

7. These and succeeding war production statistics from *The Bigelow Weaver,* Oct., 1945, p. 5, and Nov., 1945, p. 5; Bigelow-Sanford Annual Report, 1945; also *The Bigelow Weaver,* June and Sept., 1945.

8. Conversation, J. S. Ewing with Willard Furey, Thompsonville, June 13, 1951.

9. *Journal of Commerce*, Oct. 22, 25, 29, 1945.

10. Bigelow-Sanford Annual Report, 1945, p. 5.

11. Bigelow-Sanford, Manufacturing Dept. files, Manufacturing Dept. Report, 1942.

12. Bigelow-Sanford, Executive files, R. G. Knowland to John A. Sweetser, July 1, 1942; Bigelow-Sanford, Manufacturing Dept. files, Manufacturing Dept. Report, 1944.

13. *Springfield Union*, Mar. 9, 1942; *Journal of Commerce*, Mar. 17, 1942; *Springfield Union*, May 7, 1942; *The Thompsonville Press*, June 2, 1942; Bigelow-Sanford, Manufacturing Dept. files, Manufacturing Dept. Report, 1942.

14. Bigelow-Sanford, Minutes of the Directors' meeting, Aug. 5, 1942.

15. Richard A. Lester and Edward A. Robie, *Constructive Labor Relations* (Princeton, 1948), pp. 17–18.

16. *Hartford Courant*, May 10, Aug. 30, 1944; *Springfield Republican*, *Springfield Union*, Jan. 31, 1945.

17. Bigelow-Sanford, Manufacturing Dept. Report, 1944; *Hartford Courant*, *Springfield Republican*, Sept. 20, 1944; *Springfield Union*, Jan. 31, 1945.

18. *Journal of Commerce*, Apr. 2, 1943; Bigelow-Sanford, Thompsonville, Plant Manager's files, "Old Experimentals," W. R. Murry to E. I. Petersen, Oct. 9, 1942.

19. *Journal of Commerce*, May 13, 1942; Bigelow-Sanford, Sales Dept. files, J. J. Delaney to John A. Sweetser, Jan. 16, 1942; *ibid.*, J. J. Delaney to Oliver Collins, Topton Rug Mills, Topton, Pennsylvania, Apr. 22, 1942.

20. *Journal of Commerce*, Sept. 23, 1943; Mar. 16, June 14, 1944; Dec. 30, 1944.

21. Bigelow-Sanford, Sales Dept., J. J. Delaney, Special Reports, 1942, J. J. Delaney to Bigelow executive group, June 22, 1942; *ibid.*, J. J. Delaney to J. D. Wise, Feb. 21, 1945.

22. Conversation, Ewing with J. J. Kenny, New York, Apr. 16, 1952; conversation, E. Y. Bricker with Talbot Rantoul, New York, Apr. 24, 1951.

23. The Sweetser-Knowland correspondence during the years from 1940 to 1943 has numerous examples of such clashes. The data in the succeeding paragraphs are from this correspondence (Executive Files, Bigelow-Sanford, New York).

24. *Ibid.*, John A. Sweetser to R. G. Knowland, Aug. 5, 1943.

25. Conversations, Ewing with R. G. Knowland, New York, Apr. 15, 1952, and with J. J. Kenny, Apr. 16, 1952.

26. Bigelow-Sanford, Thompsonville, Plant Manager's files, E. W. Stone to F. H. Deknatel, June 14, 1941.

27. Harvard Business School, M. T. Copeland's files, John A. Sweetser to M. T. Copeland, July 8, 1942.

28. *Ibid.*, Nov. 25, 1942; Bigelow-Sanford, Sales Dept., Delaney correspondence, J. J. Delaney to John A. Sweetser, Jan. 22, 1943.

29. Bigelow-Sanford, J. D. Wise's files, Sales Dept. organization data.

30. Various correspondence files, particularly those of M. T. Copeland, provide ample evidence of these attempts and conflicts.

31. *Journal of Commerce*, Dec. 29, 1944.

32. Conversation, Ewing with B. K. MacLaury, New York, Mar. 13, 1951.

33. *Springfield Daily News*, Sept. 5, 1944.

34. Bigelow-Sanford, Directors' minutes, May 5, Aug. 4, 1943.

35. *Ibid.*, Mar. 1, 1943.

36. Bigelow-Sanford, Sales Dept. files, July 2, 1943.

37. Harvard Business School, M. T. Copeland's files, memorandum, P. F. O'Neil to John A. Sweetser and Bigelow executive group, Oct. 14, 1941.

38. Bigelow-Sanford, Sales Dept. files, Report of conference of M. T. Copeland, J. J. Delaney, and B. K. MacLaury, Aug. 17, 1943.

39. Harvard Business School, M. T. Copeland's files, B. K. MacLaury to M. T. Copeland, Aug. 18, 1944.

40. Bigelow-Sanford, Sales Dept. files, Report of conference of M. T. Copeland, J. J. Delaney, and B. K. MacLaury, Aug. 17, 1943.

41. Harvard Business School, M. T. Copeland's files, John A. Sweetser to M. T. Copeland, Feb. 23, 1943.

42. Bigelow-Sanford, Sales Dept. files, J. J. Delaney to J. D. Wise, Sept. 25, 1944.

43. *Ibid.*, Report, Bigelow Distribution of Kind of Store and Grade of Floor Covering Handled, Based on 1943 Dealer Surveys, Commercial Research Dept., Apr. 21, 1944.

44. *Ibid.*, John A. Sweetser to J. J. Delaney, June 6, 1944.

CHAPTER 15: Administrative Reorganization and Postwar Adjustment, 1945–1949

1. Letter, J. D. Wise to J. S. Ewing, Dec. 19, 1952; conversation, T. R. Navin with Samuel Welldon, New York, Nov. 14, 1950; F. S. Moseley & Co., Boston, Neal Rantoul's files, correspondence.

2. *Ibid.*; conversations, Ewing with J. D. Wise, New York, Sept. 17, Nov. 14, Dec. 19, 1951.

3. Bigelow-Sanford, Minutes of the Directors' meeting, Feb. 14, 1945; *Springfield Union*, Feb. 16, 1945.

4. *Ibid.*; *The Thompsonville Press*, Feb. 23, 1945.

5. Bigelow-Sanford, R. E. Failing's files, Booz, Allen & Hamilton reports.

6. Bigelow-Sanford, J. D. Wise's files, Speech, J. D. Wise to Booz, Allen & Hamilton, Chicago, Dec. 12, 1947.

7. Letter, J. D. Wise to Ewing, Dec. 19, 1952.

8. Bigelow-Sanford, J. D. Wise's files, Speech, J. D. Wise to Booz, Allen & Hamilton, Chicago, Dec. 12, 1947.

9. Conversation, J. S. Ewing with James Jackson, plant manager, Thompsonville, Mar. 28, 1951.

10. These appointments were generally announced in the employee magazine, *The Bigelow Weaver*, in newspapers, and in Management Newsletters. They have been supplemented here by data from Directors' and Executive Committee minutes and from interviews by the author.

11. Letter, J. D. Wise to Ewing, Dec. 19, 1952.

12. Bigelow-Sanford, executive files, Delaney correspondence, 1945–1946; conversation, Ewing with J. D. Wise, Sept. 17, 1951; conversations, E. Y. Bricker with Talbot Rantoul, Aug. 2, 1951, and with George Cayce, Aug. 29, 1951; conversations, Ewing with Willys Monroe, New York, Sept. 19, 1951, and with J. J. Kenny, Mar. 13, Apr. 5, 1951, Oct. 16, 1952; letter, J. D. Wise to Ewing, Feb. 24, 1953.

13. Bigelow-Sanford, Personnel Administration Dept. files, Survey, Opinion Research, Inc., Aug. 27, 1948.

14. Bigelow-Sanford, J. D. Wise memorandum, "Organization and Purpose of Bigelow-Sanford's Major Committees," May 8, 1953, p. 2.

15. Bigelow-Sanford, J. D. Wise's files, Bigelow's objectives from 1948 Yearbook.

16. Management Newsletter, Oct. 24, 1951.

17. Bigelow-Sanford, Sales Dept. files, memorandum, J. J. Delaney to Operations Committee, undated.

18. *The Bigelow Weaver*, Nov., 1948, p. 1.

19. Bristol Mills data from Manufacturing Board minutes, Sept. 5, Nov. 22, 1946, Bigelow-Sanford, Thompsonville, plant manager's files; Bigelow-Sanford, Directors' and Executive Committee minutes, Feb. 14, 1947.

20. *The Thompsonville Press*, Aug. 23, 1945; *The Bigelow Weaver*, Sept., 1945, p. 1.

21. *The Bigelow Weaver*, Oct., 1945, p. 2.

22. *Ibid.*, Jan.–Feb., Sept., 1947, Nov., 1948; Bigelow-Sanford, J. D. Wise's files, Wise speech, 1948; *ibid.*, Wise Community Talk, Sept. 25, 1950.

23. Bigelow-Sanford, J. D. Wise's files, memorandum, J. D. Wise to Operations Committee, Oct. 30, 1947.

24. *Business Week,* May 26, 1951, pp. 121–2.

25. Bigelow-Sanford, J. D. Wise's files, Wise speech at Atlantic City, May 8, 1950.

CHAPTER 16: Progress Under Adversity, 1950–1953

1. Bigelow-Sanford, Minutes of the Research and Development Board, Oct. 9, 1947.

2. *New York Times,* Nov. 5, 1951.

3. *Ibid.,* Mar. 8, 1952.

4. Information on Alexander Smith Incorporated is from *Journal of Commerce* (New York), Jan. 16, 1953.

5. Conversation, J. S. Ewing with J. D. Wise, Dec. 19, 1951; *The Bigelow Weaver,* June, 1952, p. 2; conversations, Ewing with J. J. Kenny and B. K. MacLaury, Oct. 16, 1952.

6. *The Bigelow Weaver,* Dec., 1952, p. 1.

7. Bigelow-Sanford, Personnel Administration Dept. files, Opinion Survey, Manufacturing Supervisory Personnel, 1950; conversation, Ewing with Willys Monroe, Sept. 19, 1951.

8. Letter, J. D. Wise to Ewing, Dec. 19, 1952, for information on the proposed changes in distribution.

9. Bigelow-Sanford, executive files, memorandum, J. J. Delaney to Operations Committee, Feb., 1946; *ibid.,* Executive Committee minutes, Dec. 5, 1950; *ibid.,* company press release, Dec. 4, 1950.

10. Bigelow-Sanford Annual Report, 1952.

11. Letter, J. D. Wise to Ewing, Dec. 19, 1952.

12. Bigelow-Sanford, Minutes of the Directors' meeting, Dec. 20, 1950.

13. *Ibid.,* Jan. 19, 1951; *Retailing Daily* (New York), Mar. 7, 1951; *New York Times,* Mar. 29, 1951; letter, J. D. Wise to Ewing, Feb. 24, 1953.

14. Management Information bulletin, Aug. 3, Oct. 31, 1951; Bigelow-Sanford, Directors' minutes, Nov. 28, 1951; letter, J. D. Wise to Ewing, Dec. 19, 1952.

15. Bigelow-Sanford, Directors' minutes, July 27, 1949; Management Newsletter, July 26, 1950.

16. Bigelow-Sanford, Directors' minutes, Sept. 15, 1951; Management Newsletter, Sept. 14, 1951.

17. Letter, J. D. Wise to Ewing, Dec. 19, 1952.

18. Conversations, Ewing with Samuel Welldon, New York, May 8, 1951, and with Neal Rantoul, Boston, Aug. 27, 1951.

19. *Retailing Daily,* May 5, 1951.

INDEX